T0334608

LIVING ORIGINALISM

LIVING ORIGINALISM

Jack M. Balkin

The Belknap Press of Harvard University Press

Cambridge, Massachusetts

London, England

For Reva Siegel and Robert Post

Copyright © 2011 by Jack M. Balkin
All rights reserved

First Harvard University Press paperback edition, 2014

Library of Congress Cataloging-in-Publication Data

Balkin, Jack M., 1956–
Living originalism / Jack M. Balkin.
p. cm.
Includes bibliographical references and index.
ISBN 978-0-674-06178-1 (cloth : alk. paper)
ISBN 978-0-674-41692-5 (pbk.)
1. Constitutional law—United States—Philosophy. 2. Constitutional law—United
States—Interpretation and construction. 3. Law—United States—Interpretation
and construction 4. Origin (Philosophy) I. Title.
KF4552.B35 2011
342.73001—dc22   2011016124

CONTENTS

III

CHANGE

I

FIDELITY

1

FIDELITY TO TEXT AND PRINCIPLE

Is our Constitution a living document that adapts to changing circumstances, or must we interpret it according to its original meaning? For many years people have debated constitutional interpretation in these terms. But the choice is a false one. Properly understood, these two views of the Constitution are compatible rather than opposed. Once we see why they are compatible, we will also understand how legitimate constitutional change occurs in the American constitutional system.

This book offers a constitutional theory, *framework originalism,* which views the Constitution as an initial framework for governance that sets politics in motion, and that Americans must fill out over time through constitutional construction. It also offers an associated theory of interpretation and construction, the method of *text and principle*. The method of text and principle requires fidelity to the original meaning of the Constitution, and in particular, to the rules, standards, and principles stated by the Constitution's text. It also requires us to ascertain and to be faithful to the principles that underlie the text, and to build out constitutional constructions that best apply the constitutional text and its associated principles in current circumstances.

The method of text and principle is both originalist and living constitutionalist. It is faithful to the original meaning of the constitutional text and to its underlying purposes. It is also consistent with a basic law whose reach and application evolve over time, a basic law that leaves to each generation the task of how to implement the Constitution's words and principles. In each generation the American people are charged with the obligation to flesh out and implement text and principle in their own time. They do this through building political institutions, passing legislation, and creating precedents, both judicial and nonjudicial. These constitutional constructions, in turn, shape how succeeding generations will understand and apply the Constitution in their time. That is the best way to understand the interpretive practices of our constitutional tradition and the work of the many political and social movements that have transformed our understandings of the Constitution's guarantees.

The text of our Constitution is a framework. It is a basic plan for politics. The ratification of the Constitution begins a constitutional project that spans many generations.[1] Each generation must do its part to keep the plan going and to ensure that it remains adequate to the needs and the values of the American people. Americans fill the project out over time through constitutional politics. People contend with each other, trying to persuade each other about the best way to realize the constitutional plan and further its goals.

Keeping the plan going over time—especially given the many disagreements—requires faith in the constitutional project. This is a faith that the constitutional system as a whole is legitimate and worthy of our respect, or will come to be so over time, despite its many faults and imperfections. Thus, fidelity to the constitutional project—and to the Constitution itself—requires faith that the Constitution can and will eventually be redeemed. Fidelity to the Constitution requires that we believe that the project is worth continuing and struggling over, even if we also believe that many current interpretations are wrong or misguided.

Constitutional change is the product of this process of debate and striving over how to continue the plan. Americans try to persuade each other about the best meaning of constitutional text and principle in current circumstances. These debates and political struggles also help generate Americans' investment in the Constitution as their Constitution, even if they never officially consented to it; and they create a platform for the possibility—but not the certainty—of the Constitution's redemption in history.

What people call "constitutional interpretation" involves more than one activity. The first is the ascertainment of meaning. For example, in the First Amendment, does the word *speech* refer only to speaking, or does it point to a more general category of expression that might include writing, music, and painting? The second activity is constitutional construction—implementing and applying the Constitution using all of the various modalities of interpretation: arguments from history, structure, ethos, consequences, and precedent.[2] We might call the first activity "interpretation-as-ascertainment" and the second "interpretation-as-construction."

Much of what people call constitutional interpretation—especially by judges—is actually interpretation-as-construction. Judges build up systems of precedent that implement constitutional purposes and give the Constitution's guarantees and structures meaning in practice, and then they apply these systems of precedent to particular controversies. In the process they often create new doctrinal distinctions that will apply to future cases. The political branches also develop precedents over time through practices that flesh out the respective powers of the different branches of government. In this book I will often draw on the distinction between interpretation-as-ascertainment and interpretation-as-construction. When I speak of "interpretation" generally, I will include both types, as do most people.

Constitutional construction, however, involves far more than developing doctrines and precedents that implement the Constitution. All three branches of government build institutions and create laws and doctrines that serve constitutional purposes, that perform constitutional functions, or that reconfigure the relationships among the branches of the federal government, the states, and civil society. These activities build out the American state over time.

For example, Congress has created the various parts of the executive branch—like the Defense Department and the Justice Department—to help the president carry out his duties to faithfully execute the laws and perform other constitutional functions. As a result, the president is far more powerful today than anyone could have imagined in 1787. The Administrative Procedure Act of 1946 helps the courts review federal administrative actions for conformity to law. The Federal Reserve Act of 1913 and later amendments shifted the responsibility for monetary policy to an independent federal agency. The Civil Rights Act of 1964, the Voting Rights Act of 1965, and later civil rights measures created an enduring framework of national civil rights protection. The Social Security Act of 1935 and later social welfare laws constructed a social safety net administered by the federal government and the states. We might call these "state-building constructions." They build out the Constitution as they build out the country.

Not all of these state-building constructions look like interpretations of specific constitutional provisions, but they rely on assumptions about the Constitution's larger purposes and about what the Constitution permits or requires. Moreover, these constructions, once accepted in practice, may create durable expectations about what the Constitution means.

Courts often shape constitutional doctrines to make sense of these state-building exercises. In fact, the construction of the administrative state during the New Deal was the occasion for a major debate about constitutional interpretation that transformed how lawyers and judges understood the Constitution's guarantees. The New Deal and the civil rights revolution also changed how ordinary Americans understood the purposes and responsibilities of government and the rights of individual citizens.

To understand constitutional interpretation and the processes of constitutional change, we must pay as much attention to institutional development and state building as we do to judicial doctrines and decisions. To understand our Constitution, we must consider not only original meaning and judicial precedents, but also a wide variety of other state-building constructions that rely on interpretations of the Constitution and that provoke new interpretations.

Original Meaning versus Original Expected Application

Constitutional interpretations are not limited to applications specifically intended or expected by the framers and adopters of the constitutional text. For example, the First Amendment today does not protect only speech that people in 1791 would have protected from censorship. The Eighth Amendment's prohibitions on "cruel and unusual punishments" ban punishments that are cruel and unusual as judged by contemporary application of these concepts and principles, not by how people living in 1791 would have applied them.

The text of our Constitution contains different kinds of language. It contains determinate rules (the president must be thirty-five, there are two houses of Congress). It contains standards (no "unreasonable searches and seizures," a right to a "speedy" trial). And it contains principles (no prohibitions of the free exercise of religion, no abridgments of the freedom of speech, no denials of equal protection). If the text states a determinate rule, we must apply the rule because that is what the text offers us. If it states a standard, we must apply the standard. And if it states a general principle, we must apply the principle. Perhaps technically we should call this the method of "text, rule, standard, and principle," but "text and principle" is a far simpler shorthand.

The method of text and principle argues that we should pay careful attention to the reasons why constitutional designers choose particular kinds of language. Adopters use fixed rules because they want to limit discretion;

they use standards or principles because they want to channel politics through certain key concepts but delegate the details to future generations. When the Constitution uses vague standards or abstract principles, we must apply them to our own circumstances in our own time. When adopters use language that delegates constitutional construction to future generations, fidelity to the Constitution requires future generations to engage in constitutional construction. This is the essence of the method of text and principle.

This assumption marks the major difference between my approach and the one popularized by one of originalism's most prominent champions, Justice Antonin Scalia.[3] Justice Scalia agrees that we should interpret the Constitution according to "the original meaning of the text, not what the original draftsmen intended."[4] He also agrees that the original meaning of the text should be read in light of its underlying principles. But he insists that the concepts and principles underlying those words must be formulated and applied in the same way that they would have been formulated and applied when they were adopted. As he puts it, the principle enacted in the Eighth Amendment "is not a moral principle of 'cruelty' that philosophers can play with in the future, but rather the existing society's assessment of what is cruel. It means not . . . 'whatever may be considered cruel from one generation to the next,' but 'what we consider cruel today [i.e., in 1791]'; otherwise it would be no protection against the moral perceptions of a future, more brutal generation. It is, in other words, rooted in the moral perceptions *of the time.*"[5]

Scalia's version of "original meaning" is not original meaning in my sense, but a more limited interpretive principle, *original expected application*. Original expected application asks how people living at the time the text was adopted would have expected it would be applied using language in its ordinary sense (along with any legal terms of art). Thus, the original expected application includes not only specific results, but also the way that the adopting generation would have expected the relevant constitutional principles to be articulated and applied.

Justice Scalia can accommodate new phenomena and new technologies— like television or radio—by analogical extension with phenomena and technologies that existed at the time of adoption. But this does not mean, Scalia insists, that "the *very acts* that were perfectly constitutional in 1791 (political patronage in government contracting and employment, for example) may be *un*constitutional today."[6]

Mistakes and Achievements

Scalia realizes that his approach would allow many politically unacceptable results, including punishments that would clearly shock the conscience today. So he frequently allows deviations from his interpretive principles, making him what he calls a "faint-hearted originalist."[7] For example, Scalia accepts the New Deal settlement that gave the federal government vast powers to regulate the economy that most people in 1787 would never have dreamed of and would probably have strongly rejected.[8]

Scalia's originalism must be "faint-hearted" precisely because he has chosen an unrealistic and impractical principle of construction, which he must repeatedly leaven with respect for precedent and other prudential considerations. The basic problem with looking to original expected application for guidance is that is inconsistent with so much of our existing constitutional traditions. Many federal laws securing the environment, protecting workers and consumers—even central aspects of Social Security—go beyond original expectations about federal power. So too do independent federal agencies like the Federal Reserve Board and the Federal Communications Commission, and federal civil rights laws that protect women and the disabled from private discrimination. Even the federal government's power to make paper money legal tender probably violates the expectations of the founding generation.[9] The original expected application is also inconsistent with constitutional guarantees of sex equality for married women,[10] with constitutional protection of interracial marriage,[11] with the constitutional right to use contraceptives,[12] and with the modern scope of free-speech rights under the First Amendment.[13]

The standard response to this difficulty is that courts should retain "nonoriginalist" precedents (i.e., those inconsistent with original expected application) if those precedents are well established, if they promote stability, and if people have justifiably come to rely on them. Interpretive mistakes, even though constitutionally illegitimate when first made, can become acceptable because we respect precedent. As Scalia explains, "[t]he whole function of the doctrine" of *stare decisis* "is to make us say that what is false under proper analysis must nonetheless be held true, all in the interests of stability."[14]

There are four major problems with this solution. First, it undercuts the claim that legitimacy comes from adhering to the original meaning of the text adopted by the framers and that decisions inconsistent with the original expected application are illegitimate. It suggests that legitimacy can come from public acceptance of the Supreme Court's decisions, or from considerations of stability or economic cost.

Second, under this approach, not all of the "incorrect" precedents receive equal deference. Judges will inevitably pick and choose which decisions they will retain and which they will discard based on pragmatic judgments about when reliance is real, substantial, justified, or otherwise appropriate. These characterizations run together considerations of stability and potential economic expense with considerations of political acceptability—which decisions would be too embarrassing now to discard—and political preference—which decisions particularly rankle the jurist's sensibilities. Thus, one might argue that it is too late to deny Congress's power under the commerce clause to pass the Civil Rights Act of 1964 but express doubts about the Endangered Species Act. One might accept that states may not engage in sex discrimination but vigorously oppose the constitutional right to abortion or the unconstitutionality of antisodomy statutes. This play in the joints allows expectations-based originalism to track particular political agendas and allows judges to impose their political ideology on the law—the very thing that the methodology purports to avoid.

Third, allowing deviations from original expected application out of respect for precedent does not explain why we should not read these mistakes as narrowly as possible to avoid compounding the error, with the idea of gradually weakening and overturning them so as to return to more legitimate decisionmaking. If the sex equality decisions of the 1970s were mistakes, courts should try to distinguish them in every subsequent case with the goal of eventually ridding us of the blunder of recognizing equal constitutional rights for women. If the New Deal settlement was thoroughly illegitimate, courts should find ways to strike down federal statutes, chip away at existing understandings, and ultimately overturn federal laws guaranteeing environmental quality, nondiscrimination, and workplace safety.

This brings us to the final and more basic problem: Our political tradition does not regard decisions that have secured equal rights for women, greater freedom of speech, federal power to protect the environment, and federal power to pass civil rights laws as mistakes that we must unhappily retain; it regards them as genuine achievements of American constitutionalism and sources of pride. These decisions are part of why we understand ourselves to be a nation that has grown freer and more democratic over time. No interpretive theory that regards equal constitutional rights for women as an unfortunate blunder that we are now simply stuck with because of respect for precedent can be adequate to our history as a people. It confuses achievements with mistakes, and it maintains them out of a grudging acceptance. Indeed, those who argue for limiting constitutional interpretation to the original expected application are in some ways fortunate that previous judges rejected their theory of interpretation; this allows them to accept as a starting point nonoriginalist precedents that would now be far too embarrassing for them to disavow.

An originalism that focuses on original expected applications cannot account for how political and social movements and post-enactment history shape our constitutional traditions. It cannot explain how succeeding generations build out the Constitution through constitutional construction. Original expectations originalism argues that social movements and political mobilizations can change constitutional law through the amendment process of Article V. They can also pass new legislation, as long as that legislation does not violate original expected application—as much federal post–New Deal legislation might. But no matter how significant social movements like the civil rights movement and the women's movement might have been in our nation's history, no matter how much they may have changed Americans' notion of what civil rights and civil liberties belong to them, they cannot legitimately alter the correct interpretation of the Constitution beyond the original expected application.

The model of text and principle views the work of political and social movements and post-enactment history quite differently. The constitutional text does not change without Article V amendment. But each generation of Americans can seek to persuade each other about how text and principle should apply to their circumstances, their problems, and their grievances. And because conditions are always changing, new problems are always arising and new forms of social conflict and grievance are always emerging, the process of argument and persuasion about how to apply the Constitution's text and principles is never-ending.

When people try to persuade each other about how to interpret the Constitution, they naturally identify with the generation that framed the constitutional text and they claim that they are being true to its deepest principles. They can and do draw analogies between the problems, grievances, and injustices the adopters feared or faced and the problems, grievances, and injustices of our own day. They also can and do draw on the experiences and interpretive glosses of previous generations—like the generation that produced the New Deal or the civil rights movement—and argue that they are also following in their footsteps.

Most successful political and social movements in America's history have claimed authority for change in just this way: either as a call to return to the enduring principles of the Constitution or as a call for fulfillment of those principles. Thus, the key tropes of constitutional interpretation by social movements and political parties are restoration, on the one hand, and redemption, on the other. Constitutional construction changes by arguing about what we already believe, what we are already committed to, what we have promised ourselves as a people, what we must return to, and what commitments remain to be fulfilled.

When political and social movements succeed in persuading other citizens that their interpretation is the right one, they replace an older set of implementing constructions and doctrines with a new one. These constructions and implementations may not be just or correct judged from the standpoint of later generations, and they can be challenged later on. But that is precisely the point. In every generation, We the People of the United States make the Constitution our own by calling upon its text and its principles and arguing about what they mean in our own time. That is how each generation connects its values to the commitments of the past and carries forward the constitutional project of the American people into the future.

From the standpoint of text and principle, it matters greatly that there was a women's movement in the 1960s and 1970s that convinced Americans that both married and single women were entitled to equal rights and that the best way to make sense of the Fourteenth Amendment's principle of equal citizenship was to apply it to women as well as men, despite the original expected application of the adopters. The laws and judicial decisions crafted in this period that ban sex discrimination are not "mistakes" that we must grudgingly live with. They are *applications* of text and principle that have become part of our constitutional tradition. They might be good or bad applications; they might be incorrect or incomplete. That is for later generations to judge. But when people accept them, as Americans accept the notion of equality for women today, they do not do so simply on the basis of reliance interests—that we mistakenly gave women equal rights in the 1970s and now it's just too late to turn back. They do so in the belief that this is what the Constitution *actually means;* that this is the best, most faithful interpretation of constitutional text and principles.

Originalism based on original expected applications fails because it cannot comprehend this feature of constitutional development except as a series of errors that it would now be too embarrassing to correct. Justice Scalia correctly notes that his reliance on nonoriginalist precedents is not consistent with his originalist commitments, but is rather a "pragmatic exception."[15] And that is precisely the problem with his view: The work of political and social movements in our country's history is not a "pragmatic exception" to fidelity to the Constitution. It is the lifeblood of fidelity to our Constitution—it is how Americans vindicate their Constitution's text and principles in history.

None of this means that the original expected application is irrelevant or unimportant either to interpretation or construction. It helps us understand the original meaning of the text and the general principles that animated the text. For example, in Chapters 9 through 11, which apply the method of text and principle to the commerce clause and the Fourteenth Amendment, I draw heavily on the history of adoption to resolve ambiguities in original meaning and to suggest the best constructions. The point, however, is that original expected applications are not part of the text and they are not themselves binding law. Rather, like other aspects of pre- and post-ratification history, they are a method or modality of interpretation, one among many others. They do not control how we should apply the Constitution's guarantees today, especially as our world becomes increasingly distant from the expectations and assumptions of the adopters' era.

The Meaning of Original Meaning

The term *original meaning* can be confusing because we use the word *meaning* to refer to at least five different kinds of things: (1) semantic content ("What is the meaning of this word in English?");[16] (2) practical applications ("What does this mean in practice?"); (3) purposes or functions ("What is the meaning of life?"); (4) specific intentions ("I didn't mean to hurt you"); or (5) associations ("What does America mean to me?"). Thus, when we ask about the "meaning" of the equal protection clause, we could be asking (1) what concepts the words in the clause point to;

(2) how to apply the clause; (3) the purpose or function of the clause; (4) the intentions behind the clause; or (5) what the clause is associated with in our minds or, more generally, in our culture.[17]

Fidelity to "original meaning" in constitutional interpretation refers only to the first of these types of meaning: the semantic content of the words in the clause. Fidelity to original meaning does not, however, require fidelity to any of the four other types of original meaning, although these forms of meaning may be quite relevant pieces of evidence of original semantic content. Moreover, these other kinds of meaning may be important for purposes of constitutional construction.

Fidelity to original meaning as original semantic content does not require that we must apply the equal protection clause the same way that people at the time of enactment would have expected it would be applied. It does not require that we must articulate the purposes or functions of the clause in exactly the same way the framers and ratifiers would have, or that we apply it only according to their intentions.[18] Finally, it does not mean that the clause can only have the same associations for us that it had for the adopting generation. Today, for example, the clause is associated with many things in our minds and our political culture—like Dr. Martin Luther King Jr. and the civil rights revolution—that the adopting generation could not have known about. These four other types of original meaning may be quite relevant to constitutional construction, and to how we should create and apply legal doctrines. But they are not dispositive on these questions.

To be faithful to original meaning in the sense I am concerned with, we need to know the concepts that the words in the equal protection clause referred to when the clause was originally enacted. This is not purely an investigation into semantic definitions. We also want to know if words in the clause were understood nonliterally—for example, as a metaphor or a synecdoche—and we want to know whether some words referred to generally recognized terms of art.

For example, the copyright clause in Article I, section 8, refers to "writings," which is a nonliteral use. It refers to more than written marks on a page but also includes printing and (probably) sculpture, motion pictures, and other media of artistic and scientific communication. Similarly, the word *speech* in the First Amendment is a synecdoche: it is an example that stands for a larger category of expression, just as the term *press* may stand for both a technology (or a class of technologies) and for a set of social institutions.[19]

Implementing Text and Principles

Although the original expected application is not binding, the constitutional text is. That is because we have a written Constitution that is also enforceable law. We treat the Constitution as law by viewing its rules, standards, and principles as legal rules, standards, and principles. If the text states a determinate rule, we must apply the rule because that is what the text provides. If it states a standard, we must apply the standard. And if it states a general principle, we must apply the principle.

When the text provides an unambiguous, concrete and specific rule, the principles or purposes behind the text cannot override the textual command. For example, the underlying goal of promoting maturity in a president does not mean that we can dispense with the thirty-five-year age requirement. The language creates a rule and must be applied accordingly. On the other hand, where the text is ambiguous or vague, we look to the principles and purposes behind the text to help us understand how to apply it. And where the text offers an abstract standard or principle, we must try to determine what principles underlie the text in order to build constructions that are consistent with it. Articulating underlying principles is one of the tasks of constitutional construction. We can and should use history to articulate these constitutional principles. But the principles we derive from history must be at roughly the same level of abstraction as the text itself. The question is not what principles people specifically intended but what principles the text enacts. Indeed, the fact that adopters chose text that features general and abstract concepts is normally the best evidence that they sought to embody general and abstract principles of constitutional law, whose scope, in turn, will have to be worked out and implemented by later generations.

In some cases the constitutional text itself states a principle, like "equal protection" or "freedom of speech," that we must flesh out by articulating subsidiary principles that explain it. In other cases we infer principles from the constitutional structure as a whole. Articulating these principles is also the task of constitutional construction. For example, there is no single separation of powers clause in the Constitution; rather we derive the principle of separation of powers from how the various institutions and structures outlined in the constitutional text relate to each other. The same is true of the constitutional principle of checks and balances. We infer a general principle from text, structure, and history.

The principle of democracy—which includes the subprinciple that courts should generally defer to legitimate majoritarian decisionmaking—is nowhere specifically mentioned in the constitutional text, and yet it may be the most frequently articulated principle in constitutional argument. It is, ironically, the principle that people most often use to object to courts' inferring constitutional principles not specifically mentioned in the text. Although the principle of democracy does not directly appear in the text, we infer it from various textual features that presume democracy and from the basic character of our government as a representative and democratic republic. The principle of democracy is a structural principle that also informs our construction of other principles, like freedom of speech or the guarantee of equal protection of the laws.[20]

Finally, many other materials gloss text and principles and help apply them to concrete circumstances. These include not only the original expected application but also post-enactment history, including the work of political and social movements that have changed our constitutional common sense, and other constitutional constructions, including judicial and nonjudicial precedents. These materials offer a wide range of theories and interpretations that help us understand and apply the Constitution. They are entitled to considerable weight. Precedents not only implement and concretize principles, they also help settle difficult legal questions where reasonable people can and do disagree. Precedents also help promote stability and rule-of-law values. However, because glosses and precedents accumulate and change over time, and because they often point in contrasting directions, they are not always dispositive of constitutional meaning.

Constitutional doctrines created by courts, and institutions and practices created by the political branches, flesh out and implement the constitutional text and underlying principles. But they are not supposed to replace them. Doctrines, institutions, and practices can implement the Constitution well or poorly, depending on the circumstances, and some implementations that seem perfectly adequate at one point may come to seem quite inadequate or even perverse later on. Because the Constitution, and not interpretations of the Constitution, is the supreme law of the land, later generations may assert—and try to convince others—that the best interpretation of text and principle differs from previous implementing glosses, and hence that we should return to the best interpretation of text and principle, creating new implementing rules, practices, and doctrines that will best achieve this end. The tradition of continuous arguments about how best to implement constitutional meaning generates changes in constitutional doctrines, practices, and law. That is why, ultimately, there is no conflict between fidelity to text and principle and practices of constitutionalism that evolve over time. Indeed, if each generation is to be faithful to the Constitution and adopt the Constitution's text and principles as its own, it must take responsibility for interpreting and implementing the Constitution in its own era.

Fidelity and Institutional Constraints

Expectations-based originalists may object that the text-and-principle approach is indeterminate when the text refers to vague standards or abstract principles like "equal protection" rather than to concrete rules. Therefore it does not sufficiently constrain judges. That might be so if text and principle were all that judges consulted when they interpreted the Constitution. But in practice judges (and other constitutional interpreters) draw on a rich tradition of sources that guide and constrain interpretation, including pre- and post-enactment history, original expected application, previous constitutional constructions, structural and intertextual arguments, and judicial and nonjudicial precedents. In practice, judges who look to text and principle face constraints much like those faced by judges who purport to rely on original expected application. As we have seen, the latter cannot and do not use original expected applications for a very large part of their work, because a very large part of modern doctrine is not consistent with original expected application. So even judges who claim to follow the original understanding are, in most cases, guided and constrained by essentially the same sources and modalities of argument as judges employing the method of text and principle.

I think there is a deeper problem with the objection that the method of text and principle does not sufficiently constrain judges. Many theories of constitutional interpretation conflate two different questions. The first is the question of what the Constitution means and how to be faithful to it. The second asks how a person in a particular institutional setting—like an unelected judge with life tenure—should interpret the Constitution and implement it through doctrinal constructions and applications. The first is the question of *fidelity;* the second is the question of *institutional responsibility.*

Theories about constitutional interpretation that conflate these two questions tend to view constitutional interpretation from the perspective of judges and the judicial role; they view constitutional interpretation as primarily a task of judges, and they assess theories of interpretation largely in terms of how well they guide and limit judges. For example, one of the standard arguments for original expectations originalism is that it will help constrain judges in a democracy. From the perspective of these theories, nonjudicial interpreters are marginal or exceptional cases that we explain in terms of the standard case of judicial interpretation.

I reject this approach. Theories of constitutional interpretation should start with interpretation by citizens as the standard case; they should view interpretation by judges as a special case with special considerations created by the judicial role. In like fashion, constitutional interpretations by executive officials and members of legislatures are special cases that are structured by their particular institutional roles. The political branches must do more than simply not violate the Constitution; they have affirmative obligations to construct institutions and laws that will carry out the Constitution's purposes. Much of the most important constitutional work does not come from courts. It comes from acts of constitutional construction by executive officials and legislatures, both at national and local levels, building institutions, programs, and practices that flesh out and implement constitutional text and principles in ways that courts cannot.

Why emphasize the citizen's perspective? People in each generation must figure out what the Constitution's promises mean for themselves. Many of the most significant changes in constitutional understandings (such as the New Deal, the civil rights movement, the second wave of American feminism) occurred through mobilizations and countermobilizations by social and political movements that offered competing interpretations of what the Constitution really means. Social and political movements argue that the way that the Constitution has been interpreted and implemented by judges or other political actors is wrong and that we need to return to the Constitution's correct meaning and redeem the Constitution's promises in our own day.

Often people do not make these claims in lawyerly ways, and usually they are not constrained by existing understandings and existing doctrines in the way that we want judges to be constrained. In fact, when social movements initially offer their constitutional claims, many people regard them as quite radical or "off-the-wall." There was a time, for example, when the notion that the Constitution prohibited what we now call sex discrimination seemed quite absurd. Yet it is from these protestant interpretations of the Constitution that later constitutional doctrines emerge. Many of the proudest achievements of our constitutional tradition have come from constitutional interpretations that were at one point regarded as crackpot and off-the-wall.

I hasten to add that most of these arguments go nowhere. Only a few have significantly changed how Americans look at the Constitution. Successful social and political movements must persuade other citizens that their views are correct, or, at the very least, they must convince people to compromise and modify their views. If movements are successful, they change the minds of the general public, politicians, and courts. This influence eventually gets reflected in new laws, in new constitutional doctrines, and in new constitutional constructions. Successful social and political mobilization changes political culture, which changes constitutional culture, which in turn changes constitutional practices outside of the courts and constitutional doctrine within them.

The causal influences, of course, do not run in only one direction. Judicial interpretations like those in *Brown v. Board of Education*[21] or *Miranda v. Arizona*[22] can become important parts of our constitutional culture; they can be absorbed into ordinary citizens' understandings of what the Constitution means, and they can act as focal points for citizen reaction. Nevertheless, we cannot understand how constitutional understandings change over time unless we recognize how social movements and political parties articulate new constitutional claims, create new constitutional regimes, and influence judicial constructions.

To understand how these changes could be faithful to the Constitution, we must have a theory that makes the citizen's perspective primary. I do not claim that all mobilizations that produce new constitutional constructions are equally faithful or equally admirable. But some are both faithful and admirable, and a theory of constitutional interpretation—which is also a theory of constitutional fidelity—must account for them. Expectations-based originalism is virtually useless for this purpose, because it views many of the most laudatory changes in our understandings of the Constitution as not faithful to the Constitution and therefore illegitimate.

For similar reasons, expectations-based originalism cannot really constrain judges because too many present-day doctrines are simply inconsistent with it; as a result, judges must pick and choose based on pragmatic justifications that are exceptions to the theory. Indeed, the exceptions threaten to swallow the theory in many areas of the law. Because original expectations originalism conflates the question of constitutional fidelity with the question of judicial constraint, it offers the wrong answer to both questions.

Constraining judges in a democracy is important. But in practice most of that constraint does not come from theories of constitutional interpretation. It comes from institutional features of the political and legal system. Some of these are internal to law and legal culture, like the various sources and modalities of legal argument listed above. Others are "external" to legal reasoning but nevertheless strongly influence what judges produce as a group.

First, judges are subject to the same cultural influences as everyone else—they are socialized both as members of the public and as members of particular legal elites. Second, the president's ability to pick jurists with views roughly similar to his own and the Senate's countervailing advise and consent power determine and limit who gets to serve as a judge, helping to ensure that most successful judicial candidates come from within the political and legal mainstream. Third, lower federal courts are bound to apply Supreme Court precedents. Fourth, the Supreme Court is a multimember body whose decisions in contested cases are usually decided by the median or "swing" justices. Over time, this helps to keep the Court's work near the center of public opinion.

This combination of internal and external features constrains judicial interpretation in practice far more effectively than any single theory of interpretation ever could; it helps construct which constitutional interpretations are reasonable and available to judges and which are off-the-wall. Equally important, it helps keep judicial decisions in touch with popular understandings of our Constitution's basic commitments, continually translating, shaping, and refining constitutional politics into constitutional law.

Fidelity to the Constitution means applying its text and its principles to our present circumstances, and making use of the entire tradition of opinions and precedents that have sought to vindicate and implement the Constitution. Reasonable people may disagree on what those principles mean and how they should apply. But the larger point about constitutional interpretation remains. We decide these questions by reference to text and principle, applying them to our own time and our own situation, and in this way making the Constitution our own. The conversation between past commitments and present generations is at the heart of constitutional interpretation. That is why we do not face a choice between living constitutionalism and fidelity to the original meaning of the text. They are two sides of the same coin.

2

FRAMEWORK ORIGINALISM

In Chapter 1, I argued that fidelity to the original meaning of the Constitution and living constitutionalism are compatible positions, two sides of the same coin. Although not all versions of originalism and living constitutionalism are compatible, the most intellectually sound versions of each theory are. Recognizing why they are compatible helps us understand how legitimate constitutional change occurs in the American constitutional system. In this chapter I show how fidelity to original meaning promotes a constitution's central purposes: setting up a basic structure for government, making politics possible, and creating a framework for future constitutional construction.

Framework Originalism and Skyscraper Originalism

I begin by contrasting two ideal types of originalism—one I will call framework originalism, and the other skyscraper originalism.[1] As the names imply, these two types of originalism differ in the degree of constitutional construction and implementation that later generations may engage in. Skyscraper originalism views the Constitution as more or less a finished product, albeit always subject to later Article V amendment. It allows ample room for democratic lawmaking to meet future demands of governance; however, this lawmaking is not constitutional construction. It is ordinary law that is permissible within the boundaries of the Constitution. Framework originalism, by contrast, views the Constitution as an initial framework for governance that sets politics in motion and must be filled out over time through constitutional construction. The goal is to get politics started and keep it going (and stable) so that it can solve future problems of governance. Later generations have a lot to do to build up and implement the Constitution, but when they do so they must always remain faithful to the basic framework. Put in terms of Article V, skyscraper originalism views amendment as the only method of building the Constitution; by contrast, framework originalism sees a major role for constitutional construction and implementation by the political branches as well as by the judiciary.

For the same reasons, skyscraper originalism and framework originalism offer different accounts of the democratic legitimacy of constitutional construction. In skyscraper originalism, the political branches do not construct the Constitution; they engage in ordinary politics within its boundaries (unless they self-consciously pursue Article V amendment). Similarly, judicial review is consistent with democracy when and only when it enforces the original bargain laid out in the Constitution and subsequent amendments, and otherwise leaves ordinary politics alone. In framework originalism the story is quite different. The political branches and the judiciary work together to build out the Constitution over time. Their authority to engage in constitutional construction comes from their joint responsiveness to public opinion over long stretches of time while operating within the basic framework. In doing so, they inevitably reflect and respond to changing social demands and changing social mores.

Finally, framework originalism and skyscraper originalism offer contrasting accounts of how to constrain judicial behavior. In skyscraper originalism, judges are constrained when they apply the original constitutional bargain using the proper methodology for ascertaining it; when they fail to do this, they are unconstrained and are simply imposing their own beliefs. Thus skyscraper originalism views following correct interpretive methodology as the central constraint on judges. Framework originalism also requires that judges apply the Constitution's original meaning. But it assumes that this will not be sufficient to decide a wide range of controversies and so judges will have to engage in considerable constitutional construction as well as the elaboration and application of previous constructions. Hence, fidelity to original meaning cannot constrain judicial behavior all by itself. The most important restraints on judges engaged in constitutional construction will come not from following proper interpretive theories but rather from *institutional* constraints. These include the moderating effects of multimember courts, in which the balance of power rests in moderate or swing judges, the screening of candidates through the federal judicial appointments process, social and cultural influences on the judiciary that keep judges attuned to popular opinion, and professional legal culture and professional conceptions of the role of the judiciary.

Let me connect the distinction between framework and skyscraper originalism to the interpretive theory offered in Chapter 1. The method of text and principle holds that interpreters must be faithful to the original meaning of the constitutional text and to the principles that underlie the text. But fidelity to original meaning does not require fidelity to original expected application. Original expected application is merely a resource for deciding how best to apply text and principle. Each generation is charged with the obligation to flesh out and implement text and principle in their own time. They do this through building political institutions, passing legislation, and creating precedents, both judicial and nonjudicial. Thus, the method of text and principle is a version of framework originalism, and it views living constitutionalism as a process of permissible constitutional construction.

I will say more about the idea of a "living Constitution" in Chapters 13 and 14. For the moment, note that my version of living constitutionalism looks different from what most advocates and critics of living constitutionalism have assumed. First, it is primarily a theory about constitutional construction, including what I have called "state-building" constructions. Second, it is primarily addressed not to judges but rather to all citizens. Third, it does not give detailed normative advice about how to decide particular cases but instead explains how constitutional change occurs through interactions between the political branches and the courts; and it endeavors to explain why and to what extent this process is democratically legitimate.

Designers and the Citizens Who Succeed Them

Framework originalism pays attention to the reasons why constitutional designers choose particular types of language. Sometimes drafters choose to express themselves in clear rules, creating hardwired features that are relatively determinate. Sometimes they use standards, and sometimes they articulate principles. These standards and principles can be broad, abstract, or vague. Then we have to implement them through practice, through state building, or through precedents. And sometimes the drafters of a constitution deliberately say nothing at all about a particular issue. Then we must fill in the details where they were silent.

Constitutional drafters use rules because they want to limit discretion; they use standards or principles because they want to channel politics but delegate the details to future generations. They leave things silent for any number of reasons: because certain matters go without saying, because they are implicit in the structure of the constitutional system, because the adopters could not decide among themselves how to resolve a particular issue and therefore handed the problem off to the future, or because the adopters simply wanted to leave space for later generations to design and build institutions appropriate to the situations they would face.

A very familiar argument for constitutionalism is that it seeks to limit future discretion and prevent future generations from making bad decisions or straying from good values. Although some constitutional features have this purpose and effect, I do not believe that this is the best general argument for constitutionalism. Constitutions are designed to create political institutions and to set up the basic elements of future political decisionmaking. Their basic job is not to prevent future decisionmaking but to enable it. The job of a constitution, in short, is to make politics possible. This is why constitutions normally protect rights and create structures.

Both rights protections and structural protections are necessary to construct a workable political sphere and to support a civil society in which politics—and everyday life—can occur. Not every form of politics is equally acceptable; together rights and structure shape social and political relations and the kinds of things that people can do to each other and the duties they owe to one another. Similarly, without some structural or rights protections for institutions of civil society, a decent form of politics is not possible. Moreover, the Constitution's ability to maintain a peaceful and stable politics ultimately depends on civil society and its related institutions; hence the Constitution must do its part to help protect and foster them. Finally, some people, perhaps most, may not want to be actively engaged in political life except perhaps for voting at regular intervals; ordinarily they may not be roused to political action unless they feel that the country has gone seriously wrong or that rights they regard as very important have been violated. A political constitution helps them to live peacefully in civil society with others by requiring the state—and other people—to respect their rights and to act fairly and nonarbitrarily toward them.

From a design perspective, the use of different types of legal norms and silences makes perfect sense. Sometimes designers use rules to set up the basic framework of institutions. They do this not merely to assign roles and tasks or to conclusively limit or grant power. Rather, as the American Constitution imagines, designers might place different parts of the government in competition with each other, producing an indeterminate result. As I will discuss in Chapters 13 and 14, this is how the American system of living constitutionalism works in practice.

Constitution makers from the American Constitution to the present day have also included rights guarantees that use the vague and abstract language of principles. This choice of language makes little sense if the purpose of constitutionalism is to strongly constrain future decision-making. It makes far more sense if the goal is to channel politics, by articulating a collection of key values and commitments that set the terms of political discourse and that future generations must attempt to keep faith with. Abstract rights provisions are valuable even if their contours are not fully determined in advance. They shape the way that political actors understand and articulate the values inherent in the political system; they shape the beliefs of political actors about what they can and cannot do, what they are fighting for and what they are fighting against.

Finally, constitutional silences and open spaces reflect the fact that adopters are not omniscient and cannot prepare for every eventuality. Future generations must build up institutions and practices to make politics and governance possible and successful in changing circumstances; they must adapt as the country faces new problems and new opportunities created by changes in foreign threats, technology, economic conditions, culture, and demographics.

To see how these ideas about constitutional language work in practice, consider the different sections of the Fourteenth Amendment, sent to the states in 1866 and ratified in 1868.[2] Section 1 of the amendment is the most familiar to us today: its first sentence offers a fairly clear and determinate rule for citizenship, which was added at the last minute.[3] But most of section 1 is written in abstract and vague language that employs standards and principles. It speaks of "privileges or immunities of citizens of the United States," "due process of law," and "equal protection of the laws."[4] The reason for this is clear: The framers of the Fourteenth Amendment understood section 1 as a statement of general principles, and they wanted to leave open certain questions—including the tricky questions of racial segregation, miscegenation, and black suffrage—to a later time.[5] They wanted to offer a general statement of principles about the rights of citizens—not limited to questions of black equality—that would no doubt be filled out by courts and especially by Congress, acting under its enforcement powers under section 5.

Congress chose general phrases in section 1 because of the conflicting interests and values of moderates and radicals within the Republican Party and because of concerns about how more specific guarantees of rights for blacks would play in the 1866 elections and the ratification campaign. The Fourteenth Amendment served as the Republicans' platform for the elections of 1866, and "[l]ike all American party platforms, the Republican Platform for 1866 had to be sufficiently ambiguous and broad to attract quite divergent segments of the nation's electorate."[6] Moderates and radicals chose open-ended "language capable of growth"[7] that papered over their differences and allowed them to present a unified front that would appeal to a wide range of constituencies. Moderates could report to their constituents that phrases like "privileges or immunities" and "equal protection" did not require integrated facilities and did not threaten laws against interracial marriage; radicals could point to the broad guarantees of equal citizenship to push for future reforms.[8] By deliberately using language containing broad principles, specific applications would be left to future generations to work out.[9]

With the glittering generalities of section 1 contrast the more rule-bound and hardwired features of sections 2, 3, and 4. Section 2 finesses the problem of black suffrage in a compromise: states that denied black men the right to vote would have a proportionate share of their population uncounted for purposes of calculating representation in the House and in the Electoral College.[10] Section 3 bars former rebels from holding federal and state offices unless Congress, "by a vote of two-thirds of each House, remove[s] such disability."[11] Section 4 guarantees the validity of the debt of the Union and prohibits the government from paying off any of the debt of the Confederacy; it also extinguishes any property claims of former slaveholders.[12]

Why would the very same Congress that used abstract standards and principles in section 1 use such different language in sections 2, 3 and 4? The Fourteenth Amendment was an armistice that set out the new rules of politics following the Civil War. It was truly a "Reconstruction" amendment in every sense of the word. Therefore, it set up relatively clear rules about how to resolve key unsettled issues of the war in sections 2, 3 and 4, while declaring (and thus leaving open for future specification) the scope of the rights protected in section 1.

The Fourteenth Amendment, which is part of our country's second founding, contains in a microcosm the various uses of constitutional language—and the purposes behind them—that exist in most constitutions, including our own. The choice of rules, standards, principles, and silences in this amendment makes sense when we look at it from the perspective of the drafters, who constrained some things and left others open in the hope that politics could flourish in the wake of a devastating Civil War.

So too, the 1787 Constitution is a framework for government responding to the widely acknowledged failures of the Articles of Confederation and the need to confront a panoply of dangers and problems, some foreign and some domestic. It was a blueprint for a "more perfect union"[13] that left much to be worked out in time; and indeed, controversies about how to build out the country's political and governing institutions began at the outset. Within three decades, for example, the new country had to figure out, among other things, whether it had the power to acquire new territory, whether it could spend for the relief of citizens in particular localities rather than the country as a whole, and whether it could create financial institutions like a national bank.[14] In some cases, such as the 1800 election,[15] the blueprint proved inadequate and so new amendments were necessary. Even before this, a declaration of rights, phrased in suitably vague and abstract terms, was the price of ratification.

John McGinnis and Michael Rappaport have recently argued that construing the Constitution according to its original meaning leads to superior consequences because the Constitution was passed according to a supermajority rule. A supermajority rule leads to superior consequences because it requires the concurrence of many different people with many different viewpoints.[16]

In order to take advantage of the superior consequences of laws passed by a supermajority, we must preserve their meaning over time. McGinnis and Rappaport argue that the people who adopt supermajority rules are likely to be risk averse and they would not have agreed to delegate the application of constitutional provisions to future generations.[17] Hence it follows that there can be no strong divergence between original meaning and original expected application.

Contrary to their assumptions, constitutional framers and ratifiers very often use open-ended language that deliberately delegates questions of application to future interpreters; the example of the Fourteenth

Amendment shows us why. Precisely because laws passed by a super-majority must appeal to a broad range of people, framers will sometimes use abstract and general language to paper over disagreements that would emerge if more specific language were chosen. In the alternative, consti-tutional framers will remain silent about particular issues to avoid de-stroying a supermajority coalition.

The 1787 Constitution contains many artful silences and decisions by its framers to agree to disagree. These ambiguities were necessary to its ratification, and as soon as the ink was dry on the document its framers and ratifiers began disagreeing about many of its central features, in-cluding most prominently the scope of powers given to the new federal government. For example, James Madison and Alexander Hamilton, both of whom attended the Federal Convention—and who coauthored the *Federalist Papers*!—immediately began to disagree about Congress's ability to charter a national bank.

McGinnis and Rappaport's assumption that supermajority rules lead to risk-averse adopters who demand fidelity to original expected appli-cations has it almost exactly backward. Supermajority requirements make it so easy to scuttle a proposed amendment that rights guarantees are likely to be framed in broad abstract terms that different parties can read according to their own understandings and expectations. Superma-jority rules, in short, are sometimes more likely to produce delegations to the future—whether through silences or vague abstractions—than rules that require only simple majority support.

In fact, there are several reasons why constitutional drafters might de-liberately choose (and adopters support) open-ended standards in a con-stitution that requires supermajorities to amend. These reasons flow from the purposes for having constitutions in the first place.

Justice Scalia has argued that a constitution's "whole purpose is to prevent change—to embed certain rights in such a manner that future generations cannot readily take them away," because societies may not progress, or mature, but rather "rot."[18] If he is right, then it would be puzzling why so many constitutions—not only the U.S. Constitution, but also most post–World War II constitutions—would contain abstract and relatively open-ended rights guarantees. Of course, this incongruity is why expectation originalists argue that we must interpret these provi-sions, despite their apparent language, to prevent them from being open-ended.[19] Nevertheless, if this feature of constitutional language occurs repeatedly in constitutions in different times and places, we might conclude one of two things: either constitutional drafters and ratifiers are not as risk-averse as McGinnis and Rappaport assume they are, or they think that the best results sometimes come from using abstract principles and standards and leaving difficult issues of application for later generations to decide.

Implicit in Scalia's theory of constitutions as preventing rot is a narrative of decline: because the future may be tempted to stray from the hard-won victories of the past, later generations must be held to the concrete practices and expectations of earlier generations, who, at least by comparison, are more noble and moral.

Something important is missing in this vision, precisely because it cannot explain why constitution makers—not only the Founding Fathers, but most constitutional makers in the two centuries that followed them—would have drafted broad and abstract guarantees of rights and liberties. The widespread adoption of these open-ended rights provisions suggests that Scalia is incorrect about the goals of constitutionalism. The "whole purpose" of constitutions cannot be simply to forestall political judgment by later generations on important issues of justice, to preserve past practices of social custom or judgments of political morality, or to freeze existing assessments of rights in time. To be sure, restricting political judgments on particular questions may be a good explanation for why written constitutions contain many rule-like provisions. But this cannot be the sole purpose of a constitution, much less of all constitutional provisions. Open-ended rights guarantees, and even some structural provisions—like the Tenth Amendment—are stated in terms of standards or abstract principles. These examples suggest that some constitutional provisions may serve a different goal. They are designed to *channel* and *discipline* future political judgment, not forestall it.

There is an important difference between blocking future judgment and disciplining it, between freezing certain results in place and creating channels for future development. In the latter case, we do not necessarily assume that later generations will be either more noble or less noble than existing ones.[20] Rather, we seek to structure future political decisionmaking so that it is most likely to adapt itself to changing circumstances in ways that promote fairness, justice, political stability, and other goods of political union.[21] Even if—like America's own founders—we are optimistic that later generations will progress morally, later generations will still need such disciplining features, and these features may even assist them in achieving progress.

Channeling political judgment, as opposed to freezing moral expectations in time, inevitably delegates important questions of justice and fairness to the future. This is most obvious in the case of structural provisions, which set ground rules for everyday politics and for later state-building activities, and which may employ rules, standards, or principles. But it is also true of rights provisions. These guarantees not only serve structural goals (think about rights of jury service and political participation) but also shape the tradition of future discussion and mobilization about rights.

Structural and rights-protecting features of constitutions channel future judgments about political morality in several ways. First, structural and rights-based provisions help prevent dominant majorities from oppressing diffuse or politically weaker minorities. Federalism and separation of powers are good examples; so too are guarantees of equality and liberty. These elements may range from relatively concrete rules to more general and abstract principles and standards. Rights provisions may have to be open-ended because we do not know what kinds of majorities and minorities will develop over time or what kinds of rights future minorities will need to avoid oppression. Although freedom of political expression and suffrage are central protectors of minority rights, they may not always be sufficient—by definition, minorities are not majorities. In any case, the American Constitution as drafted did not guarantee suffrage as a positive right, and even the Constitution as amended still merely limits certain kinds of restrictions on suffrage.

Other constitutional features—like the system of checks and balances and guarantees of equal treatment, due process, and legal and political accountability—help preserve political stability and keep the enterprise of governance going when people disagree strongly about what is just or unjust. Finally, supermajority requirements on adopting and amending constitutions have an important admonitory function. Rather than preventing the exercise of political judgment, they force majorities to think hard about the consequences of what they want to do, because they and their descendants will have to live with what they put in place for a long time.[22] This keeps majorities from focusing on short-term consequences— which might threaten political stability or have undesirable path-dependent effects—over long-term consequences. It also creates a sort of temporal veil of ignorance. It encourages existing majorities to imagine themselves as potential minorities in the future. It also encourages them to imagine that their descendants may be part of different groups or regions or have different sets of interests and allegiances.

Because constitutions are not designed primarily to prevent moral rot but rather to shape, channel, and discipline future political judgment, it makes perfect sense that constitutions regularly contain open-ended rights provisions. We need not and should not assume that the scope of these provisions must stay close to original expected applications to do their work. Protection of basic rights and basic guarantees of justice may be particularly difficult because new situations continuously arise that the adopting generation cannot foresee. Moreover, our judgments of what is just and unjust are often dependent on surrounding factual assumptions about social, economic, and political life. If those assumptions change, so too will our judgments. The changes may become quite significant over time if constitutional language lasts many years.

Thus, constitution makers may reasonably decide that it is better to adopt language that shapes the future discourse of debates about rights without trying to fully determine everything in advance. In drafting constitutional rights provisions, constitution makers may not do much more than provide a constitutional grammar and vocabulary, a set of basic principles and textual commitments, and a practice of constitutional argument in which people reason about their rights. That is more or less what the American constitutional tradition has produced. In this tradition, the concrete judgments of the framing generation are quite important—in part because they set the tradition in motion and they explain the larger purposes behind guarantees of liberty and equality—but they are not decisive. Later generations have something to add to the understanding of these guarantees through the ways that they understand and apply the textual commitments and principles of earlier generations.[23] A central lesson of constitutional design is that the present cannot control everything that the future may do, and it should not try. Instead it should try to set up a system that both disciplines and nourishes the future without conclusively determining its shape.

A theory of originalism that takes the designer's perspective sees the initial versions of a constitution as primarily a framework for governance, a skeleton on which much will later be built. We look to original meaning to preserve this framework over time, but it does not preclude us from a wide range of possible future constitutional constructions that implement the original meaning and that add new institutional structures, doctrines, precedents, and political practices that are not inconsistent with it. This approach is the essence of framework originalism. In this model of originalism, the Constitution is never finished, and politics and judicial construction are always building up and building out new features.

The contrasting position, which I call skyscraper originalism, assumes that the purpose of the Constitution is to constrain foolish and unwise decisionmaking in the future. The Constitution is a bulwark, largely finished, bequeathed to future generations to prevent them from falling prey to human folly, base motivations, temptation, and decline.[24] The goal is not to create space for institutional growth but to prevent abandonment of basic norms. Given this overarching goal, we should interpret the Constitution to resolve as many of the details as possible, dividing up clearly what is left to the political process and what is not. The Constitution may in fact leave a great deal up to everyday politics; however, absent the use of the amendment process, these political decisions do not add anything significant to the constitutional plan. They occur as permissible activity within the plan.

Skyscraper originalism produces a somewhat different take on what a commitment to "original meaning" requires. For example, it becomes important to turn abstract and vague rights provisions into something as determinate and rule-like as possible. Only then will these provisions properly do their job of constraining unconstitutional action and demarcating the space in which ordinary politics—as opposed to constitution building—may proceed. One way to do this is to identify the original meaning as closely as possible with the original expected application. That way we do not have to leave the scope and application of rights provisions to later generations. Interpreting rights provisions this way may not prevent very much, and it may greatly hamstring the powers of the federal government; but at the very least it will prevent future generations from abandoning the concrete value commitments and expectations of the adopting generation.

Thus, for example, we might decide that the cruel and unusual punishments clause bans only those punishments that the generation of 1791 thought were cruel and unusual. This does not ban very much from our present-day perspective, but it does protect us from a later, crueler time.[25] If it does not aspire to moral improvement, at the very least it prevents moral rot and decay.[26] In the same way, the scope of federal power should be limited to the expectations of the 1787 Constitution. That might prevent a great deal of democratic lawmaking at the federal level—

indeed, it would render unconstitutional most of the modern administrative and welfare state and much federal civil rights protection. But at least it preserves state and local exercises of democracy, and it preserves the sort of freedom that the framers understood and expected.

These two examples suggest why nobody really adheres to skyscraper originalism, at least in its most stringent form. Most originalists today think that there has to be considerable room for development of constitutional powers and rights over time. Sometimes they achieve flexibility through the back door by arguing, as Justice Scalia does, that nonoriginalist precedents are a pragmatic exception to commitment to original meaning.[27] Thus, we accept the New Deal settlement and the vast array of federal regulatory powers to regulate health, safety, the economy, the environment, and civil rights—which are far more extensive than the framers would have dreamed of—because it is simply too late to go back now and people have come to expect that the federal government can exercise these powers.[28] This approach views the state building of the past century as a mistake that we must retain out of a combination of reliance and inertia. But if it is an exception, it is an exception that threatens to swallow the rule of fidelity to original meaning, at least if we construe original meaning in this way.

I think it is far better to see state building during the twentieth century, including both the administrative and welfare state and the civil rights revolution, not as pragmatic exceptions to originalism but as perfectly consistent with it. These are exercises in constitutional construction that have implemented and built out the skeletal system of 1787 and adapted it to contemporary problems of governance. The growth of the modern state fits poorly with skyscraper originalism, which imagines a very different sort of building entirely. It fits well, however, with framework originalism, because the latter assumes that the Constitution was never a completed thing in the first place. It was a plan of government with an initial allocation of powers, rights, and responsibilities that would be built up through collective action and political contestation over time.

It should by now be obvious why framework originalism is consistent with a wide variety of different forms of living constitutionalism, although certainly not with all of them. Framework originalism permits a great deal of contingency in how the Constitution turns out; each of these versions can still be faithful to text and principle. Put another way, framework originalism does not assume that the nature of the Constitution is fully contained in its origins in the way that the structure of an oak is contained in an acorn. It does not assume a determinate path of evolutionary development. Much is left to circumstance and chance, and this nation, like all nations, will face a wide range of unexpected upsets and challenges that will shape and alter its path and its character, sometimes irrevocably.

3

WHY ORIGINAL MEANING?

In Chapters 1 and 2 I argued that fidelity to the Constitution requires, at the very least, fidelity to the original meaning of the constitutional text, and to the choice of rules, standards, and principles stated in the text. The Constitution is a framework for politics on which later constitutional constructions will be built. This framework simultaneously constrains and enables ordinary politics and future constitutional construction.

One can object to my account from two directions: some living constitutionalists may think it is not sufficiently adaptable, and some originalists may think it is not sufficiently fixed. In this chapter, I take up objections from living constitutionalists who see themselves as opponents of originalism. They ask why we have an obligation of fidelity to the original meaning of the text when we interpret the Constitution. They might argue, for example, that the only meanings that should count are contemporary meanings. In the alternative, they might argue that the text is not always binding on later generations.

Before discussing these objections, let me make the positive case for fidelity to original meaning.

The Consequences of a Written Constitution

Constitutional interpretation in the United States requires that we look to original meaning because the American Constitution is a written legal text that constitutes a framework for governance. That is, America has a written Constitution that is also law; this law, in turn, makes possible the creation of the various constructions, institutions, laws, and practices that have grown up around the text and that we might call the Constitution-in-practice.[1] To maintain that framework over time—with its distinctive forms of constraint and delegation—we must preserve the meaning of the words that constitute the framework.

The American Constitution is a written constitution, and it is enforceable law. Both of these facts are worthy of note. Americans did not have to choose a written constitution. The most obvious model in 1787 would have been the British constitution, which consisted largely of customary practices and precedents. In addition, the American Constitution did not have to be enforceable law. It could have been just be a political statement of principles, like the Declaration of Independence. But if we consider the written Constitution to be our law today, certain consequences follow.

Treating the Constitution as our law today means that we adopt its plan for governance as our plan for governance and that we implement and build on it in ways that are consistent with the plan, including any amendments authorized by the plan.[2] Fidelity to the Constitution as law requires that we view ourselves as endeavoring to implement its scheme of governance and make it successful in practice. To do this we must be able to understand what is consistent with the basic framework and what is not consistent with it. This is one of the central tasks of constitutional interpretation.

As a plan for governance, a written Constitution simultaneously constrains and enables politics through a combination of rules, standards, principles, and silences. To stick to the plan and implement it, we must respect its particular choices about freedom and constraint for political actors, about what it decides to determine through writing and what it delegates to the future through writing (or through silence). To respect these choices, we must preserve the legal meaning of the plan over time, because the legal meaning of the plan constructs the particular types of legal norms (rules, standards, and principles) that create these degrees of freedom and constraint, decision and delegation. And to preserve legal meaning over time, we must seek to understand and apply the original meaning of the Constitution in the particular sense that I described in Chapter 1. If we do not attempt to preserve legal meaning over time, then we will not be following the written Constitution as our plan but instead will be following a different plan.

If the law states a directive, rule, or norm that is part of the framework, we must preserve the original meaning to preserve the directive, rule, or norm that the law states. Suppose we did not follow this practice. Then, if the commonly accepted meaning of the words changes over time, the legal effect of the provision will change as well, and it will change not because of any conscious act of lawmaking by anyone in particular but merely because of changes in how language assigns concepts to words.[3]

Let me give a simple example: Article IV, section 4, the guarantee clause, states that "The United States shall guarantee to every State in this Union, a Republican Form of Government, and shall protect each of them against Invasion; and on Application of the Legislature, or of the Executive (when the Legislature cannot be convened), against domestic Violence."[4] In 1787 the words "domestic Violence" generally meant riots or disturbances within a state (as opposed to foreign attack); today the words primarily refer to assaults and batteries by intimates or by persons living in the same household. If we used the contemporary meaning of the guarantee clause rather than its original meaning, the import of the clause would be completely altered. Moreover it would be altered not due to any change in public values, but simply because linguistic usage had changed. Moreover, today the word "Republican"—the word is capitalized in the original text—refers both to representative government and to the Republican Party, founded in 1854. If we were bound by contemporary meaning rather than original meaning, one could argue that the Constitution guarantees each state a "Republican Form of Government"—that is, a government controlled by Republicans.[5]

This example may be fanciful, but it helps us see something important about constitutional interpretation: namely, the kinds of commitments that flow from choosing to structure our government in the form of a written constitution. The words of the guarantee clause impose a duty on the federal and state governments, along with a delegation to work out the contours of the duty to the extent that it employs vague language. Change the concepts and you change the duty; change the duty and you change the framework; change the framework and you are no longer following the same plan for government.

In most cases, of course, the original meaning of the words in the Constitution is the same as their contemporary meaning. The words "equal protection" mean the same today as they did in 1868. But in some cases, for example, like those mentioned above, the original semantic meaning and contemporary semantic meaning differ. (Chapter 8 gives the example of "commerce," which had a broader meaning in 1787 than it does today.) And in some cases the Constitution uses terms of art, like "letters of marque and reprisal," that have fallen out of contemporary usage. These cases show us why preserving legal meaning requires fidelity to original meaning.

It is important to note that my argument for following original meaning assumes that Americans want to be faithful to the written Constitution as law and that we want to continue to accept it as our framework for governance. We do not have to do this, especially if we think that the Constitution is not a good framework for politics—for example, because it has outlived its usefulness—or if we want to accept only parts of it. True, most Americans accept and even venerate their Constitution, but that is a choice, not a requirement. Countries jettison their existing constitutions all the time.[6] Americans could discard their Constitution and adopt a new one, as they did with the Articles of Confederation in 1787. Or they could take parts of the existing Constitution, discard the rest, and build a new Constitution on top of it. These activities might be democratically legitimate. But none of these activities involves fidelity to a written Constitution.

In like fashion, the argument assumes that we are sincere when we say we accept the written Constitution as our framework for governance. But this might also be false. The text might have become merely symbolic or hortatory, more like the Declaration of Independence, although most Americans do not realize it.[7] We Americans might be deluded about our own commitments and practices. We might be clinging to a legitimating myth that obscures inconvenient facts about our system of government.[8] Later on in this chapter I will consider theories that argue that this is the case. For now, however, I will assume that Americans are not insincere or self-deluded when they claim that they have accepted and currently live under a written Constitution.

Interpreting the text of the Constitution does not automatically require that we accept the written Constitution as a plan of governance. You might want to interpret the Constitution in order to decide whether to accept it. You might interpret it to understand its historical or sociological importance or to compare it with other constitutions. But if you seek to adopt it as your Constitution, and carry it out, you have to attempt to be faithful to it, and hence you have to try to interpret it faithfully. That is why, in constitutional interpretation by people who claim to live under the written Constitution as their framework for politics, fidelity is the point of the enterprise. It is the name of the game.

The language of fidelity can make some constitutional theorists a bit nervous. "Fidelity" sounds too much like ancestor worship or dutifully obeying the commands of persons long dead.[9] But interpretation does not require obedience to particular *persons* who lived in the past. Rather, it requires fidelity to the *texts* that we claim to be implementing in the present as our plan of government.

Fidelity to the Constitution means accepting and seeking to follow its plan for government as our plan. Fidelity to original meaning follows from fidelity to a written plan as a framework for politics. That is why I call my position framework originalism. It is the kind of originalism that is required in order to accept and implement a written framework for politics over time.

How to Do Things with Written Constitutions

So far I've argued that accepting written constitutions as law requires preserving the legal meaning of the words in the Constitution over time. Doing this serves important rule-of-law values: predictability, fairness, nonretroactivity, coordination, and the restraint of arbitrary power. These values do not guarantee justice all by themselves—indeed, they may lead us to enforce very bad laws—but they can help make regimes more just than they might otherwise be, and they help contribute to a stable and decent form of political life.

Perhaps more importantly, a written constitution is a plan for conducting politics. The point of a written constitution is to use written words to set out a basic framework for government that simultaneously constrains and enables. It sets out basic norms about what you can and cannot do in governance and in political struggle. It creates basic duties and powers, including the powers to create new institutions that will also shape the contours of politics. A written constitution does this through its choice of rules, standards, principles, and silences. These words help people know the basic rules of politics in advance. They coordinate interactions so that people do not have to decide on the ground rules of political life each time they have a disagreement. They also restrain people from exercising arbitrary power, at least with respect to those constraints outlined by the constitutional text.

Adopters have choices in how they construct plans. Rules, standards, and principles are different kinds of linguistic regulations of political action. They have different effects in a plan and create different degrees of constraint and delegation.

Within the category of rules, for example, the Constitution sometimes contains default rules rather than mandatory rules; these rules are partial delegations. For example, the Twentieth Amendment states when Congress meets unless it specifies a different time.

Sometimes it is difficult to produce a rule to cover a wide variety of future situations, and so a standard or principle must do. Thus, choosing a standard or principle normally means that adopters are delegating the task of application to later generations.

Nevertheless, there are many different kinds of standards and principles. If adopters cannot use hardwired rules but do not want to delegate so much to future generations, they can choose *historical* principles or *historical* standards. These are standards and principles that require application according to a historical test stated in the text. For example, adopters can choose language like "Congress shall make no law abridging the freedom of speech as understood at time of the adoption of this Constitution" or "as secured by the common law at the time of adoption of this Constitution." Adopters could choose language that ties applications to a particular point in time, such as "No state shall deny to any person within its jurisdiction the equal protection of the laws according to the understandings of 1868."

Using language to create historical standards and principles creates a distinctive type of constraint and delegation for future politics that is different from other kinds of standards and principles. To be faithful to such a norm, later generations must ask how a principle or standard would apply according to the understandings of a previous time. It is not difficult to write historical tests like these into law. Generally speaking, however, the U.S. Constitution does not use this type of language. And this fact is quite important to constitutional construction today.

A written constitution also constrains and enables politics through the institutions that its words help set up; these institutions then create their own political powers and constraints, further shaping the possibilities of political action. For example, the U.S. Constitution sets up different branches of the federal government that coordinate and compete, and it creates a system of regular elections in which actors can gain and lose political power. These institutional features create the political playing field; they give actions certain meanings, and they shape political actors' expectations about what is politically possible and what political actors believe they can do legitimately or without sanction. Moreover, the constitutional system allows for institutional evolution—for example, through constitutional construction—well beyond what the constitutional text itself mentions. Examples include the creation of political parties, framework statutes, administrative agencies, and the national security state. These institutional developments also shape, constrain, and enable certain forms of political action and help create political meanings.

All constitutions, whether written or unwritten, create institutional constraints, which simultaneously regulate and enable various forms of political activity. A written constitution is distinctive because it contains two kinds of constraints: institutional constraints and linguistic constraints found in the constitutional text. Thus, written constitutions regulate, constrain, and enable politics in two ways: through the choice of constitutional language and through the institutions, practices, and traditions that are built around this language. Moreover, these forms of regulation may compensate for and buttress each other. Some things that appear to be relatively unconstrained by constitutional language may nevertheless be constrained in practice by institutions as they have developed over time.

Dead Hands and Delegations

Living constitutionalists might insist that we should interpret the Constitution according to its contemporary meaning because they fear that interpreting the Constitution according to its original meaning will bind present generations to the dead hand of the past. The democratic legitimacy of the Constitution depends on its acceptance by the current generation and the fact that it both reflects and accommodates the current generation's values. But the people who drafted and adopted the Constitution and most of its amendments lived long ago, and no one in the present generation was able to participate. The values and assumptions of past generations may be very different from our own, including their views about liberty, equality, and democracy, and their expectations about the proper functions and responsibilities of government. If we interpret the Constitution according to its original meaning, the argument goes, it will drastically limit the kind of laws that Congress can pass—including many important federal labor, environmental, and civil rights laws—and it will allow both the states and the federal government to violate a panoply of rights that Americans now regard as constitutionally protected and as central to democratic citizenship. In short, living constitutionalists worry that the dead hand of the past wrongfully limits contemporary democracy and allows majorities to run roughshod over important rights.

I believe that this "dead hand" argument for contemporary meaning rests on a subtle confusion. When people argue that we should look to today's meaning rather than to original meaning, they usually do not have in mind the rule-like clauses of the Constitution. Many constitutional provisions are stated in relatively precise rules. There are only two houses of Congress, each state gets two senators, the president can veto legislation when it is presented to him, the president's term lasts only four years, and the president cannot be elected to more than two full terms. In addition, when no candidate for president wins a majority of the Electoral College, the election is thrown into the House of Representatives, where each state gets one vote; in similar circumstances the vice presidency is determined by the Senate.

Most living constitutionalists do not object to following these "hardwired" features of the Constitution, and they are usually happy to apply them according to their original meanings, which in most cases are the same as their contemporary meanings. But the dead-hand objection applies equally to these hardwired provisions. Almost all of these provisions were adopted long ago by people in a very different world with very different values. Yet these provisions continue to limit what contemporary majorities can do, and in some cases they can have very bad effects.[10] Indeed, because of the relative precision of their language, these rules represent a far more powerful dead hand of the past than other parts of the Constitution.

Nevertheless, most people—including most living constitutionalists—accept these structural features of the Constitution as stating relatively precise rules that we must follow today, even if we think them unjust or unwise. So the dead-hand objection, at least as I stated it previously, proves too much. Taken to its logical conclusion, the dead-hand objection is an argument against having any constitutions (or indeed, any laws) that last more than a generation. This is a point that Thomas Jefferson famously made,[11] but it is not really the living constitutionalist objection.

When living constitutionalists raise the dead-hand objection to originalist interpretation, they usually have in mind the interpretation of abstract or vague phrases of the Constitution: "due process," "equal protection," "cruel and unusual punishments," and "freedom of speech." What they object to is being limited by the original *expected application* of these abstract terms and vague clauses. In practice, then, the dead-hand objection is not directed against original meaning—it is directed against original expected application. Once that distinction is accepted, living constitutionalists have very little reason to object to being framework originalists.

In fact, we can restate the living constitutionalist's objection in a way that makes it perfectly consistent with framework originalism. Where the original meaning of the text states a clear, unambiguous rule, we apply the rule because that is what the text offers us. But where the original meaning of the text offers us a standard or a principle, we should not necessarily be bound by how the people who adopted the text would have applied it. The reason for this, however, is not a general objection to the dead hand of the past. Rather, it is that, by offering a standard or principle, the constitutional text constrains and regulates politics *in a different way* than it does when it offers a hardwired rule. Standards and principles channel political decisionmaking without foreclosing it. They force people to justify their actions by reference to the standards and principles, but they do not constrain people in the same way that rules do. To coin a phrase, they are a different linguistic technology of regulation and constraint.

The choice of rules, standards, and principles is a choice in the constitutional plan about what to settle at the time of adoption and what to delegate to future construction. We are certainly permitted to look to original expected applications in constructing doctrines and institutions. But when we insist that we may not make our own judgments about these matters but may only apply the original expected application, we are confusing the plan with our own choices. We may claim that we are being especially faithful to the constitutional plan when we do this, but in fact we are treating standards and principles as if they were rules. We should accept political responsibility for *that* choice, and not try to blame the imposition of our values on the founders.

My restatement of the living constitutionalist concern is not an argument against constitutionalism or against the dead hand of the past in general. It is perfectly consistent with fidelity to an old constitution. Rather, it is an argument for taking seriously the Constitution's choice of rules, principles, standards, and silences. It is an argument against the imposition of a dead hand of the past that is not required or authorized by the Constitution itself. In fact, when we adhere to the Constitution's original meaning, and to the Constitution's own choices of rules, standards, and principles, we will inevitably interpret the Constitution according to contemporary "meaning" in the sense of contemporary *applications*

and contemporary *constructions*. If the original meaning of the text requires "equal protection of the laws," then we enforce that guarantee
today because the text continues to require it, just as the text continues to
require that the president must be thirty-five years old. How we apply the
principles of equal protection, however, may well be different from what
people expected in 1868, based in part on our contemporary understandings and a history of previous constitutional constructions. As a result,
vague and abstract clauses will likely reflect contemporary understandings rather than original understandings. That is the difference between
applying rules and applying principles or standards in changed circumstances, and it is consistent with the preservation of the original semantic
meaning of enacted laws over time.

One might object: Can principles really exist apart from their expected applications? Not only is this possible, it is precisely what makes
them *principles* rather a rule, a historical test (apply the words as they
would have been applied in 1791), or a laundry list of concrete expectations. Principles are norms that are normally indeterminate in reach,
that do not determine the scope of their own extension, that may apply
differently given changing circumstances, and that can be balanced against
other competing considerations. Although the persuasive power of principles may originate from how we expect they will apply when we argue for
them, their jurisdiction, their scope, their weight, and the kinds of practices
they regulate can shift over time.[12]

Historians will correctly point out that to do serious intellectual history one must understand how vague and abstract concepts were used in
their own time for particular, specific purposes, and in the context of particular, specific disputes.[13] So, for example, the principles of "freedom of
speech" in late eighteenth-century thought and of "equal protection of
the laws" in the mid-nineteenth century are inevitably embedded in a set
of expectations and assumptions about social life and political action.
For purposes of good intellectual history, then, one may not be able to
separate historical principles from their expected applications in the politics of the day. But the goals of legal interpretation are different from the
goals of intellectual history. In the study of history we are trying to uncover a world that is no longer our own, and its distinctive values, assumptions, struggles, and disputes. In legal interpretation we are trying
to understand the legal norms produced by some people for other people
who may live many years later in a completely different political and social context. That is because laws are made not only for people who

share the historical world of the adopters, but also for those who will not share that world. They are plans for social action in the future as well as in the present.[14] If we, living in the present, choose to follow these plans, we must try to figure out what degree of constraint and freedom, fixation and delegation the adopters have generated in the words they have chosen, because we know that these words will have to be applied in quite different situations.

Thus, in constitutional interpretation—in the limited sense of ascertainment of constitutional meaning—we are interested in history as it relates to this specific question. First, we want to know the generally recognized semantic meanings of words used in the Constitution, and the implications that flowed from the grammatical usage and sentence structure in the text.[15] Second, we want to know if the language uses generally recognized terms of art, and what those terms of art meant at the time. Third, we want to know whether the text is silent on a particular matter, or offers us a rule, a standard, or a principle. This may appear obvious from the face of the text, but further historical research may alter our initial assumptions.

These historical inquiries help us understand the degrees of freedom and constraint that the framework contemplates. This, of course, does not exhaust our interest in history. History is also important for the task of constitutional construction—and here we are interested in not only the history around the time of adoption, but also the history of successive constructions offered after adoption, and the tradition of claims made on the Constitution.

One might object that we should not have to make even these modest historical inquiries to determine original meaning. It should not matter whether the people who adopted the text believed that they chose a rule instead of a principle. What matters is whether people living today think that the constitutional text should state a rule or a principle. Similarly, what matters is our choice today about whether the text contains a nonliteral usage. Fidelity to the adopters' choices about language is simply another way of chaining ourselves to original expected application. It binds us to the adopters' expectations about whether the text states a rule or a principle, and whether it offers literal or nonliteral uses of language. Indeed, it is really binding us to their original intentions; in this case, whether they intended to use a rule, a standard, or a principle, and whether they intended to use literal or nonliteral language.

If we do not have to respect original expected applications, the argument goes, we should not have to respect the adopters' choice of rules, standards, and principles either. We have no obligation to be constrained by the language of the text in the way that the adopters planned for us to be constrained. If the Constitution gains its legitimacy from present-day acceptance, we should be able to decide what kinds of constraints the text contains.

Under this account, it is up to the present generation to decide that the age requirement of thirty-five years for the president, and the four-year presidential term, although superficially resembling hardwired rules, should be treated as a standard or a principle, or as involving nonliteral usages. We do this not out of a good-faith belief that this was the adopters' choice, but simply because we prefer linguistic constraints that are more flexible.

It is certainly possible to imagine this approach to using constitutional texts. But this approach is not consistent with framework originalism, because it does not take a basic feature of the framework seriously—the adopters' choices of how to constrain and delegate through language. We could also adopt a convention that every third word in the constitutional text can be discarded or modified, but this does not make the resulting practice an attempt at faithful interpretation of the basic framework. (That might be so, however, if we believed that the text was written in a special code that was *designed* to be read this way, but then we are basing our claim of fidelity on a set of presumed expectations or intentions about how the text is supposed to work.)[16]

Fidelity to a written constitution requires at the most basic level that we see the constitutional text as our plan for political conduct, so that, for purposes of interpretation, we adopt the plan as our own plan and try to further it. Hence, fidelity to a written constitution requires that we do our best to respect the text's allocation of freedom and constraint for future constitutional construction, and thus its particular allocation of trust and distrust with respect to later generations.[17] To figure out that allocation, we ask how language was generally and publicly used when the text was adopted, and we use the lawyer's traditional toolkit of modalities to make sense of the plan and resolve ambiguities, contradictions, or absurdities.

When we engage in this inquiry, we *are* interested in both the expectations and the intentions of the adopters, but of a very particular sort. We are interested in the expectations and intentions that adopters had about their choice of linguistic technologies of freedom and constraint; we are interested in the economy of trust and distrust they created through their choice of publicly available language. The reason we are interested in these expectations and intentions is that they help us understand the nature of the written plan that we, in the present, have accepted as our own. The original expected applications of abstract concepts like "equal protection," by contrast, are not part of the plan, and therefore we do not have to accept them to accept the plan, although we are certainly entitled to use them in forming constructions. Because those expectations and intentions do not form part of the plan, they are not necessarily binding on us.

Of course, it is always possible that adopters had no subjective intentions about their use of different kinds of language. Perhaps they did not think very deeply or at all about why they used rule-like and principle-like language, why they were completely silent about certain issues, and whether they used language in a literal or nonliteral sense. Consider, for example, the progress clause of Article I, section 8, which gives Congress the power to grant copyrights and patents for "writings and discoveries." The adopters may never have considered whether the word *writings* was a synecdoche, so that Congress could create copyrights for maps and charts, as the first copyright statute of 1790 provides. In that case, we must try in good faith to *ascribe* an economy of freedom and constraint, trust and distrust, from the text we have been handed, using the familiar modalities of legal argument. But we cannot begin to engage in that good-faith ascription without paying attention to historical usage where it is available to us.[18]

Reflection may alter our initial judgments of the text's economy of freedom and constraint. Take the example of the compact clause of Article I, section 10, which provides that "[n]o State shall, without the Consent of Congress . . . enter into any Agreement or Compact with another State." The language seems to state a ban on all agreements between states without congressional consent. But such a rule, Justice Field once explained, would be unwieldy, if not absurd; it would require Congress to pass on administrative or ministerial arrangements between states in which the federal government has no interest, and that pose no danger to the federal union.

Field gives the example of Massachusetts asking New York to ship an exhibit for the Chicago World's Fair along the Erie Canal, or two states deciding jointly to drain a swamp that extends across their borders to prevent disease.[19] (Another example might be Kansas and Missouri agreeing to create a trophy for the winner of the annual football game between the KU Jayhawks and the MU Tigers.) Requiring congressional consent to these agreements would make no sense. Accordingly, the Supreme Court has always treated the compact clause as stating a principle. Using the familiar lawyer's phrase, it has asked whether an arrangement is an agreement or compact "within the meaning of" the compact clause, and held that the clause prevents combinations that increase the power of the states at the expense of the supremacy of the federal government.[20] Note that in this example Justice Field and later interpreters did not understand their task as rewriting the Constitution or ignoring the linguistic constraints in the text. Rather, they sought to understand the point of the text in order to decide what kind of constraint it creates. Treating the text as a hardwired rule was absurd; therefore they assumed that the text was ambiguous and required construction. Whether or not one agrees with this decision, it is an attempt to be faithful to the framework.[21]

Compare this example with Article I, section 3's requirement of two senators for each state.[22] We have no historical evidence that a principle—say one of "adequate state representation"—rather than a rule was intended, or that the language was intended nonliterally as a metonym or synecdoche. Indeed, what evidence we have of the political compromise between the large and small states necessary to create the Union points in the opposite direction. Nor does the passage of the Seventeenth Amendment—which makes the Senate the representative of the people rather than of state legislatures—alter our assessment of whether the text states a rule, standard, or principle. If we compare the text of Article I, section 3 with other parts of the Constitution, we discover that Article V specifically states that no amendment may deny a state's equal suffrage in the Senate without its consent (which, in effect, requires unanimous consent). This seems to suggest that Article I, section 3, was a deliberate choice to limit decisionmaking by future generations through a rule (indeed, a specially entrenched rule), rather than a decision to provide a more flexible principle or standard for future construction.[23]

Often we cannot know for certain what adopters believed or intended about various aspects of the Constitution, for not only are they long dead and unable to speak to us, but there were many adopters and their subjective intentions may be various and at odds with one another. That is one reason, as I note in Chapter 6, why most contemporary originalists rather quickly moved from a theory of original intention to a theory of original public meaning. Inevitably we must, given the text bequeathed to us, and the evidence available to us, ascribe a set of purposes to the text, including its particular economy of delegation and constraint. But we can make this ascription in two different ways. First, we can accept the adopters' Constitution as our Constitution, their plan as our plan, and thus endeavor to be faithful to it, viewing ourselves as part of a transgenerational project, a project, as the Preamble says, of forming a "more perfect Union." Second, we can regard the ascription of purpose as wholly fictional. It is really a mirror of our own present purposes, in which we do not identify with the adopters' particular plan, but rather use their words, like a ventriloquist's dummy, as a mouthpiece for the particular set of constraints and delegations that we presently desire. The first approach attempts to be faithful to a preexisting plan of political action; the second does not. The second approach uses an ancient text for present political purposes. It may even be a legitimate use of the text in a particular society or cultural tradition. I do not believe, however, that it adequately describes the best account of our own practices of constitutional interpretation and construction.

Why Be Faithful to the Text?

One way to avoid the arguments I have presented is to deny that the written Constitution still forms the basic framework for politics in the United States on which subsequent constructions have been built. Perhaps the text appears to be still in force but actually it is not, or parts of it are not. Perhaps the additions and supplementations I have called constructions actually are the real Constitution, and the written text (or parts of it) have been silently overruled or are now mere surplusage.

This argument would be especially powerful if a substantial portion of our existing doctrines and institutions—what I call the Constitution-in-practice—were not consistent with the basic framework: the written text interpreted according to its original meaning. Some living constitutionalists may believe (or at least worry) that this is so. As I shall argue in this book, however, most examples of inconsistency with original meaning that people might offer are not genuine, once we understand framework originalism and its distinction between original meaning and original expected application. And in some cases, certain constitutional constructions are actually better justified under the original meaning of different clauses than the ones the courts currently employ. (For example, I shall argue that the Fourteenth Amendment applies the Bill of Rights to the states under the privileges or immunities clause rather than the due process clause.)

Although most Americans believe that the written Constitution as it has been amended from time to time is still their fundamental law, this may in fact be an illusion. The burden of proof, however, should fall on those who contend that the belief is false, simply because that contention conflicts with basic and commonsense understandings of our political order. There is another reason as well, especially if one believes that the Constitution aims to achieve a liberal society. Jeremy Waldron, following John Rawls, has called this the liberal principle of publicity: "People should not be under any misapprehension about how their society is organized, and the legitimacy of our legal and political institutions should not depend on such misapprehensions."[24] If Americans—and, indeed, most lawyers and judges—are deluded about the legal status of their written Constitution, this undermines the legitimacy of the kind of Constitution they actually do have.

David Strauss has made the best-known case against fidelity to a written Constitution. He has argued that despite appearances, the United States actually has a common law constitution comprised largely of judicial and nonjudicial precedents.[25] We follow these precedents, which have developed in a case-by-case fashion, for two reasons: First, they reflect the accumulated wisdom of many individuals—which is likely to be superior to the judgment of any individual today—and second, precedents can slowly evolve over time, incorporating new ideas and new values, and adjusting gradually to changing conditions.

For these reasons, Strauss denies that the text is an authoritative command or political decision made in the past to which we owe any duty of fidelity or obedience. The text merely serves as a focal point for political activity around which people can usefully coordinate their activities.

Strauss also denies that the text binds us today because we are part of a transgenerational American people. Saying that we are the same "We the People" that adopted the Constitution is merely a metaphor, and not everyone living today accepts that metaphor, which Strauss thinks smacks of mysticism. Many Americans today may feel no loyalty to past generations to whom they may have no relation or connection. Being an American, he argues, should not require a quasi-religious belief in the unity of the American people over time or a "quasi-ethnic American identity" that necessarily carries obligations of fidelity to past generations.[26] Rather, we adhere to the text out of present considerations of cost and convenience—because "despite its drawbacks, [it] is on balance a good thing to do because it resolves issues that have to be resolved one way or the other."[27]

The constitutional text solves problems of coordination by providing a "common ground" for politics "among people who would otherwise disagree."[28] Sometimes "it is more important that things be settled than that they be settled right. A legal provision can settle things, and sometimes the importance of settlement alone is enough to make the provision binding."[29] However, "[t]he binding force of the provision rests on its functional ability to settle disputes, and not at all on whether the entity that enacted the provision is entitled to obedience or 'fidelity.'"[30] Requiring people to accept the text also serves basic norms of fairness, because people should not be allowed to benefit from a system of political cooperation that they are unwilling to accept for themselves. In addition, if politicians could ignore the text with impunity, others will be tempted to do so in future situations, undermining the benefits of political cooperation organized around the text.[31] In any case, Strauss argues, the constitutional text rarely matters in most important constitutional litigation and in many respects it is actually irrelevant to the development of constitutional doctrine.[32] The real Constitution, he argues, is the system of precedents and doctrines that develop in common law fashion.

Several of Strauss's arguments for why we should follow the text are fully consistent with framework originalism. One reason why adopters choose hardwired rules is that they constrain power and settle some (but not all) of the basic rules of politics. Moreover, although Strauss does not emphasize this, the presence of standards and principles in the text channels public understanding and discussion about the rights of citizens and the powers of government. Finally, fidelity to the original meaning of the text serves rule-of-law norms of predictability and fairness, although, as Strauss would no doubt point out, fidelity to any generally agreed-upon set of meanings might do just as well.

The differences from framework originalism, however, are just as important as the similarities: Strauss denies that the text is a framework or plan that we currently attempt to follow. He denies that we owe any duty of fidelity to the text simply because it was created long ago. We do so instead out of a need for stability and convenience. The real Constitution consists of precedents that can be adjusted over time through common law techniques.

Strauss's distinction between text and precedent is not as clear-cut as one might at first imagine. Precedents might reflect not the accumulated wisdom of many people but only the wisdom of a small group of judges at a particular time in the past. That is because once a court decides a precedent, later courts often follow it without re-debating its original justification. That is part of what it means to follow a decision as a precedent. Precedents do the most work in legal decisionmaking when we do not ask whether they are the best solution to a problem. For if they were the best solution, we should adopt their substantive rules because they are the best rules, not because they are precedents.

Moreover, as Strauss himself notes, if we really wanted to accumulate the wisdom of people in situations similar to our own, we would not look to old American cases for guidance. We would look to contemporaneous decisions by courts in countries most similar to our own, like Canada.[33] But however "recent and relevant" Canadian law might be, "it does not have the precedential effect of even a distant American decision."[34] In fact, much of the reason why we follow precedents of American courts is conventionalist—these precedents also settle things that need to be settled and thus they also serve as a focal point for political action. Famous cases like *McCulloch v. Maryland,* for example, have articulated the scope of federal authority as much as the constitutional text. Indeed, judicial precedents function like constitutional texts in settling contested questions and coordinating political activity because they are also texts and because they also have the force of law.

Thus, a major problem with Strauss's account is that his arguments about the need for settlement and focal points do not really distinguish the text from judicial precedents, which can be altered through common law decisionmaking. One might equally say of precedents what Strauss says of the text—that it is better that they be decided than that they be decided correctly. But if so, why shouldn't our views about the binding force of precedents (including precedents that announce clear-cut rules) be the same as our views about the binding force of the constitutional text, including such hardwired rules as the length of the president's term, the number of houses of Congress, and so on?

That equivalence works in both directions. If we decide that the length of the president's term must remain four years because the text settles the question, whether or not that is a good idea, why isn't the same true of an old precedent like the 1896 decision in *Plessy v. Ferguson,* which held that "separate but equal facilities" for different races do not violate the Constitution? Even if *Plessy* is not the wisest decision, it settles a contentious issue by offering a relatively clear rule. We cannot say that *Plessy* deserves less respect because it is very unfair, for that can also be true of the constitutional text: think of various provisions of the antebellum text that accommodated slavery.

Conversely, if we think that a long-standing precedent like *Plessy* can be overturned or modified on a sufficient showing to a court that it has outlived its usefulness as a settled decision and now creates significant problems or imposes very serious injustices, why couldn't we say the same thing of the limitation on presidential terms, the presidential veto, the malapportionment of the Senate, the Electoral College, and so on? Why couldn't the Supreme Court decide, for example, that a president can serve a longer term in office than four years because the country needs him? Why couldn't it apply its equal protection precedents to require that the Senate be proportionate to population?

Once we recognize that precedents are focal points too, the focal-point theory does not really explain why courts cannot change the hard-wired rules of the Constitution through common law adjudication. Note that Strauss contends that we follow texts because they serve as a focal point (but not because they are necessarily wise or because we owe any fidelity to past decisions) but that we follow precedents because they are a focal point *and* because they represent accumulated wisdom. If so, it would seem that it should be *easier* to change constitutional texts by judicial decision than to alter previous precedents.

It is true that changes to textual rules could disrupt politics and unsettle expectations. But that is also true of changes to the many rules that appear in judicial precedents. (Voting rights decisions are one example.) In both cases, the presence of a court announcing the new law for all parties minimizes the disruptive effect to politics by announcing a new focal point for political action.

Obviously, one reason why courts might avoid overruling the hard-wired elements of the constitutional text is that they might appear to lack legitimacy in doing so. That, in turn, might cause needless political disruption and might undermine the ability of both texts *and* precedents to serve as focal points. But this simply raises the deeper question of why the public and politicians alike assume that we should not be able to change the constitutional text by common law methods of judicial decision. This is the question of why the text stands on a different and prior footing than judicial decisions.

That question leads us to still deeper issues. The common-law/focal-point approach offers no obvious connection between the law Americans live under and popular sovereignty. The text is not binding because we (or our political predecessors) adopted it as law; it is binding because it currently and conveniently settles an issue that might otherwise disrupt politics. Thus, the text could be any text produced by anyone, as long as Americans find it useful to settle matters. It could be the French constitution or the Turkish constitution. Strauss himself gives the example of how ancient Roman law served as a focal point in Europe.[35] Similarly, Strauss offers no account of why judicial decisionmaking—which, in his view, makes up most of the Constitution—has any connection to popular sovereignty. Judges are professional elites, and the precedents of previous judges are the decisions of past elites. They are not engaged in constitutional construction that implements a written plan adopted by We the People; rather they are creating the Constitution through familiar common law methods.

Framework originalism, by contrast, directly connects the reason why we follow the text as our law to past exercises of popular sovereignty. Past acts of popular sovereignty create a framework—the written Constitution—that further acts implement. Constitutional constructions are either acts of the political branches or they are in the long run responsive to popular will because of institutional features that shape and constrain federal court decisions. Chapters 13 and 14 explain these features of constitutional construction in more detail. In any case, constructions are not isolated from an otherwise irrelevant or inert text—they exist to fill out and implement the text.

In framework originalism, then, popular sovereignty is not only central to the creation of the written framework, it also underwrites the constructions built on top of the framework that flesh it out over time. This is as true of judicial constructions as it is of constructions by the political branches. Courts have neither the first word nor the last word on the interpretation of the Constitution. Instead, courts work in the middle of a long process of shaping and modifying constitutional constructions; both public protest and public acceptance of court decisions are crucial to the development of constitutional doctrine in the United States. Thus, in framework originalism, precedents do more than accumulate wisdom or settle disputes: they also respond to popular values and attitudes over time.

The generation that builds the framework soon passes away, but what they leave behind is law. Constitutional constructions develop in the legal space created by the framework. The generations that create them also pass away, and they, too, leave behind law. The people who exercised their sovereignty in the past are not the same people who are living today under the Constitution. Nevertheless, in the American system laws continue in force over time until they are repealed or amended. That is why even statutes passed many generations ago are still law today. To be sure, the continuation of law over time is not necessary to the conception of law. One could have a legal system with a generally recognized metarule that all statutes expire after fifty year's time. (Presumably, the metarule would not apply to itself.) But we do not have such a metarule for statutes in the United States.[36] One can also pass statutes that sunset after a certain specified number of years. But with one important exception, our Constitution does not have such a sunset provision. That exception is the migration or importation clause of Article I, section 9, which expired in 1808. It prevented Congress from banning the international trade of slaves for the Constitution's first two decades. The exception is important because it shows that a written Constitution can be designed with sunset provisions.

In sum, the initial authority of the text comes from the fact that it was created through successive acts of popular sovereignty, and the text continues in force today because it is law. The authority of constitutional constructions, in turn, comes from their direct or long-run responsiveness to popular will as expressed through the processes of democratic politics. Constitutional constructions continue in force today because they are also law. Continuing to view the written framework as our law today means that we continue accept its plan as our plan and we continue to seek to further it in our own time. Indeed, we build constructions on the assumption that the plan remains our law and that these constructions implement and further it.

The focal-point theory is deficient in a second way: Constitutional texts serve important functions in politics beyond being a focal point for coordination or objects of political convenience. The text is simultaneously something to build on and something to make claims on. It is something to further and something to redeem. Indeed, these two ideas are intimately related.

Because Americans have a relatively brief, written Constitution, publicly available for all to read, quote, and argue about, they regularly call on the Constitution to justify their actions in politics. This feature is deeply rooted in American political culture. As Reva Siegel has pointed out, throughout American history the public has used the constitutional text to make claims on public officials about what the Constitution means and how it should be interpreted and applied.[37] Calling on the text gives ordinary citizens, whether individually or as part of political and social movements, a sense that their views about the Constitution are just as valuable and important as those of past generations or of present-day judges and public officials.

Even more important, the ability to make claims on the text gives ordinary citizens a sense of ownership and investment in the Constitution. When citizens make claims on the text, they are asserting that it is *their* Constitution, that their opinion of its meaning counts, and that they have the right to disagree with and talk back to courts and other government officials who claim to govern in their name and the Constitution's name.[38]

The focal-point/common-law theory of the Constitution cannot comprehend this feature of our constitutional system, because a focal point is an instrument for settlement and minimization of costs, not a deep source of political meaning or political commitment. A focal point is a mere *modus vivendi*. It is not a plan for politics that people can imagine themselves as furthering over time. It is not a promise to be redeemed, or a set of principles that must be restored or fulfilled. The focal-point theory can make no sense of this aspect of the text because it begins with the assumption that the real Constitution is not the text—the precedents are. Instead, as Strauss explains, under the focal-point theory the text, if it matters at all in constitutional disputes, "serves approximately the same role as an old precedent."[39] When we modify precedents or overrule them, Strauss contends, we are not "jettisoning 'mere precedent' in favor of 'the Constitution.'" We are not returning to a text written by a long-dead generation; we are substituting one policy for another we think is better.[40]

Because the focal-point theory does not take the text seriously as a plan, Strauss tends to run together two quite different ideas: The first is fidelity to *people*—a group of long-dead framers. The second is fidelity to a constitutional *plan*. One can deny that we owe any duty or fidelity to particular people who are long dead and still have fidelity to a plan for government initially begun by those people. That is, we should not confuse ancestor worship or filial piety with a commitment to working out a plan of government.

In like fashion, Strauss runs together two other ideas: The first is that there is a transgenerational unity of the American people (which he rejects as tantamount to a quasi-ethnic identity) or a transgenerational American tradition (which he argues Americans do not have to identify with).[41] The second is that there is a transgenerational *project* of maintaining a Constitution that different generations of Americans participate in. Even if one doubts that the American people are a single cross-generational entity, one might still conclude that the American Constitution is a project that inevitably will span many generations.[42]

To be sure, many Americans do understand themselves to be part of the same "We the People" as the founders. But one can believe this quite sensibly without any mystical assumptions about peoplehood, any quasi-ethnic sense of national identity, or any requirements of biological connection to past Americans. One merely has to believe that what makes one a member of We the People and a part of the American constitutional tradition is acceptance of and commitment to realizing the American plan for self-government.

If one defines "We the People" as those who accept the Constitution as their plan for government and seek to fulfill it over time in ever-changing circumstances, then We the People surely do exist over time, because carrying out the plan requires the participation of many generations. People can easily identify with those before and after them as participants in a shared project or plan that extends over time. In this case, it is a plan of self-government that successive generations of Americans are working out. To regard myself as part of the same "We the People" as James Madison and a twenty-fifth-century person who will not be born for centuries, I do not have to assume any biological, ethnic, or mystical connections. All I need do is understand the three of us as working on a common project of self-governance.

Thus, fidelity to the Constitution requires fidelity to a plan for self-government built on a written legal framework that continues over time. Commitment to the plan and to the continuation of the legal framework does not require belief in a quasi-ethnic American identity or a mystical connection to long-dead ancestors (who may not be our ancestors in any case). It does not require ancestor worship or filial piety. Nevertheless, as I explain in the next two chapters, it does require an attitude of attachment to the project, and a belief that the project is worth taking on and continuing. Fidelity, I shall argue, is a matter of faith—belief that the Constitution is worth preserving despite its faults, and that even if the Constitution-in-practice permits serious injustices in the present, our commitment to the plan will be redeemed in the future.

4

BASIC LAW, HIGHER LAW, OUR LAW

Three Ways of Looking at a Constitution

A successful constitution like America's must serve many different and overlapping functions. For convenience, I divide them into three categories: A constitution like America's must simultaneously work as *basic law*, as *higher law*, and as *our law*.

By *basic law* I mean that the Constitution sets up a basic framework of government that promotes political stability and allocates rights, duties, powers, and responsibilities. It sets up a plan for ordering political life and offers ways of implementing, expanding, or modifying the plan over time. A constitution also serves as basic law in the sense that it is foundational law (or supreme law) that trumps other law to the contrary. To operate effectively as basic law, a constitution does not have to be just. But it must preserve political stability and channel political and legal decisionmaking so that the governmental system can sustain itself over time.

The American Constitution is far more than basic law in this sense. Americans also view their Constitution as a source of important values, including justice, equality, democracy, and human rights. They view the Constitution's guarantees as objects of aspiration; the Constitution either offers or refers to a standard that stands above ordinary law, criticizes it, restrains it, and holds it to account. Fidelity to the Constitution requires that we aspire to something better and more just than the political, social, and legal arrangements we currently maintain. Hence, the Constitution trumps ordinary law not simply because it is legally or procedurally prior to it, but because it represents important values that should trump ordinary law, supervise quotidian acts of governmental power, and hold both law and power to account. Thus, we say that the

Constitution is not merely basic law, it is also *higher law;* that is, it is a source of inspiration and aspiration, a repository of values and principles. People sometimes use the terms *basic law* and *higher law* interchangeably; for example, the German Basic Law strongly protects human dignity, and Bruce Ackerman has famously argued that constitutional amendment outside of Article V is an example of "higher lawmaking."[1] I want to separate the two expressions because they point at different constitutional functions. The German Basic Law is both basic law and higher law in my sense, and constitutional amendments—whether inside or outside of Article V—might involve the creation of both new basic law and new higher law.

Finally, it is not enough that the American Constitution serves as basic law (a framework for governance) or as higher law (a source of aspirational standards and values). It must also be *our law.* The people who live under it—the American people—must understand the Constitution as their law: not the law of Turkey, or the law of France, or the law of South Africa. The South African constitution may be widely admired as an example of contemporary constitution-making; but it is not our law. The Constitution works as our law when we identify with it and are attached to it, whether or not we consent to it in any official or legal sense. The Constitution works as our law when we view it as our achievement and the product of our efforts as a people, which involves a collective identification with those who came before us and with those who will come after us.

Viewing the Constitution as "our law" has a curious consequence: it helps us imagine ourselves as part of a collective subject persisting over time, the collective subject—We the People—whose law the Constitution is and to whom the Constitution belongs. Many features of a political culture can cause people to think of themselves as a collective subject that persists over time; but, at least in the United States, our Constitution also performs this function. There are two reasons why this might occur.

First, the Constitution is a long-term political project in which many different generations will have to participate. Hence, all of the people in these different generations can be part of the same We the People who accept and who work to further the Constitution's plan of self-government. Perhaps the framers are the opening participants in this political project, but they are surely not the only ones. The people who come after are just as important to the plan's success over time. The Constitution will not succeed without their acceptance and attachment to the constitutional plan. The generations after the founders keep the plan from foundering.

Second, thinking of the Constitution as our law—the law of We the American People—involves a narrative conception that appeals to collective memory: to a stock of stories, symbols, and understandings that bind people together and make them a people. Put another way, viewing the Constitution as "our Constitution" is a *constitutional story*—a constitutive narrative through which people imagine themselves as a people, with shared memories, goals, aspirations, values, duties, and ambitions.

Viewing the Constitution as *our* Constitution simultaneously constitutes us as the people to whom our Constitution belongs. It is a "constitution" of We the People. It accepts and endorses a constitutional story about who Americans are and what America is. We are the people who broke away from Great Britain and who created and ratified the Constitution to secure our liberty, and so too will be our successors. Viewing the Constitution as our Constitution constructs a collective subject with a collective destiny that engages in collective activities. It binds together people living in different times and different places as a single people. It allows us to see the hopes, desires, actions, ambitions, and achievements of people who lived long ago as our hopes, desires, actions, ambitions, and achievements.

The success of this constitutional story is central to the present generation's attachment to the Constitution as their Constitution—even though they never consented to it or voted for it—and therefore to the Constitution's sociological legitimacy. Attachment is a different attitude from consent. We consent to something we have a choice in; but we can become attached to something that we live with or live in over time.[2]

The method of text and principle, I believe, serves the multiple functions of a constitution—as basic law, higher law, and our law—far better than other forms of originalism. An originalism that strongly distrusts delegation to future generations and demands that open-ended provisions must be closely connected to original expected application is defective in all three respects.

Perhaps that kind of originalism makes the most sense if we think of the Constitution only as basic law. It tries to turn open-ended principles and standards into something more concrete and rule-like, something whose effects will hopefully be more predictable and (in many cases) more constraining. But that is not the only way that constitutions could serve as basic law. As I argued in Chapter 2, constitutions do not simply block or limit decisionmaking. They also channel and discipline politics; they can create incentives for useful adaptation and political stability. In fact, the latter are far better ways to understand the basic law function of a constitution.

Even if tying constitutional principles closely to original expected application works tolerably well as basic law, it fails utterly as higher law and as "our law." The idea of higher law views the Constitution as a repository of ideals morally superior to ordinary law and toward which ordinary law should strive. It makes the Constitution an object of political and moral aspiration and offers a potential for redemption. Thus the higher-law function of constitutionalism has a temporal dimension: the higher law is a set of principles that critiques present political arrangements and that we must try to realize over time.

Earlier I noted one of Justice Scalia's arguments for an expectations based originalism: the purpose of a constitution is to prevent rot and decay in our institutions, a falling away from a more just time. The very notion of aspiration presumes the opposite of this narrative of decline.[3] It presupposes that each generation should build on the past, and strive to do better than the previous ones did. The idea of redemption assumes that the political arrangements of the past have features that must be redeemed.

Aspirationalism is Janus-faced. It recognizes that a constitution always exists in a fallen condition, that it inevitably contains compromises with evil and injustice. At the same time, it maintains that the constitution and the constitutional tradition contain elements and resources that can assist in their eventual redemption.

Implicit in this notion of constitutional aspiration is a willingness to gamble on the future, and faith in the ability of future generations to work out and develop the Constitution's guarantees over time. Constitutional aspiration requires faith in the constitutional tradition's ability to grow and improve, without any guarantees of success. Far from being based on the fear that future institutions will rot or decay, an aspirational Constitution requires a steadfast belief that the evils of the present can and will be recognized and remedied, if not in our day then in the days to come.

Finally, a constitutional theory that distrusts all delegation to the future—as skyscraper originalism does—fails as "our law." The Constitution is our law when we feel attachment to it and when we feel that we have a stake in it even if we did not consent to it officially. The Constitution is our law when we feel that it reflects our values sufficiently well that we can identify with it as ours; or, because we feel have a say in what the Constitution means, we have faith that it could and will come to reflect our values better over time.[4] Thus, the idea of the Constitution as our law also has a temporal dimension. It requires an identification between ourselves, those who lived in the past, and those who will live in the future. And it requires faith that the Constitution is either good enough as it is to deserve our respect and attachment or that it eventually will be redeemed so that it is deserving.

For the Constitution to be "our law," it must do two things simultaneously. First, it must connect past generations to present ones through a process of narrative identification. It must allow us to see ourselves as part of a larger political project that stretches back to the present and forward to the future. The Constitution succeeds as our law when we can identify ourselves with those who framed and adopted it—we when are able to see ourselves as part of them and them as part of us.

Second, the Constitution must allow us to identify our present principles and commitments with the principles and commitments of those who lived before us.[5] Constitutional traditions achieve this by encouraging people in the present to call upon the past—and the struggles and commitments of the past—as their past and as their struggles and commitments. This understanding of the past frames our present situation and explains how we should go forward into the future. This identification between past and present allows us to say that we are continuing the work of those who came before us when we apply the Constitution's text and principles in light of our current circumstances.

Doing this necessarily requires delegation to the future, because each generation must see itself as given the task of applying constitutional principles in its own time. We understand our present situation and the possibilities and needs of the future through the trajectory of our interpretation of the meaning of the past—both the principles we committed ourselves to achieving and the evils we promised ourselves we would not permit again. When we in the present perform this task, we carry forward the imagined political project that metaphorically connects us to those who came before us. Their principles are our principles, and the Constitution they left us is our Constitution, reflecting not only their past commitments but also our present ones.

A theory of interpretation that refuses to allow this delegation does not allow the Constitution to be ours, because it does not allow us to see our present-day values in the Constitution as the application or fulfill-ment of past principles and commitments. If people feel that the Consti-tution's values are not their values, but simply imposed on them as a straitjacket from an alien past, the Constitution is not theirs, and it of-fers them little hope that it will come to be theirs in the future.

Democratic Legitimacy

The idea that the Constitution must be "our law" brings us to the concept of legitimacy. Concerns about legitimacy underwrite theories of constitu-tional interpretation. Conversely, we argue for or against different theories of constitutional interpretation in terms of their effects on legitimacy.

What kind of legitimacy does my theory focus on, and how do frame-work originalism and the method of text and principle further legitimacy? The American Constitution is premised on popular sovereignty—self-government by We the People of the United States. So I am interested in how a theory of constitutional interpretation helps promote the demo-cratic legitimacy of a constitutional and legal system that is based on the idea of popular sovereignty. I say "promote," and not "guarantee," be-cause a theory of constitutional interpretation is only one element of what makes a regime democratically legitimate. We want our theory of consti-tutional interpretation to do its part along with other features of the sys-tem; conversely, we do not want it to undermine legitimacy.

As I use the term, legitimacy is a property of the entire constitutional and legal system, not just individual laws or actions. *Legitimate* is also a relative term, a bit like the word *tall*. A system is more or less legitimate, although at some point we would say that the system is illegitimate, just as we might say that, at least with respect to the population of adult human beings, people who are five foot two are not tall, even if they are taller than people under five feet.

There are many different kinds of legitimacy. A constitutional and legal system is *sociologically* legitimate to the extent that people accept the sys-tem as having the right and the authority to rule them. It is *procedurally* (or legally) legitimate to the extent that people clothed with state power (which might include government officials, jurors, and voters) make deci-sions according to official legal rules and procedures. It is *morally* legiti-mate to the extent that the system is just or morally admirable. The de-mands of moral legitimacy might include, among other things, protecting the human rights of citizens and other persons that the state affects.[6]

A system is *democratically* legitimate to the extent that it allows the members of the political community to govern themselves and makes government action accountable to public will, public values, and public opinion. Thus, democratic legitimacy is intimately connected with the goal of popular sovereignty. Democratic legitimacy presupposes members of a political community to whom the state must be responsive, but the question of who actually belongs in the community (and how they belong) is itself a contested question.

Democratic legitimacy presupposes sociological legitimacy in the sense of public acceptance and approval, but it is not the same thing, because even if people accept the government's authority, they may have no power to change what the state does, elect new representatives, or hold government officials accountable. Democratic legitimacy also requires a significant degree of procedural legitimacy, because self-rule requires procedures for self-government and methods of holding government officials accountable to law. However, states may have elaborate legal procedures and still not be democratic. Finally, democratic legitimacy requires moral legitimacy to the extent that self-government requires rights of participation and presupposes the protection of other important human rights of autonomy and dignity.[7] It follows that the thicker one's conception of "democracy," the more basic rights are necessary to democratic legitimacy. Nevertheless, democratic legitimacy is less than moral legitimacy. A democratically legitimate system may not produce justice, and in fact democracies may generate and maintain laws and practices that are very unjust indeed. Constitutions may guarantee just rights and powers, but for historical reasons they may also guarantee unjust ones. In fact, most constitutions in democracies contain various compromises with injustice that were conditions of ratification. The 1787 U.S. Constitution, with its various protections for slavery, is only the most obvious example.

We should also not confuse justice with a different kind of legitimacy that people sometimes call "moral legitimacy" but that is actually a form of sociological legitimacy. People may *believe* that a state is basically fair and just (or very fair and just)—and this will increase the *sociological* legitimacy of the system—but the system may not actually be as just as they think it is and their views may be biased or parochial. We do not, after all, live at a privileged moment in history. Just as we may now believe that people living in the past were far more unjust than they believed themselves to be, people who come after us will see our moral and political failings all too readily.

People in democracies often disagree about what is just and unjust, and they try to persuade others and push the state toward their respective visions. Facilitating their ability to do so promotes moral legitimacy, all other things being equal. However, because there is no guarantee that the winners in a democratic process will be on the side of justice, there is no guarantee that the system as a whole will always be just. Indeed, leaving decisions up to democratic processes almost always guarantees that some forms of injustice will occur.

We can (and should) maintain that a sufficiently robust conception of democracy requires that the state protect a range of key human rights. A state becomes more democratically legitimate to the extent that it respects these basic guarantees. Even so, protecting these rights does not always lead to just outcomes; for example, it may not prevent states from going to war, spending money on the wrong things, misallocating resources, or making any number of errors of judgment that lead to human suffering and injustice.

We can hope that democratic systems will tend toward real justice in the long run, and that the more democratic they become, the more just they will also become. That is certainly the faith of those of us who believe that democracies, for all their defects and imperfections, are the best system of government. But the verdict of history so far has been mixed: States with a fair degree of democratic legitimacy have sometimes protected (some) people's rights, but they have also done many unjust things, both to their own citizens and to other peoples.

In this book, therefore, we ask whether theories of constitutional interpretation are consistent with popular sovereignty and promote democratic legitimacy. However, to the extent that democratic legitimacy presupposes some degree of procedural legitimacy, moral legitimacy, and sociological legitimacy, we are interested in these questions as well.

I began this chapter by noting that a constitution like America's must simultaneously function as basic law, as higher law, and as our law. These three functions connect to these three aspects of democratic legitimacy. A constitution must succeed as basic law in order to be procedurally legitimate. It must also create procedures that divert social conflict into ordinary politics, thus preserving social peace. Succeeding as basic law thus promotes sociological legitimacy in a democracy. When the constitution succeeds as higher law, people appeal to it as a source of moral critique of ordinary law and as a reason to reform the status quo. Over time this may promote the degree of moral legitimacy required in a democracy. It also gives people a sense of pride in their Constitution; this further engenders sociological legitimacy because it encourages people to believe that their system, properly interpreted and implemented, is just in their eyes or tends toward what they believe is just. Finally, when the constitution succeeds as "our law"—when people feel that it reflects and is responsive to their needs, ideals, and values—it also promotes the kind of sociological legitimacy that a democracy needs.

When we ask how a theory of constitutional interpretation contributes to democratic legitimacy, we have already assumed a set of institutions already in place, a constitution and a set of constitutional interpreters, including not only citizens and the political branches but also courts with the power of judicial review.

Democracies can have constitutions without judicial review, especially without judicial review of legislation. It is somewhat more difficult to do without judicial review of executive action (sometimes called administrative action). That is because executive officials often have considerable discretion; they can often act quickly, and without prior approval from legislatures. As a result it is important to constrain executive officials and make sure that they abide by constitutional norms and the rule of law. In the United States we tend to run judicial review of legislation and executive action together, but if we could have only one, we should opt for judicial review of executive action.

Similarly, in a federal republic there is a stronger case for judicial review of state and local governments than for judicial review of congressional statutes. That is because to preserve political union a federal system needs to coordinate state decisionmaking, settle disputes between different states, and (in many cases) make states abide by a single federal rule or standard. (This is especially important in matters concerning foreign policy and relations with foreign governments.) Because courts may also be necessary to arbitrate between state and federal governments, judicial review of federal law may also be necessary.

Finally, if the drafters of a constitution insert rights language that applies to states and local governments, courts have the additional task of enforcing these guarantees. The 1787 Constitution had only a small number of these restrictions on states, in Article I, section 10, and Article IV. As a result they produced very little litigation. The drafters of the Reconstruction amendments, and particularly the Fourteenth Amendment, imposed new rights obligations on states that they assumed both Congress and the federal courts would enforce. They simultaneously expanded the jurisdiction of the federal courts to hear these claims. To a significant extent the expansion of judicial review in the United States came from the proliferation of doctrines spawned by the Fourteenth Amendment and, eventually, by the Fourteenth Amendment's application of the Bill of Rights to the states.

Extending the Bill of Rights to cover the states greatly multiplied the number of occasions that people could complain of unconstitutional action, because every state and local official could, in theory, become a defendant. This led to the proliferation of doctrines that applied to the states and the federal government alike. These doctrines exploded in the 1960s when the Supreme Court applied most of the Bill of Rights to the states and began enforcing national standards more frequently. Because Congress did not create a federal code of criminal procedure to govern state and local officials, the courts created one to review state and local executive action.

Justifying the practice of judicial review in a democracy would take a book by itself. In this book I assume rather than argue for the benefits of judicial review. More specifically, I assume that the practice of judicial review applies both to legislative and to executive action, and both to the states and to the federal government. Equally important, however, I maintain that courts are only one constitutional interpreter among many. I specifically do not assume (and in fact I specifically reject) the idea of judicial supremacy, because judicial supremacy does not adequately describe the American experience of judicial review. Courts have neither the first nor the last word on the practical meaning of the Constitution; to the contrary, courts are always in complicated streams of mutual influence with citizens, the national political process, and the decisions of state and local governments.

Scholars sometimes call this process of mutual interaction "dialogue." But the word *dialogue* is altogether too polite. It does not capture the pushing and shoving, aggression, and threatening that occur in American constitutional politics, or the many forms of diplomacy, conflict avoidance, and face-saving measures that courts and politicians engage in to forestall politically uncertain and potentially destructive situations. A system of multiple constitutional interpreters works—when it works— partly through diplomacy and partly through aggression, partly through veiled or hidden threats and partly through concessions, partly through reasoned argument and partly through protest. Thus, in this book I ask how this interactive process of constitutional interpretation involving all the different actors in politics promotes democratic legitimacy. I am interested in what theory of interpretation best helps this system of multiple interpreters—this process of conflict, mobilization, and confrontation—to succeed as basic law, higher law, and our law.

Making the Constitution Ours: How Democratic Legitimacy Is Produced in Time

I have argued that the delegation of constitutional construction to later generations is crucial to the Constitution's democratic legitimacy. It helps makes the Constitution "our law." But the process of creating "our law" is never finished, and it cannot be as long as the Constitution continues. One generation succeeds another, with different problems, interests, and values. Moreover, at any given time there is dispute and disagreement about how to go forward in implementing the Constitution. Therefore, the process by which we make the Constitution "our law" involves a continuous critique of the way the Constitution is currently implemented.

For ease of exposition, I shall speak of the constitutional text plus the constructions, institutions, understandings, and practices that have grown up around it at any point in time as the Constitution-in-practice. I distinguish the Constitution-in-practice from "the Constitution" for two reasons.

First, much of the Constitution-in-practice cannot be found merely from inspecting the constitutional text, even as it has been amended. It includes statutory frameworks, judicial glosses, traditions of practice, cultural understandings, and political institutions. These elements can and often do change over time, and it is important to distinguish the way the Constitution has been implemented from the many ways it could be implemented.

Second, viewed from the perspective of a particular person, the Constitution-in-practice may be unjust and unfaithful to the best understanding of the Constitution. Hence it is useful to have a way of talking about the "true" or "ideal" Constitution that is distinct from the Constitution as a currently instantiated institution. When people critique the Constitution-in-practice in the name of the Constitution—or in the name of what the Constitution truly stands for—they implicitly make this distinction. They are advocating a restoration or a redemption of an ideal or true Constitution that may never have existed fully or completely in practice, but that they view as their goal.

People criticize or defend the Constitution-in-practice in the name of their vision of what the Constitution really means. Through this process the Constitution-in-practice evolves, sometimes in ways people want, but often in ways they did not expect. As the Constitution-in-practice changes, new groups of people discover that they are unhappy with some aspect of it. Perhaps they dislike the most recent changes. Perhaps changing circumstances (whether technological, economic, social, or demographic) lead them to see features in our political order they once thought acceptable as now unbearable. Or perhaps they used to believe certain undesirable features were simply unchangeable, but have come to believe that they can be modified for the better. Whatever the reasons, they now rise to critique the Constitution-in-practice, attempting to nudge it in the right direction. Others rise to contest their attempts, and so the process of contestation goes forward indefinitely.

You might think that a Constitution-in-practice that is constantly being criticized in the name of the Constitution, and that is constantly dissatisfying in ever new ways to ever new groups of people, would be the least legitimate form of government one could imagine. In fact the opposite is true: The ability of people to criticize the Constitution-in-practice in the name of the Constitution and to work to push it toward their desired vision is what helps make an ancient document newly legitimate to each generation of Americans. The Constitution-in-practice changes in response to political mobilizations and protests as various groups contend over the meaning of the Constitution and attempt to persuade others. Constitutional constructions emerge from these public debates over the meaning of the Constitution. Public disputes over the Constitution, realized in successive waves of constitutional construction, give the Constitution-in-practice its authority as a going concern. When people fight out the meaning of the Constitution in politics and in culture, they help maintain the authority of the Constitution they have. Robert Post and Reva Siegel have called these processes "democratic constitutionalism."[8] Democratic constitutionalism helps maintain the democratic legitimacy of constitutional change through constitutional construction.

The public can change the Constitution-in-practice in many ways. For example, people can work to amend the Constitution through Article V. This is an arduous task, to be sure, but one that has been accomplished a number of times in our country's history. Nevertheless, there are many other ways to make the Constitution-in-practice more responsive that do not require constitutional amendment. People can work to elect political representatives who will appoint judges that are more likely to agree with their views. This practice of *partisan entrenchment* in the judiciary has been one of the most important engines of change in constitutional construction.[9] In addition, as I discuss in Chapters 13 and 14, constitutional constructions by the political branches change the world in which judges operate. By and large the judiciary tends to legitimate the new constitutional constructions of sustained national political majorities in the long run, as it did during the New Deal in the 1930s, during the formation of the national security state in the 1940s and 1950s, and during the civil rights revolution in the 1960s and early 1970s.

Equally and perhaps even more importantly, people can work to change public values and common sense about the key issues they care about. Political and social movements have changed Americans' attitudes about racial equality, the role of women, religion in public life, permissible forms of freedom of expression, and norms concerning sexuality and sexual orientation. To succeed in changing social norms may be as powerful as changing judges and politicians, for it alters the underlying sense of what is reasonable and unreasonable for governments to do. It shifts political and professional discourse about what is off-the-wall and on-the-wall in making claims on the Constitution. This in turn changes the way that both judges and the political branches interpret the Constitution and make new constitutional constructions.

If people come to believe that the Constitution-in-practice is not responsive to their views, and that there is little chance that it will ever be responsive, people will lose respect for it and they will no longer regard it as their law. Instead it will seem to them like a law forced on them by others, like the law imposed by a tyrant or the law of an overbearing imperial power imposed on a subordinate colony. (Think, for example, of the way the American colonists viewed British taxes and policies before the Revolution.) This is not a democratic conception of law, much less a democratic conception of a constitution.

The democratic legitimacy of the Constitution depends on the people's belief that their Constitution and their government belongs to them, so that if they speak and protest and make their views known over time, the constitutional constructions of courts and the political branches will eventually respond to their political values and to the issues they care about most.[10]

To be sure, the public believes that constitutional interpretation and construction are legitimate because they involve law and not simply politics. It follows that sometimes the law, properly interpreted, will not be on one's side. Nevertheless, mere conformity to professional discourse and professional practices is not sufficient for the Constitution to be democratically legitimate. It is not enough for the Constitution-in-practice to be law. It must also be our law. It must ultimately be responsive to the public's values. There must be some way for people to express their dissatisfaction with the Constitution-in-practice and demand that courts and the political branches reform, restore, or redeem the law to make it conform with what the public believes the Constitution properly should stand for.[11]

As a result, when people talk back to the courts and the political branches, and accuse them of every form of tyranny and injustice, they are exercising their ability to claim the Constitution as their own and not as the exclusive property of those currently in power. Expressing their grievances and their felt sense of alienation from the Constitution-in-practice gives people a chance to push the law in their favored direction. That is how our system makes the Constitution-in-practice responsive to people who disagree with what courts and the political branches do and therefore prevents a far more troubling alienation that would seriously undermine the Constitution's democratic legitimacy.

Of course, democracies are full of people who disagree about these values and these issues. So people with very different views will simultaneously demand that the government respond to their vision of the Constitution. And not everybody will or can be made equally happy with the results. Americans recognize that people disagree about constitutional questions, and they also recognize that public authorities will not always adopt their preferred position. That possibility comes with the acceptance of a democratic system and a government under law. But people can nevertheless remain faithful to the constitutional project and accept the Constitution's democratic legitimacy as long as they believe that they have a fair chance to persuade other people that their views are correct, or, what is equally important, that through their efforts or those of others like them, eventually the Constitution-in-practice will be responsive to their views.[12]

This attitude, which is crucial to the Constitution's democratic legitimacy, is faith in the eventual redemption of the Constitution. As long as people have faith in the possibility of persuasion and improvement (from their political perspective), they can accept the authority of the Constitution-in-practice and they can work to change people's views within the existing political framework, however defective it might be. The belief that the Constitution is a collective project of many generations, that it makes promises to the future that are only imperfectly realized in the present, that we should have faith that the Constitution will become better over time, and that we should work for the eventual redemption of its promises in history I call *redemptive constitutionalism*. I argue that the Constitution's democratic legitimacy is connected to the concepts of faith and redemption. Why faith and redemption are so important to constitutional interpretation is the subject of the next chapter.

5

CONSTITUTIONAL FAITH AND
CONSTITUTIONAL REDEMPTION

At the close of Chapter 4 I noted that the democratic legitimacy of the Constitution depends in part on people believing that the Constitution can eventually move closer to their ideals. Different citizens, from their varying perspectives, must be able to see that the constitutional system, understood in its best light, is sufficiently just that they can accept it as theirs, or—if it is not currently sufficiently just—they must be able to have faith that it could become so in time.

In this chapter, I argue that a similar belief supports the practice of constitutional interpretation. Interpreting the Constitution as a partici-pant in the constitutional system also requires an attitude of attachment to the Constitution, a belief that the constitutional project is worthwhile, and a faith that the Constitution-in-practice will improve in time. Constitutional interpretation, in short, depends on faith in the constitutional project, which is also a faith in its redemption through history. Hence, my theory of constitutional interpretation is also a theory of *redemptive constitutionalism*.

Redemptive Constitutionalism

The Constitution announces its redemptive project in the opening words of its Preamble—it proclaims that the Constitution is a project of self-government with long-term goals to create a "more perfect union" that strives to "establish justice, insure domestic tranquility, provide for the common defense, promote the general welfare, and secure the blessings of liberty to ourselves and our posterity." These goals were not completed in 1789, when the Constitution was adopted; they are not completed to-day. And even if the 1787 Constitution did not contain a Preamble, it would still require redemption, because the Constitution's text is only a framework that needs to be filled out over time.

Redemptive constitutionalism is the claim that our Constitution is always a work in progress—imperfect and compromised, but directed toward its eventual improvement. What does it mean to say that the Constitution—which is a text, not a person—is "directed" toward its improvement?

The Constitution is an intergenerational project of politics, and the generations of We the People are the participants in the project. The Constitution contains commitments that We the People have only partially lived up to, promises that have yet to be fulfilled, and it is the task of each generation to do its part, however great or small, to help fulfill them and to achieve a more perfect union in its own day. The participants in the project will argue among themselves about how to continue the project; they will make mistakes and commit injustices, but this by itself does not detract from the point of the enterprise. As the Talmud says, we are not required to complete the Great Work, but neither are we free to refrain from it.[1]

Redemptive constitutionalism is a characteristic feature of the American constitutional tradition. In every generation people have seen injustice in their society and made claims in the name of the Constitution to remedy those injustices. The great political and social movements that secured the basic rights and liberties that Americans now take for granted are examples of redemptive constitutionalism at work.

The idea of redemption is more than adaptation to changing conditions. After all, there are many ways to adapt to change; one way is to jettison the Constitution or parts of it. That is not redemption; it is surrender. Redemptive constitutionalism means meeting the challenges of changing conditions in ways that seek to further the promises and commitments of the plan rather than abandon them in the face of difficulties and temptations.

Political life is full of contingency; we rarely know what the future holds. Wars, disasters, and threats of harm; territorial expansion and contraction; waves of immigration and settlement; new religions and technologies; cultural upheavals and sexual revolutions; economic booms and depressions constantly reshape our values and expectations. The generation of 1787 could not have foreseen today's America; nor can our generation foresee the America of two centuries hence, if our experiment in self-governance is so fortunate as to continue to that day.

Redemption, therefore, cannot mean the unfolding of preordained events, or returning to a determinate path already marked out. The proper way to redeem constitutional values cannot be known in advance; each generation must do its best, and members of each generation will fight over the right way. The constitutional tradition will grow and develop in ways that no one could have foreseen. The civil rights movement and the women's movement claimed they carried on the founders' commitments, and today most Americans would agree, but the founders could not have imagined these social movements, and if presented with their assertions, might well have recoiled from them. Today we tell a story in which one wave of redemptive constitutionalism follows the next, but that is how the story looks to us today, not the way things had to be. In hindsight the path may look like a natural progression, but when we look at the present, we quickly disagree about who is the hero of the story and who is the villain, who is redeeming the Constitution and who is scuttling it.

Redemptive constitutionalism does not assert that redemption is guaranteed. It is something We the People must strive for. And often We the People will fall short. Americans have often been unjust; they have often compromised their values and commitments. The Constitution itself is imperfect and the Constitution-in-practice is inevitably compromised. Redemptive constitutionalism does not deny these facts; it begins with them. It accepts them as the grounds for redemption.

The fulfillment of constitutional values requires effort and struggle. If Americans believe in a narrative of redemption, they will have to make that story true. They make the narrative true by believing that it can become true and working for the day when it will be true. Abraham Lincoln understood the Declaration of Independence as a document of redemption, and what he said about the Declaration applies to the Constitution with equal force: It was designed "to set up a standard maxim for free society, which could be familiar to all, and revered by all; constantly looked to, constantly labored for, and even though never perfectly attained, constantly approximated, and thereby constantly spreading and deepening its influence, and augmenting the happiness and value of life to all people of all colors everywhere."[2] In a redemptive constitutionalism, the Constitution—or more correctly, our idea of it—is both a goad and a guide.

The idea of constitutional redemption is connected to the theory of democratic legitimacy described in Chapter 4. Even if the Constitution-in-practice does not currently correspond to their vision of justice, people believe that it is worth contributing to the constitutional project in the hope that someday it may move closer to that ideal. Because people with very different views can see the possibility of constitutional redemption from their different vantage points, they can all pledge faith in the Constitution, accept the authority of the Constitution-in-practice, and work to further the constitutional project over time. This requires, however, that people with very different views can all see something in the Constitution that can be redeemed and is worth redeeming.

For this purpose, the open-ended texture of the Constitution, with its basic framework of rules, standards, principles, and silences, and its rich tradition of multiple conflicting and contending interpretations, is an advantage, not a defect. The combination of basic hardwired rules with an ample delegation to future generations allows people with very different views to claim the Constitution as their own and work for its redemption from the perspective of their "ideal" or "true" Constitution. Although people often associate indeterminacy with instability, this is not true in constitutional politics: the ability of people with strongly held views to disagree about the Constitution and see different things in it is an important source of its durability and legitimacy over time.[3]

What is the connection between the idea of constitutional redemption and the practice of constitutional interpretation? Fidelity *to* the Constitution requires faith *in* the value and ultimate success of the constitutional project. Faith in the constitutional project, in turn, requires a belief that the project is worth participating in and furthering and that its defects and deficiencies can be remedied over time by supporting the project and working on its behalf. In this way, questions of faith and redemption are at the heart of the practice of constitutional interpretation by participants in the constitutional system.

Most constitutional theorists do not speak in these terms, perhaps because they think of faith and redemption as exclusively religious concepts. Yet these ideas apply with equal force to secular projects and institutions. Indeed, with the notable exception of Sanford Levinson's *Constitutional Faith*,[4] which astutely describes the Constitution as part of America's civil religion, most constitutional scholars have not focused on the central role of faith in constitutional interpretation, much less the role of redemption.

Questions of faith and redemption transcend the usual divisions between theories like originalism or living constitutionalism. Both originalists and living constitutionalists must have faith in the Constitution, and both seek to redeem features of the Constitution. They disagree about the object of faith and the aspects of the constitutional system in need of redemption. Indeed, one of the best ways of understanding a theory of constitutional interpretation is to ask where it locates its faith—what it believes in and what it does not trust—and what aspects of the Constitution-in-practice it believes have fallen short and need to be restored or fulfilled.[5]

To interpret the Constitution presupposes a desire to be faithful to it—at least for those who claim to be governed by it. If we do not seek to be faithful to the Constitution, we may be trying to improve the Constitution, but we are not trying to interpret it.[6] To be faithful to the Constitution, we cannot view it with perpetual distrust. Quite the contrary: we must put ourselves on the side of the Constitution. We must seek to defend it from those who would abuse it or misuse it, even—and perhaps especially—if our views about what the Constitution says are not the views of the majority or of the powerful. Suspicion and doubt about the project may be an important political or intellectual activity. But it is not interpretation.

All constitutions are imperfect, in part because of the circumstances of their origin and the compromises necessary to bring them into being and maintain them over time. All constitutions are a "covenant with death and an agreement with hell," to use William Lloyd Garrison's famous phrase.[7] Precisely for that reason, fidelity to the document requires a leap of faith in the document and the institutions of government based on the document. To interpret the document faithfully, we must buy into the constitutional project, even though compromised and flawed, and make it our own project. Given the injustices we see around us every day, this faith may sometimes be difficult to muster.

The faith that constitutional interpretation requires is not blind faith. It is not idolatry, or a belief that our Constitution is the best and wisest constitution ever crafted by human hands. Rather, constitutional interpretation requires faith that even if some aspects of the document and its associated institutions are far from perfect, the latter are good enough to justify the benefits of political union (and the use of force to compel obedience to the law), and that the system of constitutional government can and will become still better over time. What if we do not believe that the Constitution-in-practice currently meets even the minimum standards of justice required for legitimacy? Then constitutional interpretation requires the faith that, if we commit ourselves to the constitutional project, the Constitution will, in time, measure up to the appropriate standards.[8] This faith, too, may be difficult to come by, especially when our views are in eclipse and people in power do terrible and shameful things in the name of the law, the Constitution, and the country.

In short, interpretive fidelity requires faith in the redeemability of an imperfect Constitution over time. That faith is threefold: faith in the possibilities contained in the document, faith in the institutions that grow up around the document, and finally, faith in the American people, who will ultimately determine the interpretation and direction of the document and its associated institutions. All three forms of faith are necessary. We must believe that the text has sufficient adaptability to remedy the injustices of the present and the challenges of the future, that our political institutions are not incorrigible, and that our nation is able to learn from its mistakes and improve itself in the long run. These elements of faith are not limited to faith in the U.S. Constitution; they are key elements of faith in constitutional democracy generally. But if we do not believe these things, debates over interpretation are pretty much pointless; it is time to start over and engage in very different kinds of political activity.[9]

The connections between interpretive fidelity and faith are clear in the etymology of the word *fidelity*, whose Latin root, *fides*, means "trust" or "faith." To have fidelity to a person or a thing is to believe in them, in what they are now or what they could be in time. Moreover, fidelity is a two-way street—we are faithful to others because we expect (or hope) that they will be faithful to us and not betray us. We believe this even though we do not know whether this will turn out to be the case; that is what makes our attitude faith rather than mere prediction based on reasonable evidence. Thus, to have faith in an institution like the Constitution is to believe that over time the Constitution will not let us down and betray our trust, that the Constitution can and eventually will live up to our hopes for it. This faith is not simply faith in the magical powers of constitutional texts, but a faith in the redeemability of political institutions and of a people over time.

Conversely, to be "faithless" means both to lack faith and to betray. The two often go together. If we do not believe in an institution, we are less likely to feel we must play by its rules. If we lack faith in other people, we expect them to let us down or even betray us, and so it may be wise to protect our interests at their expense. Sometimes, of course, lack of faith in other people—or in institutions—may be a self-fulfilling prophecy. The institutions fail, the people betray us, because we and others were unwilling to believe in them. To interpret the Constitution in good faith as a member of the political community, one must buy into the constitutional project. Constitutional interpretation cannot be premised on the attitude that we will only be faithful to the Constitution to the extent that we think it will say what we approve of. This is both a question of interpretive attitude and a question of procedural fairness to others in the community whom we also expect to obey the Constitution and the law. If I do not commit myself to playing by the rules of the game, why should I expect other people in my community to do so, and what justifies my criticism of other people if I think they have twisted or warped the Constitution to their own ends? I can certainly argue that what they have done is unjust or hypocritical. But I can hardly oppose their actions on the grounds that they have failed to abide by principles of faithful interpretation that I refuse to abide by.

Although constitutional faith is necessary to interpretation, this faith is fraught with perils. For one thing, our faith could be misplaced; we could be apologizing for a regime that does not deserve our fidelity. Buying in too easily or in the wrong way to the constitutional project can have ideological effects and lead to a form of constitutional idolatry.[10] People may come to believe that the Constitution, because it is widely revered, must be a just system of government, and that the Constitution is admirable in all its aspects. They may become blinded to the deficiencies of its rules and the legal system that has grown around them. They may assume that whatever is constitutional is presumptively just, and confuse the language of constitutionalism with the language of justice. They may bend their political ideals to conform to what they think the Constitution requires (and does not require), warping and stunting their political imaginations and their sense of justice to sanctify the status quo.

Constitutional idolatry confuses the products of politics with the ideal of justice. It short-circuits the project of constitutional redemption by assuming that it has already occurred. In this sense constitutional idolatry is the very opposite of a redemptive constitutionalism, which maintains that the Constitution-in-practice is always open to the future and must always be subject to criticism, even (and especially) if the Constitution serves as "higher law" that critiques ordinary law and holds it to a higher standard. One can avoid the dangers of idolatry only by being unstintingly honest—both about the Constitution's failings and about its resources for redemption.

Redemptive constitutionalism does not begin with unqualified acceptance of the Constitution's legitimacy. It does not assume that the Constitution is perfectly fine just as it is. That attitude leads all too easily to constitutional idolatry. Rather, it starts with the assumption that the Constitution exists, and always has existed, in a fallen condition. It is a collection of moral and political compromises placed in an imperfect document and situated in imperfect political institutions. Nevertheless, this document and these institutions form part of a project stretching throughout history, a project that contains resources for its own redemption. Redemptive constitutionalism holds that the Constitution contains commitments that we have only partially lived up to, promises that have yet to be fulfilled. The point of redemptive constitutionalism is not to overlook the Constitution's faults or its promises—but to take both with the utmost seriousness.[11] To see the Constitution as aspiring to greater justice and moral legitimacy, we must first recognize the past and present evils in our political institutions that the Constitution has supported and still supports. There can be no redemption without the recognition of sin. At the same time, we must recognize those elements in the Constitution—both in the document itself and in its associated institutions—that make this redemption possible. I argue that we can find many of these redemptive elements in the Constitution's basic structure and in its text and underlying principles. I argue, in short, that one reason why our Constitution is redeemable is that parts of it were designed to be redeemable—it contains language that not only can be adapted to changing times and circumstances but also contains political principles that demand the continual improvement of our institutions.

The Role of Political and Social Mobilizations

In the theory of democratic legitimacy described in Chapter 4, popular mobilizations play a crucial role in building the Constitution. Different groups in society contend over the practical meaning of the Constitution and seek to push it in their favored direction. This is the source both of constitutional change and the Constitution's democratic legitimacy in the long run.

There are many different kinds of mobilizations in American life, and as American politics changes, the nature of these mobilizations will probably also change. Describing all the different types of mobilizations in American history, and showing how they have evolved and have shaped constitutional construction, would require (at least) a book in itself. For simplicity's sake, I will mention three important types of mobilizations, which overlap with each other in practice: political mobilizations, social movements, and interest group advocacy.

Political mobilizations usually operate within the party system and generally seek to form, control, or at least strongly influence a political party. Two examples are the modern conservative movement and the Tea Party, which currently dominate the Republican Party. The populist movement, which eventually formed a political party and then was absorbed into the Democratic Party, is another. Political mobilizations seek electoral success and influence over governance and legal reform.

Modern political parties, however, do not merely seek electoral success. They are now embedded in much larger networks of organizations and professionals seeking policy and legal change. A host of think tanks, advocacy groups, litigation organizations, media organizations, watchdog groups, public interest firms, and other nongovernmental organizations try to persuade and influence people toward their favored policy goals and legal positions outside of election campaigns. They engage in what Steven Teles has called nonelectoral mobilization and nonelectoral party competition.[12] Many of these groups, although ideologically allied with major political parties, are only informally connected to them. Indeed, partly because of the structure of American law, they may specifically disavow being political organizations that advocate the election or defeat of particular candidates.

Social movements often overlap with political mobilizations; they tend to exist outside of organized political parties, although they often seek to influence them and in a few cases may create parties of their own. Historically there have been many different kinds of social movements, and there is a huge literature devoted to their study.[13] Often social movements try to change people's minds about mores and private behavior in addition to promoting specific legal reforms. Put another way, social movements often seek to change culture as well as law. The civil rights movement, the labor movement, the women's movement, the gay rights movement, the environmental movement, the movement for contraceptive reform in the first half of the twentieth century, the pro-life movement, and the free culture movement for reform of intellectual property law are examples. Social movements may also generate a wide variety of nongovernmental organizations and litigation campaigns.

The term *interest group* often has negative connotations in contemporary politics; people often speak of political and social movements they oppose as interest groups or special interests, but my use is not intended to be pejorative. As I employ the term here, interest groups primarily promote the economic and material interests of their members rather than seeking cultural transformation or social change; they tend to represent the relatively concentrated interests of businesses, industries, professional organizations, trade organizations, or unions. Nevertheless, social and political movements can overlap with interest groups; many business interests also identify with the conservative movement, and unions began as part of a social movement: the labor movement. Not surprisingly, interest groups may also have strong ties to major political parties.

All three of these kinds of mobilizations engage in advocacy and litigation, often against each other. All three of them make constitutional arguments in the course of promoting their favored ideals and policies. Their participation in public life can significantly affect constitutional construction and constitutional change. In this book I will refer to all of these different mobilizations collectively as "political and social movements," "movements," or "mobilizations" unless I specifically distinguish between them.

One might object that many mobilizations do not base their claims on constitutional text and principle and are not really committed to constitutional fidelity.[14] Instead they often make claims based on simple policy grounds, and they reject the constitutional arguments offered by their opponents. For example, the labor movement in the 1930s argued that the federal government had the power to guarantee collective bargaining rights and regulate wages and working conditions; their opponents argued that the federal government lacked power under the commerce clause and was restricted by the due process clause. Second, even if political and social movements claim that they are being faithful to constitutional text and principle, they are likely to get the analysis wrong because they do not see their job as maintaining fidelity to the Constitution. Their use of arguments from constitutional text and principle may be merely rhetorical. Social and political mobilizations are primarily interested in social change, electoral success, and promoting their material interests, not constitutional fidelity.

In fact, political and social movements in the United States have regularly drawn on the constitutional text and its underlying principles to justify social and legal change.[15] The American political tradition has featured a strong belief in emancipatory rights consciousness based on foundational texts, including the Declaration of Independence and the U.S. Constitution.[16] This "emancipatory vision of natural rights, rooted in the subversive and utopian messages that people read into constitutional texts 'has justified continued struggle by groups in the face of (presumably temporary) judicial and political defeats.' "[17] As Reva Siegel has pointed out in her studies of the women's movement, throughout our history ordinary citizens have called on the text of the Constitution as a foundation and source of their rights, claiming that the text has meaning that differs from official understandings.[18] Precisely because the Constitution views We the People as its authors, citizens from all walks of life have assumed the right to claim the Constitution as their Constitution and its meanings as their meanings. They have felt authorized to insist that legal officials must conform existing law to the Constitution's true meaning.

The importance of the constitutional text as the launching pad for arguments about rights in the American political tradition comes from historical contingency, not logical necessity. It arose from several different features of our history: the tradition of common law evolution in which new rights claims were viewed as naturally emerging out of older customs and commitments, the American belief in natural rights as a source of inspiration and aspiration, and the influence of Protestantism and its assertion that ordinary believers have authority to decide what the Bible and other sacred texts mean for themselves.[19]

Not only have mobilizations regularly called upon the constitutional text, they have also called upon the enduring political principles of the generations that went before them, particularly the founding generation.[20] Woman suffragists, for example, invoked the Revolutionary slogan "No taxation without representation" to explain why women deserved the vote.[21] Martin Luther King described the work of the founding generation as a "promissory note"[22] that had to be made good in the present, arguing that the struggle for civil rights was "a dream deeply rooted in the American dream."[23] The dream in King's famous speech was "that one day this nation will rise up and live out the true meaning of its creed" enunciated in the Declaration of Independence.[24] NRA president Charlton Heston identified today's gun owners with the founding generation and its commitment to liberty.[25] And Christian conservatives have invoked the founding era's commitments to religious liberty and its belief in divine providence as the basis of free government.[26]

It is hardly surprising that political and social movements have so often made arguments based on the Constitution's text and what they regard as its enduring underlying principles. The Constitution's success and its legitimacy stem from the fact that the Constitution is not only basic law but also higher law. To be successful as higher law, the Constitution must include aspirational elements that people can use to critique existing features of social life. Mobilizations naturally look for these aspirational elements in the constitutional text to support their arguments for change. When they look to the Constitution in this way, they naturally adopt the rhetorical tropes of restoration and redemption that are characteristic of our history.

Perhaps even more important, for the Constitution to be successful and legitimate, it must be not only basic law and higher law, but also "our law." Ordinary citizens must see the Constitution as something that belongs to them and that they are attached to, even if they did not formally consent to it.

First, this means that citizens must be able to interpret the document for themselves so that it speaks to their current ideals and concerns. Because the Constitution is theirs, they can speak truth to power: they can criticize officials for failing to live up to what the Constitution means, rightly interpreted.

Second, the notion that the Constitution must be "our" Constitution refers not only to the current generation but to a transgenerational "we." It requires that citizens must be able to see themselves as part of a larger political project that extends over time and of which they form a part. The Constitution's text, which each generation inherits and must expound, is the most obvious embodiment of this larger common political project. The fact that Americans see themselves as part of a transgenerational "We the People" naturally leads them to identify with people in the past, and with their hopes, struggles, principles, and commitments, in order to make sense of current controversies and the direction of legal and political change. Political and social mobilizations thus make appeals to the continuing commitments of the past in order to explain what is legitimate or illegitimate about current conditions. They do so not only because this helps them make sense of the present in terms of the past, but also because these commitments are part of what they hold in common with other members of the political community they are trying to persuade. Thus, when the suffragists used the slogan "No taxation without representation," they understood their fight for the vote as justified by the principles of the Revolution; and they were trying to persuade their contemporaries—including men who already had the vote—to live up to their common commitments and principles.

If we view movement arguments for restoration and redemption as nothing more than rhetorical tropes, we will miss how this way of talking and thinking contributes to political and social movements' self-understanding as engaged in an enterprise that is larger than themselves and their current concerns, an enterprise that unites past, present, and future generations, and an enterprise that therefore deserves to command the respect and agreement of other members of a political community that claims to be organized under the Constitution. This rhetoric is not just rhetoric, it is *just* rhetoric—appropriate rhetoric for the American constitutional enterprise, a way of talking and thinking that leads people to see the Constitution's fate and future as something that concerns them and therefore enhances the success and the legitimacy of the constitutional project.[27] Precisely because people feel they can make claims on the Constitution as *their* Constitution, even in the face of official pronouncements to the contrary, they are invested in the Constitution and in the project of its development, restoration, and redemption. That is why the rhetoric of text and principle is so familiar in the history of so many American political and social movements, and that is why the rhetoric of text and principle promotes the success and the legitimacy of the Constitution, even for generations that are increasingly distant from the founding generation.

The rhetoric of text and principle is at work both in mobilizations that claim that the Constitution protects basic rights and structures and in mobilizations that claim that the Constitution merely permits reform rather than requires it. Examples of the latter include the contemporary movement for campaign finance reform, the twentieth-century movements for school prayer and school vouchers, the antebellum movement for the abolition of slavery, and the early twentieth-century labor movement, which argued that the Constitution permitted labor legislation that protected fair working conditions and guaranteed the right of collective bargaining. In each case opponents objected that what these movements proposed was forbidden by the Constitution. Supporters of these movements responded that the Constitution, correctly interpreted, was flexible enough to allow democratic majorities to protect important rights and social interests.

In fact, both movements and their opponents—who are often movements themselves—routinely invoke a common rhetoric of text and principle against each other; that is strong evidence of the pervasive importance of text and principle in American political history. Both sides of the struggle over the New Deal invoked text and principle. It was not a contest between an old guard that believed in the Constitution's textual commitments and New Dealers who did not. Rather, Franklin Roosevelt's argument was that the Liberty League and other opponents of the New Deal had badly misconstrued the Constitution. Rightly understood, the Constitution's text and abiding principles permitted the federal government to act in the public interest. The Constitution, Roosevelt famously declared, was "a layman's document, not a lawyer's contract,"[28] and it "used generality, implication and statement of mere objectives, as intentional phrases which flexible statesmanship of the future, within the Constitution, could adapt to time and circumstance."[29]

Nevertheless, one might object that even if political and social mobilizations often use the rhetoric of text and principle, they often get the text and the principles wrong. When people talk about constitutional principles, they usually don't offer very detailed historical or structural analysis, much less provide a detailed doctrinal exegesis. Instead, they tend to talk loosely about "what the framers intended" or "what our founding fathers fought for." They offer fairly general claims about liberty, equality, and democratic government. Members of political and social movements are not professional historians, and they tend to use—or reimagine— history to suit their own often parochial ends. Moreover, even if members of these mobilizations say they are invested in the Constitution and seek to promote what the Constitution truly means, some of them may be insincere. They may simply use constitutional discourse to promote what they think is good or what serves their own interests.

To the extent that this is true, however, it does not pose a particular problem for my theory of constitutional interpretation. Political and social groups are usually composed of people with different interests, motivations, and understandings. The important question is whether we can understand the work of these movements as consistent with constitutional fidelity. To do this we must engage in interpretive charity and a sympathetic reconstruction of their claims. That means, among other things, that if mobilizations make arguments to the public premised on their and the public's common commitment to the Constitution, we should try to see whether these arguments make sense in the terms in which they are offered.

Moreover, to engage in a sympathetic reconstruction, there will inevitably have to be a division of labor between laypersons who call on the Constitution and legal professionals who bring their claims before judges and other legal decisionmakers. Lawyers will have to translate and reconstruct movement and interest group arguments in ways that judges and other legal decisionmakers can recognize as legal arguments. Put another way, lawyers and judges translate claims of constitutional politics into claims about constitutional law. In Chapters 13 and 14 I will say more about this process of "horizontal translation" between citizens and professionals, as distinguished from "vertical translation" between the past and the present.[30]

In fact lawyers and judges do more than merely passively translate, for popular and professional understandings of the Constitution mutually influence each other. Famous decisions like *Brown v. Board of Education*[31] and *Miranda v. Arizona*,[32] and well-known legal doctrines like the diversity rationale in affirmative action[33] or the doctrine of one-person-one-vote,[34] influence popular understandings of the Constitution. No doubt popular understandings of the Constitution build on what non-lawyers recognize in the work of lawyers and judges; they in turn criticize and reshape these ideas in the popular imagination, and these revisions in turn may eventually influence professional legal understandings. Thus, when we speak about constitutional interpretations by political and social movements, we actually refer to a complex set of interactions. They involve, on the one hand, ordinary individuals and legal professionals who represent them or who are otherwise sympathetic to them; and, on the other hand, the other members of the general public and other legal professionals whom the first group seeks to persuade or convince. The work of movements occurs in many different places and before many different publics; movement interpretations may combine popular and professionally mediated claims that, in turn, may influence each other.

Lawyers, judges, and other legal officials therefore inevitably play an important role in articulating and vindicating political and social movement claims about the Constitution. This should hardly be surprising: professional understandings are always in conversation with the views of ordinary citizens; and professional claims of legal obligation are inextricably connected to contemporary understandings of fair play, reasonableness, and justice. When ordinary individuals argue (for example) that the exclusion of women from public life violates the Constitution, it will probably fall to lawyers to explain in greater detail how these claims are consistent with constitutional text and principle in ways that are persuasive to courts. To do this, lawyers will probably make more detailed historical and textual arguments than most nonlawyers could make, as well as draw on all the familiar modalities of constitutional argument. (I offer examples of how one does this later on in this book.) There is nothing particularly unusual about this process of translation; it occurs regularly in the legal representation of individual and group clients. It is true that most citizens are not very good historians, but they are not very good doctrinalists either. Rather, they make claims on the Constitution in the way that citizens make such claims, and lawyers try as best they can to translate these concerns into existing legal forms. Inevitably something will be lost in the translation from politics to law, but that is the cost of a system that tries to take citizens' claims about the Constitution seriously.

Should Judges Pay Attention to Political and Social Movement Interpretations of the Constitution?

Suppose that I am right that lawyers and judges translate constitutional politics into constitutional law, that they turn political and social movement claims into legal arguments that might persuade legal decision-makers about how to interpret the Constitution. This leads to a second objection: the method of text and principle creates real dangers for constitutional fidelity because it seeks to incorporate the work of social and political mobilizations. If judges adopt the text-and-principle approach, it will make it easier for them to respond to the claims of movements who do not respect what the Constitution really means. This will lead judges to undermine important constitutional structures, deny important constitutional rights, and create new rights that have no basis in the Constitution.[35] Moreover, if the text-and-principle approach actually *requires* judges to respond to political and social movement interpretations, matters will be even worse. Judges who feel bound to listen to these mobilizations will be even more likely to stray from what the Constitution requires.

These objections, I think, rest on a misunderstanding. Nothing in my argument obligates judges to pay any attention to political mobilizations, social movements, or interest group advocacy, much less adopt these groups' claims.[36] There are two basic reasons for this. First, judges' professional conception of themselves as deciding cases according to law—the law/politics distinction—makes it very important that judges not understand themselves as being unduly influenced by, much less taking orders from, movements, interest groups, or other political factions.[37] Of course, judges have opinions about various kinds of mobilizations and about whether their claims are laudable or pernicious. But their job is to decide the legal cases that come before them, not to take instruction from the various protesters who regularly congregate outside their courtrooms or lobby in the mass media.[38] Second, even if we assumed that judges had some duty to listen to movements, there are simply too many such movements at any one time, and their demands often point in different directions. If judges had obligations to follow or even respond to movement claims, how would they know which ones to pay attention to? For example, which mobilization should judges have paid attention to in the late 1950s and early 1960s: the civil rights movement or the counter-mobilization that sought to reverse *Brown v. Board of Education* and preserve white supremacy? Historically we know that mobilizations have influenced judicial interpretations, but it is not because judges have any obligations to listen to them.

My arguments about political and social mobilizations involve claims of positive constitutional theory and normative constitutional theory. Positive constitutional theory studies how the constitutional system works and develops over time: how government and political institutions influence and interact with each other, and how features of politics and institutional structure influence the creation and development of constitutional doctrine. Normative constitutional theory focuses not on what people actually do but on what they should do.[39] One branch of normative constitutional theory concerns constitutional design, and another concerns constitutional interpretation and construction.

My positive claim is that social and political mobilizations have shaped the development of our Constitution. My normative claim is that some, but not all, of these changes are worthy objects of pride that demonstrate the best features of the American constitutional tradition. A theory of constitutional interpretation should be able to explain why the latter changes are faithful to the Constitution rather than being mistakes or deviations from constitutional fidelity that we must preserve for prudential reasons.

The political science literature from Robert Dahl in the 1950s to the present day has pointed out that the Supreme Court's constitutional doctrines tend to stay in touch with the dominant forces in American political life.[40] (Chapters 13 and 14 describe these processes in more detail.) For example, parties, social movements, and interest groups influence judicial decisionmaking through partisan entrenchment in the judiciary, replacing old judges with newer ones whose good-faith beliefs about the Constitution more closely match those of the party or group that helped secure their appointment. Mobilizations also influence judicial doctrine by changing public opinion, and particularly elite opinion. Gradually they convert views that may be initially considered off-the-wall into the political mainstream and eventually make them part of constitutional common sense. Judges are influenced by changes in constitutional culture because they live in this culture—not to mention the changing political culture of the nation—and absorb its assumptions and presuppositions. Moreover, not all judges need be equally influenced for these effects to occur. The Supreme Court is a multimember body whose decisions in the most contested cases are determined by its median or swing justices. New judicial appointments can change the median justice while leaving most of the other justices (and their preexisting views) in place. Moreover, median or swing justices are more likely to be responsive to changes in political culture than justices at the extreme ends of the political spectrum. Lower court judges in turn are bound by the decisions of the Supreme Court, and precisely because there are so many of them, a predictably large number retire and are replaced during each presidential election cycle.

In short, judicial interpretations of the Constitution can be changed in two ways: One can change the culture in which the judges decide cases, or one can change the judges. In addition, constitutional constructions by the political branches—like the creation of the administrative state—demographic shifts, technological changes, and long-term alterations in public mores shape the terrain in which judges decide cases and create constitutional doctrine.

If one accepts my normative theory of framework originalism and the method of text and principle, will judicial decisions be too easily influenced by social and political mobilizations that will misrepresent the true meaning of the Constitution? This concern seems to misunderstand the real causes of social influence on the judiciary, as well as the sources of judicial restraint. It seems to assume that interpretive theories are a major factor in why constitutional doctrines change over time. This greatly overstates the importance of theories of constitutional interpretation in explaining the product of courts. (That is particularly true of the U.S. Supreme Court, a multimember body whose members may have very different theories of interpretation, or no theory at all.) Generally speaking, judges have responded to changing social and political mobilizations for the institutional reasons I have identified above, and they have done so regardless of their normative interpretive theories. Until the end of the nineteenth century, virtually all federal judges and justices understood themselves to be what we would now call originalists.[41] This, however, did not stop courts from responding to changing political and social mobilizations, and these tendencies continued after the idea of living constitutionalism came into vogue.

I certainly do not claim that the choice of interpretive theories has no effect on judicial behavior. After all, shared basic assumptions about interpretation are part of the shared legal culture that helps constrain judicial practice. Moreover, as I will discuss in a moment, the choice of normative theories may be important because different theories may offer different normative justifications for decisions. Those justifications, in turn, may shape the available pathways of future constitutional construction. My point is that theories of interpretation are not the major causal explanation for why doctrines have changed as they have. Although law professors might want to think it so, the choice between originalism and living constitutionalism has not been the major reason why judicial doctrines changed as they did during the twentieth century. If one is worried about runaway political and social movements leading judges astray, theories of constitutional interpretation will not prevent this baleful occurrence. As I have explained previously, theories of constitutional interpretation simply cannot be expected to do most of the work of constraining judicial behavior. Those constraints come from institutional features of the judicial system.

Courts—and in particular the U.S. Supreme Court—tend to respond to political mobilizations, social movements, and interest group advocacy when these groups become so powerful that they start to significantly influence the national political process. (The influence of the railroad industry and the trusts in the nineteenth century, and the progress of blacks, women, and gays in the twentieth century are instructive examples.) When that happens, the courts' work will tend to cooperate with these political and cultural forces. At most courts can act as a drag on changes that threaten to happen very quickly, but they will eventually come around because of the appointments process and long-term changes in constitutional culture. All of this, of course, leads to the obvious question of why we care about interpretive theory in constitutional law, to which I now turn.

Constitutional Interpretation in Dark Times

I emphasize attention to positive constitutional theory and the processes of constitutional change because I do not think that one can usefully engage in normative constitutional theory without paying at least some attention to what positive constitutional theory teaches us. To put it simply: ought implies can. We should not expect from judges—or from the constitutional system, for that matter—practices of constitutional decisionmaking that they simply cannot provide. And we cannot adopt a theory of constitutional interpretation that the actual system of constitutional law could never be faithful to. We know that constitutional law and doctrine have changed markedly in many different areas over time. We also know that constitutional doctrine responds to the work of political mobilizations, social movements, and interest group advocacy, and tends to reflect the vector sum of the dominant political forces of the time. A theory of constitutional interpretation that cannot account for these features of our system of constitutional decisionmaking will be inadequate to the task. Hence normative theories of constitutional interpretation must do different work than most law professors currently think they do.

The most important function of theories of constitutional interpretation is not to constrain judges in difficult and contested cases. Constraint in these situations comes mostly from other institutional features of our political system. Rather, normative theories about constitutional interpretation are important because they help participants understand and express claims about the legitimacy or illegitimacy of their current constitutional arrangements. This enables the Constitution to serve as "our law"—as a common object of fidelity and attachment. Theories about the right way to interpret the Constitution offer people a language to defend and criticize parts of the Constitution-in-practice with the hope of moving it closer to their values and ideals. The democratic legitimacy of the constitutional system depends on the fact that people can make these claims and seek to persuade others that they are correct.

The Constitution-in-practice, however, may fall well short of people's ideals. And things may get worse, not better, over time. Therefore citizens must have ways to critique our existing arrangements, to talk back to courts and other political actors, and to persuade their fellow citizens about what the Constitution requires. They need tools to help identify which features of existing arrangements are sufficiently faithful to the Constitution and which features are not.

Theories of constitutional interpretation form part of this toolkit. They offer platforms, concepts, and languages for legitimation, critique, persuasion, dissent, and mobilization that might promote eventual constitutional reform. These activities—legitimation, critique, persuasion, dissent, and mobilization—are central parts of our shared (and perpetually contested) constitutional culture. They matter both to the legal profession and to the political life of our nation. No doubt lawyers, judges, and legal academics will probably develop more sophisticated and complicated theories about interpreting the Constitution than most ordinary citizens. But citizens in a democracy must also have their own understandings and opinions about what makes constitutional claims—and existing arrangements—faithful or faithless to the Constitution.

Thus, theories of constitutional interpretation serve two basic tasks—and the method of text and principle helps us perform both of them. First, interpretive theories should help us explain why valuable features of our existing constitutional arrangements are faithful to the constitutional project correctly understood. There are many ways that the American constitutionalism might have evolved, depending on political, social, and economic contingencies. One goal of theories of constitutional interpretation is to explain and justify our existing forms of development in hindsight.

Second, judges, politicians, movements, and interest groups may have promoted unjust and unconstitutional policies that become widely accepted and part of the Constitution-in-practice. (Think, for example, about the construction of Jim Crow as a constitutional regime that lasted for the better part of a century.) Therefore, theories of constitutional interpretation should help us produce viable critiques of existing practices in the name of a deeper constitutional fidelity.

This second criterion is particularly important: It is not enough to have a theory of constitutional interpretation that explains why everything that has happened is perfectly fine. Such a theory will be nothing more than an apology for the actual; it will abdicate our political and moral responsibilities to be faithful to and to continue the constitutional project.

We need more than a theory that explains why many of the changes in our constitutional practices have been faithful to the American constitutional project. We also need a theory of constitutional interpretation for dark times—that is, times when our views of what the Constitution really means have been submerged and disrespected by the dominant forces in society.[42] During such times citizens and members of oppositional political and social movements must obey positive law, but they do not have to accept it as correct or faithful to the Constitution. They can protest it in the name of the Constitution and work to change people's minds. But to do this, citizens need normative leverage to challenge the existing practices of constitutional law so that they can restore or redeem the Constitution's promises. Citizens need a way of grounding their claims about the Constitution that is independent from the Constitution-in-practice. Interpretive theories—and the protestant constitutional claims they underwrite—make it possible for people to pledge faith in the Constitution even though the Constitution-in-practice falls short of what they believe the Constitution is and should become.

Above all, citizens need a theory of interpretation for dark times because the present is always dark times for somebody's vision of the Constitution. Often it is dark times for both sides of an ongoing national controversy, like abortion or gay rights. For example, although I argue that the most faithful interpretation of the Constitution protects women's rights to abortion, I know that many of my fellow citizens disagree with me. For them, the continued enforcement of abortion rights makes a mockery of the Constitution, just as for me the limitation or undermining of these rights flies in the face of the Constitution's guarantees of equal citizenship and fundamental rights. Each of us, in our own way, needs ways of talking about the Constitution that do not take existing arrangements as presumptively correct; that do not require us to bow down to the idol of the Constitution-in-practice.

You will notice that the first task I set for an interpretive theory—legitimation—presumes the standpoint of someone who seeks an attractive normative account of the existing constitutional order as it has developed through the play of political and social forces. The second task—critique—presumes the standpoint of a constitutional dissenter. Both of these standpoints are necessary to a successful constitutional theory. Moreover, these two perspectives actually depend on each other. It is precisely because people in the past were dissatisfied with the constitutional order of their day, and mobilized to change people's minds about what the Constitution really means that they succeeded in producing changes in constitutional culture and constitutional doctrine. These changes have become part of the established order that we now try to explain and legitimate. Conversely, present-day constitutional dissent usually begins with the assumption that at least some of these changes in the constitutional order are justifiable, and that the dissenter is following in the footsteps of the successful and honored political mobilizations of the past. Today's constitutional dissenter hopes to create part of the dominant constitutional vision of the future, the Constitution-in-practice that future interpreters will seek to defend and legitimate.

The method of text and principle can serve both of these functions. It is a constitutional bulwark that can legitimate the best in the many transformations our constitutional system has undergone, and it is a constitutional refuge for dark times. It allows people to recognize that valued aspects of the Constitution-in-practice have kept faith with the Constitution despite the manifold changes in American life since the founding; yet it also preserves a powerful position from which people can critique features of our existing practices. It creates a space for aspirational claims and for constitutional dissent. It allows people to understand their present situation in terms of the Constitution's abiding commitments, it lets people critique the Constitution-in-practice through a return to first principles, and it helps people mobilize and persuade others by appealing to common values, symbols, and commitments. The central idea that we should be faithful to the Constitution's text and underlying principles is both intelligible and plausible to ordinary citizens, while its legal implications are sufficiently complex for constitutional lawyers and theorists to articulate and expand in theoretically satisfying ways.[43]

If the Constitution is to be "our" Constitution, we must be able to see ourselves as part of a project that unites past, present, and future generations. We must be able to see our principles and commitments as the principles and commitments of those who came before us and of those who will come after us. The Constitutional text is the perhaps most conspicuous embodiment of a constitutional project that binds past with present and stretches out into the future. And the language of restoration and redemption of constitutional principles well captures the sense of fidelity to the constitutional project over time. Hence it is not surprising that successful political and social mobilizations have looked to the constitutional text and to enduring principles as a ground for their normative critique of present-day arrangements.

Originalism and textualism, in their various forms, have been central methods for the legitimation and critique of regimes and practices of belief. And not only in America. I would venture to say that in almost every creedal community—every community that organizes itself around a set of practices and beliefs inherited from the past—a return to origins and to basic principles is a standard method for urging reform, and especially radical reform.[44]

In a creedal tradition organized around a central (or sacred) document, each generation—situated as it is and facing the problems that it faces—places glosses on the document, and these glosses are bequeathed to the future as what the document means. Later generations, finding these interpretations inadequate to their time, try to remove some of these glosses and return to the original, redeeming its promise, but what they actually do is preserve some of the older readings while adding newer glosses atop them. The history of creedal texts is the history of continuous glossing and stripping away of glosses—and continuous claims of return, restoration, and redemption that are, from the perspective of later generations, yet more readings and rereadings that must someday be critiqued, judged, and possibly undone.

I do not claim that this is true as a matter of logical necessity. I do claim it is characteristic of the American constitutional tradition and, indeed, of many other traditions as well. Repeatedly, constitutional dissenters and insurgent movements have turned to the constitutional text and to the great deeds and commitments of the past—including most particularly those of the founding generation—as a justification for their assault on the status quo.

My friend and colleague Bruce Ackerman has famously denounced what he calls the "myth of rediscovery"[45] in American constitutional law—the notion that we can justify major transformations like the New Deal as a return to original principles and commitments. In fact, Ackerman argues, American constitutional development features a succession of generations engaged in acts of constitution making that displace and build on older ones.

I agree with Ackerman that the history of American constitutional development has been one of continuous change, but I disagree that the "myth of rediscovery" is a myth in the pejorative sense that Ackerman means to convey—a false story that obfuscates the truth about social life. Rather, myths are stories that reveal deep verities about the human condition. So it is with our life as a constitutional community. The tropes of fidelity to text and principle, and of constitutional restoration and redemption, are not simply fables we tell ourselves. These tropes allow us to see the Constitution as a project that connects different generations and identifies them as a single people stretched out over time. The notion that we, like those before us, are striving to be faithful to the Constitution's text and underlying principles, and that our job is to restore and redeem them in our time, allows the Constitution to achieve simultaneously the multiple functions that a constitution like America's must perform—a basic framework for politics and lawmaking; an honored source of values and aspirations; and a cherished object of fidelity and attachment that symbolically binds different generations together and allows them to identify with each other over time.

On the surface, the theory of text and principle seems to rely on nothing more than straightforward claims about what makes a text binding law over time. But I hope I have shown in this chapter that the theory is about far more. The American Constitution is simultaneously a text, a set of political institutions, a source of values and aspirations, a repository of cultural memory, and a transgenerational political project. Lincoln famously spoke of our constitutional system as a government of the people, by the people, and for the people. But if the Constitution belongs to the American people, it also helps constitute them as a people that persists over time. It does so by constituting a common project, a common past, and a common destiny. Its legitimacy comes from the fact that it can do this successfully—that it can serve simultaneously as basic law, as higher law, and as our law.

Textual theories generally assume that the Constitution is binding law because We the People agreed to it. But the generation that ratified the original Constitution is long dead. Later generations do not consent to the Constitution; we live with it and in it. The Constitution is a culture we inhabit, an ocean we swim in, a set of institutions we grow up with. It is a project started by others that we make our own by defending it, interpreting it, arguing about it, putting ourselves on its side. Then we become part of the same We the People who wrote and ratified it. Then the Constitution becomes our Constitution, and we become the people to whom it belongs.

We can accept the Constitution as our own if it secures our rights and defends our values sufficiently that it is worthy of our respect and allegiance, if it is more than just a covenant with death and an agreement with hell. If the Constitution-in-practice is sufficiently efficacious and just, we can support the constitutional system and expect that everyone else in the political community should do so as well. But this judgment is not a simple *quid pro quo*. It requires an attitude of attachment to and faith in the constitutional project. The Constitution-in-practice will not always respect our most cherished values. It will not always protect our rights. We will often live in dark times. Rather, the Constitution is ours if we are able to have faith that over time it will come to respect our rights and our values. The Constitution is ours if we can trust in its future and in what future generations will do to realize its promises. The Constitution is ours if we can believe in its redemption.

6

ORIGINALISMS

In Chapter 1, I argued that fidelity to the Constitution requires fidelity to original meaning. So do most conservative originalists today. Most conservative originalists, at least in the legal academy, have long abandoned arguing for following either "original intentions" or the "original understanding." What differentiates my version of original meaning from theirs?

I noted earlier that although most conservative originalists claim that they seek only to follow original meaning, they tend in practice to conflate original meaning with original expected application. As I noted in Chapter 1, Justice Scalia offers the clearest example of how this conflation occurs, and he is perhaps the most prominent and public popularizer of original meaning originalism—"the proverbial 500-pound gorilla in the interpretive debate," as Vasan Kesavan and Michael Stokes Paulsen once put it.[1] Original meaning originalism is on the map today in large part because of Scalia's efforts,[2] and so it is particularly important to pay attention to how he imagines the methodology should work in practice.

Beyond Scalia's arguments, however, is the larger community of conservative original-meaning originalists. Since the 1980s, scholars have done important theoretical work done on originalism that goes beyond Scalia's initial formulation.[3] Most originalists today would emphasize that we do not simply follow what the founding generation thought was constitutional and unconstitutional; otherwise, we would not be able to adapt the Constitution to new technologies like radio or television that were not invented when the Constitution was adopted. Similarly, if inquiries into original meaning reveal that a particular constitutional provision—say, procedural due process—requires judges to look to tradition, some originalists, such as Michael McConnell, will look to developments after the founding.[4]

Nevertheless, even though conservative original-meaning originalists do not consider themselves automatically bound by original expectations, they are often strongly guided by them in practice. Although the two concepts are distinct in theory, the turn to original meaning, particularly among conservative originalists, has not emphasized the distinction, in part because the distinction is not salient to the reasons why conservatives moved from original intention to original meaning in the first place. Quite the contrary: conservative originalist practices of arguing about original meaning tend to conflate the question of original meaning with constructions based on expected applications. When originalists face a vague or abstract provision, they look to expected applications and use this data to formulate principles that they then equate with the clause's "original meaning." But these principles are not original meaning in the sense described in Chapter 1. They are constitutional constructions, just like the constructions that other lawyers and judges make. They may be good constructions or bad ones. But we are not required to follow them simply because they were offered by the adopting generation. When the text delegates the task of construction to later generations, the choice of which constructions to adopt is up to us. This basic idea is what distinguishes framework originalism from other varieties.

To explain why conservative originalists have tended to conflate original meaning with constructions derived from original expected application, a little history may be in order. Contemporary originalism arose from efforts by conservative legal scholars and politicians to combat what they saw as overreaching by liberal judicial decisions in the Warren and Burger Courts, what is sometimes referred to as liberal judicial activism.[5] In the early 1980s, conservative lawyers like Attorney General Edwin Meese argued for a return to a jurisprudence of "original intention"[6] that would push courts back toward the proper path and show appropriate respect for democratic decisionmaking. The argument for fidelity to original intention arose out of broader conservative political and social movements that sought to correct the perceived excesses of liberal policies.[7]

But even as the theory was announced by Meese and others, lawyers and legal scholars began refining it. Originalist theorists quickly moved from original intention to original understanding, and then to original meaning, in order to respond to difficulties with the original formulation.[8] The first problem was that "original intention" seemed to focus on the intentions of the persons who drafted the document, but surely it was the ratifiers' views that counted, because only they had the authority to make the proposed Constitution law. "Original understanding" better captured a focus on the authorizing audience for the text as opposed to the text's drafters. The second and more important problem was the charge of psychologism. Critics argued that we cannot identify the law with the psychological states of particular historical actors—whether framers or ratifiers—because they may not have all shared the same mental states, because their intentions might be unknowable, and because they may have had no intentions about states of affairs that did not or could not obtain when they lived.[9] In 1985 H. Jefferson Powell added another criticism: the generation that framed the Constitution did not believe that looking to framers' intentions was an appropriate interpretive strategy; they believed that purpose and intention should be derived from the public words of the text.[10]

Original meaning originalism sought to address these problems by focusing not on the mental states of framers or ratifiers but on the general and publicly shared meanings of the text at the time of enactment.[11] Spurred on by Justice Scalia and members of the Reagan Justice Department,[12] conservative lawyers and academics began to work out the details of the new theory.[13]

Original intention originalism offered conservative lawyers, judges, and legal scholars a jurisprudential account of why liberal judicial decisions from the 1960s forward had been illegitimate. It was widely assumed that many, if not most, of these decisions were inconsistent with the framers' intentions; this fact, and not mere political disagreement with the substance of these decisions, explained why they were illegitimate.[14] Adherence to original intentions would restrain judges and restore democracy.

The turn to original meaning was designed to preserve these basic insights, not to undermine them. To be sure, it brought some changes. First, original meaning originalism might cause scholars to look to new kinds of historical evidence (such as dictionaries) and to look to other historical evidence differently than before—for example, as evidence of what a reasonable and well-informed person living at the time of enactment would have understood the constitutional text to mean.[15] Second, adherents of original meaning insisted that the theory was perfectly consistent with applying constitutional guarantees to new technologies.[16] Finally, although originalists often tied their critique of the Warren and Burger Courts to calls for judicial restraint, advocates of original meaning did not oppose courts' striking down some laws—for example, laws that trenched on state sovereignty—where text, history, and structure supported it. This evolution in views on judicial restraint became particularly important as conservative judges began to dominate the federal courts in the 1980s.[17]

Nevertheless, the turn to original meaning was not designed to drive a wedge between the text's public meaning and how the framing generation would have expected the text would be applied. For example, the Reagan Justice Department's *Guidelines on Constitutional Litigation,* which articulated the new philosophy of original meaning, explained that in cases involving the Constitution's vague or abstract clauses, lawyers should look to the intended scope of a constitutional provision:

> [T]erms such as "equal protection" or "free exercise" are less easy to define, making a more detailed inquiry into the historical context or other evidence of the intent of those responsible for drafting or ratifying the provision not only useful, but necessary to discover the values and principles embodied in those terms. While there is no mechanistic formula for discovering underlying values and principles and applying them to particular issues, a genuine attempt is required to discover those values and principles and their intended scope from particular constitutional provisions (alone or in concert with other provisions), and then to apply them in a manner consistent with the original meaning.[18]

To assist lawyers in discovering these values and principles, the *Guidelines* included a helpful bibliography "of sources available for gleaning historical evidence of the Founders' intentions."[19]

Thus the distinction between original meaning and original expected application was not particularly salient in the move to original meaning. Original meaning originalism sought to put originalism on a stronger theoretical footing, not to undo the conservative critique of liberal judicial activism. Far from it: conservative lawyers and judges in the midst of a powerful social movement would hardly have turned to a theory of interpretation that they believed would subvert most of their settled views about constitutional law. They assumed that original meaning originalism, like the jurisprudence of original intention, would discipline courts and prevent them from new adventures. As Caleb Nelson put it, "our views of 'original meaning' and 'original intention' will tend to converge in practice even if the two concepts remain distinct in theory."[20] Or as Justice Scalia explained at his 1986 confirmation hearings, there was "not a big difference" between the two ideas.[21]

Nevertheless, scholars such as Ronald Dworkin,[22] Randy Barnett,[23] Kermit Roosevelt,[24] Jeffrey Goldsworthy,[25] Mark Greenberg, and Harry Litman[26] pointed out that the move to original meaning had an unintended consequence. If original meaning is original semantic meaning—the concepts that the framers employed in the words they chose—then fidelity to original meaning does not require following what the framing generation thought the consequences of adopting the words would be. That is especially so when the text employs abstract principles or vague standards. The logical consequence of moving from original intention and original understanding to original meaning is that original meaning originalism—or at least the version I offer here—becomes a form of living constitutionalism.

Needless to say, this is not what most conservative originalists were looking for. Despite the force of this critique, today's original meaning originalists often view original expected applications as very strong evidence of original meaning, even (or perhaps especially) when the text points to abstract principles or standards. That is because, in the words of the Reagan Justice Department, they are looking for evidence of the intended scope of the adopters' principles. Hence, even though conservative originalists may distinguish between the ideas of original meaning and original expected applications in theory, they often conflate them in practice.

In particular, conservative originalists tend to equate constructions offered contemporaneous with adoption with original meaning. These contemporaneous constructions may be quite important and persuasive authority, and especially powerful in the first decades after adoption.[27] But we should not confuse these constructions with original meaning, and they may (and should) have far less force many years later.

Nevertheless, conservative original-meaning originalists are simply not comfortable with accepting that the original meaning of "equal protection" is "equal protection" and then taking responsibility for constructing a series of doctrines that would implement and flesh out this abstract guarantee. They do not want the responsibility that the text seems to announce—of delegating this process of implementation to later generations. They would prefer to identify original meaning with far narrower principles (what I would call constructions) that the text does not actually state, and then claim that these constructions *are* the original meaning. The irony is that although they resist the idea that later generations have been delegated the task of constructing the text, that is precisely what they are doing: They are implementing the text in a particularly narrow way that the text does not require.

For example, consider Michael McConnell's well-known originalist defense of *Brown v. Board of Education* in 1995.[28] Before McConnell's article, most people accepted Alexander Bickel's conclusion that the framers of the Fourteenth Amendment did not intend to prohibit segregated public schools.[29] In fact, as McConnell himself notes, at the time of ratification, segregation of schools by race was widely practiced and the idea of common schools for blacks and whites was deeply unpopular in both the North and the South.[30] Nevertheless, McConnell showed that in the years following the ratification of the Fourteenth Amendment, many of the congressmen and senators who proposed the Fourteenth Amendment argued for desegregation of schools in proposed federal legislation (parts of which eventually became the Civil Rights Act of 1875).[31] Moreover, they supported this legislation on constitutional grounds, because they believed that segregated public schools violated the Fourteenth Amendment.

Although scholars have pointed out various problems with the argument,[32] my goal here is not to dispute McConnell's conclusions. My point, rather, is that his research, while admirable, is actually unnecessary if the question is whether *Brown* is consistent with *original meaning*. McConnell's research is quite valuable in creating *constructions* of the abstract principle of equal protection, but it adds little to the question of what the words "equal protection" meant in 1868; the words meant pretty much what they mean today.

In fact, McConnell's dogged investigation of post-ratification debates shows that he believed that the best way to demonstrate the original meaning of the Fourteenth Amendment was to show how the Congress that proposed it would have applied it. That is, he thought that the best evidence of original meaning was evidence of original expected application. Moreover, McConnell did not use evidence of original expected application by the *general public* and the *ratifiers* of the amendment— whom McConnell conceded probably strongly supported school segregation.[33] Instead he used evidence of original expected application by the *framers*—Republican supporters of the Fourteenth Amendment in Congress. Ironically, McConnell made his case for *original meaning* by making a case based on the *original intentions* of the framers.[34]

McConnell's example is illustrative: in their pursuit of original meaning, most conservative originalists seek to discover evidence of how people in the adopting generation applied or would have applied the constitutional text, along with the framers' and ratifiers' statements of principle and purpose. Originalists then use these materials as data points to construct principles that, not surprisingly, will usually produce results roughly similar to the data points they started with.

The goal, in short, is to identify the original meaning of abstract language with the framers' and ratifiers' principles and constructions. Recovering those principles and constructions, however, requires close attention to expected applications, even if changed circumstances might make some cases (but not too many) come out differently. By way of analogy, Michael McConnell explains how we should reconstruct the principles of Aristotle's political philosophy: The examples Aristotle offers to explain his philosophy "should not be taken as fixed or sacrosanct. It may well be that some of them would require modification in light of current circumstances," and "[i]t is even possible that Aristotle made a mistake or two, and that some of his examples should have come out the other way."[35] Nevertheless, McConnell explains, "the more examples we reject, the more likely it is that we are making mistakes about Aristotle than it is that Aristotle made so many mistakes in applying his own principles." Thus, if we want to understand the framers' original meaning, we had better choose principles that do not result in them making very many "mistakes."[36]

Similarly, John McGinnis and Michael Rappaport argue that a "strong dichotomy between original expected applications and original meaning" is "improbabl[e]."[37] "[W]hile the original meaning may not be defined by the expected applications," McGinnis and Rappaport explain, "these applications will often be some of the best evidence of what that meaning is."[38] This is true, they argue, even "when a constitutional provision is best understood as adopting a general understanding or principle," because "verbal formulations often do not tell us which particular variation of a principle was intended."[39] Hence, even if the equal protection clause enacts "an anticaste principle, ... it may not clearly indicate the version of the principle that was adopted—to what extent, and under what circumstances, the principle allowed distinctions between different groups. The expected applications will help us determine which version of the principle was adopted."[40] Thus the anticaste principle does not ban discrimination against women or homosexuals if the generation that produced the Fourteenth Amendment would not have applied the principle to these groups.

Where subsequent experience shows that the framers' generation was clearly mistaken "as a factual matter"[41]—for example, about whether certain deposits were gold—McGinnis and Rappaport agree that we are not bound by original expected applications of the text. But where we think that the framers were mistaken *morally,* a different presumption should apply, and original meaning should stay close to original expected application: "[W]here a legal provision purports to incorporate moral or policy beliefs and those beliefs are open to several interpretations, one is much less justified in concluding that the expected applications of people at the time were mistakes."[42] Quite the contrary: "It is more likely that later interpreters are mistaken about the content of the provision that was adopted than that interpreters at the time were mistaken about the meaning of the provisions they wrote."[43]

Thus, McGinnis and Rappaport argue that we settle the original meaning of abstract or ambiguous language by reference to the framers' and ratifiers' principles. We should use original expected application to define the scope of these constitutional principles so that they generally produce results consistent with the original expected application. Adopting this method predictably conflates original meaning with original expected application. And this conflation is not accidental.

McGinnis and Rappaport's concern is that without the constraining force of original expected applications, original meaning originalism will not provide the necessary constraint against interpretive changes by unelected judges. It will not do what the turn to originalism in the 1980s was designed to do—limit liberal judicial activism. As they explain, "discarding expected applications in favor of abstract principles, as influenced by social movements, transfers tremendous power from the enacters of the Constitution to future interpreters. A Constitution that was established to place limits on future government actors would not delegate power so generously."[44]

Of course, this begs the question of what abstract provisions in a constitution are designed to do—are they designed only to limit future generations, or are they also designed to delegate the articulation and implementation of important constitutional principles to the future? As I argued in Chapter 2, a central claim of framework originalism is that we should take the use of abstract language in a constitution seriously as a decision to delegate to future generations. We can see that tethering original meaning to original expected applications is designed to avoid this delegation. McGinnis and Rappaport are not worried only about runaway judges. They are also concerned that later generations will assume the authority to determine the meaning of the Constitution's abstract guarantees for themselves. "[I]t is a little difficult to see what is left of a recognizable originalism, not to mention the amendment process, if social movement[s] have such substantial discretion to apply constitutional provisions as they see fit."[45] "[W]hy," they ask, "would one adopt a fixed constitution if it can be changed so easily by social movements?"[46] Put another way, McGinnis and Rappaport object to discarding reliance on expected applications because it makes original meaning originalism a form of living constitutionalism.

Even so, conservative original-meaning originalists are living constitutionalists despite themselves. They simply achieve living constitutionalism in other ways. One of the most important of those ways is how they handle precedent.

7

PRECEDENTS AND PRAGMATIC
EXCEPTIONS

In Chapter 6, I explained how conservative original-meaning original-ism models constitutional principles and original meaning on original expected applications. This creates a serious conflict with many important features of contemporary American law that are not really consistent with original expected applications. These include the administrative and regulatory state that came with the New Deal, the expansion of modern civil rights and civil liberties that emerged from the civil rights revolution, and the transformation of the presidency in the national security state.

Taken together, the New Deal, the national security state, and the civil rights revolution constitute a good portion of the contemporary constitutional regime. We might define a constitutional regime as consisting of (1) basic principles and assumptions about constitutional rights, duties, and powers and the proper role of government; and (2) the institutions and practices that grow up around these principles and assumptions.[1] Our current regime includes, for example, Social Security and other social safety-net programs, national fair labor and consumer protection standards, federal regulations that secure environmental protection, a large federal bureaucracy to carry out these programs, centralized fiscal and monetary policies, an enormous peacetime defensive capability complete with elaborate intelligence programs and permanent standing armies positioned around the world, the Voting Rights Act, equal rights for women, and robust free-speech protections. Most elements of this regime arose from state-building constructions that were ratified or supported by the judiciary. Constitutional doctrines largely conform to the basic assumptions of the regime and mostly legitimate existing practices; in fact, these doctrines are part and parcel of the regime itself.

Because originalists disagree among themselves about what original meaning requires, different originalists will find different parts of the modern regime consistent with their version of original meaning originalism. Unless they adopt something like framework originalism, however, large parts of current practices will not be consistent. There will be innumerable nonoriginalist precedents and practices to contend with, at least if "nonoriginalist" is defined in the way noted above—inconsistent with constitutional principles derived from original expected applications. The more closely scholars employ original expected applications as the source of the constitutional principles they identify with original meaning, the greater the discrepancy there will be.

There are two possible responses: One is to acknowledge the inconsistency and argue that much of contemporary practice should be jettisoned. But although some academics may find this solution both theoretically attractive and intellectually coherent, it casts originalists out of the political and professional mainstream. No judge who announced that the New Deal and many achievements of the civil rights revolution were mistaken and should be overturned could be confirmed to the bench.

The other solution, adopted by Justice Scalia and many other originalists both in the academy and in public life, is to accept most (but not all) nonoriginalist precedents and constructions as settled and beyond dispute. As Scalia notes, "almost every originalist would adulterate it with the doctrine of stare decisis,"[2] and he treats nonoriginalist precedents as a "pragmatic exception" to the requirement of fidelity to original meaning.[3]

The difficulty is that this approach seriously undermines conservative originalist claims about why judicial review is legitimate as well as conservative originalist arguments for judicial restraint in a democracy. Most originalists, including myself, argue that the Constitution's original meaning is binding on later generations because the constitutional text is an act of popular sovereignty that creates a supreme law that continues in force over time. Opponents of originalism may object to being ruled by the hand of long-dead framers, but originalists can reply that at the very least the Constitution reflects popular will at the time of enactment. Displacing original meaning for nonoriginalist precedent, on the other hand, substitutes the work of unelected judges—many themselves long dead—for the Constitution itself.[4]

Indeed, the longer the constitutional system continues, and the longer people build on existing nonoriginalist precedents (and create still others), the more the Constitution-in-practice will likely depart from one based on the conservative version of original meaning. The pragmatic exception eventually swallows the originalist rule, and it becomes increasingly hard to explain or defend current practices based on originalism's theory of democratic legitimacy. Indeed, we are probably well past that point. The power of the modern federal government, the pervasiveness of the modern administrative and welfare state, the scope of the president's authority, both overseas and domestically, and the content of modern civil rights and civil liberties protections are well beyond what adopting generations would have dreamed of or supported, while some economic rights that previous generations might have viewed as the central examples of constitutional guarantees have been drastically limited following the New Deal.

A second problem follows from the first. Many movement conservatives found originalism attractive because they believed that adherence to original meaning constrained judges in a democracy. If judges had only adhered to originalist reasoning, they would not have developed the liberal jurisprudence of the Warren and early Burger Courts. But accepting nonoriginalist precedents rewards judges for their previous infidelities and their lack of constraint. And accepting previous errors as beyond revisiting does little to prevent new mistakes from occurring. Indeed, it helps ensure that the process will repeat itself: If later judges write nonoriginalist opinions and the public comes to accept those results as embedded in the constitutional regime, future originalist judges who want to be accepted by the political and legal mainstream will have to work those new errors into their system as additional pragmatic exceptions.

Worse yet, originalist judging thus adulterated does not really constrain judges very much, for judges can now pick and choose when to invoke originalist justifications and when to accept previous nonoriginalist precedents, or even extend them. Indeed, because they use all the standard modalities of legal argument, including precedent and consequences, the practices of originalist judges become largely indistinguishable from those of judges who do not consider themselves originalists at all. Randy Barnett acidly notes that a "faint-hearted" originalist judge like Scalia who accepts nonoriginalist precedents

> leaves himself not one but three different routes by which to escape adhering to the original meaning of the text. These are more than enough to allow

him, or any judge, to reach any result he wishes. Where originalism gives him the results he wants, he can embrace originalism. Where it does not, he can embrace precedent that will. Where friendly precedent is unavailing, he can assert the nonjusticiability of clauses [like the Ninth Amendment] that yield results to which he is opposed. And where all else fails, he can simply punt, perhaps citing the history of traditionally-accepted practices of which he approves.[5]

Armed with this panoply of options, conservative original-meaning originalists can easily craft doctrines in contested cases that largely map onto conservative political preferences while still adhering to the basic elements of the current constitutional regime—the administrative and welfare state of the New Deal, key protections of the civil rights revolution, and the powerful presidency that emerged with the national security state. And, over time, they can attempt to shift the constitutional regime in a more conservative direction. This project may be politically attractive to movement conservatives, but it has little to do with originalism's stated theory of legitimacy, and it does not really constrain judges or keep them from "legislating from the bench"—to use a favored political slogan—albeit in a conservative direction.

My point, however, is not simply to accuse conservative originalists of inconsistency, hypocrisy, or engaging in their own forms of judicial activism. Rather, I am interested in why the problem arises. The difficulties that conservative originalists face come from two sources.

The first problem comes from conflating original meaning with constructions derived from original expected applications. As we have seen, this is the standard way that conservative originalists have tried to generate constitutional principles to apply to new situations, and it is a flawed method, for the reasons given in Chapter 6. But the second and deeper problem is that the originalist theory of democratic legitimacy is seriously incomplete. Although conservative originalists cannot really be skyscraper originalists in practice, they have adopted skyscraper originalism's theory of democratic legitimacy. According to that theory, the democratic legitimacy of the Constitution arises solely from the initial act of lawmaking, either at the founding or through subsequent amendments. Everything else is ordinary politics. But responsiveness to contemporary values and contemporary expectations is an equally important source of democratic legitimacy, both for the Constitution-in-practice and for the exercise of judicial review.

The constitution-making power of We the People (sometimes called the constituent power) creates the Constitution and, through the people's representatives, amends it from time to time. According to skyscraper originalism, that is the beginning and the end of the people's participation in constitution making. Outside of this, the power of the people is exercised only through ordinary politics and the institutions of representative government.

But this assumption of skyscraper originalism is false, or at least seriously incomplete. The people's constitution-making power never really goes away. It is continually exercised through the processes of constitutional construction and by the same institutions that participate in ordinary politics.[6] Because the constitutional framework is open-ended, people with different political views can make good-faith claims for interpreting it and building on it consistent with their competing constitutional and political visions without having to argue for amending the Constitution.[7] Many (but not all) claims that could be stated as proposals for amending the Constitution are fairly easily restated as claims of constitutional interpretation or constitutional construction. This is especially true of state-building constructions like those characteristic of the New Deal, the civil rights revolution, and the national security state.

Thus, following the adoption of the basic framework, the public's constitution-making power is usually channeled into the institutions of ordinary politics in debates over constitutional construction and the best way to exercise constitutional powers and defend constitutional rights. This process of political contestation, mobilization, and countermobilization naturally causes the Constitution-in-practice to evolve in response to changing public values and long-term shifts in popular opinion. As the constitutional system develops, constitutional politics is perpetually translated into new and modified constitutional constructions.

To be sure, amendments to the United States Constitution also continue throughout history, and mobilizations for and against proposed amendments may have important effects in shaping and influencing constitutional constructions. Nevertheless, amendments themselves are comparatively rare, and most are devoted to basic structural questions. There are many reasons why amendments have been relatively infrequent in the American constitutional system, but one of the most important is that, among the constitutions of the world, the American Constitution is one of the most difficult to amend.[8] By contrast, the constitutions of the individual states, and those of many other democratic nations have much less arduous procedures. Hence, the mix of constitutional construction and amendment in these regimes is likely to be different; and this may also affect methods of constitutional interpretation as well as the exercise of judicial review.

Because the constitution-making power of the people of the United States is never suppressed or given away, constitutional construction responds to it over long periods of time. This is not an accident or an oversight; it is a condition of our Constitution's democratic legitimacy. Our Constitution is ultimately self-enforcing, and as Jefferson recognized, the people themselves are the final source of enforcement.[9] Indeed, if the public had no ability or opportunity to affect the Constitution's interpretation through construction, the Constitution-in-practice would lose its democratic legitimacy, because it could no longer serve effectively as "our law." The possibility of persuading other citizens and government officials to change their minds, and the possibility of eventually reshaping the Constitution-in-practice give citizens faith and a stake in the constitutional enterprise over time. This bestows legitimacy on a constitutional system that is decidedly imperfect and often unjust, and that may occasionally frustrate or even oppress groups who find themselves in strong and principled dissent from the Constitution-in-practice. If the Constitution is to be "our law," it must also be accepted by those whose views do not prevail. The public can respect the decisions of courts as law, even if they disagree with these decisions, as long as they believe that they have a chance to shape the law over time through political participation and constitutional construction.[10]

The constitution-making power of the people is exercised through politics; it employs and influences constitutional construction by the political branches and the courts. And because the people's constitution-making power operates through politics, the Constitution-in-practice becomes the residue or the sediment of previous acts of constitutional politics.[11] Existing constitutional constructions, in turn, are reshaped, supplemented, and displaced by later acts of constitutional politics. The perpetual contributions of popular opinion and political mobilizations generate a kind of democratic legitimacy for the Constitution-in-practice that skyscraper originalism cannot comprehend.

This is the real reason why conservative originalists must always be "faint-hearted." What conservative originalism regards as "pragmatic exceptions" or "reliance" is really the acceptance of the basic premises of the existing constitutional regime—the outcome of decades of political struggles that produced the constitutional constructions and assumptions that form the basis of contemporary politics. For what is a constitutional regime but the residue of past constitutional constructions that have been accepted and thus legitimated by the public?

Judges do not accept the activist state, the modern presidency, and the civil rights revolution because of economic cost or reliance; they accept them because doing so is necessary for the judiciary to maintain its democratic legitimacy. Judges who declared that they would not be bound by the regime's basic commitments would not simply be imposing costs or defeating reliance; they would be undermining their claim to authority in the constitutional system.

The public expects that judges will continue to enforce the principles and assumptions of the current regime unless and until a new political revolution changes the basic assumptions of politics, as happened during the New Deal and the civil rights era. That is a large part of what the public means when it expects judges to "follow the law." Judges could safely propose jettisoning these basic commitments only if the public itself comes to reject the assumptions, institutions, and principles that constitute the current regime. Conversely, if the judiciary is persistently unresponsive to the public's changing attitudes about the purposes of government and the Constitution's meaning, it will eventually lose the public's support, and partisan entrenchment will replace older judges with newer ones. This is what happened to the Supreme Court during the constitutional struggle over the New Deal.[12] Eventually the Supreme Court gave way, and new justices appointed by the president consolidated the constitutional foundations of a new constitutional regime.

The judiciary's legitimacy, in other words, comes both from its fidelity to the initial act of constitution-making power and from its indirect, long-term responsiveness to subsequent expressions of constitution-making power, albeit always through the forms and practices of law. Framework originalism, unlike skyscraper originalism, recognizes this duality: it recognizes that democratic legitimacy arises both from the act of framing a Constitution and from the processes of democratic constitutionalism that construct it.

Justice Scalia has noted the curious "fact that most originalists are faint-hearted and most nonoriginalists are moderate (that is, would not ascribe evolving content to such clear provisions as the requirement that the president be no less than thirty-five years of age) which accounts for the fact that the sharp divergence between the two philosophies does not produce an equivalently sharp divergence in judicial opinions."[13] This convergence is not accidental. Most originalists—at least those sufficiently mainstream to obtain jobs on the bench—accept the modern constitutional regime and find ways to live within it. Conversely, most living constitutionalists who also accept the regime are actually framework originalists who accept the Constitution's hardwired rules.

Although originalism often presents itself as a return to first principles, the conservative originalism that developed in the late twentieth century developed within the existing constitutional regime as a partial critique. Conservative originalism in the 1980s arose after political and legal struggles over the New Deal had legitimated the administrative and welfare state and activist government; after America had become a world superpower and created a national security state with a powerful presidency, standing armies, sophisticated intelligence and surveillance activities, and an enormous defense budget; after public acceptance of *Brown v. Board of Education* and the civil rights revolution, which secured greater equality for blacks and prohibitions on certain forms of private racial, ethnic and religious discrimination; after the revolution in criminal procedure had rationalized state and local police practices; after the sexual revolution had transformed personal behavior and social mores and led to increasing acceptance of premarital sex and contraceptive use; and after general public acceptance of equal rights for women. None of this was contemplated at the founding. Yet conservative originalists believed they could use the purposes and expectations of the founding era to explain and justify constitutional law in the twentieth and twenty-first centuries.

If conservative originalists wanted to play an important role in mainstream politics and command the respect of professional legal culture, they would have to account for central elements of that regime. Thus, although some early originalists, like Raoul Berger (a committed New Dealer), doubted the correctness of *Brown v. Board of Education,* later, more mainstream originalists, like Robert Bork and Antonin Scalia, readily accepted both *Brown* and the New Deal. The New Deal revolution in federal power was settled and there would be no going back. Indeed, the lesson of the New Deal for conservative originalists was the signal importance of judicial restraint. Advocates of New Deal constitutionalism taught that both the federal government and the states should have a free hand in social and economic regulation. Judges should not second-guess legislative judgments, and they should show a healthy respect for majoritarian decisionmaking; some New Dealers even argued that courts should rarely, if ever, exercise their power of judicial review. In this way the liberal arguments of the 1930s—which were considered quite nonoriginalist in their own day—became the conservative originalist orthodoxy of the 1980s and 1990s.

Similarly, most originalists eventually made their peace with *Brown* and the civil rights movement, although they interpreted them in more racially conservative ways. They opposed significant integrationist remedies, especially unpopular remedies like busing. *Brown* stood for desegregation, not integration.[14] *Brown* stood for facially race-neutral policies, not for equality of results. *Brown* was not about uprooting racial subordination; it was about preventing racial classification, especially when those classifications affected whites. Conservative originalists eagerly embraced a strong color-blindness theory of *Brown* to oppose race-conscious affirmative action programs, even though this theory of strict color blindness had little basis in the history of Reconstruction.[15]

For most conservative originalists who sought to be in the political mainstream, the originalism of the late twentieth century was what one might call "New Deal/*Brown* originalism." It began by assuming the legitimacy of *Brown* and the New Deal—the basic premises of the civil rights revolution and an activist state—whether or not they could be squared with original intentions, original understandings, or original meaning. It then offered conservative interpretations of the elements of the regime: The New Deal symbolized judicial restraint; *Brown* stood for the importance of formal neutrality and color blindness, for equality of formal opportunities but not for equality of results. In like fashion, modern conservative originalism assumed a powerful president of a kind unheard of in the eighteenth and nineteenth centuries, permanent standing armies, and all the tools of government necessary to run a national security state.

One might cynically insist that conservative originalism adopted these views because they were consistent with mainstream conservative political positions. But this misses the central point: *Both* mainstream conservative thought and mainstream liberal thought accepted the legitimacy of the central elements of the New Deal/national security/civil rights regime. Both sides accepted, for the most part, the constitutional constructions that came with the regime, even if they sometimes gave them very different interpretations and sought to continue them in different ways. That is because democratic legitimacy in the late twentieth century required

acceptance of these constructions, at least until a new and highly successful sustained mobilization could persuade the public otherwise.

Twentieth-century conservative originalism arose within a conservative movement that sought to change the existing constitutional regime.
It began by working within existing assumptions and sought to reform
them. Although conservative originalism began with acceptance of the
basic parameters of the current regime, over time it sought more radical
reforms. As the conservative movement grew in power and influence,
some originalists began to challenge more aspects of the regime; conservative libertarians, for example, attacked the constitutionality of the
New Deal, although they did not succeed in overthrowing it. Others
sought to roll back key features of the civil rights regime, like disparate
impact liability and voting rights protections.[16]

As time has passed, new constitutional constructions have become as
central to public legitimacy as the New Deal and *Brown*. Two of these
came from the sexual revolution of the 1960s and the women's movement: the idea that the state cannot punish premarital sex between adults
or deny access to contraception, and the idea that the government may
not discriminate against women. Later conservative originalists of the
1990s and 2000s have been faced with explaining why their methods do
not threaten *Griswold v. Connecticut* (which protects the right of married couples to use contraceptives), *Eisenstadt v. Baird* (which protects
the sexual freedom of single persons and unmarried couples), or the sex
equality decisions of the 1970s. To stay in the political mainstream, conservative originalism must accept these constructions today even though
conservative originalists opposed them as thoroughly inconsistent with
the Constitution when they were first decided.

No doubt, once gay rights are fully assimilated into American culture,
conservative originalists will add *Lawrence v. Texas* as another "mistake" that we cannot take back. (Or perhaps someone will write a very
clever article showing that the framers and ratifiers of the Fourteenth
Amendment really did mean to outlaw criminalization of same-sex relationships.) But each time conservative originalists add a new "mistake"
to the list, each time they adjust themselves to the evolving constitutional
regime, they confront a world in which more and more of the Constitution-
in-practice is in irremediable error and less and less can be made consistent with their theories of original meaning. This is a loser's game, a war
of constitutional attrition in which originalists must continuously concede
ground to the constitution-making power of the public that originalists

fail to recognize as a source of democratic legitimacy. It generates a world in which "originalism" and "what the framers wanted" become little more than political gestures alternatively adopted and discarded as conditions demand.

To be sure, there is something recognizably conservative about this approach. A certain style of conservatism tends to resist reform until it has been generally accepted by the public; then the conservative embraces and defends yesterday's reforms against new proposals. This may make some sense as a form of Burkean political conservatism. But it is not a coherent theory of fidelity to original meaning.

In order to maintain political legitimacy, conservative originalist judges must continue to create ever-new exceptions to their stated theory of legitimacy to accommodate what previous originalists have understood to be inconsistent with original meaning. Again, my point is more than an accusation of inconsistency. The problem is not simply that originalists have to do this—for it is virtually required if they want to be taken seriously in the mainstream of American politics and American law—but that their theory of what makes constitutional interpretation legitimate (fidelity to original meaning) cannot explain why they must do so. A central aspect of democratic legitimacy remains obscured by that theory. Saddled with an inadequate theory of democratic legitimacy, conservative originalists must characterize a never-ending stream of nonoriginalist decisions as mistaken concessions to reality, rather than recognizing that these constructions represent how the Constitution-in-practice is continually responsive to contemporary values and popular visions of the Constitution. By adopting skyscraper originalism's theory of legitimacy, they needlessly cut themselves off from a central source of democratic legitimacy—the constitution-making power of We the People as expressed in successive constitutional constructions that implement the Constitution's original meaning.

This is the irony of conservative originalism's theory of legitimacy. It continually mistakes the constitution-making power of the people for mere passion and assertions of will; it does not respect the Constitution's delegation of constitutional construction to later generations. Conservative originalism must continually abandon what it insists is the only proper source of democratic legitimacy in order to achieve actual democratic legitimacy in the eyes of the public.

The final irony is that the conservative movement itself, like so many other movements before it, has repeatedly invoked the constitution-making power of the people to reshape the Constitution through persuasion and through changing public sentiments. It has participated in a powerful struggle—outside the amendment process—to reshape the constitutional regime and the institutions, practices, and assumptions of modern government. The conservative movement, like other movements before it, sought to change the Constitution-in-practice by changing people's minds; to the extent it succeeded, it did so because conservative politicians and conservative advocates offered a powerful vision of the Constitution that resonated with current generations; moreover, by winning elections, conservatives were able to staff the courts with people who thought much as they did.

It is true that the conservative movement marched under the banner of returning to original intention (and later, original meaning), but much of what conservative jurists did once they got on the bench was not really consistent with either original intention or original meaning (at least in the way that they developed the theory). What gave conservative claims about the Constitution their legitimacy in the public's eyes was not that they were consistent with the founders' original expectations— for the public had no idea what these were—but that these claims appealed to present-day public sentiments about what the Constitution stands for, the limits of government power, and the rights that Americans enjoy. Conservative arguments against affirmative action and abortion and for a powerful presidency that could fight terrorism had little to do with original meaning, but a lot to do with appeals to contemporary values and current constituencies.[17]

There is perhaps no better example than the Supreme Court's recent decision in *District of Columbia v. Heller,* recognizing for the first time an individual right to bear arms in self-defense of the home. *Heller* works on two levels: Superficially, the arguments in the opinion refer to original meaning. Yet originalist arguments can be offered in both directions, and the most important evidence is not of original meaning in 1791 but of living constitutionalism in the nineteenth century.[18] In fact, the Court eventually reversed course and adopted a new construction of the Second Amendment for three reasons: (1) because the public overwhelmingly supported an individual right to bear arms, (2) because successful mobilizations dating back some forty years changed the public's mind about the meaning of the Second Amendment, and (3) because conservative politicians who won repeated elections helped appoint judges to the federal judiciary who found the individual rights claim both attractive and convincing. Moreover, the Court's articulation of the right (defense of the home) and its stated exceptions (no right to use "dangerous" weapons, no right to carry guns in "sensitive" places, no gun rights for felons) match contemporary public sentiments and expectations as much as the actual expectations of the founding generation. If the Court's construction in *Heller* enjoys democratic legitimacy today, it is due *both* to its consistency with original semantic meaning and its responsiveness to long-term changes in public opinion.[19]

All of this is hard to fathom if you maintain that the democratic legitimacy of the Constitution (and of judicial review) stems only from popular acceptance at the moment of the adoption of the constitutional text. But it makes a great deal of sense once you recognize that later constructions gain democratic legitimacy by popular acceptance garnered over longer periods of time.

What then is the proper place of precedent in an originalist theory of interpretation? Ironically, perhaps, I tend to agree with those originalists who believe that precedents inconsistent with original meaning deserve no special respect. We simply disagree about what original meaning requires. I assume, like other originalists,[20] that a common law style system of precedents was entirely foreseeable and indeed is implicit in the constitutional framework of a country with a common law tradition. Over time, judges will articulate and implement the Constitution through doctrine. Indeed, not only judges—the political branches also participate in constitutional construction by creating new institutions and practices, and by passing legislation that articulates and enforces constitutional principles. It does not follow, however, that we should retain precedents and constructions that are inconsistent with the Constitution's text and its underlying principles judged from our present perspective. A system of precedent should serve the Constitution, and not the other way around. It should implement and articulate the Constitution's textual commitments and great principles, not displace them.

We should keep the decisions of the civil rights era that guaranteed race and sex equality, expanded free speech, and imposed obligations of decency and fairness on the criminal justice systems of the federal government and the states. We should also retain the New Deal decisions that legitimated the administrative and regulatory state and gave Congress the power to protect civil rights, the environment, and the rights of workers. But we should maintain these decisions not because they are mistakes that we are stuck with, but because they are good interpretations of text and principle. We do not keep them because they are unfaithful but practically necessary or widely accepted. We keep them because they *are* faithful; we keep them because they are reasonable, if occasionally imperfect, implementations of the Constitution.

Conversely, precedents should be modified or discarded if they are no longer reasonable constructions of text and principle, and especially if they have become deeply unjust and unworkable. Directly overruling past decisions is not always necessary; precedents are much more flexible over time than most people imagine. Courts are often able to come up with new distinctions within doctrine that reshape its direction and its effects over time. Even so, Americans should feel no obligation to keep precedents that are not reasonable implementations of text and principle. Citizens should feel free to oppose these precedents and press for their reversal through lawful means.

Courts, however, have a different institutional role than citizens. They must strive to maintain rule-of-law values of predictability and nonarbitrariness; therefore they should be considerably more forgiving in assessing what constitutes a reasonable implementation of text and principle. This will require them to maintain many legal positions they would reject if presented in a case of first impression. Nevertheless, courts should modify or overturn precedents, even precedents of long standing, that they are convinced are no longer reasonable implementations of the Constitution.

When we focus on Supreme Court justices, we tend to forget that different persons in the constitutional system—inferior court judges, state judges, lawyers, political actors, and citizens—have different relationships to existing precedents. Lower court judges and state court judges must apply the Supreme Court's constructions until they are overruled. State court judges, however, may interpret their state constitutions differently, and their interpretations sometimes turn out to be quite influential in the later development of federal law. Politicians sworn to uphold the Constitution and laws must obey direct orders from courts. Nevertheless, they can offer competing interpretations in public and they can create opportunities for courts to narrow or reconsider existing precedents by passing new laws and taking actions that lead to test cases. Lawyers can bring cases to test precedents and press for their modification.

Although citizens must obey the law, they do not exercise state power. They have little or no obligation to regard the Supreme Court's precedents as correct readings of the Constitution if they believe in good faith that the Court is wrong.[21] They are free to offer protestant interpretations of the Constitution and press for their views to be accepted by legal professionals, by the political branches, and by the courts. In this way they can, over time, alter the political and constitutional culture in which professional practice and professional judgments occur. By exercising their different positions in the constitutional system, different actors shape the evolution of doctrine over time. Pressing for modifications of precedents is as important to the construction of the Constitution as maintaining existing precedents. The precedents we value today usually emerged from reframing, modifying, distinguishing, or rejecting other precedents from the past.

These views distinguish me from those living constitutionalists who support a strong theory of *stare decisis,* especially for precedents that they believe are nonoriginalist.[22] The irony is that many of the decisions that living constitutionalists fear are inconsistent with original meaning are actually consistent with it. By conceding that decisions they admire have no basis in the Constitution's text and principles, living constitutionalists face an unnecessary difficulty in justifying the legitimacy of these decisions. They must rely on a theory of superstrong protection for precedents that they concede are not faithful to the constitutional text.

Grounding living constitutionalism on respect for precedents of long standing is a weak and defensive strategy. If one is unwilling to defend decisions on the ground that they are actually faithful to the Constitution, it becomes far more difficult to argue for overturning other decisions one thinks are unjust or unwise.

To be sure, one might argue that the development of doctrine through precedent simply is the standard of fidelity to the Constitution—that the common law system of precedent is constitutive of constitutional fidelity. But this makes it difficult for living constitutionalists to deny the equal fidelity of precedents they do not like that were produced by the same common law process. This model also places the development of the Constitution in the hands of elite jurists, obscuring its connection to constitutional politics and the people's constitution-making power.

Recently, liberal politicians and scholars who are worried that conservative judges will overrule important decisions (primarily, one imagines, *Roe v. Wade*) have suggested that there is a class of "superprecedents" that have been repeatedly reaffirmed by courts and therefore should be immune to revision.[23]

I do not agree. If a precedent is truly inconsistent with original meaning, no number of reaffirmations can make it consistent. In addition, whether a precedent is a reasonable or unreasonable implementation of a larger principle can surely change over time. Some implementations of text and principle that might have seemed reasonable or adequate at one period of time may seem increasingly strained and unreasonable as time passes. Reaffirming the precedent over long periods of time cannot prevent this historical process from happening. Repeatedly citing a precedent in judicial opinions does not prevent changes in demographics, economics, technology, social customs, or other features of social life that tend to make older implementations of constitutional principles obsolete. When previous constructions no longer make sense or have become deeply unjust or unworkable, it is time to adjust them or substitute new ones.

Ironically, some of the "superprecedents" that have been repeatedly reaffirmed are the decisions most revised in practice. The more enmeshed a construction becomes in legal and political disputes, the more legal and political disputes will tend to change its practical meaning over time. Different groups will seek to recharacterize and reinterpret it for their own purposes. The practical meaning of *Brown v. Board of Education,* for example, has mutated over the years, with opposing parties asserting that it stands for different things in debates over school segregation, busing, affirmative action, housing discrimination, criminal procedure, and a range of other issues. Another frequently noted candidate for "superprecedent" status, *Roe v. Wade,*[24] may have been repeatedly reaffirmed in the face of repeated legal challenges, but there is little doubt that it has been thoroughly transformed in the course of three and a half decades. The Supreme Court has narrowed *Roe*'s holding, eliminated its trimester system, and allowed a panoply of regulations.[25]

Living constitutionalists have placed far too much reliance on the defense of precedent when they should have been focusing on the more basic question of fidelity to text and principle. This overreliance on precedent leads to my second objection: Nonoriginalists will find it very difficult to explain why they seek to overturn other precedents that they don't like. If we must preserve *Roe v. Wade*—because it was decided in 1973 and was continuously reaffirmed—why not *Washington v. Davis,*[26] which was decided only three years later? If *Roe* is a "superprecedent" in 2007, thirty-four years after it was decided, why wasn't *Plessy v. Ferguson* a "superprecedent" in 1954, some fifty-eight years after it was decided?[27]

Originalists like Justice Scalia and the living constitutionalists he criticizes find themselves in much the same situation. Both feel it necessary to argue for respecting (what they mistakenly regard as) nonoriginalist precedents. And they face a symmetrical difficulty. By accepting some nonoriginalist precedents as a "pragmatic exception" to originalism,[28] Scalia makes it more difficult to explain why he does not accord the same respect to others, such as *Roe v. Wade,* that he despises but that have been repeatedly sustained for many years. His criteria of reliance threaten to become ad hoc and a reflection of his politics. By relying so heavily on *stare decisis* to defend precedents they (incorrectly) concede are unfaithful to the Constitution's original meaning, living constitutionalists make it difficult to explain why they do not support other precedents of equal vintage. Their criteria of support also threaten to become ad hoc and a reflection of their politics.

There is something a little strange about living constitutionalism becoming so dependent on a strong theory of precedent. In part, this happened because living constitutionalists in the present generation have found themselves on the defensive against conservative political and social movement energies. Like most social movements before them, these conservative mobilizations have called for a return to the Constitution's text and to the principles of the founding generation, even if their notions of what that entails are disputable.[29] Faced with incessant demands for constitutional revolution, living constitutionalists have resorted to arguing for preserving the status quo, and for respecting older precedents created in politically more liberal times. But earlier social and political movements helped produce the doctrinal changes they now defend; those movements would not have succeeded if courts had applied so strong a theory of precedent. Arguments for respecting precedent make the most sense when directed at persons who do not share your constitutional views, but in that case they are a *modus vivendi,* not an independent criterion of constitutional fidelity. The best argument for the decisions that living constitutionalists admire is not that they are settled precedents; it is that they are faithful implementations of the Constitution's text and principles.

II

CONSTRUCTION

8

A PLATFORM FOR PERSUASION

The first part of this book described a general theory of constitutional interpretation and construction. This chapter and Chapters 9 through 12 show how to use the method of text and principle in practice; they are primarily written for lawyers and for people interested in the structure of legal doctrine who want to know how to apply the book's ideas to specific legal controversies. Chapter 9 looks at the scope of modern federal power and the commerce clause; Chapters 10 and 11 examine the Fourteenth Amendment, and Chapter 12 draws a few general lessons about constitutional construction.

These examples show that the method of text and principle offers interpreters plenty of resources to generate constructions to decide concrete legal issues. Although the constructions I offer always begin with the constitutional text, they use of all of the familiar modalities of constitutional argument and produce the same kinds of arguments that lawyers and judges normally make.

In Chapter 4 I argued that a theory of constitutional interpretation must serve two different functions. It must be able to explain why valuable features of our existing constitutional arrangements are faithful to the constitutional project correctly understood. At the same time, it must also allow us to criticize the Constitution-in-practice and argue for the redemption and restoration of constitutional values.

The method of text and principle satisfies these two conditions. Chapters 9 through 12 show that many of the constitutional achievements of the modern state are consistent with original meaning and are reasonable constructions built on the constitutional framework. But these chapters also use the same techniques to criticize existing doctrine: its methods of reasoning, its results, or both.

This last point is particularly important. Lawyers are already quite adept at sanctifying the actual and using existing doctrines to show why the world must continue to remain exactly as it is. But to criticize the legal status quo, to imagine and to articulate a Constitution different from the Constitution-in-practice, we need a place to stand outside of existing doctrines. To critique existing constructions, we need the leverage of other forms of legal authority. The method of text and principle gives us this leverage and a place to stand.

The argument of this book operates on two levels: at the level of the constitutional system as a whole, and on the level of practice by individual participants. The theory explains how, over time, constitutional politics builds constructions on top of the constitutional framework, and how this process contributes to the democratic legitimacy of the constitutional system as a whole. It shows how people and groups participate in this system, and how their collective activities promote democratic legitimacy. I continue these themes in Chapters 13 and 14.

At the same time, the method of text and principle gives individual participants in the constitutional system tools for interpreting and constructing the Constitution. Thus, the theory makes arguments from two perspectives: from the perspective of the constitutional system as a whole and from the perspective of the participants in the constitutional system who are invested in the system and want it to succeed.

People do not have to accept both aspects of the theory. People can accept my systemic theory of constitutional change and democratic legitimacy without accepting the method of text and principle, which is directed at individual participants. Or people can accept my arguments about how to use text and principle in constitutional argument but not my systemic views about constitutional change and democratic legitimacy.

Nevertheless, the theory's two different perspectives must be consistent with each other. People who have faith that the process of constitutional politics produces democratic legitimacy over time must be able to see why they should argue for change as a participant in the system rather than do nothing at all—why it is valuable and important for them to press their views on others rather than just shrug their shoulders and conclude that whatever happens is legitimate. They must be able to understand why taking a stand as an participant—either individually or in concert with other citizens—matters and helps sustain the legitimacy of the constitutional system. Conversely, people who make arguments internal to the practice of constitutional law should not have to worry that arguing that their views are correct is in any way undermined or contradicted by the theory of how the constitutional system produces legitimacy over time.

In fact, there is no contradiction between these two perspectives. Everything I say about interpretation, construction, and constitutional change from the standpoint of the constitutional system applies to my own particular views about doctrine. My general theory of how the system works and how it produces democratic legitimacy applies to and is consistent with my own individual performance as a practitioner who makes legal arguments.

I participate in a constitutional culture that includes both citizens and trained legal professionals. I try to influence both groups, and members of both groups try to influence me. The constitutional culture I live in is full of people who do not agree with me and includes many people who think my views about the Constitution are misguided, odious, or even insane. Even so, I try to persuade others to accept my views, while others, in turn, try to persuade me to accept theirs.

Some of the positions I take in Chapters 9 through 12 are "on-the-wall"—the results are largely congruent with current doctrine and current constitutional constructions, or at the very least they are consistent with the views of a substantial number of well-respected legal professionals and legal academics.[1] In some cases I reach results that are largely in accord with current doctrine but argue for them in ways that most judges and lawyers do not currently employ. For example, in Chapter 10 I argue that the Bill of Rights applies to the states through the privileges or immunities clause, not the due process clause, as the Supreme Court currently maintains. In Chapter 9 I argue that the modern state's construction of a broad power to regulate commerce among the several states is consistent with text and principle, although I analyze the key issues quite differently than courts currently do.

Nevertheless, some of the views I offer—and sincerely hold—about the best interpretation of the Constitution are currently "off-the-wall." I do not mean that these views are wrong—for I do not think they are wrong—but that at this point most courts, commentators, and legal professionals would probably not accept the reasoning and the results. On these matters I am a constitutional dissenter. There is no shame, however—or contradiction—in being a constitutional dissenter. Our Constitution was built out of the past dissent that we now call common sense. Even though many people disagree with me about some issues, I hope, whether through this book, or through other writing and advocacy, to persuade people that my views are better readings of the constitutional text and its underlying principles and that they should accept them.

When I dissent, I make arguments for the future, because I am invested in the constitutional project, and I want it to succeed. If I am successful, then my currently off-the-wall views may someday be viewed as mainstream, or will at least lead to significant changes in the legal status quo. Then, in hindsight, perhaps people will say that my views about the Constitution were correct (or more correct) even though most well-trained lawyers at the time did not agree with me. Such a change in viewpoint over a long period of time is not an unusual occurrence in American legal history; this fact gives constitutional dissenters reason for hope, and it gives them an additional reason to have faith in the constitutional system and its legitimacy even though their strongly held views are currently in eclipse.

If no one argued for the future, or made protestant arguments that others regarded as off-the-wall, it is true that we would avoid many bad and unjust arguments, but our constitutional culture would also be impoverished; and our Constitution would not be as free, equal, and democratic as it is today. Even so, the burden lies with the advocates of such arguments to reason with and persuade others. Most of these protestant arguments do not succeed, or they have little effect, because the groups and people who champion them cannot convince their fellow legal professionals or their fellow citizens. Inertia, institutions, and countermobilizations often stand in the way of successful constitutional dissent, for good and for ill.

The same burden of persuasion applies to me and to the arguments in the chapters that follow. Perhaps in time others will come to see things my way; or perhaps in time other people will persuade me that I am wrong and that I should change my mind. The latter has happened before and no doubt it will happen again. Either way, my participation in the constitutional system as legal scholar and citizen is consistent with my theory of constitutional interpretation and change. My individual performance, viewed from the participant's perspective, is part of the system that my larger theory of constitutional change seeks to explain.

By shaping public opinion and the contours of the reasonable and unreasonable, public officials, political actors, lawyers, and ordinary citizens play important roles in the system of constitutional change and constitutional construction. Indeed, courts often come to recognize that they must change or modify past constructions only because many others who are not judges have recognized this first.

That is why there is no contradiction between the systemic perspective and the perspective of the individual participant. Because individuals believe in the constitutional project and in its eventual redemption or restoration, they press their views in public and try to persuade others. Indeed, the more certain they are that their views are correct, they more fervently they press their claims on others and attempt to win converts. Their right and their ability to do so is crucial to the system's democratic legitimacy. Perhaps courts will come to accept some of their currently off-the-wall arguments. Perhaps courts will not. But the democratic legitimacy of our system of government depends on the ability of individuals in different social and institutional roles to argue about the right way to continue the constitutional project, and the possibility of their succeeding in time.

Advocates of living constitutionalism sometimes talk as if our Constitution has grown through gradual adjustment to objective changes in social conditions. More often, I think, our Constitution has grown through disagreement—disagreement about what is actually happening, disagreement about values, and disagreement about what to make of the situation given our values. Disagreement is the engine of constitutional change, and the disagreements will continue as long as the Constitution continues to live. There is no plan for politics without a continual discussion of the plan in politics. To be invested in the plan, one must be willing to stand up for one's views and persuade others about the right way to continue it. The great advantage of framework originalism and the method of text and principle is that they offer a platform for constitutional argument and constitutional politics; rather than simply settling constitutional disputes, they facilitate reason and persuasion.

Framework originalism contemplates that successive generations will produce different types of constructions, and the kinds of constructions they produce cannot be known in advance. It follows that the method of text and principle must allow for many different types of constructions, and it must be sufficiently flexible and adaptable to allow many different kinds of people to articulate their views. It must be useful to people living at different times and people living at the same time who hold different views. It must be useful not only to judges and lawyers but also to political officials and ordinary citizens.

Obviously framework originalism cannot accommodate all views—for example, the view that there are three houses of Congress or that the president serves for life. But within these necessary limitations, people on different sides of the constitutional disputes in each era must be able to express their political values and ideals in terms of the Constitution's text and principles.

Our Constitution maintains democratic legitimacy because people of different views retain the ability to persuade each other about the best reading of the Constitution, by challenging and changing ideas about what interpretations are reasonable and unreasonable, on-the-wall and off-the-wall. If so, then the best method of constitutional interpretation must be one that many different people could, in theory, use to express their divergent views. It cannot be an algorithm for decisionmaking that would require everyone who uses it to converge on a single correct answer. It must allow people plenty of room for disagreement, because if we know one thing, it is that Americans' sense of what is a reasonable or an unreasonable interpretation of the Constitution has changed greatly over the years.

Admittedly, this is not how most people imagine interpretive theories. They concede that reasonable people using the same theory will sometimes disagree, but lack of determinacy is generally thought to be a vice of a theory, not a virtue. A theory is good to the extent that it forces different people to converge on the same answer; it is less than ideal to the extent that different people can use it to justify different results. But if a good theory of constitutional interpretation must flow from what makes constitutions legitimate, then we must seriously revise our criteria for what makes an interpretive theory good.

Protest, persuasion, and argument are central to the continuing democratic legitimacy of the American Constitution, because they offer people the possibility of redeeming the Constitution in their time or in a day to come. To argue about the Constitution, one must have a common platform for arguing, first to disagree with others, then to persuade them. That is what a theory of constitutional interpretation is for.

People using the method of text and principle will often reach contrary conclusions about the best way to interpret the Constitution. Although I offer what I believe to be the best arguments for each of the doctrinal positions I take, I would hardly be surprised if others, using the methods described in this book, reached different conclusions and were just as committed to them. This is not a problem for the theory; it is an exemplification of the theory in practice.

Even so, one might criticize this approach in three ways. Although these seem to be different objections, they are actually all the same objection, because they all assume the same set of premises about constitutional interpretation that this book challenges.

The first critic asks: In this book you interpret the Constitution in ways I disagree with. If your theory does not produce the political results I like, why should I adopt it?

The second critic asks: If your theory allows judges to reach different results, it must not constrain them very much. So what is the use of a theory that does not force judges to restrain themselves or to decide controversial cases in the same way?

The third critic asks: If your theory allows people with very different political views to make arguments for their preferred views, what is the use of your theory?

Each of these three questions, in its own way, assumes that the purpose of a theory of interpretation is to offer either determinate answers or answers that strongly constrain argument and decisionmaking. The first critic wants the answers that a theory produces to agree with his politics, and he will only choose an interpretive theory if it produces them. The second critic assumes that constitutional interpretation is primarily a method to constrain judges and therefore wants a theory that will do just that. The third critic thinks that constitutional interpretation is a way to make reasonable people reach the same answers to contested questions or at least keep them within a fairly narrow range of potential answers.

Each of these critics misunderstands what we need from a method of constitutional interpretation in a liberal democracy. Chief Justice John Marshall famously said that the Constitution must endure through different generations and be adapted to various crises.[2] Justice Oliver Wendell Holmes Jr. famously argued that our Constitution was designed for people who live together and have very different views.[3] Together these two statements capture the basic requirement of theories of constitutional interpretation: they must be helpful to people who live in different periods of time when notions of what is reasonable and unreasonable will differ greatly. And they must be helpful to people who live at the same time who disagree on how to continue our common constitutional project.

A method of constitutional interpretation is not a decision procedure. It is more like a common language that allows people with very different views to reason together. In this way it connects the grounds of democratic legitimacy of a constitution to the ways that people argue about and ascertain the meaning of the constitution. It connects the possibility of legitimacy to a platform for persuasion.

If the Constitution is to be "our" law across time, it must be responsive to successive generations of Americans, reflecting their values and ideals, not just the values of the founding generation. If the Constitution is to be "our" law within a generation, it must allow dissenters to express their views in (what for them are) dark times. It must be a language of legitimation and a language of dissent, a language of criticism and a language of justification.

A method of constitutional interpretation must allow people not only to express what the law requires but also to express what *their* law requires. It must be an approach that people living at different times and within different communities at the same time can employ. It must be the kind of analysis that can be invoked by defenders of the status quo and by ascendant social movements challenging the status quo. It must be a method that both Hamilton and Jefferson might have adopted in 1796, that Franklin Delano Roosevelt and his Republican critics might have used in 1936, and that antagonists in contemporary politics can use today. It must be a common language for constitutional discussion, offered without knowing in advance what social movements may come into being or how Americans will disagree over their collective destiny in the future.

Moreover, because the same method must be available to judges on opposite sides of controversies from the founding to the present day, it must be capacious enough to allow all of them—or at least the vast majority—to express their considered judgments within it. It must be a discourse of professional reason that also allows professional reasoning to be responsive to changes in popular values and beliefs, that allows professional discourse to shift as new ideas traverse the spectrum from off-the-wall to on-the-wall.

If a theory of interpretation cannot do this, if it is so fixed in its ways that it leads to conclusions suitable for only one time or only one political set of views, it will generate the same problems as skyscraper originalism. It will create a vision of correct law that cannot adapt to a world perpetually in flux. But more important, it will lose democratic legitimacy because the Constitution that it justifies and legitimates cannot be "our law" for an increasing number of citizens. It will not give citizens a common language in which they can face each other and argue about their collective future. The dream of an interpretive method that offers fixed and determinate answers to the most heated questions that divide a republic is, ironically, the desire for a theory that condemns its own democratic legitimacy as time passes.

9

COMMERCE

A good test for the plausibility of any theory of constitutional interpretation is how well it handles the doctrinal transformations of the New Deal period. Roughly between 1937 and 1942, the Supreme Court significantly altered the law of federal–state relations, including the federal power to regulate commerce and to tax and spend for the general welfare.

The doctrinal structure that emerged by the mid-1940s was drastically different from the expectations of the founding generation. Even the most stridently nationalist members of that generation would not have expected a federal government as powerful as the one that developed in the middle of the twentieth century. It now had a robust regulatory and welfare state with jurisdiction over federal health and safety laws, laws protecting the environment, laws securing the rights of workers, and a panoply of federal civil rights guarantees. Without the New Deal transformation in constitutional understandings about national power, we could not have a federal government that provides all of the social services and statutory rights guarantees that Americans have come to expect. The government could neither act to protect the environment nor rescue the national economy in times of crisis.

The rise of the modern state poses a problem for originalist theories of constitutional interpretation. Some originalists, like Justice Antonin Scalia (or Judge Robert Bork) have simply accepted the New Deal as settled even though they believe it is inconsistent with original meaning.[1] As we have seen, Justice Scalia's "pragmatic" exception to originalism[2] includes his acceptance of a variety of nonoriginalist precedents that validate federal power. Other originalists, like Justice Clarence Thomas,[3] Randy Barnett,[4] and Richard Epstein,[5] refuse to make the same concessions to current political realities; they regard significant parts of the New Deal and the legislation that followed it as unconstitutional. For them, the question is how best to transition to a federal government that stays within its proper constitutional limits.

By contrast, Bruce Ackerman, a vigorous defender of the New Deal, agrees that it is inconsistent with the founders' Constitution.[6] He explains the legitimacy of the New Deal by arguing that starting in 1936, the American people had a quasi-revolutionary "constitutional moment," which actually amended the Constitution outside of the Article V amendment process.

I reject each of these approaches. I disagree both with originalists and with their critics because I do not believe that the New Deal is inconsistent with the Constitution's original meaning, its text, or its underlying principles. Therefore there is no need to make an exception for it, "pragmatic" or otherwise. Nor did the transition to the modern state require an Article V amendment; and therefore it also did not require an amendment outside of Article V. Rather, the New Deal, while preserving the Constitution's original meaning, featured a series of new constitutional *constructions* by the political branches that were eventually ratified by the federal judiciary. Although the scope of the change was larger than in most doctrinal transformations, the New Deal is actually a fairly standard example of how new constitutional constructions displace older ones.

The impetus for changed understandings came not from the courts but from the political branches, who led and responded to political mobilizations for change. The federal courts, attuned to an older way of thinking, and seeking to preserve older constructions, resisted at first. However, the public strongly supported the president and Congress, who continued to press for a different understanding of the Constitution. The courts, increasingly stocked with allies of the president, eventually followed popular opinion, legitimating the new constitutional constructions in a series of landmark decisions.[7]

But this simply raises the question: How *is* the modern regulatory and administrative state consistent with the original meaning of the constitutional text? In this chapter, I focus on the most important source of authority for the modern state: the commerce clause of Article I, section 8, which provides that "[t]he Congress shall have the power . . . [t]o regulate Commerce with foreign Nations, and among the several States, and with the Indian Tribes."[8] I will not be able to discuss all of the issues raised by the commerce clause in this Chapter; instead I will touch only on basic features that are central to the legitimacy of the regulatory state.

Whether they defend a broad or narrow conception of federal authority, contemporary originalist readings have tended to view the commerce power through modern eyes. Originalists defending narrow readings of federal power have identified "commerce" with the trade of commodities; originalists defending broad readings of federal power have identified "commerce" with all gainful economic activity. In the eighteenth century, however, the word *commerce* did not have such narrowly economic connotations. Instead, *commerce* meant "intercourse," and it had strongly social overtones. Commerce was interaction and exchange between persons or peoples. To have commerce with someone meant to exchange things or ideas with them, converse with them, or interact with them. Thus, commerce naturally included all trade and economic activity because economic activity involved social interaction. Defenders of commercial activity in the eighteenth century emphasized its sociality: they argued that commercial intercourse generated peace, fostered social cooperation, and ultimately forged bonds of connection. But the idea of commerce-as-intercourse was broader than economics narrowly conceived—it also included networks of transportation and communication through which people traveled, interacted, and corresponded with each other.

Defining commerce in its original sense of "intercourse" is consistent with all of the evidence offered by rival theories of commerce as trade or economic activity, but it better explains the source of Congress's powers over immigration and foreign affairs. It also better explains Congress's broad powers over transportation and communications networks, whether or not these networks are used for purposes of business or trade.

Congress's power to regulate commerce "among the several states" is closely linked to the general structural purpose of Congress's enumerated powers as articulated by the framers: to give Congress power to legislate in all cases where states are separately incompetent or where the interests of the nation might be undermined by unilateral or conflicting state action. This structural principle underlies all of Congress's enumerated powers, and we should interpret the commerce power accordingly. Properly understood, the commerce power authorizes Congress to regulate problems or activities that produce spillover effects between states or generate collective action problems that concern more than one state.

This basic structural principle explains why Congress's commerce power inevitably expanded with the rise of a modern integrated economy and society, and it explains and justifies most, if not all, of modern doctrine. In particular, this approach justifies the constitutionality of federal regulation of labor law, consumer protection law, environmental law, and antidiscrimination law; it even shows why a federal mandate for individuals to purchase health insurance is constitutional. Finally, this approach shows why there are still areas where federal commerce power does not extend—these are areas where Congress cannot reasonably claim that an activity produces interstate spillovers or collective action problems, and that do not involve networks of transportation and communication.

A Government of Federal and Enumerated Powers

The text of the commerce clause has two noteworthy features. First, the commerce clause is a *clause*—it forms one part of a very long extended sentence, which lists (most of) the enumerated powers of Congress. Second, the commerce clause uses the words "regulate" and "commerce" only once; it then applies them to three different situations: with foreign nations, with the Indian tribes, and among the several states. The same words—"regulate commerce"—apply to each situation. So, if there is a difference in Congress's constitutional powers with respect to foreign, Indian, and domestic commerce, it does not stem from the original meaning of the words "regulate" or "commerce." Rather, any differences in congressional power come from the difference between the words "with" and "among." For this reason, Akhil Amar has remarked that we should really call the commerce clause the "with-and-among clause."[9]

Why does the text read this way? Why does it yoke foreign, Indian, and interstate commerce together in a single clause, and why does it embed that clause in a very long list of enumerated powers?

The text looks the way it does because a basic structural principle underlies the text, and in fact the text was written precisely to articulate that general principle. The Tenth Amendment, added in 1791, emphasizes that the powers delegated by the people are less than a complete grant to the national government. It states that "[t]he powers not delegated to the United States by the Constitution, nor prohibited by it to the States, are reserved to the States respectively, or to the people."[10] Chief Justice Stone once described the amendment as "but a truism that all is retained which has not been surrendered."[11] But the Tenth Amendment is not a mere truism if it reflects a deeper structural principle underlying the text and its choice of enumerated powers.

A note about structural arguments: When we interpret the Constitution, we constantly make reference to structural principles, such as the separation of powers, or the principle of checks and balances, or democratic self-government, or the rule of law. These structural principles are special types of constructions. They do not simply implement abstract principles already announced in the text; rather, they explain how the Constitution works in practice and how it should work.

Many of these structural principles were intended by people who drafted the Constitution, and they explained their ideas in debates about the Constitution. We can use evidence of their reasoning to show that a structural principle exists and that it should guide our interpretation of the Constitution. But we should not confuse structural principles with original intentions. Structural principles do not have to have been intended by anyone in particular; indeed, they may only become apparent over time as we watch how the various elements of the constitutional system interact with each other. Like Minerva's owl, people may recognize structural principles in the Constitution only after the mechanisms have been working for some time, or when they threaten to stop working properly and must be repaired or redeemed.

Later constitutional amendments, subsequent constructions, and changes in circumstances might make some of the framers' assumptions about how the Constitution would work obsolete. For example, the framers did not imagine a system of political parties, or a dominant presidency, much less expect that the United States would someday be a world power with standing armies located around the globe. Americans had to figure out the structural principles that should apply (and how they should apply) given those changed circumstances. The Seventeenth Amendment sought to give the people greater control over the Senate. But it had structural consequences that were not fully understood for many years. In fact, we might say that structural arguments often arise when people disagree about whether the constitutional machine is out of joint and they have to articulate how it should work properly. If we try to ground structural principles solely in the intentions of the framers, we will miss many structural features of our Constitution as it actually works in practice.

Many people who defend the modern administrative and regulatory state following the New Deal probably think that the framers' structural assumptions about limited and enumerated powers fall into the category of ancient structural principles that have been thoroughly undermined. Perhaps they suspect this because the people who want to shrink or overthrow the modern state are always doing so in the name of the framers. The latter tell us that if we were faithful to the framers' structural principles, we couldn't have anything like the modern state.

But both sides are wrong. The defenders of the modern activist state have given up too quickly on the text of the Constitution and its underlying principles, while their opponents have confused ancient and outmoded constructions for the actual requirements of the constitutional framework. The key structural principles underlying the list of enumerated powers in Article I, section 8, are still quite relevant today. Not only are they consistent with the rise of the modern administrative and regulatory state, they also explain and justify why that state came into being.

The basic principles underlying the list of enumerated powers were well stated by one of the key founders, James Wilson, in the Pennsylvania ratifying convention in November 1787:

> Whatever object of government is confined, in its operation and effects, within the bounds of a particular state, should be considered as belonging to the government of that state; whatever object of government extends, in its operation or effects, beyond the bounds of a particular state, should be considered as belonging to the government of the United States.[12]

In saying this, Wilson was doing no more than summarizing the structural assumptions of the drafters in Philadelphia. The origins of Congress's powers go back to the sixth of the resolutions prepared by the Virginia delegation, led by James Madison and Edmund Randolph, and introduced at the constitutional convention on May 29, 1787. These resolutions were collectively called the Virginia plan. Resolution VI, introduced by Randolph, stated that the new "National Legislature" would be empowered "to enjoy the Legislative Rights vested in Congress by the Confederation & moreover to legislate in all cases to which the separate States are incompetent, or in which the harmony of the United States may be interrupted by the exercise of individual Legislation."[13] The convention initially approved this language on May 31 by a vote of nine in favor, none against, and one delegation divided.[14]

Representing the interests of smaller states, William Paterson offered his New Jersey plan on June 15, 1787, with a far weaker national government and a smaller list of enumerated powers, including the power to "pass Acts for the regulation of trade & commerce as well with foreign nations as with each other."[15] Comparing the two plans, Wilson explained that while under the Virginia plan "the Natl. Legislature is to make laws in all cases at which the separate States are incompetent," the New Jersey plan offered Congress only a minor increase of the powers it enjoyed under the existing confederation.[16] The convention reapproved the Virginia plan and rejected the New Jersey Plan on June 19, by a vote of seven states to three, with one delegation divided.[17]

On July 16, after the so-called Great Compromise that gave the small states equal representation in the Senate, the convention took up Resolution VI once again. On July 17, Roger Sherman of Connecticut, who had been the only delegate to oppose Resolution VI in the original vote, moved to amend it to ensure that the federal government would not interfere with state governments:

> To make laws binding on the People of the United States in all cases which may concern the common interests of the Union: but not to interfere with the government of the individual States in any matters of internal police which respect the government of such States only, and wherein the general welfare of the United States is not concerned.[18]

The convention defeated this proposal by a vote of eight to two.[19]

Gunning Bedford of Delaware then moved to further clarify the principles of Resolution VI: "That the national Legislature ought to possess the legislative rights vested in Congress by the confederation;"[20] "and moreover to legislate in all cases for the general interests of the Union, and also in those to which the States are separately incompetent, or in which the harmony of the United States may be interrupted by the exercise of individual legislation."[21] The Bedford amendment passed six to four, and the amended Resolution VI was adopted by a vote of eight to two.[22]

The amended version of Resolution VI, along with the other resolutions, was then handed to the Committee of Detail, which on August 6, 1787, produced the basic list of enumerated powers that now appears in Article I, section 8. It is worth noting that nobody at the Philadelphia convention seems to have objected to the transformation from general principle to enumerated list. As Jack Rakove explains, "[T]he fact that it went unchallenged suggests that the committee was only complying with the expectations of the convention."[23] It was "an effort to identify particular areas of governance where there were 'general Interests of the Union,' where the states were 'separately incompetent,' or where state legislation could disrupt the national 'Harmony.' "[24] Indeed, when Pierce

Butler of South Carolina complained that the test of state "incompetence" was far too general, Nathaniel Gorham of Massachusetts responded that "[t]he vagueness of the terms constitutes the propriety of them. We are now establishing general principles, to be extended hereafter into details which will be precise & explicit."[25]

The structural principle of Resolution VI—with its focus on state competencies and the general interests of the Union—was designed to be adaptable to changing circumstances. Putting to one side the concrete expectations of the framers, the principle seems to suggest that the federal government might grow very large and very powerful if social, economic, and technological changes meant that more and more problems required federal solutions. Indeed, if spillover effects multiplied and the United States developed a fully integrated national society and economy, something like the modern regulatory state might be entirely appropriate.

For this reason Resolution VI has always made the proponents of a weak federal government a bit nervous. Thus, in his libertarian reinterpretation of the Constitution, Randy Barnett argues that the convention actually *rejected* Bedford's language.[26] This is simply not the case. The records indicate that the convention specifically *adopted* Bedford's language. The Committee of Detail was not charged with the authority to reject resolutions voted on by the convention; rather its purpose was to articulate the general principles stated by the convention in concrete language and specific provisions.

Perhaps what Barnett really means is that the actual language of Resolution VI does not appear in the final Constitution. That is certainly true. But there is no evidence that the convention rejected the structural principle stated in Resolution VI at any point during its proceedings. Indeed, this principle was the *animating purpose* of the list of enumerated powers that appeared in the final draft, and it was the key explanation that framer James Wilson offered to the public when he defended the proposed Constitution at the Pennsylvania ratifying convention. Wilson was a member of the Committee of Detail and he would certainly have known if the Committee had abandoned the principle of Resolution VI. As Wilson explained, however, the purpose of enumeration was not to *displace* the principle but to *enact* it:

> [T]hough this principle be sound and satisfactory, its application to particular cases would be accompanied with much difficulty, because, in its application, room must be allowed for great discretionary latitude of construction

of the principle. In order to lessen or remove the difficulty arising from discretionary construction on this subject, an enumeration of particular instances, in which the application of the principle ought to take place, has been attempted with much industry and care.[27]

Advocates of a weak federal government might point to the Tenth Amendment as having rejected Bedford's (and Wilson's) principle. That is hardly the case. The Tenth Amendment is simply the mirror image of Resolution VI. It tells us that what was not delegated to the federal government was reserved to the states and to the people. And what principle explains what *was* delegated? Those situations in which "the States are separately incompetent; or in which the harmony of the United States may be interrupted by the exercise of individual legislation."[28]

In sum, the creation of a list of enumerated powers was not simply an attempt to limit the new federal government for its own sake. It was designed to realize a basic structural idea, and as we look through the list of enumerated powers, we see how each of them furthered the principle announced in Resolution VI. They allowed the new federal government to engage in a single foreign policy, a single trade policy, and a single military and defensive strategy. All this was crucial to the infant nation's survival in a dangerous geopolitical situation where it would have been easy for a foreign power to divide and conquer the states, where individual states might frequently have acted competitively or at cross-purposes, and where the actions of individual states might drag the entire Union into a conflict with foreign powers. The government also had the power to raise taxes, collect duties, and spend for the general welfare, to control a single currency, to regulate naturalization and bankruptcy by uniform laws, and last but not least, to regulate commerce with the Indian tribes, with foreign powers, and among the several states.

One might argue that we should read each of the enumerated powers strictly and narrowly so that they do not overlap; otherwise the enumeration of each would be superfluous. But this misunderstands the purpose of enumeration. Because all of Congress's powers were designed to realize the structural principle of Resolution VI, they inevitably must overlap to ensure that the new government would have the power to legislate in all areas where the states were severally incompetent. As circumstances changed, the various enumerated powers might intersect in new ways. It should hardly be surprising, for example, that the powers to raise and support armies, make war, make rules for the government and regulation of the land and naval forces, and define and punish offenses against the law of nations inevitably would overlap in practice, both among themselves and with the power to regulate foreign and Indian commerce. Likewise, there should be no difficulty if the power to regulate commerce comprehends many of the same subjects as the power to tax and spend for the general welfare, to establish post roads, to coin money, or to promote the progress of the sciences and the useful arts. What limits these powers is not that they are hermetically sealed off from each other, but that they extend only to subjects of individual state incompetence.

The list of enumerated powers was designed so that the new federal government would have power to pass laws concerning subjects and problems that are *federal* by nature; that is, problems that require a federal solution, as opposed to *national* problems that occur in many places but that do not require coordinated action and a single approach. This is the key insight of Resolution VI, and it is still true to this day.[29]

Examples of federal problems include questions of foreign and military policy where the nation needs to speak with a single voice, to marshal resources for the common defense, and to prevent foreign powers from pushing the states around or engaging in divide-and-conquer strategies— whether relating to trade, immigration, military threats, or diplomatic alliances. Domestically, federal problems are those that single states cannot unilaterally solve by themselves, because activity in one state has spillover effects in other states, or because a problem that affects multiple states creates collective action problems, so that some states may be unable or unwilling to act effectively in ways that promote the general welfare unless other states do so as well. Finally, federal problems may arise when states are likely to produce conflicting regulations over a set of activities, engage in parochial legislation favoring their own interests at the expense of the general welfare, or engage in escalating forms of provocation or retaliation against each other. Each of these might hamper economic union in the short run and threaten political and social union in the long run.[30]

It is a commonplace to say that the national government is a government of limited and enumerated powers. But it would be more correct to say that it is a government of *federal* and enumerated powers, for the purpose of enumeration is not merely to limit the scope of the powers, but to ensure that they serve a federal purpose. When we implement congressional powers through constructions, we must always keep this general principle in mind.

The text of the commerce clause reflects this basic structural principle. Article I, section 8, clause 3, gives Congress the power "[t]o regulate Commerce with foreign Nations, and among the several States, and with the Indian Tribes."[31] It focuses on relationships between the United States and foreign powers and Indian tribes, which involve foreign policy concerns, and activities among the various states, which raise problems of spillover effects and collective action. Both of these sets of concerns might require the United States to speak with a single voice, and that is why they are properly part of the list of enumerated powers.

Earlier I noted that the same words, "regulate commerce," apply to foreign commerce, Indian commerce, and interstate commerce. Whatever "regulate" and "commerce" refer to, there is a strong argument that they have the same semantic meaning with the respect to all three examples.[32] Chief Justice John Marshall made precisely this point in *Gibbons v. Ogden,* when he noted that the word "commerce" "must carry the same meaning throughout the sentence, and remain a unit, unless there be some plain intelligible cause which alters it."[33] Marshall argued that "commerce" must include navigation, because it would make no sense to think that Congress could not regulate navigation to and from foreign nations.[34]

There are three important qualifications to this argument. First, the same set of words might have different effects in combination with different words in the same sentence, so that to "regulate commerce *with*" might not mean the same thing as to "regulate commerce *among*." The difference between Congress's powers over foreign and domestic commerce reflects this difference in language.

Second, we might have good reasons to choose different *constructions* to implement congressional power to regulate foreign commerce, Indian commerce, and interstate commerce. In fact, that is exactly what happened in American history. These reasons connect to the different structural purposes for regulating foreign, Indian, and domestic commerce, as well as the linguistic differences between "with" and "among."[35] My point here, however, is about original semantic meaning—the irreducible requirement of the basic framework across different generations—and not about the constructions we choose to implement original meaning. The distinction is important because we could pick different constructions to implement the constitutional text later on as times and conditions change, and this, too, is what has happened throughout American history.

Third, the Constitution may contain additional textual restrictions on Congress's powers that may apply differently to these different types of commerce. Article I, section 8, clause 1, requires that "all duties, imposts and excises shall be uniform throughout the United States." Article I, section 9, clause 5, states that "[n]o tax or duty shall be laid on articles exported from any state," and clause 6 states that "[n]o preference shall be given by any regulation of commerce or revenue to the ports of one state over those of another: nor shall vessels bound to, or from one state, be obliged to enter, clear, or pay duties in another."

These additional texts affect Congress's powers over domestic, Indian, and foreign commerce in different ways. For example, although Congress may treat trade from different foreign countries differently, it may not discriminate between ports in different states of the Union or have different duties, imposts, or excises for different parts of the country. These provisions limit the powers that Congress might otherwise have had under the commerce clause. They also shape the most reasonable constitutional constructions for the clause. But they do not demonstrate that the words "regulate" and "commerce" have different semantic meanings when applied to terms within the same sentence.

The Original Meaning of "Commerce"

What is the original meaning of "commerce"? Samuel Johnson's dictionary, roughly contemporaneous with the founding, defines "commerce" as "Intercourse; exchange of one thing for another, interchange of anything; trade; traffick."[36] Johnson's secondary definition of commerce is "common or familiar intercourse."[37] Today we associate commerce with economics, trade, and business, but at the time of the founding, commerce included far more than purely commercial activity. It meant "intercourse"— that is, interactions, exchanges, interrelated activities, and movements back and forth, including, for example, travel, social connection, or conversation.[38] Economic transactions were only a special case of social intercourse. To have commerce with someone meant to converse with them, mingle with them, associate with them, or trade with them.[39] *Traffick* was a coarser word for "trade" (for example, to traffic in drugs);[40] later it came to mean "travel," whether or not for purposes of trade, and still later, "impediments to travel" (such as traffic jams).

The contemporary meanings of *intercourse* and *commerce* are far narrower than their eighteenth-century meanings. We no longer think of interaction, exchange, and movement when we think of intercourse—we think only of sexual intercourse, which is not the concept referred to by the commerce clause. And when we think of commerce, we no longer think of intercourse or social interaction, only business and the exchange of commodities. But it is the broader, eighteenth-century meaning and not the narrower, contemporary meaning that should determine Congress's powers today.

Some contemporary originalists like Justice Clarence Thomas have argued that the original meaning of "commerce" is very narrow, essentially limited to the trade or exchange of goods and commodities.[41] Thus, it would not include manufacturing, mining, or agriculture, much less any noneconomic activities. This reading is anachronistic; by focusing on the disposition of commodities, it reflects a *modern* conception of commerce viewed as a subset of economic activity; it completely misses the eighteenth-century dimensions of commerce as a form of social intercourse and exchange.

The concept of "commerce" in the eighteenth century had social connotations that are lost in our modern focus on commodities. It was the *exchange* of commodities *by people* that made business activity "commerce," not the commodities themselves. Commercial relations were "commerce" because they were *relations*.[42] Commerce brought people together, and caused people of different experiences and nationalities to mingle (think of port cities as an example); therefore many eighteenth-century thinkers believed that commercial relations fostered tolerance and understanding, smoothed over social, religious, and cultural differences, brought refinement of manners, and, in the long run, political and social peace. Half a century earlier, Montesquieu had coined the term *doux commerce,* meaning "sweet commerce" or "gentle commerce," to describe this phenomenon.[43]

The framers of the 1787 Constitution, influenced by these ideas, believed that commercial relations between different parts of the country would foster national connection and social cohesion, and that commercial relations with other nations would keep America peaceful, prosperous, and safe while avoiding dangerous political and military alliances.[44] We see these ideas in the 1776 Model Treaty and the nation's subsequent Treaties of Amity and Commerce with Prussia and France.[45]

A striking example of the idea of commerce as intercourse that produces social cohesion appears in George Washington's Farewell Address. Although the Address is best known for its warning against entangling alliances with foreign powers, it also offers a vision of commercial intercourse and networks of transportation and communication as social cement. Washington argued that the North and South, in an "unrestrained intercourse" benefiting manufacturing and agriculture, would grow closer together.[46] "The East, in a like intercourse with the West," he predicted, would benefit from "progressive improvement of interior communications by land and water," which would produce not only exchanges of goods and materials but "an indissoluble community of interest as one nation."[47]

If we want to capture the original meaning of "commerce," we must stop thinking primarily in terms of commodities. We must focus on the ideas of interaction, exchange, sociability, and the movement of persons that business (in its older sense of being busy or engaged in affairs) exemplifies.

I will call the contrasting view held by Justice Thomas and others—that the original meaning of "commerce" is the trade or exchange of commodities—the "trade theory." The trade theory immediately runs into difficulties, because "trade" or "exchange of goods" does not literally include methods of transportation, like navigation. However, the framers clearly sought to give the new government powers over navigation and often used the terms *commerce* and *navigation* interchangeably.[48] So in order to ensure that Congress can regulate navigation, the trade theory must treat "commerce" nonliterally as a metonym (a word that denotes one thing but also refers to a related thing).[49] Alternatively, we might argue that the necessary and proper clause gives Congress power over transportation (although the question would remain whether Congress could reach transportation that is not used for purposes of trade).[50]

Now if the word "commerce" was used nonliterally in the Constitution's text, or if the necessary and proper clause was required to give Congress the power to regulate navigation, one would think that opponents of the Constitution (or the framers at the Philadelphia convention itself) would have pointed this out. This didn't happen; as noted above, people routinely spoke of navigation as falling within commerce. This in itself should suggest that there is something wrong with the trade theory. We do not have to read the word nonliterally (or bring in the necessary and proper clause) if we adopt the actual eighteenth-century definition of commerce as "intercourse," which necessarily includes movements back and forth and therefore easily comprehends navigation and, indeed, every form of transportation and communication.

By 1824, in *Gibbons v. Ogden,* counsel for Ogden tried to argue that "commerce" meant only trade or exchange. Chief Justice Marshall bluntly rejected the argument:

> This would restrict a general term, applicable to many objects, to one of its significations. Commerce, undoubtedly, is traffic [i.e., trade], but it is something more: it is intercourse. It describes the commercial intercourse between nations, and parts of nations, in all its branches, and is regulated by prescribing rules for carrying on that intercourse.[51]

Marshall clearly did not suggest that treating navigation as commerce was a nonliteral usage or that the necessary and proper clause was required: "All America understands, and has uniformly understood, the word 'commerce,' to comprehend navigation. . . . [T]he attempt to restrict it comes too late."[52]

Another group of modern scholars, including Douglass Adair, Walton Hamilton, and William Crosskey, and more recently Grant Nelson and Robert Pushaw, have also noted that the trade theory is artificially narrow, and have offered an economic theory of commerce.[53] The economic theory accepts that the core meaning of "commerce" is trade, but expands it nonliterally in two different ways. First, it treats the term "commerce" as a synecdoche—a figure of speech in which a part stands for a larger whole. The economic theory argues that "commerce" stands for "economic behavior," or "the economy." Thus, Congress's power to regulate "commerce" extends to all forms of business and economic activity, including manufacturing, agriculture, all gainful employment, and all business contracts, including employment contracts.[54] Second, like the trade theory, the economic theory treats the term "commerce" as a metonym because it argues that commerce includes associated transportation networks used for engaging in trade and economic activity.[55]

In 2005 in *Gonzales v. Raich*[56] the Supreme Court came very close to adopting the economic theory. Without explicitly defining "commerce," the *Raich* Court argued that Congress had the power to regulate both interstate and intrastate economic activities that affected interstate commerce, and then defined "economics" as "the production, distribution, and consumption of commodities."[57] If we combine the economic theory with the idea that Congress can regulate interstate transportation networks (including intrastate networks that connect to those networks) and anything that moves (or has moved) in these networks, the federal government enjoys very wide powers.[58]

The economic theory is a definite improvement on the trade theory because it can account for a greater share of the data. As Adair, Hamilton, Crosskey, Nelson, and Pushaw successively documented, there is plenty of evidence that at the time of the founding, people used the word *commerce* to include a wide range of economic activities, sometimes called the "branches of commerce."[59] But in another sense the economic theory is also ahistorical. Viewing history through modern eyes, it focuses solely on economics rather than on the relations of exchange and the social interactions through which the economy operates. It also maintains that the Constitution uses the word "commerce" nonliterally in not one but two different ways, and that, once again, nobody in 1787 seems to have noticed this fact or remarked on it. To be sure, the Constitution has plenty of nonliteral language. The word "speech" in the First Amendment is a nonliteral usage; so too are the words "writings" and "discoveries" in the progress clause.[60] But if we start with the primary eighteenth-century definition of *commerce* as "intercourse," we do not need to treat the word as a metonym or synecdoche. We can account for all of the evidence of linguistic usage offered by proponents of the trade and economic theories, and, as we shall see shortly, we can account for examples that the other theories cannot. When people like George Washington, John Marshall, and Joseph Story use the words *commerce* and *intercourse* interchangeably, perhaps we should listen to them.

Advocates of the trade theory argue that in the Philadelphia convention and the ratification debates, delegates spoke only about questions of trade and potential barriers to trade.[61] But constitutional debates tend to focus on the key concerns that divide people at the time and not on the many possible applications of constitutional language. Even if the framers used the term "commerce" in its narrowest possible sense (which they did not, for they spoke of commerce and navigation interchangeably), the public meaning of the word to a general audience was much wider, and surely it is the general publicly understood meaning of the words used that should count.[62]

Modern defenders of the trade theory, like Justice Thomas, are quite critical of much of contemporary commerce clause doctrine. Yet, ironically, contemporary commerce clause doctrine is actually based on the trade theory. The Supreme Court adopted the distinctions between commerce, agriculture, and manufacturing in the early nineteenth century, in part to maintain distinctions between local and national power.[63] The trade theory is actually a *constitutional construction* adopted in a particular historical context that limited the scope of "commerce" in order to maintain an underlying structural principle.

Although the economic and social conditions that gave rise to this construction have vanished, the Court has never officially abandoned this nineteenth-century construction. Instead, the Court simply worked around it, adding a wide variety of doctrines that now give the federal government the power to do most of the things it wants to do. For example, without deciding that commerce includes agriculture or manufacturing, the Court held in 1941 in *United States v. Darby* that Congress can regulate intrastate activity that cumulatively and substantially affects interstate commerce.[64] The Court also repeatedly leveraged the view that Congress can regulate navigation. In the early nineteenth century, people disagreed about whether commerce included any other forms of transportation.[65] However, the Court gradually extended Congress's powers to include railroads, turnpikes, bridges, and tunnels; and new instrumentalities of transportation like cars, buses, and airplanes.[66] The Court also eventually gave Congress the power to regulate other instrumentalities of trade like telegraph, telephone, and communication networks.[67] Finally, the Court has held that all instrumentalities of transportation and all items that move or ever have moved in interstate transportation networks, or have crossed state lines, are within Congress's commerce power, whether or not they have anything to do with trade or exchange.[68] The Court has done all this without ever officially abandoning the distinctions between commerce, manufacturing, and agriculture.

Contemporary commerce clause doctrine since the New Deal has often been defended as pragmatic and realistic because it recognizes that we live in a fully integrated national economy. But in another sense the doctrine is quite formalistic and even a little bizarre.[69] The courts gave the federal government its current powers by stretching older constructions and multiplying legal fictions. The doctrine looks the way it does because courts began with a very narrow construction of "commerce" as trade plus navigation and gradually built an elaborate superstructure on top of it, expanding it beyond all recognition. It is like a vast mansion that was built with no particular rational plan around a modest bungalow. This happened in part because the Supreme Court often does not like to overrule older cases explicitly, but instead works around them,[70] and in part due to the federal courts' characteristically evolutionary and ad hoc forms of common law decisionmaking.

Contemporary critics of commerce clause doctrine—especially economic libertarians—would like to return to a narrow version of the trade theory without these many workarounds. But the trade theory remains ad hoc and formalistic even if we remove all of the later additions. That is because in today's world it is not a theory that is well designed to serve the Constitution's key structural principle: empowering the federal government to legislate in areas in which the states are separately incompetent. Rather, the trade theory is designed to limit the federal government *per se,* and it cripples the federal power to protect civil rights, employee rights, public health, public safety, and the environment in ways that the American public would find totally unacceptable. It is a construction that lacks democratic legitimacy and thus fails as "our law."

By contrast, if we returned to the original meaning of "commerce" as intercourse, the commerce clause would be perfectly adaptable to modern conditions. Call this approach the "interaction theory" of commerce. It has been offered in different forms by John Marshall, Joseph Story, Justice Hugo Black, and Akhil Amar.[71] Donald Regan and Steven Calabresi have advanced similar ideas without specifically connecting their arguments to the original meaning of the text.[72]

The interaction theory defines "commerce" according to its broadest eighteenth-century meaning as "intercourse." The primary focus of the clause, as Chief Justice Marshall explained, is "commercial intercourse between nations, and parts of nations, in all its branches."[73] Nevertheless, Congress can also regulate other forms of interaction, like communications and transportation networks, whether they are used for commercial or noncommercial purposes. What Congress can reach under the commerce clause, in short, are exchanges—whether of people, communications, or things.

Under the interaction theory, Congress has the power to regulate all interactions or affairs with foreign governments and with the Indian tribes.[74] Congress also has the power to regulate interactions or affairs among the several states. This would include activities that are mingled among the states or affect more than one state because they cross state borders, because they produce collective action problems among the states, or because they involve activity in one state that has spillover effects in other states. Thus, the interaction theory closely connects the language of the commerce clause to the structural principle of Resolution VI that underlies the enumeration of federal powers.[75]

As noted previously, the interaction theory accounts for all of the historical evidence offered by defenders of the trade and economic theories without having to resort to nonliteral usages. As I shall now show, it is also consistent with other evidence that the two other theories have difficulty explaining.

If we view the commerce clause through the lens of the central reasons for forming the Constitution and the central questions that faced the new nation—foreign affairs and dealings with Indian tribes—reading "commerce" to mean "intercourse" or "interactions" makes the most sense. The clause enabled "Congress to regulate *all* interactions (and altercations) with foreign nations and Indian tribes," which "if improperly handled by a single state acting on its own, might lead to needless wars or compromise the interests of sister states."[76]

One of the first things the new government did, for example, was to regulate its interactions with the Indian tribes, through a series of Trade and Intercourse Acts beginning in 1790. The title of these acts was apt: they not only required licenses for trade with Indians, but also punished "any crime upon, or trespass against, the person or property of any peaceable and friendly Indian or Indians."[77] These crimes did not necessarily involve trade or even economic activity; they could involve assault, murder, or rape. Note as well that even if the point of regulating these crimes was because of their likely effects on trade with the Indian tribes, the activities regulated were themselves not economic. And note finally that the 1790 and 1793 Trade and Intercourse Acts could not be justified as legislation designed to enforce treaties; they applied to crimes against Indians whether or not they had signed treaties with the United States.[78] Congress clearly believed that it could reach both economic and noneconomic activity under the Indian commerce clause;[79] at the very least it believed that it could regulate noneconomic activity in order to protect trade and diplomatic relations that would further trade.[80] This is hardly surprising. It was assumed in international law at the time of the founding that international intercourse included both commercial and noncommercial aspects that were inevitably intertwined.[81]

Neither the trade theory nor the economic theory can explain why the early Trade and Intercourse Acts would be constitutional unless we assume that Congress has the auxiliary power to regulate noneconomic (or nontrade) activity that affects foreign or Indian commerce. That is, we must assume that Congress can reach activities that do not involve trade or are not economic in order to protect its powers to regulate trade or other economic activity, perhaps under the necessary and proper clause. If so, then the two theories essentially merge into the interaction theory. Note, however, that the clause says that Congress can regulate "commerce" with foreign nations and with the Indian tribes, not "activity that affects commerce" with foreign nations and with the Indian tribes. The interaction theory is therefore more consistent with the text.

Immigration offers a second example of the limitations of the trade and economic theories. Although the 1787 Constitution bestows a power "[t]o establish an uniform Rule of Naturalization,"[82] it does not specifically mention the power to control immigration. We could infer the power from the naturalization power or from Congress's power to declare war or its powers "[t]o provide for calling forth the Militia to execute the Laws of the Union, suppress Insurrections and repel Invasions."[83] But there is a far more obvious source of the power to regulate the flow of populations across the nation's borders. It is the commerce power, which appears in the clause immediately before the naturalization power.[84] The eighteenth-century definition of commerce as "intercourse" or "exchange" among different peoples easily encompasses immigration and emigration of populations for any purpose, whether economic or noneconomic.

Article I, section 9, clause 1 limits Congress's power to prohibit "the Migration or Importation of such Persons as any of the States now existing shall think proper to admit" before 1808.[85] Where does that power to prohibit come from? The obvious source, once again, is Congress's power to regulate commerce with foreign nations and the Indian tribes. Indeed, this was assumed both in the debates in Philadelphia and at the time of the founding.[86] Note that even if the "importation" of slaves into the United States was trade narrowly defined, the "migration" of other persons—which might include free white immigrants—was not, although it still fell under the commerce power. In the period before the Civil War, the use of the commerce power to regulate immigration became increasingly bound up with disputes over Congress's powers to regulate slavery, and many different theories emerged.[87] Following the abolition of slavery, the Supreme Court returned to the original assumption that Congress had the power to regulate immigration under the commerce clause.[88] Thus, in *Chy Lung v. Freeman,* the Court argued, consistent with the structural principle in Resolution VI, that:

[t]he passage of laws which concern the admission of citizens and subjects of foreign nations to our shores belongs to Congress [under its] . . . power to regulate commerce with foreign nations: the responsibility for the character of those regulations, and for the manner of their execution, belongs solely to the national government. If it be otherwise, a single State can, at her pleasure, embroil us in disastrous quarrels with other nations.[89]

The interaction theory best explains and justifies Congress's powers over immigration. Congress could regulate immigration under the trade theory to the extent that it can regulate methods of transportation used for trade. Congress could regulate immigration under the economic theory to the extent that people pay for their travel and transportation companies engage in economic activity. But neither theory would reach a person entering the country on foot from Mexico or Canada, even if the purpose was to make a living in the United States. If these theories cannot explain why Congress has the power to control the flow of people walking into the country, they are not very plausible accounts of the power to control the country's borders. To be sure, migration of populations affects the price of goods and labor. Therefore, once again, if we postulate that Congress has the power to regulate nontrade or noneconomic activity that affects commerce (defined either as trade or economic activity), then the trade and economic theories merge into the interaction theory. In that case, the interaction theory is superior because it is simpler and it better corresponds to the actual words of the Constitution.

Today, courts would probably say that Congress's power to regulate immigration (and indeed conduct foreign affairs generally) comes from the plenary power doctrine, which was introduced in the *Chinese Exclusion Case*[90] and was stated most forcefully in *United States v. Curtiss-Wright Export Corporation*.[91] The plenary power doctrine, however, has no basis in the text. It was created in the late nineteenth century in order to give Congress a free hand in regulating foreign affairs at a time when courts held that the scope of Congress's domestic powers were very limited.[92]

If one had to defend an unenumerated plenary power to conduct foreign affairs, the best justification would be something like the structural principle stated in Resolution VI: Congress must have the power to regulate in the interests of the nation as a whole, in all areas where the states are separately incompetent or where individual actions by states might disturb the harmony of the Union. The argument for such an unenumerated power seems entirely sensible, but it also flies in the face of the claim that the federal government is a government of limited and enumerated powers and that the framers exercised considerable care in their choice of which powers to give the new federal government. Because foreign affairs were so crucial to the framers' reasons for forming a new Constitution, it seems very strange that they would have forgotten to give the federal government this power.

But they didn't forget. One doesn't need to postulate a general unenumerated power to conduct foreign affairs if one reads the commerce clause according to its original meaning of "intercourse." The commerce clause, like the powers to conduct war, make treaties, and define and punish violations of international law, is already in the text of the Constitution, and together with these other powers it gives the federal government the ability to regulate all kinds of affairs and interactions with the outside world.

Focusing on Congress's powers to regulate foreign commerce also helps settle whether the word "regulate"—i.e., prescribe rules for commerce—includes the power to prohibit.[93] Surely if Congress has the power to keep both goods and people out of the country under the foreign commerce clause, "regulation" must include prohibition. Even under the trade theory, the power to regulate must include the power to prohibit. The point of the new federal government was to promote American trade with foreign nations. It could not do this unless it could credibly threaten to block or embargo goods coming from foreign countries in order to force them to open up their borders to American goods.

I have argued that the interaction theory makes the most sense of the meaning of "commerce" because it makes the most sense of Congress's powers to regulate foreign and Indian commerce. It is true that Congress's powers to regulate domestic commerce are more constrained. My point, however, is that people who want to demonstrate that difference by limiting the meaning of the word "commerce" are looking in the wrong place. As a result, they have to come up with rather implausible theories for why the same word in the same sentence points to three different concepts.[94]

These linguistic somersaults are unnecessary if one reads just a little further in the text. The powers of foreign and Indian commerce are different from powers over interstate commerce because they serve different structural purposes that are reflected in the text. Congress can regulate commerce *with* foreign nations and the Indian tribes, but it can only regulate commerce *among* the several states.

"Among the Several States"

Operations and Effects

What does "among the several states" mean? Samuel Johnson's dictionary defines "among" as "mingled with" or "conjoined with others."[95] Randy Barnett argues that "among" means only commerce "between States" or "between people of different states," and does not reach commerce that occurs between persons in the same state.[96] Even if this activity affected other states or the nation as a whole, Congress could not reach it.[97] In *Gibbons v. Ogden,* Chief Justice Marshall properly rejected this view. He argued that "among" means "intermingled with" and that "commerce among the several states" means "commerce which concerns more States than one."[98] Thus, even commerce that occurs within a single state might be within Congress's regulatory power if it has external effects on other states or on the nation as a whole. As Marshall puts it, echoing Resolution VI:

> The genius and character of the whole government seem to be, that its action is to be applied to all the external concerns of the nation, and to those internal concerns which affect the States generally; but not to those which are completely within a particular State, which do not affect other States, and with which it is not necessary to interfere, for the purpose of executing some of the general powers of the government.[99]

Marshall warned in *Gibbons* that Congress's power would not apply to "[t]he completely internal commerce of a State."[100] But the question at issue is what commerce is "completely internal." Marshall and other nineteenth-century jurists adopted a series of constructions of "commerce among the several states" designed to limit the reach of the commerce power and preserve distinctions between local and national subjects of regulation.[101] Many of these distinctions, like the distinction between commerce and production or between direct and indirect effects on commerce, make little sense today, but they are not part of the original meaning of the text and we do not have to accept them.

Instead, we should read the phrase "among the several states" in a way that is most consistent with the structural principle behind the enumeration of powers. To use James Wilson's words, Congress can regulate interactions that extend in their *operation* beyond the bounds of a particular state, and interactions that extend in their *effects* beyond the bounds of a particular state.[102]

What kinds of *operations* extend beyond a state's boundaries? Transportation and communication are the two most obvious examples. Thus, Congress can regulate whatever crosses state lines. Equally important, it can regulate interstate networks of communication and transportation, subject always, of course, to individual rights protections like the First Amendment.[103]

Transportation and communication are not only activities; they occur as part of *networks,* which include technologies, institutions, facilities, and standards that are linked together in a system. Thus, a transportation or communications network includes not only the actual movement of people, goods, or electrons, but also an architecture of channels, nodes, and links, and the technologies, institutions, facilities, and standards that make movement possible.

Transportation and communications networks are crucial to the "commerce" of the nation, particularly when we understand "commerce" in the eighteenth-century sense of "intercourse." These networks create important externalities whose value transcends any particular state and can become more valuable as more people use them; indeed, economists give these externalities a special name—they are called network effects. Leaving regulation of these networks solely to state control might produce conflicting regulations that undermine their efficiency and interoperability and disturb the "harmony of the Union." (Imagine, for example, that the state of Arkansas required all Internet traffic to use a special protocol that no one else used.) This would reduce the value of these networks both within and without a state and impose costs on persons in other states.

The generation of 1787 did not use the term "network effects," a product of twentieth-century economic theory. But they well understood that the ability to move and communicate throughout the country was essential both to political union and to a vibrant commercial republic.[104] It follows that Congress also has the power to regulate intrastate transportation and communication networks, because they are part of larger national networks. Every element of interstate transportation and communications networks, Donald Regan has pointed out, operates within the boundaries of some state (think of telephone poles and railroad tracks), and "[t]he power to regulate some particular element" of the network "should not depend on whether that element itself ever moves across state lines or not."[105] The fact that a cellular antenna or a piece of fiber optic cable remains fixed in the ground in one state does not mean that Congress cannot regulate it.

What kinds of interactions have *effects* beyond a single state? These are interactions that create spillover effects or collective action problems. In the words of Resolution VI, commerce is "among the several states" when the states are "separately incompetent" to deal with a particular issue, "or [when] the Harmony of the United States may be interrupted by the Exercise of individual Legislation."[106] Note that the structural principle announced in Resolution VI is somewhat more restrictive than Wilson's formulation in the Pennsylvania ratifying convention.[107] It is not enough that the activity in question has effects beyond a particular state's borders; what matters is that these effects generate the sort of problem that makes a federal solution appropriate. We have already seen that transportation and communications networks can produce significant spillover effects. But many other kinds of activities can produce them as well, including environmental pollution, agriculture, manufacturing, banking, and employment relations.

Darby and Labor Regulation

Begin with federal minimum wage and maximum hour laws, upheld in the landmark case of *United States v. Darby*.[108] The Fair Labor Standards Act prohibited shipping goods made with substandard labor conditions across state lines. It also prohibited substandard labor conditions whether or not the goods crossed state lines.

Congress can ban the interstate shipment of goods made with substandard labor conditions if it believes that these goods unfairly compete with goods from states that do not have substandard labor conditions. Because Congress has the right to control interstate transportation and communications networks, it may control what goods and persons cross state lines, subject to the Constitution's individual rights guarantees. In this case, the goods are presumably not defective or dangerous in and of themselves; rather, Congress wants to control their flow across state lines because of the spillover effects that they produce.[109]

In *Darby* Justice Stone also argued that Congress had the power to ban substandard labor conditions in production in order to enforce the ban on interstate transportation.[110] This style of argument is a relic of the trade theory: Congress can control production because production affects trade. If we start with the interaction theory (or the economic theory, suitably understood), we need not entertain the legal fiction that Congress is regulating local labor conditions because it helps police the flow of goods across state lines. Rather, we can move directly to the real issue. Congress may regulate production because substandard labor conditions in some states create spillover effects in other states and create a potential collective action problem that only Congress can solve.

Suppose some states prohibit substandard conditions, while others do not. In the short run at least, firms in unregulated states will probably face lower production costs, and they can sell their goods more cheaply than firms in regulated states. In a national market, they will underprice goods from regulated firms; in particular they will be cheaper in the regulated states themselves. States that require better working conditions probably cannot constitutionally block goods from states with substandard labor conditions, because courts would view this as a forbidden discrimination against out-of-state businesses. Worse still, in the long run firms in regulated states may threaten to relocate to unregulated states to take advantage of lower costs and a friendlier business environment. All of this will put economic and political pressure on regulated states to allow substandard labor conditions.

Thus, in a national market, substandard labor conditions are not purely local matters; they have spillover effects on other states, and individual states are separately incompetent to deal with the problem.[111] (There is also a potential collective action problem if many states would like to improve working conditions but will not do so unless all the other states do so as well.) Congress may therefore regulate wages and working conditions because states face a federal problem that requires a federal solution.[112]

Note that this argument presumes that what I am calling "substandard" working conditions really are below an acceptable level—whether for moral, political, or economic reasons—and that additional regulation would be better, not worse. Often this will be a controversial claim. What some states regard as unjust violations of human dignity others will think perfectly acceptable and a protection of liberty of contract for employers and employees alike. What some states see as unfair competition that pressures them to participate in a race to the bottom others will view as a race to the top: good old-fashioned competition that promotes greater liberty, local autonomy, and productivity. What some states see as a federal problem demanding a federal solution others will see as not presenting a problem at all other than the dangers of needless federal interference with individual states' regulatory choices and their distinctive modes of life.

If the claimed spillover effects are nonexistent or insignificant or if they are outweighed by the values of liberty and local self-determination, there is no federal problem that requires a federal solution. If the states disagree among themselves about these issues, who decides the question? The answer is that Congress decides. The point of having a federal government, after all, is to resolve conflicts among the different interests in different states. All states are represented in Congress, and they can struggle among themselves about whether there really is a federal problem and, if they decide that there is, negotiate the appropriate solution. The commerce clause does not require any particular answer to this question; it simply gives Congress the ability to solve problems that it reasonably believes to exist.[113]

The advantage of this construction of "commerce" and "among the several states" is that it makes the constitutional question very similar to the policy question that Congress must debate—whether there are significant spillover effects or collective action problems and whether these present a genuine problem that is best solved by a federal solution. By resolving the policy debate, Congress also resolves the constitutional question, unless its conclusion is completely unreasonable.

Wickard and the Culmination of Individual Effects

Next consider *Wickard v. Filburn*,[114] which many people have assumed tests the limits of Congress's powers. In fact, *Wickard* is a fairly easy case, a standard example of a problem requiring a federal solution. The issue in *Wickard* is volatility in agricultural production and prices. Congress believed that farmers would go through cycles of overproduction leading to low prices, which would lead to farm bankruptcies and eventually to new agricultural shortages. Individual states could not solve this problem by limiting what their farmers could grow, because farmers in other states might overproduce—indeed, they might have incentives to do so—and this would drive down prices for all. Thus state agricultural policies have spillover effects on other states and even if all states wanted to limit production, they cannot do so unless all the other states who produce the same crops agree. Producing states might make an informal agreement to do so, but this might violate the prohibition on interstate compacts in Article I, section 10, clause 3.[115] After all, states that consumed, but did not grow, the crop in question might resent the cartel because it raised costs for their citizens, and they might try to find ways to retaliate. In any case such an agreement (like all other cartels) might be difficult to enforce, and it probably could not be enforced by blocking agricultural goods coming from defecting states.[116] (By contrast, the federal government has the power to block agricultural exports from foreign nations.) In short, states are separately incompetent to limit agricultural production. The problem, to the extent that one exists, is a federal one, and Congress has the power to decide the nature of the problem and devise an appropriate solution.

Wickard is famous for the proposition that if the sum of certain activities is within Congress's powers to regulate—because, for example, it has a sufficiently substantial effect on commerce—Congress can regulate each individual instance.[117] In *Wickard,* the activity in question was wheat grown on a family farm for private consumption, which might substitute for purchased wheat or, if prices rose, might be drawn into the national market.[118] Under the interaction theory (or the economic theory) this proposition not only makes considerable sense, it is almost inevitable.[119] Spillover effects and collective action problems are produced by the sum of many different individual activities; therefore, we must look to the aggregate to decide whether the problem is both federal and substantial. And if it is, Congress should be able to reach all the individual instances in a general scheme of regulation to get at the problem.[120]

Spillovers, Biohazards, and Environmental Regulation

Next, consider environmental and public health regulations. Air and water pollution cross state lines. So too do biohazards and epidemics. States may have sufficient incentives to prevent pollution or biohazards that fall wholly within their own jurisdictions, but they may have neither sufficient incentive nor sufficient ability to prevent pollution beyond their borders, and they may be helpless to prevent the spread of communicable diseases that affect the nation as a whole.

The interaction theory is superior to the economic theory in this case, because not all pollution, environmental damage or biohazards are caused by economic activity, even if they have economic effects. Once again, however, if we adopt the construction that Congress may regulate noneconomic activities that cumulatively affect interstate economic activity, there is little practical difference between the two theories.

What about the protection of endangered species? Many species migrate between states, so securing their survival presents a federal problem.

What about species that stay in one state? Congress can protect them if pollution or threats to their survival (such as hunters or predators) come from out of state. It can also protect them if they are threatened by business activities that have spillover effects in other states.

The value of environmental protection, however, is not completely captured by considerations of economic cost; it also concerns how Americans view their relationship to nature and the resources that nature provides us.[121] The nation's natural resources properly belong to the nation as a whole, and not to any single state. If interactions among the several states threaten those resources, the nation as a whole should have the right to protect them.

Antidiscrimination Law and the Right to Commerce

Now consider the constitutionality of antidiscrimination laws. Since the civil rights revolution of the 1960s, Congress has passed most of these laws using its commerce power. The primary reason why discrimination presents a federal problem is not because, as the Supreme Court once suggested, food served in discriminating restaurants has traveled from out of state.[122] Rather, discrimination—even in housing and local restaurants—has spillover effects on states that prohibit discrimination, which these states cannot effectively counteract on their own. In addition, discrimination affects the ability of Americans to participate fairly and fully in interstate networks of transportation and communication.

Like other labor laws, antidiscrimination laws create collective action problems that may discourage states from prohibiting discriminatory practices unless other states do so as well. Some antidiscrimination laws may increase costs for businesses, especially in the short run. Examples include laws that require accommodation of disabled employees or customers, laws that require employers to pay women and minorities as much as white men, laws that prohibit firing or demoting people for discriminatory reasons (creating problems of proof), and laws that require significant monitoring, record keeping, and compliance costs. As in the previous discussion of *United States v. Darby,* firms located in states that permit discrimination may have a competitive advantage over firms in states that prohibit discrimination. Similarly, states may shy away from passing stronger antidiscrimination laws out of fear that businesses will migrate to states with weaker laws.

Discrimination within a state may produce spillover effects on other states in a number of different ways. First, discrimination imposes costs on employers in interstate enterprises who may not be able to make the most efficient allocation of resources in their personnel decisions. For example, businesses may be less likely to assign blacks or gays to jobs that require them to move or travel to jurisdictions where housing or public accommodations discrimination will increase their costs of living, interfere with their ability to do their jobs, or otherwise make them less productive. Some businesses may not move to discriminating jurisdictions for fear of losing valuable employees or gaining a reputation as discriminatory or hostile to minorities.

Second, discrimination within a state or a region of the country (like the Jim Crow South) can have spillover effects in other jurisdictions if markets for goods and services are interconnected. Businesses in states that do not permit discrimination may alter their employment and production policies in order to cater to consumers and clients in jurisdictions that permit (or even expect) discrimination.

Third, if markets are interconnected, then credit, employment, risk, and pricing decisions by businesses in jurisdictions that permit (or expect) discrimination may affect business judgments by firms in other states. Interstate effects on business judgments can occur in many different ways. Regional or local discrimination may lower the average wealth and educational attainment (and hence expected creditworthiness) of minorities in the nation as a whole, skewing decisions in nondiscriminating jurisdictions. If regional patterns of discrimination lead to high rates of poverty and incarceration for racial minorities, this affects nationwide assessments of criminality, creditworthiness, healthiness, expense, and other risks. Sex discrimination that limits women's job histories affects their ability to compete when they travel to nondiscriminating jurisdictions. In this way, patterns of subordination in one area of the country lead to informational heuristics and biases that may limit housing, employment, and other opportunities for women and minorities in other parts of the country. In sum, if people economize on information when they make decisions, and they make decisions based on risk pools, the effects of discrimination against women and minorities can move with them across state lines.

Fourth, minorities, unhappy with poor treatment and limited opportunities, may leave states that allow discrimination for states that prohibit discrimination (or have greater protections against discrimination).

Gays may leave socially conservative rural areas to enjoy freer lives in large urban centers. Jim Crow policies in the South led to the Great Migration of blacks to cities in the North. Immigration from discriminating states will put pressure on housing, wages, and working conditions in more egalitarian states, especially if the new immigrants are used to working at lower wages and under inferior working conditions. Accordingly, the flow of cheap labor into the state and the influx of minority groups into neighborhoods and schools may exacerbate discrimination against minorities by majority groups, undermining the state's nondiscrimination policies and increasing costs for public and private sectors alike.

Many people—including members of Congress during the debates over the 1964 Civil Rights Act—have pointed out that Congress's powers to enforce the Reconstruction amendments are a better vehicle for combating discrimination than the commerce power, because the former powers directly concern equality and the latter power, in their view, concerns only issues of business and trade.[123] In one sense, this is correct: the Reconstruction amendments are and should be an important source of congressional power to regulate private discrimination.[124] In another sense, however, this criticism misses the deeper purpose of the power to regulate interactions among the states in a federal system. This may be in part because people still view the commerce power through the lens of the nineteenth-century trade theory, which defines "commerce" as solely about the exchange (and transportation) of goods and not in its broader sense of "intercourse," which includes ideas of social interaction, intermixture, and, to use more modern language, integration.

The commerce clause empowers Congress to prevent states from exporting elsewhere the problems they create through unwise and unjust social policies. To do this, Congress inevitably must make judgments of morality and policy. That is because one state's externality is another state's liberty. Activities in different states often affect other states, but not all of them justify a federal solution as a matter of sound policy. Congress therefore must decide whether state policies impose real and undesirable effects on other parts of the Union or whether these policies actually preserve local autonomy, economic liberty, and individual choice. One cannot do this unless one makes judgments of what effects are good or bad and what liberties are worth preserving.

Antidiscrimination laws involve Congress's judgment that private discrimination is not a liberty worth protecting, and that the practice of discrimination is a poison that affects and undermines other parts of the

Union. Jim Crow may have impoverished the South by denying many of its citizens the chance to become healthy, happy, and productive, but in an integrated economy it impoverished the North as well. Congress was entitled to decide that in undermining human dignity, the South was dragging other states down with it.[125]

Moreover, the commerce clause gives Congress the power to give Americans access to networks of transportation and communication, and to allow them to enjoy the benefits of commerce (that is, commercial and noncommercial intercourse) among the several states. Discrimination discourages minorities from using these networks fully and fairly. Racial discrimination discouraged blacks from traveling in the South, and it denied them economic opportunities nationwide. Because discrimination has multiple ripple effects in an integrated economy, it hinders the ability of minorities to compete fully and fairly in public life and discourages their use of the instrumentalities and networks of interstate commerce. Antidiscrimination laws, in short, protect both freedom of commerce (in its eighteenth-century sense) and equality in commerce.

These are not simply questions about gross national product. They are questions of personal liberty—including economic liberty, to be sure—but also of the rights to travel, meet, interact, and live with others throughout the country. These issues concern the rights to participate in the social and economic intercourse of the nation. Congress has to decide what are fair terms of access and fair opportunities of enjoyment with respect to the networks, channels, and instrumentalities of interstate commerce. These judgments of fairness are inevitably political and moral; they are inevitably judgments of what both liberty and equality require.

Federalism and Experimentation

A familiar defense of federalism is that it preserves traditional mores and local ways of life against national homogenization. This argument has a checkered pedigree: not only valuable traditions but also discrimination against blacks, women, and homosexuals have been defended on these terms. When states differ about these matters, the argument goes, the harmony of the Union and individual freedom are best served by letting each state decide these questions without federal interference. That may be so where tradition imposes costs only within a single state. But where discrimination imposes costs on other states, the harmony of the Union is already disturbed, and Congress may step in.

When subordination of social groups in the name of tradition has spill-over effects elsewhere, tradition may be too costly for the federal government to ignore.

A second and more important defense of federalism is that it promotes innovation and experimentation in different localities. Almost every important antidiscrimination principle began with states and local governments. Indeed, this justification for federalism is in some tension with a defense based on tradition: experiments mean rejecting customary ways of doing business. It is hard to see Jim Crow as an experiment. If it was, it was an experiment that failed.

We should take the language of experimentation seriously rather than as a rhetorical excuse for nonregulation or as a way to resist the application of federal constitutional rights. Experiments should be encouraged if they work to the benefit of the entire nation. But if these are genuine experiments, experiments generally end at some point and the results are tabulated; somebody has to decide whether the experiment is a success or a failure, and, if a success, adopt best practices nationwide.

Second, some experiments can blow up in your face, and, more importantly, in your neighbor's. You don't let your neighbor experiment with nuclear fission next door, because his actions might harm you and others. Where state experiments throw off harms to other states, Congress may regulate them.

Finally, some types of innovation are best achieved when the federal government ensures a basic platform of uniform standards on which both states and private parties can innovate. *Gibbons v. Ogden* is a good example.[126] New York sought to promote and reward technological innovation by awarding a monopoly to a new technology, steamship transportation. The problem was that the monopoly interfered with the transportation network along the East Coast of the United States. By establishing a single national coastal licensing scheme, the federal government allowed many different parties to innovate and compete with each other. This promoted technological development in the long run.

Telecommunications regulation is another example. States might allow (or require) broadband companies to block or filter Internet traffic. This may assist broadband companies' own attempts at innovation, but it can squelch innovation by third parties. A federal requirement of either network nondiscrimination or open access to telecommunications facilities decentralizes innovation so that many different people can create new technologies and applications that can be layered on top of national telecommunications networks. Federal regulation that creates a platform for innovation may benefit many different states, businesses, and individuals.

Antidiscrimination law also provides a platform for innovation, although we do not often think of it this way. Jim Crow kept the South backward and undermined its economic development. It is no accident that port cities and centers of commerce and immigration also tend to be most tolerant of differences. In recent years, cities that have welcomed homosexuals have benefited from cultural and economic innovation. In these situations a national "platform" of tolerance and antidiscrimination can benefit creativity and innovation as well as civil rights.

These claims are surely controversial. I can think of fairly obvious counterexamples. But the point is that if there is controversy about whether regulation stifles or promotes innovation, someone has to decide. Congress is best suited to decide these questions.

Lopez and Limits

Is anything beyond Congress's commerce powers? Yes, if Congress cannot reasonably conclude that an activity presents a federal problem. Note, however, that Congress may still be able to reach the activity through its other powers to tax and spend for the general welfare or its powers to enforce the Reconstruction amendments.

In *United States v. Lopez,* the Supreme Court struck down the Gun-Free School Zones Act of 1990, which made it a federal crime to possess a firearm within one thousand feet of a school.[127] Putting aside the Court's reasoning in *Lopez,* the result makes some sense. The possession of guns near schools does not look like a federal problem that produces significant spillover effects in other states, and Congress, at least at the time it passed the bill, did not provide any evidence that this activity created a federal problem.[128] Gun possession in or near schools might be a serious problem around the nation, but one whose dangers individual states would be motivated to address. That is, it might be a *national* problem—one that occurs in many states—but not a *federal* problem that states are incompetent to address individually.[129]

The Gun-Free School Zones Act appeared to be legislative grandstanding, a freestanding prohibition unconnected to a larger federal scheme of regulation of education, on the one hand, or gun trafficking, on the other. Thus, Chief Justice Rehnquist noted that "[s]ection 922(q) is not an essential part of a larger regulation of economic activity, in which the regulatory scheme could be undercut unless the intrastate activity were regulated."[130] More correctly put, it was not part of a larger scheme of regulation of *interstate* activity that would be undercut unless intrastate activity were included.[131] It follows that Congress may be on surer constitutional footing if it displaces more state law than if it displaces less. But the apparent paradox is illusory: the issue is not the amount of federal regulation but rather whether it is reasonably directed at a federal problem. *Lopez* therefore makes the most sense if we understand it as announcing an "antigrandstanding" principle. This principle requires that in close cases Congress must demonstrate a genuine federal problem by detailed findings or else Congress must make its desired regulation an integral part of a more comprehensive scheme that does address a genuine federal problem.

The justices in the *Lopez* majority, however, did not stop here. Instead, they offered two new constructions to explain why the Gun-Free School Zones Act was beyond federal power. Neither is well connected to the structural purposes of the commerce clause.

First, the Court suggested that the federal government could not reach what it called "traditional" areas of state regulation, including education, crime, and family law.[132] The argument is based on a false premise: the federal government has regulated family law since at least Reconstruction, and it has regulated education heavily in the last fifty years.[133] And of course, the federal government has attacked crime since the beginning of the Republic and with increasing frequency in the twentieth century. Perhaps more important, the argument from tradition is the same argument that was rejected during the New Deal: The *Lochner*-era Court viewed manufacturing and labor relations as traditional areas of state regulation; the justices eventually realized that this made little sense in an integrated economy. If an area of concern has significant spillover effects on other states, or begins to do so, it shouldn't matter that it was the traditional concern of state regulation.

Education is a good example. The federal government became increasingly interested in educational policy after World War II because conditions changed; both economic productivity and democracy required a well-educated workforce. The evolution of an information economy in the late twentieth century made these requirements all the more important. As transportation networks have improved, so has mobility, and given easy mobility, some states may increasingly underinvest in education. Poorer and rural states may not be able to recoup the long-term benefits of a good educational system because educated persons will leave for large urban areas. Conversely, people may flock to states with better educational systems, putting strains on their resources and preventing them from delivering quality services. Because poorly educated people are less able to be productive in an information economy and participate in an information-rich public sphere, states with poor educational systems may impoverish not only themselves but other states as well.

Crime offers a second example. Much crime presents a national problem but not necessarily a federal problem. But two varieties are federal concerns. The first type are crimes that make use of interstate transportation and communication networks or that cross state lines for their preparation and execution. An example is the federal power to regulate wire fraud. The second type are crimes in which the enterprise is organized in more than one state; states may be less effective in investigating and prosecuting out-of-state participants and may need federal assistance. Hence, the federal government may reach different varieties of organized and white-collar crime.[134] On the other hand, the constitutionality of the Violence Against Women Act, struck down in *United States v. Morrison*,[135] is better defended not in terms of crime that has spillover effects but as Congress's attempt to guarantee women's equal treatment in the justice system. Despite the Court's remarkably cavalier treatment of the issue, the Violence Against Women Act is a straightforward application of Congress's powers under section 5 of the Fourteenth Amendment to guarantee the equal protection of the laws.[136]

The *Lopez* Court offered a second construction to justify its decision: it argued that Congress should not be able to regulate noneconomic activity even if it cumulatively affected interstate commerce.[137] But it should not matter that air pollution comes from a backyard incinerator or a factory, that a dangerous virus spreads through personal contact or escapes from a biotech company, or that a migratory bird is shot by a lone hunter or a corporate operative.[138] If noneconomic activity creates a federal problem that states cannot individually handle, it should fall within the commerce power.[139]

There is a far more sensible limiting construction. Instead of asking whether the activity that produces the spillover effects is "economic," we should focus instead on whether the spillover has economic effects. Air or water pollution may not come from a factory or economic enterprise, but the effects may still cost money to the invaded state. We might sensibly require that Congress measure the spillover effects in economic terms and not simply in terms of the degree of moral or ethical disapprobation by individuals in other states. Moral or ethical objections to how a state handles its resources or governs its populations would not count as a spillover effect; but economic consequences for other states would. Of course, one can always cash out moral objections by asking hypothetically how much people in other states would be willing to pay to persons in the state to stop these activities or to adopt different ones, but under the construction suggested here the possibility of a hypothetical transfer payment does not make the spillover effects economic.

The *Lopez* majority recognized and accepted that in a modern, integrated economy, there will be very few things that the federal government cannot regulate, especially if it does so through general comprehensive programs. It also recognized that the federal government can often reach these subjects through its other powers, like the power to tax and spend for the general welfare. Thus, despite all the controversy that accompanied the decision, the practical effect of *Lopez* was very modest: only a very small class of possible statutes would be beyond Congress's power to enact. For this reason the doctrinal distinctions that *Lopez* created did not really further any of the traditional goals of federalism, whether they be individual liberty, respect for traditional subjects of state regulation, or local experimentation, precisely because Congress could regulate the same activities in other ways.

Nevertheless, like other courts before it, the *Lopez* Court sought a limiting principle to federal commerce power so that it could claim that the commerce clause did not bestow a general federal police power to regulate on all subjects in any part of the Union. The irony of the decision is that there *is* such a structural limiting principle in the text, backed by impeccable historical sources. The commerce power does not extend to situations where Congress cannot reasonably claim to be solving a federal problem.

The Individual Mandate for Health Insurance: *Lopez* or *Wickard?*

The recent debate over health care reform has revived the debate over limits on the commerce power. The Patient Protection and Affordable Care Act features an "individual mandate" that is designed to coax uninsured persons into purchasing health insurance.[140]

The term "individual mandate" is misleading for two reasons. First, the law does not actually require all individuals to purchase insurance. The mandate does not apply to persons receiving Medicare or Medicaid, military families, persons living overseas, persons with religious objections, or persons who already get health insurance from their employers under a qualified plan.[141] Second, it is not actually a mandate. It is a tax, which people do not have to pay if they have purchased health insurance. As amended, the Patient Protection and Affordable Care Act imposes a penalty tax for each month an individual fails to pay premiums into a qualified health plan.[142]

The tax is part of a comprehensive reform of health care and health insurance that insures more people and prevents them from being denied insurance coverage because of preexisting conditions. Successful reform requires that uninsured persons—most of whom are younger and healthier than average—join the national risk pool; this helps lower the costs of health insurance premiums nationally.

The tax gives uninsured people a choice. If they stay out of the risk pool, they effectively raise other people's insurance costs; and Congress taxes them to give them additional incentives to purchase insurance and recoup some of the costs if they don't. If they join the risk pool, they save the system money and so they do not have to pay the tax. A good analogy would be a tax on polluters who fail to install pollution-control equipment: they can pay the tax or install the equipment.

It is likely that the individual mandate is fully constitutional under Congress's powers under the general welfare clause "[t]o lay and collect Taxes, Duties, Imposts and Excises, to pay the Debts and provide for the common Defence and general Welfare of the United States."[143] The tax clearly promotes the general welfare under existing precedents.[144] Moreover, the tax is not a direct tax that must be apportioned by state population.[145]

Nevertheless, the tax is also constitutional as an exercise of Congress's commerce power. Congress has two goals in reforming health care: The first goal is universal coverage—to make health insurance as widely available as possible. The second goal is "guaranteed issue," which is essentially a requirement of nondiscrimination. Such a rule makes insurance coverage portable when people change jobs, prevents insurance companies from denying coverage because of preexisting conditions, and prohibits insurance companies from imposing lifetime caps on insurance or imposing other arbitrary limitations on health care coverage.

The goals of universal coverage and guaranteed issue are connected because markets for health insurance face a problem of adverse selection. Younger and healthier people have incentives to stay out of health insurance markets, while the elderly and people with greater health care needs have incentives to stay in. Because the latter are more expensive to insure, adverse selection increases the total cost of insurance for everyone in the pool. Guaranteed issue requirements exacerbate the difficulty; many people will wait until they become ill to purchase health insurance, knowing that they cannot be turned down.

To solve the adverse selection effects and lower insurance costs, health reform must bring younger and healthier persons into the risk pool. Some kind of universal coverage requirement is necessary to make guaranteed issue rules work. Congress sought to achieve this result through a tax on those who do not purchase insurance.

Does health insurance reform present a regulatory problem where states are individually incompetent and a national solution is required? Only one state so far (Massachusetts) has attempted something like the Affordable Care Act, combining an individual mandate with a guaranteed issue rule. It is not difficult to see why. States that unilaterally impose strict guaranteed issue requirements face obvious collective action problems. People with health problems will have incentives to move to a state where they cannot be turned down, raising health care costs for everyone, while insurers will prefer to do business in states where they can avoid more expensive patients with preexisting conditions, and younger and healthier people may leave for jurisdictions where they can avoid paying for health insurance.

If all states imposed an individual mandate, there would be no incentive for businesses or younger and healthier people to exit and the costs of guaranteed issue reforms would be subsidized by a broader risk pool in each state. But without a guarantee that all states will adopt similar reforms, individual states may not want to reform their insurance practices if this would result in significantly higher health insurance premiums for their citizens.

For this reason Congress might reasonably conclude that few states will be able to adopt guaranteed issue/individual mandate reforms on their own. Only a national solution can solve the collective action problems that states face while simultaneously creating a broader risk pool than any individual state could manage. Thus, the regulatory question is quite similar to those in *Darby* and *Wickard*.

The regulatory problem is also similar to that in *Katzenbach v. McClung*[146] and *Heart of Atlanta Motel, Inc. v. United States*,[147] which upheld the federal Civil Rights Act of 1964. Guaranteed issue rules prevent insurers from discriminating against people with preexisting conditions. Like states without antidiscrimination laws, states without guaranteed issue rules may inhibit interstate migration. People with preexisting conditions will be less willing to seek new opportunities in states that allow insurers to discriminate against them and deny them health insurance. To remove these burdens on interstate migration, Congress may reasonably conclude that a national solution is needed, and that an individual mandate is necessary to make guaranteed issue rules work.

But is the individual mandate a regulation of "commerce"? One objection to the individual mandate is that it regulates people who don't buy insurance. They cannot be engaged in commerce if they are literally doing nothing.[148] In fact, this is not accurate. People who do not buy health insurance are self-insuring and obtaining health care in other ways. When they get sick, they rely on their families for financial support and they purchase over-the-counter health care remedies. They also go to emergency rooms where they cannot be turned away, increasing costs for everyone in their community. (In 2008 alone, the cost of such uncompensated care was estimated at 43 billion dollars.) Indeed, emergency room care may be far more expensive than preventative care or care by a regular physician. These practices involve borrowing, purchasing, and consuming goods and services; their cumulative economic effect is substantial, and they impose significant economic costs on the rest of the country. Because uninsured persons contribute to a national health care problem, Congress may regulate them as part of a national solution.[149]

An Aside on "Necessary and Proper"

I have said relatively little about the necessary and proper clause so far because most contemporary understandings of federal regulatory power can be justified without it. The interaction theory derives Congress's foreign and domestic powers directly from the original meaning of the clause coupled with basic structural principles. Under the trade or economic theories, however, one might need the necessary and proper clause to explain why Congress can reach nontrade or noneconomic activity that affects trade or economic activity, respectively. Because Congress has the power to make its regulations of commerce effective, the argument goes, it may reach at least some activity that is neither trade nor economic activity.

Much ink has been spilled on the meaning of "necessary" and to what extent it limits federal regulatory power. Does "necessary" mean "absolutely required" or "indispensable," or does it mean "convenient" or "designed to achieve a particular end," as Alexander Hamilton and Chief Justice John Marshall maintained? The answer becomes clear when we look at the text of the entire clause: "The Congress shall have Power . . . To make all Laws which shall be necessary and proper for carrying into Execution the foregoing Powers, and all other Powers vested by this Constitution in the Government of the United States or in any Department or Officer thereof."[150]

Most writers have focused on what we might call the "vertical" aspect of the clause: laws that affect the interests of states. But an equally important function of the clause is its "horizontal" aspect. It empowers Congress to organize the executive and judicial branches to carry out federal governmental functions.[151]

The power to create new cabinet departments and organize or reorganize existing ones, for example, comes from Congress's powers "[t]o make all Laws . . . for carrying into Execution" the "Powers vested . . . in the Government of the United States, or in any Department or Officer thereof."[152] This horizontal aspect of the necessary and proper clause gives Congress the power to shape the structure and organization of coordinate branches of the federal government.[153]

Congress has used its horizontal powers under the necessary and proper clause throughout the nation's history. For example, Congress created the Department of Justice in 1870 to administer and prosecute federal laws following the Civil War. Following World War II, it merged the Departments of the Army and the Navy into the Department of Defense and created the Central Intelligence Agency and the National Security Council in the National Security Act of 1947. It combined various federal programs and agencies into a Department of Health, Education and Welfare in 1953 and later split that into a Department of Education (created in 1979) and a Department of Health and Human Services (officially renamed in 1980). It created a Department of Homeland Security in 2002 following the September 11, 2001, terrorist attacks. And of course, within each department Congress has created and modified various offices and agencies, and assigned to each its respective duties, jurisdictions, and obligations.

According to the text of the Constitution, each creation or reorganization of these federal departments had to be "necessary and proper" for carrying out powers granted to the federal government. But was each of them *indispensable* to "carry[] into execution" the Constitution's enumerated powers? Obviously not. Nor could we always say that these laws were always the most efficient, most straightforward, or most direct means of exercising federal powers. Rather, in each case Congress simply judged the legislation a convenient or appropriate way of organizing the executive branch. That is all that the word "necessary" requires.

If "necessary" only means "convenient" or "designed to achieve a particular end" when Congress regulates horizontally (that is, when it creates laws that affect the other branches), it means the same thing when it regulates vertically (that is, when it creates laws that affect the interests of the states). There is, after all, only one necessary and proper clause. In fact, the bill creating the Second Bank of the United States upheld in the famous case of *McCulloch v. Maryland*[154] had both horizontal and vertical aspects. It created a new federal agency (with a mixture of public and private ownership and control), and the agency affected state banks and state economic activities.

The word "proper" is equally important to understanding the scope of the necessary and proper clause. A regulation is "proper" if it is consistent with the Constitution, including its underlying structural principles. An otherwise convenient law might not be proper, for example, because it violates individual rights protected by the Constitution. An otherwise convenient law might not be proper because it violates the Tenth Amendment, which, as we have seen, is just the flip side of the structural principle in Resolution VI. (For example, the law might not seek to solve a genuine federal problem but merely be an exercise in congressional grandstanding.) Finally, a law might not be proper because it violates the separation of powers or undermines important checks and balances between the different branches.

Construction and Change

The original meaning of the commerce clause is consistent with the modern activist state and gives the federal government wide latitude to pass civil rights, employment, consumer protection, health, and environmental laws. Courts, however, have read it far more narrowly for much of the nation's history. Original meaning did not compel them to do so.

Judicial doctrines were constructions designed to implement the constitutional text and underlying structural principles. These doctrines were premised on assumptions about economic and social life in the early nineteenth century that were not sustainable as national markets developed and transportation and communications networks expanded. There is nothing surprising about this: constitutional constructions are always attempts at implementation—often imperfect and provisional—premised on background assumptions about social and political life. When those assumptions prove outmoded or unreasonable, fidelity to text and principle not only allows but requires that we abandon older constructions and replace them with new ones.

Nineteenth-century courts sought to preserve a distinction between national and local power by making distinctions between national and local subjects of regulation, and they created a series of doctrinal structures to accomplish this goal. These included distinctions between commerce and agriculture or manufacturing, and between direct and indirect effects on commerce. Thus, as noted earlier, the trade theory is less an adequate account of original meaning than a *construction* designed to demarcate separate spheres of federal and state power. Ironically, it achieves this goal by defining "commerce" narrowly—with predictable problems for Congress's powers to regulate foreign and Indian affairs—when the real point of these distinctions was to narrowly define what commerce was "among the several states" and therefore subject to federal regulation.

Lawyers often associate these distinctions with the *Lochner*-era Court that sat between 1897 and 1937, but they actually date from a bit earlier in the nineteenth century. They grow out of John Marshall's dicta about state inspection laws in *Gibbons v. Ogden,* and they were developed in a series of cases that gave the states freer rein to regulate in areas that the federal government was unlikely to enter.[155] Judges who supported state autonomy before the Civil War advocated narrow constructions of interstate commerce because they hoped to limit federal power generally. But it is important to remember that even strongly nationalist judges like John Marshall and Joseph Story had good reasons to offer narrow constructions of interstate commerce during this early period. It was not settled until the 1850s whether the states or only the federal government had the power to regulate interstate commerce.[156] Nationalists argued that federal power to regulate was exclusive; but if so, a broad construction of interstate commerce might have prevented reasonable (and even valuable) state regulations.[157]

In the late eighteenth and early nineteenth centuries, people well understood that many activities, including noneconomic activities, could affect more than one state, particularly if they used interstate networks of transportation and communication. But the lack of a truly integrated national society and economy meant that these spillover effects were likely not to be significant in most cases. Travel between different parts of the Union was often difficult and sometimes even dangerous. In a nonintegrated society and economy, spillover effects between states might often be attenuated. Moreover, the structural principle behind enumerated powers was double-sided; it assumed that states would have regulatory authority in cases where federal solutions were not needed. Therefore, it made sense for politicians and judges to argue for constructions that would act as rules of thumb to divide up the realms of state and federal regulatory power.

Although many of the nineteenth-century constructions purported to define "commerce," they were really ways of articulating and implementing what commerce was "among the several states"—that is, situations that presented a federal problem that required a federal solution. Where foreign nations and the Indian tribes were concerned, the problem was presumptively federal, and so courts usually gave Congress fairly wide latitude. But where domestic legislation was concerned, the distinction between direct and indirect effects, or between commerce, manufacturing, and agriculture, arguably had a heuristic or functional justification. They helped maintain a rough, albeit imperfect, division between activities that might have significant spillover effects or create significant collective action problems and activities that did not.

Nevertheless, these nineteenth-century constructions became increasingly unrealistic as the twentieth century proceeded. The problems began years earlier when telegraphs and railroads began to connect previously isolated parts of the country, later assisted by automobiles, trucks, and airplanes. As the industrial revolution took off and telecommunications and transportation networks grew, spillover effects multiplied. Courts responded by creating an elaborate series of crosscutting doctrines, distinctions, and subdistinctions to get around the straitjacket imposed by these early nineteenth-century constructions.

By the early twentieth century, this doctrinal structure had lost most of its usefulness. Distinctions between manufacturing, agriculture, and commerce, or between direct and indirect effects, no longer served the function of implementing the structural principle of Resolution VI and demarcating areas where intrastate activities had few spillover effects. Instead, in a changed world, these older constructions frustrated the Constitution's purposes by limiting federal power in arbitrary ways. In this context, the structural principle behind the doctrine of enumerated powers justified replacing older constructions with newer ones. These changes inevitably meant a much greater potential federal power to regulate private intrastate activity. But that is the consequence of applying an abstract text and an abstract principle to profoundly changed circumstances. The generation of 1787 would never have dreamed of a federal government as powerful as the one we have today. But they lived in a different world. Although we must remain faithful to the original meaning of the constitutional text, we are not bound by the framers' expected applications of text and principle.

10

PRIVILEGES OR IMMUNITIES

The Fourteenth Amendment may be the Constitution's most important source of civil rights and civil liberties. Yet it presents a genuine problem for expectations-based originalism, including versions of originalism that try to construct principles from how the generation of 1868 would have applied the constitutional text. Deriving constitutional principles from original expected application cannot account for the modern protection of constitutional civil rights and civil liberties. For example, the generation that ratified the Fourteenth Amendment would not have accepted our modern notions of sex equality and believed that states should be able to ban marriage between blacks and whites. Because the achievements of the civil rights revolution are a crucial source of the Constitution's current legitimacy, this is an important argument in favor of framework originalism.

Conversely, critics of originalism, confronted with examples of the framers' and ratifiers' views about race and sex, have feared the worst; they have assumed that the history of Reconstruction is inconsistent with the civil rights advances of the modern era. As a result, they have forgotten much of the history that actually supports our modern civil rights regime.

The method of text and principle helps us recognize that the modern civil rights regime has kept faith with the great promises of liberty and equality contained in the text of the Fourteenth Amendment. Even so, modern constitutional doctrine is hardly perfect. Legal doctrines developed and applied by courts are makeshift, historically conditioned attempts at realizing larger constitutional principles; they have been different before, and they will be different again. (In Chapter 9, for example, I noted that current commerce clause doctrines are built awkwardly on top of older nineteenth-century constructions.) In some respects today's Four-teenth Amendment doctrines do not adequately implement the text of the Fourteenth Amendment. Moreover, courts sometimes protect rights under the due process and equal protection clauses of the Fourteenth Amend-ment that should actually be implementations of the privileges or immuni-ties clause or the guarantee clause of Article IV, section 4. The method of text and principle gives us a critical perspective for understanding both the strengths and the weaknesses of current doctrine.

The text of section 1 of the Fourteenth Amendment begins with a definition of citizenship, the citizenship clause, which was added near the very end of congressional debates in the spring of 1866. Following this is a very long sentence, divided into three clauses: the privileges or immu-nities clause, the due process clause, and the equal protection clause. Section 5 is a grant of power to Congress to enforce all of the provi-sions of the Fourteenth Amendment by appropriate legislation. It is similar to the grant of enumerated powers in Article I, section 8. I have written about section 5 elsewhere.[1] In this chapter and the next, I will focus on section 1.

Why does the text of the Fourteenth Amendment look the way it does? Just as the enumerated powers of Article I, section 8, of the 1787 Constitution share an underlying structural principle, so too do the vari-ous parts of the Fourteenth Amendment.

As we saw in Chapter 9, the enumerated powers in the 1787 Consti-tution were designed to give the federal government the power to regu-late where states were separately incompetent or where the harmony of the Union would be disturbed by the exercise of individual legislation. This principle said little about the states' protection of civil rights or civil liberties. It was assumed that the new federal government was a more dangerous threat to liberty than the state governments. State con-stitutions had their own bills of rights, and although state governments could impose oppressive and inegalitarian policies on their populations, they were more or less known quantities.

The struggle over slavery and the Civil War changed these understand-ings. In order to protect slavery, the Southern states had repeatedly and routinely suppressed civil liberties, including the rights of free persons as well as slaves.[2] After the Civil War, former slave states had passed the "Black Codes," which, in effect, denied the freedmen much of their prac-tical liberty and reduced them to a state little better than slavery.[3] Al-though the Civil War began as a struggle over preservation of the Union, by its end Republicans understood the point of the war as the preservation of freedom, not only for the freed slaves but also for all citizens. In the eyes of the Reconstruction Congress, the states, and not the federal government, now posed the greatest threat to liberty and equality.

The central purpose of the Fourteenth Amendment was to recognize and protect the twin principles of equal citizenship and equality before the law. Equal citizenship meant that there was a basic template of civil rights and civil liberties enjoyed equally by all United States citizens. It was simultaneously a guarantee of liberty and equality. Equality before the law meant that governments must treat all persons equally in their enjoyment of rights, and that governments could not make arbitrary or invidious distinctions among persons, including noncitizens.

Each of these themes featured prominently in a famous speech given by Senator Jacob Howard of Michigan introducing the Fourteenth Amendment to the Senate on May 23, 1866.[4] Senator Howard was a member of the Joint House-Senate Committee on Reconstruction (the Committee of Fifteen) that drafted the amendment. He acted as the floor manager for the amendment in the Senate, presenting it with a speech that stated the Committee's official views about the amendment's purposes. Howard's speech was widely reported in the press, and portions of it were reprinted in newspapers.[5] Senator Howard explained that the basic purpose of section 1 of the Fourteenth Amendment was to "disable [the states] from passing laws trenching upon those fundamental rights and privileges which pertain to citizens of the United States, and to all persons who may happen to be within their jurisdiction."[6] Thus, the amendment secured the rights of both citizens and noncitizens. The amendment "establishes equality before the law, and it gives to the humblest, the poorest, the most despised of the race the same rights and the same protection before the law as it gives to the most powerful, the most wealthy, or the most haughty."[7]

The Reconstruction Congress assumed that Congress would be the primary protector of these rights. Today we tend to think of the courts in this role, but the Reconstruction Congress had very different assumptions. The antebellum Supreme Court had often protected the interests of slaveholders, and the example of *Dred Scott v. Sandford*,[8] which held that blacks could never be citizens, was still fresh in everyone's mind. The Reconstruction Congress believed that it was a far more reliable institution for protecting civil rights than the Supreme Court.[9] The enumerated powers of Article I, section 8, gave Congress the power to pass laws where states were separately incompetent; its new powers under the Fourteenth Amendment allowed Congress to secure equal citizenship and equality before the law. These powers were not given because individual states could not protect rights in a federal system, but rather because over a period of eighty years some states had demonstrated that they would not.

The first draft of section 1, debated in Congress from February 26–28, 1866, reflects these ideas. Introduced in the House by its most important framer, Representative John Bingham of Ohio, the February draft stated that "The Congress shall have power to make all laws which shall be necessary and proper to secure to the citizens of each State all privileges and immunities of citizens in the several States, and to all persons in the several States equal protection in the rights of life, liberty, and property."[10]

The February draft gave Congress broad powers to protect equal rights; the "necessary and proper" standard was taken directly from Article I, section 8, and it reflected the broad construction of congressional powers announced in Chief John Marshall's opinion in *McCulloch v. Maryland.*[11]

In the debates that followed, critics raised two basic objections. First, the language seemed too broad. It might be construed to say that Congress could pass any laws concerning life, liberty, and property as long as the rights created were equal. This was not John Bingham's intention, but both supporters and opponents of the amendment noted that it might be understood this way.[12]

Representative Giles Hotchkiss of New York made a second objection. The draft gave Congress the power to protect equal rights, but it said nothing about judicial enforcement. But what if Republicans lost their majority in both houses of Congress?

This was no idle concern. Two months before, in December 1865, the Reconstruction Congress had refused to seat southern senators and congressmen. They argued that the southern states, full of former rebels, had systematically oppressed blacks through the Black Codes and other devices; in the view of the Reconstruction Republicans, they were not republican (representative) governments consistent with the guarantee clause of Article IV, section 4.[13]

Once these states were readmitted to the Union, the South might have an even greater majority than it did before the war, because blacks in the South would no longer count as three-fifths of a person but would count as whole persons, even though they could not vote or enjoy many other rights. Ironically, by granting blacks freedom, the Reconstruction Congress had increased the political power of the former Confederacy in the House of Representatives and the Electoral College.[14] A coalition of southerners and northern conservatives might make genuine reform impossible, preventing both a new civil rights act and a new amendment (the latter, of course, would require a two-thirds vote of both houses). To hold off this possibility, Congress decided in December 1865 to keep the southern states out of Congress until new southern governments had formed that guaranteed black civil rights and black suffrage and would ratify a constitutional amendment guaranteeing basic civil rights. Congress simultaneously formed the famous Joint House-Senate Committee of Fifteen to investigate conditions in the South, to consider what legislation or amendments should be proposed to secure the rights of freedmen going forward, and to decide the conditions under which southern states would be readmitted to the Union.[15] The proposed Fourteenth Amendment before the House was the work of that Committee.

If the purpose of the new amendment was to protect equal rights, Hotchkiss argued:

> It should be a constitutional right that cannot be wrested from any class of citizens, or from the citizens of any State by mere legislation. But this amendment proposes to leave it to the caprice of Congress; and your legislation upon the subject would depend upon the political majority of Congress, and not upon two thirds of Congress and three fourths of the States. . . .
>
> Now I desire that the very privileges for which the gentleman is contending shall be secured to the citizens; but I want them secured by a constitutional amendment that legislation cannot override. . . .
>
> . . . [N]ow, when we have the power in this Government, the power in this Congress, and the power in the States to make the Constitution what we desire it to be, I want to secure those rights against accidents, against the accidental majority of Congress. Suppose that we should have here the influx of rebels that the gentleman predicts; suppose a hundred rebels should come here from the rebel States. Then add to them their northern sympathizers, and a reasonable percentage of deserters from our side, and what would become of this legislation? . . .
>
> . . . Why not provide by an amendment to the Constitution that no State shall discriminate against any class of its citizens; and let that amendment stand as a part of the organic law of the land, subject only to be defeated by another constitutional amendment. We may pass laws here to-day, and the next Congress may wipe them out. Where is your guarantee then?[16]

Hotchkiss's point was that the new amendment had to give *the judiciary* the power to enforce equal rights regardless of the civil rights laws that a future Congress might pass (or repeal). His words proved prophetic: the Democrats regained control of the House of Representatives in 1875, and no civil rights legislation was passed again until 1957.[17] Instead, during Reconstruction, Congress empowered the federal judiciary, giving birth to the modern conception of judicial review. It increased the number of federal judges, expanded federal jurisdiction, and passed a federal removal statute, all designed to give federal courts the ability to supervise states.[18]

Because it had become clear that there were too many objections to the February draft to meet the necessary two-thirds requirement for passage of a constitutional amendment, the House voted to postpone consideration of the measure, and the Committee of Fifteen returned to its deliberations.[19]

In the meantime, Congress had passed the 1866 Civil Rights Act over President Johnson's veto. The Act guaranteed black citizenship and equal civil rights and the "full and equal benefit of all laws and proceedings for the security of person and property" regardless of race.[20] Johnson's veto angered Congress and demonstrated the potential vulnerability of civil rights laws. Thaddeus Stevens and James Garfield pointed out that the 1866 Act might be repealed if the Democrats took control. A new Fourteenth Amendment would lock in its protections permanently.[21]

When the Fourteenth Amendment was reintroduced in the House on April 30, 1866, its language had been significantly altered.[22] The amendment was now divided into five sections, with the fifth section bestowing congressional power to enforce all of the amendment's provisions. Language protecting civil rights and liberties was now contained in a new self-enforcing section 1, giving the federal judiciary power to protect constitutional rights and liberties without the aid of congressional legislation.

The language of section 1 had also changed significantly from the previous version. The first part of the February draft gave Congress the power to pass laws "secur[ing] to the citizens of each State all privileges and immunities of citizens in the several States." This language had tracked the comity clause of Article IV, section 2.[23] Under the standard judicial construction, the comity clause protected citizens living temporarily in other states from discrimination. As described below, however, many Republicans, including John Bingham himself, believed that Article IV, section 2, also protected substantive constitutional rights such as habeas corpus and the Bill of Rights.

The new language of section 1, "No State shall make or enforce any law which shall abridge the privileges or immunities of citizens of the United States," tracked the 1787 Constitution's direct prohibitions on states in Article I, section 10 ("No State shall"), as well as the First Amendment's prohibition on Congress ("Congress shall make no law").[24] In 1871 Bingham explained that he had been guided by Chief John Marshall's opinion in *Barron v. Baltimore*,[25] which held that the Bill of Rights did not apply to the states. In *Barron*, Chief Justice Marshall explained that if Congress wished to bind states by constitutional amendments, it should use language of the form "No state shall."[26] Therefore Bingham wrote section 1 in precisely this way. In addition, the words "make or enforce" ensured that the language of the privileges or immunities clause applied to all branches of state government: legislative, executive, and judicial.

The new language now protected the "privileges or immunities of Citizens *of the United States*" instead of guaranteeing "the citizens *of each State* all privileges and immunities of citizens *in the several States.*" This language focused attention on the rights of *national* citizenship, that is, rights possessed by all United States citizens regardless of whether they lived in a state or in a federal territory. The new language made clear that these rights of national citizenship did not depend on state citizenship or state law; they applied equally to citizens in their own state, to citizens of one state living temporarily in another state, and to citizens in federal territories (who were not citizens of any state) who resided temporarily in a state or were otherwise affected by state law.

The second half of the February draft had protected persons, not just citizens. Modeled on the Fifth Amendment's due process clause,[27] it gave Congress the power to guarantee "to all persons in the several States equal protection in the rights of life, liberty, and property." The reference to "equal protection" was a gloss on the Fifth Amendment's due process clause; as we will see later on, the Reconstruction Congress believed that the idea of due process of law included a guarantee of impartiality, equal treatment, and equality before the law. The new language of section 1 divided this part of the February draft into two clauses, one tracking the precise language of the Fifth Amendment's due process clause ("No State shall . . . deprive any person of life, liberty, or property, without due process of law") and one specifically guaranteeing equal protection

("No State shall . . . deny to any person within its jurisdiction the equal protection of the laws").[28]

Congressional power to enforce the Fourteenth Amendment was placed in a new section 5, with only minor changes in language that did not substantially affect the meaning. "[S]ecure" became "enforce." "[N]ecessary and proper" became "appropriate," if anything an even more obvious reference to the test of *McCulloch v. Maryland*.[29] The new section 5 tracked the language of the enforcement clause in section 2 of the Thirteenth Amendment, which Congress had already interpreted quite broadly (in accordance with the rule of *McCulloch*) when it passed the Civil Rights Act of 1866.

Finally, on May 30, 1866, Senator Jacob Howard moved to amend section 1 to add a citizenship clause that clarified who was a citizen and therefore enjoyed the rights of equal citizenship: "All persons born or naturalized in the United States, and subject to the jurisdiction thereof, are citizens of the United States and of the State wherein they reside."[30] Howard stated that the citizenship clause was merely declaratory of existing understandings,[31] and Congress had already given blacks citizenship in the 1866 Civil Rights Act. Nevertheless, when Senator Doolittle of Wisconsin pressed him on why the clarification was necessary, Howard replied that it was integral to the protection of the rights of equal citizenship: "We desired to put this question of citizenship and the rights of citizens and freedmen under the civil rights bill beyond the legislative power of [those] who would pull the whole system up by the roots and destroy it, and expose the freedmen again to the oppressions of their old masters."[32] The text of the citizenship clause applied to both the national government and the states. It overturned the *Dred Scott* decision, which had held that blacks born in the United States could never be citizens; it placed in the Constitution the rule that citizenship, and equal enjoyment of all of the rights of citizenship, attached upon birth in the United States or naturalization. Finally, it made clear that United States citizenship was primary and did not depend on state citizenship, because persons born or residing in federal territories were citizens even if they were not the citizens of any state.

The Privileges or Immunities Clause

When courts consider issues of constitutional liberty and equality today, they generally look to the due process clause and the equal protection clause, but not to the privileges or immunities clause, which the framers of the Fourteenth Amendment designed to be its central guarantor of civil rights and civil liberties. The reason is the Supreme Court's initial misinterpretation of the Fourteenth Amendment in the *Slaughter-House Cases*[33] in 1873 and *United States v. Cruikshank*[34] in 1875. The *Slaughter-House Cases* severely limited the privileges or immunities clause by sharply distinguishingly between the rights of national citizenship that the clause protected and all other rights, which were left to protection by state governments. In essence, the Court held that rights were either rights of national citizenship or rights of state citizenship, and the two sets of rights did not overlap.[35] It held that the privileges or immunities of citizens of the United States were confined to a seemingly narrow class of rights, including, among other things, the rights to travel to the nation's capitol, to protection on the high seas and in foreign lands, and to free access to the nation's ports and federal administrative offices.[36] Two years later, in *United States v. Cruikshank*,[37] the Court asserted that various Bill of Rights protections were not privileges or immunities of national citizenship because these were natural rights subject to state protection.[38]

Slaughter-House, Cruikshank, and their progeny mangled the constitutional text and caused enormous mischief in subsequent years. Because the privileges or immunities clause was effectively read out of the Constitution, litigators and courts turned instead to the due process clause (and still later to the fundamental rights doctrines arising out of the equal protection clause) to do much of the work that the privileges or immunities clause should have performed. Thus, in *McDonald v. City of Chicago,* which applied the Second Amendment to the states through the due process clause, eight justices stated that they did not wish to disturb either *Slaughter-House* or *Cruikshank;* only Justice Thomas argued that the right to keep and bear arms should be considered a privilege or immunity of national citizenship.[39]

Fidelity to the original meaning of the Fourteenth Amendment, however, requires us to take the text of the privileges or immunities clause seriously and restore it to its rightful place as the central guarantor of constitutional civil liberties. Read free of the glosses of present-day doctrines, the declaration that states may not "make or enforce any law which shall abridge the privileges or immunities of citizens of the United States" looks like a guarantee of basic civil liberties against state abridgment, and the reason it reads this way is because that is precisely what it was designed to do. Even if courts stick with the due process clause as the source of basic liberties, as they probably will for the foreseeable future following *McDonald,* they could learn a great deal about how the Constitution protects fundamental rights by applying the theory and history of the privileges or immunities clause to their constructions of the due process clause.

The Original Meaning of "Privileges" and "Immunities"

In 1868, "privileges" and "immunities" were both synonyms for rights. Generally speaking, a privilege was a right to do something; an immunity was protection against invasions of a legally protected interest.[40] During the nineteenth century, federal treaties acquiring new territory from foreign governments or Indian tribes often included promises that the inhabitants would enjoy the "privileges," "rights," "advantages," and "immunities" (or some combination of these terms) of citizens of the United States. These rights generally included the Bill of Rights and other constitutional protections that citizens enjoyed in existing federal territories.[41]

Thus, "the privileges or immunities of citizens of the United States" are the basic rights that people enjoy by virtue of being United States citizens. This phrase, however, contains a crucial ambiguity. It might refer to the rights that all citizens enjoy whether or not noncitizens enjoy them as well; or it might refer only to the rights that citizens enjoy but that noncitizens do not enjoy.[42] This second, restrictive interpretation would exclude the right to habeas corpus in Article I, section 9, the jury trial right in Article III, and many of the guarantees in the Bill of Rights, because they do not protect only citizens.

Congressional debates over the Fourteenth Amendment resolve this ambiguity in original meaning. Framers like Bingham and Howard spoke of various rights that apply to all persons—like those in the Bill of Rights—as characteristic privileges or immunities of citizens. Speaking in 1871, Bingham explained that "the privileges and immunities of citizens of the United States, as contradistinguished from citizens of a State, are chiefly defined in the first eight amendments to the Constitution," and he proceeded to read the text of the first eight amendments into the record, including many rights that both citizens and noncitizens enjoy.[43] Similarly, in introducing the Fourteenth Amendment before the Senate in May 1866, Senator Howard specifically listed rights in the Bill of Rights that protect noncitizens as privileges or immunities of citizens of the United States.[44] This is hardly surprising: Congress was concerned that loyal citizens in the South had been denied free-speech rights, freedom of religion, and rights to a fair criminal process, and these parts of the Bill of Rights apply to citizens and noncitizens alike. Excluding these rights from privileges or immunities would not have made much sense.

The best reading, therefore, is that the phrase "privileges or immunities of citizens of the United States" does not refer to rights *exclusive* to citizens; rather it assumes that citizens' rights necessarily include the rights that the Constitution bestows on noncitizens. Put another way, the rights that all United States citizens enjoy because they are citizens form *a basic template of rights* guaranteed by the Constitution. If noncitizens enjoy some or all of these rights, it is because the due process and equal protection clauses require states to give them the same rights as citizens. Senator Howard explained that section 1 would prevent states "from passing laws trenching upon those fundamental rights and liberties which belong to every citizen of the United States and to all persons who happen to be within their jurisdiction." Thus, even though the privileges or immunities clause speaks of citizens, the framers of the Fourteenth Amendment designed the text of section 1 to protect the rights of both citizens and noncitizens.[45]

The Privileges or Immunities Clause and the Privileges and Immunities Clause

As noted earlier, the phrase "privileges or immunities" was based on the language of the comity clause, Article IV, section 2, which provides that "[t]he Citizens of each State shall be entitled to all Privileges and Immunities of Citizens in the several States." This clause was particularly important in Republican and antislavery thought. The February draft copies the language of the comity clause directly, and Republican ideas influenced the final language.

Republican and antislavery interpretations of the comity clause differed from the mainstream reading in the antebellum period. Many courts and commentators maintained that Article IV, section 2, was solely an equality provision; it required states to treat out-of-state visitors as well as they treated their own citizens with respect to basic or fundamental rights.[46] It followed that states could deny these rights to visitors if they also denied them to their own citizens. A year after the ratification of the Fourteenth

Amendment, the Supreme Court affirmed this equal treatment position in *Paul v. Virginia*.[47]

Before the Civil War, however, many Republicans and antislavery activists argued that Article IV, section 2, was also a substantive guarantee of basic rights that states could not deny.[48] John Bingham, for example, read "citizens in the several States" to mean "citizens of the United States in the several States;" so that the clause protected basic rights enjoyed by virtue of United States citizenship.[49] In particular, Bingham argued that the Bill of Rights and other enumerated federal constitutional rights applied to the states through Article IV, section 2.[50] Nevertheless, Republicans disagreed among themselves about whether Congress had the power to enforce Article IV, section 2 rights by legislation.[51]

Republicans also had distinctive views about the Bill of Rights. Even though the Supreme Court had held in *Barron v. City of Baltimore* that the Bill of Rights did not apply to state governments, leading Republicans like Howard and Bingham—and indeed, most of the Republicans in the 39th Congress—disagreed. They believed that the states had a duty to obey the Bill of Rights and other enumerated rights in the Constitution because these were basic rights of United States citizens.[52] Bingham, for example, argued that state officials were required to enforce the Bill of Rights because the supremacy clause of Article VI required them to take oaths to support and defend the Constitution.[53] Once again, however, Republicans disagreed about whether Congress had the power to enforce any of these obligations against the states.[54] Bingham himself denied that Congress had the power to enforce the Bill of Rights either directly or through Article IV, section 2, and that is one reason why he opposed the Civil Rights Act of 1866.[55]

The importance of federal territories in American politics in the years before the Civil War made these interpretations of Article IV and the Bill of Rights seem plausible and even natural to Republicans. Citizens of the original thirteen colonies lived in states that had existed before the 1787 Constitution and had long histories of constitutional government. By 1866, however, many congressmen and senators lived in states that had begun as federal territories. For them, federal rights and federal citizenship naturally came before state citizenship, and they naturally regarded the federal government as the central protector of basic rights. By contrast, slaveholding states had regularly denied basic rights in order to shore up slavery.[56]

Before a territory became a state, citizens and noncitizens alike were protected by the Bill of Rights and other constitutional guarantees from interference by the territorial government. To Republicans like John Bingham, gaining statehood should not mean the loss of basic federal constitutional rights.[57] Hence, it seemed natural to argue that states (and state officials bound by oath to defend the Constitution) still had an obligation to protect these rights even if Congress lacked the power to enforce them. The rights enumerated in the Constitution—like habeas corpus and the rights contained in the Bill of Rights—were declaratory; they stated the basic kinds of liberties that all republican governments should protect. Thus, in the February debate, Bingham repeatedly insisted that there was nothing in his draft that was not already in the Constitution and that the new amendment did not impose any obligations on the states that they did not already have.[58] What he meant was that states were already required to obey the Bill of Rights and other constitutional guarantees, but now Congress could enforce this obligation.

The Central Purposes of the Privileges or Immunities Clause

These distinctive Republican theories about the Constitution help us understand why Bingham and the Committee of Fifteen wrote the Fourteenth Amendment the way they did. It also explains why they changed Bingham's original language into the present version of section 1 when it became clear that Bingham's February draft might be misunderstood as creating a general federal power to legislate on life, liberty, and property. The goal was not a general federal police power; it was a judicially and congressionally enforceable guarantee that no state could deny the basic liberties (i.e., the privileges or immunities) of citizens of the United States, and that no state could deny persons equality before the law (i.e., due process and equal protection).

Introducing the amendment before the Senate in May, Senator Howard made these points explicitly. There was "a mass of privileges, immunities, and rights, some of them secured by [Article IV, section 2], some by the first eight amendments of the Constitution."[59] Nevertheless, "the course of decision of our courts and the present settled doctrine is, that all these immunities, privileges, rights, thus guarantied by the Constitution or recognized by it . . . do not operate in the slightest degree as a restraint or prohibition upon State legislation" because "there is no power given in the Constitution to enforce and to carry out any of these guarantees."[60] "[T]hey stand simply as a bill of rights in the Constitution, without power on the part of Congress to give them full effect; while at the same time the States are not restrained from violating the principles embraced in them except by their own local constitutions, which may be altered from year to year."[61]

Therefore, explained Howard, "[t]he great object of the first section of this amendment is . . . to restrain the power of the States and compel them at all times to respect these great fundamental guarantees."[62]

Howard emphasized that the privileges and immunities of citizenship "cannot be fully defined in their entire extent and precise nature."[63] Many of them were unenumerated. He began by looking to the list produced by Justice Bushrod Washington in *Corfield v. Coryell*,[64] interpreting the privileges and immunities clause of Article IV, section 2. Washington stated that these privileges and immunities were those "which are fundamental, which belong of right to the citizens of all free governments."[65] Washington also noted that the privileges and immunities of citizenship could not be exhaustively enumerated, but that they included, among other things:

> Protection by the government; the enjoyment of life and liberty, with the right to acquire and possess property of every kind, and to pursue and obtain happiness and safety; subject nevertheless to such restraints as the government may justly prescribe for the general good of the whole. The right of a citizen of one state to pass through, or to reside in any other state, for purposes of trade, agriculture, professional pursuits, or otherwise; to claim the benefit of the writ of habeas corpus; to institute and maintain actions of any kind in the courts of the state; to take, hold and dispose of property, either real or personal; and an exemption from higher taxes or impositions than are paid by the other citizens of the state.[66]

Although this list of fundamental rights was not limited to those specifically mentioned in the Constitution, and although Justice Washington had included suffrage in his list,[67] Howard cautioned that the new privileges or immunities clause did not guarantee the right to vote: "The right of suffrage, is not, in law, one of the privileges or immunities thus secured by the Constitution."[68]

"[T]o these," Howard, explained, "should be added the personal rights guaranteed and secured by the first eight amendments to the Constitution."[69] He then proceeded to list specific individual rights in the Bill of Rights as examples of the privileges or immunities of citizens of the United States protected against state abridgment:

> the freedom of speech and of the press; the right of the people peaceably to assemble and petition the Government for a redress of grievances, a right

appertaining to each and all the people; the right to keep and to bear arms; the right to be exempted from the quartering of soldiers in a house without the consent of the owner; the right to be exempt from unreasonable searches and seizures, and from any search or seizure except by virtue of a warrant issued upon a formal oath or affidavit; the right of an accused person to be informed of the nature of the accusation against him, and his right to be tried by an impartial jury of the vicinage; and also the right to be secure against excessive bail and against cruel and unusual punishments.[70]

Likewise, John Bingham stated repeatedly during and after the debates over the Fourteenth Amendment that the purpose of the Fourteenth Amendment was to give Congress the power to enforce rights listed in the Constitution (including the Bill of Rights) against the states.[71] Other Republicans agreed with Bingham and Howard on this point.[72]

The text says "privileges or immunities" and not "Bill of Rights" for an obvious reason. As Howard explained, there were "a mass of privileges, immunities, and rights" in the Constitution, only some of which were listed in the first eight amendments. For example, the privilege of habeas corpus was in Article I, section 9; the right to jury trial was in Article III; equal treatment for sojourning citizens was in Article IV, section 2; and a new right against enslavement was in the recently enacted Thirteenth Amendment. Additional fundamental rights recognized at common law—perhaps some of those contained in Judge Washington's list in *Corfield v. Coryell,* like the right to travel, or to protection by the government—might also qualify as privileges or immunities of national citizenship, either as substantive rights or as a guarantee of equal treatment.[73] Senator Howard's explanation of the purposes of the Fourteenth Amendment—as well as the text of the Ninth Amendment—suggested the possibility of still other, unenumerated privileges and immunities of citizens of the United States. The only formula that could capture all of these rights would have been something like "privileges or immunities of citizens of the United States," and that is precisely what the proposed Amendment said.

Equality as a Privilege or Immunity of Citizens

John Harrison and David Currie have argued that the privileges or immunities clause did not enforce substantive rights and was only a guarantee of equality.[74] They point out that the Fourteenth Amendment was widely acknowledged to lock in the protections of the Civil Rights Act of 1866, and it is hard to see how a substantive provision could accomplish that end, because the Civil Rights Act is an equality guarantee.[75]

There are several difficulties with this argument. First, the Civil Rights Act of 1866 is not a pure equality measure. It calls for the "*full and equal* benefit of all laws and proceedings for the security of person and property, as is enjoyed by white citizens."[76] This language is both a substantive and an equality guarantee;[77] therefore a substantive constitutional guarantee is necessary to match its scope. Second, the scope of the Civil Rights Bill is also covered by the equal protection clause, which guarantees equality of civil rights for citizens as well as persons. Third, the language of the privileges or immunities clause—"No State shall make or enforce any law which shall abridge the privileges or immunities of citizens of the United States"—reads like a substantive guarantee of rights, not a simple guarantee of equality. The language of the clause echoes the First Amendment, which says that "Congress shall make no law . . . abridging the freedom of speech."[78] Even the majority opinion in the *Slaughter-House Cases*, which greatly limited the privileges or immunities clause, held that it protected a set of substantive rights; the dissenters maintained that it protected even more rights.[79]

Nevertheless, Harrison and Currie raise an important point. There is no reason why the privileges or immunities clause could not protect *both* fundamental rights *and* equality before the law. That makes particular sense if one believes, as the Reconstruction Republicans did, that equality before the law is one of the most important rights of citizens and persons.[80] Therefore, we should view the privileges or immunities clause as not simply a guarantee of liberty or a guarantee of equality, but a guarantee of both.

One might object that this makes the equal protection clause redundant, but the equal protection clause ranges more broadly, covering noncitizens as well. We might make the same point about the due process clause: Surely due process is a privilege or immunity of United States citizens, but that does not make the clause redundant, because it specifies that aliens enjoy due process protections.[81]

In fact, there is no reason why the three clauses should not overlap substantially in their coverage: together they were designed to serve the structural goals of equal citizenship and equality before the law. Just as the enumerated powers of the national government listed in Article I, section 8, often overlap, so too do the Constitution's civil rights and civil liberties protections; in both cases this ensures that there are no significant gaps in coverage and that the Constitution's larger structural purposes are achieved.[82] When important constitutional provisions overlap in their coverage, this is often a feature, not a bug.

What Rights Does the Privileges or Immunities Clause Protect? The Declaratory Theory

If the privileges or immunities clause guarantees substantive rights, which rights does it protect? The privileges or immunities clause is *declaratory*—its language does not specify the rights it protects but merely asserts their existence.[83] The declaratory aspect of privileges or immunities was quite important: it allowed Republicans like Bingham to insist that states were *already* bound by the privileges or immunities of citizenship, and that all free governments were *already* required to provide equal protection and respect basic rights like habeas corpus, freedom of speech, and freedom of religion, regardless of the actual history of enforcement of these rights in the South.

The declaratory idea presupposes that certain rights preexist governments, and that all free governments have an obligation to respect them whether or not they actually do so. Indeed, the very fact that some governments have failed to respect these rights in the past is the very reason for present-day protest, and the justification for clarifying and enforcing these rights through positive law.[84] Nevertheless, a declaratory approach does not ignore positive law but instead treats it as a resource. It uses a common law method to identify rights, looking to past customs, practices, and laws as evidence of larger principles of freedom to be applied to present-day circumstances. Persons employing a declaratory approach might look to documents like Magna Carta, the English Bill of Rights of 1689, the Declaration of Independence, landmark decisions and statutes, and provisions in federal and state constitutions as evidence of preexisting rights and as sources of maxims or principles that might be generalized to new questions and situations.[85]

The declaratory model of rights thus relies on tradition, but the tradition is often an invented tradition, or, at the very least, it is a tradition selectively viewed and interpreted from the standpoint of the present. It asserts the existence of rights that We the People "have always" had, even if the understanding of and need for these rights has only recently become apparent or salient. It treats tradition not as providing fixed rules but rather as offering legal and rhetorical resources for making arguments about justice in the present.

For example, one could understand the traditions of liberty in antebellum America in at least two ways: In one story, Southern governments had violated the preexisting liberties of free persons and citizens and the great traditions of American freedom by abridging rights of freedom of speech, freedom of religion, and trial by jury; denying due process and equal protection of the laws; and imposing cruel and unusual punishments. In the second story, there were no such preexisting rights that states were obligated to respect and there was no such tradition of freedom. Instead, existing laws and understandings allowed Southern governments to act as they did. The existence of a so-called tradition of freedom is belied by the very fact that these rights were not respected.

When John Bingham insisted that the Fourteenth Amendment "takes from no state any right that ever pertained to it," he adopted the first story of history and tradition and rejected the second. He offered a declaratory account of fundamental rights and described an invented tradition: "No State," he asserted, "ever had the right, under the forms of law or otherwise, to deny any freeman the equal protection of the laws or to abridge the privileges or immunities of any citizen of the Republic, although many of them have assumed and exercised that power, and that without remedy."[86]

How should we apply a declaratory theory of privileges or immunities today? We can divide this question into two parts. First, does the privileges or immunities clause protect textually enumerated rights in the Constitution? Second, does it protect any unenumerated rights, and if so, how do we determine what they are?

Enumerated Rights

As we have seen, the privileges or immunities clause was designed to enact a basic principle: states should be bound by those fundamental rights of American citizenship that already bound the federal government. If we apply this principle today, we will reach a result very similar to the assumptions of key framers like John Bingham and Jacob Howard. The clause will enforce the individual rights guarantees found in the 1787 Constitution (like the Article I, section 9 right to habeas corpus), in the Bill of Rights, and in all subsequent amendments.[87] Although we are not bound by original expected applications, in this case applying the underlying principles that we derive from history leads us to a similar result. Simply put, if we asked for a list of fundamental rights that all United States citizens enjoy by virtue of their citizenship, we would almost certainly begin with textually enumerated rights. Under a declaratory theory, the fact that We the People have put these rights in the Constitution is powerful evidence that they are the fundamental rights of citizens.

The Supreme Court has achieved similar results through different methods. Because of the *Slaughter-House Cases* and *United States v. Cruikshank,* it has ignored the privileges or immunities clause and asked instead whether parts of the Bill of Rights are incorporated in the due process clause. Employing a theory called "selective incorporation," the Supreme Court has considered rights one by one and asked whether they are among those "fundamental principles of liberty and justice which lie at the base of all our civil and political institutions,"[88] whether they are "basic in our system of jurisprudence,"[89] or whether they are "fundamental to the American scheme of justice."[90] By now the Supreme Court has incorporated most of the Bill of Rights except for the Third Amendment, the grand jury clause of the Fifth Amendment, the right to jury trials in civil cases in the Seventh Amendment, and the prohibition against excessive fines in the Eighth Amendment.[91]

Nevertheless, the Court's selective incorporation doctrine has always been a makeweight necessitated by the original wrong turn in *Slaughter-House* and *Cruickshank.* Fidelity to original meaning requires taking the text of the privileges or immunities clause seriously.

How would this make a difference for existing doctrine? Our basic assumption should be that all individual rights specifically mentioned in the text are presumptively privileges or immunities because We the People have placed them in the Constitution, and the burden is on the interpreter to prove why they are not really part of the basic rights of citizens. The selective incorporation model starts with the presumption that none of the textually enumerated rights are privileges or immunities, and requires proof that these rights are necessary to ordered liberty or essential to the American system of democracy. As Justice Hugo Black once said, the selective approach is better than nothing, but it is not the best approach.[92]

Nevertheless, taking the privileges or immunities clause seriously does not necessarily mean that every part of the Bill of Rights automatically applies to the states. Justice Hugo Black's model of "total incorporation" is not necessarily the best account of the clause.[93] Akhil Amar has pointed out, for example, that many parts of the Bill of Rights—like many other parts of the Constitution—serve structural goals of federalism and separation of powers.[94] For example, Article I, section 9 includes a guarantee of the privilege of habeas corpus, which is a privilege or immunity of citizenship. However, Article I, section 9 also includes a requirement that capitation taxes must be apportioned according to state population. The capitation clause protects individual interests, but it is not an individual right. It is a structural guarantee of federalism designed to regulate permissible tax burdens among states.[95] To apply the privileges or immunities clause today, we must decide which elements of the Constitution (including the Bill of Rights) protect individual rights and which are structural guarantees.

To give one example, the Seventh Amendment's guarantee that "[i]n Suits at common law, where the value in controversy shall exceed twenty dollars, the right of trial by jury shall be preserved" might or might not be a privilege or immunity of citizenship, depending on the theory of the clause. The Supreme Court has held that the amendment guarantees the right to a jury trial in federal civil cases involving legal rights akin to those protected by the common law in 1791.[96] It is more likely, however, that the Seventh Amendment is a federalism provision that requires that federal courts preserve the right of trial by jury in any case where the state in which the federal court sits would preserve it. The idea is that parties cannot escape the right to jury trial by fleeing to a federal court.

This interpretation would adjust federal practice to evolving state practices regarding jury trials, ensuring that federal courts never offered less protection for civil jury trial rights than states did; it would make the Seventh Amendment operate somewhat like the Rules of Decision Act in the 1789 Judiciary Act, which requires that federal courts apply state laws of decision in diversity cases unless there is a conflict with federal law.[97] Nevertheless, it would still require federal courts to create their own evolving common law doctrines—like those in the states— that would apply to civil trials in the District of Columbia and other federal territories.

There are a few other complicated cases in the Bill of Rights. Consider the establishment clause, which says that "Congress shall make no law respecting an establishment of religion." The word "respecting" means "concerning." At the time of the founding, several states had established churches and the clause prevented Congress from interfering with them. This aspect of the clause is a structural guarantee of federalism and cannot be a privilege or immunity of citizens.[98] Therefore it does not apply to state governments.

In addition to requiring *noninterference* with state establishments, however, the establishment clause also embodied a principle of *nonestablishment* that independently limited the federal government even where the states were not concerned. Otherwise, the federal government would be able to establish a national church in federal territories, hire clergymen to run it, and require that federal tax money be devoted to its maintenance.[99]

This aspect of the establishment clause was not a federalism guarantee, and it became particularly important as the country expanded and the federal government took over governance of increasing amounts of new federal territory, where an increasing number of American citizens lived.[100] Here the establishment clause prevented federal territorial governments from making any laws respecting an establishment of religion. Not surprisingly, the citizens in these territories understood the establishment clause primarily as a ban on religious establishments rather than a federalism provision, and when they formed new state governments, they included establishment clauses of their own in their new state constitutions.[101] Meanwhile the older states gradually abolished state support of their established churches.[102]

Even so, does the constitutional guarantee of nonestablishment create an individual right of citizens that could be applied to the states? Yes. The guarantee of nonestablishment has two elements: one concerns civil liberty, and the other civil equality. The establishment clause protects individual liberty because it prevents the federal government from coercing anyone to adhere to or participate in a favored religious belief or to contribute money toward the maintenance of a church or religion. The establishment clause also protects civil equality because it prohibits government from designating a preferred religion or a preferred set of religious beliefs, and therefore it prohibits government from making distinctions among citizens depending on whether they agree or disagree with the government's religious viewpoint.[103] The establishment clause bans practices that convey the message that there is a favored group of citizens, or "real" Americans, who share the government's stated religious views and other citizens whose religious beliefs are merely tolerated. The idea that the government may not create first- and second-class citizens when it comes to matters of religion is strongly connected to the Fourteenth Amendment's general purpose of securing equal citizenship.[104] These privileges of liberty and equality belong to all United States citizens, and states may not violate them.

The establishment clause presents another textual problem, however, which it shares with the rights of religious exercise, speech, press, assembly, and petition guaranteed by the First Amendment. The First Amendment appears to be only a limitation on Congress instead of a general right against government action. Does this mean that these First Amendment privileges and immunities only provide rights against state legislation? No, it does not.

Begin by noting that even if the establishment clause were *only* a federalism guarantee, it would still have to limit more than Congress. A promise of federal noninterference would mean little if the president or the federal courts could undermine state establishments. The word "Congress" in the First Amendment must be a nonliteral usage, a synecdoche or metonym that stands for all of the lawmaking and law enforcement operations of the federal government.

This argument becomes even more powerful when we think of the First Amendment in terms of individual rights of freedom of speech, assembly, and religion. If the First Amendment applied only to "Congress," territorial legislatures and federal sheriffs could punish people for speaking out against the government or practicing their religion. Federal judges could issue prior restraints against books distributed in the nation's capitol, federal post offices could refuse to deliver mail the president did not like, and the president, acting in his capacity as commander in chief, could order all U.S. soldiers to pray to the same god for victory.[105]

We should not read the constitutional text to permit such results if we can help it, because we should try to interpret constitutional language to fulfill the purpose of the text as best we can determine it. As noted in Chapter 1, the words "speech" and "press" in the same amendment are clearly nonliteral usages; it is perfectly reasonable to read "Congress" in the same way.

In the alternative we can imply a structural principle to supplement the text. To prevent important rights from being so easily abridged, individual rights that bind Congress must also limit coordinate branches and all agencies and individuals acting under color of federal power that make or enforce federal law. Under either approach, First Amendment rights are privileges and immunities of national citizenship that apply to all branches of state and local governments.

One might object that both of these arguments contradict the text because it refers only to "Congress." I disagree. We cannot know whether a proposed reading contradicts the text until we decide whether the text uses a term nonliterally; this requires us to understand the principle or principles the text attempts to vindicate. In the same way, we need to know these principles in order to decide whether a proposed structural argument supplements or contradicts the text.

To understand the text, we need to put ourselves "on its side," honestly attempting to further what we believe to be its purposes as best we can understand them. To do this we can and should bring to bear all of the traditional modalities of constitutional argument, including history, structure, and consequences. Structure and consequences argue in favor of a nonliteral reading. So too does history: Historical sources do not suggest that significant numbers of people in the founding generation—or later generations, for that matter—thought that the First Amendment limited only actions by Congress and that there were good reasons to allow other branches of the federal government to violate people's rights of speech, assembly, and religion. Quite the contrary, the earliest federal decision even to imagine that there was an issue simply assumed that the First Amendment applied to all branches of the federal government.[106]

We can certainly imagine principles that would distinguish congressional power to censor from judicial and executive power, but none of those principles makes particular sense either at the time of the founding or today, and a very long history of practice rejects the idea. Therefore, we are entirely justified in treating "Congress" as a nonliteral usage that includes all branches of government, or implying a structural principle to the same effect.

The Second Amendment presents a different set of problems. History presents us with two readings of the amendment: one that makes the right to bear arms a privilege or immunity of national citizenship, and one that does not; we must decide which reading makes the most sense today.

The text of the Second Amendment connects "the right of the people to keep and bear arms" with "the security of a free State" through the maintenance of "[a] well-regulated militia." The Second Amendment was premised on a civic republican idea. The people, organized as a militia, would check potential federal tyranny and help preserve republican government.[107] The Amendment also served federalism goals by preventing the federal government from disarming state militias. The text explains, however, that the Second Amendment protected the right of "the people" to serve in militias, whether organized by states or not. At the time of the founding, "the people" referred to those with the right to govern—free adult males.[108]

This version of the right to keep and bear arms is a structural guarantee against tyranny and usurpation. It was a collective duty of the people as much as a right. The great mass of the people, consisting of all free adult male citizens, had a civic obligation to protect the republic from tyrants and usurpers by being ready and able to bear arms in defense of liberty. Because women and minors were not part of "the people" who could serve in militias, the amendment did not bestow rights on all citizens. Thus, the right to keep and bear arms was more akin to the political rights to serve on juries, vote, or hold office, which were also restricted to the governing class of adult males and also served structural purposes of checking and regulating government power.[109] This version of the right to keep and bear arms, therefore, is not a civil right and is not a privilege or immunity of citizens of the United States that applies to state governments.

The common law right of self-defense, on the other hand, is an individual right. At the time of the founding, there is some indication that the Second Amendment was designed to secure the common law right of self-defense, but the evidence is far more ambiguous and inconclusive than evidence of the civic republican right.[110] By the time of Reconstruction, however, there is plenty of evidence that people—including the congressional Republicans who wrote the privileges or immunities clause—understood the right to keep and bear arms as an individual guarantee of self-defense.[111] In the decades since the founding the right to keep and bear arms had been transformed from a civic republican, structural guarantee of community protection against usurpation and tyranny into a liberal, individualist guarantee of self-defense against marauders and terrorists. Congressional Republicans believed that the freedmen and their political allies needed to bear arms to protect themselves from Klansmen and members of southern militias that were now terrorizing them. That is why the right to bear arms appears in Senator

Howard's list of privileges or immunities of citizens of the United States and why the 1866 Freedman's Bureau Act specifically listed "the constitutional right to bear arms" as one of the rights it protected.[112]

In *Heller v. District of Columbia,* the Supreme Court used evidence from the nineteenth century to show that the ratifying public in 1791 sought to protect an individual right to self-defense.[113] This use of history is anachronistic. Although some members of the public may have believed that the Second Amendment protected an individual right to self-defense, the most likely purpose of the 1791 text was civic republican—securing the right to serve in citizen militias from federal interference and protecting the ability of citizens to check an overweening federal government. Nevertheless, the nineteenth-century evidence helps show why Reconstruction Republicans believed that the right to keep and bear arms was a liberal individual right and a privilege or immunity of national citizenship that should be enforced against the states. Ironically, then, the historical case for a Second Amendment individual right of self-defense is stronger with respect to state governments than with respect to the federal government.

From the standpoint of framework originalism, however, the question is not what the generation of 1791 or 1868 intended or expected. The text states an abstract principle, which delegates construction to future generations. The question therefore is what constructions make the most sense today. To answer this question we can draw on principles articulated throughout American history, including Reconstruction as well as the founding. Although the text speaks of militias, the self-defense reading is consistent with the text and it was actually a preferred construction when the Fourteenth Amendment was proposed and ratified. It is therefore a permissible construction today, even if it were absolutely clear that the public in 1791 intended only a civic republican right of adult males to serve in militias to check federal tyranny. After all, the principles stated in the First Amendment and the equal protection clause may protect rights that framing generations never expected; we should treat the Second Amendment no differently.

But if it is a permissible construction, is it also the best construction? The argument for recognizing an individual right to keep and bear arms in self-defense is very similar to the argument for recognizing unenumerated rights such as the rights to travel or to use contraceptives, to which I now turn.

Unenumerated Rights

The privileges and immunities clause protects some rights that are not enumerated. As Senator Howard explained, the privileges or immunities clause guarantees those "fundamental rights and privileges which pertain to citizens of the United States, and to all persons who may happen to be within their jurisdiction."[114] The list of such fundamental rights "cannot be fully defined in their entire extent and precise nature,"[115] so that it is no objection that some of them are not specifically mentioned in the Constitution. Indeed, every Justice in the *Slaughter-House Cases* assumed that the privileges or immunities clause protected at least some unenumerated rights. They simply disagreed about what those rights were, with the dissenters offering a more capacious list.[116]

Senator Howard's speech introducing the Fourteenth Amendment explained that the rights protected by Article IV, section 2, were privileges or immunities of citizens of the United States, pointing to Justice Washington's partial list of privileges and immunities in *Corfield v. Coryell*. Most of these rights would not be listed in the Constitution. Nevertheless, fidelity to original meaning does not require us to assume that the list of unenumerated rights protected by the privileges or immunities clause today must be identical to those the framers of the Fourteenth Amendment would have expected. Moreover, it is by no means clear that there was consensus among the framers of the Fourteenth Amendment about what those unenumerated rights were and whether all of them were *substantive guarantees* or some were simply *rights of equal treatment* that could be limited or abridged if all citizens were treated the same and subjected to reasonable regulation.

For example, some Republicans, relying on language in *Corfield*, might have argued that the privileges or immunities clause protected substantive economic rights, like the common law rights of property and contract.[117] Other moderate and conservative Republicans, however, would have rejected this interpretation for a very simple reason: its effect on Congress's powers to enforce the privileges or immunities clause under section 5. If the privileges or immunities of national citizenship included substantive property and contract rights, Congress would have the power to pass national laws regulating and protecting them. This possibility was the very reason why the February draft was rejected. It is unlikely, therefore, that most of the framers believed that common law rights of contract and property were fully constitutionalized as privileges or immunities of citizens of the United States. Instead, Republican moderates and conservatives would have assumed that these Article IV, section 2, privileges or immunities were simply guarantees of equal treatment.[118]

Nevertheless, most congressional Republicans would probably have agreed that other rights listed in *Corfield* should be viewed as substantive constitutional rights and not simply as rights of equal treatment;— because otherwise these rights could be completely abrogated if they were eliminated for all. These substantive rights would probably include the right to habeas corpus, the right against bills of attainder, and the right to travel. The first two of these are textually enumerated rights, while the right to travel, recognized by the Supreme Court a year later in *Crandall v. Nevada*[119] as a basic right of citizens, is unenumerated.[120]

The language of the privileges or immunities clause is a far more logical source of unenumerated fundamental rights (like the right to contraception) than the due process clause, where courts currently locate them. Instead of asking whether an interest is a fundamental right or a protected liberty that cannot be taken without due process of law, the more natural and sensible question is whether it is a privilege or immunity of national citizenship, part of a basic template of rights that all citizens enjoy.

As we have seen, the privileges or immunities clause is *declaratory*— its language does not specify the rights it protects but merely asserts that these are rights We the People always have (or should always have) enjoyed. Especially where unenumerated rights are concerned, federal courts must play a different role in articulating the privileges or immunities of national citizenship than legislatures and the general public. Courts should generally proceed with caution, recognizing unenumerated rights only after there is very substantial evidence of their fundamental character from the states and from the people.

When Congress passes legislation to protect the privileges or immunities of national citizenship, it can announce that, in its view, these rights belong to all citizens.[121] And when individuals or social movements interpret the Constitution in pressing for social change, they can make arguments that certain rights heretofore unrecognized or insufficiently protected are fundamental guarantees of citizenship that deserve special protection. When a *court* seeks to protect declaratory rights, however, it must do something in addition to making substantive arguments for why the rights are important; it needs evidence that the rights in question have achieved a special status as fundamental. If the rights are specifically mentioned in the text, or can easily be implied from specific references in the text, the task is far easier. But if not, then courts need another way to establish that the rights already exist and deserve judicial protection. One way to do this—although not the only way—is to look at the kinds of rights that have historically or traditionally been protected by states, or rights that almost all of the states have recognized or protected. The idea is that when lots of different states from different parts of the country agree that these rights deserve protection, they are more likely to be rights with special constitutional value that all governments are supposed to protect. That is, they become the (expected or assumed) privileges or immunities of citizens of the United States.

This approach creates a reciprocal relationship between the states and the federal courts. Declarations by federal courts of national privileges or immunities limit state governments, but the development of rights claims in the states and local governments guides the federal courts in recognizing fundamental rights. Mobilization for and recognition of rights at the state and local levels therefore matter greatly to the kinds of rights that federal courts eventually protect. This bottom-up approach also has the effect of requiring sustained mobilization and broad support among the states in different parts of the country before federal courts recognize a right as fundamental.

It follows that the list of unenumerated fundamental rights may change over time as political parties or social movements mobilize to protect certain rights and convince their fellow citizens that these rights are indeed important, even if previous generations had not felt particularly endangered or upset by their lack of protection.[122] Conversely, sustained political or social mobilization may eventually persuade courts to allow democratic regulation of unenumerated rights previously considered fundamental.

A good example of the ebb and flow of unenumerated rights in constitutional doctrine is the right of freedom of contract protected by the federal courts during the *Lochner* era between 1897 and 1937. During the late nineteenth and early twentieth centuries, politicians appointed judges who interpreted Reconstruction-era ideas of free labor, personal liberty, and inherent limits on government to restrict the ways that governments could regulate businesses. During the *Lochner* era, courts struck down legislation regulating maximum hours or regulating the right to join labor unions because it interfered with an unenumerated right to free contact. Decades of social and political mobilization, culminating in the New Deal, and new judicial appointments led the federal courts to reject the fundamental status of freedom of contract. The moral of the story is that sustained and successful constitutional politics can subtract from as well as add to unenumerated fundamental rights. Some unenumerated fundamental rights that courts recognize today may no longer be considered fundamental fifty or a hundred years from now. Those who wish to preserve these rights must perpetually work in their defense, a piece of advice that applies to all important rights.

The example of freedom of contract shows that there is no one-way ratchet in favor of ever more unenumerated rights constricting the operations of democracy. Unenumerated rights will come and go over very long periods of time. Textually specified rights, by contrast, can be added or removed only through Article V amendment; nevertheless, the scope of these rights will depend on constitutional constructions that may also change over time. Indeed, because social and political mobilizations will affect how courts construe even enumerated rights like those contained in the First Amendment, perpetual vigilance in the political process is still necessary to protect them.

There is nothing particularly strange or unusual about a dynamic conception of declaratory rights. People press for rights when they begin to feel aggrieved by their absence, and their aggrievement does not come all at once, but is triggered by new problems and changed circumstances.[123] Then people press for protection of these rights, arguing that governments always should have protected them, whether or not this was in fact the case and whether or not the claim even made sense in an earlier era. Thus, a declaratory conception of rights is almost always a dynamic conception that uses history and tradition as a powerful justificatory rhetoric. Rights become fundamental and timeless, in short, when the time is right for them.

This approach to privileges and immunities sees the scope of the privileges or immunities clause as dynamic, depending on the emerging customs, expectations, and traditions of the American people as a whole. The clause's "declaratory" nature invites individuals throughout the country to press for reforms at the state, local, and national levels to protect rights that they believe are due to them as citizens and to explain to and convince their fellow citizens why these rights are so important. When enough people around the country have been convinced, and enough legal protections have spread throughout the country, federal courts are entitled to pronounce that these rights have become expected and customary rights of American citizens and therefore should be binding on the small remainder of the states that have become outliers. Rights become privileges or immunities of citizenship as a result of a sustained period of constitutional politics in which the people speak through mobilization, protest, discussion, and legal reform, arguing that certain rights are important basic protections of American citizenship and winning over a large number of people to their views.

This approach to privileges and immunities of citizenship makes sense of much of the Court's "substantive due process" doctrines, which developed after the Court improperly truncated the privileges or immunities clause. These doctrines developed in response to social and political demands for rights over a sustained period of time that drew on existing traditions of practice, or that eventually convinced many people in many different parts of the country.

From this perspective, it is not difficult to see why the right to use contraceptives, first recognized in *Griswold v. Connecticut*[124] in 1965, and extended in *Eisenstadt v. Baird*[125] and *Carey v. Population Services International*,[126] would qualify as a privilege or immunity of citizens of the United States. A social movement for contraceptive rights had been ongoing throughout most of the twentieth century, and had eventually convinced most of the country, as evidenced by almost universal decriminalization. By 1965 when *Griswold* was decided, only one state, Connecticut, still outlawed the use of contraceptives, and the law was only fitfully enforced. As the sexual revolution proceeded, more and more people assumed that basic elements of sexual autonomy were guarantees of citizenship and the Supreme Court soon extended the right from married couples to all individuals in *Eisenstadt* and *Carey*. In 1987 Judge Robert Bork's confirmation to the Supreme Court failed in part because he refused to accept that the decision in *Griswold* protected a basic right of American citizens.[127]

The declaratory theory of the privileges or immunities clause also makes sense of the Court's 2003 decision in *Lawrence v. Texas*.[128] By 2003 only thirteen states criminalized same-sex sodomy, and the law was almost never enforced in criminal prosecutions. Instead, it was used to deny homosexuals rights to employment, adoption, and other civil privileges.[129] As a result, it also acted as a contemporary form of class legislation that singled out a group and declared its expressions of love and intimacy criminal. A sustained social movement for reform changed public attitudes and made heterosexuals recognize that homosexuals were individuals who were equally citizens and therefore deserved the same rights of sexual intimacy that heterosexuals had long enjoyed. This changed the social meaning of sodomy laws and hence their constitutional meaning under the Fourteenth Amendment.

This analysis also shows why the issue in *Lawrence* presented a more difficult case for courts in 1986 when *Bowers v. Hardwick,*[130] which upheld Georgia's sodomy law, was decided. In 1986 only half of the country had abolished its same-sex sodomy laws, although the trend was toward decriminalization.[131] The AIDS crisis of the early 1980s temporarily complicated the picture but not the long-run result. *Bowers v. Hardwick,* rather than being the last word on the subject, stimulated further debate and political mobilization: it caused more homosexuals to announce their sexual orientation openly and fight for their rights.

The example of *Bowers* shows that if we wish to understand the wellsprings of fundamental rights in the American system, focusing on court decisions can be seriously misleading. Far from crushing the gay rights movement, *Bowers* gave it renewed energy; social mobilization for gay rights in civil society, culture, and politics proceeded unabated and led to ever greater social acceptance. By 2003, *Lawrence v. Texas* confirmed what most Americans already believed—that criminalizing sexual relations between gays was fundamentally unfair. *Lawrence* is declaratory in precisely this sense. Indeed, by the time *Lawrence* was decided, the terms of political debate had already shifted well past the issue of criminalization to the issue of gay marriage.

This form of analysis explains descriptively why courts come to recognize unenumerated rights. It also offers a form of normative legal argument that lawyers might address to courts to explain why it is consistent with the judicial role to recognize unenumerated rights. Finally, it helps signal to courts when certain positions are no longer off-the-wall and should be seriously considered. The above analysis is not, however, a test that nonjudicial actors need employ when they consider what rights Americans have. Citizens are not required to count states or jurisdictions to justify their opinions about basic rights. Citizens must think for themselves and then attempt to persuade others; without their input, unenumerated rights would never be recognized in the first place. It was entirely appropriate for ordinary citizens and politicians to insist in 1970 that the Constitution guaranteed sexual autonomy for gays, just as people may argue for a revival of freedom of contract jurisprudence today. Unenumerated rights begin in the judgments of the public about the rights that Americans should have and always should have had. The judgments of judges arrive later on and generally should arrive later on.

Under a declaratory model of implied fundamental rights, the decisions of courts are often less important than they seem. Courts ratify public attitudes about basic rights and conserve these attitudes over time, offering resistance to changes in public understandings of basic rights but ultimately not preventing them if they are sufficiently powerful and sustained. Indeed, as we saw in the case of *Bowers,* judicial resistance can sometimes spur successful social mobilizations in response.

The most important fundamental rights case of the second half of the twentieth century, of course, is *Roe v. Wade.*[132] I have written about the case extensively, arguing that the right to abortion is a requirement of sex equality guaranteed by the equal protection clause and a personal freedom guaranteed by the privileges or immunities clause. It is not guaranteed by the Fourteenth Amendment's due process clause, as the court held in *Roe* itself. (Ironically, however, with respect to the *federal* government, the proper source of the abortion right is the Fifth Amendment's due process clause. That is not because the clause protects substantive rights, but because it guarantees equal protection, as discussed in Chapter 11.) Like many fundamental rights, the right to abortion is simultaneously a guarantee of liberty and equality. The close relationship between liberty and equality is implicit in the text of the Fourteenth Amendment itself: the privileges or immunities clause is simultaneously a guarantee of liberty and equality; it secures equal liberty and therefore equal status.

I have argued that the right to abortion is actually two rights. The first is the right not to be forced by the state to sacrifice life or health in order to bear children. The second is the right of women to have a reasonable time to choose whether or not to become mothers and take on the life-altering responsibilities and social obligations of motherhood. Without a right to safe and legal abortion as a backstop to contraception, many women will not be able effectively to choose the number and timing of their children; the state can force them to become mothers against their will, imposing life-altering obligations on them. The right to abortion is the right to motherhood by choice. It allows women to take on the responsibilities of motherhood as a result of their own decision, rather than being forced into this role—along with its accompanying burdens and obligations—by the state. Although the right to abortion is not sufficient by itself to guarantee women equality, it is a necessary condition for sex equality, at least in a society like our own. I invite readers interested in the details of the argument and, more generally, in how to apply the method of text and principle to abortion rights, to consult my two articles on the subject.[133]

How does the right to abortion fit into the declaratory model of privileges or immunities of national citizenship I described earlier? In one respect the answer is easy: I have argued that the right to abortion follows from the Constitution's guarantee of sex equality. Therefore it must be a privilege or immunity of citizenship because the right to equal protection of the laws is also a privilege or immunity of national citizenship. But what if we focus instead on the abortion right as a substantive liberty separate from the argument from sex equality?

In 1960 all states criminalized abortion with very few exceptions. In the next decade, however, because of the sexual revolution, changing views about women's equality, and a long social movement for contraceptive rights, attitudes toward abortion changed dramatically, and by 1972 a significant majority of Americans—including American Catholics—believed that the question of abortion should be left to the woman and her doctor.[134] At the same time a wide range of prominent organizations—ranging from the AMA to the YMCA to the ABA to a presidential commission—called for reform of the nation's abortion laws.[135] Nevertheless, by January 1973, when *Roe* was decided, only thirteen states had passed abortion reform statutes, which gave doctors greater leeway to perform abortions in cases where life or health was threatened, and only four states had passed abortion repeal statutes that left the decision up to the woman and her doctor in the first half of pregnancy.[136] Thus, when *Roe* was decided, the Court imposed constitutional rules that had been adopted by only four states out of fifty. It is possible that a wave of abortion repeal statutes might have swept the country in the 1970s, but we will never know because the Supreme Court interrupted the trend. Both David Garrow and Gene Burns have argued, to the contrary, that the pro-life movement was rapidly gathering steam even before *Roe* and might have stopped or at least greatly slowed the pro-choice movement's advance in state legislatures.[137]

Applying the declaratory theory to *Roe v. Wade* thus depends on how we understand the attitudes of Americans about the right to abortion in 1973. If we look only to state legislative action, the right to abortion had not yet gained the status of a privilege or immunity of national citizenship, when the Court decided *Roe* in 1973. If we look to public attitudes, by contrast, the public had already moved significantly toward the view that women have a right to end their pregnancies through abortion. This shift in attitudes accompanied the sexual revolution and the success of the movement for women's equality. In *Roe* itself, the Supreme Court did not understand abortion rights in terms of women's rights and equal status in society; instead it understood abortion through a medical frame, speaking of the rights of women and their doctors. Nevertheless, the rest of the country recognized the connection between women's rights and abortion rights. Since the 1970s, abortion has been generally understood as a right of women that allows them to choose the terms under which they will become mothers.

A different question is whether the right to abortion has become a privilege or immunity of citizenship in the past forty years. If *Roe v. Wade* were overruled today, it is likely that an overwhelming majority of the states would protect some kind of right to abortion, especially in the first trimester or first half of normal pregnancies. Perhaps less than ten states would outlaw abortion in virtually every case. Both pro-life and pro-choice groups, for complementary reasons, have incentives to argue that the number would be much higher. Pro-life groups want to show that their side is gaining converts, while pro-choice groups want to emphasize the need for pro-choice appointments to the courts to keep state legislatures at bay. Both sides, however, tend to neglect the fact that *Roe v. Wade* limits the set of possible legislative proposals for regulating abortion. Without *Roe* in place, pro-life politicians would face a very different set of political choices than they currently do. Instead of being able to champion relatively popular measures like requiring parental notification for minors seeking abortions, or banning partial-birth abortions, they would have to vote on whether to criminalize abortion in the first trimester. Without *Roe v. Wade* as a backstop, such laws would immediately become very unpopular in most jurisdictions.

Despite moral qualms about abortion among much of the public, opinion polls regularly show strong public resistance to overturning *Roe v. Wade*.[138] The reason is not hard to see: In the forty years since *Roe* was decided, two generations of women have come of age expecting that they will be able to obtain abortions if they need them. Moreover, by the beginning of the twenty-first century, approximately a third of American women have had abortions at some point in their lives, greatly altering women's understanding of what choices are effectively available to them.[139] People may praise women for deciding not to have abortions, for example, if women decide to have a child with a known birth defect. But that moral praise is premised on the fact that women can make the choice; they are not forced by the state to give birth against their will.

If American women have come to expect that abortions will always be available to them in cases of need, then in the early twenty-first century, abortion may be a privilege or immunity of citizens of the United States in addition to a requirement of sex equality. This right is important not merely for women who choose not to become mothers, but especially for those who do plan to become mothers, those who already have children, and those who also seek to work outside the home. Now more than ever, American women believe that their freedom as women means having control over the number and timing of their children. That expectation cannot be sustained without effective access to abortion when contraception fails.

Critics might respond that widespread support for *Roe* today is due to the Court's bootstrapping: making the right to abortion the legal status quo unfairly allowed the country (and American women) to get used to having the right and the additional freedoms that come with it. If *Roe* had never been decided, women would never have expected that they would have abortion as a fail-safe, and social attitudes (not to mention social structures) might be very different. We cannot be sure how much of current public acceptance of abortion rights is due to the Court's decision in *Roe* and how much is due to much larger features in American society, including changing social and economic conditions and the success of the women's movement. In the case of a exhaustively debated decision like *Roe,* however, this bootstrapping effect is not likely to be great. Political scientists have long pointed out that the Court does not oppose popular majorities over a sustained period, particularly on salient and controversial subjects like abortion.[140] (I discuss these points in more detail in Chapter 14.) Despite forty years of pro-life mobilization, the political success of the Republicans as a pro-life party, the election of several pro-life presidents, and decades of Republican judicial appointments, the basic right to abortion is still standing. Instead of being completely overturned, the original *Roe* decision was cut back in the 1992 decision in *Planned Parenthood of Southeastern Pennsylvania v. Casey,* a compromise that, not at all coincidentally, also better reflected public opinion.[141] Whether or not one believes that the right to abortion is a privilege or immunity of national citizenship, the case for it is perhaps even stronger today than it was when *Roe* was originally decided.

Finally, consider how this analysis applies to the individual right to keep and bear arms. By the time the Supreme Court decided *Heller v. District of Columbia,* over forty state constitutions guaranteed an individual constitutional right to keep and bear arms in self-defense, subject to reasonable regulations designed to promote public safety.[142] Public support for a basic right to own guns subject to reasonable regulation was overwhelming,[143] and both the president and Congress supported it, as did many political leaders in both parties. (See Chapter 14 for more discussion.) Obviously, supporters of the right argued that it was also specifically required by the text, but of course the whole point of the dispute was whether the text referred to an individual right of self-defense. Courts concluded that the right of self-defense was in the text in 1791 only after the right enjoyed widespread *contemporary* public support as a right that Americans have "always" enjoyed; at this point the courts confirmed that the text meant what supporters claimed it always had meant.

The examples of abortion and gun rights are well worth considering together, for two reasons. First, they provide a useful corrective to the notion that fundamental rights reflect a virtually universal social consensus, and that rights become forever fixed in the constitutional firmament thereafter. Rather, rights of national citizenship are the product of previous social disagreement, in which sustained majorities express their views over long periods of time.

Second, these examples show that judicial recognition of fundamental rights does not end disagreement, but instead shapes how political disagreements will proceed thereafter. In the case of abortion and gun rights, many Americans still believe strongly that courts should not have protected one or the other of these rights; they find the notion that these rights are somehow fundamental and consistent with the best traditions of the American people a mockery and an abuse of the Constitution. Perhaps equally important, many of the people who believe that abortion is not a fundamental right nevertheless feel quite certain that the right to bear arms in self-defense is a fundamental right, and vice versa. The examples of abortion and gun rights show that recognizing fundamental rights can make Americans constitutional dissenters just as much as the failure to recognize them, and these constitutional dissenters are quite important to the long-term development of constitutional law. Even after the recognition of a right of national citizenship, the fight over its scope and contours continues. We have seen this before in the case of abortion rights, and we will probably see a similar process in the case of the right to bear arms.

11

EQUALITY BEFORE THE LAW

The next two clauses of the Fourteenth Amendment protect all persons, not just citizens. The equal protection clause, together with the due process clause, Senator Howard explained, was designed to "abolish[] all class legislation in the States and do[] away with the injustice of subjecting one caste of persons to a code not applicable to another."[1] Section 1 of the Fourteenth Amendment "establishes equality before the law, and it gives to the humblest, the poorest, and the most despised of the race the same rights and the same protection before the law as it gives to the most powerful, the most wealthy, or the most haughty."[2]

Equal Protection of the Laws

John Harrison has argued that the equal protection clause does not regulate legislation at all: Emphasizing the word "protection," he argues that the equal protection clause was designed to guard against discriminatory remedies and protections or discriminatory enforcement by executive officials. It imposed a duty to apply and enforce the law fairly and evenhandedly, for example, by requiring southern states to punish and prosecute crimes against blacks as seriously as crimes against whites.[3]

The language of the equal protection clause surely reaches executive enforcement, but it is not limited to it. The prohibition says "No State," which includes all three branches of government. Laws that arbitrarily discriminate or that selectively abridge basic rights also "deny" the "equal protection of the laws."[4] The language of the equal protection clause is not particularly vague or ambiguous on this question; even if it were, statements made by the Fourteenth Amendment's framers support this obvious and natural construction; and this evidence is valuable evidence both of original meaning and of how one should construe the clause. Senator Howard's speech introducing the amendment before the Senate, for example, argued that the equal protection clause would "abolish[] all class *legislation* in the States and do[] away with the injustice of subjecting one caste of persons to a *code* not applicable to another."[5] No one in the debates responded that Howard was mistaken and that the clause did not apply to legislation. Similarly, Senator Timothy Howe argued that the new amendment was necessary because some states had "an appetite so diseased" that they sought to "deny to all classes of [their] citizens the protection of equal laws."[6] Howe's remarks anticipate the famous dictum of *Yick Wo v. Hopkins,* that "the equal protection of the laws is a pledge of the protection of equal laws."[7] Probably the most famous use of the term *equal protection* in the antebellum era was Andrew Jackson's justification for his veto of legislation renewing the Second Bank of the United States. Jackson did not complain about lax enforcement; after all, he was the nation's chief executive officer. Instead, he argued that the legislation rechartering the bank denied "equal protection" between rich and poor.[8] Finally, the February draft of the Fourteenth Amendment gave "Congress . . . power to make all laws which shall be necessary and proper to secure to . . . all persons in the several States equal protection in the rights of life, liberty, and property."[9] Congressional civil rights statutes would do more than create remedies to secure equal enforcement; they would also preempt contrary state laws.

Harrison's argument is based on his assumption that the privileges or immunities clause is a pure equality provision; hence, if the equal protection clause dealt with legislation, it would be redundant.[10] This assumption is incorrect: As noted previously, the original meaning of the privileges or immunities clause does not require a pure equality reading. Moreover, the equal protection clause is not redundant. The privileges or immunities clause protects citizens' substantive rights, including the right to equal treatment; and the equal protection clause extends its protections to noncitizens. Section 1's clauses overlap in many ways; this is a characteristic feature of an amendment that was designed to secure equal citizenship and equality before the law for citizens and noncitizens alike.

Equal Protection and the Tripartite Theory of Citizenship

What constructions should we use to articulate the principle of equal protection of the law? In the debates on the Fourteenth Amendment, the framers articulated a number of different and overlapping conceptions of equality before the law. Taken together, they prohibited four different types of unequal treatment.[11] The first was legislation that made arbitrary and unreasonable distinctions between persons.[12] The second was "class legislation," consisting of "special" or "partial" legislation that unjustifiably singled out a group for special benefits or special burdens.[13] The third was "caste" legislation—that is, legislation that created or maintained a disfavored caste or subordinated a group through law.[14] The fourth was legislation that selectively restricted or abridged basic rights of citizenship and that therefore treated people as second-class citizens.[15]

These four conceptions are principles underlying the equal protection clause. They do not exhaust the scope of the equal protection clause or the principle of "equal protection of the laws" that it contains. Each of them, however, is a reasonable construction of the purposes of the clause derived from an examination of historical sources, articulated at roughly the same level of abstraction as the language of the clause, and each is still relevant today.

The original expected application of the equal protection clause, and several other principles offered by the framing generation, limited the reach of these four principles in important ways. These constructions are not reasonable today and we do not have to accept them. Indeed, these constructions create very serious problems for any form of originalism that identifies original meaning with the constructions of the founding era or tries to create principles that match original expected applications.

For example, during the debates over the Reconstruction amendments, members of Congress distinguished between *civil, political,* and *social* equality. Civil equality meant equal enjoyment of what were then called "civil rights." These included the right to contract and own property; the right to testify, sue, and be sued in courts; the right to freedom of speech and freedom of religion; and the right to due process of law and the basic protections of the civil and criminal process. Political equality meant equality of political rights, which included the rights to vote, to hold political office, to serve on juries, and to serve in a militia. Social equality, by contrast, meant equal social status in civil society; it concerned whom people associated with and considered their social equals; for the same reason it also concerned whom people could marry.[16] For convenience, I will call these views the *tripartite theory of citizenship.*

The concepts of civil, political, and social equality were contested, and the boundaries changed over time.[17] Nevertheless, the key point of the tripartite theory was that equal citizenship and equality before the law meant something less than it does for us today: civil equality, but not political or social equality.

The tripartite theory helped explain and justify the racial attitudes of the generation that ratified the Fourteenth Amendment. Congressional Republicans as a group were probably more racially egalitarian than much of the public. Nevertheless, many Republicans did not want to give blacks the right to vote and they did not want to challenge state laws banning racial intermarriage; to do so in 1866 would have been politically explosive. Instead, they maintained that the Fourteenth Amendment guaranteed "equality before the law"—that is, equal protection and equal civil rights—but not political or social equality. The rights listed in the Civil Rights Act of 1866 are classic examples of what generally counted as "civil rights": equal rights "to make and enforce contracts, to sue, be parties, and give evidence, to inherit, purchase, lease, sell, hold, and convey real and personal property, and to full and equal benefit of all laws and proceedings for the security of person and property."[18] They did not include far more controversial guarantees concerning interracial marriage and voting.

The tripartite theory also helps us understand why the Fourteenth Amendment did not include a textual ban on racial discrimination in the way that the Fifteenth Amendment does. Although the most radical Republicans in Congress may have favored a general guarantee of racial equality, moderates in the party did not wish to go this far; as we have seen, they did not want to give blacks the right to vote and they did not want to disturb laws against miscegenation. Thus, the Joint Committee on Reconstruction defeated a color-blindness proposal when it was offered to them.[19] Conversely, congressional Republicans wanted to benefit the freedmen through a variety of race-conscious legislation. They also gave money to destitute blacks, especially women and children, regardless of whether they were newly freed slaves.[20]

Finally, as the Joint Committee's report explained, southern states had abridged the civil rights of whites who opposed slavery and supported black interests. A ban on racial discrimination would not remedy these injustices. Therefore, Congress agreed on broader language that guaranteed equal civil rights for citizens and equality before the law for all persons.[21]

The tripartite theory also justified the existing treatment of women. Women were by definition men's social equals—they were men's wives, mothers, and daughters—but they did not enjoy political equality. In most states they could not vote, serve on juries, hold public office, or serve in state militias. The theory of "virtual representation" argued that women were adequately represented by their husbands and fathers.[22]

The Congress that drafted the Fourteenth Amendment believed that men and women were civil equals.[23] Nevertheless, they accepted a wide range of laws and practices that effectively kept women in a subordinate condition and economically dependent on men. In particular, they did not expect that the new amendment would disturb the common law coverture rules, under which married women surrendered most of their common law rights under the fiction that they consented upon marriage to the merger of their legal identity into their husband's.[24] In theory single women should have enjoyed all the civil rights of adult males. Because it was assumed that almost all adult women were either married or lived in households headed by males, however, states effectively had no constitutional obligation to treat women the same as men.

The Supreme Court confirmed these understandings in 1875 in *Minor v. Happersett*,[25] holding that women did not have the right to vote, and in 1873 in *Bradwell v. Illinois*, holding that Illinois could exclude women from the practice of law.[26] Justice Bradley's concurrence in *Bradwell* pointed out that, as a married woman, Myra Bradwell might not have the right to make contracts in her own name, which would greatly inhibit her ability to represent clients; hence, Illinois was justified in concluding that only men could be admitted to the bar.[27]

Section 2 of the Fourteenth Amendment also reflects the distinction between civil and political equality. It is a compromise between supporters and opponents of voting rights for black men. It says that if states deny the right to vote "to any of the male inhabitants of such State, being twenty-one years of age," representation in the House of Representatives (and the Electoral College) would be reduced accordingly. The implicit logic of section 2 is that women and minors are citizens but not political equals. Under the theory of virtual representation, the interests of women and minors were protected by the votes of their adult male relatives.

In 1866, moderates were reluctant to give black men the right to vote, but subsequent events quickly altered the political landscape. By 1870, military reconstruction had reorganized southern governments with black suffrage.[28] Republicans recognized that their political success in the South and the border states depended on the black vote. Attitudes quickly changed on the question of black suffrage, and the Fifteenth Amendment was adopted in 1870.[29] This effectively eliminated the distinction between civil and political equality for black men, although the distinction still mattered for women, minors, aliens, and a variety of other groups denied the right to vote. By 1896 the Supreme Court could state confidently that "the Constitution of the United States, in its present form, forbids, so far as civil and political rights are concerned, discrimination by the General Government, or by the states against any citizen because of his race."[30]

This said nothing, however, about social equality. In *Pace v. Alabama*,[31] a unanimous Supreme Court upheld an Alabama statute that punished interracial sex more than sex between persons of the same race and also prohibited interracial marriage.[32] The 1896 decision in *Plessy v. Ferguson*,[33] which upheld separate accommodations for whites and blacks on Louisiana railroads, also rests on the distinction between civil and social equality. The majority argued that equal access to public accommodations was a question of social, not civil, equality.[34] The Court had reached the same conclusion in the 1883 *Civil Rights Cases*.[35] Justice Harlan, the lone dissenter in the *Civil Rights Cases,* was also the lone dissenter in *Plessy,* arguing, as he had before, that equal access to public accommodations was a civil, and not a social, right.[36]

Because the majority treated segregated railway carriages as a question of social equality, it analogized Louisiana's law to bans on interracial marriage upheld in *Pace v. Alabama* and separation of whites and blacks in public schools; these were questions of social equality beyond the scope of the Fourteenth Amendment.[37] Because Justice Harlan believed that access to public accommodations was a civil and not a social right, he dissented in *Plessy* and joined the majority in *Pace v. Alabama*.

We must understand Harlan's famous dictum that "our Constitution is colorblind" in this light.[38] He was not criticizing the tripartite theory; he was applying it. All the justices, including Harlan, agreed that the Fourteenth Amendment did not make blacks social equals with whites. "The white race deems itself to be the superior race," Justice Harlan explained, "[a]nd so it is, in prestige, in achievements, in education, in wealth, and in power. So, I doubt not, it will continue to be for all time, if it remains true to its great heritage, and holds fast to the principles of constitutional liberty."[39] But "[i]n respect of civil rights, all citizens are equal before the law."[40] Treating blacks differently with respect to *civil* rights would violate the constitutional principle against caste legislation. That is why Harlan argued that "[t]here is no caste here" in America.[41]

The majority did not disagree with this principle; they disagreed only with its application to public accommodations.[42]

Although Harlan introduces the language of color blindness into the *Supreme Court Reports,* he did not actually believe in color blindness in the modern sense. Our modern conception of "color blindness" rejects the tripartite model; it is the product of the success of the civil rights movement and the struggle over the legacy of *Brown v. Board of Education* between racial liberals and conservatives.[43]

Conservative Originalism and the Tripartite Theory

As I mentioned in Chapter 6, Michael McConnell has shown that many congressmen and senators who voted for the Fourteenth Amendment also voted several years later for a provision that would have desegregated public schools. He also shows that they did so because they believed that access to public education was a civil right and that the Fourteenth Amendment required equal treatment.[44] This provision was originally part of what eventually became the Civil Rights Act of 1875 but was deleted from the final bill because it could not gain sufficient support.[45] On this basis, McConnell argues that *Brown v. Board of Education* follows from original public meaning.

McConnell's excellent historical work nevertheless shows the great difficulties that the Fourteenth Amendment presents for modern conservatives. McConnell has demonstrated that many of the framers of the Fourteenth Amendment would have agreed with the result in *Brown* because they regarded education as a civil right; but he has not shown that the general public would have agreed that the Fourteenth Amendment had this effect. Indeed, the historical evidence points in the opposite direction; as McConnell explains, "school desegregation was deeply unpopular among whites, in both North and South, and school segregation was very commonly practiced."[46]

Strictly speaking, then, McConnell has not offered an argument about the original public meaning of the Fourteenth Amendment in the sense normally employed by conservative originalists. Rather, he has offered an argument about the original construction and original understanding of the Fourteenth Amendment by some of its framers, views that Mc-Connell acknowledges were strongly at variance with the constructions and understandings of the general public and the persons who ratified the amendment. Conservative originalists often look to the statements of the framers as a proxy for the views and understandings of the ratifiers and the general public, but in the specific case of school segregation we know that the views of the Fourteenth Amendment's framers are *not* a good proxy.

Indeed, McConnell maintains that the public's conception of the amendment and its likely consequences is actually irrelevant, because "a political minority, armed with the prestige of victory in the Civil War and with military control over the political apparatus of the rebel states, imposed constitutional change on the Nation as the price of reunion, with little regard for popular opinion."[47] Rejecting contemporaneous public understandings about the effect of constitutional provisions is not how conservative original public meaning arguments generally work, nor is it consistent with the reasons why conservative originalists maintain that original public meaning is authoritative. In particular, if the ratifiers would have rejected a particular understanding of equal protection, it is not clear why that understanding is supported by popular sovereignty.

But even putting arguments about *Brown* to one side, there are deeper problems. McConnell's evidence does not show that Congress rejected the distinction between civil, political, and social equality; instead, he shows that people argued within the terms of the tripartite theory. Everyone in the debates over the 1875 Civil Rights Act accepted the basic distinction, and the two sides were merely arguing over whether access to public education was a civil or a social right.[48] The really important question, then, is not whether *Brown* can be squared with original public meaning; it is whether conservative originalists can reject the civil/political/social distinction.

As Chapter 6 described, conservative originalists argue that fidelity to original public meaning requires following principles that the ratifying public intended to express through the text. These principles, articulated at the correct level of generality, are not optional; they are part of original meaning.[49] Where the framers and ratifiers stated their principles abstractly, we should fix the appropriate level of generality by asking how the framers and ratifiers would have applied the amendment and what justifications and explanations they would have offered in applying it. Evidence of expected applications and more concrete statements of principle help us understand the contours of the principles the framers and ratifiers were trying to enact. If we treat too many of their explanations and expected applications as mistakes, we have probably misunderstood these principles.[50]

The problem is that if we use these methods, we must accept the tripartite theory as part of original meaning. The historical record is clear that constitutionally protected equality was limited by the distinction between civil, political, and social rights, and the expected applications of the framers and ratifiers are consistent with this tripartite division. Indeed, the tripartite theory was offered in order to explain and justify giving blacks and women a limited form of equality. If we follow the precepts of conservative original-meaning originalism, we should still apply the civil/social distinction today. This means that *Loving v. Virginia* is wrong and that states can still ban blacks and whites from marrying.[51] Moreover, it also means that states may retain the common law coverture rules, under which women lose all their rights upon marrying (other than the right to vote).[52] Therefore, *Frontiero v. Richardson*[53] and the Court's modern sex equality jurisprudence are incorrect.

To be sure, most conservative originalists today would not accept these results; instead, they would probably argue that *Loving* and the modern sex equality cases are settled precedents that courts should not disturb. The point, however, is that the methodology described above requires treating these precedents as mistakes rather than as faithful interpretations of the equal protection clause.

Framework Originalism and the Uses of History

These examples aptly demonstrate the difference between the assumptions of modern conservative originalism and framework originalism. Framework originalism denies that the original meaning of the text includes principles stated at a level that captures most of the public's—or the framers'—expected applications. The civil/social distinction is not in the text, and we do not have to accept it today. Nor do we have to accept the constitutionality of common law coverture rules. Previous constructions, even statements of principle by the framers, are not themselves part of original meaning, and although some previous constructions are entitled to great weight, others are simply not worth following today.

The method of text and principle does not consider this evidence irrelevant. It is deeply interested in the history of ratification, and the justifications, statements of principle, and expected applications of the framers and ratifiers. But the method of text and principle uses all of this material in a different way. This material is not part of original meaning, but is evidence that can help resolve ambiguities in original semantic meaning. Perhaps even more important, this material constitutes a valuable resource from which interpreters can generate underlying principles and constitutional constructions to implement the constitutional text. The difference between framework originalism and conservative originalism is the difference between viewing history as a *resource* and viewing it as a *command*.

Constitutional construction is inevitably a presentist endeavor, drawing on the resources of the entire constitutional tradition that precedes the interpreter. Interpreting the equal protection clause today means interpreting it after the New Deal, after the civil rights revolution, and after the second wave of American feminism. Our task, viewing the constitutional tradition from where we stand, is to decide how to use the tradition's resources to face our fellow citizens and argue for the best way to continue the constitutional project. The history of previous understandings and constructions is one of the modalities of constitutional argument. It is a common cultural resource for present-day construction.

We must decide in the present which constructions are most faithful to the text; history cannot decide this question for us. If we decide that we want to adopt certain constructions and expectations of the framing generation, that is our choice and, equally important, our responsibility. It is not something compelled by fidelity to the constitutional plan.

Thus, framework originalism treats history differently than conservative originalists do, and it sees the relationship between law and history differently. Conservative originalists argue that principles derived from framing-era understandings are not simply resources for building constructions; they are actually part of original meaning and bind present generations as law. That is why the civil/social distinction and the constitutionality of common law coverture pose such a problem for conservative originalism; by the same logic these principles should also be part of the law that future generations must accept.

By contrast, when I argue that the principles underlying the equal protection clause include a ban on class and caste legislation, I am not restating an authoritative command from the past; I am arguing that accepting this construction from the past is the best way to be faithful to the principles stated in the text in the present. I appeal to common resources in our constitutional tradition and argue that this is the right way to continue the constitutional project. When I argue that we should not accept the civil/social distinction or the constitutionality of coverture rules, I make the same sort of argument. Both my acceptance of certain features of the constitutional tradition *and* my rejection of others are attempts to be faithful to the constitutional project.

Contemporary constitutional understandings reject the distinction between civil and social equality, at least in its nineteenth-century form.[54] Americans today do not understand this distinction as a valuable constitutional principle that should guide contemporary law; quite the contrary, they see it as an obsolete political compromise that justified giving blacks and women less than full equality.

To be sure, some political compromises—like the different rules of representation in the House and the Senate—are binding because they are required by the text. But the civil/social distinction has no such basis in the text. Moreover, from our modern vantage point, the civil/social distinction is deeply in tension with principles against class legislation, caste legislation, arbitrary discrimination, and selective protection of basic rights.

Today we live in the wake of two great egalitarian shifts in American politics that changed basic constitutional understandings about equality and about the practices of ordinary politics—the New Deal and the civil rights revolution. The New Deal emphasized substantive economic equality and equality of opportunity over formal equality and the formal liberty of contract. The civil rights revolution emphasized substantive equality and equality of opportunity between whites and blacks. It sought to eliminate not only government discrimination but also discrimination by private parties in employment, housing, and public accommodations. Its ideal of equal citizenship was so powerful that it influenced other movements for equality for women, Latinos, the disabled, gays, and other groups. For this reason the civil rights revolution has justly been called the nation's Second Reconstruction. The constitutional regime we live in today is built on the constitutional assumptions of these two eras of constitutional transformation.[55]

The civil rights revolution rejected the nineteenth-century version of the civil/social distinction. This issue was at the heart of two important cases: *Brown v. Board of Education* and *Loving v. Virginia*. Each involved what most people in the nineteenth century would have considered questions of social equality—the right of blacks and whites to attend the same public schools, and the right of blacks and whites to marry. *Brown* rejects the holding in *Plessy v. Ferguson,* and *Loving* rejects the holding in *Pace.*[56]

The civil rights revolution was so successful in altering understandings of equality that the tripartite theory seems strange to us today; it seems odd that equal citizenship and equality before the law would not require the results in *Brown* and *Loving.* That is why we read Justice Harlan today anachronistically as asserting a general color-blindness principle in *Plessy,* when in fact he was simply asserting the principle of civil equality.

The constitutional assumptions of the New Deal and the civil rights revolution and the success of subsequent social movements for equality have become so thoroughly embedded in our contemporary understandings of the Constitution that they influence what we consider easy cases of constitutional equality and inequality. If we wanted to offer uncontroversial examples of arbitrary discrimination, or class legislation, or subordinating legislation, laws segregating public schools or prohibiting interracial marriage would seem to be obvious examples.

Brown and *Loving,* in short, seem today to be obvious and uncomplicated applications of the principles underlying the Fourteenth Amendment. In fact, decisions like *Brown* and *Loving* help make sense of these abstract principles as much as the principles justify *Brown* and *Loving.* Cases like *Brown* and *Loving* seem almost like postulates from which we reason, rather than conclusions to which we reason from the text of the Fourteenth Amendment.

In Chapters 13 and 14 I call cases like *Brown* and *Loving* "durable" and "canonical" constructions. In any ongoing constitutional regime, certain constitutional constructions become widely regarded as easy, paradigmatic, or obvious applications of the Constitution's abstract principles and vague standards. People use them to articulate principles and policies that explain the constitutional text and to reason about how to apply the constitutional text to other, more controversial cases. Constitutional politics has made constructions like *Brown* and *Loving* not only easy cases, but foundational to our understanding of the equal protection clause. Yet they were not always so central; at one point they would have been highly controversial or even clearly wrong constructions; and perhaps at some point in the distant future people will understand *Brown* and *Loving* very differently than we do now.

Caste and Class Legislation and Modern Doctrine

Loving is important for another reason. It exemplifies the new doctrinal regime that replaced the tripartite theory of citizenship. Today lawyers and law students learn a complicated set of rules about different levels of judicial scrutiny that distinguishes between "ordinary social and economic legislation," on the one hand, and certain "suspect classifications" or "fundamental rights," on the other. These doctrinal categories are comparatively recent and cannot be found in the constitutional text. They implement the basic principles underlying the equal protection clause.[57]

In *Loving,* for example, the Supreme Court held that courts should apply what is now known as "strict scrutiny" to racial classifications.[58] In today's law this means that a challenged classification must be narrowly tailored to achieve a compelling state interest and the government must show that it cannot achieve its ends in other ways.[59] Legislation that does not employ suspect classifications need only meet a very relaxed test of "rational basis": it must be rationally related to some hypothetical legitimate interest the government might have had.[60] Thus, the modern equal protection regime treats classifications as its central concern, and it treats most classifications as either presumptively illegitimate or presumptively legitimate. Sex classifications are the exception: they receive an intermediate form of scrutiny, effectively a balancing test. Recently the Supreme Court has argued that governments must offer an "exceedingly persuasive justification" for any sex classifications,[61] but, interestingly, classifications on the basis of pregnancy are generally not treated as sex classifications at all.[62]

This model of scrutiny rules arose in the wake of the civil rights revolution in the 1960s and 1970s. *Brown v. Board of Education* says nothing about scrutiny or suspect classifications. It merely says that the "separate but equal" rule of *Plessy v. Ferguson* does not apply to public elementary and secondary education.

Modern doctrines that focus on suspect classifications attempt to identify situations that are most likely to involve arbitrary and unreasonable distinctions, class legislation, or legislation that helps maintain group subordination. The list of suspect classifications began with race, national origin, and religion; it quickly expanded in the 1960s and 1970s to include alienage, illegitimacy, and (as described above) gender, because the civil rights revolution changed people's minds about what kinds of legal distinctions are likely to be inherently unfair and unrelated to any legitimate or public-regarding purpose.[63]

Just like nineteenth-century constructions, modern equal protection doctrine articulates and implements the text and underlying principles of the equal protection clause. And just like its nineteenth-century counterpart, it is imperfect, limited, and contestable.[64] The method of text and principle gives us a perspective outside of doctrine that we can use to evaluate it, instead of simply reasoning within the existing body of rules and looking for minor adjustments. Just as we can ask whether the tripartite theory and police powers jurisprudence of the nineteenth century failed fully to enforce the Constitution's text and underlying principles, we can critique the doctrines learned in law school classrooms and cited in legal briefs today.

Here are a few examples in which underlying principles give us additional leverage to critique doctrine.

First, current equal protection law focuses on classifications. It treats as democratically legitimate facially neutral laws that foreseeably burden women and minorities.[65] The law makes an exception if one can prove that these laws were enacted with a purpose to discriminate, but it defines discriminatory purpose very narrowly, essentially requiring proof of something like malice or a deliberate intent to harm a group.[66] Put another way, the law imagines that deliberate or malicious classification by government is the chief way that law contributes to inequality in contemporary American society. But a focus on *classifications* is not the same thing as a focus on second-class citizenship, class legislation, or group subordination through law.

Governments don't have to engage in overt classification to subordinate a group or impose special benefits or burdens. Consider, for example, the seminal use of the concept of "equal protection" in American public law: President Andrew Jackson's constitutional objections to the rechartering of the Second Bank of the United States.[67] The charter did not make any suspect classifications in today's terminology; nevertheless, Jackson believed that in practice it would create an aristocracy of wealth for bankers and financiers who could leverage their government-created powers in ways that would work to the detriment of ordinary citizens. "Many of our rich men," Jackson argued, "have not been content with equal protection and equal benefits, but have besought us to make them richer by act of Congress."[68] If the bank bill violated equal protection, it is not because it engaged in forbidden classifications, but because it unjustifiably created special privileges for a small group of already powerful Americans.

Jackson's concern was probably limited to white males,[69] but the logic behind his objection is still relevant today. Not all state action that subordinates employs explicit group-based classifications, and not all inequality is produced by evil minds. Rather, we must decide whether law subordinates a group by looking at its social meanings and its effects within existing social and political structures. Sometimes focusing on overt classification or deliberate intent to harm is the right way to protect against government action that promotes social subordination and the maintenance of caste, but at other times it will be seriously deficient. Bias often plays a role in fostering inequality, but perhaps even more important are institutional arrangements and rules that entrench unequal resources and opportunities. Looking only for overt classifications based on a limited set of criteria will often completely miss these effects.

For similar reasons, the principles against caste and class legislation do not necessarily require a showing of specific intent to harm a group. Criminal and tort law feature many different kinds of *mens rea* or intent, ranging from specific purpose to knowledge of consequences to recklessness about consequences to foreseeable negligence. To secure equal protection, we might have to apply different tests of intent to different factual situations, like employment, criminal penalties, land use, and jury selection.[70] In some cases, a significant disparate impact on minority groups might require government to offer some form of explanation or justification, as it does in employment discrimination law and jury selection cases.[71]

Focusing on classification and deliberate purpose to harm largely fights the last war: It prevents the kind of openly hostile laws that legislatures passed in the Jim Crow South—which, of course, governments no longer enact after the civil rights revolution. It leaves in place laws that subordinate individuals in other ways, and gives these laws an almost irrebuttable presumption of democratic legitimacy.

Next consider affirmative action policies designed to promote integration and remedy social inequality. Current law treats them the same way it treats Jim Crow laws. Thus, we get the bizarre result that government can create college admissions preferences for the children of Wall Street investment bankers if there is a hypothetical rational basis for the policy, because there is no classification on the basis of race; but if governments try to use preferences to increase the number of African Americans or Latinos in higher education, they must overcome strict scrutiny.

The ideas of caste and class legislation can offer a useful corrective. Policies that seek to integrate citizens from diverse backgrounds and ensure that important educational and employment opportunities are open to all groups in society do not subordinate majority groups or treat them as less worthy citizens. Nor do they make blacks or Latinos into a favored caste. Quite the contrary: these programs are necessary to the extent that minority groups still enjoy less status and less equality of opportunity in American society. As noted previously, the Reconstruction Congress passed race-conscious laws that granted educational benefits to blacks, whether or not they themselves had formerly been held in slavery. These laws made racial classifications, but they did not subordinate or oppress whites or make them into second-class citizens.

This does not mean, however, that race-conscious affirmative action policies deserve no constitutional scrutiny. If they are not appropriately structured, affirmative action policies can violate the principle against class legislation because they bestow special benefits on groups without adequate public justification. Poorly structured preferences can also treat people arbitrarily and unfairly. But if race-conscious policies are properly designed to diffuse the costs to individual members of dispreferred groups, they need not violate any constitutional principle. Badly designed policies can create a sense of unfairness and undermine social solidarity. But well-designed policies may help integrate social, economic, and political institutions, create opportunities for leadership and influence for members of all groups in society, and thereby promote equal opportunity and equal citizenship.[72]

Finally, the creation of a bifurcated all-or-nothing regime of strict and rational basis scrutiny has subverted the principles underlying the equal protection clause. Strict scrutiny gives judges relatively little discretion to evaluate classifications, so judges often cheat and apply something less than strict scrutiny—or insist that there is no classification at all—when they want to uphold a law. Because strict scrutiny intrudes so heavily on democratic decisionmaking, judges have resisted extending equal protection doctrine to new groups, even groups widely acknowledged to have suffered long histories of discrimination and invidious treatment. In fact, the Supreme Court has not created any new suspect classifications since the 1970s. Yet the principles against class, caste, and arbitrary legislation were not limited to laws affecting blacks; they applied to any laws that violated equal respect for persons. The bifurcated system of strict and rational basis scrutiny defeats this larger goal.

The ideas of caste and class legislation continue to be central to understanding the Fourteenth Amendment, even though existing doctrinal categories sometimes fit them only awkwardly. When faced with the question whether a previously unchallenged law or practice is a forbidden classification—such as the use of race in census questionnaires—courts often look to antisubordination principles. They ask (and should ask) whether the law unfairly keeps a group down.[73]

The ideas of caste and class legislation appear in still other ways. For example, the courts will sometimes invalidate laws that they declare are motivated by "irrational prejudice," whether or not an officially recognized suspect classification is involved.[74] A good example is *Romer v. Evans,* in which the Supreme Court struck down a state constitutional amendment passed by referendum aimed at gays and lesbians. Colorado's Amendment 2 prevented any government action that would protect people from discrimination based on their "homosexual, lesbian or bisexual orientation, conduct, practices or relationships."[75] Under existing doctrine, sexual orientation was not a suspect category, so the amendment should have been upheld under the test of minimal scrutiny. But the Supreme Court recognized that "Amendment 2 fails, indeed defies . . . conventional inquiry."[76] It was a textbook example of class or caste legislation translated into a late twentieth-century context. Colorado's rural voters, angered by the proliferation of antidiscrimination ordinances in gay-friendly cities, decided to repeal these ordinances and put them beyond the reach of ordinary legislation. Notably, they made it illegal to protect gays and lesbians, but not straights, from sexual orientation discrimination.

The Supreme Court held that even under rational basis, the law violated equal protection because it was motivated by anti-gay "animus." But the Court had no direct proof of the mental states of the people in voting booths. Rather, it understood that Amendment 2 was legislation designed to single out a particular unpopular group for special burdens— the essence of class legislation—and render them second-class citizens by law, a marker of caste legislation. The Court saw the amendment as marking gays and lesbians and declaring them unworthy of equal rights. The Court therefore *ascribed* invidious motivation to the voters because it interpreted the social meaning of Amendment 2 as class legislation.

Seven years later, in *Lawrence v. Texas,* the Supreme Court struck down a law criminalizing same-sex but not opposite-sex sodomy. The Court argued that the statute violated a "liberty interest" protected under the due process clause.[77] As noted in Chapter 10, Texas's law might have run afoul of the privileges or immunities clause. But it also violated principles underlying the equal protection clause: principles against arbitrary and unreasonable distinctions, class legislation, caste legislation, and selective abridgments of basic rights.[78]

Another important example of the principles against class and caste legislation is the 1942 decision in *Skinner v. Oklahoma,* in which the Court struck down an Oklahoma statute requiring forced sterilization for persons convicted of certain types of theft but not white-collar crimes like embezzlement. The Court was concerned that the criminal law was being used to promote spurious ideas of genetic inferiority and held that the statute violated the equal protection clause: "When the law lays an unequal hand on those who have committed intrinsically the same quality of offense and sterilizes one and not the other, it has made as invidious a discrimination as if it had selected a particular race or nationality for oppressive treatment."[79]

The Fourteenth Amendment and Political Equality

If we need not adopt the civil/social distinction today, what about the civil/political distinction? The question is a bit trickier because there is some support for the distinction in the text of the Fourteenth and Fifteenth Amendments. The Fifteenth Amendment was necessary because the framers of the Fourteenth Amendment did not intend to give blacks the right to vote. Section 2 of the Fourteenth Amendment says that states lose representation in House (and the Electoral College) if they deny the vote to males above the age of twenty-one. This presumed that states could deny the vote to women and to males younger than twenty-one without penalty.

Nevertheless, there are two reasons why the Fourteenth Amendment might protect at least some equality in political rights today. First, the operation of the Fourteenth Amendment has been altered by the Fifteenth, Nineteenth, Twenty-Fourth, and Twenty-Sixth Amendments, which increasingly expanded the franchise and suggest that, at least for adults, civil and political equality are strongly linked. The Fifteenth Amendment said that race was not an appropriate ground for denying adult citizens the right to vote, the Nineteenth said the same of sex, the Twenty-Fourth said the same of poverty (by outlawing the poll tax in federal elections), and the Twenty-Sixth said the same of age (eighteen is generally thought to be the beginning of adulthood). Changes in the constitutional text interact with previous portions of the Constitution; they alter structural assumptions and the scope of underlying principles, just as the Fourteenth Amendment itself reshaped the federalism principles underlying the 1787 Constitution. Reading these five amendments together points to a general structural principle: there should be no distinction between political and civil equality for adult citizens without a compelling justification.

This conclusion does not mean that states may not impose voting qualifications or regulate voting generally. After all, states may make reasonable distinctions in the enjoyment of civil rights. Rather, it means that the principles against caste and class legislation, arbitrary and unreasonable classification, and selective abridgments of basic rights should apply to this sphere as well. The question is whether legislation makes arbitrary or unreasonable distinctions, unjustifiably singles out persons for special disabilities or subordinates them. Imagine, for example, a law that prevented homosexuals or persons with a net worth less than $100,000 from voting. Arbitrarily denying a group of people the right to participate in the political process or have their votes counted may not have been deemed class or caste legislation in 1868, but it certainly seems so today.[80]

Earlier I argued that Colorado's Amendment 2 violated the class legislation principle. So too would a state constitutional amendment disenfranchising gays and making it illegal for them to serve on juries or hold political office. Stripping gays of their ability to vote for candidates who would support civil rights laws protecting them, preventing them from holding any political positions where they could press for civil rights measures, and excluding them from juries (especially in cases where gays were criminal defendants or were the victims of crimes) would seem to be an even more powerful example of subordinating legislation than Amendment 2 managed. According to the principles against class and caste legislation, states must offer special justifications for laws that make a group of adult citizens politically powerless.

The Supreme Court suggested this basic idea in the famous footnote 4 of its *Carolene Products* decision.[81] The Court argued that "legislation which restricts those political processes which can ordinarily be expected to bring about repeal of undesirable legislation" might justify "more exacting judicial scrutiny under the general prohibitions of the Fourteenth Amendment" and gave as examples restrictions on the rights to vote and form political associations.[82] Similarly, it argued that "prejudice against discrete and insular minorities may be a special condition, which tends seriously to curtail the operation of those political processes ordinarily to be relied upon to protect minorities."[83] Both ideas are modern articulations of the principles against class and caste legislation, although they do not capture everything in these principles.

As the above example suggests, the concept of political equality extends beyond voting to jury service, militia service, and the right to hold political office. The text of the Fifteenth, Nineteenth, Twenty-Fourth, and Twenty-Sixth Amendments says nothing about these rights. The right to hold office actually appeared in an earlier draft of the Fifteenth Amendment but was eventually removed.[84] Despite this complication, we might argue that the rights to officeholding and jury and militia service are governed by these amendments.[85] However, an equally suitable textual home is the equal protection clause of the Fourteenth Amendment and its principles against class and caste legislation.

These arguments do not completely abolish the distinction between political and civil rights; they argue that the two concepts have merged for adult citizens. The civil/political distinction still matters for minors and for noncitizens.

The Twenty-Sixth Amendment suggests that states may reserve political decisionmaking to adults. There are two reasons why this distinction still makes sense. First, minors will eventually gain political rights when they reach the age that most people's brains are fully developed and they can exercise (relatively) mature judgment. Second, in the meantime, it is reasonable to assume that adults as a group will want to legislate in the interests of their children and the children of their friends and relatives. The Nineteenth Amendment rejected the notion that adult women were virtually represented by their husbands, but the law still assumes that children's interests are appropriately represented by their parents, adult relatives, and guardians.

The civil/political distinction also continues to make sense for noncitizens. Although states may not generally discriminate against aliens, and aliens generally enjoy Bill of Rights protections, states do not have to give aliens equal political rights. (In the nineteenth century, some states did give aliens the right to vote in return for a promise to become citizens, but this choice was not required by the Constitution.)[86]

Second, there is an important analogy between the right to marry (recognized in *Loving*) and political rights. Civil marriage, as opposed to marriage as a religious sacrament, is a set of special legal privileges the state grants to couples; it is not so much a fundamental right as a *fundamental interest*. Fundamental interests are rights or privileges that, once provided by the state, must be provided equally. A principle underlying both the privileges or immunities clause and the equal protection clause is that states may not selectively restrict or abridge basic rights of citizenship. It is a reasonable construction to apply this principle to fundamental interests that, like marriage and voting, owe their existence to state law.

In *Harper v. Virginia Board of Elections*,[87] the Supreme Court struck down the use of poll taxes in state elections. The Twenty-Fourth Amendment had abolished poll taxes in federal elections in 1964, and by 1966 only four states still levied poll taxes in state elections. In addition, Congress asked the Court to overturn state poll taxes in section 10 of the Voting Rights Act of 1965.[88] Employing the methodology described earlier for identifying privileges or immunities of national citizenship, these four states were outliers; and Congress had articulated its view, through the amendment process, and through section 10 of the Voting Rights Act, that poll taxes were a form of invidious discrimination. It was therefore reasonable for the Court to conclude that, by the middle of the twentieth century, voting had become a fundamental interest of adult citizens. The Court protected this interest through the equal protection clause; it might also have done so through the equality guarantees of the privileges or immunities clause.

This conclusion does not mean that states may not regulate voting, any more than it means they may not regulate marriage. It means only that they may not make arbitrary distinctions in who gets to vote.

The Fourteenth Amendment and the Guarantee Clause

We should read the Fourteenth Amendment—and all of the subsequent amendments expanding suffrage rights—together with the guarantee clause of Article IV, section 4, of the 1787 Constitution. The guarantee clause requires the United States to guarantee each of the states a "Republican Form of Government." The word *republican* in 1787 meant a representative government with regular elections. The guarantee of republican government protected popular sovereignty and the right of people to govern their affairs through majority rule.[89] John Bingham pointed out that although the Fourteenth Amendment does not give Congress the power to regulate suffrage in the states generally, it does reach situations where a State has denied a republican form of government, because "the right of the people of each State to a republican government and to choose their Representatives in Congress is [one] of the guarantees of the Constitution."[90]

The guarantee clause protects the abstract principles of popular sovereignty and representative government; these principles, like the principle of equal protection, must be articulated and applied by later generations. As in the case of equal protection, we are not bound by the original expected application of the guarantee clause. We must ask what the guarantees of representative government and popular sovereignty mean today in our world. In 1787, only a small number of citizens, mostly white male property owners, had the right to vote in most of the states. These states were considered republican governments. But nobody today would consider such a system representative, just as nobody today would think that the race or sex equality views of 1868 would be equal protection of the law.

The guarantee clause is mostly a dead letter today because of the 1849 case of *Luther v. Borden*,[91] which has been read (incorrectly, in my view) to hold that all questions arising under the guarantee clause are political questions that are not suitable for judicial resolution, and hence for doctrinal development. But the case does not actually stand for so broad a proposition, and even if it did, that proposition is incorrect.

For many years after independence, Rhode Island continued to be governed by its royal charter. The charter was impossible to amend, and many thought its provisions unjust and unrepresentative. In 1842, without the state legislature's permission, a group of citizens led by Thomas Dorr called a state constitutional convention. They wrote a new constitution, held elections, and proceeded to form a new government with Dorr as the new governor. Dorr and his followers then sought to take political power in the state. In response, the charter government arrested many of Dorr's followers, and Dorr fled the state. Luther, a follower of Dorr, sued members of the charter government for arresting and imprisoning him, arguing that they were not the real government of Rhode Island. Subsequently the charter government called for a new constitutional convention, and in 1843 a new constitution was ratified that expanded the right to vote and offered more equitable representation.

No one doubted that by 1849 the only government of Rhode Island was the government under the new state constitution. The Dorr legislature sat for only two days in May 1842 and then adjourned and never reassembled. The question before the Court was which government was legitimate at the time of Luther's arrest in August 1842. Chief Justice Taney noted that the Rhode Island state courts had treated the charter government as legitimate, and the president of the United States had agreed and noted that he would send troops to assist the charter government if it became necessary. Moreover, Taney pointed out, Congress had effectively delegated the decision of who was the lawful government to the president in the 1795 Militia Act, which gave the president authority to respond to rebellions following application for aid by the legislature or the executive of a state. It would be very difficult for a court, five years later, to disagree with these decisions, and throw the legitimacy of all of the acts of the charter government into legal dispute. Therefore the Court treated the judgment of the president as conclusive on this question.[92]

Given its facts, *Luther* does not stand for the general proposition that courts may not enforce any claims under the guarantee clause. It holds only that some kinds of claims—those involving recognition of governments and deciding when domestic violence requires intervention by federal troops—are best determined by the political branches, and in particular by the president. If Luther had brought his claim under any other provision of the Constitution, the Court would have refused to hear it as well, and for the same reasons.

This narrower holding of *Luther v. Borden* makes particular sense. First, generally speaking, the president decides whether to recognize new foreign governments as legitimate, and courts should usually respect this decision. Second, the president, as commander in chief of the armed forces, is far better situated than the courts to decide whether insurrection or widespread civil disobedience threatens republican government in an individual state so that a federal response is necessary.

It does not follow, however, that all guarantee clause issues are within the discretion of Congress or the president. This is not consistent with the text of the clause, which says that "*The United States* shall guarantee . . . a Republican Form of Government." The constitutional text does not differentiate between the different branches of government; it places a constitutional duty on all of them. Therefore, federal courts, as part of the government of the United States, are also required to guarantee republican government where it is institutionally appropriate for them to do so. In *Baker v. Carr,* the Supreme Court held that questions of apportionment were appropriate for judicial resolution.[93] In *Reynolds v. Sims,*[94] the Court chose not to disturb the conventionally broad reading of *Luther v. Borden;* instead, it argued that questions of apportionment were governed by the equal protection clause (and by Article 1, section 2, in the case of apportionment for the House of Representatives).[95] As a result, constitutional voting rights jurisprudence since the 1960s has generally proceeded under the equal protection clause. But if judges are institutionally equipped to pass on reapportionment and other voting rights questions under these provisions, they should be equally able to consider them under the guarantee clause.

Although both the equal protection clause and the guarantee clause protect political rights, they do not apply equally well to all situations. Consider four different kinds of voting rights claims. The first type of claim asks who has the right to vote and who may be properly excluded from voting in a particular kind of election.[96] The second type of claim asks whether state officials have used a fair method for counting votes or whether the method used is likely to neglect lawful votes, reject them improperly, or misread them.[97] The third type of claim asks whether the method of apportionment is fair or whether legislative districts are malapportioned.[98] The fourth type of claim asks whether legislative apportionment has been unfairly gerrymandered either to unfairly limit or to unfairly bolster the influence of a particular group.[99]

All four of these voting rights claims are appropriate under the guarantee clause because all concern the integrity and the structural fairness of the electoral process. The goal of the guarantee clause is to protect popular sovereignty; it seeks to ensure that majorities rule and prevent aristocracy or oligarchy, whether the aristocracy or oligarchy is due to birth, concentration of economic power, or the result of political machination.

The guarantee clause seeks to counteract frequent tendencies in republican government that may lead to its undoing and to the usurpation of government by persons who do not adequately represent popular majorities. In republican government, politicians are supposed to serve as agents of the people; nevertheless, their natural tendency is to try to keep themselves in power as long as possible, regardless of changes in their constituents' preferences. Similarly, republican government is designed to allow newer majorities to replace older ones through regular elections. When the nature and sentiments of political majorities change, their representatives should change accordingly through elections. Nevertheless, temporary majorities and political incumbents usually seek to ensure that they continue to remain in power, regardless of changes in demographics and public sentiments.

The principle of republican government prohibits political incumbents and temporary majorities from trying to entrench themselves in power unfairly through manipulating voter qualifications, vote counting, fixing the size of different legislative districts, and drawing district boundary lines. For this reason, we could reinterpret much of current voting rights doctrine through the guarantee clause rather than the equal protection clause, although the focus would be on the structural integrity and fairness of the political process rather than on whether the state had denied particular individual rights to equal treatment.[100]

In some ways, this would be a welcome change. The equal protection clause vindicates different principles than the guarantee clause. Its job is not so much to ensure that majorities rule, but rather to ensure that minorities in a democratic society are treated equally and fairly by those in power and that existing majorities do not engage in class or caste legislation, or selectively and arbitrarily deny basic rights. Disenfranchisement claims make particular sense as equal protection claims when governments single out particular persons or groups for special burdens and selectively deny them a basic right. Vote-counting claims also make sense as equal protection claims: when executive officials use arbitrary methods to count or discard votes, they deny equal protection of the laws.

By contrast, although courts have also treated apportionment and gerrymandering claims as equal protection claims, they are sometimes a bit more difficult to state in terms of individual rights to equal treatment. Some apportionment and gerrymandering claims can be viewed as attempts by majorities to render minorities politically powerless, and so they would violate the principles against class and caste legislation. Often, however, apportionment and gerrymandering claims are better understood as attempts at self-entrenchment by politicians or by temporary majorities. These claims primarily concern the structural integrity and fairness of the political system. Constitutional requirements based on notions of individual equality—like the Supreme Court's "one person, one vote" requirement—can be a means for achieving these goals, but they are not the goal itself; sometimes the goal of political fairness and representativeness might better be achieved by focusing directly on the structure of representation rather than translating all concerns into concerns about individual equality.[101]

Due Process

The due process clause of the Fourteenth Amendment says that "[n]o state . . . shall . . . deprive any person of life, liberty, or property, without due process of law."[102] After the *Slaughter-House Cases* and *United States v. Cruikshank* greatly limited the privileges or immunities clause, lawyers and judges turned to the due process clause to serve most of the purposes for which the privileges or immunities clause was originally designed. As a result, it became a major source for protections of constitutional liberty.

The text of the clause prohibits deprivations "without due process of law," and therefore seems to focus on fair procedures rather than on substantive guarantees. Despite this, there is a long history of decisions holding that the due process clause also protects fundamental rights of life, liberty, and property against certain types of government action abridging them. Several state courts and legal commentators developed the idea before the Civil War, using the idea of due process of law to protect vested rights of property, to prevent property being taken for a private purpose, and to invalidate special or partial legislation.[103] The Supreme Court also argued that the due process clause prevented interference with vested property rights in two antebellum decisions, *Bloomer v. McQuewan*[104] in 1852 and *Dred Scott v. Sanford*[105] in 1857. (Thus, *Bloomer*, and not *Dred Scott*, marks the first appearance in a Supreme Court opinion of what we now call "substantive due process.")[106]

Beginning in the 1890s, federal courts increasingly adopted the concept of due process to review state and federal legislation. They used the due process clause to protect freedom of contract, property rights, and other natural rights against state and federal regulation during the so-called *Lochner* era, running from 1897 to the New Deal. This period was named for the 1905 decision in *Lochner v. New York*,[107] which struck down a maximum hour law for bakers on the grounds that it denied bakers their right to contract.

Late nineteenth and early twentieth-century doctrines of freedom of contract, in turn, were repudiated during the New Deal. Advocates of the New Deal settlement associated the concept of "substantive due process" with the discredited jurisprudence of the *Lochner* era.[108] At the same time, however, the Supreme Court began incorporating parts of the Bill of Rights through the due process clause. Incorporation of substantive rights like freedom of speech was also a form of substantive due process because the Court argued that these rights are part of the "liberty" protected by the due process clause.[109] One might distinguish this version on the ground that, unlike the freedom of contract, the rights protected are enumerated in the Bill of Rights. However, in 1965 the Supreme Court once again began to employ the concept of substantive due process to protect unenumerated rights. In *Griswold v. Connecticut*, it recognized a fundamental right to marital privacy, and, still later, general rights of contraceptive use, the right to abortion, and homosexual rights.[110]

Two opposing views of the due process clause have emerged in response to these decisions. The first view seeks to legitimate the long history of judicial constructions, arguing that, despite its reference to "process," the due process clause guarantees more than fair procedures: it also protects substantive liberties, including implied fundamental rights and most, if not all, of the Bill of Rights. The second view draws historical lessons from the (mis)use of substantive due process in *Dred Scott v. Sandford, Lochner v. New York,* and modern cases like *Roe v. Wade.* It argues that the due process clause does not protect any substantive rights, but merely guarantees fair procedures.

Both views are incorrect. The best construction of the clause lies somewhere in between.

First, the language of the clause seems to state a principle of procedural fairness. Virtually everyone agrees that at the very least the due process clauses of the Fifth and Fourteenth Amendments require fair procedures before individuals can be deprived of life, liberty, or property.[111] In fact, in 1856, in *Murray's Lessee v. Hoboken Land & Improvement Co.,* the Supreme Court argued that the best way to articulate the idea of due process of law in the Fifth Amendment is to look to the procedural rights contained in the federal Bill of Rights.[112] Note that this construction does not make the due process clause superfluous, because the clause protects more than this. Rather, *Murray's Lessee* argued—and reasonably so—that a good way of fleshing out a general obligation of procedural fairness is to look at other procedural protections that We the People have insisted on in the text of the Constitution.

Everything *Murray's Lessee* says about the Fifth Amendment's due process clause should also be an appropriate construction of the Fourteenth Amendment. Indeed, when John Bingham was asked by Andrew Jackson Rogers what he meant by "due process of law," he famously (and curtly) responded, "courts have settled that long ago, and the gentleman can go and read their decisions."[113] Reading *Murray's Lessee* suggests that the Fourteenth Amendment's due process clause includes the procedural protections of the Bill of Rights, and that these rights apply not only to citizens, but to all persons. Ironically, then, parts of the Bill of Rights are "incorporated" into the due process clause after all, not as a matter of substantive due process but because these rights help us make sense of the more general principle of "due process of law."

Second, early accounts of the idea of due process during the late eighteenth and early nineteenth centuries included some guarantees that we would now consider substantive. The reason for this, however, is not that the due process principle was a general guarantee of liberty, but that people connected procedural fairness with the separation of legislative and judicial powers.

"Due process of law" was often viewed as synonymous with the idea of "law of the land" from Magna Carta; that is, the principle that no one could be punished by the state except according to the law of the land.[114] What connected these two formulas was the idea that individuals would not be deprived of their legal rights (that is, of life, liberty, and property) except in accordance with laws duly promulgated by the legislature in advance and following a judicial process and decree. Legislatures (or the executive) would violate due process of law if they attempted to short-circuit this process. For example, if a legislature simply announced in a law that the property of private party A was now the property of another private party B, it would be acting like a court adjudicating a private dispute, but without the procedural guarantees normally provided by the judicial process. Similarly, if legislatures tried to destroy established property rights through legislation, they would be usurping judicial functions without providing fair warning, presentment, indictment, trial by jury, and other elements of the judicial process.

The notion that due process of law protected "vested" rights—for example, rights of property—from being destroyed by government or transferred from one private party to another may look substantive to us today, but it was deeply connected to the idea of separation of powers, which, from another perspective, was both a structural and a procedural concern.[115] Similar concerns underlay the constitutional prohibitions against ex post facto laws and bills of attainder. In each case, legislatures seemed to be acting like courts and imposing judicial sentences. In fact, the related idea that certain kinds of decisions affecting people's rights cannot be made by legislative or executive fiat, but only after an individual hearing, still undergirds the construction of modern administrative law.[116] At the time of the founding, however, the paradigmatic concern was the state taking property from private party A and bestowing it on another private party B; this was thought to be beyond the power of legislatures and therefore not due process of law.[117]

A second conception of "due process of law" developed during the early nineteenth century from the ideas of vested rights and separation of powers. It distinguished between general rules (the province of legislatures) and "special" laws directed at particular persons or groups of people (which were the province of judicial determinations). Due process of law required legislatures to create laws of general scope, which did not single out groups of persons for special favor or disfavor. The classic statement, often cited by courts and commentators during the nineteenth century, was offered by Daniel Webster in his famous argument in the *Dartmouth College* case before the United States Supreme Court. Citing Magna Carta, Lord Coke's discussion of the principle of "due course and process of law," and the New Hampshire Constitution's law of the land clause, Webster argued that

> By the law of the land is most clearly intended the general law; a law, which hears before it condemns; which proceeds upon inquiry, and renders judgment only after trial. The meaning is, that every citizen should hold his life, liberty, property, and immunities, under the protection of the general rules which govern society. Every thing which may pass under the form of an enactment, is not, therefore, to be considered the law of the land. If this were so, acts of attainder, bills of pains and penalties, acts of confiscation, acts reversing judgments, and acts directly transferring one man's estate to another, legislative judgments, decrees, and forfeitures, in all possible forms, would be the law of the land."[118]

From this line of reasoning developed the notion that due process of law guaranteed equality before the law and prohibited special or partial laws. The principle of due process of law required that laws should be impartial and not for the benefit of any particular class.[119]

As Mark Yudof points out, "[t]he idea that laws should be general and not tainted by considerations of class or caste was widely recognized and accepted before the fourteenth amendment was enacted. It was part-and-parcel of the presumed fairness of governmental processes, of due process of law."[120] Thus, the guarantee of equality in the due process clause was an additional restraint on class and caste legislation. That is why Senator Howard's speech introducing the Fourteenth Amendment before the Senate mentioned the equal protection and due process clauses together.[121] And that is why John Bingham could say of the February draft—which first introduced the language of equal protection—that it simply secured guarantees already in the Fifth Amendment. The guarantee of equal protection simply made more overt what was already implicit in the concept of due process.[122]

This history suggests that the due process clause of the Fourteenth Amendment has often been misunderstood and misapplied in the modern era. Although the text clearly points to a principle of procedural fairness, early nineteenth-century constructions show that this principle also required equality before the law; it prevented legislatures from engaging in caste and class legislation, or engaging in the sort of legislative decrees that were appropriate only for courts. These constructions look substantive to us today only because we have forgotten the history behind the principle.

Even so, the due process clause is not a general guarantee of substantive liberty, and therefore it is not the appropriate vehicle for most implied fundamental rights. To the extent that the Constitution guarantees these fundamental rights, they are protected by the privileges or immunities clause of the Fourteenth Amendment in conjunction with the Ninth Amendment.[123]

There are three important qualifications to this conclusion. First, as noted before, some fundamental rights—for example, some of those in the Bill of Rights—protect fair procedures; they are secured by the due process clause as well as the privileges or immunities clause. Because the due process clause protects "persons," these rights apply to citizens and noncitizens alike.

Second, both the equal protection clause and the due process clause require equality before the law for noncitizens. Therefore these clauses extend nonpolitical but fundamental rights to noncitizens. This means, for example, that if states must guarantee free-exercise rights or contraceptive rights to citizens, they must extend the same rights to noncitizens.[124]

Third, some claims about implied fundamental rights might actually be equality claims in disguise, and if these claims are valid, they would be protected by the due process clause because it secures equality before the law. For example, courts may have viewed some of the *Lochner*-era decisions protecting freedom of contract as a way of preventing class legislation, although we would not agree with this application of the principle today.[125] Some modern versions of implied fundamental rights, like the rights to abortion and sexual autonomy, might actually be designed to guarantee sex equality or prevent discrimination against sexual orientation minorities. If so, these rights would be secured by the equal protection clause and the due process clause.

Federal Guarantees of Equality before the Law and *Bolling v. Sharpe*

The Fourteenth Amendment says that "no state" shall deny equal protection of the laws. Does this mean that the federal government has no constitutional obligation to provide equal protection or equality before the law? When the Fifth Amendment was ratified in 1791, most blacks were held in slavery and most women had hardly any rights. Yet in 1954, in *Bolling v. Sharpe*,[126] the Supreme Court held that the Fifth Amendment embodied a constitutional guarantee of equality that prohibited segregated schools in the District of Columbia. *Bolling* was a companion case to *Brown v. Board of Education* and was decided on the same day. "[T]he concepts of equal protection and due process," Chief Justice Warren, explained, "both stemming from our American ideal of fairness, are not mutually exclusive."[127] Furthermore, given that *Brown* held "that the Constitution prohibits the states from maintaining racially segregated public schools, it would be unthinkable that the same Constitution would impose a lesser duty on the Federal Government."[128]

Many scholars have viewed *Bolling* as an uncomfortable demonstration that the Constitution's original meaning cannot account for important features of modern civil rights law, and nonoriginalists have argued that *Bolling* shows why originalism is simply untenable as a theory of constitutional interpretation.[129] Even noted originalists like Robert Bork and Michael McConnell have agreed that *Bolling* is inconsistent with original meaning. Bork provocatively compares *Bolling* to *Lochner v. New York* and *Dred Scott v. Sandford* as examples of judicial overreaching using the doctrine of substantive due process, and denounces the decision as "not law but social engineering from the bench."[130] McConnell argues that there might be good reasons to give the federal government more leeway than the states to treat people unequally.[131]

Both originalists and their critics are incorrect. When we employ the method of text and principle, we discover that *Bolling* is not a particularly difficult case and that Chief Justice Warren's reading is actually quite reasonable.

In *Bolling*, Chief Justice Warren offers two reasons why the federal government must guarantee equality. The first is that the concepts of due process and equal protection are connected. The second is that the state guarantee of equal protection presupposes a similar obligation for the federal government. Although Chief Justice Warren does not mention it in his brief opinion, both of these reasons are actually consistent with the text of the Fifth Amendment and with the assumptions of the Reconstruction Congress that drafted the Fourteenth Amendment.

As we have seen, by the time the Fourteenth Amendment was ratified, the concept of due process embodied in the Fifth Amendment required equality before the law and banned special, partial, or class legislation. Although this construction probably developed a few decades after the ratification of the Fifth Amendment, antebellum lawyers did not see any conflict between the equality principle and the words "due process of law"; rather, as suggested by Webster's speech in the *Dartmouth College* case, they saw equality as simply an elaboration of the basic principles of procedural fairness and the separation of the judicial role from the legislative.

This construction of the Fifth Amendment clearly informed the drafting of and the debates over the Fourteenth Amendment. To put the point still more strongly, the very words "equal protection" were added to the Constitution *based on a widely accepted construction of the Fifth Amendment's due process clause.* Moreover, the Committee of Fifteen's notes explicitly reference the Fifth Amendment as the source of this language, and John Bingham explained to Congress that the language was based on "a portion of the fifth amendment."[132]

Today lawyers worry that the original semantic meaning of "due process of law" is inconsistent with the idea of equality, because they think that procedural fairness has nothing to do with equality, which is a substantive principle. But early nineteenth-century lawyers did not reason this way. Although we do not know precisely what people thought in 1791, we do know that lawyers in the decades following ratification of the Fifth Amendment thought that the equality reading was perfectly consistent with the text. And if an equality reading was consistent with the text in the early 1800s, it should be a permissible construction today. Indeed, during the nineteenth century the equality reading was not only a permissible construction; it was a generally accepted one.

Evidence of the connection between due process and equality is everywhere in Reconstruction-era debates. John Bingham and other congressional Republicans believed that equal protection in the rights of life, liberty, and property followed from the guarantee of due process.[133] Introducing the Fourteenth Amendment in the Senate, Senator Howard insisted that equality was presupposed by a republican form of government; indeed, there could be no republican government without it.[134] Representative John Farnsworth of Illinois made the same point in the House debates. The idea of equal protection, he argued, was already presupposed by the text of the Constitution, "[b]ut a reaffirmation of a good principle will do no harm." "'Equal protection of the laws'; can there be any well-founded objection to this?" he exclaimed. "Is not this the very foundation of a republican government? Is it not the undeniable right of every subject of the Government to receive 'equal protection of the laws' with every other subject?"[135]

Reading the Fifth Amendment through modern eyes, we may tend to forget its central role in constitutional arguments against slavery before the Civil War. Antislavery advocates argued that due process required equal access to judicial processes and equal protection of the laws.[136] The federal government, like all republican governments, was obligated to give blacks the same protection from public and private violence that it offered to white persons (the Fifth Amendment speaks of persons, not citizens). The institution of slavery denied basic features of due process because it allowed people to be deprived of their liberty without criminal charges or a right to trial by jury; the institution of slavery also allowed private actors to deprive slaves of their liberty without providing a remedy for false imprisonment or any procedural protections. It followed that slavery could not legally exist in federal territories and the duty of equal protection required Congress to eliminate it. Accordingly, both the 1856 and the 1860 Republican Party platforms argued that the Fifth Amendment made slavery unconstitutional in the federal territories and that Congress had an affirmative duty to abolish it.[137] In 1862, three years before the ratification of the Thirteenth Amendment, Congress repudiated the *Dred Scott* decision by abolishing slavery in the District of Columbia and shortly thereafter in all federal territories using its powers under the territory clause.[138] Speaking in favor of the District of Columbia bill, John Bingham based his arguments on the Fifth Amendment's due process clause: the American Constitution, he explained, "proclaimed that all men in respect of the rights of life and liberty and property were equal before the law."[139]

If due process already includes ideas of equal protection, why does the Fourteenth Amendment include both a due process and an equal protection clause? Isn't the equal protection clause redundant? As Representative Farnsworth's comments suggest, at least one supporter of the amendment thought so.[140] But the most likely reason is the one offered by Akhil Amar: "the Equal Protection Clause was in part a clarifying gloss on the due process idea."[141] It was directed at opponents of equal rights for the freedmen to ensure that there could be no doubt of Congress's enforcement powers. As we saw in Chapter 10, the citizenship clause was added at the last minute for much the same reason.[142]

In offering this clarification, the framers of the Fourteenth Amendment probably cared less about future judicial decisions than about

Congress's section 5 powers to enforce equality in the immediate aftermath of the Civil War. One cannot understand the choices made in drafting the text without recognizing that Congress believed it would take the lead in enforcing the amendment through new civil rights acts. As Chapter 10 explained, a key purpose of the Fourteenth Amendment was to provide constitutional backup to the 1866 Civil Rights Act, which secured equal civil rights for blacks and whites. In the debates over the 1866 Act, James Wilson, the chairman of the House Judiciary Committee, argued that the Fifth Amendment's due process clause gave Congress the power to pass the Civil Rights Bill.[143] Although most congressional Republicans believed the act was perfectly constitutional (to enforce either the Fifth Amendment or the Thirteenth Amendment), adding an explicit guarantee of equal protection of the laws to section 1 made unmistakably clear that Congress had power to enact the measure under section 5. In fact, Congress repassed the text of the 1866 Act (with a few changes) in the Enforcement Act of 1870, invoking its new powers under the Fourteenth Amendment.[144]

Congress was also particularly concerned about selective protection by law enforcement officials in Southern states. Immediately following the Civil War, groups of marauding Southern whites terrorized blacks and white unionists; victims were murdered, raped, and lynched; their property was stolen and their houses were burned. Local law enforcement officials, either frightened or complicit, simply looked the other way. This violence—and the lack of official response to it—was a major concern of the Report on the Joint Committee on Reconstruction that led to the adoption of the Fourteenth Amendment.[145] This concern led to the passage of the 1866 Civil Rights Act, the 1870 Enforcement Act, and the 1871 Ku Klux Klan Act. Congress wanted to ensure that it had authority to pass laws that would remedy policies of state neglect, which denied equal protection of the laws in the most literal sense.[146] A specific guarantee of equal protection in addition to a due process clause would firmly establish Congress's power to act.

Whether or not the framers of 1791 thought that the principle of due process of law included equal protection of the law, the framers of 1868 certainly did. In this respect, the issue is similar to the construction of the Second Amendment: whether or not the 1791 framers believed that the Second Amendment guaranteed an individual right of self-defense, this construction was widely accepted at the time the Fourteenth Amendment was adopted.

Scholars unfamiliar with this history have tried to justify *Bolling* through a "reverse incorporation" argument, arguing that the Fifth Amendment's due process clause somehow "incorporates" the Fourteenth Amendment's equal protection clause.[147] Framework originalism makes this sort of argument unnecessary. The expected application of 1791 does not control modern-day constructions. Nor do we have to assume that the Fourteenth Amendment implicitly amended the Fifth Amendment.

The question we should ask today is whether a proposed construction is one that the text can bear and makes the most sense of the clause in the context of the larger constitutional plan. History shows us that the Fifth Amendment's language can easily bear this construction, for it was widely held throughout the nineteenth century. History also shows that the Fourteenth Amendment was designed to hold the states to the same fundamental rights guarantees as the federal government, which included guarantees of equality before the law.[148] The structural purposes behind the Fourteenth Amendment assumed what was at the time a widely accepted equality construction of the Fifth Amendment. In fact, the same year that the Supreme Court decided *Plessy v. Ferguson,* it asserted this view in a unanimous opinion by Justice Harlan, which stated that "the constitution of the United States, in its present form, forbids, so far as civil and political rights are concerned, discrimination *by the General Government, or by the states,* against any citizen because of his race. All citizens are equal before the law."[149]

Nevertheless, one might insist, the Fifteenth Amendment specifically mentions the federal government, while the Fourteenth does not. Because the Reconstruction Congress knew how to limit the federal government through the text, Congress's failure to make a specific reference to the federal government in the Fourteenth Amendment means that no limitation on federal power was intended.

This argument is anachronistic; it neglects the distinction between civil and political equality. Congressional Republicans did not forget to include a federal equality guarantee in the Fourteenth Amendment. They assumed that a guarantee of civil equality was already present in the Fifth Amendment. A guarantee of federal voting rights, however, was a different matter. The due process clause of the Fifth Amendment guaranteed equality before the law—civil equality, and not political equality— and that is why a right against the federal government had to be specifically mentioned in the Fifteenth Amendment.[150]

In sum, nothing in the constitutional text prevents us from reading the Fifth Amendment's due process clause to secure equality before the law, and when we read the due process clause of the Fifth Amendment in the way that the framers of the Reconstruction Amendments read it, it is not only a permissible construction, it is the best construction.

12

TEXTS AND PRINCIPLES

Resources for Construction

The last several chapters have shown how to apply the method of text and principle in particular legal controversies. They use of all of the modalities of constitutional argument, which are familiar to all lawyers and available to all citizens. These include arguments about text; pre-enactment history, including original purposes, original principles, original intentions, and original expected applications; post-enactment history, including constitutional arguments and constitutional constructions by prominent individuals, social movements, and public officials; judicial precedents; precedents by nonjudicial actors; structural considerations; consequences; national ethos; and narrative understandings of the trajectory and meaning of national history.

Described in the abstract, framework originalism might not seem to leave us much to work with. But when we add all of the modalities of constitutional interpretation and all the features of ordinary legal argument, we will discover that there are often plenty of resources for constitutional construction. No doubt people using these resources will still disagree about many constitutional controversies, but that is true of the ordinary practice of constitutional argument and, indeed, virtually all methods of constitutional interpretation.

Constitutional construction is as much art as science, as much legal practice as logical proof. The familiar modalities of constitutional argument are tools for building constructions and offering reasons to justify them. They are methods for understanding what the Constitution means in practice and for persuading other people to your point of view.

Common rhetorical resources are crucial to an intergenerational project of constitution building. When I describe these resources as "rhetorical," I do not mean that they are tools to obfuscate or mislead; I mean rhetoric in the classical sense of resources we use to argue about things that cannot be known for certain. We persuade others to agree with us by stating our views through a common language; we put things in ways that others can understand and that can help them see the truth of what we say.

Arguments using the method of text and principle look very much like the standard legal arguments that lawyers make. That is precisely the point. Framework originalism is not an algorithm for correct decision. It is a platform for ordinary legal argument about the Constitution. Hence the term *framework originalism* is doubly appropriate, for it describes a framework for politics and a framework for legal arguments to construct the Constitution.

Nevertheless, the constructions in the last several chapters have a few distinctive characteristics. They do not begin, as lawyers' arguments often do, with the latest pronouncements from the Supreme Court and the lower federal courts. Instead they begin with an examination of the constitutional text. Because the Constitution as a whole is a plan for politics, we do not look at a particular text or clause in isolation but try to view the Constitution holistically, as a coherent project of governance—or one that at least strives for coherence. We place the relevant text in the context of the entire Constitution, and we try to understand its structural relationship to other parts of the Constitution. In doing this, we may also compare and contrast its words with words in other parts of the document (a practice that Akhil Amar has called intertextualism).[1]

We consider whether the language of the text is ambiguous and whether it might involve a nonliteral usage or a term of art. Where we find ambiguity, we use all the standard resources of legal argument to discern the original meaning of words and concepts like "commerce," and terms of art like "bills of attainder." In short, we try to begin with the text, using the familiar modalities to ascertain original meaning and basic structural considerations; then we use these resources to build constructions to implement the text's rules, standards, and principles. In this way, we end up with the familiar forms of legal argument.

Although I emphasize the distinction between original meaning and original expected applications, the constructions in Chapters 9, 10, and

11 make plenty of use of original expected applications, as well as original intentions, original understandings, original statements of principle and purpose, and constructions roughly contemporaneous with the adoption of constitutional provisions. These are merely resources, not binding commands; even so, they may be particularly valuable to construction. Not only do they offer evidence that can resolve ambiguities about original meaning, they also offer us evidence about *permissible constructions,* because constructions and statements of purpose and principle contemporaneous with the adoption of the text are likely to be consistent with the text.

Why is this important if we would not want to adopt many of these constructions today? It is important because people so easily forget or misremember history. Seeing language through modern eyes, they incorrectly assume that some constructions are simply off the table if they wish to be faithful to the text. Chapters 9 through 11 offer many examples: Knowing that the framers spoke of navigation and commerce interchangeably helps us see that "commerce" must have a broader meaning than trade or exchange. Understanding the role of Resolution VI in the Philadelphia convention helps us understand that the doctrine of enumerated powers embraces an important structural principle that can adapt with changing circumstances and is fully consistent with the modern state. Knowing that various framers of the Fourteenth Amendment believed that both the equal protection clause and the due process clause prohibited caste and class legislation helps us see that modern antisubordination theories of equality are not only consistent with the text but entirely reasonable approaches to constitutional equality. Finally, knowing that nineteenth century lawyers believed that the concept of due process of law included equality before the law and that the equal protection clause was actually based on the Fifth Amendment significantly changes our views about the correctness of *Bolling v. Sharpe,* the companion case to *Brown v. Board of Education* that banned racial segregation in the District of Columbia.[2]

Modern scholars, and especially modern political liberals, have often tended to reject originalism out of hand because they assume that original expectations, purposes, and principles are hopelessly regressive and irrelevant. But the assumptions, purposes, and principles we find in historical materials are often far more complex, surprising, and sophisticated than many nonoriginalists assume. Sometimes they do reflect values and factual assumptions that Americans no longer hold; but sometimes they are particularly farsighted and relevant to contemporary concerns.

What Are Underlying Principles?

The constructions in Chapters 9 through 11 repeatedly refer to *underlying principles,* a concept I have mentioned throughout this book. Underlying principles do not appear in the constitutional text; they are constitutional constructions. In fact they are often the first step in construction, a special set of heuristics or aids to construction.

Underlying principles are helpful guides to implementing the constitutional plan, explaining the point of present and future construction. Examples are principles such as separation of powers or checks and balances. There is no "separation of powers" or "checks and balances" clause in the Constitution. Rather, we ascribe these principles to the Constitution. Therefore we say that they "underlie" the text, in the sense of supporting it and making sense of it.

Depending on their relationship to the text, underlying principles can perform at least two functions. Some underlying principles are structural. They explain the functions of government and how the constitutional system is supposed to operate. Often they do not correspond to any specific part of the text but are implied from various parts of the text. In addition to separation of powers and checks and balances, other examples of underlying principles include federalism, democracy, equal citizenship, equality before the law, and the rule of law. There may be no single clause in the text that corresponds to these principles; instead we assume that these principles are part of the plan of government and underlie many different aspects of the text. Conversely, the principle of separation of powers (or the principle of checks and balances) is not exhausted by the particular examples of the principle stated in the text. Rather, we apply this principle to new situations in which the text is silent and to new state-building constructions that implement the Constitution. Resolution VI, described in Chapter 9, is a structural principle. It explains the structural purpose of Congress's enumerated powers and why the text is written the way it is.

Underlying principles serve a second function. In some cases the text itself states a standard or a principle, like equal protection or freedom of speech, and we must decide what the text requires. In one sense the answer is quite simple. If the words say that states may not deny "equal protection of the laws," the principle is that states must not deny the equal protection of the laws. But what does *that* mean? To answer this question, we will have to cash out the principle of "equal protection of the laws" in terms of subsidiary principles. These subsidiary principles are aids or heuristics that help explain or flesh out the textual commitment. We might call them explanatory or implementing principles. The principles against class and caste legislation are examples of this kind of underlying principle. They explain what kinds of inequalities the equal protection clause prohibits.

These underlying principles are not identical with the words of the text—they do not *constitute* the text, as the words "equal protection of the laws" do. They are constructions that support and help explain the point of the text, and they do not exhaust either its meaning or its effect.

In sum, constitutional construction requires us to ascribe certain principles to the text, either to explain the purposes of constitutional structures and the ways that government should work or to explain particular abstract principles and standards we find in the text. I call these ascribed principles *underlying principles* because they support and illuminate the text.

Using History to Construct Underlying Principles

If underlying principles are constructions, where do we find them and how do we construct them? The most obvious source is history. Sometimes we find statements of these principles in historical materials or in the history of constructions of the Constitution. Thus, Resolution VI appears in the Philadelphia debates, and a similar principle appears in the ratification debates. The principles against class and caste legislation appear in the debates over the Fourteenth Amendment and were familiar both before and after the Civil War.

Nevertheless, underlying principles are not limited to specific principles that the framers and ratifiers actually sought to endorse. Rather, we construct underlying principles from an assessment of the structural functions and purposes of the constitutional text. Even so, it is very important to look to history to derive underlying principles, even (and perhaps especially) principles that nobody in particular intended.

As I noted in Chapter 9, there can be new principles underlying the text that the framers and ratifiers did not think of, but that we may fairly ascribe to the text today. That is most obvious in the case of structural principles that are not necessarily tied to a specific piece of text but that we infer from the interaction of various parts of the Constitution and from the structure and logic of the constitutional system. Some of these structural principles—like the separation of powers—were surely recognized and promoted by various framers and ratifiers. But others could not be, in part because they were not salient to the persons who wrote and ratified the document, and in part because some important structural issues arose only as the constitutional system developed over time. The members of the generation that produced the 1787 Constitution were quite talented, but they were not fortune-tellers; they began what they understood to be a great experiment in self-governance, and they could only offer their best guesses as to how things would operate in practice.

Sometimes one only figures out how a machine or a system or any other complex structure works—and should work—by watching it operate over time. Charles Black once famously argued that even if there had been no free-speech clause in the Constitution, the Constitution's structure and its commitment to representative government demanded protection of at least speech on topics related to public governance.[3] That would be so whether or not any framers or ratifiers of the 1787 Constitution specifically believed that a principle of free expression undergirded the Constitution prior to the adoption of the Bill of Rights.

In addition, the Constitution was not drafted at a single time. Currently its various amendments stretch over two hundred years. New amendments may alter the relationships between other parts of the Constitution, sometimes in expected ways, but sometimes in quite unexpected ways. The Reconstruction amendments altered the relationships between the federal government and the states, and between the federal courts and state legislatures, in ways that did not become clear for generations. Subsequent constitutional constructions can have path-dependent effects on how the constitutional system operates. Four good examples are the creation of the party system (which the framers originally opposed), the creation of the federal civil service in the nineteenth century, the rise of the administrative state in the first half of the twentieth century, and the development of permanent standing armies and naval forces stationed around the world in the second half of the twentieth century.

Indeed, because of the cumulative effects of later developments, some principles that the founding generation would have rejected or conceived narrowly can be underlying principles today. For example, today democracy is one of the most important principles underlying the

Constitution. Nevertheless, the generation of 1787 did not fully trust the idea of democracy; they were comfortable with limited suffrage and constrained participation, and preferred to speak of republicanism or representative government.[4] Although they believed in majority rule, their notion of who counted as the governing people was quite limited, and they accepted a civil society with strongly inegalitarian features in which many, if not most, people were largely or completely excluded from governance. Over time, however, our Constitution has become increasingly democratic in many dimensions; not merely through expanding the right to vote and hold office but through breaking down powerful hierarchies of status in civil society, and through making opportunities for leadership and political participation more widely available. Even if democracy in its modern sense of egalitarian participation in public life and public affairs was not an intended principle in 1787, it has become one of the central principles underlying our Constitution today.

For all of these reasons, structural principles might emerge from the constitutional system that no single person or generation intended. We should always look to history to see how the generation that produced a constitutional text expected that the constitutional system would operate in light of the text. But this does not exhaust all of the structural ideas behind the Constitution. We must look to other generations as well as the founding generation to understand how constitutional structures should work (and how they might fail to work).

Similar considerations apply to underlying principles that explain standards or principles explicitly stated in the text, like the equal protection clause, the free-speech clause, or the guarantee of security against unreasonable searches and seizures. These explanatory or implementing principles do not have to be specifically intended by the adopters. At the same time history remains quite important to discovering and articulating these principles.

We need history because it can help us resolve ambiguities in the text and decide whether the text employs nonliteral usage or a term of art. We must also decide what subsidiary principles best explain and implement the abstract principles in the text. We can look to contemporaneous statements of principle, and we can also look to the aspirations of supporters and advocates of the text. We can also look to the general evils or problems that the generation that produced the text sought to address. This evidence helps us construct principles that explain textual commitments such as "equal protection of the laws." I use the term "construct" advisedly; we cannot always simply plug in the statements of various framers and ratifiers as the relevant principles. Their statements may merely be statements about their expected applications of the text.

Framing Underlying Principles

The principles underlying the text should be at roughly the same level of generality as the text (understood to include any generally recognized terms of art). If the text uses general language, the underlying principles that support and explain the text should as well. The reason is simple. The adoption of a constitution like the 1787 Constitution required the cooperation of a very large number of people who are geographically dispersed; hence, idiosyncratic meanings are very unlikely, and we may assume that the words of a Constitution should be used and understood in their ordinary, everyday sense.[5] Absent strong evidence to the contrary, we assume that people choose general language if they want to endorse general principles, and more specific language if they want to commit themselves to narrower principles. Generally speaking, the best way to commit yourself to abstract principles and open-ended standards is to put abstract principles and open-ended standards in the text; the best way to prevent that sort of commitment is to avoid using that sort of language.

There has been a very long debate in American constitutional theory about the proper level of generality at which to construe the framers' and ratifiers' purposes, presumably on the grounds that these purposes are somehow controlling.[6] This debate asks the wrong question if it focuses on psychology and not on what the text enacts. The proper level of generality for the constitutional principles in the text is the one we find in the text itself.

For example, people have long debated whether the equal protection clause prohibits only racial classifications—because a primary object of the amendment was to secure equal citizenship for blacks—or whether it protects other groups (for example, women) from state discrimination. I regard this as an easy question. Obviously the framers of the Fourteenth Amendment sought to give the freedmen equality. But if the Fourteenth Amendment's framers had wanted to institute a principle that banned all racial classifications—and no more—they could have said so. They would have chosen different words than they did. Indeed, if you look at the Fifteenth Amendment, you can see that they knew exactly how to ban certain classifications based on race and prior condition of servitude. However, they did not do this in the case of the Fourteenth Amendment. They sought to establish principles of equal citizenship, which they saw as something both more and less than a total ban on racial classifications. In fact, as noted in Chapter 11, the Committee of Fifteen that drafted the Fourteenth Amendment rejected the color-blindness principle when it was offered to them.[7] Instead the framers of the Fourteenth Amendment used the very general language of "equal protection of the laws" and "privileges or immunities of citizens of the United States." Any underlying principles we associate with those texts must be as general as the words themselves. Racial classifications are prohibited by the text of the Fourteenth Amendment to the extent that such classifications violate the principles behind the text—in this case, the principles guaranteeing equal citizenship and prohibiting class and caste legislation.

To give another example: a person supporting the Fourteenth Amendment may have stated that the purpose of the amendment was to constitutionalize certain features of the Civil Rights Act of 1866.[8] Even if many people made this claim, it does not follow that the equal protection clause (or section 1 of the Fourteenth Amendment) is limited to this function. The words chosen are "equal protection of the laws," which are stated at a much higher level of generality. To be sure, the principles we construct should probably protect as much as the 1866 Civil Rights Act protects.[9] But the language of the equal protection clause suggests that these principles should protect far more than that. It is entirely correct to say that one of the purposes of the Fourteenth Amendment was to constitutionalize the Civil Rights Act of 1866. But we should not say that this purpose was *the* principle underlying the words chosen.

The examples I just gave are fairly easy ones. In practice it may be difficult to know whether a principle is at roughly the same level of generality as the text. First, talking about comparable levels of generality offers a metaphor, not a mathematical formula. Second, our initial assumptions about the generality of a standard or principle may be altered by historical knowledge about how language was used at the time—for example, whether the text uses commonly accepted terms of art. As a result there will usually be a kind of reflective equilibrium between our assessment of the generality of the text's language and our assessment of the historical evidence of the context that produced it. There will often be controversy when we use history to discern underlying principles. Nevertheless, we must do the best we can with what we have.

In Chapter 11 I argued that the equal protection clause prohibits class legislation, caste legislation, "special" or "partial" legislation, and arbitrary and unreasonable distinctions between persons or citizens. Each of these principles, I claim, is at roughly the same level of generality as the words of the clause, and although they overlap, each has a slightly different focus. My evidence for these principles comes from the public explanations that the people who drafted the Fourteenth Amendment gave for what they were trying to do. I noted previously that we cannot necessarily identify these statements of purpose with the principles underlying the text if these statements of purpose are relatively concrete and the text is quite general. However, in the case of the Fourteenth Amendment, the persons who drafted and supported the amendment spoke about their purposes in quite general terms, and they repeatedly and deliberately used very abstract language to explain their goals. They matched their explanations to the text's level of generality. They spoke about equal citizenship, about ending caste and class legislation, about equality before the law, and about protecting basic rights of citizenship. People defending the amendment stated their goals in terms of very general principles, and that helps explain why they chose such general language in the first place.

Not every part of the Constitution offers such a rich historical record. The First Amendment's speech clause lacks the same degree and type of evidence that we have for the Fourteenth Amendment. We have evidence about official legal protection for speech in 1791 that is not very speech protective. We have evidence of historical practices of speech protection that run contrary to the law on the books and are far more libertarian.[10] And we have some general statements of principle by the generation that produced the First Amendment. Nevertheless, in comparison to the Fourteenth Amendment, the historical record is far sparser. History gives us relatively little help in determining what principle or principles underlie the words "freedom of speech." And for some clauses and portions of the Constitution, the historical record is sparser still.

Nevertheless, our task is the same: we must still try to figure out what principle or principles the text enacts using whatever sources and forms of reasoning are available to us. Where the history is available, as in the case of the Fourteenth Amendment, we should certainly use it. But we do not look to history because we are bound by the original or intended purposes of either the framers or the ratifiers. We look to history because we want to know what standard or principle the text they produced enacts. If we faced a piece of constitutional text where historical evidence of purpose was completely lacking, we could not do what I have tried to do with the Fourteenth Amendment. We would be thrown back on other resources. We would try to figure out the underlying principles by reasoning from the text and from other parts of the Constitution, from any historical context we could discover, from structural considerations, from later interpretations of the text, and from considerations of justice and political morality. Our conclusions would no doubt be subject to dispute and uncertainty, but that is hardly unusual in constitutional interpretation even when we have a very rich historical record.

In Chapters 10 and 11 I used history to offer a series of principles underlying the Fourteenth Amendment's text, principles that I claim have roughly the same level of generality as the text. But the text does not say "no class legislation"; it says "equal protection of the laws." That means that the principles I find in history do not exhaust the meaning of the clause.[11] They are particular attempts, situated in history, for figuring out what principles the clause enacts. Think of them as heuristics, aids to understanding the text and its principled commitments. Given the history, my best guess is that a commitment to equal protection of the laws includes a commitment against class legislation, caste legislation, arbitrary and unreasonable distinctions, and special or partial laws. But there could be other constitutional principles embodied by the equal protection clause that no particular person living in 1868 intended but that we come to recognize through our country's historical experience. Although we may use history to recognize these principles, they need not have been originally intended principles.

Moreover, the text itself might point to the possibility of new principles. The Fourteenth Amendment's privileges or immunities clause and the Ninth Amendment's reservation of unenumerated rights are declaratory texts. They contemplate the protection of rights that the American people come to regard as fundamental, even if they were not specifically recognized as protected in 1868 (or 1791). Assuming that these rights involve substantive constitutional principles, those principles were not specifically intended when these texts were adopted.

Nevertheless, I suspect that living constitutionalists are worried about using history to articulate underlying principles because they associate history with original expected applications. Hence, they might insist that the Constitution continually needs a fresh supply of "new" underlying principles derived from present-day values and concerns because they assume that whatever underlying principles we discover through historical investigation will have to be stated at a fairly low level of generality and closely tied to the expected applications of the framers or ratifiers. For example, how can women be protected by the equal protection clause if we discover that the framers of the Fourteenth Amendment did not wish to disturb the common law rules of coverture, which robbed married women of almost all of their common law rights? How can agnostics or atheists be protected by the free-exercise clause if we discover that the clause was originally intended to prevent discrimination among religious believers?[12] This is nothing more than the tired old debate about the level of generality at which we should construe the framers' and ratifiers' purposes, a debate that is still beholden to the theory of original intention or original understanding. If what matters to us is the original meaning of the text, then the principles underlying the constitutional text should be as general as the text itself. And how we apply those principles cannot be settled by an inquiry into original expectations.

Many cases where nonoriginalists assume we need "new" principles to explain the text actually involve nothing more than contemporary applications of underlying principles stated at a level of generality that matches the text. For example, I think that the principle against class legislation protects homosexuals from discrimination even if nobody knew there were such things as homosexuals in 1868, or, if they knew what homosexuals were, would have opposed the extension of the principle to that social group. One does not need a "new" principle for this case; rather, one needs to apply the principle against class legislation appropriately to present-day circumstances given present-day understandings.

The framers and ratifiers may have stated a wide variety of principles at various levels of scope and generality, or they may have stated no principles at all that have come down to us. The proper question, however, is what principles we should ascribe to the text the framers and ratifiers made into law. Thus, for me the key issue is encapsulated in Mitch Berman's suggestion that constitutional principles must be ones "that the text can bear."[13] We want to make sure that in our eagerness to articulate new principles we do not wind up with a play on words. The reason we look to history—where it is available—is to act as a check on our assumptions about what "the text can bear." We use history to see whether the issues or problems that concerned the framing generation are structurally or analogically similar to ones we face today. If so, then we can have somewhat more confidence that the principles we articulate are principles that the text can bear.

We must avoid a play on words because rule-of-law values require that we preserve semantic meaning over time. But there is another, deeper reason. The Constitution must not only serve as basic law, it must also serve as higher law and as "our law." It must be more than a law created by framers that binds us in the present; it must also be a law that connects our present political aspirations and commitments with the aspirations and commitments of previous generations, including not only the adopting generation but all that succeed it.

For the Constitution to succeed as "our law," we must be able to see ourselves as embarked on a common project that begins in the past and that we bring into the future. The fact that we share a common text certainly helps connect past to present. But shared political aspirations involve more than common texts; looking to history helps us articulate a narrative that allows us to view ourselves as continuing the commitments of the past in present-day circumstances.

Constitutional Redemption and Constitutional History

In order to see the commonality between our aspirations and those of previous generations, it is not necessary that we articulate constitutional principles in precisely the way that previous generations would have. Rather, we try to interpret the past in the present as articulating principles which we are still committed to today. When we pledge fidelity to the past, we always do so from the standpoint of the present. Fidelity to the past is a present-day decision about what we are committed to seen through the lens of a present-day perspective. There is no time in which we can pledge faith but in the present, and there is no other perspective available to us than the one we now inhabit. And as the present is always changing into the future, so too does our situation and hence our perspective. These are the inextricable circumstances of fidelity to an ongoing creedal tradition and a continuing political practice.

Even if the facts of history do not change, and even if we uncover no new historical sources, what history means to us and the way it appears to us continually do change, because we ourselves are moving through history and continually see what happened in the past through new perspectives. (Indeed, the source materials we think relevant may change based on those changing perspectives.) We inevitably recognize and conceptualize what happened in the past from the standpoint of our own cultural memories and experiences. These are always changing—new things happen to us or become important to us, while older events and memories are reinterpreted or forgotten. Hence, elements of the past always look salient to us in ever-new ways, even if specific source materials do not change.

History seems freshly (and differently) relevant as time passes, not because the facts of history have altered, but because what facts are important to us and what they mean to us change as we and our country go through various crises, conflicts, controversies, and transformations. We see the problems and the difficulties, the fears and the commitments, the goals and the aspirations of people in the past in terms of our present controversies and experiences. So the past always seems relevant to us, in ways that may differ markedly from how previous generations apprehended our common history. History always looks new to us because we ourselves are constantly changing; our perspectives are constantly shifting under our feet. We are always moving through history and viewing the past from ever-new perspectives, in light of contemporaneous events that are themselves ever receding before us. You cannot step into the same Constitution twice, but this is not because the Constitution is always changing; it is because you and the position from which you interpret the Constitution are always changing.

I suspect that many living constitutionalists are suspicious of any form of originalism because they worry that the past offers insufficient resources for vindicating our values in the present. Opponents of originalism, I suspect, fear that the past is really against us, and that the aspirations and principles of those who lived in the past are insufficient to do justice in the present, because they were created by people who were very unjust to each other, and who held many views—about social equality, for example—that we today would think outmoded, wrongheaded, and reactionary.

But when we enter into an appropriate spirit of charity toward the past, when we see it as striving or aspiring to the goals of the Preamble— "to form a more perfect Union, establish justice, insure domestic tranquility, provide for the common defense, promote the general welfare, and secure the blessings of liberty to ourselves and our posterity"—we get a very different view of the resources of history.[14] Viewed sympathetically as people attempting a feat of political change unheard of in prior human history, the 1787 framers were putting in place the most democratic constitution of their time; the radical Republicans of 1868 were casting aside a system of chattel slavery and replacing it with a new system premised on the foundation of free and equal citizens. Their larger principles, expressed in the abstract language they chose, offer resources for articulating our present concerns, if we are willing to view these aspirations with sympathetic eyes, and in a spirit of magnanimity. We should understand these great principles as promising their eventual redemption in history, and we should understand our role as helping to move that redemption forward.[15] When we engage in a project of redemptive constitutionalism, their principles are our principles, their project is our project, and their Constitution is our Constitution.

Earlier I noted that the Fourteenth Amendment's prohibition on class legislation might justify constitutional protection of homosexuals. The historical materials I drew on in Chapter 11 to argue that the Fourteenth Amendment prohibits class legislation have been known to legal historians for many years. But the idea that they might say something about the struggle of homosexuals for equal rights was not obvious to most people in 1940 or 1960. It becomes possible to see this in the history only after one lives in a world in which homosexuals assert themselves, demand equal civil rights, and claim that they are being unfairly singled out for special burdens and discriminations by society. Indeed, understanding that this is what the gay rights movement is doing is the product of an imaginative interaction between past memories and present meanings. Similarly, as genetic engineering develops and as the possibility of genetic discrimination becomes increasingly salient to us, what the history of the Fourteenth Amendment means to us will also change as we move forward in time. It is perfectly plausible that some day the equal protection clause— and its prohibition on class legislation—might limit the state's ability to engage in genetic discrimination and impose special burdens on people who share a common genetic marker, even if they correspond to no social group that existed in 1868.[16] Indeed, I think that day is already here.

Consistency with the Text: Articulation and Supplementation

Framework originalism requires that constitutional constructions must be consistent with the text. We may articulate and supplement the constitutional text through construction, but we may not contradict it. Thus, whenever we argue from principles underlying the text, we must always return to the text to check our arguments.

It may sometimes be difficult to know whether a given implementation of a principle contradicts the constitutional text or merely articulates it. Randy Barnett offers an easy case: suppose that a principle underlying the Second Amendment's right to bear arms is the promotion of public safety.[17] One can promote public safety in many ways, however, including confiscating all privately held arms from the citizenry. Nevertheless, that would contradict the textual grant of a right to bear arms and so it is not a permissible application of the underlying principle.

To the extent that the text is vague, however, it may not offer very much of a check on construction. Suppose, for example, that a legislature agrees that the right to bear arms protects the principle of public safety and the individual's right to possess weapons. Nevertheless, it insists that these principles are perfectly consistent with imposing reasonable regulations on the sale, purchase, possession, and use of firearms, and even with banning the private ownership of particularly dangerous weapons. Does this implementation of the principles behind the text contradict the textual grant of "the right to bear arms" or does it merely articulate it? In close cases, it may be difficult to tell. If we think the legislature's implementation is unreasonable, we will say that it contradicts the text. But if we think the implementation is reasonable, we will say that it merely articulates it, even if we do not think it is the best implementation.

Indeed, precisely because the constitutional text may be vague, deciding how best to implement underlying principles may be the best guide to what the text requires of us. In some cases—perhaps the most controversial cases—whether an implementation of a constitutional principle contradicts the constitutional text will largely depend on (1) whether we think we have correctly identified the proper principle, (2) whether we think we have correctly identified the principle's appropriate scope and reach, and (3) whether we think the particular application at issue is a reasonable implementation of the principle.

Moreover, a particular text may enact more than one constitutional principle, and these principles may sometimes conflict. Suppose for example, that we discover that the free-speech clause protects both the principle of democratic deliberation and the principle of individual self-expression. These principles may not conflict in a wide range of cases, but they may in some cases. Here are two examples: In the first, Congress seeks to limit campaign contributions to preserve democratic deliberation and prevent corruption of democratic self-government. The democracy principle may conflict with the self-expression principle if we think that the latter includes the right to make campaign contributions of any size. In the second example, Congress seeks to ban indecent art that has no relationship to democratic deliberation. The self-expression principle will conflict with the democracy principle if we think that the latter protects only speech related to democratic deliberation and leaves other expression to the democratic political process. The text of the free-speech clause will not resolve this conflict for us—it says that Congress can make no law that abridges the freedom of speech, but we must figure out the contours of the "freedom of speech." We can resolve the conflict by preferring one principle over the other or by interpreting their scope and reach so that they do not conflict. The text may give us considerable help in some situations, but in many other cases, perhaps most cases, it will not. That is why we so often need recourse to other modalities of constitutional argument—including history, structure, precedent, consequences, and ethos—to help us out.

Similar considerations apply to structural principles that may not be tied to any particular text but that we infer from the interaction of many different texts. For example, the principle of checks and balances is advanced by specific institutional instantiations in the constitutional text. The president may veto legislation, the Senate must advise and consent to the appointment of federal judges and senior executive officers, and so on. But the principle of checking and balancing power—like the principle of separation of powers—extends beyond these specific instantiations and may apply to situations not specifically mentioned in the text. Can the president exit from treaties without congressional consent? Can Congress limit the president's ability to remove officers in independent administrative agencies, like the Federal Communications Commission or the Federal Reserve Bank? No matter which way we decide these questions, we will be extending one principle or the other to cases the text does not contemplate or provide for. In these situations, it is not clear whether the application of the principle *contradicts* the text or merely *supplements* it. Once again, the text may not be of much help, and we must turn to the other modalities to resolve the question.

Next, consider the First Amendment, whose language limits Congress. Does the First Amendment apply to the other branches of government? Can the president establish a church, or the judiciary freely issue prior restraints on publication? In Chapter 10 I argued that for structural reasons we must read "Congress," like "speech" itself, as a nonliteral usage; in the alternative, a structural principle requires that the First Amendment applies to other branches of government. Does this construction *supplement* the constitutional text or *contradict* it? The text cannot decide this question for us; instead the conclusion must follow from our judgment about the proper scope of the free-speech principle and structural assumptions about how the constitutional system should function.

I do not pretend that the distinction between contradiction and supplementation is always clear in practice. Literary theory teaches us that supplements can sometimes be "dangerous supplements"; they can either undermine or displace what they supplement, or take on a life of their own.[18] At the same time, the same literary theories teach us that we cannot always easily do without supplements; they may seem optional or extraneous but are not actually so. What appears to be merely a supplement can also prove central or crucial to the thing it supplements. This is the lesson of the First Amendment: applying the First Amendment only to "Congress" and not to the president or the courts would seriously undermine the Constitution's guarantees of religious freedom, and the protections of freedom of speech, press, petition, and assembly necessary for democratic legitimacy. Here the supplement turns out to be essential to the thing it supplements.

We should not think of the method of text and principle as a simple model in which individual principles sit beneath specific clauses or texts. Rather, constitutional principles play multiple roles, with multiple relationships to the text. A text can point to more than one principle, and sometimes these principles can conflict. Some principles derive from the interaction of multiple texts, and some principles emerge from the structure and logic of the constitutional system.

Principles undergird the constitutional text, they articulate it, they supplement it; they give unity to the entire Constitution and preserve its logic and its stability over time. The method of text and principle honors the text by recognizing the text's intimate connection to principles of many different kinds. It recognizes that one cannot do without principles in constitutional argument, even—and especially—when we seek to ground our constitutional arguments in the text's original meaning.

CHANGE

13

RETHINKING LIVING
CONSTITUTIONALISM

I began this book with a central claim: fidelity to original meaning and the idea of a living Constitution that adapts to changing times and conditions are not rival theories of constitutional interpretation; they are actually compatible positions. When we understand how and why they are compatible, we will also understand how democratically legitimate constitutional change that is faithful to the Constitution's original meaning occurs in the American constitutional system. To this end I have offered what I believe is the best account of fidelity to original meaning, framework originalism, and an approach for interpretation and construction that is faithful to original meaning, the method of text and principle. By this point I hope I have convinced you that there is a version of originalism that is consistent with the great achievements of American constitutional development: the protection of modern civil rights and civil liberties and the creation of a modern state.

Just as we need to rethink originalism, however, we also need to rethink the idea of a living Constitution. Living constitutionalism has often been more of a slogan than a theory: the claim that the Constitution adapts—and should adapt—to changing times and conditions, and reflect the evolving values of the American people.

Defenders and critics alike have generally assumed that living constitutionalism is a philosophy of judging that explains and justifies how courts should interpret the Constitution. Defenders assume that it must be a distinctive interpretive approach or method—opposed to originalism—that judges could and should consciously follow to produce better or more just decisions.[1] Critics have responded that living constitutionalism is a bad methodology that gives judges too much discretion to impose their personal preferences.[2]

I believe this way of talking is a serious mistake. The best account of a living Constitution cannot be a sort of mirror image of originalism. It cannot be a countertheory that offers particularized advice to judges about how to decide cases.

The expression "living" Constitution compares the Constitution to a living organism growing and changing in response to its environment.[3] This metaphor presupposes a process of change that involves larger social, political, and economic forces in which the Constitution-in-practice is situated. Judges cannot be at the center of this account because they do not control these forces and they could not successfully control them even if they tried. Moreover, the process of change must involve all of the various actors in the constitutional system and their responses to (and advocacy of) social, political, and economic change.

Therefore, a theory of living constitutionalism that focuses primarily on what judges should do is at odds with the very assumptions behind the idea of a living Constitution.

To rethink living constitutionalism, then, we have to begin by jettisoning the idea that it is primarily a theory about good judging. We must recognize that it is an account, to borrow a phrase, of the processes of constitutional decisionmaking,[4] and their basis in democracy and in the ideals of popular sovereignty.

Understood as an account of the processes of constitutional decisionmaking, living constitutionalism makes a great deal of sense. It also has the advantage of describing the actual history of our nation. Understood as a doctrine for correct judging, however, "living constitutionalism" is an undertheorized concept. One popular formula of living constitutionalism is that judges should adapt to changing conditions, reflect changing values, and generally keep up with the times. But such advice, directed at individual judges, is substantively empty. When judges leave issues up to the political process, they can view themselves as allowing that process to respond to changing values and times. (Think of the New Deal.) When judges discipline the political process through judicial review, they can view themselves as maintaining constitutional commitments in order to respond to changing values and times. (Think of debates about free expression or privacy.) No matter what judges do, then, they can see themselves as responding appropriately to change.

In any case, it is by no means clear why individual judges have any such obligation or responsibility to "keep up with changing times" or "reflect changing values" instead of doing what they are supposed to do, which is to interpret and apply the law as best they can. But even if judges had such a responsibility, there are many possible ways that one can "adapt to changing conditions," "reflect changing values," and "keep up with the times." One can "keep up with the times" as a liberal or as a conservative, as a secular person or as a religious person, as a technophile or as a technophobe. One simply does so in different ways. One can respond to changing times by changing one's values in the face of recalcitrant events, or by maintaining one's values in the face of trials and temptations. Civil libertarians argue for the latter position all the time, and there are many living constitutionalists among their number.

Moreover, whose account of "changing conditions," whose interpretation of "changing times," and whose version of "changing values" should judges look to? To my interpretation or to yours? Should they look to the values of contemporary liberals or contemporary conservatives? Both sets of values are constantly changing, and both of them are doing their very best to respond to changing times and circumstances.

These questions have no useful answers. If we want the idea of a living Constitution to do useful work, we must change our assumptions.

First, a theory of living constitutionalism must focus not on constitutional interpretation—ascertainment of original meaning—but on constitutional construction. Second, it must explain how constitutional construction occurs in response to constitutional politics. Third, it should not be a theory about how particular judges should decide particular cases, but rather an explanation of the role that judges and judicial review play in the process of constitutional construction. Fourth, it should not be a theory about how individual decisions are consistent or not consistent with the judicial role, but rather a theory about how the entire system of constitutional construction—including the work of the political branches, courts, political parties, social movements, interest groups, and individual citizens—is consistent with democratic legitimacy. Thus, living constitutionalism is not a theory primarily addressed to judges; it is addressed to all citizens who want to know how the Constitution-in-practice changes through constitutional construction and why these processes of constitutional change are democratically legitimate.

Throughout this book I have alluded to the processes of constitutional change. In these final two chapters I describe them in more detail.

In this chapter I offer a descriptive and interpretive account of how the processes of constitutional change occur and how they build on the framework of original meaning.

In Chapter 14, I consider whether this account is consistent with the theory of democratic legitimacy offered in Chapters 4 and 5. I argue that the processes I describe are examples of what Robert Post and Reva Siegel have called "democratic constitutionalism."[5] These processes have been built up over long periods of time; they allow citizens to take ownership of their Constitution and, although they are far from perfect, they further democratic legitimacy. Viewed from the standpoint of participants in the constitutional project, they allow the Constitution to be "our law." They give people a stake in the constitutional project, and allow them to change the Constitution-in-practice through persuasion and sustained social and political mobilizations. They create pathways for constitutional redemption and allow for the possibility of constitutional faith.

What is the connection between the idea of a living Constitution and redemptive constitutionalism? When people seek to redeem or restore the Constitution, they succeed or fail through the processes of living constitutionalism. All reform movements make use of these processes, including, perhaps ironically, the modern conservative movements associated with the philosophy of originalism that have viewed the very idea of a "living Constitution" as their mortal enemy.

In fact the debate between living constitutionalism and originalism as rival philosophies has often been a debate between liberals and conservatives *as both participate in the processes of living constitutionalism.* Constitutional liberals have used the term *living Constitution* as a way of describing their commitment to the preservation of liberal precedents and the promotion of liberal values through judicial review. Conservatives, in turn, have used the term *originalism* to explain their own constitutional commitments and vision. Politics and political visions have often driven choices about which methodology to champion. That is why contemporary liberals have tended to abhor originalism in all of its forms, fearing that it is merely a rhetorical device that allows conservatives judges to reach results they like; and contemporary conservatives have repeatedly attacked the idea of a living Constitution, concerned that it is merely cover for liberal judicial activism.

But the concepts of fidelity to original meaning and a living Constitution, correctly understood, do not correspond to either liberal or conservative ideologies. In previous chapters I have shown that original meaning originalism is perfectly consistent with the development of the modern state and the civil rights revolution. And in this chapter and the next I show that the idea of a living Constitution that adapts to changing times, conditions, and values is perfectly consistent with conservative constitutional constructions. Indeed, because conservatives have dominated American political life for the last several decades, and conservative presidents have appointed most of the federal judiciary, much of the living constitutionalism of this period has promoted conservative values and a conservative political vision.

Many of the processes that allow for constitutional constructions were themselves built through previous constitutional constructions. Like the Constitution-in-practice, they are flawed and imperfect. Like the Constitution-in-practice, we might well wonder whether they are adequate, and whether they can be improved over time. And so the questions of constitutional faith and redemption that apply to the Constitution also apply to the processes of constitutional change that Americans have developed.

Constitutional faith is crucial to a system of living constitutionalism precisely because we do not know what the future holds. There are no guarantees that the processes of constitutional change will not lead to great injustices or even political disaster. This is a consequence of the Constitution's openness to the future.[6] Advocates of conservative originalism may believe that if judges faithfully adhered to original meanings (and original expected applications), the country will be insulated from disaster. I disagree. As I have argued in this book, contemporary conservative originalism is not an alternative to the processes of living constitutionalism; it is the living constitutionalism of contemporary conservatives.

The same resources that allow for constitutional adaptation and constitutional redemption also allow for the American people to commit great injustices and bring the constitutional project to ruin. The Constitution creates a platform for a decent politics, but it cannot guarantee that politics will have a happy ending. We know from human history that institutions do not last forever; our Constitution is no different. The goal, rather, is to make the project work as long as possible in a way that is faithful to constitutional values and particularly the goals of the Preamble. We are not sure that our constitutional project will continue to succeed, but for it to succeed, we must have faith: not only in the Constitution's text, and not only in the processes of constitutional development we have inherited, but also in the work of present and future citizens. The Constitution belongs not to the dead but to the living, and the burden of securing the Constitution's success rests not on the generations that have passed away but on the present generation and the generations to come.

Living Constitutionalism as Constitutional Construction

The basic concern of living constitutionalism is constitutional construction—implementing and applying the Constitution in practice, and building out institutions to perform constitutional functions.[7] We must create doctrines and laws to concretize principles and decide cases, and we must build institutions to make the constitutional system work in practice.

We need construction in two situations. The first is when the terms of the Constitution are vague or silent on a question, and we must develop doctrines or pass laws to make its words concrete or fill in gaps.[8] The second is when we need to create laws or build institutions to fulfill constitutional purposes.[9] Both of these practices are the work of living constitutionalism.

Framework originalism requires that we interpret the Constitution according to its original meaning. Living constitutionalism concerns the process of constitutional construction. Framework originalism leaves space for future generations to build out and construct the Constitution-in-practice. Living constitutionalism occupies this space. It explains and justifies the process of building on and building out. That is how the two ideas are related, and why they do not conflict but in fact are inextricably connected.

Put this way, you might think that the original meaning and constitutional construction do not overlap at all. One simply builds on where the other leaves off. But it is not so in practice. Because constitutional construction occurs in the same political space and time as the amendment process, the two processes can sometimes substitute for each other. Vague clauses can be built out through doctrine and institution building in ways that might also be achieved through amendment. (The same is also true with various silences and gaps in the original Constitution.) Multiple pathways for change are a characteristic feature of our constitutional system. Nevertheless, the processes of amendment and construction are not identical, and what each can achieve in practice does not always overlap.

Some kinds of changes—like the abolition of the Electoral College or altering the length of the president's term of office—cannot easily be

achieved through construction; they require amendment. Constructions may be less durable than amendments: interbranch understandings can be altered through practice, statutes can be repealed and
doctrinal constructions overturned, distinguished, or made irrelevant.
Conversely, amendment may be an awkward and cumbersome way to
respond to certain problems, revise previous doctrinal constructions,
create new rules, or promote wholesale changes in government. Constructing doctrine gradually through case-law development and creating framework statutes and new institutions may be a more nimble
and effective method.

Today people generally associate "living constitutionalism" with judicial decisions; but the political branches actually produce most living
constitutionalism. Most of what courts do in constitutional development
responds to these political constitutional constructions. Courts largely
rationalize, legitimate, and supplement what the political branches do,
creating new doctrines along the way.[10]

The very concept of a "living" Constitution arose in the early twentieth century due to innovations by Congress and by state and local
governments in constructing early versions of the regulatory state.[11] At
first federal courts resisted these changes, but eventually rationalized
and legitimated them in a series of landmark decisions that are now
foundational to modern constitutional law.[12] But such judicial decisions are only the tip of the iceberg. We should understand these changes—
and living constitutionalism itself—both as a series of doctrines and as
a set of new laws and institutions that the doctrines upheld. Living
constitutionalism in the New Deal required adjusting older constitutional doctrines to explain and justify these changes in how governments governed.[13]

Landmark precedents like the New Deal decisions became durable precisely because so much of the developing structure of governance depended on their construction of the Constitution. This is the central insight of living constitutionalism: state building by the political branches
and judicial constructions are, generally speaking, mutually productive
and mutually supportive. To use the metaphor of the living constitution,
they grow up together. That is why the New Deal precedents are durable.
We have not built upon them because we think they are correct; we think
they are correct because we have built so much upon them.

The example of the New Deal is hardly exceptional. Living constitutionalism is usually as much the product of the political branches

(including administrative agencies and state and local governments) and changing social and cultural practices as it is the product of federal judicial decisions. Social and political movements express values and press for change both in culture and in politics. The political branches create new laws and institutions, and courts make sense of these constructions. Courts also ratify changes in social mores and institutional practices, some of which are already reflected in new laws and institutions, or in the abolition and reform of older ones. The sexual revolution and the movement for women's liberation are two obvious examples of how constitutional change is prefigured by changes in civil society. Courts can usually do little to block widespread cultural change. Courts may slow down drastic political change in the short run, especially if their members were appointed by different parties or in different regimes; but generally they rationalize and authorize these changes over time. The political branches, in turn, continue to build out the state based on the justifications offered by the judiciary.

The New Deal Court legitimated the creation of the administrative and welfare state, particularly after Franklin Roosevelt was able to appoint new justices. It did so by reinterpreting and expanding federal and state power to regulate the economy and engage in redistributive programs, and by creating new procedures to rationalize the expansion of administrative agencies. The members of the Warren Court were largely in sync with the bipartisan liberal coalition that emerged in the 1960s. The Warren Court upheld new federal laws that prohibited local discrimination, supervised state voting practices, and brought regional majorities (especially in the South) in line with the dominant liberal values of national politics in the 1960s.[14] After the political mood of the country changed, the Rehnquist Court cooperated with the ascendant conservative movement, promoting state regulatory autonomy and making it easier for government to support majority religions.[15]

When federal courts exercise judicial review to strike down laws, they often work in cooperation with the dominant national political coalition or promote the values of national political elites. Federal courts often impose national values on regional and local majorities, and strike down statutes passed by older political regimes that are inconsistent with the current national political coalition's values.[16] Federal courts also respond, over long periods of time, to significant changes in constitutional culture produced by successful social and political mobilizations.

When most states have adopted a social policy, the Supreme Court tends to ratify these dominant values in new constitutional constructions.

The Court's 2003 decision in *Lawrence v. Texas*[17] protected the rights of homosexuals under the due process clause only after the vast majority of states had decriminalized sodomy and new attitudes about homosexuality had swept the country.[18] The Court decided *Brown v. Board of Education*[19] only after significant changes in race relations following World War II, and after most states had already ended *de jure* racial segregation in public schools.[20] The Truman administration had desegregated the armed forces and pushed for civil rights in 1948; it had asked the Supreme Court to overrule *Plessy v. Ferguson*[21] in 1950 and again in 1952 in the first round of litigation in *Brown v. Board of Education*.[22] After the Republicans took office in 1953, Dwight Eisenhower's Justice Department, led by Attorney General Herbert Brownell, supported the Truman administration's position, demonstrating to the Court that administrations from both major political parties concurred.[23]

Just as federal courts usually cooperate, in the long run, with the dominant forces in national politics, national politicians have regularly buttressed and supported the institution of judicial review and the judiciary's work of constitutional construction. Keith Whittington points out that only a small number of presidents have openly resisted the Supreme Court's ability to interpret the Constitution,[24] and these arguments generally cease as soon as these presidents have placed like-minded jurists on the bench.[25] Most presidents have actively supported judicial review, or at least have seen it as a better choice than the alternatives. In fact, presidents have regularly delegated constitutional constructions and even substantial amounts of policymaking to the courts.[26]

Although presidents routinely assert their right to interpret the Constitution in the normal exercise of their powers, they hardly ever compete with the courts for final authority over the Constitution's meaning except in rare historical circumstances: This occurs when a new president, like Thomas Jefferson or Franklin Roosevelt, seeks to repudiate a previous and discredited constitutional regime and faces a judiciary controlled by adherents of the old order.[27] The attack on judicial authority, however, is only temporary. As soon as the president can stock the judiciary with ideological allies, presidential challenges to the courts tend to cease because the courts generally support and legitimate what the president is doing.[28] As a result, Whittington explains, "Presidents and political leaders have generally preferred that the Court take the responsibility for securing constitutional fidelity."[29]

When presidents like Harry Truman or Martin Van Buren are affiliated with the existing constitutional regime of their predecessors

(Franklin Roosevelt, Andrew Jackson) and try to further its goals, they usually face a court already stocked with political allies. Hence, they generally support the federal courts' powers of judicial review and constitutional construction. In fact, courts generally help presidents enforce the regime's constitutional values against political outliers and local and regional majorities.[30] Lyndon Johnson strongly supported the Warren Court for precisely this reason.

Finally, when presidents (like Bill Clinton, Richard Nixon, or Grover Cleveland) face a hostile political environment and/or a Congress controlled by the other party, they usually find that it is better to ally themselves with the power of the courts to restrain Congress and protect their prerogatives than to try to challenge two different branches of government at the same time. In difficult political environments "the law and the judiciary may be the best defense that a president has."[31]

Mark Graber puts the point succinctly: "[a]n institution that routinely promotes presidential ambitions is no more countermajoritarian than the presidency" itself.[32] And even during the rare moments when the president attacks judicial authority, important parts of the national political process, including members of Congress, often support the courts against the president, because they prefer judicial construction to complete presidential control over constitutional meaning.[33]

When Alexander Bickel famously argued that "judicial review is a deviant institution in the American democracy,"[34] he gave insufficient weight to these majoritarian features of judicial review. One of the great ironies of Bickel's famous formulation of the "counter-majoritarian difficulty"[35] is that he offered it during a period when the Supreme Court was working hand in hand with the national political coalition and imposing its values on regional majorities.[36] The Supreme Court may have been nationalist, but it was not particularly countermajoritarian.

Equally ironic is that Bickel offered his diagnosis in 1962, at the beginning of a wave of popular constitutionalism that revolutionized American constitutional doctrines. America was in the early stages of powerful political mobilizations for civil rights on behalf of blacks and women, and significant changes in public attitudes about free expression and sexuality. In hindsight, it is difficult to see the work of the federal courts in this period as standing apart from these popular movements. These mobilizations, in turn, were met by countermobilizations, especially after the 1968 election, leading to new judicial appointments that once again strongly affected the shape of constitutional doctrine. Whatever else one can say about this tumultuous period, the courts were clearly responding to changes in constitutional culture created by sustained political mobilizations. Thus, ironically, the period in which Bickel asserted that the courts were countermajoritarian featured some of the most powerful examples of democratic constitutionalism in American history.

Writing at the very beginning of the civil rights and sexual revolutions, however, Bickel did not fully recognize these trends. His model of a countermajoritarian Court was no doubt influenced by the constitutional struggle over the New Deal, which was among the most salient examples for constitutional scholars of his generation. He imposed that model on the events of his day. Yet even here Bickel drew the wrong lesson from history: The struggle over the New Deal is not the story of a countermajoritarian Court; it is the story of a federal judiciary that gradually adjusts in response to changing political circumstances, sustained popular mobilizations, and new judicial appointments. As we have seen, judicial resistance to the New Deal was relatively short-lived. Within the space of a few years, the Supreme Court backed down from its initial opposition and began to legitimate the new constitutional regime.

The Supreme Court Is a Player, Not a Mirror

The practice of judicial review is integrated into democratic processes and does not stand fully outside them. Courts work in conjunction with other parts of the national political system to create new constitutional constructions. But we should not confuse these facts with a simplistic claim that federal courts (or the Supreme Court) "mirror" or "reflect" popular opinion or are simply the faithful servants of a dominant national coalition. The metaphors of "mirror" and "reflection" are highly misleading, suggesting passivity and mere reproduction. Although courts are surely influenced by the same changes that influence the public generally, I certainly do not claim that judicial decisions will always move in lockstep either with popular opinion (however measured) or with the wishes of the president or Congress. Federal courts with life tenure remain relatively independent from day-to-day political influences, but not from long-run political trends. They are independent actors that mutually influence other actors in the political system, and in the long run this system of mutual influence helps maintain democratic legitimacy. Thus, neither Bickel's model of countermajoritarian intransigence nor a simple model of mirroring or following public opinion grasps how courts and the political branches interact in producing constitutional constructions. Here are eight reasons why the mirror metaphor oversimplifies:

First, one of the most important mechanisms by which the political branches influence the federal judiciary is what Sanford Levinson and I have called *partisan entrenchment*.[37] When a party wins the White House, the president can seek to stock the federal judiciary with like-minded jurists. (The president's choices, of course, are also shaped by the balance of power in the Senate, which must confirm judicial appointments.) Because judges enjoy life tenure, they will normally serve for many years, extending the influence of the political forces that produced their appointment.

Presidents engage in partisan entrenchment for at least four reasons. First, they seek judicial partners who will support their policy initiatives, as Franklin Roosevelt did during the New Deal. Second, presidents seek a judiciary that will enforce national values against state and local outliers. This was President Johnson's goal during the civil rights revolution. Third, presidents may want a judiciary that will take on difficult questions—like slavery or abortion—that would split their governing coalitions, and that will resolve contentious issues like school prayer, pornography, or campaign finance so that the president and his party can avoid direct responsibility. Examples include President George W. Bush's decision to sign the McCain-Feingold campaign finance act while leaving it to a conservative federal judiciary to strike down parts of it. Fourth, presidents want judges who will protect their constitutional and policy goals after they leave office or their party loses electoral power, and will check new political insurgencies. This was the goal of John Adams and the Federalist Party after the 1800 election, when the Republicans took power.

Partisan entrenchment is an imprecise strategy, and often it is only partially successful. Presidents may lack qualified candidates who match their desired combination of goals. The Senate—or presidential obligations to various constituencies—may strongly shape presidents' choice of candidates. Given the contingencies of when judges retire or die, some presidents may not be able to make many Supreme Court appointments, and the appointments they do make may not alter the identity of the swing or median justices. As time passes, the effects of partisan entrenchment weaken, because new issues arise that were not salient at the time an appointment was made. Justices' and judges' views may also shift somewhat over time as the political context evolves. In addition, changed circumstances may sometimes make judicial views that once seemed liberal quite conservative, and vice versa. For example, Felix Frankfurter, the liberal apostle of judicial restraint during the 1930s, was regarded as a conservative by the 1950s because he applied his philosophy of restraint in the civil liberties cases that were central to that period.

Nevertheless, appointments by successive presidencies eventually change the direction of the Supreme Court—sometimes slowly, sometimes more quickly, depending on circumstances. Over time these appointments help produce the Supreme Court's tendency to cooperate, in the long run, with the dominant political forces of the day. But partisan entrenchment does not make the Court simply a mirror of public opinion. Because of life tenure, the federal judiciary is staffed by persons appointed over many years by different presidents and different parties. This means that the federal judiciary, and especially the Supreme Court of the United States, represents the values and commitments of national political elites stretched over a generation or more, rather than those of current political forces. Put simply, the federal judiciary represents a temporally extended majority rather than a current majority. This feature of judicial appointments is often important in understanding why a majority of the Supreme Court sometimes resists, delays, or inhibits what national majorities want to do. A Supreme Court majority dominated by conservative appointments from past administrations may look skeptically on legislation passed by a later, more liberal president and Congress: this is what happened during Franklin Roosevelt's first term. On the other hand, a Supreme Court majority consisting of liberal justices appointed over many years may find it easy to cooperate with a newly empowered political coalition of liberal politicians. This is what happened during the civil rights revolution of the 1960s.

In short, the phenomenon of partisan entrenchment leads courts to cooperate with the dominant forces of American politics only in the long run; they may sometimes resist in the short run, depending on who appointed them. Faced with rapid changes in basic assumptions or governing practices, courts can act as conservators of past constitutional values. The system of federal courts often slows down and temporizes change until ascendant forces have shown sustained support over time. Then, partly as a result of changed political circumstances and partly as a result of new judicial appointments, courts make sense of and rationalize the new regime, working out the details in new constitutional doctrines.

The second reason the mirror metaphor oversimplifies is that federal judges are more responsive to political elites than to public opinion; that is because federal judges are generally drawn from elites and regularly interact with them.[38] Sometimes there is a difference between what political elites want and what a majority of the public wants. Despite their claim to stand for all of the people of the nation, presidents may not accurately represent mainstream public opinion; instead they may seek to promote their ideological goals through judicial appointments and through control over the federal bureaucracy.[39] This may lead to judicial appointments that are significantly more conservative or liberal than the center of public opinion.

Third, in addition to promoting partisan entrenchment, civil society organizations and social and political mobilizations affect federal judicial decisionmaking in other ways. Scholars like Charles Epp and Steven Teles have emphasized that successful legal change needs more than opportunities to appoint new judges. It also needs a support structure with various institutions in civil society—like think tanks, foundations, churches, religious groups, political groups, universities, law schools, law firms, and public interest organizations. These institutions generate concepts, people, and legal strategies. They offer new ideas and theories for litigators, administrators, and politicians; they produce potential judicial candidates for presidents to appoint; and they generate test cases for courts to consider.[40]

Civil society organizations also shape popular and elite opinion, and especially the views of legal professionals, who are often the most influential reference group for federal judges. Success in the federal courts by groups as disparate as the women's movement, the gay rights movement, religious conservatives, and corporate interests has often depended on the resources available to civil society organizations.

The breadth and diversity of this support structure—or the lack of a support structure—may importantly affect who becomes a federal judge, what kinds of cases judges hear, how often they hear them, and how they decide them. The better funded and organized these civil society organizations are, the more influence they can bring to bear in shaping constitutional culture, the opinions of political elites, the pool of judicial candidates, and the dockets of the federal courts.

Fourth, federal courts are active participants in the national political coalition of their day rather than simply servants of national political elites. When control of the national government is divided, a Supreme Court majority has greater discretion to tilt in the direction of one branch or another. Usually the Supreme Court tilts toward the presidency, but not always. After the Republicans gained control of both houses of Congress following the 1994 election, for example, the Rehnquist Court's conservative majority became increasingly active in reshaping doctrine in the areas of federalism and religion, cooperating with the values and interests of congressional Republicans.

During some periods of American history, one party has dominated national politics, and/or parties have been ideologically heterogeneous, so that it was possible for a cross-party coalition to dominate. (An example is the bipartisan coalition of racial liberals that dominated national politics in the middle of the twentieth century during the civil rights revolution.) In both cases, it is possible to speak of a dominant national coalition subsisting for periods of time. But in other periods, like the present, the parties may be sharply polarized and intensely competitive, and neither party may be able to dominate politics for very long. In such highly polarized and competitive periods, the federal courts have comparatively more slack.[41] Both houses of Congress and the president can claim to represent popular will, and, depending on its membership, the Supreme Court may tilt toward one group of political elites rather than another.

For the same reason, however, during periods of intense political competition where neither party dominates national politics, the federal courts will be filled with judges of very different persuasions. When politics is polarized, a Supreme Court staffed by jurists of different parties (and judges appointed when polarization was less marked) is likely to produce positions more moderate than those of the two major parties.[42] Although this will make neither side's partisans entirely happy, it may tend to produce more centrist results. At the very least it may produce constructions that check the most energetic or radical assertions by either side until one party or another is able to win a sufficient number of elections to staff most of the federal judiciary.

Fifth, although we tend to identify "federal courts" with the U.S. Supreme Court (and therefore sometimes speak of "the Court" as if it were the judiciary), there is not a single federal court in the United States, but a system of federal courts, whose membership results from successive waves of presidential appointments. At any point in time, therefore, federal judges may hold a variety of different views about important constitutional issues. For example, individual federal district court judges, who do not have to deliberate with anyone else, may be strongly ideological and reach strongly opposed results. In the long run, conformity in federal law occurs because district courts must work within the parameters set by higher-court precedents, and because litigants can appeal district court judgments to multimember panels of circuit court judges (with the further possibility of *en banc* review) and, in a small number of cases, to a multimember U.S. Supreme Court. At the same time, ideologically diverse lower federal courts play an important role in considering new kinds of legal claims and legal arguments, bringing them before the Supreme Court, and thus helping to shape its agenda.[43] When we speak about what "courts" do in the long run, therefore, we are talking about the systemic effects of the federal judiciary as a whole, rather than the actions of individual federal judges.

Sixth, federal courts, like federal government bureaucrats generally, enjoy greater slack and can exercise greater discretion in areas where there is not significant public attention; decisions in some of these technical areas may not fall along ideological fault lines. Indeed, the public may have no decided opinion on many of the technical issues of law that federal courts routinely decide but that significantly shape constitutional construction in the long run. Political entrepreneurs, nevertheless, may attempt to focus public attention on some of these decisions, in an attempt to change constitutional culture and put pressure on the courts.

Seventh, the political branches, and especially the president, delegate policymaking to the federal courts on a range of issues—such as criminal procedure—because they do not want direct responsibility for them.[44] The very fact of this delegation means that members of the dominant national coalition will not always be happy with each and every decision rendered.

Eighth, Supreme Court decisions do not simply mirror popular or elite opinion because they influence politics, creating new political opportunities and shaping political and social movement agendas. Court decisions give politicians legitimating excuses, on the one hand, and political targets for mobilization, on the other. They reshape the terrain of political combat and social movement activism.

Politicians—and especially presidents—can leave certain questions up to courts (and conveniently blame them for doing what politicians themselves are unwilling to do); in the alternative, they can use courts to legitimate their actions (or their failures to act).

Political and social movements can use recent court decisions—especially decisions where they appear to have lost—to mobilize the public and energize constituents. When political entrepreneurs make court decisions highly salient, they can sometimes influence voter preferences and the results of elections.

Finally, federal court decisions affect future political struggles because they often have symbolic significance that changes people's understandings of politics; or political entrepreneurs can give decisions symbolic significance after the fact. (Examples might include *Roe v. Wade*, *Miranda v. Arizona*, and *Lochner v. New York*.) Equally important, federal court decisions can change the law. Changing the law, in turn, may undermine certain strategies of legal and political action while opening up new possibilities for others. Moreover, by deciding cases in a particular order and at particular times, courts affect the agendas of social movements and politicians. They affect people's understandings of what is politically possible and politically legitimate.

Institutional Constraints on the Judiciary

Even though federal court decisions do not precisely mirror public opinion, the same institutional features of American law and politics outlined above significantly constrain the direction of judicial construction.[45] These institutional features explain why, in practice, living constitutionalism does not give judges unfettered discretion. It is not because legal materials prevent innovation, for the history of American constitutional law demonstrates that, over long periods of time, they can be quite flexible. Rather, it is because institutional and structural elements in the political system tend to hem in judicial constructions.

I noted some of these constraints in Chapters 1 and 5: The Supreme Court is a multimember body whose decisions in close cases tend to be resolved by the median or swing justices, whose identity (and position at the median), in turn, is produced by successive judicial appointments. Justices and lower federal court judges are legal professionals, and professional culture demands that their decisions remain in the political and cultural mainstream and that their opinions manifest coherent professional reasoning from case to case. Lower courts are further hemmed in by appellate court and Supreme Court precedents. Additional constraints include the symbiotic relationship between courts and the political branches just described, elite and popular opinion, and above all, control of the appointments process by the president and Senate.[46]

Collectively, these factors tend to guarantee that judicial innovations are likely to occur only within certain boundaries. That is why the process of judicial construction of doctrine is constrained despite the Constitution's vague clauses and ambiguous silences. The Constitution's open-ended language may seem indeterminate, but at any point in time it is a constrained indeterminacy.

The fact that judicial decisions occur within certain boundaries, however, does not mean that the boundaries themselves may not change over time. And they do change, moving professional legal conceptions of reasonableness along with them. Social movements, political parties, and interest groups vie with each other to influence popular and elite views about the Constitution. Social and political mobilizations seek to alter what is off-the-wall and on-the-wall in constitutional culture and eventually in professional legal thought.[47] The federal judicial appointments process also reflects a tug-of-war between different social and political constituencies. Partisan entrenchment in the judiciary, combined with changing popular attitudes and shifts in constitutional culture, eventually affects judicial decisionmaking using vague texts. Thus, as I describe in more detail in Chapter 14, the processes of living constitutionalism gradually translate constitutional politics into constitutional law.

These political and cultural influences can push doctrine to the left as well as to the right. Some of the most powerful political and social mobilizations in the past forty years have been conservative, and therefore it is no surprise that many constitutional doctrines reflect contemporary conservative ideas. Political conservatives have influenced political culture for the past generation, and have enjoyed sufficient political clout to staff most of the federal judiciary and a majority of the positions on the Supreme Court. The same basic features of constitutional politics that led courts to recognize the rights of gays in *Lawrence v. Texas* also produced recognition of an individual right to bear arms in *District of Columbia v. Heller.*[48] Indeed, the very same weather vane, the swing justice, Anthony Kennedy, was the fifth and deciding vote in both decisions.

In short, the judiciary cooperates with the political branches because of institutional features of democratic politics. Living constitutionalism is a process of argument and persuasion in politics and culture that is eventually reflected in law. If you don't like the living Constitution you get, you should be working harder to get the national politics you like, because that is the engine of constitutional construction and constitutional change.

The system of living constitutionalism does not depend on judges of impeccable character any more than it depends on the good character of legislators and presidents. Indeed, as critics of the federal judiciary often remind us, the members of the federal judiciary may not be wiser or more moral than the political process itself. Even so, the framers of our Constitution recognized that multiple institutions that compete with and check each other can add to the legitimacy of the political system. Different institutional roles foster different role moralities and perspectives. The clash of these positions restrains all of the participants in the constitutional system. We can best understand the judiciary not as a special font of wisdom or political morality but as an institution of constitutional development with a distinctive institutional role and professional ethos that competes and cooperates with constitutional development by the other branches. The judiciary generally cooperates with policies that demonstrate sustained popular support at the national level, but it also usually acts as a check on radical constitutional innovation that lacks sustained support. These judicial functions serve the larger goals of constitutionalism and thus contribute to the democratic legitimacy of the political system as a whole, even if particular members of the judiciary do not possess judgment superior to that of most members of the national political process.

The system of living constitutionalism that has developed in the United States is hardly without its flaws. It may produce very unjust results, especially in the short run. In addition, its long-run democratic responsiveness is imperfect and could be improved. For example, I have argued that partisan entrenchment is one of the most important mechanisms that helps ensure democratic responsiveness in the long run. But the effects of partisan entrenchment depend on judges regularly leaving the bench. Lower federal court judges have incentives to take senior status, freeing up spots for new appointments, and helping to ensure more or less continuous appointments of new judges by new presidents. A similar system, however, does not apply to the Supreme Court, and since the 1970s Supreme Court justices have tended to be appointed younger, live longer, and remain longer on the bench than at any other point in the nation's history. For instance, for most of the nation's history, a new slot opened up on the average every two years or so; but from 1994 to 2005 there were no vacancies at all.[49] These changes give contemporary presidents fewer opportunities to affect the composition of the Supreme Court; they increase the role of luck in determining which presidents will have a chance to make appointments, and they make the Supreme Court more of a drag on constitutional change. Fewer and less regularly spaced Supreme Court appointments mean that other institutional features of the system must do more of the work of keeping the federal court system in line with national values.

I believe that it is possible to reform these practices consistent with the constitutional text. For example, Congress could give each president a Supreme Court appointment every two years and specify that the quorum for deciding appeals will consist of the nine justices most junior in service. Nothing in the constitutional text prevents Congress from structuring the Supreme Court more like the circuit courts, in which the panels that hear and decide cases consist of subsets of the total number of judges in a circuit. Under the proposed reforms, the more senior justices would continue to hold their federal judicial appointments until retirement; they would help select cases for the docket, sit on lower courts by designation, and hear Supreme Court appeals when more junior justices were disqualified or recused.[50]

These reforms would encourage justices to retire earlier. They would also encourage presidents to pick judges based on their ability rather than their youth. This would open up a much broader range of possible candidates who might serve the nation. Currently presidents rarely consider anyone older than their mid-fifties for a Supreme Court appointment, because they want their appointees to stay on the Court as long as possible. Finally, if national politicians know that each president will receive two appointments per term and that the justices selected will decide most cases in their first eighteen years of service, this may lower the political stakes of Supreme Court appointments; and it may help make them less politically fraught and polarizing events.[51]

Although I believe these reforms are constitutional, they may not be realized for some time, if at all. My arguments about the democratic legitimacy of the current system of living constitutionalism should not be confused with the claim that the system could not be made more legitimate. It can, and it should.

Varieties of Constitutional Construction

Living constitutionalism, I have argued, is primarily a theory about the processes of constitutional development produced by the interaction of the courts with the political branches. It is a descriptive and normative theory of the processes of constitutional construction. It explains how change occurs, and it gives an account of why that process is democratically legitimate. To understand living constitutionalism, therefore, we need to understand constitutional construction. And we must begin not with courts—which usually react and respond—but with constitutional constructions by the people's elected representatives.

Political actors engage in constitutional construction when they elaborate and enforce constitutional values by creating new institutions, laws, and governing practices. Constitutional construction by political actors overlaps with the ordinary processes of policy and lawmaking, and it may be futile to try to separate them out in every case.[52] A particular piece of legislation may simultaneously promote the political agenda of a party and implement constitutional values; a new institution may simultaneously promote policy goals and flesh out constitutional structures.

For example, the acts that created the various parts of the executive branch to carry out programs and administer laws are constitutional constructions; so too is the creation of the Office of the Attorney General[53] (and later the Department of Justice) to advise the president on legal matters and to defend the government in court.[54] The construction of the national security state in the late 1940s and early 1950s involved the transformation of American defense policy: a permanent standing army, the dispersal of American troops throughout the globe, and the creation of the Department of Defense, the National Security Council, the Central Intelligence Agency and other institutions for surveillance and intelligence gathering.[55] These innovations had constitutional overtones: they changed expectations about how and when Congress and the president would use military force and exert influence overseas.

Political actors also engage in constitutional construction when their decisions and actions create precedents for constitutionally permissible activities, like the Louisiana Purchase, the First and Second Banks of the United States, or the creation of the Federal Reserve System. Political actors can also create precedents about what is not constitutionally permitted, like understandings about when filibusters may be used, when laws or budget appropriations may be kept secret, or the proper grounds for impeachment.[56] Some of the most important constitutional constructions create precedents by articulating constitutional values in new legislation or new institutions, like Congress's passage of New Deal legislation, the chartering of a national bank, and the creation of independent federal agencies. Each of these reinterpreted the scope and reach of federal powers.

Political actors also engage in constitutional construction when they create or modify constitutional norms and understandings. Examples include whether it is permissible for the president to veto legislation based on policy disagreement or only constitutional objections, what practical standards Congress will use for impeachments, and how much deference Congress should give to cabinet and judicial nominations. Sometimes constitutional construction involves filling in constitutional silences through constitutional practice, like the decision to adopt first-past-the-post voting systems or secret ballots.

Some constitutional construction involves forging compromises between different parts of the federal government—or between the states and the federal government—about their respective duties, obligations, and prerogatives. These compromises may lead to new understandings about federalism and the separation of powers.[57] As different parts of the government struggle with each other, push back at each other, and develop new expectations, they construct new constitutional norms or modify old ones. Examples might include the multiple compromises about protective tariffs during the antebellum era, the admission of states to the Union, and the regulation of slavery in the territories. More recent examples are the president's increasing authority to initiate legislation and control the budgeting process, the creation of a vast range of classified intelligence activities with secret budgets to pay for them and secret regulations to govern them, and the change in relative authority between Congress and the president in the conduct of foreign affairs and the use of military force.

The political branches build out the Constitution through everyday politics—passing legislation, issuing regulations, and striking political deals. In addition, constitutional culture and constitutional understandings evolve through arguments and mobilizations occurring in ordinary politics. This means that in practice it is useless to try to draw clear boundaries between activities that in hindsight we would label constitutional construction and ordinary political activity. Potentially almost all political and governmental activity could be constitutional construction.

Often we may only know what counts later on when institutions become settled and practices and precedents become established. The very notion of constitutional construction involves an interpretive understanding of previous political activity as helping to build out the Constitution and its related institutions.

For example, Congress engages in construction when it passes laws that interpret the Constitution. However, every congressional enactment passed under the commerce power, and every appropriation under the general welfare clause, involves an implicit interpretation of these clauses, whether or not any court ever considers them. Every appointment of an inferior officer, indeed, even the purchase of a new stapler in a regional office of the Social Security Administration, presumes the political power to act. Should we regard all of these activities as constitutional constructions? As an interpretive matter, we would not, if the legality of these practices seems clearly established. The purchase of the stapler presumes constitutional power to act, but the activity now seems routine as opposed to a practice of institution building.

Nevertheless, the continuous repetition of actions and tasks believed to be uncontroversially authorized (and self-conscious forbearance from actions generally believed to be unconstitutional) is not unimportant. It helps reproduce expectations about the authority of constitutional constructions and helps make constitutional constructions durable over time. The everyday activities of administrative agencies or the institutions of national security continuously enmesh these constitutional constructions in lived political experience; they reproduce understandings and expectations about their continued existence and their continued authority. Long-lived constitutional constructions—like those involved in the regulatory state or the national security state—are not simply established in a single moment. They are repeatedly performed in practice, and expectations about them are continuously reproduced in constitutional culture, confirming and reinforcing their durable character.

It follows that even minuscule tasks and quotidian legislation could in theory contribute to constitutional construction, if they help forge new understandings of the relative powers of the different branches or of the federal and state governments under the Constitution. The president's power, for example, has sometimes increased by slow accretion over two centuries. Expectations about what presidents and their administrations can do (and must do) have expanded through a series of acts great and small, some of which were actively challenged but most of which were not. In hindsight we might see the collection of these activities as part of a long-term process of constitutional construction of the executive branch.

In like fashion, the everyday micropractices of race relations, gender roles, and sexuality in civil society cumulatively may change the public's attitudes about the cultural meaning of equality; in turn this may reshape the American people's understandings of equal protection and constitutionally protected liberty. In hindsight these practices may form part of—or significantly influence—a long-term practice of constitutional construction.

In sum, it is best not to worry too much about where constitutional construction leaves off and merely ordinary politics begins. The key point, instead, is to recognize how practices within the constitutional scheme can subtly adjust the scheme itself in addition to the formal processes of constitutional amendment.

The Role of Courts in Constitutional Construction

Courts also build institutions through creating the federal judiciary's administrative structure, and through developing rules of standing, justiciability, evidence, and procedure.[58] But perhaps the most important role of federal courts in the system of constitutional construction is legitimating and rationalizing the work of the national political process and its constitutional constructions. Generally speaking, the practice of living constitutionalism by courts is a process of doctrinal construction that rationalizes and supplements constitutional constructions by the political branches, and responds to changes in political and cultural values in the nation as a whole. Although courts sometimes push back at what Congress and the president do, their constitutional constructions are usually more cooperative than competitive.

Courts engage in constitutional construction in several ways. First, courts rationalize new constitutional constructions by the political branches through creating new doctrines. Rationalization has a dual meaning. On the one hand, it means providing reasons why the constructions are faithful to the Constitution; on the other, it means subjecting these constructions to reasons—articulating rules and principles of judgment—that will presumably be binding on the political branches in the future. Rationalization is thus both a form of legitimation and a form of policing. Courts express and articulate the constitutional norms and values of the dominant national coalition in constitutional doctrine and thereby help justify and constrain them. They redescribe political values in terms of legal rules and principles that will apply to future cases. They synthesize new values and institutions with the past by reinterpreting the past constitutional commitments of previous generations, showing how what the political branches are doing is actually faithful both to the Constitution and to the past. To do this, courts may describe past commitments in new ways or at a higher level of generality, often drawing on the entire history of readings of the Constitution by political and judicial actors.

In giving reasons and synthesizing present with past, courts also set boundaries on what the political branches can do. Thus, the process of rationalization is Janus-faced. It justifies constitutional construction by the political branches, but that justification comes with a price: The courts require the political branches to act within a set of principles, rules, and reasons that courts construct in order to maintain their legitimacy and the legitimacy of the political system.

Many of the most important decisions of the federal courts rationalize constructions by the political branches in precisely this way: They make sense of these constructions and legitimate them while subjecting them to legal authority created by courts; this, in turn, legitimates similar actions politicians may take in the future. Thus, following the New Deal the Supreme Court responded to the passage of the Social Security Act, the Fair Labor Standards Act, and other legislation by upholding these new assertions of federal power. It legitimated the emerging regulatory and welfare state that had already been created in politics, and gave doctrinal explanations for how new legislation could also pass constitutional muster.[59] The Administrative Procedure Act,[60] in turn, helped articulate the values of due process and the relationship of Article III courts to the explosion of federal administrative agencies. During the civil rights revolution the Court upheld new civil rights statutes, once again explaining why Congress's actions were permissible and establishing how future civil rights laws would be judged. Many of the landmark decisions of American constitutional history, from *McCulloch v. Maryland*[61] to *United States v. Darby*[62] to *Katzenbach v. Morgan*,[63] have this dual character. Over time, courts work out the logical consequences of the value commitments of the new regime, as well as its landmark precedents, and synthesize them with the work of previous regimes, making them appear as coherent as possible.

Even when the Supreme Court seems to disagree with the president and Congress, it can ultimately rationalize and legitimate their constructions. During the 2000s the Supreme Court repeatedly rejected parts of the Bush administration's detention policies in the war on terror.[64] But the ultimate effect of these decisions was to legitimate the president's power to detain enemy combatants with only minimal due process protections; and Congress responded to the Court's invalidation of the Bush administration's military commissions by creating new military commissions in the Military Commissions Acts of 2006 and 2009.

Second, as noted previously, much federal judicial review is directed at state and local government officials. Federal courts cooperate with the dominant forces in national politics by policing and disciplining those who do not share the dominant coalition's values; they impose the values of national majorities on regional or local majorities. These decisions are countermajoritarian only from a local or regional perspective.

Two examples of this phenomenon that I noted previously are *Brown v. Board of Education* and *Lawrence v. Texas*. *Brown* required southern majorities to accept the constitutional values of the dominant North; *Lawrence* required the remaining thirteen states to decriminalize same-sex sodomy. In enforcing national values, the Supreme Court often looks to the direction of change in state practices to determine the meaning of vague clauses like the Eighth Amendment's cruel and unusual punishments clause. Not surprisingly, disputes in these cases often turn on whether the Court has adequately recognized a genuine trend, and whether the trend marks a truly enduring constitutional value or merely reflects a temporary and revisable policy preference.[65]

Along the same lines, courts apply vague clauses and fill in gaps and silences in the Constitution in response to long-term changes in social attitudes that have become reflected in national politics. During the sexual revolution, for example, the federal courts promoted liberal values by loosening legal restraints on pornography[66] and by protecting the right of married couples and single persons to use contraceptives.[67] After social and religious conservatives began to dominate American politics in the 1980s, the Supreme Court revised its establishment clause doctrines, making it easier for governments to support religious schools and create voucher programs.[68] It interpreted the free-speech clause to allow private religious groups to hold prayer services after hours in public schools and to engage in religious expression on government property.[69]

Third, federal courts sometimes cooperate with the reigning national political coalition by limiting or striking down laws that reflect an older coalition's values. Following the Republican takeover of Congress in 1995, the conservative majority on the Rehnquist Court tilted toward the views of the Congress led by House Speaker Newt Gingrich. It created a new set of doctrines promoting federalism. It also began to limit or strike down civil rights statutes passed by the previous Democratic-controlled Congress, including parts of the 1994 Violence Against Women Act, which had been passed just before the Republican takeover.[70] People often point to *Dred Scott v. Sandford*[71] as a rare example of the Supreme Court holding a federal law unconstitutional in the period before the Civil War.[72] Not surprisingly, it invalidated an older law: the Missouri Compromise of 1820, a statute that reflected an older set of political assumptions about slavery, and that had been repealed by Congress in the Compromise of 1850.[73]

Fourth, federal courts cooperate with national politicians by taking responsibility—and thus the political heat—for decisions that members of the dominant coalition cannot agree on and that would potentially split the coalition.[74] Decisions on abortion and Internet pornography are recent examples. Moderate and conservative politicians, particularly in the Republican Party, may want to avoid casting votes that would criminalize abortion entirely; *Roe v. Wade*[75] takes that question off the table. Instead, they are perfectly happy to cast votes limiting abortion funding or partial-birth abortions because these policies are popular both with moderates and with conservatives. Some moderate and liberal politicians, particularly in the Democratic Party, may not want to be blamed for opposing the criminalization of Internet pornography but are happy to have the courts strike such measures down.[76] In this way, the Court promotes their values while taking legal responsibility for the outcome.

Fifth, the Supreme Court often takes direction about how to construct doctrine from contemporaneous expressions of constitutional values by political majorities. It does so not out of compulsion but because Supreme Court majorities happen to agree with these values and find it useful to defer to Congress or the president in order to justify their decisions. I have already noted the Roosevelt Court's legitimation of the New Deal. During the 1960s the Warren Court took direction from the national political process to further the civil rights revolution. Bruce Ackerman and Jennifer Nou have pointed out that following the ratification of the Twenty-Fourth Amendment, which banned poll taxes in federal elections, section 10 of the 1965 Voting Rights Act urged the attorney general to challenge the constitutionality of poll taxes in state elections.[77] Taking its cue from the political branches, the Warren Court held these taxes unconstitutional in *Harper v. Virginia Board of Elections.*[78]

The Supreme Court's sex equality decisions provide an even more powerful example. During the 1960s, Congress passed a series of acts promoting gender equality, including the Equal Pay Act, Title VII of the Civil Rights Act of 1964, and the 1972 Amendments to Title VII, culminating in passage of an Equal Rights Amendment (ERA) sent to the states in 1972. The Supreme Court recited this history in *Frontiero v. Richardson,* offering it as a reason why sex discrimination violated the equal protection clause even before the ERA was ratified.[79] In fact, the Court's development of sex equality doctrine under the equal protection clause made the ERA largely superfluous. Even so, these doctrines followed the judgments of Congress and the president that sex discrimination already violated constitutional values, as well as large-scale changes in public attitudes about sex equality. More recently, after Congress and the president passed a ban on partial-birth abortions, the Supreme Court upheld the Partial Birth Abortion Act of 2003, effectively reversing a seven-year-old decision striking down similar laws.[80] In each of these examples, judicial constructions either ratified or meshed with recent constitutional constructions offered by the president and Congress.

Critics of the federal judiciary often complain that judges are elites who are influenced by elite values.[81] This is certainly true. But it is also true of the political elites who operate the national political process. Both sets of elites respond to changes in national public opinion, but both sets also favor elite values to the extent that they differ from the values of non-elites.[82] When political elites are liberal, as they were in the mid 1960s, the work of courts will also tend to be more liberal; when political elites are more conservative, as they were in the late twentieth century, the work of courts will tend to shift to the right. Complaints about federal judicial decisions as "elite" and antidemocratic often better express concerns about federalism—they reflect complaints by representatives of regional majorities (and regional elites) about the contrasting values of the dominant forces in the national political process. Conversely, although judicial doctrine tends to stay in sync with the views of national political elites, in some cases these political elites are actually less responsive to changes in national public opinion than the federal judiciary because of the many veto points in the political system. For instance, seniority and voting rules in the Senate prevented federal civil rights legislation for generations despite popular support for reform; *Brown v. Board of Education* responded to changing views about race following World War II in ways that Congress could not until the middle of the 1960s.[83]

Constitutional Constructions and Constitutional Revolutions

A similar analysis applies to constitutional revolutions. Lawyers often associate them with famous court decisions, but in fact these transformations usually involve significant cooperation between courts and the national political branches. Twentieth-century constitutional revolutions, like the New Deal revolution of the 1930s or the civil rights revolution of the 1960s, have not primarily been led by the federal judiciary. Rather, they have mostly involved judicial responses to changes in reigning political coalitions and in the values of the dominant regime in American politics. During the early years of the New Deal, the Supreme Court mostly resisted changing political and constitutional assumptions, leading President Roosevelt to make increasingly broad and sweeping claims about federal power to regulate the economy. The New Deal "revolution" consisted largely of the Supreme Court's decision to get behind the emerging political realities and cooperate with the political branches and especially with the president's program. Although Roosevelt attacked the Court when it disagreed with him, he largely stopped attacking it—and its powers of judicial review—as soon as the Court began to agree with and cooperate with his administration. Once Roosevelt had stocked the Supreme Court with friends of the New Deal, the Court responded with a series of precedents legitimating and rationalizing the new constitutional regime and constructing a new constitutional common sense about federalism and economic regulation.[84]

The Warren Court, by contrast, needed little prodding to act in concert with the dominant liberal political consensus of the 1960s. By the 1950s the Supreme Court had been stocked with justices who were liberal on racial issues, reflecting the dominance of racial liberals in the presidential wings of both parties.[85] *Brown v. Board of Education* was the result. A regional majority in the South blocked any congressional action on racial segregation, but a national majority of states favored the result in *Brown,* as did foreign policy elites and lawyers in administrations of both parties.[86] *Brown* was not an example of a Court striking out on its own against the wishes of a national majority; as noted previously, in *Brown* the Court that sided with key elements of the dominant national political coalition, with a wide range of national political elites—including the Justice Departments of both the Truman and Eisenhower administrations—and with a majority of state legislatures.

In the 1960s a liberal Democratic president, Lyndon Johnson, led a coalition of political liberals and moderates in both parties to enact an ambitious civil rights agenda, passing the Civil Rights Act of 1964, the Voting Rights Act of 1965, and the Fair Housing Act of 1968. The Supreme Court strove to uphold the new civil rights legislation from constitutional challenge, expanded congressional powers to protect civil rights, and struck down state poll taxes after Congress requested it do so in the 1965 Voting Rights Act.[87] The Warren Court's criminal procedure revolution imposed national standards of fairness on state and local law enforcement officials whose practices disproportionately burdened blacks and the poor.[88] As Congress and the president began the War on Poverty, the Court began constitutionalizing protections for the poor;[89] several years after Congress passed a revolutionary new immigration act in 1965, the Court protected resident aliens from discrimination by state governments.[90]

The twentieth century's constitutional revolutions have largely been revolutions in constitutional construction. They have involved alterations in constitutional common sense produced through political mobilization and judicial cooperation. Constitutional revolutions are changes in expectations about what constitutional provisions mean and how they are likely to be applied; changes in what kinds of positions are thought reasonable and unreasonable, off-the-wall and on-the-wall. These changes are prompted by the contemporaneous work of the political branches and by social mobilizations.

Most of what courts do in constitutional construction is normal science, working out the consequences of previous commitments (and countercommitments) and reasoning from previous precedents. During periods of significant constitutional change, however, courts face a different task: making sense of new political realities, significant shifts in public sentiment, and new constitutional constructions created by the political branches. Courts play their supporting role by shifting what is off-the-wall and on-the-wall in constitutional doctrines and expectations about the likely application of constitutional doctrines. They do this in order to make sense of the facts on the ground created in ordinary politics. During these periods of constitutional transformation the Supreme Court and the lower federal courts must decide whether and how to legitimate changes or innovations in statecraft and whether and how to cooperate with the newly ascendant forces in national politics, particularly the presidency. How courts react often depends on their composition: who appointed their members and when they were appointed.

Courts are by nature conserving, if not conservative, institutions; their composition tends to reflect the political values of the times when their various members were appointed. For this reason, sometimes courts will resist significant changes in governing assumptions promoted by the president or Congress. They will ally themselves with those parts of the national political process that oppose change. The federal judiciary acts as a check on the political branches, just as Congress and the president check each other. This checking function occurs not because courts are wiser than the political branches but because of their institutional configuration: judges are appointed by politicians from the past, and they decide cases based on past precedents and prior conventions. Nevertheless, in successful constitutional transformations, like the New Deal, advocates of change maintain political power and eventually stock the courts with their allies. At this point courts begin to cooperate, and they resume their standard function: they legitimate and rationalize new constitutional constructions by the political branches, and they impose norms of procedural regularity and new forms of civil liberties protections to make sense of the new regime's innovations. Courts will not uphold everything the national political process does, but they will uphold the major aspects of the new regime's program and articulate its values in judicial decisions. These doctrinal developments cannot be explained solely as the normal or ordinary working-out of the details of previous doctrines, particularly when old judges are replaced by newer judges who are more in sync with dominant political forces. These new judges reject a significant amount of previous assumptions, remaking constitutional common sense.

To respond to changes in the national political process, courts may have to discard a substantial proportion of existing doctrine. They must create new rights and powers where none existed before, overrule existing decisions, or distinguish them into irrelevance. Courts do this by ascending to the general—by going back to first principles and rearticulating those higher-order principles in a new way. In *West Coast Hotel v. Parrish,*[91] a key decision in the legitimation of the New Deal, the Supreme Court cast a skeptical eye on an entire generation of due process jurisprudence:

> [T]he violation alleged by those attacking minimum wage regulation for women is deprivation of freedom of contract. What is this freedom? The Constitution does not speak of freedom of contract. It speaks of liberty and prohibits the deprivation of liberty without due process of law. In prohibiting that deprivation, the Constitution does not recognize an absolute and uncontrollable liberty. Liberty in each of its phases has its history and connotation. But the liberty safeguarded is liberty in a social organization which requires the protection of law against the evils which menace the health, safety, morals, and welfare of the people. Liberty under the Constitution is thus necessarily subject to the restraints of due process, and regulation which is reasonable in relation to its subject and is adopted in the interests of the community is due process.[92]

Here, the Court claims fidelity to basic constitutional principles stated at a high level of generality. Claiming fidelity to principles of higher generality that remain consistent with the text is the easiest way for courts to synthesize revolutionary changes in doctrine with past commitments. Constitutional construction in revolutionary times ascends to the general in order to bless the actual. Appeals to text and principle allow courts to maintain continuity with the past even as their constructions change considerably.

Basic principles often appear differently to later generations than to previous generations that articulated them. The perspective of later generations is likely to be different because they stand in a different relation to the past. And because later generations see different things in the past, they will understand themselves to be faithful to the past differently.

Although constitutional construction by courts involves the articulation, elaboration, and application of constitutional principles, my account of constitutional construction differs from Ronald Dworkin's model of the Court's principled function. Dworkin's model of constructive interpretation tries to make sense of the whole of past judicial decisions, justified by the best theory of political morality available.[93] My model argues that courts try to make sense of recent innovations in state building and constitutional culture, redescribing past principles and precedents in the process. The New Deal Court did not try to make sense of the entire history of federalism and due process doctrine; instead it tried to shape doctrines to fit new forms of statecraft by the political branches.

Moreover, the principles employed in constitutional construction are not limited to those available at the time of adoption. New constitutional principles (including, for example, structural principles) can emerge over time as constitutional constructions of the text. Doctrine consists of a wide variety of different principles at different levels of generality and specificity. New constitutional constructions can be inconsistent with many prior constructions and with a wide variety of principles of varying levels in existing doctrine. For example, during the period from 1934 through 1950, the Supreme Court largely abandoned an elaborate theory of the scope of state police powers that it had developed over a period of seventy years.[94] In its place it constructed a new theory of judicial scrutiny for cases involving economic and social legislation.[95]

My account of constitutional construction has much in common with Bruce Ackerman's theory of constitutional moments, particularly in light of his recent revision of the theory to account for the civil rights revolution.[96] Nevertheless, there are six important differences, which produce a different account both of constitutional revolutions and of living constitutionalism.

First, Ackerman's theory focuses only on the very largest changes in constitutional development that produce new constitutional regimes like Reconstruction or the New Deal. In addition, Ackerman's model of change is not gradual, but revolutionary. Regime changes must occur in a very short space of time, normally within ten years.[97] Thus, Ackerman's model does not purport to explain midlevel or smaller changes within regimes or between great regime shifts, except to the extent that he can describe these changes as the working-out of the regime's larger commitments or as a synthesis with the commitments of previous regimes.[98] By contrast, my model assumes that constitutional constructions come in many different sizes, from very great to very small. Moreover, constitutional constructions have no set time limit. Some very important shifts have emerged from modest changes that culminate over time.

Second, Ackerman argues that regime changes are democratically legitimate because they enjoy the self-conscious, mobilized, and broad support of the American people.[99] This means that the American people, or at least the vast majority of them, must understand that the Constitution is being amended and previous constitutional commitments are being discarded, and they must actively support these changes. By contrast, I argue that the American people do not need to have—and generally do not have—a self-conscious understanding of new constitutional constructions as revolutionary constitutional amendments. Many constitutional constructions go largely unnoticed by the public. Moreover, when members of the public actively support them (which they may not), they tend to understand these changes as restorations or redemptions of constitutional text and principle rather than as displacements or amendments. Even during the height of the controversy over the New Deal, Franklin Roosevelt insisted that his proposals for reform were fully consistent with the constitutional text; he wanted the right to appoint new justices who would read the Constitution correctly.[100] In any case, much constitutional construction, especially smaller and midlevel changes, occurs without self-conscious mobilization or assent by the American people. Instead it reflects the passage of new legislation and administrative regulations by the national political coalition, and the judiciary's adjustment, rationalization, and extension of these efforts.

Third, Ackerman's constitutional moments usually have some tincture of illegality that signals that a revolution is taking place. They involve "unconventional adaptations" of existing constitutional machinery that the people accept or reject.[101] By contrast, constitutional constructions in my model present themselves as perfectly legal articulations of text and principle; at most they discard previous constructions that advocates claim are no longer faithful to the best understandings of text and principle and have otherwise lost connection with changed social and political realities.

Fourth, in order to ensure that regime change enjoys the mobilized support of the American public, Ackerman requires that change must traverse a five-stage process: a signaling event, a proposal, a triggering election, a ratifying election, and consolidation.[102] If change does not correspond to this sequence of events, it is not legitimate. By contrast, I argue that constitutional constructions emerge through many different methods, and there is no necessary sequence they must follow to create valid law.

Fifth, Ackerman's model has a place for what I call constitutional construction, but he explains its democratic legitimacy differently. The commitments of a new regime, he argues, must be worked out over time and synthesized with the commitments of previous regimes. For example, he assumes that the sex equality jurisprudence of the 1970s is not part of the civil rights revolution, which Ackerman believes was centrally about racial equality.[103] Instead he argues that this jurisprudence is a judicial elaboration of the 1960s civil rights regime synthesized with the commitments of previous regimes like Reconstruction.[104] The democratic legitimacy of these judicial elaborations derives from the democratic legitimacy of each of the regimes whose commitments judges synthesize. The legitimacy of these decisions does not come from their contemporaneous connection to national public opinion about sex equality or to the values of national politicians and political elites. By contrast, I argue that the judicial recognition of sex equality in the 1970s emerged from significant changes in popular opinion spurred on by the second wave of American feminism, from the efforts of state legislatures and the political branches of the federal government—who began to put sex equality guarantees into legislation and administrative regulations—and from Congress's submission of the Equal Rights Amendment to the states in 1972. The federal courts' sex equality decisions in the 1970s recognized and rationalized these shifts in constitutional culture; the decisions gained their legitimacy from their connection to changes in constitutional culture and contemporaneous constitutional constructions by the political branches.

Sixth, Ackerman's model argues that the central artifacts of regime changes, especially in the twentieth century, are landmark decisions and landmark statutes. One of his most controversial claims is that these decisions and statutes are full-fledged constitutional amendments[105]— that they have the same legal status as other constitutional amendments passed through Article V. Moreover, Ackerman argues that courts should reason from their text and principles in the same way that they reason from newly enacted constitutional texts.[106] By contrast, I do not regard either the Social Security Act of 1935 or Title VII of the Civil Rights Act of 1964 as constitutional amendments. They are acts of ordinary legislation that can be amended (and have been amended) or even repealed through the ordinary political process. If Congress does not repeal the Social Security Act or Title VII, it is not because it lacks the formal authority to do so. It is rather because these constructions are durable in practice and it would be politically difficult, if not impossible, to repeal them in our current political culture.[107] Even so, landmark statutes like the Social Security Act, the National Labor Relations Act, the Voting

Rights Act, and the Civil Rights Act of 1964 have been repeatedly altered through ordinary legislation throughout their history, and these legislative amendments are not unconstitutional, even if they are unwise or inconsistent with the spirit of the original enactments.

In like fashion, key doctrines created by courts are not amendments to the Constitution, as Ackerman contends, but constitutional constructions that can be limited, distinguished, or even overturned by later courts in the same way that any other decisions can be limited, distinguished, or overturned. Landmark decisions like *United States v. Darby* and *Wickard v. Filburn* could, in theory, be significantly limited or jettisoned tomorrow, if courts found them unworkable or completely inhospitable to the needs of the national political coalition, but this is unlikely to happen because so much depends on their continuation.[108] Perhaps the most famous of all landmark decisions, *Brown v. Board of Education,* has been continuously reinterpreted since it was first handed down, and there is a strong argument that it has been significantly modified, if not wholly transformed, by later decisions.[109] This has happened, in part, because courts have reinterpreted and reshaped *Brown* in concert with the shifting values and agendas of successful countermobilizations and changes in national politics.

Durability, Canonicity, and the Emergence of New Secondary Rules

According to the model of constitutional construction described in this book, many things cannot be changed without constitutional amendment. For example, the "hardwired" features of the Constitution are fixed; so too are those rules that follow directly from the original meaning of the text. This is the point of framework originalism.

In addition, constitutional constructions—both those created by the political branches and those created by courts—can also become *durable* or *canonical.* Durability means that constitutional constructions—whether in the form of statutes, practices, or decisions—are not easy to change, however easy this might appear as a formal matter. Canonicity means that constitutional constructions are important to legal understanding—and especially professional legal understanding—in the current constitutional culture.[110] Canonical constructions set the parameters for what is considered reasonable and unreasonable, central and peripheral, in the constitutional culture. They also set agendas for current debates about constitutional development. Legal thought is distinctive in that it has both a canon of constructions that are currently valued (or important) in constitutional culture and an anti-canon of prior, rejected constructions that legal professionals now regard as characteristic examples of how not to reason about the Constitution.[111] *Dred Scott v. Sandford* is a well-known example of an anti-canonical decision.

Constructions become durable in part because they are useful to everyday political life and because successive generations build on them and depend on their continuation. Constitutional constructions become durable because they are embedded in political, economic, and social practices, and people continuously build on those practices. Dependence in use not only makes these constructions durable; it also causes people to view them as correct or even obvious interpretations of the Constitution.

Constitutional constructions become canonical because their meaning is salient and important to our political regime. Canonical constructions pose agendas and problems to solve; they symbolize important commitments, values, and controversies; and therefore people feel the need to rationalize and explain their positions with respect to these constructions. Conversely, people feel the need to show why their positions are inconsistent with or repudiate constructions that are anti-canonical in the current regime. Some constitutional constructions can be more canonical—in the sense of being salient and important to current understandings and debates—than parts of the constitutional text. The Social Security Act,[112] *Brown v. Board of Education,* and even *Roe v. Wade* are more canonical in the present constitutional regime than the import-export clause of Article I.[113]

Many constitutional constructions are both durable and canonical, and these characteristics often reinforce each other. *Brown v. Board of Education* is both durable and canonical. So too are the Civil Rights Act of 1964[114] and the Social Security Act. They are durable in the sense that people rely on them and build on them. They are canonical in the sense that people see them as articulating important values and commitments.

Constitutional constructions can be durable but not canonical. Many statutes that promote constitutional values are not central to the meaning of the existing constitutional regime, and so too are many precedents embedded in the fabric of the law that nobody pays much attention to.

Constructions can be durable but not canonical if they lack cultural meaning or salience. They can become newly salient, of course, if someone challenges them.

Conversely, constitutional constructions can be canonical but not durable, if, for example, they are canonical because they are controversial, like *Brown* before 1964 or *Roe v. Wade* today, or if they become part of the anti-canon, like *Lochner v. New York*[115] or *Dred Scott*. (Although *Dred Scott* has a prominent place in the anti-canon, it is not currently important to everyday political practice.)

Durability does not mean resistance to all alteration. Landmark statutes are often amended, and courts and administrative agencies put many glosses on them. Rather, durability means that people build on a construction, and by building on it, depend on its continuation. Precisely because the construction serves as a building block for future improvements, it may be altered in the process so that it better meshes with the interests, values, and understandings of the existing constitutional regime.

Likewise, canonicity does not require that social meaning remains constant. Quite the contrary: canonical constructions are often protean—they seem to mean new things as they are introduced into new political and legal contexts. For example, the meaning of cases like *Brown, Marbury, Roe,* or *Lochner* may change greatly over time as a result of political contestation or in the context of successive regimes.[116]

Moreover, a principle associated with a constitutional construction can be durable or canonical, but how the principle would apply to specific applications or facts can change. For example, the principle of *West Coast Hotel v. Parrish* in 1937—deference to legislative judgments in social and economic legislation—is durable. Yet the actual statute upheld in *West Coast Hotel*—a minimum wage law for women but not for men—would no longer be considered ordinary social and economic legislation. It would violate the equal protection clause under the Supreme Court's 1970s sex equality jurisprudence.[117]

Conversely, certain basic applications of a canonical construction like *Brown* to its original facts might remain constant—*de jure* racial segregation is still illegal—but the construction's meaning and the principles it stands for can change as people fight over its legacy and invoke it for different purposes. Later generations can also blunt its practical effects in some areas—such as school integration—while expanding it in others, such as limitations on affirmative action plans.[118]

How and why do constitutional constructions become durable or canonical? There are four basic reasons:

1. Constitutional constructions become durable when people stop fighting about them and accept them in practice.[119]
2. Constitutional constructions become durable when they become embedded in practice and people build on them. The New Deal cases—*United States v. Darby*,[120] *Wickard v. Filburn*,[121] and *Steward Machine Company v. Davis*[122]—are durable in this way.
3. Constitutional constructions become canonical when people stop fighting over whether to accept them and start fighting over their meaning and legacy. This is what happened to *Brown* and the 1970s sex equality decisions.
4. Constitutional constructions become canonical when fights over their meaning become important to resolving constitutional disputes in the present. They set the agenda of constitutional reasoning and debate. This is true of *Roe v. Wade* today. It will likely also be true of *Lawrence v. Texas,* which recognized gay rights, and *District of Columbia v. Heller,* which recognized an individual right to bear arms in the home for purposes of self-defense.

Both durability and canonicity are features of constitutional culture: they concern which practices and understandings become normal, expected, essential, compulsory, or simply go without saying; which issues are salient; and which fade into the background of concern. Durable and canonical constructions help shape what kinds of claims are off-the-wall and on-the-wall at a given time and what legal professionals regard as reasonable and unreasonable positions. One can characterize a constitutional culture like our own in terms of what is durable and what is canonical at a particular time in history.

Durable and canonical constructions can be limited, overthrown, repealed, or made irrelevant. But this takes sustained effort over periods of time. This is the connection between durability, canonicity, and the processes of constitutional change I identify with living constitutionalism. The process of living constitutionalism features not only durable and canonical constructions in particular eras, but also the gradual replacement or supplementation of some constructions with new ones over time. Thus, one way of understanding living constitutionalism is as the process by which some durable or canonical constructions become embedded, extended, and supplemented in constitutional culture, while others are slowly limited, expunged, or made practically irrelevant.

Griswold v. Connecticut[123] and *Eisenstadt v. Baird*[124] are durable and canonical constructions, in part because of the success of the sexual revolution. Likewise, the Voting Rights Act[125] is durable and canonical: even though parts of it must be renewed by Congress, it is currently unthinkable that Congress would not renew it. (Similarly, the Supreme Court avoided a recent constitutional challenge to section 5 of the Act by reinterpreting one of its provisions.[126] If the Court ever does strike down the Voting Rights Act, it would mark a significant change in American politics.) Because of changes in social attitudes about homosexuality, and new social practices around which people have organized their lives, *Lawrence* is clearly canonical, as mentioned above, and is probably already durable. Like *Griswold* and *Eisenstadt*, *Lawrence* is an example of how living constitutionalism and the concepts of durability and canonicity are always in dialogue with social norms and mores. People are not actively trying to overturn *Lawrence;* no major political figure in 2011 seeks to reinstate the sort of criminal penalties for homosexual conduct that politicians might have supported in the past. Instead, the debate over gay rights has moved on to issues of same-sex marriage and employment discrimination.

Durable and canonical constitutional constructions like *Griswold* or the Voting Rights Act become part of the "constitutional catechism" that all Supreme Court justices who seek confirmation must accept as valid.[127] The constitutional catechism is important because it suggests that there is a series of decisions, institutions, and statutes that have become so accepted by the public and by political elites that no judicial nominee can be confirmed if he or she would threaten their continuation. Judge Robert Bork failed confirmation in 1987 in part because people could not be sure that he accepted the legitimacy of *Griswold*.[128] Canonical and durable constructions shape judicial appointments, a key element of the process of living constitutionalism; their effects on judicial appointments, in turn, reinforce their canonical and durable character.

Canonical constructions that are not durable can affect judicial appointments in a different way: social and political movements press to reshape them or even overturn them. *Roe v. Wade* is clearly canonical, because it creates problems that people feel they must discuss and resolve. But it is not yet durable, because people have not given up fighting about whether to overrule it. Every Supreme Court appointment since the 1980s has occurred in the shadow of the struggle over this most canonical of contemporary constructions.

Living constitutionalism is a system of constitutional development that produces new constitutional constructions. This system of constitutional development did not emerge all at once; rather, it evolved through the interaction of the basic framework created by the Constitution and its amendments with constitutional constructions that were added at various points in time. The system of living constitutionalism not only produces new doctrines and institutions; it also creates its own set of secondary rules—that is, ways for building new constitutional constructions. Bruce Ackerman has pointed out, for example, that our methods of constitutional development have become increasingly nationalist over time.[129] Constitutional amendment under Article V requires the concurrence of three-quarters of state legislatures, almost all of which are bicameral, thus creating many different ways to defeat amendments. In the twentieth century, America has increasingly shifted toward nationalist forms of constitutional construction as the central method of constitutional development: judicial decisions by federal courts, federal framework statutes, and the creation of new federal institutions.

These emerging forms of constitutional construction developed together in response to each other. For example, the development of federal judicial doctrine greatly accelerated after the Civil War—and especially during the twentieth century—because of five key features. The first was the ratification of the Fourteenth Amendment, which required that state and local governments adhere to basic rights guarantees. The Fourteenth Amendment made it easier for the federal courts to supervise local and regional majorities and keep them in line with the values of the national political coalition. During the late nineteenth century, the federal courts promoted economic nationalism; during the middle of the twentieth century, they promoted federal civil rights.

A second and related phenomenon was the Republican Party's decision to expand the jurisdiction of the federal courts after the Civil War. This increased the number of times that federal courts would pass on constitutional issues and thus, in the long run, increased the chances for doctrinal development, elaboration, and proliferation.[130]

A third feature was the development during the twentieth century of new institutions of civil society that promoted constitutional litigation as a method of social change and the appointment of judges as a key goal of electoral politics. These civil society institutions, as Steven Teles has described, created new forms of ideological and partisan competition outside the electoral system that helped change constitutional culture and professional reasoning.[131]

A fourth key element was the rise of the administrative and welfare state during the twentieth century. This greatly increased the amount of legislation as well as the number of administrative regulations. Statutes and administrative decisions are the building blocks of new constitutional constructions by the political branches. Rising amounts of legislation and regulation, in turn, increased the number of possible occasions for litigants to raise constitutional and administrative challenges and the number of opportunities for federal courts to develop and proliferate doctrine.

Finally, the rise of an administrative and welfare state also meant that Congress and the president increasingly created new agencies, institutions, and practices that changed the structures of government on the ground. New landmark and framework statutes created an elaborate legal and institutional infrastructure that shaped the Constitution-in-practice. Following their customary role, courts were called on to rationalize, legitimate, and regulate this burgeoning regime, not only leading to increased work for themselves but also increasing their responsibility and their power. The New Deal, for example, created a large federal bureaucracy, new social programs, and new institutional structures. Courts justified and legitimated these changes in governance, but in the process began to subject them to procedural and constitutional norms, thus proliferating judicial precedents and constitutional constructions.

Continuous interaction, cooperation, and contest between the judiciary and the political branches have created ever-new opportunities for new constitutional constructions outside the amendment process. Thus, although the twentieth century has featured no less than twelve Article V amendments, focusing only on these amendments does not offer an accurate portrait of the key changes in American constitutionalism of the past hundred years. For example, these amendments say little about the growth of the administrative and welfare state, the expansion of presidential power, the creation of a national security state, or the civil rights revolution.[132] Constitutional construction has become the dominant form of constitutional development today, because previous constructions during the twentieth century have made available so many new methods of constitutional change that can be more efficient, narrowly tailored, and agile than Article V amendment.

14

CHANGE AND LEGITIMACY

In Chapter 13 I explained that the processes of constitutional change are primarily the work of constitutional construction, involving both the political branches and the courts. What we call a "living Constitution" is really the product of constitutional construction and changes in constitutional construction over time. It is a "democratic constitutionalism," to use Post and Siegel's expression, because constitutional doctrine is responsive, over time, to a wide variety of political and cultural forces. Constitutional change occurs (1) because of changes in constitutional culture—what ordinary citizens and legal and political elites believe the Constitution means and who they believe has authority to make claims on the Constitution; (2) because of changes in political institutions and statecraft, which federal courts eventually rationalize and legitimate; and (3) because of changes in judicial personnel (and hence their views of the Constitution). The latter changes, in turn, are caused by the judicial appointments process, which is controlled by elected officials—particularly the president and the Senate—who in turn respond to existing political pressures and incentives.

One might make two objections to this account of the processes of living constitutionalism. The first is that it is insufficiently legal—that it gives too much power to cultural and political influences, the national political process, political mobilization, and partisan entrenchment, rather than reasoned development of doctrine by courts. The second is that the account is insufficiently political. If the Supreme Court responds to changes in public opinion and political configurations, why not eliminate the middleman and dispense with judicial review entirely? These two objections push in opposite directions, and I consider each of them in turn.

Courts Are Bad at Tackling, Good at Piling On[1]

One might argue that courts should be, in Ronald Dworkin's words, "the forum of principle."[2] They should take the lead on questions of rights, justice, and constitutional structure, rather than letting constitutional development be guided or pushed by social movements and political mobilizations. But this is a false dichotomy. The locus of constitutional change occurs simultaneously in the courts, in the political branches, and in the public sphere. History teaches us that courts normally do not engage in significant changes in constitutional doctrine without lengthy prodding from a sustained campaign by political parties, social movements, and interest groups.[3] Such campaigns generally employ not only litigation but also political mobilization and cultural and social persuasion. The long march of progressivism that led to the New Deal revolution, and the even longer march that led to the civil rights revolution, are two obvious examples, but the same could be said of almost every important transformation in constitutional doctrine in the country's history. If one admires these achievements of living constitutionalism, one must pay proper respects to the social and political mobilizations that preceded them.

Brown v. Board of Education did not arise full-blown from the head of Earl Warren; it was the result of a decades-long campaign, well documented by historians, in which the Supreme Court made only sporadic and not always helpful appearances.[4] As noted in Chapter 13, World War II and the Truman administration's support for civil rights were crucial factors, and President Truman asked the Court to overrule *Plessy v. Ferguson*[5] four years before it actually got around to doing so.[6] State courts and state legislatures, especially in the North, were also particularly important in the lengthy process of changing American constitutional culture in the years before *Brown*.[7] Constitutional innovations in state and local law usually precede the U.S. Supreme Court's entrance into a new area.

One might worry that social movements, political parties, and interest group advocates will shape constitutional culture poorly without the careful and regular guidance of wiser courts. But whether one likes it or not, courts generally do not pay much attention to constitutional claims until social and political mobilizations get behind them; this is true of claims that are now the foundation of many of today's constitutional doctrines. The work of social and political mobilizations in making claims, taking positions, and trying to persuade others that their views are correct is crucial to constitutional development. That is because courts generally will not engage in constitutional innovation until political success changes the composition of the judiciary or alters the political and constitutional culture in which courts make their decisions.

Courts usually do not get involved in developing new constitutional doctrines—whether about gun rights or gay rights—until political forces are strong enough to make them sit up and take notice. The famous *Carolene Products*[8] case argued that the proper role of courts is to look out for the interests of "discrete and insular minorities." But the irony of *Carolene Products* is that no group gets recognized as "discrete and insular," and therefore deserving of judicial protection, until it has gained the attention of political majorities.[9] Until it gains some political clout, a minority group is usually simply ignored. Blacks got increasing attention from the courts after black migration to the North and to urban areas made them swing voters who could influence elections,[10] and after Jim Crow became an embarrassment to the American foreign policy establishment during the Cold War.[11] Blacks made progress in the courts, in other words, because they made political progress through a halting and agonizingly slow process. (Of course, the one place blacks made little or no progress was in the South, and the civil rights revolution essentially imposed a national majority's views about race on the entire country, displacing those of a regional majority in the South.)

The Court's sex discrimination decisions of the 1970s followed an enormous groundswell of support for sex equality in popular culture and social movement mobilization (not to mention passage of the ERA by overwhelming margins in both houses of Congress in 1972).[12] From 1921 in *Adkins v. Children's Hospital*[13] until the 1970s, the U.S. Supreme Court pretty much stayed out of the gender equality business (there are two cases, *Goesaert v. Cleary*[14] in 1948 and *Hoyt v. Florida*[15] in 1961, both treating sex equality claims dismissively).

Finally, the Supreme Court's 2008 decision in *District of Columbia v. Heller*,[16] although written in the language of originalism, is actually a classic example of the processes of living constitutionalism in operation. Doctrinal recognition of an individual right to own guns for self-defense arose only after both political culture and political elites supported the right. For many years the conventional wisdom following the passage of the 1934 National Firearms Act[17] during the New Deal was that the Second Amendment did not guarantee an individual right to use guns for self-defense. In 1991, for example, retired chief justice Warren Burger, a conservative establishment Republican, insisted that the individual rights view of the Second Amendment was "one of the greatest pieces of fraud—I repeat the word 'fraud'—on the American public by special interest groups that I have ever seen in my lifetime."[18] Burger cast particular scorn on the efforts of the National Rifle Association (NRA) and other groups—which he pejoratively labeled "special interest groups"—to convince Americans otherwise.[19]

The modern movement for gun rights arose in reaction to increased political mobilization for stricter gun control laws, particularly after passage of the 1968 Crime Control and Safe Streets Act,[20] which Congress enacted following the assassinations of Martin Luther King Jr. and Robert F. Kennedy.[21] Beginning in the 1970s the NRA, which had previously acquiesced in some gun control legislation and formed alliances with hunters and conservation groups, changed its leadership. It began aggressive national lobbying efforts to oppose gun control legislation. It negotiated the tension between gun rights and conservative demands for "law and order" by distinguishing between law-abiding citizens who had rights to guns for self-defense and criminals who had no rights.[22]

The NRA's new position on gun rights quickly gained influence within the Republican Party, as New Right leaders like Richard Viguerie recognized that gun rights could play a key role in the emerging culture wars over abortion, women's rights, homosexuality, affirmative action, and pornography.[23] Movement conservatives who had previously used originalism to attack liberal judicial decisions now turned to originalism to defend Second Amendment rights.[24] As conservatives gained increasing political influence during the last decades of the twentieth century, the NRA's constitutional position gained increasing public support and convinced members of a newer generation of conservative legal elites. In 1994 the Republicans took control of both houses of Congress by making their opposition to recent gun control laws passed by a Democratic-controlled Congress a key campaign issue.[25]

In her study of the contemporary constitutional movement for gun rights, Reva Siegel has pointed out that during the 1980s the NRA emphasized a republican or insurrectionist theory of the Second Amendment—that protected the right of citizens to resist a tyrannical government—and had flirted with the radical militia movement.[26] Following the Oklahoma City terrorist bombings in 1995, however, the militia movement came under strong public criticism.[27] The NRA quickly distanced itself from the militia movement; it promoted gun rights as an element of the culture wars and increasingly emphasized that law-abiding citizens had the right to have weapons for self-defense in the home to protect themselves against criminals.[28] This also became the view of the conservative movement in the Republican Party. In May 2002 Attorney General John Ashcroft announced the Bush Justice Department's official position that the Second Amendment protected an individual right to use arms in self-defense.[29]

Justice Scalia's majority opinion in *Heller* largely followed the emerging public vision of gun rights, the NRA's shift away from the insurrectionist theory, and the NRA's emphasis on the distinction between law-abiding citizens and criminals.[30] Thus, his opinion effectively elevated the self-defense theory over the insurrectionist theory of the Second Amendment, although the latter theory has far more historical support in the period leading up to ratification.[31] The evidence for a constitutional right of self-defense becomes stronger during the nineteenth century.[32] In fact, as Chapter 10 explained, perhaps the strongest originalist argument comes not from the original understanding of the Second Amendment but from its subsequent incorporation in the privileges or immunities clause of the Fourteenth Amendment.[33]

Scalia's majority opinion in *Heller* emphasized the right of law-abiding citizens to keep guns in their homes and strongly suggested that felons will have no Second Amendment rights.[34] In fact, near the end of his opinion he acknowledged that modern developments in weaponry may have made the Second Amendment's original purpose of allowing citizen militias to overthrow a tyrannical government completely irrelevant.[35] Nevertheless, he insisted that the Second Amendment remains necessary to protect the right of self-defense in the home.[36] This conclusion perfectly reflects the transformation of the NRA's arguments following the Oklahoma City terrorist attack.

In this respect the result in *Heller* was not entirely surprising. As in *Brown v. Board of Education,* the 1970s sex equality cases, and *Lawrence v. Texas,* the Supreme Court has kept its interpretation of the Constitution in line with changing public values. Another name for this phenomenon is living constitutionalism.

There is no plausible account of living constitutionalism that does not involve the federal court system responding to popular culture, social movement mobilization, and electoral politics. Popular constitutionalism and partisan entrenchment drive doctrinal development. Doctrinal development, in turn, shapes the direction of social movements and political activism. It does this sometimes by changing facts on the ground, sometimes by shaping popular consciousness, sometimes by opening up new channels and opportunities for constitutional claims, and sometimes by spawning backlash and countermobilizations that attempt to discipline the courts and change their direction. Constitutional politics influences constitutional courts; and in turn constitutional courts influence constitutional politics—both by what courts do and by what they refrain from doing.

Not all of the action occurs in the political arena. Courts have plenty to do in shaping constitutional culture. They have to hear cases and decide them, creating new doctrinal distinctions that become the basis for later litigation and contestation. Through their opinions, courts influence public opinion, but not always as they intend. They may provoke reaction as much as they educate or enlighten. By declaring what is legal and illegal, which claims are plausible and which are off-the-wall, court decisions reshape the terrain of politics and political meanings; they create new opportunities for political entrepreneurs, both those who support judicial decisions and those who oppose them.

Above all, courts translate constitutional politics into constitutional law. They really cannot help themselves, or more correctly, the work of a collection of justices on a multimember court like the U.S. Supreme Court cannot help but produce this effect. The justices do this not because they are more intelligent, more noble, more farsighted, more principled, or more sober than the rest of us. Rather, they translate constitutional politics into constitutional law because of how they get their jobs and because they inhabit professional roles in which they must continually hear claims and articulate their answers in terms of the forms, practices, and arguments of professional legal culture.

Eliminate the Middleman?

The democratic legitimacy of living constitutionalism rests on the fact that, in the long run, it is democratically responsive. In this way the process of constitutional construction, mediated through the three branches of the federal government and the states, respects popular sovereignty. Nevertheless, this raises a second objection: If constitutional change responds to political mobilizations, social movement activism, interest group advocacy, new forms of governance, presidential appointments strategies, and shifts in popular opinion, what is the purpose of having constitutional courts in the first place? Why not just get courts out of the business of holding anything unconstitutional and exercise judicial restraint in almost every case?[37] If the system of living constitutionalism gains its legitimacy from its democratic responsiveness, why not eliminate the middleman? Why not leave all constitutional development to the majoritarian political process?

To answer this question, consider some key features of the system of living constitutionalism. First, its effects tend to be conservative (in a prudential rather than ideological sense) because justices tend to reflect the views of political coalitions that put them in office when they were appointed. On a multimember court, that means that its members represent a variety of different positions, strewn across time. Partisan entrenchment in the judiciary tends to prevent quick and drastic changes in governance, because it requires that political majorities win for sustained periods of time before they can change the legal culture and appoint new judges who will go along with their innovations.

Second, these features add an additional supermajoritarian requirement to already supermajoritarian features of American democracy. They create an additional veto point in the system: laws must pass not only Congress and the president (or the state legislature and the governor) but also the scrutiny of a court whose members were appointed by people at different times with very different political views.

Due to these conserving and supermajoritarian features, living constitutionalism creates a bias toward preserving the constitutional values of the political status quo. If the vector sum of political forces changes swiftly on a constitutional issue, the courts will tend to hold back and resist the views of the day until the change in constitutional culture proves lasting, in part because it will take time for new judges to replace older ones.

These features of living constitutionalism share something in common. They are basic features of constitutionalism generally. Constitutionalism channels and disciplines present-day majorities through supermajoritarian rules that they cannot easily change overnight (but can change eventually); this prevents drastic changes in governance and keeps temporary majorities from altering or subverting the constitutional values of more temporally extended supermajorities. The system of living constitutionalism—like all constitutionalism—channels and disciplines ordinary politics by restraining simple majoritarianism.[38]

Living constitutionalism sits squarely between two extremes: It incorporates significant aspects of democratic politics in producing constitutional constructions over time, yet it also maintains the benefits of supermajoritarian constitutionalism. First, it requires fidelity to the hardwired features of the Constitution absent an Article V amendment. Second, it requires political victories sustained over a long period of time to change existing understandings of the Constitution's text and structure that have been filled out through past constitutional construction.

Living constitutionalism allows social and political mobilizations gradually to shift the interpretation and application of abstract clauses and open-ended features of the Constitution. It allows new constructions to make sense of vagueness and ambiguity in the text, and it allows for building new institutions to carry out constitutional functions. But for the most part, living constitutionalism has not altered the hardwired features of the constitutional text. (To the extent that this has happened, it is really quite exceptional, and, I think, quite wrong.)[39] This approach is consistent with what I have called framework originalism: It is faithful to the Constitution's original meaning but not necessarily the original expected application of the text. Long-term changes in constitutional culture can move us from *Plessy v. Ferguson* to *Brown v. Board of Education,* but they won't allow a thirty-four-year-old president, or three houses of Congress, or a simple majority of one house to overturn a presidential veto. While Article V amendment is necessary for changing these hardwired features of the Constitution, the interpretation, implementation, and application of vague and abstract terms like "equal protection" can and do change through sustained political mobilization.

Under this model of living constitutionalism, successive generations may not reject the Constitution's text and principles, but they may decide how best to honor, implement, and apply them through constitutional constructions and doctrinal implementations. We can reject *Plessy v. Ferguson,* which is simply one generation's attempt at implementing the Constitution, but not the words of the equal protection clause.

This model produces a system of judicial interpretation that is responsive to democratic politics in the long run but not directly controlled by it in the short run. It preserves constitutional law's relative autonomy from everyday politics while making it ultimately responsive to constitutional politics.

The system of living constitutionalism thus maintains the benefits of constitutionalism while allowing adjustments in interpretation over time in the face of sustained democratic mobilization. It features a system of judicial review but not a system of judicial supremacy. This distinction is crucial: Courts act as a stabilizing force, and hold officials—and especially executive officials—accountable to law, but they never have the last word. The purpose of judicial review in this model is to represent and protect, in as legally principled a way as possible, the constitutional values of temporally extended majorities, and to prevent drastic changes in those constitutional values unless there has been extended and sustained support for change that is reflected in long-term changes in constitutional culture.

Judges do not have to do anything special or out of the ordinary to participate in the processes of living constitutionalism. They do not have to be politicians or moral theorists or divinities like Ronald Dworkin's Hercules.[40] They do not have to be Platonic guardians[41] or philosopher kings. They don't have to be smarter, wiser, more moral, or more far-sighted than anyone else. All they have to do, once they get appointed, is to try to decide the cases according to law, in the best way they can. If they just go about doing their jobs, they will, in spite of themselves, participate in the gradual translation of constitutional politics into constitutional law. Meanwhile the job of members of the political community is to criticize how judges interpret the law and to try to persuade judges and other citizens that their interpretations of the Constitution are the best ones.

Individuals and Systems

This account of living constitutionalism is neither merely descriptive nor purely external. To the contrary, it is normative and takes an internal perspective on the constitutional system, treating its norms as legally binding. It focuses on the entire system of constitutional development, of which courts are only one part, and considers that system's role in promoting democratic legitimacy.

In evaluating a constitutional and political system, we can focus our normative judgments on what individuals in a system should do within the system or on how the system operates as a whole. Sometimes we should focus on improving individual behavior, but sometimes the system is the proper focus. Suppose, for example, that we want to solve a problem of social coordination by designing an efficient market. We ask how its design and incentives produce certain types of results, and if they do not, we redesign the market and reshape the incentives. We do not spend very much time giving advice to people in the market about how to behave so as to produce efficiency; rather, we assume that efficiency arises from the sum of their interactions and not from each of them following our advice about how to behave. In fact, it may be a mistake to focus primarily on advising individual people about how to behave in the market, although educating people about costs and benefits might be a good idea; so too might be educational campaigns to shape people's values and preferences.

Another example of a focus on systems is our Constitution's separation of powers. The Constitution tries to preserve republican government by balancing contrasting interests, under the assumption, as Madison put it, that enlightened statesmen (that is, the sort who would respond to good advice) will not always be at the helm.[42] My account is of the same sort: it asks whether and how the structural features of the system of constitutional change—many of which developed over time—promote or detract from democratic legitimacy and popular sovereignty. It asks whether the system works, regardless of whether judges, lawyers, or political actors are wise or foolish, noble or base.

Advice to Judges or Theory of Legitimacy?

To be sure, most people have assumed that a theory of living constitutionalism must be a theory that tells judges, "Here's how to decide cases that come before you. Do this and don't do that." Why do people think this? Possibly it is because they think that originalism is just such a theory, and so they assume that living constitutionalism must be of the same kind, its mirror image. They are wrong about living constitutionalism. They are also wrong about originalism.

Originalism offers directives to judges about how to decide cases because it is a theory of what makes the constitutional system—and the institution of judicial review—legitimate. It argues that fidelity to the Constitution is necessary for democratic legitimacy. There are several different theories for why that is so, but perhaps the most familiar version is that the Constitution was created through an act of popular sovereignty and therefore we must preserve the meaning of the Constitution over time in order to respect the rule of law and preserve the democratic legitimacy of the initial act of lawmaking. If judges must adhere to original meaning, they will do their part to maintain the system's legitimacy.[43]

Skyscraper originalism closely connects what makes the constitutional system legitimate with instructions to individual judges about how to decide particular cases. But living constitutionalism may not work in the same way. Indeed, precisely because it is compatible with (and supplements) framework originalism, living constitutionalism may not offer much additional advice to the judiciary beyond what framework originalism requires.

It certainly does not offer contradictory advice: judges in a system of living constitutionalism should, at a minimum, respect the original meaning of the Constitution and try to apply its underlying principles to present-day conditions. Nevertheless, the focus of living constitutionalism lies elsewhere. It concerns how the system as a whole works over long periods of time—why the cumulative processes that produce changing interpretations of the Constitution promote democratic legitimacy.

I emphasize how the constitutional system actually changes because we cannot expect actors to do what is not possible for them to do. A causal and structural account of the constitutional system is a necessary precursor to any normative account of constitutional legitimacy.[44] Sadly, much normative constitutional theory seems to ignore this crucial question. It assumes that if we just give judges the correct advice, and they follow this advice, the system as a whole will produce legitimate results. Conversely, any problems of legitimacy come from judges not following the theorists' advice. This approach does not always stop to ask whether individual judges on a multimember court could or would actually take the advice being offered, or, if they took it, whether the constitutional system as a whole would respond in the right way.

The work of a multimember court will not correspond to any coherent theory of advice directed at one individual. The cases will go all over the place: they will not correspond to any consistent methodology. To be sure, they may be consistent with the relatively modest requirements of framework originalism. But that version of originalism does not dictate the results of constitutional construction, and for a very large number of disputed cases, construction is the name of the game.

This does not mean that normative criticisms of judges and their decisions are useless or irrelevant to constitutional legitimacy. Quite the contrary: criticizing courts and pushing for different constitutional constructions is crucial to the legitimacy of the system. My point, rather, is that normative arguments about good judging and correct constitutional construction are not external to the system of constitutional change. They are part of the process through which change occurs, and they help secure its democratic responsiveness. In a constitutional democracy like our own, citizens, judges, lawyers, and government officials continually make constitutional claims, continually contend for their preferred vision of the Constitution, and continually argue about how judges should behave. The clash of opposed views about what the Constitution means, and the clash of opposed positions about the authority of different actors in the system, drives the system forward.

When people argue with each other and try to persuade each other, they are helping to shape the constitutional culture in which citizens live and in which judges hear and decide cases. When people make arguments about judges' authority to interpret the Constitution, they are trying to influence their fellow citizens as well as judges. They are shaping the boundaries of the reasonable, the notion of what sorts of claims are off-the-wall and on-the-wall in the constitutional culture in which they live. Similarly, when political officials make legal arguments in public life, or when lawyers argue before courts, they are trying to persuade judges to rule their way, thus reshaping professional judgments and the constitutional culture of legal professionals. Indeed, we can define a constitutional culture to a significant extent by what claims ordinary citizens and professionals regard as reasonable and unreasonable, off-the-wall and on-the-wall. Citizens and professionals may differ in these judgments from time to time, but this is also an important aspect of constitutional culture, because it means that popular opinion and popular mobilizations may, over time, alter professional judgments.

Thus, in my account of living constitutionalism, normative argument about the Constitution is hardly futile. It is a central element of what makes a living Constitution live. Arguments about what the Constitution means and who has the authority to say what it means are important because they can persuade the actors in the system to think differently. They influence public opinion, the work of litigators and social movements, and the positions of politicians and political parties. These forms of influence—together with regular elections—produce new judicial appointments and can shape the views of judges who are already on the bench. Normative arguments about what the Constitution means occur in mobilization, political disputes, electoral politics, debates about judicial selection, and litigation campaigns. They are the stuff of constitutional culture and the drivers of constitutional change.

The Translation of Constitutional Politics into Constitutional Law: On Horizontal and Vertical Translation

In our constitutional system, lawyers and judges translate constitutional politics into constitutional law through their everyday professional tasks of litigating and deciding cases. This concept of translation is somewhat different from Lawrence Lessig's famous comparison between original- ist judging and translating.[45] Lessig argued that the right way for judges to be originalists was to analogize interpretation to the translation of an ancient text in a foreign language. Given changed circumstances, we should try to enter into the world of the past and translate the expecta- tions of the framers into our present-day concerns.[46] Because I don't think we are bound by original expected applications, I don't accept Lessig's thesis on precisely the terms he offered it. Nevertheless, I think the meta- phor of translation is powerful and evocative.

Lessig's model of translation was *vertical,* moving from past to pres- ent: we translate the thick set of beliefs and expectations surrounding an ancient text into today's meanings and applications. My account of translation is *horizontal:* judges respond to the political and constitu- tional culture of their day and recognize it in their work, whether con- sciously or unconsciously. In Lessig's model, translation was something that judges *should do;* in my model, it is something that judges *actually do,* whether they intend to or not. Judges engage in horizontal transla- tion because of the way they are selected and the way that democratic politics shapes professional legal culture, legal argument, and legal deci- sionmaking. An originalist like Justice Scalia may insist that he is only following the commands of long-dead framers, but, willy-nilly, he is channeling the values of the contemporary conservative movement. He has done so overtly in his many dissents, making direct appeals to the public and decrying the values of liberal elites, who, he believes, are out of touch with the contemporary sensibilities of ordinary Americans.[47]

The word *translate* means "to carry across," and lawyers' arguments and judges' decisions carry ideas, values, and commitments from the realm of politics to the realm of law. The work of judges and lawyers perpetually traverses the membrane that separates law from politics while simultaneously preserving that boundary by operating through professional rhetoric and norms. Judges and lawyers reconceptualize the claims of constitutional politics in the materials of the law, transform- ing, professionalizing, and rationalizing them in the process. This process is horizontal translation, the translation of constitutional politics into constitutional law.

I emphasize the contributions of lawyers as well as judges because lawyers shape the claims of litigants and members of interest groups, political mobilizations, and social movements and present them before the judiciary. Litigation—and the resources devoted to litigation—shape the direction of constitutional construction, for judges cannot hear cases that are not brought to them.[48] Lawyers are the great translators of our political life, collecting the stories, claims, and grievances of Americans and spinning them into the discourse of power that we call legal reason.

The past—and the meaning of the past—matters greatly in horizontal translation. Judges, lawyers, and their fellow citizens often reason with each other by invoking the past—not only the values, concerns, and hopes of the framers, but also those of those of succeeding generations, like the generations of the New Deal, World War II, or the civil rights revolution. In fact, it often seems that between precedent and history, constitutional argument appears to be about nothing other than the past, albeit the nation's entire past, not just the moment of the founding. But people invoke the memory of the past in order to face each other in the present, and to reason about how to apply the Constitution in their own time. In a democracy like ours, moral and political disagreement is a fact of life. The past serves a crucial function: it provides a common stock of intellectual resources, values, and commitments that people with very different views can draw upon to reason with each other in a political community so that they can decide what to do and how to go forward.[49] People preserve democratic community and democratic legitimacy by using the past to decide what to do in the present. Constitutional doctrine translates these arguments and counterarguments into constitutional law.

Courts must think and act in terms of legal forms and practices; they must make legal arguments and write legal opinions. Their job is not to do politics but to do law. Nothing in what I have said suggests that judges should do anything but interpret and construct law. They should be faithful to text and principle and use the various modalities of argument—text, structure, history, precedent, prudence, and national ethos—to decide the cases before them. The work of translation and change will take care of itself without much effort on their part. They will disagree among themselves, often heatedly, about the direction in which doctrine should travel, but that by itself does not make the process of change illegitimate. To the contrary: this process of disagreement about the law over time—and the mutual recognition of opposing positions—is itself part of the process of horizontal translation that helps secure the democratic legitimacy of constitutional change through constitutional construction.

Through doing law (not politics) and working in tandem and in opposition with each other, successive generations of lawyers and judges inevitably translate changes in constitutional politics into constitutional law. They do so because new judges replace older ones, and because the judges who hear cases and decide them are influenced and shaped by the constitutional culture in which they live. This culture includes not only professional norms of what is off-the-wall and on-the-wall legally, but also popular notions of constitutional values that influence professional judgments. In this way living constitutionalism produces change that preserves legitimacy in a democratic society while allowing judges to continue being judges.

The Role of Dissent in a System of Living Constitutionalism

Individuals within the constitutional system will not always like how judges or the political branches engage in constitutional construction, because the system will often produce constitutional changes that they do not agree with. Many people, perhaps most, instinctively associate "living constitutionalism" with whatever is liberal or progressive and therefore support or oppose it. But this characterization is incorrect. As noted previously, a Constitution that grows and changes in response to social and political mobilizations is as likely to move to the right as to the left. Indeed, it has moved in many different directions over the course of our nation's history. Moreover, what we call "left" and "right" today are the products of coalition building—a configuration of contingent forces and events. The content of these ideas has been different and will be different again. Someday they may be replaced by other ideas and labels that will better describe the political disputes of the future.

The conservative dominance of the last forty years is an important example of the process of living constitutionalism at work, even though many of its proponents have fought under the banner of originalism. There is no contradiction here. Appeals to the values of the framers or founders are a pretty standard way that people call for restoration or redemption. Appeals to origins are a familiar way that people justify constitutional change outside of Article V (and change within it, too).

Like many revolutionary movements before it, the conservative movement of the late twentieth century has been predicated on a return to an imagined origin, a restoration of proper principles it claims that later generations have abandoned. Of course, revolutions often use the tropes of return and restoration to promote what is actually change. The conservative originalism of the past several decades has been an attempt to replace a more liberal constitutionalism with a more conservative one. In many ways it has succeeded. Whether liberal critics like it or not, this change is also an example of the living Constitution. In a conservative era, the positive constitutional law of a living Constitution will become more conservative in many respects. That is how the Constitution "keeps up with the times" and "reflects changing values."

Why should citizens recognize the legitimacy of this process, if it generates constitutional constructions that citizens disagree with? They should recognize and respect it because it is the same process that produced constitutional constructions they also respect and admire. Each of us will find some decisions of the courts to disagree with, and others that we truly despise. But we must accept these decisions as law while working to change them over time through the processes of legal persuasion in the courts and political mobilization outside the courts. I can argue that these decisions are bad interpretations of the law and work to distinguish or overrule them, just as people who disagree with me can work to limit or overturn decisions that they do not like. The ability of citizens to talk back to courts—their ability to redraw the boundaries of what is reasonable and unreasonable through persuasion, protest, and political action—is crucial to democratic legitimacy. Faced with a deeply unjust decision, *Dred Scott v. Sandford*, Abraham Lincoln once said that *Dred Scott* was law and should be respected until it was altered or overturned, but "we mean to do what we can to have the Court decide the other way."[50] Here Lincoln articulated the basic premise of a living Constitution as a process: the Supreme Court's decisions deserve respect as positive law, but not respect as proper interpretations of the Constitution, unless, in fact, they are the right interpretations. People can and should work to overturn decisions that, in their opinion, are contrary to the Constitution's spirit, and to its text and principles, through political mobilizations, through the appointments process, and through legal arguments directed at judges and legal officials.

People who disagree with particular decisions must accept them as positive law, but need not accept them as correct. A system of living constitutionalism means that I can always dissent during "dark times" when my views are in the minority. I can try to persuade other people that my views are correct and work for the restoration or the redemption of important constitutional values. Through this agonistic process of mobilizations and countermobilizations of groups who seek the restoration and redemption of constitutional values, the Constitution maintains its public acceptability.

Moreover, this process provides its own constraints on runaway construction by the courts and the political branches. As Reva Siegel has pointed out, both sides of a constitutional controversy must appeal to common values and common political goods in order to persuade the public that their views are correct. They must modify their positions to appeal to the values of the (imagined) center, and in the process they often acknowledge and incorporate aspects of each others' views.[51] The clash of mobilization and countermobilization, the necessities of everyday politics, and the need to compromise and make positions palatable provide yet another checking function in our constitutional system, like the separation of powers itself. This does not make constitutional politics either principled or unprincipled; the point, rather, is that the content, scope, and effect of the constitutional principles that the political process produces are continually being reconceptualized and reconfigured in the crucible of democratic politics. We can see the reshaping of constitutional claims in the context of debates over racial equality, sex equality, free speech, and even the right to bear arms.[52] Contemporary liberal claims about the Constitution have been shaped by the conservative constitutional culture of our era, just as today's conservative constitutionalism reacted to and absorbed important features of the more liberal constitutional culture that preceded it.

The Problem of Constitutional Evil[53]

One might accept that I have accurately described how constitutional change occurs in the United States but object on a different ground. The objection is not that my theory of constitutional development is false but that it is morally unsatisfactory or even dangerous, because the process I describe might lead to very bad and unjust results. The process of constitutional change may possess sociological legitimacy because it roughly follows public opinion and is supported by it. It may possess procedural legitimacy because constitutional construction employs standard forms of legal argument and because it is democratically responsive in the long run. Yet it may lack moral legitimacy because constitutional constructions can be very unjust; they can oppress minority groups and individual citizens, and undermine or even destroy democratic values.

A system of framework originalism and living constitutionalism may be democratically legitimate and still produce or countenance very unjust results that well-trained lawyers can defend using plausible legal arguments. This well describes most of American constitutional history. Throughout our history minorities have been badly treated and individual rights denied in ways that we would find completely unacceptable in a constitutional democracy today. This is not to assume that we inhabit a privileged position: no doubt future generations may think the same of some practices in our current political order.

As an example of what the processes of constitutional change might lead to, consider an example from our recent history: the Bush administration's claim—most often associated with Vice President Dick Cheney, David Addington, and John Yoo—that when the president acts in his capacity as commander in chief, he cannot be bound by congressional enactments that seek to limit his powers. This includes, among other things, laws against domestic surveillance and even laws against torture and cruel and inhumane treatment.[54]

The famous "torture memos" produced by the Bush administration's Office of Legal Counsel articulate this theory; they sound quite lawyerly, and they make coherent legal arguments, even if they are not very good arguments. They exemplify an important fact about legal discourse—that well-trained lawyers can make truly bad legal arguments that argue for very unjust things in perfectly legal-sounding language. No one should be surprised by this fact. Today lawyers make arguments defending the legality of torture and, indeed, claiming that laws that would prevent the president from torturing people are unconstitutional.[55] In the past lawyers have used legal-sounding arguments to defend the legality of slavery,[56] Jim Crow,[57] and compulsory sterilization.[58]

Elsewhere I have asserted that the Cheney/Addington/Yoo theory of presidential power, taken to its logical conclusions, allows presidents to rule by decree (or indeed without decree) and in this sense is tantamount to presidential dictatorship.[59] If the president cannot be limited by congressional statutes when he acts as commander in chief, he is not very limited at all, especially when the United States is engaged in a war on terror with no geographical boundaries and no foreseeable conclusion.

Such a theory has little basis in the original understanding of the founding period, which feared the rise of a new Caesar or Cromwell; it is a product of the modern era.[60] But even if we stipulate that it is a bad interpretation of the Constitution, could the courts adopt such a theory through the processes of living constitutionalism described in this book? It is certainly possible that they could, for President Bush and his lawyers pushed it vigorously on several occasions.

Suppose that President Bush had been a far more successful president than he actually was, that his adventures in Iraq had gone much better than they actually did, that the economy did not implode in his second term, and that the public rewarded his party by repeatedly returning his political allies to office. A few more Supreme Court appointments who saw things President Bush's way, and we might be well on our way to a conception of presidential power that would have been unimaginable only ten years before. As noted above, courts have made many bad and unwise decisions in our nation's history. Nobody should underestimate what lawyers in high places can do armed with legal language. But the more important question is whether the constitutional system as a whole can correct the excesses of such lawyers.

Ultimately it is a question of design and faith in that design: whether a system of living constitutionalism such as we have can set ambition against ambition, mobilization against countermobilization, and judicial conservation against political zeal in a way that preserves a decent society or at least helps us move haltingly toward a more decent one. The question is whether the system of living constitutionalism we have generated through years of construction is a worthy successor to the framers' idea of separation of powers and checks and balances—a system that moderates, tests, and checks; and one that makes politics both possible and accountable to prudence and reason. This is a question of reason and faith; of practical knowledge and of moral commitment to preserving just institutions and working for better ones.

It is possible, but very unlikely, that five justices of the Supreme Court would adopt reasoning like that of the torture memos. Unlikely, because it would require the justices to overturn a lot of precedent and disregard basic principles of the constitutional system. Possible, because the history of our country shows that constitutional culture can change greatly, given enough time. But the fact that courts make bad decisions, and even evil decisions, does not mean that the constitutional system as a whole becomes illegitimate. It just means that a particular decision is very wrong. The more important question is whether our constitutional system offers opportunities to correct bad judicial decisionmaking— through sustained criticism and protest, through changing people's minds about what our Constitution requires, through political responses, mobilizations and workarounds, and through the judicial appointments process. These features of political practice are part of the checks and balances of our constitutional system. We recognize them easily when the president and Congress are in conflict, but perhaps less easily when the courts are involved—perhaps because we think incorrectly that they have the last word on the meaning of the Constitution.

The system of living constitutionalism we have created has produced new checks and balances to buttress the ones provided in our original Constitution. It is a good thing, too. National power has increased, and with the blessing and support of the political branches the courts have become more important and more powerful. Institutions have grown, politics has become more complex, and power can be asserted through ever-new means. We are always in need of new ways for power to check power, and hold off the destruction of free government.

These same features of our political system offer us the means to prevent bad decisions from occurring in the first place. Today nobody can be appointed to the Supreme Court who thinks that Jim Crow policies are constitutional. But that was not true through most of our country's history. It became true only because of years of political and legal struggle.

If the Supreme Court adopted a theory of presidential dictatorship, it might send us spiraling down toward the end of our two-centuries-old constitutional experiment with democracy—a possibility that the framers imagined but tried to forestall. Or it might not. The next administration might come along, take very different positions, and appoint new justices who would distinguish the bad decision, or even overrule it. But in any case, it would not simply be a question of us waiting passively for the Supreme Court to decide our fates. There are always things we can do to promote the redemption of constitutional government. The fact that the Constitution is in all of our hands, and not simply the hands of the justices, is the reason why our Constitution still lives.

NOTES

1. Fidelity to Text and Principle

1. On the notion of the Constitution as a project that simultaneously constitutes the American people, see Mark V. Tushnet, *Taking the Constitution Away from the Courts* 11–12 (Princeton University Press 1999).

2. On the idea of constitutional construction, see Keith E. Whittington, *Constitutional Construction: Divided Powers and Constitutional Meaning* 5 (Harvard University Press 1999). See also Keith E. Whittington, *Constitutional Interpretation: Textual Meaning, Original Intent, and Judicial Review* (University Press of Kansas 1999). Whittington defines constitutional interpretation as the "process of discovering the meaning of the constitutional text," whereas constitutional construction is "essentially creative, though the foundations for the ultimate structure are taken as given. The text is not discarded but brought into being." Id. at 5.

In Whittington's model, all branches may engage in constitutional interpretation, but constitutional construction is reserved only for the political branches. Id. at 9, 11–12, 221 n. 3. In contrast, Randy Barnett and I have argued that all branches may engage in constitutional construction. See Randy Barnett, *Restoring the Lost Constitution: The Presumption of Liberty* 118–27 (Princeton University Press 2004); Jack M. Balkin, "Abortion and Original Meaning," 24 *Const. Comm.* 291, 293–94, 300–307 (2007).

On the modalities of constitutional argument, see Philip Bobbitt, *Constitutional Interpretation* (Blackwell 1993); Philip Bobbitt, *Constitutional Fate: Theory of the Constitution* (Oxford University Press 1982). Bobbitt argues that these modalities of argument are equal in importance; where they conflict, individuals must rely on their conscience to decide between them. My view is slightly different. Interpretations and constructions may not contradict original meaning, therefore once we know the original meaning of the text, it trumps any other form of argument. Nevertheless, people can and should use all of the modalities of argument to resolve any uncertainties or ambiguities in original meaning and to build constitutional constructions that are consistent with original meaning.

Bobbitt emphasizes that people use the modalities to deliberate and exercise individual conscience in deciding between them. I emphasize that the modalities of constitutional argument are also forms of shared public rhetoric. Constitutional disagreements are aired in public among fellow citizens; constitutional understandings change over time through persuasion. The modalities of constitutional argument are common resources that help us explain to others what we think the Constitution means and why they should agree with us.

3. See Antonin Scalia, "Originalism: The Lesser Evil," 57 *U. Cin. L. Rev.* 849, 862–64 (1989); Antonin Scalia, "Common Law Courts in a Civil Law System: The Role of United States Federal Courts in Interpreting the Constitution and Laws," in *A Matter of Interpretation: Federal Courts and the Law* 17 (Amy Gutmann ed., Princeton University Press 1997).

4. Scalia, "Common Law Courts," supra note 3, at 38.

5. Scalia, "Response," in *A Matter of Interpretation,* supra note 3, at 145 (emphasis in original).

6. See id. at 140–41 (emphasis in original).

7. Scalia, "Originalism," supra note 3, at 861–64.

8. See, e.g., Gonzales v. Raich, 545 U.S. 1, 17 (2005) (Scalia, J., concurring).

9. See Kenneth Dam, "The Legal Tender Cases," 1981 *Sup. Ct. Rev.* 367, 389 ("difficult to escape the conclusion that the Framers intended to prohibit" use of paper money as legal tender); *Hearings before Senate Comm. on the Judiciary 100th Cong., 1st Sess. Nomination of Robert H. Bork to Be Associate Justice of the Supreme Court of the United States: Part 1,* at 84–85 (1987).

10. See Frontiero v. Richardson, 411 U.S. 677 (1973).

11. Loving v. Virginia, 388 U.S. 1 (1967).

12. Griswold v. Connecticut, 381 U.S. 479 (1965); Eisenstadt v. Baird, 405 U.S. 438 (1971).

13. E.g., Cohen v. California, 403 U.S. 15 (1971) (protecting public expressions of profanity); Brandenburg v. Ohio, 395 U.S. 444 (1969) (protecting advocacy of sedition and law violation); New York Times v. Sullivan, 376 U.S. 254 (1964) (holding unconstitutional aspects of common law of defamation); Scalia, "Response," supra note 5, at 138 (contemporary First Amendment protections are "irreversible" "whether or not they were constitutionally required as an original matter").

14. Scalia, "Response," supra note 5, at 139.

15. Id. at 140.

16. See Lawrence B. Solum, *Semantic Originalism* (Illinois Pub. Law Research Paper No. 07-24, 2008), available at papers.ssrn.com/sol3/papers.cfm?abstract_id=1120244.

17. Solum identifies three of these forms of meaning. See id. at 2–3. I also include meaning as intention and meaning as association because they are important to culture in general and constitutional culture in particular.

18. That we are not bound by the specific purposes of the adopters is especially important in the case of structural arguments, and in the case of textual commitments to unenumerated rights, for example, in the Ninth Amendment and the privileges or immunities clause of the Fourteenth Amendment. Some structural arguments depend on events that occurred after enactment, and unenumerated rights by their nature cannot be specified in advance. See Chapters 9 and 12, infra.

19. See Scalia, "Common Law Courts," supra note 3, at 37–38 (the text of the First Amendment must be construed as a synecdoche in which "speech" and "press" stand for a whole range of different forms of expression, including handwritten letters).

20. See John Hart Ely, *Democracy and Distrust: A Theory of Judicial Review* (Harvard University Press 1980). Ely famously argued against a "clause-bound textualism" and in favor of larger structural principles derived from the text as a whole.

21. 347 U.S. 483 (1954).

22. 384 U.S. 486 (1966).

2. Framework Originalism

1. Cf. Thomas K. Seung, *Intuition and Construction: The Foundation of Normative Theory* 194–99 (Yale University Press 1993) (distinguishing between "bedrock" and "skyscraper" accounts of political ideals). Although drawn for quite different purposes, this distinction, and Seung's related concept of the "constrained indeterminacy" of human values, is quite relevant to how originalism works. See Thomas K. Seung, *Plato Rediscovered: Human Value and Social Order* 291–92 (Rowman and Littlefield 1996) (noting concept of "constrained indeterminacy" of meaning).

2. U.S. Const. amend. XIV.

3. U.S. Const. amend. XIV, § 1.

4. Id.

5. See William E. Nelson, *The Fourteenth Amendment: From Political Principle to Judicial Doctrine* 143–45 (Harvard University Press 1988) (arguing that framers of the Fourteenth Amendment deliberately used language containing broad principles, leaving specific applications to future generations to work out); Alexander M. Bickel, "The Original Understanding and the Segregation Decision," 69 *Harv. L. Rev.* 1, 59–63 (1955) (moderates and radicals chose open-ended "language capable of growth" that papered over their differences and allowed them to present a unified front that would appeal to a wide range of constituencies).

6. Nelson, *The Fourteenth Amendment,* supra note 5, at 143.

7. Bickel, "The Original Understanding," supra note 5, at 59–63.

8. Id.; see also *Cong. Globe,* 39th Cong., 1st Sess. 3148 (1866) (Remarks of Rep. Stevens) (describing the Fourteenth Amendment as a "mutual concession" and compromise "among men as intelligent, as determined, and as independent as myself, who, not agreeing with me, do not choose to yield their opinions to mine").

9. Nelson, *The Fourteenth Amendment,* supra note 5, at 143–45.

10. U.S. Const. amend. XIV, § 2. The Fourteenth Amendment's silence on the question of black suffrage left open space for congressional action. In 1867 and 1868, while the Fourteenth Amendment was still before the states, Congress passed a series of Reconstruction acts (Act of March 2, 1867, ch. 153, 14 Stat. 428; Act of March 23, 1867, ch. 6, 15 Stat. 2; Act of July 19, 1867, ch. 30, 15 Stat. 14; Act of March 11, 1868, ch. 25, 15 Stat. 41). These required states in the former Confederacy to hold new constitutional conventions in which blacks could vote for delegates, leading to new state constitutions that secured black suffrage in the South. The Fifteenth Amendment finally granted black males the right to vote throughout the United States in 1870. U.S. Const. amend. XV, § 1.

11. U.S. Const. amend. XIV, § 3.

12. U.S. Const. amend. XIV, § 4.

13. U.S. Const. pmbl.

14. David P. Currie, *The Constitution in Congress: The Jeffersonians 1801– 1829,* at 87–107, 250–58, 290–95 (University of Chicago Press 2001).

15. Bruce Ackerman, *The Failure of the Founding Fathers: Jefferson, Marshall, and the Rise of Presidential Democracy* (Harvard University Press 2005).

16. John O. McGinnis and Michael Rappaport, "Original Interpretive Principles as the Core of Originalism," 24 *Const. Comment.* 371, 374 (2007); McGinnis and Rappaport, "A Pragmatic Defense of Originalism," 101 *Nw. U.L. Rev.* 383 (2007).

17. McGinnis and Rappaport, "Original Interpretive Principles," supra note 16, at 372, 380.

18. Antonin Scalia, "Common Law Courts in a Civil Law System: The Role of United States Federal Courts in Interpreting the Constitution and Laws," in *A Matter of Interpretation: Federal Courts and the Law,* n. 3, 40 (Amy Gutmann ed., Princeton University Press 1997). Thus, Scalia argues that we should look to the original expected application of the cruel and unusual punishments clause because we need protection against "the moral perceptions of a future, more brutal generation." Scalia, "Response," in *A Matter of Interpretation,* supra, at 129, 145.

19. See McGinnis and Rappaport, "Original Interpretive Principles," supra note 16, at 378–81 (arguing for reading abstract principles close to original ex-

pected applications); Scalia, "Response," supra note 18, at 129, 135 (arguing against reading the Bill of Rights as aspirational); id. at 145 (arguing for reading the Eighth Amendment according to original expected application).

20. In any case, the framers of the American Constitution were optimists who believed in Enlightenment values of human progress, although they well understood the recurrent temptations of power, selfishness, and avarice in the political struggles of history.

21. For a good discussion, on which the next few paragraphs are based, see Christopher L. Eisgruber, *Constitutional Self-Government* 12–20 (Harvard University Press 2001); Christopher L. Eisgruber, "Should Constitutional Judges Be Philosophers?" in *Exploring Law's Empire: The Jurisprudence of Ronald Dworkin 5*, 19–21 (Scott Hershovitz ed., Oxford University Press 2006).

22. Lawrence G. Sager, "The Incorrigible Constitution," 65 *N.Y.U. L. Rev.* 893, 951–53 (1990).

23. We might look to original expected applications as a floor for rights that protect the equality and liberty of individuals and minorities. This is the point of Jed Rubenfeld's constitutional theory, which has both a descriptive and a normative claim. Rubenfeld's descriptive claim is that the American constitutional tradition has continued to uphold certain paradigm cases of rights and equality protections although these protections have sometimes greatly expanded. His normative claim is that this should be so, because maintaining paradigm cases is part of what it means to make a normative commitment. Jed Rubenfeld, *Revolution by Judiciary: The Structure of American Constitutional Law* (Harvard University Press 2005); Jed Rubenfeld, *Freedom and Time: A Theory of Constitutional Self-Government* (Yale University Press 2001).

The role that original expected application plays in forming later constructions suggests why Rubenfeld's descriptive and normative claims make considerable sense. As time and circumstances change, future generations might want to retain these paradigm cases as central examples of what they see themselves as committed to. Maintaining those central examples helps establish that they have constitutional commitments and helps ground and channel the development of these commitments over time.

Nevertheless, an important difference between Rubenfeld's position and my own is that he claims that the paradigm cases enjoy a legal status similar to the constitutional text; like the text, paradigm cases cannot be disregarded or repudiated without amending the Constitution. In contrast, I regard the adopters' choice of rules, standards, principles, and silences in the text as the constitutional framework that cannot be changed without amendment, and on which later generations must build.

Even so, I believe that Rubenfeld's paradigm cases should have very strong weight in creating modern-day constructions. If present-day constructions do not protect what the adopting generation thought was the most central example of a right, or the most central example of what powers the federal government possessed, that is a good reason to ask whether a construction is faulty. Nevertheless, moral and political commitments—even the most deeply held ones—always exist against the background of assumptions about how society is organized, what is technologically feasible, and how the world works. Social, economic, and technological changes might undermine these background assumptions. Thus, unlike Rubenfeld, I do not treat paradigm cases as necessarily binding in all circumstances. Instead, I regard them as strong evidence about how to construct provisions faithfully.

Rubenfeld makes a further, more controversial claim about paradigm cases, which I also do not necessarily accept. He argues that understandings that a constitutional provision *would not* apply to certain situations cannot, by stipulation, be either a paradigm case or a constitutional commitment. Rubenfeld, *Revolution by Judiciary*, at 15. If the framers believed that a certain rights provision would never apply to a certain situation, this is not a constitutional commitment; if they believed that a constitutional power would never allow the government to perform a certain action or pass a certain type of law, that is also not a constitutional commitment.

This definition of commitment meshes well with post–New Deal understandings of the Constitution: the federal government has expansive powers, and rights have expanded to limit government. But it does not seem to capture the vision of the framers, in which limitations on government power were an important method for securing liberty. Similarly, the adopting generation did not want the President to have the same powers as George III because too great an executive power might undermine liberty or lead to despotism. Under Rubenfeld's definition of commitment, however, it is hard to see how the 1787 framers could have committed themselves to creating a set of limited federal powers (or limited Presidential powers) except by explicitly listing all the things that the federal government—or the President—could not do. See id. at 49.

24. See, e.g., Jon Elster, "Intertemporal Choice and Political Thought," in *Choice Over Time* 35 (George Loewenstein and Jon Elster eds., Russell Sage Foundation 1992) (discussing constitutions as precommitment devices); Stephen Holmes, "Precommitment and the Paradox of Democracy," in *Constitutionalism and Democracy* 195 (Jon Elster and Rune Slagstad eds., Cambridge University Press 1988) (discussing historical arguments for and against the use of precommitment devices in constitutions); Antonin Scalia, "Common-Law Courts," supra note 18, at 3, 40–41 ("[A constitution's] whole purpose is to prevent change—to embed certain rights in such a manner that future generations cannot readily take them away").

25. Scalia, "Response," supra note 18, at 129, 145 (arguing that we should look to the original expected application of the cruel and unusual punishments

clause because we need protection against "the moral perceptions of a future, more brutal generation").

26. Scalia, "Common Law Courts," supra note 18, at 40.

27. Scalia, "Response," supra note 18, at 140.

28. See Gonzales v. Raich, 545 U.S. 1, 17 (2005) (Scalia, J., concurring); *Nomination of Judge Robert H. Bork: Hearings before the Senate Committee on the Judiciary,* 100th Cong. 112–13, 264–65, 292–93, 465 (1987), reprinted in 14 *The Supreme Court of the United States: Hearings and Reports on Successful and Unsuccessful Nominations of Supreme Court Justices by the Senate Judiciary Committee, 1916–1987,* at 292–93, 444–45, 472–73, 645 (Roy M. Mersky and J. Myron Jacobstein eds., William S. Hein and Co. 1989) (testimony of Robert H. Bork from Sept. 15, 1987–Sept. 19, 1987); Antonin Scalia, "Originalism: The Lesser Evil," 57 *U. Cin. L. Rev.* 849, 861–64 (1989); Philip Lacovara, "A Talk with Judge Robert H. Bork," *District Law.,* May/June 1985, at 29, 32; cf. John O. McGinnis and Michael B. Rappaport, "Reconciling Originalism and Precedent: A Constitutional and Normative Analysis," 103 *Nw. U. L. Rev.* 803 (2009) (offering a consequentialist analysis for determining when nonoriginalist precedents should be retained).

3. Why Original Meaning?

1. See the discussion in Chapter 4.

2. Scott Shapiro's theory of law as social planning explicitly compares legal systems—including constitutions—to social plans. Scott Shapiro, *Legality* (Harvard University Press 2011).

3. This argument is hardly original with me. James Madison himself made an early version:

> I entirely concur in the propriety of resorting to the sense in which the Constitution was accepted and ratified by the nation. In that sense alone it is the legitimate Constitution. And if that be not the guide in expounding it, there can be no security for a consistent and stable, more than for a faithful, exercise of its powers. If the meaning of the text be sought in the changeable meaning of the words composing it, it is evident that the shape and attributes of the government must partake of the changes to which the words and phrases of all living languages are constantly subject. What a metamorphosis would be produced in the code of law if all its ancient phraseology were to be taken in its modern sense! And that the language of our Constitution is already under-going interpretations unknown to its founders will, I believe, appear to all unbiased enquirers into the history of its origin and adoption.

Letter from Madison to Henry Lee (June 25, 1824), in 9 *The Writings of James Madison* 191–92 (Gaillard Hunt ed., G. P. Putnam's Sons 1910). For modern versions, each with a slightly different emphasis, see Randy Barnett, *Restoring the Lost Constitution,* 100–107 (Princeton University Press 2004) (emphasizing the lock-in function of writings); Joseph Raz, "Intention in Interpretation," in *The Autonomy of Law: Essays on Legal Positivism* 249, 258 (Robert P. George ed., Oxford University Press 1996) (arguing that "it makes no sense to give any person or body law-making power unless it is assumed that the law they make is the law they intended to make"); Steven Smith, "Law without Mind," 88 *Mich. L. Rev.* 104, 117 (1989) ("Present-oriented interpretation . . . makes law substantially the product of historical accident").

4. U.S. Const. art. IV, § 4 (the capitalization is as in the original).

5. I have often joked that this was the underlying basis of Bush v. Gore, 531 U.S. 98 (2000).

On a more serious note, Mark Stein points out that if the original meaning of "domestic violence" was not "riots and insurrections" but any "violence internal to a state," then spousal abuse would literally fall within the original semantic meaning of the guarantee clause. Mark S. Stein, "The Domestic Violence Clause in 'New Originalist' Theory," 37 *Hastings Const. L. Q.* 129, 133–34 (2009). Applying the clause only to riots and insurrections would limit it to original expected applications.

If Stein's reading were correct, it would have given the United States the constitutional responsibility to protect the states from all violent crime within their borders. Therefore, his theory of the clause's original semantic meaning is very unlikely. Moreover, even if his reading were correct, it says nothing about the best construction of the guarantee clause today. Although we are not limited to original expected applications, we are certainly permitted to use them to create constructions, especially if they are reasonable. Contemporary interpreters might well conclude that instead of giving the federal government the constitutional duty to prevent all violent crime occurring within the United States, it would be more sensible to limit the application of "domestic violence" to "riots and insurrections."

6. Zachary Elkins, Tom Ginsburg, and James Melton, *The Endurance of National Constitutions* (Cambridge University Press 2009) (noting a half-life of nineteen years).

7. See David A. Strauss, *The Living Constitution* 116 (Oxford University Press 2010) (arguing that Article V amendments "are actually not a very important way of changing the Constitution"); David A. Strauss, "The Irrelevance of Constitutional Amendments," 114 *Harv. L. Rev.* 1457, 1467 (2001) (arguing that constitutional amendments now have largely symbolic value and comparing them in this respect to "congressional resolutions, presidential proclamations, or declarations of national holidays").

8. See Bruce Ackerman, "Constitutional Politics/Constitutional Law," 99 *Yale L. J.* 453, 458–59, 488, 491 (1989) (describing the "myth of rediscovery" that Americans return to the Constitution in constitutional transformations when in

fact they are making profound changes); Bruce A. Ackerman, 1 *We the People: Foundations* 43, 62 (Harvard University Press 1991) (same).

9. David A. Strauss, "Common Law, Common Ground, and Jefferson's Principle," 112 *Yale L. J.* 1717, 1724 (2003).

10. For a bill of particulars, see Sanford Levinson, *Our Undemocratic Constitution: Where the Constitution Goes Wrong (and How We the People Can Correct It)* (Oxford University Press 2006).

11. Letter from Thomas Jefferson to James Madison (September 6, 1789) in 15 *The Papers of Thomas Jefferson* 392, 396 (Julian P. Boyd and William H. Gaines Jr. eds., Princeton University Press 1958).

12. See Jack M. Balkin and Reva B. Siegel, "Principles, Practices, and Social Movements," 154 *U. Pa. L. Rev.* 927, 928, 930–33 (2006). In this book I speak of three basic kinds of legal norms: rules, standards, and principles. Rules are distinguished from standards by how much practical or evaluative judgment they require to apply them to concrete situations. Legal norms that are more standard-like require people to engage in considerable practical reasoning (which includes moral reasoning) in order to apply the legal norm to specific circumstances. Legal norms that are more rule-like offer comparatively less discretion and therefore require less practical reasoning to apply. In comparison with rules, standards normally involve a greater degree of delegation to the future.

When rules and standards apply to a situation, they are normally conclusive in deciding a legal question, although decisionmakers can make exceptions later on. Principles, by contrast, are norms that, when relevant, are not conclusive but must be considered in reaching a decision. Decisionmakers may balance them against other considerations, and sometimes the principle does not prevail. Thus, Ronald Dworkin has argued that principles have "weight." Ronald Dworkin, *Taking Rights Seriously* 26–27 (Harvard University Press 1978). Robert Alexy argues that principles are "optimization conditions": when they apply, we must try to realize them as much as possible to the extent that they are not outweighed by other relevant considerations. Robert Alexy, *A Theory Of Constitutional Rights* 47–48 (Julian Rivers trans., Oxford University Press 2002).

In addition to being nonconclusive, many principles—like the guarantees of freedom of speech and the equal protection of the laws—are also vague or abstract: hence, it may take considerable practical reasoning to decide whether they apply to a given situation. Scott Shapiro has pointed out, however, that some principles can appear very "rule-like": it is fairly easy to know whether they apply, but they are nevertheless principles because they are not conclusive and can be outweighed by other considerations. One example might be the compact clause of Article I, section 10, which says, "No state shall, without the consent of Congress, . . . enter into any agreement or compact with another state." It might be easy to tell whether states have entered into an agreement or compact, and whether Congress has consented; even so, the norm might not prevail, for example, if the compact or agreement is on a very minor issue, does not threaten federal supremacy, and does not undermine federal power. As noted in the discussion of the compact clause infra in this chapter, this is how the Supreme Court has interpreted the clause.

Thus, applying principles involves two dimensions of concern. First, does the principle apply at all? (For example, in the case of the free speech principle, is challenged statute directed at "speech" or merely nonspeech conduct?) Second, if we decide that the principle applies, how much weight should it have and how should we balance the principle against other considerations? (For example, under what conditions should we allow the government to restrict access to streets and parks for protests?) Another way to put this is that principles do not determine the scope of their own jurisdiction, and they do not determine the weight they will have in application. (Rules and standards also may not determine the scope of their own jurisdiction, but when they apply, their "weight" is more or less conclusive.)

Because principles do not determine the scope of their jurisdiction and they do not determine their own weight in particular circumstances, they require considerable practical reasoning to apply; therefore, like standards, they usually involve some degree of delegation to the future.

Moreover, because both constitutional standards and principles require considerable practical judgment to apply, they create incentives for people to engage in further constructions in order to make sense of them and apply them. For example, both the Fourth Amendment's standard of "unreasonable" searches and seizures and the First Amendment's principle of 'freedom of speech' have led to the creation of entire bodies of law. These constructions, in turn, may consist of other explanatory rules, standards, and principles. These explanatory standards and principles, in turn, may lead to still further constructions, and so on. In short, when standards and principles appear in constitutional texts, doctrines, and discourse, they often impel a process of construction, reconceptualization, and reconstruction.

One of the best-known accounts of principles is Ronald Dworkin's. I agree with Dworkin that principles have an indeterminate scope and jurisdiction, and that principles are not conclusive, so that decisionmakers must balance principles against other considerations.

Even so, my account of principles is motivated by different concerns from those in Dworkin's account.

First, as a matter of terminology, Dworkin calls all legal norms "standards," and he divides standards into rules, on the one hand, and principles, on the other. What motivates his distinction between rules and principles is whether the norm in question is mandatory or whether it merely has weight. Dworkin, *Taking Rights Seriously,* at 22, 24–25.

My concern, by contrast, is the degree of delegation that a legal norm offers to later decisionmakers; that is why I distinguish, as many other scholars do, between rules and standards. Note, moreover, that what I call "standards" Dworkin also places in the category of "rules." For example, Dworkin says that a norm that "unreasonable contracts are void" is a rule because it cannot be balanced away by other considerations. I would say it is a standard (because it requires considerable practical reasoning to apply) whose jurisdiction is limited to the subject of contracts. Id. at 28, 79.

Second, Dworkin distinguishes two subcategories of principles: principles proper, and policies. Policies are norms that set out economic, political, or social goals to be reached. Reducing automobile accidents is a policy. Principles proper are norms that we should observe not because they help us reach economic, political, or social goals, but because of considerations of justice or morality. The idea that no one should profit from his or her own wrong is a principle. Id. at 22.

The distinction between principles and policies is important for Dworkin's jurisprudential theory because principles state moral imperatives for judges. Dworkin believes that these principles are part of the materials of the law and judges must use them (but not policies) to decide hard cases.

My interest in principles is quite different. I wish to explain the processes of constitutional construction and the degree of delegation to the future that a constitution provides. So my primary focus is not on judges, but on construction by all constitutional actors. Principles are important features of constitutional language because they may encourage or require further construction to apply them. My account does not require that constitutional principles must state norms of justice or moral values. Many constitutional principles (as I define the term), like the principles of federalism or the separation of powers, state policies or goals within particular institutions. Nor do I maintain, as Dworkin does, that judges must decide cases (hard or otherwise) based on moral principles or principles of justice as opposed to policies.

Throughout this book I also speak of "underlying principles." These do not appear in the constitutional text. Rather, they are constitutional constructions that officials and citizens attribute to the Constitution and use to make sense of the constitutional text or the structural scheme of government. (See the discussion in Chapter 12.) Like the principles that appear in the text, these constructions may be employed either by judges or by other constitutional actors, and they may or may not state moral values or principles of justice. Like the principles in the text, they may also lead people to create further constructions to explain and apply them.

Third, principles are important to Dworkin's jurisprudential theory because he argues that, in general, judges do not have discretion to make new law in deciding cases. Instead, judges are required to consider all relevant legal materials—including principles—and produce the best account of law, given the constraints of fit with previous materials and moral justification according to the best available theory. See Ronald Dworkin, *Law's Empire* (Harvard University Press 1987).

Framework originalism has a very different concern: the choice of rules, standards, principles, and silences in a constitution shapes the degree of constraint and discretion that future participants will have in building out the Constitution-in-practice. Framework originalism assumes, rather than denies, that constitutional construction requires discretionary authority to create new law and government institutions.

Presumably Dworkin would distinguish between judicial constructions, on the one hand, and constructions by the political branches, on the other. Although the former do not involve discretion, he would argue, the latter may. I reject this account. At any point in time there may be several different ways for judges to build out constitutional doctrine consistent with their constitutional duties. This is especially the case when judges are responding to new state-building constructions by the political branches.

Chapters 13 and 14 explain how judges play both a dialectical and a cooperative role in state building, limiting and legitimating constructions by the political branches that create new conventions, capacities, and institutions. Judges work in the midst of a series of transformations in how governments operate, some larger and some smaller, some sudden and some gradual. In these constitutional revolutions, far from being constrained by Dworkin's notions of fit, judges may sweep away significant bodies of previous doctrine in order to legitimate new state practices. This activity would not be possible without considerable discretion.

In short, the distinction between rules, standards, and principles does very different work in my theory than the distinction between rules and principles does in Dworkin's. Dworkin employs his distinction to show why the body of legal materials is much thicker than it appears: he believes that it contains numerous background principles that, when properly considered, significantly limit judicial discretion. I use the distinction between rules, standards, and principles to show the economies of constraint and delegation in the constitutional system, and why not only judges but all constitutional actors possess discretion to build out the Constitution-in-practice over time.

13. See Quentin Skinner, 1 *Visions of Politics: Regarding Method* 3, 57–89 (Cambridge University Press 2002).

14. See Scott Shapiro, *Legality*, supra note 2.

15. Lawrence B. Solum, *Semantic Originalism*, SSRN, at papers.ssrn.com/sol3/papers.cfm?abstract_id=1120244 (November 22, 2008).

16. The above argument is not an argument about the inherent or universal nature of interpretation or texts, but rather an argument about American legal

culture and its traditions. Legal interpretation of texts always occurs against the background of a legal culture, with its own assumptions about which texts are authoritative and what are the permissible and impermissible argumentative moves and operations on authoritative texts. Although permissible interpretive moves and operations are often similar across different legal cultures and at different points in history, they can also be quite different.

For example, in the traditions of rabbinic interpretation, it is sometimes permissible to use Gematria to discover hidden meanings in the Torah and other parts of the Hebrew Bible. Gematria involves counting up the numbers assigned to the Hebrew letters in a word or phrase in the text, comparing them with the numbers assigned to other words or phrases, and drawing interpretive conclusions. Arguments using Gematria are bona fide textual arguments in a particular religious culture; one of the reasons why they are valid moves is that the religious culture assumes that God has placed certain coded meanings in divinely ordained texts for later interpreters to discover.

In American legal culture, by contrast, these textual moves are not permissible. Generally speaking, legislatures do not deliberately place hidden numerical codes in texts for later interpreters to uncover; conversely, legal interpreters generally do not believe that it is permissible to make use of hidden numerical codes to discover hidden meanings in authoritative legal texts. The reason why these moves are not valid in American constitutional interpretation is not because of the inherent or transhistorical nature of texts or of interpretation, but because of a history of practices of reading and communication, and the development of a particular form of professional legal culture.

17. See Shapiro, *Legality,* supra note 2 (arguing that law, as a form of social planning, involves an economy of trust and distrust).

18. Behind this example is a larger issue: At the time of the founding, there was no generally agreed-upon set of conventions for interpreting constitutional language. See Larry Kramer, "Originalism and Pragmatism: Two (More) Problems with Originalism," 31 *Harv. J. L. & Pub. Pol'y* 907, 912–13 (2008). This means that when textual issues arise, constitutional construction may be required, and modern interpreters must do the best they can, using textual exegesis, structural reasoning, and historical evidence (where it is available) to resolve ambiguities and build workable solutions.

Saul Cornell has argued powerfully that at the time of the founding, there was no generally accepted way to interpret a written constitution precisely because the idea was so novel in Anglo-American political thought. As a result, different groups offered conflicting visions of constitutional interpretation, which were often connected to their politics, their social position, and their professional training. See Saul Cornell, "The People's Constitution versus the Lawyers' Constitution: Popular Constitutionalism and the Original Debate over Originalism," *Yale J. Law & Hum.* (forthcoming 2011). See also Caleb Nelson,

"Originalism and Interpretive Conventions," 70 *U. Chi. L. Rev.* 519, 555–56, 561, 571–73 (2003) (noting lack of consensus on interpretive conventions for the new federal Constitution). Different participants in the ratification debates and the early Congresses proposed competing rules of construction from various sources, often tied to particular substantive agendas. See id. at 570–76. Put another way, in these early debates people sometimes offered rules of construction based on the results they would likely produce, rather than reasoning to the results from neutral, apolitical, and generally agreed-upon rules of construction.

At the time of the founding, people also disagreed about what kind of text the Constitution most resembled. Competing analogies produced different rules of construction. For example, if the Constitution were analogized to a statute, it should be construed generously and equitably to effectuate its purposes, a position that would appeal to proponents of a strong national government. If it were analogized to a treaty or compact, it should be construed strictly to preserve the antecedent rights and sovereignty of its signatories, a position that appealed to proponents of a weak federal government. Id. at 575–76.

One might have thought that the natural analogy would be to the construction of existing state constitutions, but, as Caleb Nelson points out, "state counterparts were still too young to have generated a canonical set of interpretive rules, and in some respects the federal Constitution was a different creature anyway" because it had been "adopted for a federal system" that "raised interpretive questions not presented by any of the existing state constitutions." Id. at 570.

This history suggests serious flaws in John McGinnis and Michael Rappaport's project of "original methods originalism," which argues that "the Constitution should be interpreted using the interpretive methods that the constitutional enactors would have deemed applicable to it." John McGinnis and Michael Rappaport, "Original Methods Originalism: A New Theory of Interpretation and the Case against Construction," 103 *Nw. U. L. Rev.* 751 (2009). As the title of their article implies, McGinnis and Rappaport adopt this method to avoid the delegation to later generations implicit in theories of constitutional construction. There are four problems with their approach.

First, McGinnis and Rappaport claim that original interpretive methods are part of original meaning because when people voted for the Constitution they assumed that everyone would employ these methods forever to interpret the document. See id. at 783–84. But if there was no consensus on the proper methods of interpretation, or if the advocacy of different methods was tied to political disputes about the Constitution, this aspect of "original meaning" was inherently disputable from the outset and lacked the supermajoritarian consensus that is essential to McGinnis and Rappaport's theory. Therefore, modern interpreters still must choose among interpretive methods today to clarify and implement the Constitution's original meaning.

Second, McGinnis and Rappaport make the familiar error of speaking as if the Constitution had been adopted at a single point in time rather than over the course of two centuries. Many of the most controversial judicial constructions concern the Fourteenth Amendment. But McGinnis and Rappaport provide no evidence of original interpretive methods during Reconstruction or, for that matter, during the twentieth century, when many other amendments were adopted. They do not explain how one would employ their approach if interpretive practices at the time of the ratification of the Fourteenth Amendment were different from those used at the time of the founding. This might be especially important, for example, in cases involving application of the Bill of Rights to state and local governments through the Fourteenth Amendment. During Reconstruction one can find a variety of rules of construction, including appeals to underlying purpose and intention and what is essentially framework originalism. See *Cong. Globe*, 42nd Cong., 1st Sess. 370 (1871) (statement of Rep. Monroe)(arguing that free constitutions have a "natural growth" caused by "the more extended application of" constitutional principles to new situations. "Principles have commonly a much wider application than we suspect" and what seem like innovations "may only be the application of known and admitted principles to new circumstances").

Third, McGinnis and Rappaport advocate original methods originalism in part to constrain judges. Unless judges are bound by original interpretive methods, they argue, later interpretations will not have gone through the supermajoritarian process of ratification, and judges will create constructions of the Constitution's abstract and vague clauses based on their own views rather than the views of the adopters. See McGinnis and Rappaport, "Original Methods Originalism," supra, at 783. Following original interpretive methods will require later interpreters to hew more closely to original expected applications. That is because, McGinnis and Rappaport contend, "there is little or no evidence supporting dynamic interpretation or living constitutionalism." Id. at 788.

McGinnis and Rappaport offer little evidence themselves to back up this bare assertion. In fact, the history suggests otherwise, whether we focus on the founding or, equally important, on Reconstruction (as the above quote from Representative Monroe suggests). Saul Cornell points out that if our concern is the interpretive understandings of the general ratifying public (as opposed to the much smaller class of professionally trained lawyers), the most common interpretive method at the founding would have been something like framework originalism and it would be consistent with the idea of a living Constitution. Legislatures and juries (as opposed to judges) would be the primary interpreters of constitutional meaning; they would apply the Constitution's text to their understanding of current circumstances. See Cornell, "The People's Constitution versus the Lawyers' Constitution," supra note 18. Cornell notes that such a plain-meaning approach was championed by various Anti-Federalists, who feared that a cabal of elite lawyers using esoteric methods might threaten American freedoms through their interpretation of the new Constitution. Id. McGinnis and Rappaport simply assert that popular understandings of the Constitution should be preempted by the understandings of professional lawyers at the time of the founding where the two conflict, thus adopting one position among many in this debate. McGinnis and Rappaport, "Original Methods Originalism," supra, at 770–72. They do not appear to recognize that this very question was a major issue of contention at the founding.

Finally, and perhaps most important, McGinnis and Rappaport's theory is unworkable because it seeks to reject the distinction between interpretation-as-ascertainment-of-meaning and interpretation-as-construction. See id. at 773. McGinnis and Rappaport want to derive as much of the Constitution-in-practice as possible from "original meaning" and make as little as possible a matter of discretionary construction and adjustment. But this is not how constitutional development works, either today or at the time of the founding.

Canons of statutory construction, then as now, were rules of *construction;* they were employed to resolve vagueness or ambiguity in legal texts and to develop workable doctrines and conventions. They did not prevent discretion; rather, they invited judgment. They were maxims and rules of thumb that, like legal principles, could be balanced away by competing canons and competing considerations. Different sides in political and legal debates employed these canons—as well as other kinds of arguments—in order to promote different constructions of vague, ambiguous, or abstract constitutional texts.

In short, politicians during the founding and in the first Congresses did something very similar to what people do today when faced with an unclear legal text. They offered competing constructions of the Constitution, trying to build it out in ways they favored. The specific tools they used—how they built out the Constitution—are not themselves part of original meaning, although it is certainly helpful to know these maxims and methods when we create our own modern-day constructions.

McGinnis and Rappaport assert that they can find no evidence of "construction" in my sense of the word at the time of the founding. Id. But evidence of construction is everywhere: in the ratification debates, in the debates over the First Bank of the United States—indeed, in almost every contested constitutional question in the early federal period. See generally David P. Currie, *The Constitution in Congress—The Federalist Period, 1789–1801* (University of Chicago Press 1997) (describing these initial debates). Institutions had to be built, conventions had to be established, and disputed political questions had to be resolved. By attempting to collapse interpretation-as-construction into interpretation-as-ascertainment-of-meaning, McGinnis and Rappaport do not recognize that construction, then as now, was essential to making a constitutional plan operate in practice.

19. See Virginia v. Tennessee, 148 U.S. 503, 518 (1893).

20. Id. at 519 (holding that the compact clause is "directed to the formation of any combination tending to the increase of political power in the States, which may encroach upon or interfere with the just supremacy of the United States"). The Court, employing the interpretive canon of *noscitur a sociis* (one is known by one's neighbors) argued that the words "Agreement or Compact" should be read in the context of Article I, section 10's ban on states entering into any "treaty, alliance, or confederation" that also involved threats to federal authority. Justice Field argued that while the latter refer to political agreements between sovereigns, the former concern "mere private rights of sovereignty; such as questions of boundary; interests in land situate [sic] in the territory of each other, and other internal regulations for the mutual comfort and convenience of States bordering on each other." Id. (citing Joseph Story, 3 *Commentaries on the Constitution of the United States* § 1403 (Brown, Shattuck, & Co. 1833). See also the discussion in United States Steel Corp. v. Multistate Tax Comm'n, 434 U.S. 452, 460–67 (1978).

21. Another way to understand the compact clause would be to view it as a rule with a number of judicially created exceptions. A familiar practice of common-law judging allows decisionmakers to create exceptions to rules to avoid absurdity or disastrous consequences. Nevertheless, this practice requires a normative assessment of whether the consequences of a particular application are sufficiently absurd or disastrous to justify an exception. These judgments are not always obvious and may often be quite controversial.

If the number of situations that seem to call for an exception proves sufficiently large, this is a strong argument for treating the norm as a principle rather than a rule with exceptions. I believe this is the best account of the compact clause. See also the discussion of the compact clause in note 12, supra.

22. See Larry Solum's amusing April Fool's Day parody of the method of text and principle, "Balkin on the Senate," Legal Theory Blog (April 1, 2010), at lsolum.typepad.com/legaltheory/2010/04/balkin-on-framework-originalism-and-the-senate.html.

23. The example of Senate apportionment creates a number of puzzles that are beyond the scope of this book. For example, could Congress amend Article V to remove the requirement of unanimous consent by a vote of three-fourths of the states? By a vote of three-quarters of the states, could an Article V amendment create a new body with representation based on population (call it Senate 2.0) and transfer most, if not all, of the original Senate's powers to that body? The answer to these questions is not immediately clear from the text; it requires constitutional construction that will inevitably draw on structural assumptions about the nature of the plan. For my purposes it is sufficient to note that, however these questions are resolved, they do not allow courts to treat the current texts regarding Senate apportionment as nonliteral usages, abstract principles, or vague standards.

24. Jeremy Waldron, "Principles of Legislation," in *The Least Examined Branch: The Role of Legislatures in the Constitutional State* (Richard W. Bauman and Tsvi Kahana eds., Cambridge University Press 2006), at 22, citing John Rawls, *Political Liberalism* (Columbia University Press 1993), at 66ff.

25. David A. Strauss, *The Living Constitution,* supra note 7; Strauss, "Common Law, Common Ground," supra note 9; David A. Strauss, "Common Law Constitutional Interpretation," 63 *U. Chi. L. Rev.* 877 (1996).

26. David A. Strauss, "Common Law, Common Ground," supra note 9, at 1725.

27. Id. at 1734.

28. Id. at 1725.

29. Id.

30. Id.

31. Id. at 1735.

32. David A. Strauss, *The Living Constitution,* supra note 7; David A. Strauss, "The Irrelevance of Constitutional Amendments," 114 *Harv. L. Rev.* 1457 (2001); David A. Strauss, *Common Law Constitutional Interpretation,* supra note 25.

33. Strauss, "Common Law, Common Ground," supra note 9, at 1738.

34. Id.

35. Id. at 1734.

36. Although Judge Guido Calabresi famously suggested that we should adopt special interpretive rules for older, outmoded statutes. See Guido Calabresi, *A Common Law for the Age of Statutes* (Harvard University Press 1982).

37. Reva B. Siegel, "Text in Contest: Gender and the Constitution from a Social Movement Perspective," 150 *U. Pa. L. Rev.* 297 (2001).

38. These points are elaborated in Jack M. Balkin, *Constitutional Redemption: Political Faith in an Unjust World* (Harvard University Press 2011), ch. 8.

39. Strauss, "Common Law, Common Ground," supra note 9, at 1751.

40. Id. at 1752.

41. Id. at 1724 ("it is difficult to see why people who do not feel themselves part of that tradition—who identify primarily with a different ethnic, religious, or cultural tradition, or with no tradition at all—should . . . have to identity with this particular American tradition as well").

42. Mark V. Tushnet, *Taking the Constitution Away from the Courts* 11–14 (Princeton University Press 1999) (describing the Constitution as a transgenerational project of realizing the principles of the Declaration of Independence); Jed Rubenfeld, *Freedom and Time: A Theory of Constitutional Self-Government* 176–77 (Yale University Press 2001) (describing the Constitution as a temporally extended project of self-governance).

4. Basic Law, Higher Law, Our Law

1. See Bruce A. Ackerman, 1 *We the People: Foundations* (Harvard University Press 1991).

2. Jack M. Balkin, "The Declaration and the Promise of a Democratic Culture," 4 *Widener L. Symp. J.* 167 (1999). It is worth noting here that the argument in this chapter is directed to the *American* constitutional tradition and may not be readily generalizable to the constitutions of other countries, including democracies.

First, the sociological legitimacy of constitutions in some other democratic traditions may not be strongly connected to a national narrative, much less an imagined transgenerational project of constitutional politics. In many cases, a country's current constitution may play only a minor role in the construction of national identity, whereas it plays a significant role in America's self-understanding.

Second, national narratives and forms of collective memory in different countries may be very different from the American experience, affecting how people tell the story of their constitution and understand their relationship to it. Not all constitutions emerged from a revolutionary tradition or a revolutionary narrative; Australia's and Canada's constitutions developed through longer, more gradual, and relatively peaceful transitions from colonial status. Some countries have had multiple constitutions in relatively short periods of time, their constitutions are viewed as a patchwork or a complicated mix of enactments, or their constitutions have been repeatedly suspended or disregarded. As a result, these constitutions do not receive the same sort of veneration as the U.S. Constitution does in the American political tradition.

Finally, because of their distinctive political histories, constitutions in other countries may not function either as "higher law" or as "our law" in the same way that the American Constitution functions in America's distinctive political culture. For an illuminating comparative analysis, see Gary Jacobsohn, *Constitutional Identity* (Harvard University Press 2010).

3. Not surprisingly, Scalia himself has little tolerance for the notion that constitutional guarantees could be aspirational. Antonin Scalia, "Response," in *A Matter of Interpretation: Federal Courts and the Law* 134–36 (Amy Gutmann ed., Princeton University Press 1997).

4. For a more extensive discussion, see Jack M. Balkin, *Constitutional Redemption: Political Faith in an Unjust World* (Harvard University Press 2011); Jack M. Balkin, "Respect Worthy: Frank Michelman and the Legitimate Constitution," 39 *Tulsa L. Rev.* 485, 498–501 (2004).

5. This is the basic assertion of Jed Rubenfeld's work on the Constitution as a practice of temporally extended self-government. Jed Rubenfeld, *Revolution by Judiciary: The Structure of American Constitutional Law* (Harvard University

Press 2005); Rubenfeld, *Freedom and Time: A Theory of Constitutional Self-Government* (Yale University Press 2001).

6. Richard H. Fallon Jr., "Legitimacy and the Constitution," 118 *Harv. L. Rev.* 1787 (2005); Jack M. Balkin, "The Legitimacy of the 2000 Election," in *Bush v. Gore: The Question of Legitimacy* (Bruce Ackerman ed., Yale University Press 2002).

7. See, e.g., Ronald Dworkin, *Freedom's Law: The Moral Reading of the American Constitution* 15–35 (Harvard University Press 1996) (arguing for a thick conception of constitutional democracy with significant rights protections, contrasted with pure majoritarianism).

8. See Robert C. Post and Reva B. Siegel, "Democratic Constitutionalism," in *The Constitution in 2020* (Jack M. Balkin and Reva B. Siegel eds., Oxford University Press 2009). See also Robert C. Post and Reva B. Siegel, "Roe Rage: Democratic Constitutionalism and Backlash," 42 *Harv. C.R.–C.L. L. Rev.* 373 (2007). Although Post and Siegel's account is primarily descriptive, in this book I use the idea of democratic constitutionalism as a normative account of why the processes of constitutional construction possess democratic legitimacy.

9. See Jack M. Balkin and Sanford Levinson, "The Processes of Constitutional Change: From Partisan Entrenchment to the National Surveillance State," 75 *Fordham L. Rev.* 489 (2006); Jack M. Balkin, "How Social Movements Change (or Fail to Change) the Constitution: The Case of the New Departure," 39 *Suffolk U. L. Rev.* 27 (2005); Howard Gillman, "How Political Parties Can Use the Courts to Advance Their Agendas: Federal Courts in the United States, 1875–1891," 96 *Am. Pol. Sci. Rev.* 511–24 (2002); Jack M. Balkin and Sanford Levinson, "Understanding the Constitutional Revolution," 87 *Va. L. Rev.* 1045 (2001).

10. See Balkin, *Constitutional Redemption,* supra note 4, ch. 3; Post and Siegel, "Democratic Constitutionalism," supra note 8; Balkin, "Respect Worthy," supra note 4.

11. People must not only believe that government institutions are sufficiently just; they must also believe that these institutions are sufficiently efficacious to secure the benefits that come from political union. If people believe that the constitutional system can no longer guarantee the rule of law, enforce social cooperation, or protect their rights, the system also loses legitimacy.

12. Balkin, *Constitutional Redemption,* supra note 4, ch. 3; Post and Siegel, "Democratic Constitutionalism," supra note 8; Balkin, "Respect Worthy," supra note 4.

5. Constitutional Faith and Constitutional Redemption

1. *Pirke Avot* 2:21.

2. Abraham Lincoln, "Speech on The Dred Scott Decision at Springfield, Illinois," in *Lincoln: Speeches and Writings, 1832–1858,* 390, 398 (Don E. Fehrenbacher ed., Library of America 1989).

3. See Frank I. Michelman, "Ida's Way: Constructing the Respect-Worthy Governmental System," 72 *Fordham L. Rev.* 345, 364–65 (2003); Jack M. Balkin, "Respect Worthy: Frank Michelman and the Legitimate Constitution," 39 *Tulsa L. Rev.* 485, 492 (2004).

4. Sanford V. Levinson, *Constitutional Faith* (Princeton University Press 1988).

5. Many originalists—and especially conservative originalists—may be suspicious of the idea of constitutional redemption. If "redemption" means perpetual revision of the Constitution by unelected judges acting on behalf of social and political movements, the Constitution does not need to be "redeemed." If only judges would restore the Constitution's original meaning and enforce it, all would be well. Yet this is actually a powerful example of redemptive constitutionalism and constitutional faith. The Constitution must be redeemed from glosses produced by generations of nonoriginalist judges and political officials who have strayed from the Constitution's original meaning. Restoring original meanings will redeem the Constitution from those who have abused it and reassert proper constitutional values.

In addition, conservative originalists have faith that a political process governed by original meanings will produce a legitimate and desirable form of government. For many conservative originalists, fidelity to original meanings will also constrain the judiciary so that it behaves according to its appropriate role. Perhaps some originalists might see this not as a question of faith but as a matter of constitutional and legal requirement. Nevertheless, it presupposes faith—faith in the wisdom of the Constitution and faith in a democratic process constituted by original meanings. For if originalists did not have such faith, they would be tempted to engage in judicial elaboration to correct the Constitution's deficiencies—in other words, engage in what conservative originalists sometimes call "judicial activism." Robert Bork's famous defense of originalism is therefore appropriately entitled *The Tempting of America*. See Robert Bork, *The Tempting Of America: The Political Seduction Of The Law* (Macmillan 1990). The temptation is to try to obtain a better Constitution by straying from original meanings. One must have plenty of faith to stick to original meanings and seek to redeem them in the face of political temptation.

Conversely, living constitutionalists also have constitutional faith, but they locate it in other aspects of the constitutional system. Some living constitutionalists may lack faith in the Constitution's original meaning, and they may doubt whether the originalist version of the Constitution contains sufficient resources to command contemporary assent and maintain democratic legitimacy. See Ethan Leib, "The Perpetual Anxiety of Living Constitutionalism," 24 *Const. Comment.* 353, 354, 359 & n. 19, 360–63 (2007). Nevertheless, living constitutionalists seek to redeem the Constitution by making doctrine conform more closely to social realities and evolving social values, and they must have faith that these processes of constitutional development (however defined) will produce a more just Constitution over time.

6. See Jack M. Balkin, "Agreements with Hell and Other Objects of Our Faith," 65 *Fordham L. Rev.* 1703, 1705 (1997). ("To claim to interpret the Constitution is already to claim to be faithful to it. . . . When we say that fidelity is not important to us, we are no longer interpreting the Constitution, we are criticizing it.")

7. The phrase comes from a resolution Garrison introduced before the Massachusetts Anti-Slavery Society in 1843, arguing that the Union should be disbanded: "That the compact which exists between the North and South is 'a covenant with death, and an agreement with hell'—involving both parties in atrocious criminality; and should be immediately annulled." Walter M. Merrill, *Against Wind and Tide: A Biography of Wm. Lloyd Garrison* 205 (Harvard University Press 1963).

8. These points are developed in Jack M. Balkin, *Constitutional Redemption: Political Faith in an Unjust World* (Harvard University Press 2011).

9. One reason to start over is if the constitutional framework blocks necessary reforms in ways that are not easily susceptible to later constitutional construction or statutory workarounds. At the close of his 1988 book, *Constitutional Faith,* Sanford Levinson explained that he was willing to sign the Constitution of the United States out of the belief that the constitutional conversation would develop into institutions that would respect human rights. Sanford Levinson, *Constitutional Faith,* supra note 4, at 193. By 2006 Levinson had given up his constitutional faith. He does not think the problem is with the open-ended clauses of the Constitution—the ones that most people fight about most of the time. Indeed, Levinson believes that the Constitution contains sufficient resources to provide whatever citizens might want for the protection of human rights. Rather, Levinson objects to the "hardwired" features of the constitutional system embodied in determinate rules—like the presidential veto, equal suffrage in the Senate, and the Electoral College. These, he argues, are the real reason why we should abandon our Constitution. See Sanford Levinson, *Our Undemocratic Constitution: Where the Constitution Goes Wrong (and How We the People Can Correct It)* (Oxford University Press 2006).

10. On the idea of idolatry in constitutional law and in law generally, see Jack M. Balkin, *Constitutional Redemption,* supra note 8, chs. 4 and 5.

11. Id., ch 5. See also Amy Kapczynski, "Historicism, Progress, and the Redemptive Constitution," 26 *Cardozo L. Rev.* 1041, 1113 (2005) (arguing that progressive accounts of history "commit themselves to a narrative of improvement that blinds them to both the threats and possibilities of today. By cutting themselves loose from the aspects of the past that appear disastrous, progressives also fail to see that some of the historical forces they think have been overcome in fact still operate").

12. See Steven M. Teles, *The Rise of the Conservative Legal Movement: The Battle for Control of the Law* 6–21 (Princeton University Press 2008).

13. For an introduction, see Charles Tilly and Lesley J. Wood, *Social Movements, 1768–2008* (2d ed., Paradigm Publishers 2009); Sidney Tarrow, *Power in Movement: Social Movements and Contentious Politics* (2d ed., Cambridge University Press 1998).

14. See Mitchell N. Berman, "Originalism and Its Discontents (Plus a Thought or Two about Abortion)," 24 *Const. Comment.* 383, 393–94 (2007).

15. Hendrik Hartog, "The Constitution of Aspiration and 'The Rights that Belong to Us All,'" 74 *J. Am. Hist.* 1013, 1014 (1987) ("Constitutional rights consciousness suggests a faith that the received meanings of constitutional texts will change when confronted by the legitimate aspirations of autonomous citizens and groups"); Reva B. Siegel, "Text in Contest: Gender and the Constitution from a Social Movement Perspective," 150 *U. Pa. L. Rev.* 297 (2001) (discussing why textual arguments have been so important to citizens and social movements throughout history).

16. Hartog, "The Constitution of Aspiration," supra note 15, at 1016.

17. Jules Lobel, "Losers, Fools & Prophets: Justice as Struggle," 80 *Cornell L. Rev.* 1331, 1356 (1995) (quoting Hartog, "The Constitution of Aspiration," supra note 15, at 1016).

18. Siegel, "Text in Contest," supra note 15, at 322–23.

19. See Hartog, "The Constitution of Aspiration," supra note 15, at 1016–17. ("An American emancipatory tradition of constitutional meaning must be rooted in the subversive and disruptive and utopian messages that people read into constitutional texts and drew from diverse and contradictory sources, including English common law, liberalism, Enlightenment philosophy, post-Reformation theology, and the medieval peasant's vision of self-ownership and freedom.")

20. See Siegel, "Text in Contest," supra note 15, at 337.

21. Id.

22. Martin Luther King Jr., "I Have a Dream," in *A Testament of Hope: The Essential Writings of Dr. Martin Luther King, Jr.* 217 (James M. Washington ed., Harper Collins 1986).

23. Id. at 219.

24. Id.

25. Charleton Heston, NRA Keynote Address (May 2, 1999), available at www.varmintal.com/heston4.htm. ("The Founding Fathers guaranteed this freedom, because they knew no tyranny can ever arise among a people endowed with the right to keep and bear arms. That's why you and your descendants need never fear fascism, state-run faith, refugee camps, brain-washing, ethnic cleansing, or especially submission to the wanton will of criminals.")

26. See, e.g., David Barton, *Original Intent: The Courts, the Constitution and Religion* (3d ed., Wallbuilder Press 2004); CBN.com, *Faith of Our Fathers: God*

and the American Revolution, www.cbn.com/spirituallife/churchandministry/churchhistory/faith_fathers. aspx; David Brody, *Finding God's Signature in Washington,* www.cbn.com/ cbnnews/cwn/070204washington.aspx.

27. See Robert C. Post and Reva B. Siegel, "Roe Rage: Democratic Constitutionalism and Backlash," 42 *Harv. C.R.–C.L. L. Rev.* 373 (2007) (describing democratic constitutionalism as the legitimacy-enforcing relationship between ordinary citizens and their Constitution).

28. Franklin D. Roosevelt, "Address on Constitution Day, Washington, D.C., September 17th, 1937," in John Woolley and Gerhard Peters, The American Presidency Project [online], available at www.presidency.ucsb.edu/ws/?pid=15459.

29. Id.

30. This "horizontal" translation between professionals and laypersons contrasts with Larry Lessig's "vertical" concept of translation. Lawrence Lessig, "Fidelity in Interpretation," 71 *Tex. L. Rev.* 1165 (1993); Lawrence Lessig, "Understanding Changed Readings: Fidelity and Theory," 47 *Stan. L. Rev.* 395 (1995); Lawrence Lessig, "Fidelity and Constraint," 65 *Fordham L. Rev.* 1365 (1997). Lessig was interested in how to translate the concrete expectations of the framers into decisions related to present circumstances. My interest here is in how popular claims about the Constitution—which may not respect a clear division between law and politics—are translated into forms of constitutional discourse that judges and legal decisionmakers would recognize as plausible legal arguments. I discuss these points further in Chapters 13 and 14.

31. 347 U.S. 483 (1954).

32. 384 U.S. 436 (1966).

33. Regents of the Univ. of Cal. v. Bakke, 438 U.S. 265, 313–15 (1978) (opinion of Powell, J.).

34. Reynolds v. Sims, 377 U.S. 533, 558 (1964) (quoting Gray v. Sanders, 372 U.S. 368, 381 (1963)).

35. See Mitchell N. Berman, "Originalism and Its Discontents," supra note 14, at 394; John O. McGinnis and Michael Rappaport, "Original Interpretive Principles as the Core of Originalism," 24 *Const. Comment.* 371, 376–81 (2007).

36. See Jack M. Balkin, "How Social Movements Change (or Fail to Change) the Constitution: The Case of the New Departure," 39 *Suffolk U. L. Rev.* 27, 29 (2005) ("the notion that judges are not supposed to take instruction from social movements—or 'factions,' as they might have been called by the founding generation—seems to be one of the basic assumptions of American constitutionalism").

37. Id.

38. See, e.g., William H. Rehnquist, "Constitutional Law and Public Opinion," 20 *Suffolk U. L. Rev.* 751, 752, 768–69 (1986) (noting that judges may be

influenced by public opinion but they are not supposed to take direction from politics).

39. Jack M. Balkin, "What *Brown* Teaches Us about Constitutional Theory," 90 *Va. L. Rev.* 1537, 1537 (2004); Barry Friedman, "The Importance of Being Positive: The Nature and Function of Judicial Review," 72 *U. Cin. L. Rev.* 1257, 1257–58 (2004); Mark A. Graber, "Constitutional Politics and Constitutional Theory: A Misunderstood and Neglected Relationship," 27 *Law & Soc. Inquiry* 309, 312, 317–18 (2002).

40. The arguments in the following two paragraphs draw on Jack M. Balkin and Sanford Levinson, "The Processes of Constitutional Change: From Partisan Entrenchment to the National Surveillance State," 75 *Fordham L. Rev.* 489 (2006); Balkin, "How Social Movements Change," supra note 36; Jack M. Balkin and Sanford Levinson, "Understanding the Constitutional Revolution," 87 *Va. L. Rev.* 1045 (2001).

41. Howard Gillman, "The Collapse of Constitutional Originalism and the Rise of the Notion of the 'Living Constitution' in the Course of American State-Building," 11 *Stud. Am. Pol. Dev.* 191 (1997).

42. Cf. *I Ching: The Book of Changes* 159 (Richard Wilhelm and Cary Fink Baynes trans., Princeton University Press 1950) ch. 36, "Darkening of the Light"; Hannah Arendt, *Men in Dark Times* 11 (Harcourt Brace and Company 1968) ("History knows many periods of dark times in which the public realm has become obscured and the world become so dubious that people have ceased to ask any more of politics than that it show due consideration for their vital interests and personal liberty").

43. In Bruce Ackerman's terms, it is a constitutional theory that can make sense from the perspectives of both ordinary observation and scientific policy-making. Bruce A. Ackerman, *Private Property and the Constitution* 10–15 (Yale University Press 1977).

44. H. Jefferson Powell, "Parchment Matters: A Meditation on the Constitution as Text," 71 *Iowa L. Rev.* 1427, 1433 (1986); Lawrence B. Solum, "Originalism as Transformative Politics," 63 *Tul. L. Rev.* 1599, 1626–27 (1989).

45. Bruce A. Ackerman, 1 *We the People: Foundations* 43, 62 (Harvard University Press 1991); Bruce A. Ackerman, "Constitutional Politics/Constitutional Law," 99 *Yale L. J.* 453, 488, 491 (1989).

6. Originalisms

1. Vasan Kesavan and Michael Stokes Paulsen, "The Interpretive Force of the Constitution's Secret Drafting History," 91 *Geo. L. J.* 1113, 1140 (2003).

2. Id.

3. E.g., Kermit Roosevelt III, *The Myth of Judicial Activism: Making Sense of Supreme Court Decisions* (Yale University Press 2006); Randy Barnett, *Restoring*

the Lost Constitution: The Presumption of Liberty (Princeton University Press 2004); Keith E. Whittington, *Constitutional Interpretation: Textual Meaning, Original Intent, and Judicial Review* (University Press of Kansas 1999); Ronald Dworkin, "Comment," in *A Matter of Interpretation: Federal Courts and the Law* 115 (Amy Gutmann ed., Princeton University Press 1997); Lawrence B. Solum, *Semantic Originalism,* SSRN, at papers.ssrn.com/sol3/papers.cfm?abstract_id=1120244 (November 22, 2008); John F. Manning, "The Eleventh Amendment and the Reading of Precise Constitutional Texts," 113 *Yale L. J.* 1663 (2004); Caleb Nelson, "Originalism and Interpretive Conventions," 70 *U. Chi. L. Rev.* 519 (2003); Kesavan and Paulsen, "Interpretive Force," supra note 1; Gary Lawson, "Delegation and Original Meaning," 88 *Va. L. Rev.* 327 (2002); Mark D. Greenberg and Harry Litman, "The Meaning of Original Meaning," 86 *Geo. L. J.* 569 (1998); Steven G. Calabresi and Saikrishna B. Prakash, "The President's Power to Execute the Laws," 104 *Yale L. J.* 541 (1994); Lawrence B. Solum, "Originalism as Transformative Politics," 63 *Tul. L. Rev.* 1599 (1989).

4. See Michael W. McConnell, "The Importance of Humility in Judicial Review: A Comment on Ronald Dworkin's 'Moral Reading' of the Constitution," 65 *Fordham L. Rev.* 1269 (1997).

5. See Dennis J. Goldford, *The American Constitution and the Debate over Originalism* (Cambridge University Press 2005); Johnathan O'Neill, *Originalism in American Law and Politics: A Constitutional History* (Johns Hopkins University Press 2005); Robert C. Post and Reva B. Siegel, "The Right's Living Constitution," 75 *Fordham L. Rev.* 545 (2006); Keith Whittington, "The New Originalism," 2 *Geo. J. L. & Pub. Pol'y* 599, 601 (2004).

6. See Edwin Meese III, "Address before the American Bar Association," in *The Great Debate: Interpreting Our Written Constitution* 9 (Paul G. Cassell ed., The Federalist Society 1986); Edwin Meese III, "Address before the D.C. Chapter of the Federalist Society Lawyers Division," in *Original Meaning Jurisprudence: A Sourcebook* 91 (Office of Legal Policy, U.S. Department of Justice 1987); Edwin Meese III, "Construing the Constitution," 19 *U. C. Davis L. Rev.* 22, 25–26 (1985). Meese sometimes used the terms *original intention* and *original meaning* interchangeably. See, e.g., Edwin Meese III, "The Supreme Court of the United States: Bulwark of a Limited Constitution," 27 *S. Tex. L. Rev.* 455, 465–66 (1986) ("It has been and will continue to be the policy of this administration to press for a jurisprudence of original intention. In the cases we file and those we join as amicus, we will endeavor to resurrect the original meaning of constitutional provisions and statutes as the only reliable guide for judgment").

7. Post and Siegel, "The Right's Living Constitution," supra note 5; Whittington, "The New Originalism," supra note 5; Barry Friedman, "Originalism and Judicial Activism" (2007) (unpublished manuscript).

Before Meese, Raoul Berger had advocated interpretation according to original intention. Raoul Berger, *Government By Judiciary: The Transformation of the Fourteenth Amendment* (Harvard University Press 1977). Berger's originalism, however, arose not from political objections to contemporary liberalism but from his positivism, formalism, and hostility to natural rights jurisprudence. O'Neill, *Originalism,*, supra note 5, at 112–13. Berger saw in both the *Lochner*-era Court and in the later Warren and Burger Courts natural law and moral ideals overriding constitutional limitations and judicial restraint. Id.

8. For accounts of the shift from original intentions to original meaning, see Kesavan and Paulsen, "Interpretive Force," supra note 1, at 1137–40; Barnett, *Restoring the Lost Constitution,* supra note 3, at 90–91. See also O'Neill, *Originalism,* supra note 5, at 158 ("Originalists responded tactically by de-emphasizing the word *intent,* though of course not the jurisprudential approach associated with it") (emphasis in original).

9. For early and influential discussions, see Paul Brest, "The Misconceived Quest for the Original Understanding," 60 *B. U. L. Rev.* 204 (1980); Mark V. Tushnet, "Following the Rules Laid Down: A Critique of Interpretivism and Neutral Principles," 96 *Harv. L. Rev.* 781, 793–804 (1983). For a response defending original intention originalism, see Richard S. Kay, "Adherence to the Original Intentions in Constitutional Adjudication: Three Objections and Responses," 82 *Nw. U. L. Rev.* 226, 244 (1988).

10. H. Jefferson Powell, "The Original Understanding of Original Intent," 98 *Harv. L. Rev.* 885, 887–88 (1985); H. Jefferson Powell, "Rules for Originalists," 73 *Va. L. Rev.* 659 (1987).

11. Scholars have offered various formulations over the years. See, e.g., Calabresi and Prakash, "The President's Power," supra note 3, at 552 (meaning of the Constitution and other legal writings like statutes, contracts, wills, and judicial opinions "depends on their text, as they were objectively understood by the people who enacted or ratified them"); Gary Lawson, "Legal Theory: Proving the Law," 86 *Nw. U. L. Rev.* 859, 875 (1992) (defining "originalist textualism" as "a method which searches for the ordinary public meanings that the Constitution's words, read in linguistic, structural, and historical context, had at the time of those words' origin" (citing Gary Lawson, "In Praise of Woodenness," 11 *Geo. Mason U. L. Rev.* 21, 22 (1988))); Kesavan and Paulsen, "Interpretive Force,", supra note 1, at 1131 (originalist textualism requires "faithful application of the words and phrases of the text in accordance with the meaning they would have had at the time they were adopted as law, within the political and linguistic community that adopted the text as law").

12. Antonin Scalia, "Address Before the Attorney General's Conference on Economic Liberties (June 14, 1986)," in *Original Meaning Jurisprudence: A Sourcebook,* supra note 6, at 101; Office of Legal Policy, Department of Justice, *Original Meaning Jurisprudence: A Sourcebook,* supra note 6, at 14

("Our fundamental law is the text of the Constitution as ratified, not the subjective intent or purpose of any individual or group in adopting the provision at issue"); Office of Legal Policy, U.S. Department of Justice, *Guidelines on Constitutional Litigation* 3–6 (U.S. Department of Justice 1988). For a discussion, see Nelson, "Originalism and Interpretive Conventions," supra note 3, at 555 (2003).

13. Robert Bork's *The Tempting of America* represents a transitional document between original understanding and original meaning. One of his research assistants was Stephen Calabresi, who would later help champion the new textualism. See Robert Bork, *The Tempting of America: The Political Seduction of the Law,* at xvii (Macmillan 1990). Thus the work contains pronouncements that endorse original meaning originalism (see, e.g., id. at 144–45), while Bork's substantive views in the book reflect his previous attachment to the philosophy of original intention and original understanding. Kesavan and Paulsen, "Interpretive Force," supra note 1, at 1141 & n. 96; Robert H. Bork, "Neutral Principles and Some First Amendment Problems," 47 *Ind. L. J.* 1 (1971) (offering positivist and majoritarian justifications for originalism); Robert H. Bork, "The Constitution, Original Intent and Economic Rights," 23 *San Diego L. Rev.* 823, 823 (1986) ("I wish to demonstrate that original intent is the only legitimate basis for constitutional decisionmaking").

Bork argued that judges were bound by the principles intended by the framers, a formula that allowed judges to take into account technological changes and to apply the document to conditions unforeseen by the framers. Id. at 826. This did not mean that "judges will invariably decide cases the way the Framers would if they were here today" but "many cases will be decided that way." Id. He argued that the framers' principles should be discovered and applied "by choosing no level of generality higher than that which the interpretations of the words, structure, and history of the Constitution fairly support." Id. at 828. Hence, the equal protection clause could not protect homosexuals because "equality on matters such as sexual orientation was not under discussion." Id. In essence, Bork claimed that the scope of constitutional principles was defined by the framers' original expected application, but that such principles, once defined, could be applied to circumstances that the framers did not foresee, such as "apply[ing] the first amendment's Free Press Clause to the electronic media," or "the Commerce Clause to state regulations of interstate trucking." Id. at 826. At the same time Bork argued that sufficient reliance had grown up around the construction of the administrative and regulatory state that courts had to retain New Deal commerce clause decisions that were inconsistent with the framers' intentions; the same might be true of many other features of current doctrine. Philip Lacovara, "A Talk with Judge Robert H. Bork," *District Lawyer,* May/June 1985, at 29, 32; "Nomination of Judge Robert H. Bork: Hearings before the Senate Committee on the Judiciary," 100th Cong. 112–13, 264–65, 292–93,

465 (1987), reprinted in 14 *The Supreme Court of the United States: Hearings and Reports on Successful and Unsuccessful Nominations of Supreme Court Justices by the Senate Judiciary Committee, 1916–1987,* at 292–93, 444–45, 472–73, 645 (Roy M. Mersky and J. Myron Jacobstein eds., W. S. Hein 1989) (testimony of Robert H. Bork from Sept. 15, 1987–Sept. 19, 1987).

Bork gives no evidence in *The Tempting of America* that the change in terminology from original intentions of the framers to original understanding to original meaning would require a shift in his previous substantive positions. This conflation of original meaning and what I would call adherence to original expected application is hardly unique to Bork, although his example suggests why the conflation would occur.

14. Meese, "Construing the Constitution," supra note 6, at 29; Edwin Meese III, "Dialogue: A Return to Constitutional Interpretation from Judicial Law-Making," 40 *N.Y.L. Sch. L. Rev.* 925, 930–33 (1996); Whittington, *Constitutional Interpretation,* supra note 3, at 599; O'Neill, *Originalism,* supra note 5, at 133–60. The Office of Legal Policy's *Original Meaning Jurisprudence: A Sourcebook,* supra note 6, listed several examples of recent cases that employed "non-interpretive jurisprudence," id. at 58–64, including Mapp v. Ohio, 367 U.S. 643 (1961) (announcing the exclusionary rule); Engel v. Vitale, 370 U.S. 421 (1962) (striking down practice of nondenominational school prayer in public schools); Griswold v. Connecticut, 381 U.S. 479 (1965) (holding unconstitutional the prohibition on use of contraceptives by married couples); Miranda v. Arizona, 384 U.S. 436 (1966) (requiring specific procedures governing police interrogation of all criminal suspects); Katzenbach v. Morgan, 384 U.S. 641 (1966) (upholding features of the 1965 Voting Rights Act on grounds of Congress's authority to interpret the Fourteenth Amendment); Shapiro v. Thompson, 394 U.S. 618 (1969) (holding that the constitutional right to travel prevented denial of welfare benefits to those who did not meet one-year residency requirement); Perez v. United States, 402 U.S. 146 (1971) (upholding federal crime of "loan sharking" under commerce clause); Furman v. Georgia, 408 U.S. 238 (1972) (striking down then-existing capital punishment statutes under Eighth Amendment); Roe v. Wade, 410 U.S. 113 (1973); and Bd. of Educ. v. Pico, 457 U.S. 853 (1982) (holding that public school students had a constitutional "right to receive ideas" in public school libraries). The *Sourcebook* cautioned, however, that "[t]he ultimate results reached in these cases do not necessarily differ from the meaning, but the analysis in each case is both illegitimate and representative of the jurisprudence advocated by non-interpretivists today." *Original Meaning Jurisprudence: A Sourcebook,* supra at 6.

15. See Kesavan and Paulsen, "Interpretive Force,", supra note 1, at 1143–49. Gary Lawson's version of original meaning originalism is particularly worthy of note because he takes this premise further that most contemporary originalists. He argues that originalism "is a hypothetical inquiry that asks how a fully

informed public audience, knowing all that there is to know about the Constitution and the surrounding world, would understand a particular provision. Actual historical understandings are, of course, relevant to that inquiry, but they do not conclude or define the inquiry—nor are they even necessarily the best available evidence." Gary Lawson, "Delegation and Original Meaning," 88 *Va. L. Rev.* 327, 398. Lawson's "ideal observer" approach to original meaning gives him a different focus from other originalists; it means, for example, that the political statements and decisions of early politicians are not necessarily trustworthy guides to original meaning. In particular, "members of Congress, even those who participated in the drafting and ratification of the Constitution, are not disinterested observers. They are political actors, responding to political as well as legal influences, who are eminently capable of making mistakes about the meaning of the Constitution." Id. Hence, early congressional acts were "postenactment legislative history that ranks fairly low down on the hierarchy of reliable evidence concerning original meaning" and "whatever evidence can be gleaned from early statutes—and there is evidence in both directions—is minimally relevant." Id.

16. See *Original Meaning Jurisprudence: A Sourcebook,* supra note 6, at 24–25.

17. Whittington, *Constitutional Interpretation,* supra note 3, at 167–68; Whittington, "The New Originalism," supra note 5.

18. *Guidelines on Constitutional Litigation,* supra note 12, at 5.

19. Id. at 11.

20. Nelson, "Originalism and Interpretive Conventions," supra note 3, at 558.

21. "Nomination of Judge Antonin Scalia: Hearings before the Senate Committee on the Judiciary," 99th Cong. (1986), reprinted in 13 *Hearings and Reports,* supra note 13, at 89, 142 (testimony of Antonin Scalia on Aug. 5, 1986).

22. Dworkin, "Comment," supra note 3, at 115, 116, 119; Ronald Dworkin, *Freedom's Law: The Moral Reading of the Constitution* 13, 291–92 (Harvard University Press 1996); Ronald Dworkin, "The Arduous Virtue of Fidelity: Originalism, Scalia, Tribe, and Nerve," 65 *Fordham L. Rev.* 1249, 1255–58 (1997); Ronald Dworkin, "Reflections on Fidelity," 65 *Fordham L. Rev.* 1799, 1803–8 (1997).

23. Randy E. Barnett, "An Originalism for Nonoriginalists," 45 *Loy. L Rev.* 611 (1999).

24. Kermit Roosevelt, *The Myth of Judicial Activism,* supra note 3.

25. Jeffrey Goldsworthy, "Originalism in Constitutional Interpretation," 1 *Federal Law Review* 1–50 (1997) (offering theory of moderate originalism).

26. Greenberg and Litman, "The Meaning of Original Meaning," supra note 3.

27. Richard Primus, "When Should Original Meanings Matter?" 107 *Mich. L. Rev.* 165 (2008); Adam Samaha, "Originalism's Expiration Date," 30 *Car-*

dozo L. Rev. 1295 (2008); David A. Strauss, "Common Law, Common Ground, and Jefferson's Principle," 112 *Yale L. J.* 1717 (2003).

28. Michael W. McConnell, "Originalism and the Desegregation Decisions," 81 *Va. L. Rev.* 947 (1995); Michael W. McConnell, "The Originalist Justification for *Brown*: A Reply to Professor Klarman," 81 *Va. L. Rev.* 1937 (1995).

29. Alexander M. Bickel, "The Original Understanding and the Segregation Decision," 69 *Harv. L. Rev.* 1 (1955).

30. McConnell, "Originalist Justification for *Brown*," supra note 28, at 1938–39; see also Earl M. Maltz, "Originalism and the Desegregation Decisions—A Response to Professor McConnell," 13 *Const. Comment.* 223, 228–29 (1996); Michael J. Klarman, "*Brown,* Originalism, and Constitutional Theory: A Response to Professor McConnell," 81 *Va. L. Rev.* 1881, 1885–94 (1995).

31. McConnell, "Originalism and the Desegregation Decisions," supra note 28, at 953. The Civil Rights Act of 1875 was struck down in the Civil Rights Cases, 109 U.S. 3 (1883).

32. Maltz, "Originalism and the Desegregation Decisions," supra note 30, 224–28; Klarman, "*Brown,* Originalism, and Constitutional Theory," supra note 30, 1901–28.

33. McConnell, "Originalist Justification for *Brown,*" supra note 28, at 1938–39.

34. One reason he did so is that McConnell believed that the Fourteenth and Fifteenth Amendments were ratified "with little regard for popular opinion." McConnell, "Originalist Justification for *Brown,*" supra note 28, at 1939; see also McConnell, "Originalism and the Desegregation Decisions," supra note 28, at 1109 ("When an Amendment obtains its supermajority through congressional exercise of its power to condition readmission of states to the Union, it is a fiction to treat the opinions of the people of the various states as controlling"). But this simply raises the question whether McConnell's methodology is consistent with the theory of popular sovereignty that justifies original meaning originalism.

35. McConnell, "The Importance of Humility," supra note 4, at 1284.

36. Id.

37. John O. McGinnis and Michael Rappaport, "Original Interpretive Principles as the Core of Originalism," 24 *Const. Comment.* 371, 378 (2007).

38. Id.

39. Id. at 379.

40. Id. This resembles the argument made in the Reagan Justice Department's 1988 *Guidelines on Constitutional Litigation,* supra note 12.

41. McGinnis and Rappaport, "Original Interpretive Principles," supra note 37, at 379.

42. Id.

43. Id.

44. Id. at 378.
45. Id. at 381.
46. Id.

7. Precedents and Pragmatic Exceptions

1. On the idea of a constitutional regime, see Mark V. Tushnet, *The New Constitutional Order* (Princeton University Press 2003); Bruce Ackerman, 1 *We The People: Transformations* (Harvard University Press 1998).

2. Antonin Scalia, "Originalism: The Lesser Evil," 57 *U. Cin. L. Rev.* 849, 861 (1989).

3. Antonin Scalia, "Response," in *A Matter of Interpretation: Federal Courts and the Law* 140 (Amy Gutmann ed., Princeton University Press 1997).

4. Randy Barnett, "Scalia's Infidelity: A Critique Of 'Faint-Hearted' Originalism," 75 *U. Cin. L. Rev.* 7, 13 (2006).

5. Id. at 13–14.

6. Stephen M. Griffin, "Constituent Power and Constitutional Change in American Constitutionalism," papers.ssrn.com/sol3/papers.cfm?abstract_id=928493 (September 5, 2006).

7. Id.

8. See Donald S. Lutz, "Toward a Theory of Constitutional Amendment," in *Responding to Imperfection: The Theory and Practice of Constitutional Amendment* 237, 261, 265–267 (Sanford Levinson, ed., Princeton University Press 1995) (noting that in comparison with other countries, "the U.S. Constitution is unusually, and probably excessively, difficult to amend," and arguing that the strategies of judicial revision are the likely consequence of such a constitution).

9. Larry Kramer, *The People Themselves: Popular Constitutionalism and Judicial Review* (Oxford University Press 2004).

10. See Jack M. Balkin, *Constitutional Redemption: Political Faith in an Unjust World* (Harvard University Press 2011), ch. 3; Robert C. Post and Reva B. Siegel, "Democratic Constitutionalism," in *The Constitution in 2020* 27–28 (Jack M. Balkin and Reva B. Siegel eds., Oxford University Press 2009).

11. Barry Friedman and Scott B. Smith, "The Sedimentary Constitution," 147 *U. Pa. L. Rev.* 1 (1998).

12. Post and Siegel, "Democratic Constitutionalism," supra note 10.

13. Scalia, "Originalism: The Lesser Evil," supra note 2, at 862.

14. See, e.g., Missouri v. Jenkins, 515 U.S. 70, 115 (1995) (Thomas, J., concurring); Keyes v. School District No. 1, Denver, Colo., 413 U.S. 189, 258 (Rehnquist, J., dissenting) (1976).

15. See the discussion in Chapter 11, supra; Andrew Kull, *The Colorblind Constitution* (Harvard University Press 1992); Stephen A. Siegel, "The Federal

Government's Power to Enact Color-Conscious Laws: An Originalist Inquiry," 92 *Nw. U. L. Rev.* 477, 560 (1998); Jed Rubenfeld, "Affirmative Action," 107 *Yale L. J.* 427, 430–32 (1997); Eric Schnapper, "Affirmative Action and the Legislative History of the Fourteenth Amendment," 71 *Va. L. Rev.* 753 (1985).

16. See, e.g., City of Rome v. United States, 446 U.S. 156, 193, 200–201 (1980) (Powell, J., dissenting); id. at 207 (Rehnquist, J., dissenting) (arguing for constitutional limitations on Congress's power to protect voting rights); NAMUDNO v. Holder, 129 S. Ct. 2504 (2009) (noting potential problems with constitutionality of section 5 of Voting Rights Act); Ricci v. DeStefano, 129 S. Ct. 2658 (2009) (Scalia, J., concurring) (questioning constitutionality of disparate impact liability).

17. See the discussion in Robert C. Post and Reva B. Siegel, "The Right's Living Constitution," 75 *Fordham L. Rev.* 545 (2006).

18. See Chapter 10; Jack M. Balkin, "Is Heller an Original Meaning Decision?" *Balkinization,* July 2, 2008, at balkin.blogspot.com/2008/07/is-heller-original-meaning-decision.html.

19. See Reva B. Siegel, "Heller & Originalism's Dead Hand—In Theory and Practice," 56 *UCLA L. Rev.* 1399 (2009).

20. John O. McGinnis and Michael Rappaport, "Original Interpretive Principles as the Core of Originalism," 24 *Const. Comment.* 371, 376 (2007).

21. See Mariah Zeisberg, "Frederick Douglass, Citizen Interpreter," SSRN, at papers.ssrn.com/sol3/papers.cfm?abstract_id=1583683 (April 2, 2010).

22. David Strauss, for example, has argued that "the common law approach, not the approach that connects law to an authoritative text, or an authoritative decision by the Framers or by 'we the people,'" simultaneously "best explains, and best justifies, American constitutional law today." David A. Strauss, "Common Law Constitutional Interpretation," 63 *U. Chi. L. Rev.* 877, 879 (1996). Although an approach that makes precedent central allows us to reject "morally unacceptable traditions," we "should be very careful about rejecting judgments made by people who were acting reflectively and in good faith, especially when those judgments have been reaffirmed or at least accepted over time." Id. at 891, 895. Indeed, Strauss has argued provocatively that adding text to the Constitution through Article V amendment is generally "either unnecessary or ineffective." David A. Strauss, "The Irrelevance of Constitutional Amendment," 114 *Harv. L. Rev.* 1457, 1468 (2001). On the other side of this debate is Michael Stokes Paulsen, who argues that reliance on precedent is "intrinsically corrupting" and essentially incompatible with a theory of original meaning. Michael Stokes Paulsen, "The Intrinsically Corrupting Influence of Precedent," 22 *Const. Comment.* 289 (2005). McGinnis and Rappaport and I fall somewhere between these two positions: we assume that some common law development of constitutional doctrine was implicit in creating a system of federal courts that would construe the meaning of the Constitution.

23. Michael Gerhardt, "Super Precedent," 90 *Minn. L. Rev.* 1204 (2006).

24. 410 U.S. 113 (1973).

25. See, e.g., Planned Parenthood of Southeastern Pennsylvania v. Casey, 505 U.S. 833 (1992); Gonzales v. Carhart, 550 U.S. 124 (2007).

26. 426 U.S. 229 (1976).

27. See Michael Stokes Paulsen, "*Brown, Casey*-style: The Shocking First Draft of the Segregation Opinion," 69 *N.Y.U. L. Rev.* 1287 (1994).

28. Scalia, "Response," supra note 3, at 140.

29. See Post and Siegel, "The Right's Living Constitution," supra note 17, at 558–68.

8. A Platform for Persuasion

1. For a discussion of the concepts of "on the wall" and "off the wall," see Jack M. Balkin, *Constitutional Redemption: Political Faith in an Unjust World* (Harvard University Press 2011), ch. 7.

2. McCulloch v. Maryland, 17 U.S. 316, 415 (1819).

3. Lochner v. New York, 198 U.S. 45, 76 (1905)(Holmes, J., dissenting).

9. Commerce

1. See Gonzales v. Raich, 545 U.S. 1, 37 (2005) (Scalia, J., concurring in judgment); Robert H. Bork, *The Tempting of America: The Political Seduction of the Law* 158–59 (Macmillan 1990); "Nomination of Robert H. Bork to be Associate Justice of the Supreme Court of the United States: Hearings before the S. Comm. on the Judiciary," 100th Cong. pt. 1, 112–13, 264–65, 292–93, 465 (1987), reprinted in 14 *The Supreme Court of the United States: Hearings and Reports on Successful and Unsuccessful Nominations of Supreme Court Justices by the Senate Judiciary Committee 1916–1987,* at 292–93, 444–45, 472–73, 645 (Roy M. Mersky and J. Myron Jacobstein eds., W. S. Hein & Co. 1990) (testimony of Robert H. Bork, Sept. 15, 1987–Sept. 19, 1987); Antonin Scalia, "Originalism: The Lesser Evil," 57 *U. Cin. L. Rev.* 849, 861–64 (1989); Philip Lacovara, "A Talk with Judge Robert H. Bork," *District Law.,* May/June 1985, at 29, 32.

2. Antonin Scalia, "Response," in *A Matter of Interpretation: Federal Courts and the Law* 129, 140 (Amy Gutmann ed., Princeton University Press 1997); id. at 139.

3. United States v. Lopez, 514 U.S. 549, 584 (1995) (Thomas, J., concurring).

4. Randy E. Barnett, *Restoring the Lost Constitution: The Presumption of Liberty* 317–18, 348–53 (Princeton University Press 2004).

5. Richard A. Epstein, "The Proper Scope of the Commerce Power," 73 *Va. L. Rev.* 1387 (1987).

6. Bruce Ackerman, 1 *We the People: Foundations* (Harvard University Press 1998).

7. See the discussion in Chapter 13, supra; Jack M. Balkin and Sanford Levinson, "The Processes of Constitutional Change: From Partisan Entrenchment to the National Surveillance State," 75 *Fordham L. Rev.* 489, 490–92 (2006).

8. U.S. Const. art. I, § 8, cl. 3.

9. Akhil Reed Amar, *America's Constitution: A Biography* 108 (Random House 2005).

10. U.S. Const. amend. X.

11. United States v. Darby, 312 U.S. 100, 124 (1941).

12. 2 *The Debates in the Several State Conventions on the Adoption of the Federal Constitution as Recommended by the General Convention at Philadelphia* 424 (Jonathan Elliot ed., 2d ed. 1836) [cited hereafter as Elliot].

13. 1 *The Records of the Federal Convention of 1787* 21 (Max Farrand ed., rev. ed., Yale University Press 1966).

14. Id. at 47; see id. at 53–54.

15. Id. at 243.

16. Id. at 252, 277.

17. Id. at 322.

18. 2 *The Records of the Federal Convention of 1787,* supra note 13, at 21 (internal quotation marks omitted); see id. at 25. James Wilson seconded the motion, understanding it as a friendly amendment, but Gouverneur Morris objected, arguing that "[t]he internal police, as it would be called & understood by the States ought to be infringed in many cases, as in the case of paper money & other tricks by which Citizens of other States may be affected." Id. at 26.

19. Id. at 26.

20. Id. at 14; see id. at 16–17.

21. Id. at 21, see id. at 26, 131–32.

22. Id. at 21, 27.

23. Jack N. Rakove, *Original Meanings: Politics and Ideas in the Making of the Constitution* 178 (Knopf 1996).

24. Id.; accord Robert L. Stern, "That Commerce Which Concerns More States Than One," 47 *Harv. L. Rev.* 1335, 1340 (1934).

25. 2 *The Records of the Federal Convention of 1787,* supra note 13, at 17 (Madison spells Gorham's name "Ghorum"). John Rutledge of South Carolina then moved "that the clause should be committed to the end that a specification of the powers comprised in the general terms, might be reported." Id. The motion failed by an equally divided vote of the state delegations. But as it turned out, this was only a temporary delay, for by the middle of August the Committee of Detail, on which Rutledge served, had done precisely what he had asked for in July. Also see the May 31 discussion of the delegates, in which they argued for framing general principles that would later be articulated or enumerated in

precise terms. 1 *The Records of the Federal Convention of 1787*, supra note 13, at 53–54, 59–60.

26. Barnett, *Restoring the Lost Constitution*, supra note 4, at 155 (arguing that the Committee of Detail rejected the language); id. at 167 (arguing that "the Convention" rejected the language). See the discussion of Barnett's views in note 27 infra.

27. 2 Elliot, supra note 12, at 424–25.

Despite this evidence, Barnett argues that when the Philadelphia Convention voted to accept a list of enumerated powers drafted by the Committee of Detail, it specifically intended to reject the principle of Resolution VI (and the Bedford Resolution that elaborated it). The only evidence he offers for this assertion comes from his reading of Joseph Lynch, *Negotiating the Constitution: The Earliest Debates over Original Intent* (Cornell University Press 1999). See *Restoring the Lost Constitution*, at 156–57. But even assuming that Lynch's account of the convention is accurate, it contradicts Barnett's argument.

Lynch argues that following the Great Compromise that gave small states equal suffrage in the Senate, Virginia turned against the Virginia Plan, which gave Congress power to legislate in all cases where the states were severally incompetent. He therefore infers that a compromise was struck in the Committee of Detail, featuring the enumeration of powers and a necessary and proper clause. The combination of enumerated powers plus a suitably vague necessary and proper clause, Lynch argued, kicked the issue of congressional power down the road. The necessary and proper clause was "a provision of indeterminate authority, whose scope, in practice, would be for Congress to determine." Lynch, *Negotiating the Constitution*, at 19. "Since initially the northern states," who favored federal power, "would control both houses of Congress, they would determine the extent of authorization." Id. And that, Lynch argues in the remainder of the book, is precisely what happened in the first Congresses, who for the most part adopted broad constructions of federal power consistent with the principle of Resolution VI.

This was a compromise, Lynch argues, that kept the structural principle of Resolution VI intact. If the Committee of Detail "had meant to disregard the proposal to confer on Congress the power to legislate in the general interests of the United States or to preserve harmony among the states," Lynch explains, "we should expect to read of a discontented Bedford protesting the committee's betrayal of his handiwork, and of a happy [Pierce] Butler [of South Carolina] supporting the report. This did not happen." Id. at 20. Instead, "[t]he framers had left it to Congress to determine whether, pursuant to that clause, they could legislate in the general interests of the country or whether they could merely implement the specifically enumerated powers." Id. at 100.

I do not agree in all respects with Lynch's account of the convention; in particular, I do not agree with his view that the necessary and proper clause is the source of congressional power to legislate in the interests of the Union. In my view, the principle of Resolution VI underlies and should inform the proper construction of all of Congress's enumerated powers. But in any case, Lynch's book is the source of Barnett's argument that the Convention rejected Resolution VI, and it undermines Barnett's claims.

Faced with these difficulties, Barnett argues that the compromise Lynch describes is part of original intentions; therefore it can form no part of original meaning. (On this point, Barnett and I are in agreement. The views of the framers are evidence of original expected applications.) On the other hand, various federalists made representations that the necessary and proper clause would only give Congress power to pass legislation incidental to enumerated powers; these public representations, Barnett argues, should inform the construction of original meaning. Barnett, *Restoring the Lost Constitution*, at 157. (Once again, I believe these representations are evidence of original expected applications and do not form part of original meaning.)

Nevertheless, the disagreement here is not over original semantic meaning; it is over the structural principles that underlie and best explain the enumeration of congressional powers in Article I, section 8. I have argued that Resolution VI provides the proper structural principle and the best explanation for the list of enumerated powers, and, moreover, that this principle was intended by the Philadelphia Convention. Barnett denies this, contending that the Convention rejected the Bedford Resolution because the resolution does not appear in the Constitution's text. This *is* a claim about original intentions, and Barnett's sole evidentiary source argues against him.

Even if Barnett is correct that public representations in ratification debates gloss original semantic meaning, James Wilson, who was a member of the Committee of Detail and one of the first justices appointed to the Supreme Court, publicly represented that the principle of Resolution VI *was* the basis for the choice of enumerated powers. In any case, Barnett can hardly deny that the principle of Resolution VI is *consistent* with the original meaning of the text; otherwise, according to Lynch's account (which Barnett relies on), the northern and small states would never have voted for the enumeration of powers.

The central question, in my view, is what structural principle best accounts for the choice of enumerated powers in the Constitution. As I noted earlier in my discussion of structural principles, this could be a principle specifically intended by the framers or ratifiers of the document, or it could be a principle that nobody intended but that makes the most sense of the constitutional plan today. (See also the discussion in Chapter 12.) There is plenty of evidence that the principle of Resolution VI was the reason for the list of enumerated powers chosen by the Constitution's framers; it also happens to make the most sense of the constitutional plan to this day.

28. 2 *The Records of the Federal Convention of 1787,* supra note 13, at 21; see id. at 131–32.

29. Robert Cooter and Neil Siegel reach a similar conclusion using economic analysis. Robert D. Cooter and Neil S. Siegel, "Collective Action Federalism: A General Theory of Article I, Section 8," 63 *Stan. L. Rev.* 115 (2011). Cooter and Siegel explain that public goods benefiting the entire nation are best produced nationally, and that many activities originating within states produce positive and negative interstate externalities. Costs and benefits that spill over state lines create incentives for states to free ride on the efforts of other states. This leads to less than optimal investments in interstate or national public goods and more negative interstate externalities. In theory, states could band together to achieve interstate benefits and avoid interstate harms, but the more states that are affected, the higher the transaction costs and the greater the possibility of hold-outs. As a federation of states grows in size, the transaction costs quickly become prohibitive. A federal government allows states to solve these problems by majority rule in a national legislature rather than by requiring unanimous consent through an interstate compact. Plenary federal power over all subjects, however, allows a majority of states to exploit a minority in cases where there is no genuine interstate good or collective action problem. Therefore, Cooter and Siegel argue, national powers should extend only to (1) problems where the federal government is likely to be best at internalizing interstate externalities and (2) situations involving the provision of national or interstate public goods. Id. at 135–44.

30. See also id. at 42, 55 (offering a list of appropriate federal concerns including securing national defense, facilitating and protecting national markets, building and maintaining infrastructures that create beneficial network effects, providing media of economic exchange, setting standards, developing nationally enforceable intellectual property rights, preventing regulatory races to the bottom, and protecting natural resources of benefit to the nation).

31. U.S. Const. art I, § 8, cl. 3.

32. Saikrishna Prakash calls this "the presumption of intrasentence uniformity." Saikrishna Prakash, "Our Three Commerce Clauses and the Presumption of Intrasentence Uniformity," 55 *Ark. L. Rev.* 1149 (2003). For a response, see Adrian Vermeule, "Three Commerce Clauses? No Problem," 55 *Ark. L. Rev.* 1175 (2003). Vermeule's arguments, however, go primarily to how best to construct the Constitution through doctrine, and not to original meaning.

33. Gibbons v. Ogden, 22 U.S. (9 Wheat.) 1, 194 (1824).

34. Id. at 197.

35. In an 1829 letter to Joseph Carrington Cabell, James Madison explained that although the literal meaning of "commerce" is the same for foreign and interstate commerce, the scope of the two powers should be construed differently because they serve different structural purposes:

I always foresaw that difficulties might be started in relation to that power which could not be fully explained without recurring to views of it, which, however just, might give birth to specious though unsound objections. Being in the same terms with the power over foreign commerce, the same extent, if taken literally, would belong to it. Yet it is very certain that it grew out of the abuse of the power by the importing States in taxing the non-importing, and was intended as a negative and preventive provision against injustice among the States themselves, rather than as a power to be used for the positive purposes of the General Government, in which alone, however, the remedial power could be lodged. And it will be safer to leave the power with this key to it, than to extend to it all the qualities and incidental means belonging to the power over foreign commerce, as is unavoidable. . . ."

Letter from James Madison to Joseph C. Cabell (Feb. 13, 1829), in 4 *Letters and Other Writings of James Madison* 14–15 (1865) (citation omitted). Madison's basic assumption—that the powers over foreign and domestic commerce are different—is sound even today, although one might dispute his views about the best contemporary construction of Congress's powers over domestic commerce.

36. Samuel Johnson, *A Dictionary of the English Language* (9th ed. 1805, 1790) (unpaginated) (defining *commerce* as a noun); id. (4th ed. 1773) (unpaginated) (same); id. (1st ed. 1755) (unpaginated) (same). Johnson's first edition offered the following examples of proper usage:

Places of publick resort being thus provided, our repair thither is especially for mutual conference, and, as it were, *commerce* to be had between God and us. *Hooker,* [*Ecclesiastical Polity,*] b[ook].v.s., [Chapter] 17 [18].

How could communities,
Degrees in schools, and brotherhoods in cities,
Peaceful *commerce* from dividable shores,
But by degree stand in authentick place? Sh[akespeare],
    Troil[ius]. and Cress[ida].

Instructed ships shall sail to quick *commerce*,
By which remotest regions are ally'd;
Which makes one city of the universe,
Where some may gain, and all may be supply'd.
Dryden.

These people had not any *commerce* with the other known parts of the world. *Tillotson*

In any country, that hath *commerce* with the rest of the world, it is almost impossible now to be without the use of silver coin. *Locke.*

All of these are examples of exchange, some social, some economic. The primary example is not economic: Hooker's "places of publick resort" are not inns but churches for public preaching, and presumably our commerce with God is communication and prayer, not the trade of commodities. In the fourth edition of 1775, Johnson's example of the second definition of *commerce*, "common or familiar intercourse," also concerns social interactions: "Good-nature, which consists of overlooking of faults is to be exercised only in doing ourselves justice in the ordinary *commerce* and occurrences of life. *Addison.*" Id.

37. Id. (4th ed. 1775).

38. Conversely, Johnson's primary definition for *intercourse* is "Commerce; exchange." The secondary definition is "Communication, followed by *with*." Id. If the primary definition of *commerce* is "intercourse," and the primary definition of *intercourse* is "commerce," this suggests that, at the time of the founding, *commerce* and *intercourse* were either synonyms, or very closely related in meaning, just as Chief Justice John Marshall argued in *Gibbons v. Ogden.* See Gibbons, 22 U.S. (9 Wheat.) at 189–90; see also Amar, *America's Constitution,* supra note 9, at 107–8 (the commerce clause gives Congress powers to regulate "all forms of intercourse in the affairs of life, whether or not narrowly economic . . . if a given problem genuinely spilled across state or national lines").

39. See Johnson, *A Dictionary of the English Language,* supra note 36 (9th ed. 1790) (definition of *commerce* as verb).

40. See id. (defining *traffick*).

41. United States v. Lopez, 514 U.S. 549, 585–86 (Thomas, J., concurring); see Barnett, *Restoring the Lost Constitution,* supra note 4, at 280–88; Epstein, "The Proper Scope of the Commerce Power," supra note 5.

42. The Latin cognate from which the word *commerce* is derived, *commercium,* meant not simply the exchange of goods but a variety of forms of social exchange, interaction, and participation. In Roman law, the rights of *commercium* included the basic civil rights of citizens to make transactions, inherit and convey property, and have access to courts to defend their rights. In his *Critique of Pure Reason,* Immanuel Kant equates *commercium* with the German word *Gemeinschaft* (community) and explains that it refers to a "dynamical community." Immanuel Kant, *Critique of Pure Reason* A213/B260–A214/B261, at 235–36 (Norman Kemp Smith trans., Macmillan Press 1929) (1784); see also Howard Caygill, *A Kant Dictionary* 117 (Wiley-Blackwell 1995) (explaining that when Kant uses *commercium* he means "free exchange and respect between individuals rather than in terms of shared characteristics or space"). *Commercium* came to refer to traditional academic feasts, where *commercium* songs were sung around the table. Finally, *commercium* meant "correspondence"; thus the Royal Society's famous account of the dispute about the invention of calculus between Sir Isaac Newton and Leibniz is called the *Commercium Epistolicum,* i.e., a "correspondence of letters." Jason Socrates Bardi, *The Calculus Wars: Newton, Leibniz, and the Greatest Mathematical Clash of All Time* 198–99 (Basic Books 2006).

43. See Albert O. Hirschman, *The Passions and the Interests: Political Arguments for Capitalism before Its Triumph* 60–63 (Princeton University Press 1977).

44. Felix Gilbert, *To the Farewell Address: Ideas of Early American Foreign Policy* 62–72 (Princeton University Press 1961).

45. Id. at 48–62. Treaty of Amity and Commerce Between the United States of America and His Most Christian Majesty, U.S.–Fr., Feb. 6, 1788, 8 Stat. 12 (annulled July 7, 1798) (treaty with France); Treaty of Amity and Commerce Between his Majesty the King of Prussia and the United States of America, U.S.–Prussia, July 9–Sept. 10, 1785, 8 Stat. 84; see also Treaty of Peace and Friendship Between the United States of America, and His Imperial Majesty the Emperor of Morocco, U.S.–Morocco, July 15, 1786–Jan. 25, 1787, 8 Stat. 100; Treaty of Amity and Commerce, Concluded between his Majesty the King of Sweden and the United States of North America, U.S.–Swed., Apr. 3, 1783, 8 Stat. 60; Treaty of Amity and Commerce between their High Mightiness the States General of the United Netherlands, and the United States of America, to wit: New Hampshire, Massachusetts, Rhode-Island and Providence Plantations, Connecticutt, New-York, New-Jersey, Pennsylvania, Delaware, Maryland, Virginia, North-Carolina, South-Carolina, and Georgia, U.S.–Neth., Oct. 8, 1782, 8 Stat. 32. The famous Jay Treaty of 1794 was styled a "Treaty of Amity, Commerce and Navigation." Treaty of Amity, Commerce and Navigation Between His Britannic Majesty and the United States of America, by their President, with the Advice and Consent of their Senate, U.S.–U.K., Nov. 19, 1794, 8 Stat. 116. The Jay Treaty became controversial in part because of concerns that it would tilt the United States politically toward Britain.

46. George Washington, "Farewell Address" (Sept. 19, 1796), available at avalon.law.yale.edu/18th_century/washing.asp.

47. Id.

48. For the discussion of navigation acts in the Philadelphia convention on August 29, 1787, see 2 *The Records of the Federal Convention of 1787,* supra note 13, at 449–53; id. at 631 (remarks of George Mason).

49. Justice Thomas does not appear to recognize that under the eighteenth-century dictionary definitions he offers to prove his case, including navigation would be a nonliteral usage. Instead, he simply adds "as well as transporting for these purposes" to his own definition of commerce. See United States v. Lopez, 514 U.S. 549, 585–86 (1995) (Thomas, J., concurring). Perhaps he assumes that "traffick" includes travel, as it does today, although in the eighteenth century it was a synonym for trade. Randy Barnett, to his credit, immediately sees the difficulty. Barnett, *Restoring the Lost Constitution,* supra note 4, at 291–93. He notes that the framers might have used words "which did not accurately express their intentions." Id. at 292. He proposes that navigation might be included in commerce "because of its intimate connection to the activity of trading," id., and because the framers seem to have spoken of navigation and commerce together frequently. Id. at 292–93. That is, he proposes a metonymic extension of the word.

50. Barnett, *Restoring the Lost Constitution,* supra note 4, at 293.

51. 22 U.S. (9 Wheat.) 1, 189–90 (1824).

52. Id. at 190; see also Joseph Story, 2 *Commentaries on the Constitution of the United States* §§ 1057–62 (5th ed., William S. Hein and Co. 1994) (expanding on Marshall's arguments and maintaining that commerce "comprehend[s] navigation and intercourse").

53. See William Winslow Crosskey, 1 *Politics and the Constitution in the History of the United States* (University of Chicago Press 1953); Walter H. Hamilton and Douglass Adair, *The Power to Govern* (W. W. Norton and Co. 1937); Grant S. Nelson and Robert J. Pushaw Jr., "Rethinking the Commerce Clause: Applying First Principles to Uphold Federal Commercial Regulations but Preserve State Control over Social Issues," 85 *Iowa L. Rev.* 1 (1999).

54. See Crosskey, 1 *Politics and the Constitution in the History of the United States,* supra note 53, at 288–92; Nelson and Pushaw, "Rethinking the Commerce Clause," supra note 53, 9–10, 14–21, 35–42; Robert J. Pushaw Jr. and Grant S. Nelson, "A Critique of the Narrow Interpretation of the Commerce Clause," 96 *Nw. U. L. Rev.* 695, 700 (2002).

55. See Nelson and Pushaw, "Rethinking the Commerce Clause," supra note 53, at 37. Robert Natelson takes a position between the trade theory and the economic theory, arguing that "commerce" is a legal term of art that refers to "the sort of [economic] activities engaged in by merchants" but does not include all gainful economic activity. Robert G. Natelson, "The Legal Meaning of 'Commerce' in the Commerce Clause," 80 *St. John's L. Rev.* 789, 845 (2006). Natelson argues that in legal documents "commerce" referred to "buying and selling products made by others (and sometimes land), associated finance and financial instruments, navigation and other carriage, and intercourse across jurisdictional lines." Id. The evidence Natelson provides is actually consistent with Marshall's theory of commerce as "commercial intercourse," but he does not recognize that all of his examples are united by the general concept of "intercourse."

56. 545 U.S. 1 (2005).

57. Id. at 25–26 (quoting Webster's *Third New International Dictionary* 720 (1966)).

58. Not all advocates of the economic theory, however, would accept these extensions. See Pushaw and Nelson, "A Critique of the Narrow Interpretation," supra note 54, at 698, 698–99 & nn. 28–29 (arguing for purely economic meaning). Cf. Natelson, "The Legal Meaning of 'Commerce' in the Commerce Clause," supra note 55, at 845 (same).

59. See, e.g., Crosskey, 1 *Politics and the Constitution in the History of the United States,* supra note 53, at 84–89, 96–113; Hamilton and Adair, *The Power to Govern,* supra note 53, at 52–63, 79–81, 89–100; Herbert Hovenkamp, "Judicial Restraint and Constitutional Federalism: The Supreme Court's *Lopez* and *Seminole Tribe* Decisions," 96 *Colum. L. Rev.* 2213, 2229–30 (1996)

(quoting Adam Smith, *The Wealth of Nations* 690–716 (3d ed. 1784)); Nelson and Pushaw, "Rethinking the Commerce Clause," supra note 53, at 16–21.

Around the time of the founding, there are many examples of people speaking of "agriculture, manufacturing and commerce" or "manufactures and commerce," which might suggest these terms were differentiated from each other. Yet it was equally common to speak of "navigation and commerce" or "trade and commerce": this suggests that the conjoined terms were strongly connected. See Pushaw and Nelson, "A Critique of the Narrow Interpretation of the Commerce Clause," supra note 54, at 705–6.

Thus, Tench Coxe, a political economist who served as assistant secretary of the Treasury in the Washington administration, argued that agricultural production, manufacturing, and trade were necessarily interconnected, and that the federal government should encourage all of them. Tench Coxe, *A View of the United States of America* 4–33 (William Hall; Wrigley and Barriman 1794). Perhaps more important from the standpoint of original meaning, he argued that "[t]he commerce of America, including our exports, imports, shipping, manufactures and fisheries, may be properly considered as forming one interest." Id. at 7.

Similarly, responding to Thomas Jefferson's argument against the First Bank of the United States, Alexander Hamilton argued that the federal government's power to regulate commerce necessarily included more than simply prescribing rules for buying and selling, as Jefferson had contended. It included policies like the creation of a national bank that regulated the economy at the national level. Such policies were designed to encourage "navigation and manufactures," which he described as "general relations of commerce":

> Prescribing rules for *buying* and *selling* . . . is indeed a species of regulation of trade, but it is one which falls more aptly within the province of the local jurisdictions than within that of the general government, whose care must be presumed to have been intended to be directed to those general political arrangements concerning trade on which its aggregate interests depend, rather than to the details of *buying* and *selling*. Accordingly, such only are the regulations to be found in the laws of the United States, whose objects are to give encouragement to the enterprise of our own merchants, and to advance our navigation and manufactures. And it is in reference to these general relations of commerce that an establishment which furnishes facilities to circulation, and a convenient medium of exchange and alienation, is to be regarded as a regulation of trade.

Alexander Hamilton, "Opinion as to the Constitutionality of the Bank of the United States," February 23, 1791, in 3 *The Works of Alexander Hamilton* 445, 481 (Henry Cabot Lodge ed., G. P. Putnam and Sons 1904) (emphasis in original).

See also Nelson and Pushaw, "Rethinking the Commerce Clause," supra note 53, at 15–16 (citing examples from the writings of Adam Smith, Malachy Postlethwayt, and Daniel Defoe in which the branches of commerce include manufacturing, mining, grazing, agriculture, fisheries, banking, insurance, and the maintenance of corporations).

60. The word "speech" in the First Amendment is both a synecdoche—where a part stands for a larger whole—and a metonym—where a word stands for something related to it. Thus, "speech" refers to a larger category of communication including writing, singing, painting, drama, moviemaking, and broadcasting. It also protects media of communication and various activities associated with communication. Similarly, "writings," for purposes of the progress clause, are not limited to written marks on paper, but include many other forms of fixed communication, like maps, drawings, sculptures, even software programs. And "discoveries" in the same clause refers to new inventions and new technology, not to scientific discoveries about the laws of nature, which are not patentable.

As one might expect, nonliteral usage presents many problems for constitutional interpretation. First, we must have evidence that a nonliteral usage was understood by the general public. For example, although in theory "thirty five," the minimum age for presidents, could be a nonliteral usage, the historical context does not support this. Second, assuming the usage is nonliteral, we must figure out what set of concepts the text refers to. This makes the question of original meaning very difficult to disentangle from original expected application; nevertheless our goal is not to recover original expected application, but to figure out the animating principles or policies that naturally led people to use words nonliterally. Third, some nonliteral usages at the time of enactment eventually become generally accepted meanings of a word, which makes it difficult to know what the original meaning was.

61. See, e.g., Barnett, *Restoring the Lost Constitution,* supra note 4, at 282–89. But see Nelson and Pushaw, "Rethinking the Commerce Clause," supra note 53, at 13–42; Pushaw and Nelson, "A Critique of the Narrow Interpretation," supra note 54, at 709–11 (providing counterexamples in the debates).

62. Pushaw and Nelson, "A Critique of the Narrow Interpretation," supra note 54, at 700.

63. Howard Gillman, "More on the Origins of the Fuller Court's Jurisprudence: Reexamining the Scope of Federal Power over Commerce and Manufacturing in Nineteenth-Century Constitutional Law," 49 *Pol. Res. Q.* 415, 421–23 (1996).

64. See 312 U.S. 100, 113 ("While manufacture is not of itself interstate commerce, the shipment of manufactured goods interstate is such commerce").

65. See, e.g., Veazie v. Moor, 55 U.S. (14 How.) 568, 573–74 (1852) (explaining that Congress's powers under the commerce clause do not include "control over turnpikes, canals, or railroads").

66. Boris I. Bittker with Brannon P. Denning, *Bittker on the Regulation of Interstate and Foreign Commerce* 3-8 to 3-16, 3-20 to 3-24 (Aspen Publishers 1999) (tracing the evolution of the Court's doctrines).

67. Id. at 3-30 to 3-39.

68. See, e.g., Scarborough v. United States, 431 U.S. 563 (1977); United States v. Bass, 404 U.S. 336 (1971).

69. Donald H. Regan, "How to Think about the Federal Commerce Power and Incidentally Rewrite *United States v. Lopez,*" 94 *Mich. L. Rev.* 554, 562 (1995) (labeling current doctrine "a new formalism" that is "'pragmatic' only in the sense that it can always serve the goal of justifying federal power").

70. Akhil Reed Amar, "The Supreme Court, 1999 Term—Foreword: The Document and the Doctrine," 114 *Harv. L. Rev.* 26, 40–41 & n. 44 (2000).

71. Gibbons v. Ogden, 22 U.S. (9 Wheat.) 1, 190 (1824) (opinion of Marshall, C. J.); Story, 2 *Commentaries on the Constitution of the United States,* supra note 52, at §§ 1057–62; United States v. Se. Underwriters Ass'n, 322 U.S. 533, 549–53 (1944) (opinion of Black, J.); Amar, *America's Constitution,* supra note 9, at 107–8.

72. See Steven G. Calabresi, "'A Government of Limited and Enumerated Powers': In Defense of *United States v. Lopez,*" 94 *Mich. L. Rev.* 752, 781–84, 805–7, 814–30 (1995) (arguing that externalities produced by state policies justify the scope of federal power); Regan, "How to Think about the Federal Commerce Power," supra note 69, at 555–59 (arguing that federal power is justified in order to solve problems that states cannot solve individually).

73. Gibbons v. Ogden, 22 U.S. (9 Wheat.) at 189–90 (opinion of Marshall, C. J.).

74. At Philadelphia, the convention originally voted to give Congress the power to regulate "affairs" with the Indian tribes. 2 *The Records of the Federal Convention of 1787,* supra note 13, at 321. When it prepared the list of enumerated powers, the Committee of Detail attached this power to the end of the commerce clause. Id. at 367; see also id. at 569 ("Report of the Committee of Style"). There is no evidence, however, that the shift from "affairs" to "commerce" was thought to change the meaning or the scope of the powers granted. Amar, *America's Constitution,* supra note 9, at 107 & n. 17.

Under the Articles of Confederation, Congress had the power of "regulating the trade and managing all affairs with the Indians, not members of any of the States, provided that the legislative right of any State within its own limits be not infringed or violated." Articles of Confederation, art. IX, ¶ 4. Because under Resolution VI Congress was to have at least the powers of the old confederation, we may assume that "commerce" included both "trade" and "affairs."

75. As Justice Black explained:

The power confided to Congress by the Commerce Clause is declared in The Federalist to be for the purpose of securing the "maintenance of harmony and proper intercourse among the States." . . . It is the power to legislate concerning transactions which, reaching across state boundaries, affect the people of more states than one;—to govern affairs which the individual states, with their limited territorial jurisdictions, are not fully capable of governing.

Se. Underwriters Ass'n, 322 U.S. at 551–52 (quoting *The Federalist* no. 41 (James Madison)).

76. Amar, *America's Constitution,* supra note 9, at 107.

77. An Act to Regulate Trade and Intercourse with the Indian Tribes, Act of July 22, 1790, ch. 33, 1 Stat. 137 (1790) (expired 1793). Congress passed new versions repeatedly during the antebellum era, with changing provisions. Act of Mar. 1, 1793, ch. 19, 1 Stat. 329 (repealed 1796); Act of May 19, 1796, ch. 30, 1 Stat. 469 (expired 1799); Act of Mar. 3, 1799, ch. 46, 1 Stat. 743 (expired 1802); Act of Mar. 30, 1802, ch. 13, 2 Stat. 139 (repealed 1834); Act of June 30, 1834, ch. 161, 4 Stat. 729. The current version of the Trade and Intercourse Acts is 25 U.S.C. § 177 (2006), which now covers only purchases and grants of land from Indian tribes.

The first such statute, the 1790 Act, does regulate economic transactions with Indians and the Indian tribes. For example, it requires a license to do business with Indian tribes, and it holds that sales of lands by Indians are not valid unless "made and duly executed at some public treaty, held under the authority of the United States." 1 Stat. 137 § 3. But section 5 of the Act also regulates ordinary crimes committed against members of the Indian tribes:

> Sec. 5: *And be it further enacted,* That if any citizen or inhabitant of the United States, or of either of the territorial districts of the United States, shall go into any town, settlement or territory belonging to any nation or tribe of Indians, and shall there commit any crime upon, or trespass against, the person or property of any peaceable and friendly Indian or Indians, which, if committed within the jurisdiction of any state, or within the jurisdiction of either of the said districts, against a citizen or white inhabitant thereof, would be punishable by the laws of such state or district, such offender or offenders shall be subject to the same punishment, and shall be proceeded against in the same manner as if the offence had been committed within the jurisdiction of the state or district to which he or they may belong, against a citizen or white inhabitant thereof.

Id. at § 5.

The reason for section 5 of the 1790 Act is fairly clear: Congress wanted to keep the peace with nonbelligerent Indian tribes; if Americans attacked Indians or trespassed on their property, this might damage foreign relations. In fact, the 1796 Act is specifically entitled "An Act to regulate Trade and Intercourse with the Indian Tribes, and to preserve Peace on the Frontiers." Congress's power to regulate "commerce" (i.e., intercourse or interactions) with the Indian tribes is the natural source of the prohibitions in the 1790 Act.

The Trade and Intercourse Act of 1793, which succeeded the 1790 Act, made even clearer that noneconomic transactions were covered: it prohibited "murder, robbery, larceny, trespass or other crime, against the person or property of any friendly Indian or Indians." 1 Stat. 329 § 4.

78. Beginning in 1796 the Trade and Intercourse Acts do enforce treaty obligations—for example, they limit hunting and cattle drives on Indian lands—although they continue to prohibit ordinary crimes against Indians whether or not there is a treaty. 1 Stat. 469 § 2. (The ban on crimes against the person of Indians was not removed until the 1834 version.)

79. Another example is Congress's attempt to protect Indians from the influence of alcohol. Congress made it a crime not only to sell alcohol to Indians, but to give it away to them, or even to bring it into Indian Country. Section 20 of the Trade and Intercourse Act of June 30, 1834, made it a crime to "sell, exchange, give, barter, or dispose of any spiritous liquor or wine to an Indian (in the Indian Country)" or "to introduce, or attempt to introduce, any spiritous liquor or wine into the Indian Country" except as required by the War Department. Indian Intercourse Act, 4 Stat. 729 (1834). The Act was amended in 1862 to protect Indians who were not in Indian Country as long as they were "under the charge of any Indian superintendent or Indian agent appointed by the United States." Act of February 13, 1862, 12 Stat. 339 (1862).

The Court upheld the 1862 act in United States v. Holliday, 70 U.S. (3 Wall.) 407 (1865) and United States v. Forty-Three Gallons of Whiskey, 93 U.S. 188 (1876). *Holliday* involved a sale to an Indian, while *Forty-Three Gallons* involved transportation "with intent to sell, dispose of, and distribute." 93 U.S. at 189. In *Holliday*, Justice Miller held that the law properly regulated not only "buying and selling and exchanging commodities, which is the essence of all commerce," but also "the intercourse between the citizens of the United States and those tribes, which is another branch of commerce, and a very important one." 70 U.S. (3 Wall.) at 417.

80. In United States v. Kagama, 118 U.S. 375, 378 (1886), Justice Miller argued that criminal laws that regulated Indians living on reservations might not fall within the Indian commerce clause, if they were not part of a larger set of "trade and intercourse laws." This is consistent with the notion that Congress's power is regulating commerce *with* the Indian tribes, rather than simply regulating the Indian tribes per se.

81. See, e.g., Adam M. McKeown, *Melancholy Order: Asian Migration and the Globalization of Borders* 91 (Columbia University Press 2008) ("At the turn of the nineteenth century, intercourse was generally conceived as the entwined relationships of trade and diplomacy between nations"); see also Gilbert, *To the Farewell Address*, supra note 44, at 92 (arguing that in eighteenth-century conceptions of power politics, diplomacy, trade, and military strategy were inseparable).

82. U.S. Const. art. I, § 8, cl. 4.

83. Id. at cl. 15.

84. Id. at cl. 3.

85. Id. at § 9, cl. 1.

86. In the Virginia ratifying debates, Edmund Randolph noted, "To what power in the general government is the exception made respecting the importation of negroes? Not from a general power, but from a particular power expressly enumerated. This is an exception from the power given them of regulating commerce." 3 Elliot, supra note 12, at 464.

87. See David L. Lightner, *Slavery and the Commerce Power* (Yale University Press 2006). The South was firmly opposed to any suggestion that Congress might regulate the interstate slave trade under the commerce clause, even though, if slavery were not involved, the question would be fairly easy. (Moreover, no one doubted Congress's ability to regulate or even ban the foreign slave trade after 1808.) The Supreme Court debated the questions in a trio of cases: The Passenger Cases, 48 U.S. (7 How.) 283 (1849); Groves v. Slaughter, 40 U.S. (15 Pet.) 449 (1841); and New York v. Miln, 36 U.S. (11 Pet.) 102 (1837).

88. See, e.g., The Head Money Cases, 112 U.S. 580, 591 (1884); New York v. Compagnie Generale Transatlantique, 107 U.S. 59, 60 (1883); Henderson v. Mayor of New York, 92 U.S. 259, 270 (1875).

89. 92 U.S. 275, 280 (1875).

90. Chae Chan Ping v. United States (The Chinese Exclusion Case), 130 U.S. 581 (1889).

91. United States v. Curtiss-Wright Export Corp., 299 U.S. 304, 315–18 (1936).

92. Justice Sutherland's argument rested on the fiction that the states were never really sovereign in foreign affairs and therefore "the investment of the federal government with the powers of external sovereignty did not depend upon the affirmative grants of the Constitution." Id. at 318. This would no doubt have come as a surprise to the framers, especially in those jurisdictions that debated whether to join the new Constitution.

93. Samuel Johnson's definition of *regulate* is "to adjust by rule or method." Johnson, *A Dictionary of the English Language,* supra note 36 (9th ed. 1805) (unpaginated); id. (1st ed. 1755) (unpaginated) (same). Champion v. Ames (The Lottery Case), 188 U.S. 321 (1903), considered whether Congress could prohibit the shipment of lottery tickets between states as a regulation of interstate commerce.

The four dissenting judges argued that the power to regulate commerce gave Congress only the power to "free[] such commerce from state discrimination, and not to transfer the power of restriction." Id. at 372 (Fuller, C. J., dissenting). They conceded that their theory "does not challenge the legislative power of a sovereign nation to exclude foreign persons or commodities, or place an embargo, perhaps not permanent, upon foreign ships or manufactures." Id. at 374. Thus, they were forced to maintain that the word "regulate" had two different meanings for foreign and domestic commerce, when the more sensible reading would be to distinguish "commerce with" from "commerce among."

The majority held that Congress had the power to prohibit undesirable or wrongful commerce from moving across state borders. Because states might not be able to ban such commerce—this might be forbidden discrimination against out-of-state business—the federal government was "the only power competent to that end." Id. at 358. Note especially the Court's use of the word "competent," echoing Resolution VI's basic structural principle that the federal government has the power to act where states are separately incompetent. The *Champion* Court correctly understood that the power to "regulate"—that is, to prescribe a rule for commerce—includes the power to determine what commerce is wrongful or undesirable and therefore may be restricted or excluded. Congress may do more than protect commerce among the states. It may use its powers to promote particular social or economic policies by regulating commerce that produces spillover effects or creates collective action problems.

94. Randy Barnett, for example, notes that ascribing three meanings to the same word raises potential difficulties with his theory of objective meaning, because that theory focuses on what an ordinary speaker of the language would understand a word to mean. See Barnett, *Restoring the Lost Constitution,* supra note 4, at 92–93, 97, 103. However, he argues that "when a group of people agrees to use one word to connote, depending on the circumstances, two different meanings, they have objectively manifested their intentions, albeit in an awkward manner that makes the objective meaning of their words sometimes difficult to discern." Id. at 310. What Barnett has not demonstrated is that there was an agreement by the ratifiers to assign three different meanings to the same word in the same sentence. Such an agreement among such a widely dispersed population would have been very difficult to negotiate and form. Perhaps more importantly for his theory of objective original public meaning, he has not shown that members of the general public who were not involved in the debates would have understood that there was an agreement to use one word in three different ways. Instead of attributing an "awkward manner" to the constitutional text, we might simply look for other ways in the text to distinguish foreign, Indian, and domestic commerce.

95. Johnson, *A Dictionary of the English Language,* supra note 36 (9th ed. 1805) (unpaginated); id. (1st ed. 1755) (unpaginated) (same).

96. Barnett, *Restoring the Lost Constitution,* supra note 4, at 297.

97. Id. at 300.

98. Gibbons v. Ogden, 22 U.S. (9 Wheat.) 1, 194–95 (1824).

99. Id. at 195.

100. Id.

101. See infra Part V.

102. 2 Elliot, supra note 12, at 424.

103. See Regan, "How to Think about the Federal Commerce Power," supra note 69, at 571–75.

104. That is one reason why Congress was given the power in Article I, section 8, clause 7 "[t]o establish Post Offices and post Roads." U.S. Const. art I, § 8, cl 7.

105. Regan, "How to Think about the Federal Commerce Power," supra note 69, at 574; see also Houston, E. & W. Tex. Ry. v. United States (The Shreveport Rate Case), 234 U.S. 342 (1914) (upholding federal rate regulation of intrastate railroad transportation that affects interstate commerce); The Daniel Ball, 77 U.S. (10 Wall.) 557 (1870) (upholding federal safety regulation of a steamship moving entirely within a single state).

106. 2 *The Records of the Federal Convention of 1787,* supra note 13, at 21, 26, 131–32.

107. Elliot, supra note 12, at 424.

108. 312 U.S. 100 (1941).

109. See id. at 113–17 for Justice Stone's version of this argument.

110. Id. at 117–21.

111. See id. at 122 (arguing that legislation is necessary to prevent unfair competition from firms implementing substandard labor conditions that harms businesses implementing acceptable labor conditions).

112. One might object that some businesses, like laundries and restaurants, do not sell goods that regularly cross state lines. Regan, "How to Think about the Federal Commerce Power," supra note 69, at 588–89 (arguing that the federal government should not be able to regulate businesses that produce goods primarily for local consumption). However, these businesses compete for labor with businesses that do interstate business. Moreover, labor, like capital, is mobile and may leave for states with better working conditions, thus putting downward pressure on wages and working conditions in those states. Congress may therefore include both businesses that ship interstate and those that do not in a comprehensive federal solution.

113. Note that a reasonableness test applies to two different questions: The first is whether there is a sufficient spillover effect, collective action problem, or other effect on interstate commerce to justify regulation. The second is whether Congress's choice of regulation is sufficiently adapted to achieving its purposes in regulating.

The test of reasonableness is not required by the original meaning of the constitutional text. It is a construction that originates in one of the earliest judicial constructions of Congress's enumerated powers. McCulloch v. Maryland, 17 U.S. (4 Wheat.) 316 (1819). In *McCulloch*, Chief Justice Marshall argued that "the sound construction of the constitution must allow to the national legislature that discretion, with respect to the means by which the powers it confers are to be carried into execution." Id. at 421. Such discretion requires that courts defer to Congress's judgment where reasonable minds may differ. Hence, Marshall concluded that all means that are appropriate and adapted to legitimate constitutional ends are constitutional exercises of Congress's enumerated powers. Id.; see also id. at 413–14 (explaining that "necessary" means convenient or useful to achieving an end); id. at 415–16 ("[Congress must not be] deprive[d] . . . of the capacity to avail itself of experience, to exercise its reason, and to accommodate its legislation to circumstances"); id. at 419 (explaining that even without the necessary and proper clause, Congress may employ means "which, in its judgment, would most advantageously effect the object to be accomplished"); id. at 420 ("[The necessary and proper clause] cannot be construed . . . to impair the right of the legislature to exercise its best judgment in the selection of measures to carry into execution the constitutional powers of the government").

In *United States v. Darby*, the Supreme Court followed *McCulloch* by requiring a reasonable relationship between Congress's choice of means for regulating commerce and its legitimate ends:

> Congress, having by the present Act adopted the policy of excluding from interstate commerce all goods produced for the commerce which do not conform to the specified labor standards, it may choose the means reasonably adapted to the attainment of the permitted end, even though they involve control of intrastate activities. Such legislation has often been sustained with respect to powers, other than the commerce power granted to the national government, when the means chosen, although not themselves within the granted power, were nevertheless deemed appropriate aids to the accomplishment of some purpose within an admitted power of the national government.

Darby, 312 U.S. at 121 (citing *McCulloch* and later cases).

114. 317 U.S. 111 (1942).

115. The compact clause states that "No State shall, without the Consent of Congress . . . enter into any Agreement or Compact with another State." U.S. Const. art. I, § 10, cl. 3.

116. See Regan, "How to Think about the Federal Commerce Power," supra note 69, at 583–85.

117. 317 U.S. at 127–29.

118. Id. at 127–28.

119. *See* Regan, "How to Think about the Federal Commerce Power," supra note 69, at 583–84.

120. See, e.g., Gonzales v. Raich, 545 U.S. 1, 17–22 (2005) (upholding federal regulation of intrastate manufacture and possession of marijuana); Perez v. United States, 402 U.S. 146, 154 (1971) ("Where the class of activities is regulated and that class is within the reach of federal power, the courts have no power 'to excise, as trivial, individual instances' of the class" (emphasis omitted)); United States v. Wrightwood Dairy Co., 315 U.S. 110, 118–19 (1942) ("Congress . . . possesses every power needed to make [its] regulation [of interstate commerce] effective. . . . [Its power] extends to those intrastate activities

which in a substantial way interfere with or obstruct the exercise of the granted power"); cf. United States v. Lopez, 514 U.S. 549, 561 (1995) (invalidating a statutory section that was "not an essential part of a larger regulation of economic activity, in which the regulatory scheme could be undercut unless the intrastate activity were regulated").

121. See Jedediah Purdy, "The Politics of Nature: Climate Change, Environmental Law, *and Democracy,*" 119 *Yale L. J.* 1122 (2010).

122. Katzenbach v. McClung, 379 U.S. 294, 298–300 (1964).

123. See, e.g., "A Bill to Eliminate Discrimination in Public Accommodations Affecting Interstate Commerce: Hearing on S. 1732 Before the S. Comm. on Commerce," 88th Cong. 190–93 (1963) (statement of Sen. John Cooper). At the same hearing, Senator John Pastore stated: "I believe in this bill, because I believe in the dignity of man, not because it impedes our commerce. . . . I like to feel that what we are talking about is a moral issue. . . . And that morality, it seems to me, comes under the 14th amendment . . . about equal protection of the law." Id. at 252; see also Heart of Atlanta Motel, Inc. v. United States, 379 U.S. 241, 291 (1964) (Goldberg, J., concurring) ("The primary purpose of the Civil Rights Act of 1964 . . . as the Court recognizes . . . is the vindication of human dignity and not mere economics"); id. at 292 ("Discrimination is not simply dollars and cents, hamburgers and movies; it is the humiliation, frustration, and embarrassment that a person must surely feel when he is told that he is unacceptable as a member of the public because of his race or color") (quoting S. Rep. No. 872, at 16 (1964)); Robert C. Post and Reva B. Siegel, "Equal Protection by Law: Federal Antidiscrimination Legislation After *Morrison* and *Kimel,*" 110 *Yale L. J.* 441, 504–5 (2000) ("No one at the time had the slightest doubt but that the antidiscrimination statutes enacted by Congress during the 1960s were implementing the equality norms of Section 1 of the Fourteenth Amendment"); cf. Seth P. Waxman, "Twins at Birth: Civil Rights and the Role of the Solicitor General," 75 *Ind. L. J.* 1297, 1312–13 (2000) (noting that choice to use the commerce power to defend the 1964 Civil Rights Act was based on litigation strategy, not the purpose of the Act).

124. See Jack M. Balkin, "The Reconstruction Power," 85 *N.Y.U. L. Rev.* 1801 (2010) (arguing that Congress has ample authority to pass modern civil rights laws—including those affecting private parties—under its powers to enforce the Reconstruction amendments).

125. Racial discrimination also made our relations with foreign powers more difficult during the Cold War, which was one motivation for Brown v. Board of Education, 347 U.S. 483 (1954) and the passage of national civil rights laws. Mary L. Dudziak, *Cold War Civil Rights: Race and the Image of American Democracy* 79–114 (Princeton University Press 2000). Here, however, I focus only on domestic effects. I do not reach the interesting question of whether Congress may, under its powers to regulate foreign commerce, reach intrastate activity

that would embarrass the nation diplomatically. At least where no treaty obligations are involved, there might be good reasons to adopt a limiting construction of Congress's ability to regulate intrastate activities to further the regulation of foreign commerce or to define and punish offenses against the law of nations.

126. Gibbons v. Ogden, 22 U.S. (9 Wheat.) 1 (1824).

127. 514 U.S. 549 (1995).

128. Indeed "neither the statute nor its legislative history contain[s] express congressional findings regarding the effects upon interstate commerce of gun possession in a school zone." Id. at 562 (quoting Brief for United States at 5–6). Congress later provided legislative findings about effects on interstate and foreign commerce in section 320904 of the Violent Crime Control and Law Enforcement Act of 1994, Pub. L. 103-322, 108 Stat. 1796 (1994). See Lopez, 514 U.S. at 563 n. 4.

129. See the discussion in Paul Brest, Sanford Levinson, Jack M. Balkin, Akhil Reed Amar, and Reva B. Siegel, eds., *Processes of Constitutional Decisionmaking* 621–23 (5th ed., Aspen L. & Bus. 2006).

130. Lopez, 514 U.S. at 561.

131. See Brest et al., *Processes of Constitutional Decisionmaking,* supra note 129, at 626.

132. Lopez, 514 U.S. at 564–65; see also United States v. Morrison, 529 U.S. 598, 615–16 (2000).

133. Kristin A. Collins, "Federalism's Fallacy: The Early Tradition of Federal Family Law and the Invention of States' Rights," 26 *Cardozo L. Rev.* 1761, 1767 (2005) (arguing that prior to the Civil War, the federal government was actively engaged in creating law concerning family relations); Jill Elaine Hasday, "Federalism and the Family Reconstructed," 45 *UCLA L. Rev.* 1297 (1998) (arguing that the federal government has been heavily involved in regulating domestic relations since Reconstruction). Federal regulations of health, safety, and welfare that seek to promote "family values" are only the most obvious examples. It is true that the federal government has primarily used the taxing and spending powers to regulate education and family life. But the question is not which federal power is being used; it is whether the states have traditionally had more or less exclusive control in the area with no significant history of federal intervention.

134. See, e.g., Perez v. United States, 402 U.S. 146 (1971) (upholding federal loan-sharking statute). The federal government may also have special regulatory competence where weapons or other dangerous items that are portable, easily concealed, and often used in crime regularly cross state lines in ways that are hard for individual states to police. Regan, "How to Think about the Federal Commerce Power," supra note 69, at 569–70.

135. 529 U.S. 598 (2000).

136. See Jack M. Balkin, "The Reconstruction Power," 85 *N.Y.U. L. Rev.* 1801 (2010). The basic idea is that if state and local law enforcement officials do not

take violence against women seriously, they are, quite literally, denying women "the equal protection of the laws." Therefore, Congress may pass both corrective and prophylactic legislation that directly prohibits gender-motivated violence by private actors, just as Congress is empowered to protect blacks from racially motivated violence when local law enforcement looks the other way. See David P. Currie, *The Constitution in the Supreme Court: The First Hundred Years, 1789–1888* 397 (University of Chicago Press 1985) ("A strong argument can be made, on the basis of the origins of the equal protection clause, that private lynching was among the evils that Congress was meant to have power to forbid"); Laurent B. Frantz, "Congressional Power to Enforce the Fourteenth Amendment against Private Acts, 73 *Yale L. J.* 1353, 1357, 1377–78 (1964) (explaining that Congress assumed the Fourteenth Amendment gave it authority to protect blacks from private violence).

137. Lopez, 514 U.S. at 561; accord Morrison, 529 U.S. at 613.

138. See Regan, "How to Think about the Federal Commerce Power," supra note 69, at 564.

139. In particular, the notion that ordinary household activity that contributes to pollution or to other social problems is not economic is particularly ironic. The word *economic* comes from the words *oikos,* meaning "household," and *nomos,* meaning "rules" or "ordering" (or in this case, "management" or "control"); one of its earliest meanings was "household management." See *Oxford English Dictionary* (2d ed. 1989). The first economic treatise, Xenophon's *Oeconomicus,* is a Socratic dialogue about how to manage an estate. The household was the source of production throughout most of human history and still is the source of the vast majority of budgetary decisions.

140. Patient Protection and Affordable Care Act, Pub. L. No. 111-148, 124 Stat. 119 (2010), amended by Health Care and Education Reconciliation Act, Pub. L. No. 111-152, 124 Stat. 1029 (2010). The individual mandate is § 1501(b) (codified at 26 U.S.C § 5000A).

141. See id. § 1501(b) (codified at 26 U.S.C. §5000A(d), (e)). Persons listed as dependents on another's tax return are not directly liable for the penalty; however, the taxpayer listing them as a dependent is responsible for their health care coverage. See 26 U.S.C § 5000A(b)(3)(A).

142. The amount of the penalty is the greater of a flat dollar amount (which is calculated according to a complicated formula) and a percentage of adjusted gross income, which rises to 2.5 percent for taxable years beginning after 2015; this figure, in turn, is capped at the average national premium. See id. (codified at 26 U.S.C. § 5000A(c)(3)).

143. U.S. Const. art. I, § 8, cl. 1.

144. See Jack M. Balkin, "The Constitutionality of the Individual Mandate for Health Insurance," 362 *New Eng. J. Med.* 482 (2010); Jack Balkin, "The Constitutionality of an Individual Mandate for Health Insurance," Parts I and

II, in David B. Rivkin Jr., Lee A. Casey, and Jack M. Balkin, Debate, "A Healthy Debate: The Constitutionality of an Individual Mandate," 158 *U. Pa. L. Rev. PENNumbra* 93, 102–5, 114–16 (2009), www.pennumbra.com/debates/pdfs/HealthyDebate.pdf.

145. See Balkin, "The Constitutionality of the Individual Mandate for Health Insurance," supra note 144, at 2; Balkin, "A Healthy Debate," supra note 144, at 114–16.

146. 379 U.S. 294 (1964).

147. 379 U.S. 241 (1964).

148. Balkin, "A Healthy Debate," supra note 144, at 99; Memorandum from Randy Barnett et al., The Heritage Foundation, "Why the Personal Mandate to Buy Health Insurance Is Unprecedented and Unconstitutional" (Dec. 9, 2009), available at www.heritage.org/research/legalissues/lm0049.cfm.

149. Under current doctrine, Congress may regulate economic activity that has a cumulative and substantial effect on interstate commerce. Wickard v. Filburn, 317 U.S. 111, 117 (1942); United States v. Wrightwood Dairy Co., 315 U.S. 110, 121–22 (1942); United States v. Darby, 312 U.S. 100, 118–24 (1941). Congress may also regulate local behavior when doing so is "an essential part of a larger regulation of economic activity, in which the regulatory scheme could be undercut unless the intrastate activity were regulated." Gonzales v. Raich, 545 U.S. 1, 24 (2005) (quoting United States v. Lopez, 514 U.S. 549, 561 (1995)). Indeed, as Justice Scalia has explained, under the necessary and proper clause "Congress may regulate even noneconomic local activity if that regulation is a necessary part of a more general regulation of interstate commerce." Id. at 37 (Scalia, J., concurring in the judgment).

The constitutionality of the individual mandate is a straightforward application of *Wickard* and *Raich*. In *Wickard,* the Supreme Court held that Congress could regulate wheat grown for home consumption as part of a more general regulation of farm production. People who grew wheat at home substituted it for wheat products they would otherwise purchase in the market; cumulatively, this practice had a substantial effect on interstate farm prices and undermined Congress's regulation of farm production. In *Gonzales v. Raich*, the Court held that Congress could regulate marijuana grown for home consumption as part of a general ban on controlled substances, because Congress reasonably concluded that people would substitute homegrown marijuana for other marijuana purchased in black markets, and this would undermine Congress's more general regulation of controlled substances.

As noted in the text, uninsured persons actually self-insure; they rely on their families for financial support, go to emergency rooms (often passing costs on to others), or purchase over-the-counter remedies. They substitute these activities for paying premiums to health insurance companies. All these activities are economic, and they have a cumulative effect on interstate commerce. Moreover, like people who substitute homegrown marijuana or wheat for purchased crops, the cumulative effect of uninsured people's behavior undermines Congress's regulation—in this case, its regulation of health insurance markets. Because Congress believes that national health care reform will not succeed unless these people are brought into national risk pools, it can regulate their activities in order to make its general regulation of health insurance effective.

150. U.S. Const. art. I, § 8, cl. 18.

151. See Amar, *America's Constitution,* supra note 9, at 110–11. The idea of the clause's "horizontal" effect comes from William W. Van Alstyne, "The Role of Congress in Determining Incidental Powers of the President and of the Federal Courts: A Comment on the Horizontal Effect of the Sweeping Clause," 40 *Law & Contemp. Probs.* 102 (1976).

152. U.S. Const. art. I, § 8, cl. 18.

153. In *United States v. Comstock,* the Supreme Court held that Congress had the power to create a civil commitment procedure for mentally ill sexually dangerous federal prisoners beyond the date they would otherwise be released. United States v. Comstock, 560 U.S., 130 S.Ct. 1939 (2010). Justice Breyer's majority opinion held that the test is "whether the statute constitutes a means that is rationally related to the implementation of a constitutionally enumerated power." Id. at 1956. *Comstock* is a good example of the basic principle behind Congress's Article I, section 8 powers. *Comstock* presents a classic collective action issue, a NIMBY (not in my back yard) problem. As Justice Alito puts it, "The statute recognizes that, in many cases, no State will assume the heavy financial burden of civilly committing a dangerous federal prisoner who, as a result of lengthy federal incarceration, no longer has any substantial ties to any State." Id. at 1969 (Alito, J., concurring in the judgment). Without a federal solution, states will attempt to deny responsibility for dangerous mentally ill sex offenders, hoping that some other state will assume the costs. Hence a federal solution becomes appropriate. See Jack M. Balkin, "*Comstock,* Health Care Reform, and Federalism," *Balkinization,* May 17, 2010, http://balkin.blogspot.com/2010/05/comstock-health-care-reform-and.html.

154. 17 U.S. (4 Wheat.) 316 (1819).

155. Gibbons v. Ogden, 22 U.S. (9 Wheat.) 1, 203 (1824) (inspection laws "act upon the subject before it becomes an article of . . . commerce . . . and prepare it for that purpose. . . . No direct general power over these objects is granted to Congress"); Veazie v. Young, 55 U.S. 568, 573–74 (1852) (holding that regulation of commerce does not include regulation of manufactures and agriculture); McCready v. Virginia, 94 U.S. 391, 396–97 (1877) ("Commerce has nothing to do with land while producing, but only with the product after it has become the subject of trade"); James Kent, *Commentaries on American Law* 436 (John M. Gould ed., 14th ed. 1896) (noting that commerce does not

include preparation of articles for export); Gillman, "More on the Origins of the Fuller Court's Jurisprudence," supra note 63, at 421–22.

156. See Cooley v. Board of Wardens, 53 U.S. 299 (1852) (holding that states have power to regulate certain aspects of interstate commerce).

157. See Gibbons, 22 U.S., at 209 (noting "great force" in the argument that the power to regulate interstate commerce is exclusive to the federal government); id. at 227 (Johnson, J., concurring) (arguing that federal power is exclusive).

10. Privileges or Immunities

1. Jack M. Balkin, "The Reconstruction Power," 85 *N.Y.U. L. Rev.* 1801 (2010).

2. See Akhil Reed Amar, *The Bill of Rights: Creation and Reconstruction* 160–62 (Yale University Press 1998); Michael Kent Curtis, *No State Shall Abridge: The Fourteenth Amendment and the Bill of Rights* 30–34, 37–41 (Duke University Press 1986); see also Michael Kent Curtis, *Free Speech, "The People's Darling Privilege": Struggles for Freedom of Expression in American History* (Duke University Press 2000) (describing Southern suppression of free speech before the Civil War).

3. See Walter L. Fleming, 1 *Documentary History of Reconstruction* 255–312 (Arthur H. Clark Co. 1906); Eric Foner, *Reconstruction: America's Unfinished Revolution, 1863–1877* 198–209 (Peter Smith Publisher 2002); *Cong. Globe,* 39th Cong., 1st Sess. 588–89 (statement of Rep. Donnelly) (describing the legislation passed by various Southern states); id. at 474 (1866) (statement of Senator Trumbull) (southern legislatures "still impose upon [the freedmen] the very restrictions which were imposed upon them in consequence of the existence of slavery, and before it was abolished").

4. *Cong. Globe,* 39th Cong., 1st Sess. 2764–68 (1866) (statement of Sen. Howard).

5. See Amar, *The Bill of Rights,* supra note 2, at 187 (noting coverage of Howard's speech in the front page of the *New York Herald,* the most widely read newspaper in the nation in 1866, as well the reprinting of portions of the speech on the front page of the *New York Times*); Michael Kent Curtis, "The Bill of Rights and the States: An Overview from One Perspective," 18 *J. Contemp. Legal Issues* 3, 7–8 & n. 18 (2009) (noting coverage by the *Philadelphia Inquirer, Washington, D.C., National Intelligencer, Hillsdale* (Michigan) *Standard,* and the *Boston Daily Advertiser*); Bryan H. Wildenthal, "Nationalizing the Bill of Rights: Revisiting the Original Understanding of the Fourteenth Amendment in 1866–67," 68 *Ohio St. L. J.* 1509, 1564 (2007) (collecting papers discussing or reprinting Howard's speech). As early as 1954, William Crosskey had pointed to coverage of Howard's speech in both the *New York*

Times and the *New York Herald.* William W. Crosskey, "Charles Fairman, 'Legislative History,' and the Constitutional Limitations on State Authority," 22 *U. Chi. L. Rev.* 1, 102–3 (1954).

6. *Cong. Globe,* 39th Cong., 1st Sess. 2766 (1866) (statement of Sen. Howard); see also id. at 2765 ("The first section . . . relates to the privileges and immunities of citizens of the several States, and to the rights and privileges of all persons, whether citizens or others, under the laws of the United States").

7. Id. at 2766. Thaddeus Stevens, introducing the final version in the House of Representatives, made similar points: "[T]he Constitution limits only the action of Congress, and is not a limitation on the States. This amendment supplies that defect, and allows Congress to correct the unjust legislation of the States, so far that the law which operates upon one man shall operate *equally* upon all." *Cong. Globe,* 39th Cong., 1st Sess. 2459 (1866).

8. 60 U.S. (19 How.) 393 (1857).

9. See Michael W. McConnell, "Institutions and Interpretation: A Critique of *City of Boerne v. Flores,*" 111 *Harv. L. Rev.* 153, 182 (1997) ("Section Five of the Fourteenth Amendment was born of the fear that the judiciary would frustrate Reconstruction by a narrow interpretation of congressional power"); Laurent B. Frantz, "Congressional Power to Enforce the Fourteenth Amendment Against Private Acts," 73 *Yale L. J.* 1353, 1356 (1964) (the "federal judiciary . . . was looked on with considerable distrust"); Robert Harris, *The Quest for Equality: The Constitution, Congress, and the Supreme Court* 30 n. 15, 53–54 (Louisiana State University Press 1960) (Radical Republicans "did not trust the judiciary in general and the Supreme Court in particular").

10. *Cong. Globe,* 39th Cong., 1st Sess. 1034 (1866). The bill was introduced in the Senate on February 16, 1866 , id. at 806, and debated in the House of Representatives from February 26–28, 1866, id. at 1034–35, 1054–67, 1083–95. Although I refer to it as the February draft, a version of it was first read in the House of Representatives on December 6, 1865. Id. at 14.

11. McCulloch v. Maryland, 17 U.S. (4 Wheat.) 316, 421–22 (1819); see Balkin, "The Reconstruction Power," supra note 1.

12. See *Cong. Globe,* 39th Cong., 1st Sess. 1095 (1866) (Representative Hotchkiss) ("I understand the amendment as now proposed by its terms to authorize Congress to establish uniform laws throughout the United States upon the subject named, the protection of life, liberty, and property"); id. at 1064 (Representative Hale) ("[I]t is a grant of power in general terms—a grant of the right to legislate for the protection of life, liberty, and property, simply qualified with the condition that it shall be equal legislation").

13. Akhil Reed Amar, *America's Constitution: A Biography* 366–76 (Random House 2005); William M. Weicek, *The Guarantee Clause of the U.S. Constitution* 194–200 (Cornell University Press 1972).

14. See *Cong. Globe,* 39th Cong., 1st Sess. 3–5 (1865); *Report of the Joint Committee on Reconstruction* xiii (1866); Bruce Ackerman, 2 *We The People: Interpretations* 183–85 (Harvard University Press 1998).

15. *Cong. Globe,* 39th Cong., 1st Sess. 6–7 (1865).

16. *Cong. Globe,* 39th Cong., 1st Sess. 1095 (1866) (statement of Rep. Hotchkiss).

17. The Democrats won control of the House in the 1874 elections. The last Reconstruction-era civil rights bill, the Civil Rights Act of 1875, was passed by a lame-duck session of the Republican-controlled Congress and signed into law on March 1, 1875. 18 Stat. 335 (1875).

18. See Howard Gillman, "How Political Parties Can Use the Courts to Advance Their Agendas: Federal Courts in the United States, 1875–1891," 96 *Am. Pol. Sci. Rev.* 511 (2002) (arguing that economic nationalism drove expansion of federal judicial power even more than protection of civil rights).

19. *Cong. Globe,* 39th Cong., 1st Sess. 1095 (1866); see also *Cong. Globe,* 42d Cong., 1st Sess. App. 151 (1871) (statement of Rep. Garfield) ("[I]t became perfectly evident . . . that the measure could not command a two-thirds vote of Congress, and for that reason the proposition was virtually withdrawn").

20. Act of Apr. 9, 1866, ch. 31, § 1, 14 Stat. 27. (An Act to protect all Persons in the United States in their Civil Rights, and furnish the Means of their Vindication.) Section 1 of the Act provided:

> That all persons born in the United States and not subject to any foreign power, excluding Indians not taxed, are hereby declared to be citizens of the United States; and such citizens, of every race and color, without regard to any previous condition of slavery or involuntary servitude, except as a punishment for crime whereof the party shall have been duly convicted, shall have the same right, in every State and Territory in the United States, to make and enforce contracts, to sue, be parties, and give evidence, to inherit, purchase, lease, sell, hold, and convey real and personal property, and to full and equal benefit of all laws and proceedings for the security of person and property, as is enjoyed by white citizens, and shall be subject to like punishment, pains, and penalties, and to none other, any law, statute, ordinance, regulation, or custom, to the contrary notwithstanding.

21. See *Cong. Globe,* 39th Cong., 1st Sess. 2459 (1866) (statement of Rep. Stevens) ("[T]he first time that the South with their copperhead allies obtain the command of Congress [the Civil Rights Act] will be repealed. The veto of the President and their votes on the bill are conclusive evidence of that"). In response to Representative Finck's taunt that support for the amendment proved that Congress had no power to pass the Civil Rights Act of 1866, id. at 2461, Representative Garfield replied that supporters did not doubt the Act's constitutionality; instead, the purpose was to "fix it in . . . the eternal firmament of the Constitution itself," because "every gentleman knows it will cease to be a part

of the law whenever the sad moment arrives when that gentleman's party comes into power." Id. at 2462.

22. See *Cong. Globe,* 39th Cong., 1st Sess. 2286; Benjamin B. Kendrick, *Journal of the Joint Committee of Fifteen on Reconstruction* 106 (Columbia University Press 1914).

23. Kendrick, *Journal of the Joint Committee of Fifteen,* supra note 22. The committee's notes confirmed the basis of the language used:

> The Congress shall have power to make all laws which shall be necessary and proper to secure to the citizens of each state all privileges and immunities of citizens in the several states (Art. 4, Sec. 2); and to all persons in the several States equal protection in the rights of life, liberty, and property (5th Amendment).

Id. John Bingham made the same point in explaining the February draft before the House: "The residue of the resolution, as the House will see by a reference to the Constitution, is the language of the second section of the fourth article, and of a portion of the fifth amendment." *Cong. Globe,* 39th Cong., 1st Sess. 1033 (1866) (statement of Rep. Bingham).

24. See Amar, *The Bill of Rights,* supra note 2, at 163–65.

25. 32 U.S. (7 Pet.) 243 (1833).

26. Id. at 248–49; *Cong. Globe,* 42d Cong, 1st, Sess. App. 84 (1871) (statement of Rep. Bingham).

27. See supra note 23; Kendrick, *Journal of the Joint Committee,* supra note 22, at 60; *Cong. Globe,* 39th Cong., 1st Sess. 1033 (1866) (statement of Rep. Bingham).

28. *Cong. Globe,* 39th Cong., 1st Sess. 2286 (1866).

29. See, e.g., Jack M. Balkin, "The Reconstruction Power," supra note 1; Robert J. Kaczorowski, "Congress's Power to Enforce Fourteenth Amendment Rights: Lessons from Federal Remedies the Framers Enacted," 42 *Harv. J. on Legis.* 187, 200–203 (2005); Akhil Reed Amar, "Intratextualism," 112 *Harv. L. Rev.* 747, 822–27 (1999); Michael W. McConnell, "Institutions and Interpretation," supra note 9, at 178 n. 153.

30. *Cong. Globe,* 39th Cong., 1st Sess. 2890 (1866) (Sen. Howard). The original language ended "and of the States wherein they reside."

31. Id.

32. *Cong. Globe,* 39th Cong., 1st Sess. 2896 (1866) (Sen. Howard).

33. 83 U.S. (16 Wall.) 36 (1873).

34. 92 U.S. 542 (1875).

35. 83 U.S. (16 Wall.) at 74–75.

36. Id. at 79–80.

37. 92 U.S. 542 (1875).

38. Id. at 551–54. Later cases confirmed these understandings about the privileges or immunities clause, although in 1897 the Supreme Court argued that the

due process clause included the prohibition against takings of property without just compensation. See Maxwell v. Dow, 176 U.S. 581 (1900) (rejecting the claim that the individual rights protected by the Bill of Rights, and, in particular, the Fifth and Sixth Amendments, were privileges and immunities of citizenship, on the authority of *Slaughter-House* and *Cruikshank*); Chicago, Burlington & Quincy R. R. Co. v. City of Chicago, 166 U.S. 226, 233–41 (1897) (holding that the Fourteenth Amendment's due process clause incorporated the Fifth Amendment's prohibition against takings without just compensation). For arguments that later cases misread *Slaughter-House,* which did not actually reject incorporation of the Bill of Rights, see Gerard N. Magliocca, "Why Did the Incorporation of the Bill of Rights Fail in the Late Nineteenth Century?" 94 *Minn. L. Rev.* 102 (2009); and Kevin Christopher Newsom, "Setting Incorporationism Straight: A Reinterpretation of the *Slaughter-House* Cases," 109 *Yale L. J.* 643 (2000).

39. McDonald v. City of Chicago, 130 S. Ct. 3020 (2010); compare id. at 3031 (plurality opinion of Justice Alito) ("We . . . decline to disturb the *Slaughter-House* holding"); id. at 3089 (Stevens, J. dissenting) (agreeing with plurality on this question); and id. at 3132 (Breyer, J., dissenting, joined by Ginsburg and Sotomayor, JJ.) ("the Court today properly declines to revisit our interpretation of the Privileges or Immunities Clause") with id. at 3058, 3086 (Thomas, J., concurring) (rejecting elements of *Slaughter-House* and arguing that *Cruikshank* should be overruled).

40. See Amar, *The Bill of Rights,* supra note 2, at 166–69; Curtis, *No State Shall Abridge,* supra note 2, at 42–44; Michael Kent Curtis, "Historical Linguistics, Inkblots, and Life After Death: The Privileges and Immunities of Citizens of the United States," 78 *N.C. L. Rev.* 1071, 1089–1136 (2000); see also Joel Tiffany, *Treatise on the Unconstitutionality of American Slavery* 55–58, 84–96, 139–40 (Miami, Mnemosyne Publishing Co. 1969) (1849) (privileges or immunities include the Bill of Rights and the privilege of habeas corpus).

41. Amar, *The Bill of Rights,* supra note 2, at 167–68; Kurt Lash, "The Origins of the Privileges or Immunities Clause, Part I: 'Privileges and Immunities' as an Antebellum Term of Art," 98 *Geo. L. J.* 1241 (2010).

42. See, e.g., Maxwell v. Dow, 176 U.S. 581, 595–96 (1900); Louis Henkin, "'Selective Incorporation' in the Fourteenth Amendment," 73 *Yale L. J.* 74, 78 n. 16 (1963); Philip Hamburger, "Privileges or Immunities," 105 *Nw. L. Rev.* 61 (2011); Amar, *The Bill of Rights,* supra note 2, at 170–71 (responding to Henkin).

43. *Cong. Globe,* 42d Cong., 1st Sess. App 84 (1871).

44. *Cong. Globe,* 39th Cong., 1st Sess. 2765 (1866).

45. *Cong. Globe,* 39th Cong., 1st Sess. 2766. (1866) (statement of Sen. Howard); see also id. at 2765 ("The first section . . . relates to the privileges and immunities of citizens of the several States, and to the rights and privileges of all persons, whether citizens or others, under the laws of the United States"); id. at

2542 (1866) (statement of Rep. Bingham) (remarking that the new Fourteenth Amendment gives the federal government the power "to protect by national law the privileges and immunities of all the citizens of the Republic and the inborn rights of every person within its jurisdiction whenever the same shall be abridged or denied by the unconstitutional acts of any State").

46. For a survey of antebellum sources, see Lash, "The Origins of the Privileges or Immunities Clause, Part I," supra note 41.

47. 75 U.S. (8 Wall.) 168 (1869).

48. Curtis, *No State Shall Abridge,* supra note 2, at 47–48.

49. *Cong. Globe,* 35th Cong., 2d Sess. 984 (1859) (statement of Rep. Bingham) ("There is an ellipsis in the language employed in the Constitution, but its meaning is self-evident that it is 'the privileges and immunities of citizens of the United States in the several States' that it guaranties"); see also William W. Crosskey, "Charles Fairman, 'Legislative History,' and the Constitutional Limitations on State Authority," 22 *U. Chi. L. Rev.* 1, 15–16 (1954) (attributing this view generally to the Republicans who framed the Fourteenth Amendment).

50. Curtis, *No State Shall Abridge,* supra note 2, at 61–63.

51. See Richard L. Aynes, "Enforcing the Bill of Rights Against the States: The History and the Future," 18 *J. Contemp. Legal Issues* 77, 83–85 (2009). The reason for the disagreement is that the fugitive slave clause also appears in Article IV, section 2. Although the full faith and credit clause of Article IV, section 1 gives Congress power to enforce its provisions, there is no specific grant of power for Article IV, section 2. Hence, many antislavery lawyers argued that Congress had no power to enforce any part of Article IV, section 2. See Richard L. Aynes, "On Misreading John Bingham and the Fourteenth Amendment," 103 *Yale L. J.* 57, 74–78 (1993). Despite the lack of explicit textual authority, the Supreme Court held in Prigg v. Pennsylvania, 41 U.S. 539 (1842), that Congress had the power to enforce the fugitive slave clause of Article IV, section 2, clause 3. Almost twenty years later, in Kentucky v. Dennison, 65 U.S. 66, 107 (1861), it reached the opposite conclusion, holding that Congress had no power to enforce the fugitive from justice clause of Article IV, section 2, clause 2.

When the Reconstruction Congress considered new legislation to protect civil rights, many Republicans argued that they no longer had to adopt the old antislavery theory; if the Supreme Court held that Congress had the power to protect the rights of slaveholders, Congress should also have the right to protect the rights of freedmen. See Balkin, "The Reconstruction Power," supra note 1; Aynes, "Enforcing the Bill of Rights," supra note 51 at 83–84; Robert J. Kaczorowski, "Congress's Power to Enforce Fourteenth Amendment Rights," supra note 29, at 200. For example, Representative James Wilson, chairman of the House Judiciary Committee, argued that Congress had ample authority to pass the Civil Rights Act of 1866 based on the theory of *Prigg. Cong. Globe,* 39th Cong., 1st Sess. 1118, 1294–95 (1866).

52. Curtis, *No State Shall Abridge,* supra note 2, at 49–54; Amar, *The Bill of Rights,* supra note 2, at 181–87; Richard L. Aynes, "Enforcing the Bill of Rights," supra note 51, at 81. Akhil Amar points out that this view was not limited to Republicans; it was held by many distinguished lawyers and judges before the Civil War. Amar, *The Bill of Rights,* supra note 2, at 145–62.

53. See, e.g., *Cong. Globe,* 39th Cong., 1st Sess. 1034 (1866) (statement of Rep. Bingham); id. at 1090, 1291–92; Curtis, *No State Shall Abridge,* supra note 2, at 63–64.

54. Aynes, "Enforcing the Bill of Rights," supra note 51, at 83–85.

55. See *Cong. Globe,* 39th Cong., 1st Sess. 1291–92 (1866) (statement of Rep. Bingham); id. at 1367 (Bingham's vote against the bill).

56. See Amar, *The Bill of Rights,* supra note 2, at 156–62.

57. Hence, Bingham objected to the proposed 1859 Oregon Constitution. Upon becoming a state, Oregon's new constitution would ban blacks from entering the state, owning property, or having access to the courts to enforce their rights. See *Cong. Globe,* 35th Cong., 2d Sess. 984 (1859) (statement of Rep. Bingham) ("This guaranty of the Constitution of the United States [found in Article IV, section 2] is senseless and a mockery, if it does not limit State sovereignty").

58. *Cong. Globe,* 39th Cong., 1st Sess. 1034, 1089, 1090, 1095 (1866) (statement of Rep. Bingham).

59. *Cong. Globe,* 39th Cong., 1st Sess. 2765 (1866) (statement of Sen. Howard).

60. Id.

61. Id. at 2766.

62. Id. Howard speaks of the "first section," but in context it is clear that he is referring to the "great fundamental guarantees" of the privileges or immunities clause, because in the following paragraph he turns to discuss "[t]he last two clauses of the first section," the due process and equal protection clauses.

63. Id. at 2765.

64. Corfield v. Coryell, 6 F. Cas. 546 (C.C.E.D. Pa. 1823) (No. 3,230).

65. Id. at 551. Justice Washington added "and which have, at all times, been enjoyed by the citizens of the several states which compose this Union, from the time of their becoming free, independent, and sovereign." Id. As explained below, we must regard this language as hortatory, because various states sometimes denied these rights to outsiders and sometimes even to their own citizens.

66. Id. at 551–52.

67. Id. at 552 ("to which may be added, the elective franchise, as regulated and established by the laws or constitution of the state in which it is to be exercised").

68. *Cong. Globe,* 39th Cong., 1st Sess. 2766 (1866) (statement of Sen. Howard).

69. Id. at 2765.

70. Id.

71. See *Cong. Globe,* 39th Cong., 1st Sess. 1088–94 (1866); id. at 1291–93; *Cong. Globe,* 39th Cong., 2d Sess. 811 (1867); *Cong. Globe,* 42d Cong., 1st Sess. 84 App. (1871); Aynes, "On Misreading John Bingham," supra note 51, at 71–74.

In the February 1866 debate Bingham sometimes speaks of Article IV, section 2 as if it were part of the Bill of Rights. See *Cong. Globe,* 39th Cong., 1st Sess. 1034 (February 13, 1866); id. at 1089 (February 28, 1866). Because Bingham held that the Bill of Rights and other enumerated rights applied to the states through Article IV, section 2, this way of speaking would make perfect sense. It would be like a modern lawyer treating the Fourteenth Amendment as part of the Bill of Rights because it enforces these rights against state governments.

72. See Curtis, *No State Shall Abridge,* supra note 2, at 82–91, 112; Amar, *The Bill of Rights,* supra note 2, at 181–87; Aynes, "Enforcing the Bill of Rights," supra note 51, at 81–99; see also *Cong. Globe,* 38th Cong., 1st Sess. 1202–3 (1864) (statement of Rep. Wilson) ("[P]rivileges and immunities of citizens of the United States" include rights of religion, speech, press, assembly and petition included in the First Amendment; "With these rights no State may interfere"); *Cong. Globe,* 39th Cong., 1st Sess. 2459 (1866) (statement of Rep. Stevens) (arguing that the Fourteenth amendment remedies the "defect" that "the Constitution limits only the action of Congress, and is not a limitation on the States").

73. See Amar, *The Bill of Rights,* supra note 2, at 226–30 (describing common law conception of privileges or immunities); Spies v. Illinois, 123 U.S. 131, 151 (1887) (oral argument of John Randolph Tucker).

74. See John Harrison, "Reconstructing the Privileges or Immunities Clause," 101 *Yale L. J.* 1385, 1387–88 (1992); David Currie, *The Constitution in the Supreme Court: The First Hundred Years* 342–51 (University of Chicago Press 1985). Harrison argued that equality of treatment with respect to civil rights could not have been guaranteed by the equal protection clause because the clause applies to noncitizens as well as citizens, and the use of the word *protection* "suggests either the administration of the laws or, if it is about their content, laws that protect as opposed to laws that do other things." Harrison, "Reconstructing the Privileges or Immunities Clause," supra, at 1390; see also Currie, *The Constitution in the Supreme Court,* supra, at 349. I discuss this argument in Chapter 11.

75. Harrison, "Reconstructing the Privileges or Immunities Clause," supra note 74, at 1389–92.

76. Civil Rights Act of 1866, § 1, 14 Stat. 27, 27 (1866) (emphasis added); see Curtis, *No State Shall Abridge,* supra note 2, at 71–74.

77. Curtis, *No State Shall Abridge,* supra note 2, at 72. Similar language in section 14 of the Freedmen's Bureau Act of 1866 spoke of "full and equal benefit of all laws and proceedings for the security of person and estate, including the constitutional right of bearing arms," suggesting that Bill of Rights provisions were included. Act of July 16, 1866, ch. 200, 14 Stat. 173, 176 (1866). See

Aynes, "Enforcing the Bill of Rights," supra note 51, at 81–85 (describing congressional purpose to enforce the Bill of Rights in debates over the Freedman's Bureau Act and the Civil Rights Act of 1866).

In *McDonald v. City of Chicago*, the Supreme Court noted this history as evidence that the Reconstruction Congress believed that the individual right to bear arms in self-defense was a fundamental right. See 130 S. Ct. at 3040–41. However, it is also evidence that the Reconstruction Congress believed that it had enforced the protections of the Bill of Rights against the states in passing the Civil Rights Act of 1866. See also id. at 3074–75 (Thomas, J., concurring in part and concurring in the judgment) ("Both proponents and opponents of this Act described it as providing the "privileges" of citizenship to freedmen, and defined those privileges to include constitutional rights, such as the right to keep and bear arms").

78. Harrison concedes that the clause "reads like the First Amendment, which forbids Congress from abridging the freedom of speech," id. at 1391, but argues it should nevertheless be read as an equality provision.

However, when the Constitution uses "abridge" in a provision to secure equality, it always explains the purpose for which abridgment is forbidden. Thus, the Fifteenth Amendment says "abridged . . . on account of race, color, or previous condition of servitude"; the Nineteenth Amendment says "abridged . . . on account of sex"; the Twenty-Fourth Amendment says "abridged . . . by reason of failure to pay poll tax or any other tax"; the Twenty-Sixth Amendment says "abridged . . . on account of age."

Finally, section 2 of the Fourteenth Amendment says that state representation is reduced in the House of Representatives if a state "abridge[s]" the right to vote for adult males for any reason other than "participation in rebellion, or other crime." That is, states may only abridge the substantive right for certain purposes, if they want to avoid the penalty.

79. 83 U.S. (16 Wall.) 36 (1873); id. at 76 (Miller, J.) (noting that privileges or immunities clause protects "those rights which are fundamental"); id. at 79–80 (listing various rights protected by the privileges or immunities clause); Richard L. Aynes, "Ink Blot or Not: The Meaning of Privileges and/or Immunities," 11 *U. Pa. J. Const. L.* 1295, 1298–99 (2009). Harrison concedes that not all of the framers of the Fourteenth Amendment might have ascribed to a pure equality theory, only that some did. Harrison, "Reconstructing the Privileges or Immunities Clause," supra note 74, at 1396–97. That point seems plausible. See William E. Nelson, *The Fourteenth Amendment: From Political Principle to Judicial Doctrine* 123–24 (Harvard University Press 1988) (arguing that the intentions of the framers of the Fourteenth Amendment were unclear and that there is evidence for both a substantive and an equality reading). It does not, however, require that we give the clause a pure equality reading today.

80. Equality before the law was a basic right of citizens because it was a basic right of persons in general. See Amar, *The Bill of Rights,* supra note 2, at 283; Harrison, "Reconstructing the Privileges or Immunities Clause," supra note 74, at 1411–13; William W. Crosskey, "Charles Fairman, 'Legislative History,' and the Constitutional Limitations on State Authority," 22 *U. Chi. L. Rev.* 1, 16–17 (1954). Indeed, there does not seem to be any serious dispute among Republicans during this period that equality before the law was a basic right of citizens of the United States and a central purpose of the Fourteenth Amendment. Even in the *Slaughter-House Cases,* which read the privileges or immunities clause quite narrowly, Justice Miller's majority opinion argued that the rights guaranteed by the equal protection clause were among the privileges or immunities of citizens of the United States. 83 U.S. (16 Wall.) at 80 (privileges or immunities include the "rights secured by . . . the other clause of the fourteenth"). Justice Bradley's dissent, pointing to Article IV, section 2, agreed that "equality before the law is undoubtedly one of the privileges and immunities of every citizen." Id. at 118 (Bradley, J., dissenting).

81. See *Cong. Globe,* 39th Cong., 1st session, at 2542 (1866) (statement of Rep. Bingham) (arguing that the new Fourteenth Amendment gives the federal government the power "to protect by national law the privileges and immunities of all the citizens of the Republic and the inborn rights of every person within its jurisdiction whenever the same shall be abridged or denied by the unconstitutional acts of any State"); id. at 2765–66 (statement of Sen. Howard) (stating that the Fourteenth Amendment protects "rights and privileges of all persons, whether citizens or others, under the laws of the United States"); id. at 2766 ("[The Fourteenth Amendment] disable[s] [the states] from passing laws trenching upon those fundamental rights and liberties which belong to every citizen of the United States and to all persons who happen to be within their jurisdiction").

82. See Aynes, "Ink Blot or Not," supra note 79, at 1305–7; Jacobus ten-Broek, *Equal under Law* 239 (Collier 1965) ("The three clauses of section 1 of the Fourteenth Amendment are mostly but not entirely duplicative. . . . All three, however, refer to the protection or abridgment of natural rights").

83. On the declaratory ideas behind the Fourteenth Amendment and declaratory theories generally, see Amar, *The Bill of Rights,* supra note 2, at 147–56.

84. In *Corfield v. Coryell,* Justice Washington spoke of "those privileges and immunities which are, in their nature, fundamental; which belong, of right, to the citizens of all free governments; and which have, at all times, been enjoyed by the citizens of the several states which compose this Union, from the time of their becoming free, independent, and sovereign." 6 F. Cas. 546, 551 (C.C.E.D. Pa. 1823) (No. 3230). Washington's statement that these rights "have at all times been enjoyed" must be taken as aspirational rather than as an accurate

account of history; the comity clause was necessary precisely because states had not always respected these rights and might not in the future.

85. See Amar, *The Bill of Rights,* supra note 2, at 147–49.

86. See *Cong. Globe,* 39th Cong., 1st Sess. 2542 (1866) (statement of Rep. Bingham).

87. Such rights might include, in addition to the individual rights listed in the Bill of Rights, the privilege of habeas corpus in Article I, section 9; rights against bills of attainder, ex post facto laws, and impairments of contract that already bind states in Article I, section 10; the jury trial right in Article III; the rights to equal treatment protected by Article IV, section 2; the individual rights listed in the Bill of Rights; and other individual rights created by the Thirteenth, Fourteenth, Fifteenth, Nineteenth, Twenty-Fourth, and Twenty-Sixth Amendments. (The last five of these amendments specifically bind states and also give Congress independent power to enforce them.)

88. Powell v. Alabama, 287 U.S. 45, 67 (1932).

89. In re Oliver, 333 U.S. 257, 273 (1948).

90. Duncan v. Louisiana, 391 U.S. 145, 149 (1968). *Duncan* emphasized that the proper question is whether "a procedure is necessary to an Anglo-American regime of ordered liberty" because a right in question might "not necessarily [be] fundamental to fairness in every criminal system that might be imagined but [it] is fundamental in the context of the criminal processes maintained by the American States." Id. at 149 n. 14. Thus, the Court has not asked whether a right is fundamental to all free governments, because American liberties emerged from a common law system; not all legal systems are common law legal systems, and Anglo-American traditions of criminal procedure are not universal. The Continental or European tradition does not share the American assumption that an adversarial system with trial by jury is the best way to protect the rights of accused persons.

91. For an exhaustive list, see McDonald v. City of Chicago, 130 S. Ct. at 3034 n. 12. In each of these cases protections against the state and federal government are identical, in accord with the purposes of the Fourteenth Amendments' framers.

The Sixth Amendment's right of trial by jury in criminal cases has been incorporated differently than other rights because of Apodaca v. Oregon, 406 U.S. 404, 406 (1972) (plurality opinion) (approving non-unanimous 11–1 or 10–2 verdicts for state criminal juries). See also Johnson v. Louisiana, 406 U.S. 356 (1972) (due process clause does not require unanimous state criminal jury verdicts). In *Apodaca,* eight justices agreed that the Sixth Amendment's jury trial rules should apply equally for federal and state criminal juries. See Johnson, 406 U.S. at 395 (Brennan, J., dissenting). However, the four justices in the dissent argued that unanimity was necessary for both federal and state criminal trials, while the four justices in the plurality argued that unanimity was not necessary for either. Justice Powell's concurrence in the judgment and deciding vote in *Apodaca* held that unanimity was required in federal but not state jury trials. Apodaca, 406 U.S. at 369–77 (Powell, J., concurring in the judgment);

The Court has assumed without deciding that the Eighth Amendment's prohibition on excessive bail is incorporated. See Schilb v. Kuebel, 404 U.S. 357, 365 (1971). However, it has left open the question of excessive fines. See Browning-Ferris Indust. v. Kelco Disposal, 492 U.S. 257, 276 n. 22 (1989).

92. Duncan v. Louisiana, 391 U.S. 145, 171 (1968) (Black, J., dissenting); Hugo LaFayette Black, *A Constitutional Faith* 39 (Knopf 1968).

93. Adamson v. California, 332 U.S. 46, 68–123 (1947) (Black, J., dissenting); see also Duncan v. Louisiana, 391 U.S. 145, 162–71 (1968) (Black, J., dissenting).

94. This is one of the central claims of Amar, *The Bill of Rights,* supra note 2.

95. See id. at 179–80.

96. See, e.g., Chauffeurs, Teamsters & Helpers, Local No. 391 v. Terry, 494 U.S. 558, 564–65 (1990).

97. See 28 U.S.C. 1652 (2006); Amar, *The Bill of Rights,* supra note 2, at 88–91.

98. Amar, *The Bill of Rights,* supra note 2, at 32–35, 246; Kurt T. Lash, "The Second Adoption of the Establishment Clause: The Rise of the Nonestablishment Principle," 27 *Ariz. St. L. J.* 1085, 1085, 1089–92 (1995).

99. Earlier drafts of the establishment clause in the Senate made clear that the federal government should not be able to make its own establishments of religion: Congress could "make no law establishing one religious sect or society in preference to others," "make no law establishing religion," and "make no law establishing articles of faith or a mode of worship." See 1 *Documentary History of the First Federal Congress of the United States of America* 151, 166 (L. De Pauw ed., Johns Hopkins University Press 1972) (Senate Journal). In the House, Madison's original version stated that "no religion shall be established by law," 1 *Annals of Cong.* 757 (Joseph Gales ed., 1789), and at one point he offered to clarify it to read that "no national religion shall be established by law," but this was rejected because it might suggest that the government was a "national" rather than a "federal" one. Id. at 758.

100. Amar, *The Bill of Rights,* supra note 2, at 247–57.

101. Id. at 249–52.

102. Michael W. McConnell, "The Origins and Historical Understanding of Free Exercise of Religion," 103 *Harv. L. Rev.* 1409, 1437 ("By 1834, no state in the Union would have an established church"). Nevertheless, as Kurt Lash points out, slaveowning states passed a series of laws strictly controlling black religious practices and religious instruction to blacks in order to avoid religiously inspired slave insurrections. The result, in Lash's words, was "the most comprehensive religious establishment to exist on American soil since Massachusetts Bay." Lash, "The Second Adoption of the Establishment Clause," supra

note 98, at 1137. Several of the framers of the Fourteenth Amendment, including John Bingham, sought to put an end to these practices, which they viewed as violations of the rights of conscience. Id. at 1141–45.

103. See Amar, *The Bill of Rights,* supra note 2, at 253–54 (citing Thomas M. Cooley, *A Treatise on the Constitutional Limitations Which Rest upon the Legislative Power of the States of the American Union* 469 (Little, Brown and Co. 1868)) (The American system of government establishes religious equality, not merely religious toleration, and religious liberty cannot exist "where any one sect is favored by the State").

104. Justice Sandra Day O'Connor's endorsement test, first announced in her concurrence in Lynch v. Donnelly, 465 U.S. 668 (1984), is an elaboration of the idea of civic equality in the establishment clause. "Endorsement," Justice O'Connor argued, "sends a message to nonadherents that they are outsiders, not full members of the political community, and an accompanying message to adherents that they are insiders, favored members of the political community. Disapproval sends the opposite message." Id. at 688 (O'Connor, J., concurring).

105. See David A. Anderson, "The Origins of the Press Clause," 30 *U.C.L.A. L. Rev.* 455 (1983) (supporting a nonliteral reading by pointing out that "nothing in the legislative history indicates that the framers attached controlling significance to the opening words" and that the focus was on limiting federal power rather than legislative power). For two scholars who are willing to take the literal interpretation to its logical conclusion, see Gary Lawson and Guy Seidman, "The Jeffersonian Treaty Clause," 2006 *Ill. L. Rev.* 1, 16–20 (2006) (arguing that the First Amendment does not reach executive and judicial action and also does not reach treaties, which require the concurrence of the president and the Senate).

106. Magill v. Brown, 16 F. Cas. 408, 427 (C.C.E.D. Pa. 1837) (Baldwin, J.) (holding that the First Amendment "wholly prohibits the action of the legislative or judicial power of Union on the subject matter of a religious establishment, or any restraint on the free exercise of religion").

107. See Sanford Levinson, "The Embarrassing Second Amendment," 99 *Yale L. J.* 637, 646–51 (1989).

108. See Amar, *The Bill of Rights,* supra note 2, at 47–49, 51–52.

109. Id.

110. The scholarly literature defending the individual rights theory is extensive, and many of the key pieces of pre-ratification evidence are ably summarized in Justice Scalia's opinion in District of Columbia v. Heller, 554 U.S. 570, 592–605 (2008); unfortunately, Justice Stevens's dissent, also drawing on a hefty volume of scholarly literature, counters each claim. Id. at 639–665 (Stevens, J., dissenting). For another summary of the key evidence, pointing out its ambiguities, see Mark V. Tushnet, *Out of Range: Why the Constitution Can't End the Battle over Guns* 16–26 (Oxford University Press 2007).

111. See Amar, *The Bill of Rights,* supra note 2, at 257–66 (collecting sources leading up to the Civil War and pointing out the shift in emphasis from militia service to self-defense of blacks). Justice Scalia is therefore quite correct when he states that "[i]t was plainly the understanding in the post–Civil War Congress that the Second Amendment protected an individual right to use arms for self-defense." Heller, 554 U.S. at 616. See also the sources cited in McDonald v. City of Chicago, 130 S. Ct. at 3038–42; id. at 3080–83 (Thomas, J., concurring in the judgment).

112. See *Cong. Globe,* 39th Cong., 1st Sess. at 2765 (statement of Sen. Howard); Freedman's Bureau Act of July 16, 1866, § 14, 14 Stat. 176, 176–77 (1866).

113. Heller, 554 U.S. at 605–19.

114. *Cong. Globe,* 39th Congress, 1st Sess. at 2766 (statement of Sen. Howard).

115. Id. at 2765.

116. See Slaughter-House Cases, 83 U.S. 36, 79 (1873) (Miller, J.) (listing as examples the right to travel to the nation's capitol, the right to access to seaports, the right to access to federal facilities, the right to protection on the high seas or in foreign lands, and the right to use the navigable waters of the United States); id. at 96–97 (Field, J., dissenting, joined by Chase, C. J., Swayne, J., and Bradley, J.) (listing as examples common law rights of contract and property, rights of access to courts, and Justice Washington's list of privileges and immunities in *Corfield v. Coryell*); id. at 113–14, 117–19 (Bradley, J., dissenting) (listing the "right of any citizen to follow whatever lawful employment he chooses to adopt," "the privilege of buying, selling, and enjoying property; . . . the privilege of resorting to the laws for redress of injuries" and other rights listed in *Corfield v. Coryell*); id. at 128 (Swayne, J., dissenting) (stating his agreement with Bradley).

In this respect the privileges or immunities clause corresponds to the rule of construction offered by the Ninth Amendment, which states that "[t]he enumeration in the Constitution, of certain rights, shall not be construed to deny or disparage others retained by the people." The Ninth Amendment, originally designed to restrain federal power, suggests that certain unenumerated rights limit the federal government even if they are not specifically mentioned in the text; if some of these rights are privileges or immunities of citizens of the United States, they limit state governments as well. Reconstruction Republicans understood the Ninth Amendment in much the same way. See *Cong. Globe,* 39th Cong. 1st Sess. 1072 (1866) (statement of Sen. James Nye) ("[L]est something essential in the specifications [of natural and personal rights in the Constitution] should have been overlooked, it was provided in the ninth amendment. . . . This amendment completed the document. It left no personal or natural right to be invaded or impaired by construction").

117. See Randy E. Barnett, *Restoring the Lost Constitution: The Presumption of Liberty* 61–67 (Princeton University Press 2004); Slaughter-House

Cases, 83 U.S. 36, 96–97 (Field, J., dissenting, joined by Chase, C. J., Swayne, J., and Bradley, J.) (citing *Corfield v. Coryell* and including common law rights of contract and property as among the privileges or immunities of national citizenship).

118. See Kurt T. Lash, "The Origins of the Privileges or Immunities Clause, Part II: John Bingham and the Second Draft of the Fourteenth Amendment," 99 *Geo. L. J.* 329 (2011).

119. 73 U.S. 35 (1867).

120. Justice Miller, the author of *Crandall,* used language from that case in his 1873 *Slaughter-House* opinion, describing various unenumerated rights protected by the privileges or immunities clause. Compare id. at 43–44 *with Slaughter-House Cases,* 83 U.S. at 79 (Miller, J.).

121. To be sure, that is not how the Supreme Court currently understands the operation of section 5 of the Fourteenth Amendment, but that is in part because the Court's understanding of the text and principles behind the Fourteenth Amendment is not very good. For a discussion based on the history surrounding the adoption of the Fourteenth Amendment, see Michael W. McConnell, "Institutions and Interpretation," supra note 9, at 182–83; see also Balkin, "The Reconstruction Power," supra note 1.

122. For a discussion of how social movements draw on existing materials to fashion rights claims, see Jim Pope, "The Role of Social Movements in Constitutional Interpretation and Enforcement" (August 2007) (unpublished manuscript on file with author).

123. See Reva B. Siegel, "Text in Contest: Gender and the Constitution from a Social Movement Perspective," 150 *U. Pa. L. Rev.* 297, 340–45 (2001) (noting how suffragists reframed arguments as constitutional claims given the particular problems they faced).

124. 381 U.S. 479 (1965).

125. 405 U.S. 438 (1972).

126. 431 U.S. 678 (1977).

127. At the very least, Bork's opponents believed that his opposition to *Griswold* helped undermine his case. See Lackland H. Bloom, "Twenty Fifth Anniversary of *Griswold v. Connecticut* and the Right to Privacy: The Legacy of *Griswold,*" 16 *Ohio N.U. L. Rev.* 511, 542–43 (1989).

128. 539 U.S. 558 (2003).

129. See id. at 572.

130. 478 U.S. 186 (1986).

131. See Lawrence, 539 U.S. at 572.

132. 410 U.S. 113 (1973).

133. See Jack M. Balkin, "Abortion and Original Meaning," 24 *Const. Comment.* 291 (2007); Jack M. Balkin, "Original Meaning and Constitutional Redemption," 24 *Const. Comment.* 427, 515–23 (2007).

134. See David J. Garrow, *Liberty and Sexuality: The Right to Privacy and the Making of* Roe v. Wade 539 (MacMillan 1994) (noting a January 1972 Gallup poll stating that 57 percent of Americans, and 54 percent of American Catholics agreed that the abortion decision should be left to a woman and her doctor). See also Linda Greenhouse and Reva B. Siegel, *Before* Roe v. Wade: *Voices That Shaped the Abortion Debate before the Supreme Court's Ruling* (Kaplan Publishing 2010) (demonstrating the significant shift in public opinion in favor of abortion, including among American Catholics).

135. Barry Friedman, *The Will of The People: How Public Opinion Has Influenced the Supreme Court and Shaped the Meaning of the Constitution* 297–98 (Farrar, Straus and Giroux 2009); Gerald Rosenberg, *The Hollow Hope: Can Courts Bring About Social Change?* 184 (University of Chicago Press 1991).

136. Rosenberg, *The Hollow Hope,* supra note 135, at 184; see Rachel Benson Gold, "Lessons from Before Roe: Will Past Be Prologue?" *Guttmacher Report on Public Policy* 8 (2003), available at www.guttmacher.org/pubs/tgr/06/1/gr060108.html.

137. Gene Burns, *The Moral Veto: Framing Contraception, Abortion and Cultural Pluralism in the United States* 214–28 (Cambridge University Press 2005) (reasoning that a shift from a medical frame to a moral frame, exacerbated by associations between abortion and the feminist movement, limited the success of abortion repeal statutes by the early 1970s); David Garrow, "Abortion before and after *Roe v. Wade:* An Historical Perspective," 62 *Alb. L. Rev.* 833, 840–41 (1999) (arguing that the 1970 New York liberalization law, and not *Roe v. Wade*, energized the right-to-life movement).

138. In an ABC/Washington Post poll taken April 22–25, 2010, 59 percent of respondents wanted the next justice appointed to uphold *Roe v. Wade*. A CBS News/New York Times poll conducted June 12–16, 2009, found that 64 percent of Americans would not "like to see the Supreme Court overturn its 1973 Roe versus Wade decision concerning abortion." See PollingReport.com, *Abortion,* www.pollingreport.com/abortion.htm. Depending on how the question is phrased, support for retaining *Roe v. Wade* has remained around 60 percent for years.

139. See "Facts on Induced Abortion in the United States" (May 2010), at www.guttmacher.org/pubs/fb_induced_abortion.html.

140. The canonical statement is Robert A. Dahl, "Decision-Making in a Democracy: The Supreme Court as a National Policy-Maker," 6 *J. Pub. L.* 279 (1957). Dahl noted that "the policy views dominant on the Court are never for long out of line with the policy views dominant among the lawmaking majorities of the United States." Id. at 285. For later versions, see Barry Friedman, *The Will of the People,* supra note 135, at 297–98 (2009); Jack M. Balkin and Sanford Levinson, "The Processes of Constitutional Change: From Partisan Entrenchment to the National Surveillance State," 75 *Fordham L. Rev.* 489 (2006); Teri Jennings Peretti, *In Defense of a Political Court* 80–132 (Princeton Univer-

sity Press 1999). Among other things, *Roe v. Wade* allowed the Republican Party to gain majority status and remain pro-life without losing the support of moderate and suburban voters who do not want abortion fully criminalized. See Mark A. Graber, "The Nonmajoritarian Difficulty: Legislative Deference to the Judiciary," 7 *Stud. Am. Pol. Dev.* 35, 36 (1993) ("[J]ustices . . . declare state and federal practices unconstitutional only when the dominant national coalition is unable or unwilling to settle some public dispute . . . [and] prominent elected officials consciously invite the judiciary to resolve those political controversies that they cannot or would not address").

141. See Planned Parenthood of Southeastern Pa. v. Casey, 505 U.S. 833 (1992). Neal Devins argues that post-*Casey* legislation in the states effectively recognizes a right to abortion subject to various devices designed to dissuade women from exercising the right. Neal Devins, "How *Planned Parenthood v. Casey* (Pretty Much) Settled the Abortion Wars," 118 *Yale L. J.* 1318 (2009).

142. See Adam Winkler, "Scrutinizing the Second Amendment," 105 *Mich. L. Rev.* 683, 686 (2007) (counting forty-two states currently recognizing an individual right and finding that "the courts of every state to consider the question apply a deferential 'reasonable regulation' standard in arms rights cases"); Eugene Volokh, "State Constitutional Rights to Keep and Bear Arms," 11 *Tex. Rev. L. & Pol.* 191, 205 (2006) (counting forty state constitutions with right to bear arms provisions that protect an individual right of self-defense, two states with provisions interpreted to recognize only a collective right, and two where courts have not yet interpreted the provision); David B. Kopel, "What State Constitutions Teach about the Second Amendment," 29 *N. Ky. L. Rev.* 827, 851 (2002) (counting forty-four states with constitutional provisions, with forty-three recognizing some form of individual right, and one, Massachusetts, recognizing only a collective right).

143. See Polling Report, "Guns," www.pollingreport.com/guns.htm (citing a May 14–17, 2009, CNN/Opinion Research Corporation poll reporting that 77 percent of Americans believed the Second Amendment "was intended to give individual Americans the right to keep and bear arms for their own defense"); id. (reporting in the same poll that 54 percent believed that the Second Amendment allows "some restrictions" on gun ownership, while 22 percent did not believe it protected an individual right); Tushnet, *Out of Range,* supra note 110, at 127–28 (noting simultaneous support for abstract right combined with various regulations).

11. Equality before the Law

1. *Cong. Globe,* 39th Cong., 1st Sess. 2766 (1866) (statement of Sen. Howard). Although Howard began by referring to both the equal protection clause and the due process clause in his account, his reference to "equal protection of

the law" suggests the equal protection clause was expected to take the lead in securing equality. Nevertheless, as discussed infra, the due process clause also protected against class legislation, because the antebellum idea of due process also included the notion that laws should be general and impartial and not for the benefit of any particular class. See Ryan C. Williams, "The One and Only Substantive Due Process Clause," 120 *Yale L.J.* 408, 425, 462–64 (2010); James W. Ely Jr., "The Oxymoron Reconsidered: Myth and Reality in the Origins of Substantive Due Process," 16 *Const. Comment.* 337–38 (1999); Melissa L. Saunders, "Equal Protection, Class Legislation, and Colorblindness," 96 *Mich. L. Rev.* 245, 258–59 & n. 58 (1997); Mark G. Yudof, "Equal Protection, Class Legislation and Sex Discrimination: One Small Cheer for Mr. Herbert Spencer's Social Statics," 88 *Mich. L. Rev.* 1366, 1376 (1990).

2. *Cong. Globe,* 39th Cong., 1st Sess. 2766 (1866) (statement of Sen. Howard).

3. See John Harrison, "Reconstructing the Privileges or Immunities Clause," 101 *Yale L. J.* 1385, 1390, 1396, 1435–38 (1992); David Currie, *The Constitution in the Supreme Court: The First Hundred Years* 349 (University of Chicago Press 1985); for an original meaning argument along these lines, see Christopher R. Green, "The Original Sense of the (Equal) Protection Clause: Pre-Enactment History" 19 *Geo. Mason U. Civ. Rts. L. J.* 1 (2008).

4. See Virginia v. Rives, 100 U.S. 313, 318 (1880). ("[A] State may act through different agencies, either by its legislative, its executive, or its judicial authorities; and the prohibitions of the amendment extend to all action of the State denying equal protection of the laws, whether it be action by one of these agencies or by another.")

5. See *Cong. Globe,* 39th Cong., 1st Sess. 2766 (1866) (statement of Sen. Howard) (emphasis added).

6. See *Cong. Globe,* 39th Cong., 1st Sess. S. app. 219 (1866) (statement of Sen. Howe).

7. 118 U.S. 356, 369 (1886). See Saunders, "Equal Protection, Class Legislation, and Colorblindness," supra note 1, at 288–93 (citing evidence in pre- and post-enactment debates that the equal protection clause was designed to enforce the antebellum prohibition on special or partial legislation).

The earliest construction of the equal protection clause by the Supreme Court likewise assumed that the equal protection clause reaches state legislation. See Strauder v. West Virginia, 100 U.S. 303, 307–8 (1880) (striking down a West Virginia statute limiting jury service to whites under the equal protection clause and stating that if whites were excluded by statute from jury service "we apprehend no one would be heard to claim that it would not be a denial to white men of the equal protection of the laws").

8. Andrew Jackson, "Veto Message" (July 10, 1832), in 2 *Messages and Papers of the Presidents* 576–89 (James D. Richardson ed., Government Printing Office 1897).

9. *Cong. Globe,* 39th Cong., 1st Sess. 1034 (1866).

10. Harrison, "Reconstructing the Privileges or Immunities Clause," supra note 3, at 1387–89.

11. The various strands are described in William E. Nelson, *The Fourteenth Amendment: From Political Principle to Judicial Doctrine* 115–47 (Harvard University Press 1988), and in Yudof, "Equal Protection, Class Legislation and Sex Discrimination," supra note 1 (reviewing Nelson).

12. See Nelson, *The Fourteenth Amendment,* supra note 11, at 115, 138–42.

13. See *Cong. Globe,* 39th Cong., 1st Sess. 2766 (1866) (statement of Sen. Howard) (noting that the purpose of the equal protection and due process clauses is to "abolish[] all class legislation"); *Cong. Globe,* 40th Cong., 2d Sess. 883 (1868) (statement of Sen. Howe) (Fourteenth Amendment "[protects] classes from class legislation. That is really what the constitutional amendment meant").

The idea of "class legislation" had its roots in Jacksonian ideology. See Howard Gillman, *The Constitution Besieged: The Rise and Demise of Lochner Era Police Power Jurisprudence* 46–60, 62 (Duke University Press 1993); Nelson, *The Fourteenth Amendment,* supra note 11, at 115, 149; Saunders, "Equal Protection, Class Legislation, and Colorblindness," supra note 1, at 251–68, 289–90 & n. 198; Yudof, "Equal Protection, Class Legislation and Sex Discrimination," supra note 1, at 1376–77. In his 1832 veto message concerning the charter of the second national bank, Andrew Jackson gave a canonical account of the equal protection principle: The law should make no "artificial distinctions, to grant titles, gratuities, and exclusive privileges, to make the rich richer and the potent more powerful." "If [law] would confine itself to equal protection, and, as Heaven does its rains, shower its favors alike on the high and the low, the rich and the poor, it would be an unqualified blessing." Andrew Jackson, "Veto Message," supra note 8, at 576–89.

The Jacksonian concept of "class legislation" was originally designed to oppose corporate charters and business monopolies, because of the fear that these would create a new class of economic "nobility" elevated above the ordinary white working man. By the end of the Civil War, however, the framers of the Fourteenth Amendment understood the concept as encompassing the converse phenomenon: legislation that denigrated or demeaned a group of persons and held them as less equal than others. On the transformation of the Jacksonian idea of class legislation, see Eric Foner, *Free Soil, Free Labor, Free Men* 90–91 (Oxford University Press 1970); and Yudof, "Equal Protection, Class Legislation and Sex Discrimination," supra note 1, at 1379. Cf. Nelson, *The Fourteenth Amendment,* supra note 11, at 18 (noting use of class legislation idea in antislavery rhetoric).

14. See *Cong. Globe,* 39th Cong., 1st Sess. 2766 (1866) (statement of Sen. Howard) (equal protection and due process clauses "do[] away with the injustice of subjecting one caste of persons to a code not applicable to another"); id.

at 674 (statement of Sen. Sumner) (proposed joint resolution for Reconstruction—a predecessor of the Fourteenth Amendment—would abolish "Oligarchy, Aristocracy, Caste, or Monopoly invested with peculiar privileges and powers"); see also Adamson v. California, 332 U.S. 46, 51 n. 8 (1947) (quoting Sumner's joint resolution as evidence of meaning of Fourteenth Amendment); Andrew Kull, *The Color-Blind Constitution* 74–75 (Harvard University Press 1992) (also quoting Sumner's joint resolution as evidence of meaning of Fourteenth Amendment).

15. *Cong. Globe,* 39th Cong., 1st Sess. 2459 (1866) (statement of Rep. Stevens) ("This amendment . . . allows Congress to correct the unjust legislation of the States, so far that the law which operates upon one man shall operate *equally* upon all"); id. at 2766 (statement of Sen. Howard) (Fourteenth Amendment "protects the black man in his fundamental rights as a citizen with the same shield which it throws over the white man").

16. On the distinction between civil, political, and social rights, see, for example, *Cong. Globe,* 42d Cong., 2d Sess. 901 (1872) (statement of Sen. Trumbull) (the Civil Rights Act of 1866 was "confined exclusively to civil rights and nothing else, no political and no social rights"); Akhil Reed Amar, *The Bill of Rights: Creation and Reconstruction* 216–18, 258–61, 271–74 (Yale University Press 1998) (civil versus political rights); Harold M. Hyman and William W. Wiecek, *Equal Justice under Law: Constitutional Development, 1835–1875* 276–78, 394–402 (Harper and Row 1982); Michael W. McConnell, "Originalism and the Desegregation Decisions," 81 *Va. L. Rev.* 947, 1024 (1995); and Mark Tushnet, "Civil Rights and Social Rights: The Future of the Reconstruction Amendments," 25 *Loy. L.A. L. Rev.* 1207 (1992).

17. See Richard A. Primus, *The American Language of Rights* 154–56 (Cambridge University Press 1999) ("The many political and legal actors who spoke and wrote about rights using these terms did not always employ the categories in the same way"). During the debate over the Civil Rights Act of 1866, for example, John Bingham objected to language in the draft bill prohibiting "discrimination in civil rights or immunities among citizens of the United States . . . on account of race, color, or previous condition of slavery." *Cong. Globe,* 39th Cong., 1st Sess. 1291 (1866). Bingham argued that this guaranteed "civil rights," which he defined broadly to include "political rights" to vote and hold office. Id. Bingham also objected that "civil rights" included the protections of the Bill of Rights, and although Bingham believed that state officials were bound by oath to protect the Bill of Rights, Congress lacked the power to compel them to do so. Id. at 1292–93.

At Bingham's urging, the "civil rights or immunities" language was struck from the bill. *Cong. Globe,* 39th Cong., 1st Sess. 1296, 1366 (1866). Even so, Bingham voted against the amended bill, id. at 1367, and did not vote on the override of President Johnson's veto. Id. at 1861. Despite this, Bingham's draft of section 1 of the Fourteenth Amendment guaranteed the "Privileges or Immunities of Citizens of the United States," which was not thought to include the right to vote. See id. at 2766 (statement of Sen. Howard).

18. Act of Apr. 9, 1866, ch. 31, § 1, 14 Stat. 27.

19. Instead, the Joint Committee chose more general language that did not mention race. Andrew Kull, *The Color-blind Constitution,* supra note 14, at 82–87; Benjamin B. Kendrick, *The Journal of the Joint Committee of Fifteen on Reconstruction* 82–85, 106–7 (Columbia University Press 1914). Section 1 of Thaddeus Stevens's proposal stated that "No discrimination shall be made by any state, nor by the United States, as to the civil rights of persons, because of race, color or previous condition of servitude." Section 2 would have prohibited discrimination in voting on the basis of race after July 4, 1876. Id. at 83–84. Note that even this proposal initially distinguished between civil and political rights, with blacks gaining the right to vote ten years later.

20. See Act of July 28, 1866, ch. 296, 14 Stat. 310, 317, which appropriated funds for "the 'National association for the relief of destitute colored women and children,'" a corporation created by Congress three years earlier "for the purpose of supporting . . . aged or indigent and destitute colored women and children." Act of Feb. 14, 1863, ch. 33, 12 Stat. 650, 650; Resolution of Mar. 16, 1867, No. 4, 15 Stat. 20, 20, which appropriated $15,000 "for the relief of freedmen and destitute colored people in the District of Columbia."

Congress also appropriated money for black servicemen. See Act of Mar. 3, 1869, ch. 122, 15 Stat. 301, 302, which appropriated $145,000 for "collection and payment of bounty, prize-money, and other legitimate claims of colored soldiers and sailors"; and Act of Mar. 3, 1873, ch. 227, 17 Stat. 510, 528, which appropriated $50,000 for the same purpose. See generally Jed Rubenfeld, "Affirmative Action," 107 *Yale L. J.* 427, 430–32 (1997) (identifying and discussing these statutes). Congress also created a bank, the Freedman's Saving and Trust Company, for "persons heretofore held in slavery in the United States, or their descendants," Act of Mar. 3, 1865, ch. 92, § 12 Stat. 510, 511. See Stephen A. Siegel, "The Federal Government's Power to Enact Color-Conscious Laws: An Originalist Inquiry," 92 *Nw. U. L. Rev.* 477, 560 (1998). The addition of the words "their descendants" meant that the bill was not restricted to assisting only former slaves.

The Freedmen's Bureau Acts, Act of July 16, 1866, ch. 200, 14 Stat. 173; Act of Mar. 3, 1865, ch. 90, 13 Stat. 507, were also designed to aid blacks, although the legislative formula generally used was relief to "freedmen and refugees," which was a fig leaf to appease conservatives who did not want benefits to go exclusively to blacks. See Paul Moreno, "Racial Classifications and Reconstruction Legislation," 61 *J. S. Hist.* 271 (1995) (arguing that the classifications were formally race-neutral); Eric Schnapper, "Affirmative Action and the Legislative History of the Fourteenth Amendment," 71 *Va. L. Rev.* 753 (1985) (arguing that the bills were race-conscious and that their purpose and effect was over-whelmingly to benefit blacks even if they also benefited some whites); Siegel, "The Federal Government's Power to Enact Color-Conscious Laws," supra, at 560 (arguing that references to "freedmen" and "previous condition of servi-tude" were racial categories).

21. See, for example, the exchange between Rep. Hale and Rep. Bingham, *Cong. Globe,* 39th Cong., 1st Sess. 1065 (1866), in which Bingham emphasizes that the new amendment was designed to protect the rights of "loyal white citi-zens" as well as blacks, and to apply to States "that have in their constitutions and laws to-day provisions in direct violation of every principle of our Constitution."

22. See Reva B. Siegel, "She the People: The Nineteenth Amendment, Sex Equality, Federalism, and the Family," 115 *Harv. L. Rev.* 947, 981–87 (2002).

23. Thus, Akhil Amar notes that "[t]he Fourteenth Amendment, in some ways, was designed to give everyone—all persons, all citizens—certain civil rights. These rights were largely defined by the status of unmarried white women." Akhil Reed Amar, "Women and the Constitution," 18 *Harv. J. L. & Pub. Pol'y* 465, 468 (1995). However, as Amar also notes, when women married, they lost most of these rights. See id. at 468 n. 14.

24. See *Cong. Globe,* 39th Cong. 1st Sess. 1089 (1866) (statement of Rep. Bingham) (noting that states would retain the ability to regulate married wom-en's ownership of property because property rights were governed by local law while "[t]he rights of life and liberty are theirs [i.e., women's] whatever States may enact"); id. at 1064 (statement of Rep. Stevens) ("When a distinction is made between two married people or two *femmes sole,* then it is unequal legis-lation; but where all of the same class are dealt with in the same way then there is no pretense of inequality"). See generally Ward Farnsworth, "Women under Reconstruction: The Congressional Understanding," 94 *Nw. U. L. Rev.* 1229, 1241 (2000) ("Until she joined a family as a wife and mother, a femme sole [i.e., an unmarried woman] was a family of one and could hold property; but once she married, her property rights yielded to the order of the family circle. She then enjoyed vicariously the rights held by the men in the family"). Similar rea-soning was used to justify women's exclusion from the franchise. See Siegel, "She the People," supra note 22, at 981–84 (noting that both common law coverture rules and the theory of virtual representation of women by their husbands and fathers stemmed from the republican theory of the household as the unit of soci-ety, and the head of the household as the representative of its dependents).

25. 88 U.S. (21 Wall.) 162 (1875).

26. 83 U.S. (16 Wall.) 130 (1873).

27. Id. at 141.

28. The Reconstruction Act of Mar. 2, 1867, ch. 153, 14 Stat. 428, which re-quired former Confederate states to create new constitutions, also required black suffrage for adult males. See id. at 429 § 5; see Gabriel J. Chin, "The 'Vot-

ing Rights Act of 1867': The Constitutionality of Federal Regulation of Suffrage During Reconstruction," 82 *N.C. L. Rev.* 1581 (2004).

29. Akhil Reed Amar, *America's Constitution: A Biography* 396–99 (Random House 2005).

30. Gibson v. Mississippi, 162 U.S. 565, 591 (1896).

31. 106 U.S. 583 (1883).

32. To the extent that the law discriminated, it did so as a prohibition on certain forms of association (a question of social equality), but it did not offer different pains and penalties for the two races (a question of civil equality). Writing for a unanimous Court, Justice Field explained that the law did not violate civil equality, because both blacks and whites were subject to equal penalties for violating the statute: "Indeed, the offence against which this latter section is aimed cannot be committed without involving the persons of both races in the same punishment. Whatever discrimination is made in the punishment prescribed in the two sections is directed against the offence designated and not against the person of any particular color or race. The punishment of each offending person, whether white or black, is the same." Id. at 585.

33. 163 U.S. 537 (1896).

34. Id. at 544. ("The object of the amendment was undoubtedly to enforce the absolute equality of the two races before the law, but in the nature of things it could not have been intended to abolish distinctions based upon color, or to enforce social, as distinguished from political equality, or a commingling of the two races upon terms unsatisfactory to either.")

35. In the Civil Rights Cases, 109 U.S. 3 (1883), decided the same year as *Pace v. Alabama*, the Court struck down the Civil Rights Act of 1875, which prohibited racial discrimination in public accommodations. The Court distinguished Congress's power to pass the Civil Rights Act of 1866, which also banned private racial discrimination, on the ground that the 1866 Act was designed to remedy violations of civil rights and not social rights. Id. at 23.

36. See The Civil Rights Cases, 103 U.S. at 59 (Harlan, J., dissenting) ("The rights which congress, by the act of 1875, endeavored to secure and protect are legal, not social, rights"); Plessy, 163 U.S. at 562 (Harlan, J., dissenting) ("The arbitrary separation of citizens, on the basis of race, while they are on a public highway, is a badge of servitude wholly inconsistent with the civil freedom and the equality before the law established by the Constitution").

37. Plessy, 163 U.S. at 544–45. Because civil equality was not involved, the only question was whether separating whites and blacks on railway carriages was a reasonable exercise of the police power to promote health, safety and welfare. Justice Brown noted, however, that if the law were designed for the harassment or annoyance of a particular class, it would be constitutionally suspect as class legislation. Id. at 549–50.

38. Id. at 559 (Harlan, J., dissenting).

39. Id.

40. Id.

41. Id. Moreover, Harlan insisted that giving blacks civil equality would not create a slippery slope to social equality. "for social equality no more exists between two races when traveling in a passenger coach or a public highway than when members of the same races sit by each other in a street car or in the jury box, or stand or sit with each other in a political assembly, or when they use in common the streets of a city or town, or when they are in the same room for the purpose of having their names placed on the registry of voters, or when they approach the ballot box in order to exercise the high privilege of voting." Id. at 561.

42. See 163 U.S. at 550 ("[E]very exercise of the police power must be reasonable, and extend only to such laws as are enacted in good faith for the promotion for the public good, and not for the annoyance or oppression of a particular class").

43. See Reva B. Siegel, "Equality Talk: Antisubordination and Anticlassification Values in Constitutional Struggles over *Brown*," 117 *Harv. L. Rev.* 1470 (2004).

44. Michael W. McConnell, "Originalism and the Desegregation Decisions," supra note 16.

45. Id. at 1098.

46. McConnell, "The Originalist Justification for *Brown*: A Reply to Professor Klarman," 81 *Va. L. Rev.* 1937, 1938–39 (1995).

47. Id. at 1939.

48. See McConnell, "Originalism and the Desegregation Decisions," supra note 16, at 1016 (noting that all sides accepted the tripartite theory); see also McConnell, "The Originalist Justification for *Brown*," supra note 46, at 1951 ("The two sides in the 1875 Act debates argued about whether education is a civil right").

49. See McConnell, "Originalism and the Desegregation Decisions," supra note 16, at 1151 ("the level of generality is itself an historical question, susceptible of reasoned historical inquiry"); Michael W. McConnell, "The Importance of Humility in Judicial Review: A Comment on Ronald Dworkin's 'Moral Reading' of the Constitution," 65 *Fordham L. Rev.* 1269, 1284 (1997) (arguing that mainstream originalists agree that we should "read the Constitution in light of the moral and political principles [the framers] intended to express" by using history to determine the correct level of generality); see also the discussion of McConnell's views in Chapter 6, supra.

50. See John O. McGinnis and Michael Rappaport, "Original Interpretive Principles as the Core of Originalism," 24 *Const. Comment.* 371, 379 (2007); Cf. McConnell, "The Importance of Humility in Judicial Review," supra note 49, at 1285 ("[T]he more examples we reject, the more likely it is that we are

making mistakes about Aristotle than it is that Aristotle made so many mistakes in applying his own principles").

51. See Michael J. Klarman, "*Brown,* Originalism, and Constitutional Theory: A Response to Professor McConnell," 81 *Va. L. Rev.* 1881, 1919–20 (1995). McConnell suggests that opposition to the 1875 Act was based on the principle "that 'social rights' and 'social equality' are not fitting subjects for regulation—a position that, logically, extends to statutes mandating, as well as statutes prohibiting, segregation." McConnell, "Originalism and the Desegregation Decisions," supra note 16, at 1099; see also id. at 1122–23. This is incorrect. The social rights argument asserted that the new Fourteenth Amendment did not give the *federal government* the power to legislate on matters of social equality, but states could certainly do so, for it was widely accepted that states could ban interracial marriage. McConnell also argues that congressional Republicans in the 1870s generally avoided the subject when pressed on miscegenation, id. at 1018–20; but this is not the same thing as saying that they believed in 1866 that the Fourteenth Amendment prohibited antimiscegenation laws.

52. See Ward Farnsworth, "Women under Reconstruction: The Congressional Understanding," 94 *Nw. U. L. Rev.* 1229 (2000).

53. Frontiero v. Richardson, 411 U.S. 677 (1974) (plurality opinion) (holding unconstitutional a law that treated married servicewomen differently from married servicemen).

54. It is possible that the civil/social distinction still continues, but in a greatly attenuated form; for example, in rules that treat certain private race-based decisions about friends, sexual partners, and family formation as beyond the reach of civil rights law. A law that prohibited persons from choosing marriage partners because of their race might still be unconstitutional today, also because of *Loving v. Virginia.* Put differently, the principle of *Loving* prohibits the state from banning types of certain marriage choices and protects, to some degree, the liberty of persons to choose whom they will marry.

55. This is the point of Bruce Ackerman's constitutional history of the New Deal and the civil rights revolution. Bruce A. Ackerman, 2 *We The People: Transformations* (Harvard University Press 1998); Bruce A. Ackerman, "The Living Constitution," 120 *Harv. L. Rev.* 1737 (2007).

56. See also McLaughlin v. Florida, 379 U.S. 184 (1964), which concerned an antimiscegenation statute and had already overruled *Pace.*

57. See Jack M. Balkin, "*Plessy, Brown,* and *Grutter:* A Play in Three Acts," 26 *Cardozo L. Rev.* 1689 (2005) (tracing the historical shift from the tripartite theory to the modern theory of fundamental rights and suspect classifications). Along with the tripartite theory of citizenship, the nineteenth century developed a police power jurisprudence designed to explain and limit legislative power. Constitutionally valid legislation had to fall within the states' police power: it had to be public-regarding legislation that reasonably furthered the health,

safety, and welfare of the public. Conversely, legislation primarily for purposes of advantaging a particular group or shifting income or power from one group to another was likely to be class legislation and constitutionally objectionable. See Howard Gillman, *The Constitution Besieged,* supra note 13, at 19–60. Police power jurisprudence meshed with the tripartite theory: Class legislation and laws that made arbitrary and unreasonable distinctions violated constitutional guarantees of equality before the law.

The constitutional politics of the New Deal transformed police power jurisprudence into a new set of doctrinal categories. It introduced a strong, almost irrebuttable presumption that ordinary social and economic legislation was public-regarding—and therefore constitutional—as long as the state could offer a plausible reason for its action. Moreover, even legislation with strongly redistributive purposes could further the public interest. The ratification of the Sixteenth Amendment symbolized this change in thinking. Although the amendment nominally concerned only the federal government's power to tax income, it presumed that Congress could legitimately engage in redistribution in the public interest. At least where economic rights were concerned, the category of forbidden class legislation shrunk almost to the vanishing point. Nevertheless, the constitutional principles against class and caste legislation did not disappear; they reemerged through a new idea: "suspect" classifications.

58. 388 U.S. 1, 11 (1967) ("most rigid scrutiny").

59. Adarand Constructors v. Pena, 515 U.S. 200, 227 (1995); Richmond v. J. A. Croson Co., 488 U.S. 469 (1989).

60. Dandridge v. Williams, 397 U.S. 471, 485 (1970); Lindsley v. Natural Carbonic Gas Co., 220 U.S. 61, 78–79 (1911).

61. United States v. Virginia, 518 U.S. 515, 524 (1996).

62. Geduldig v. Aiello, 417 U.S. 484, 496–97 (1974).

63. See, e.g., United States v. Carolene Prods. Co., 304 U.S. 144, 153 n. 4 (1938) (special scrutiny for laws that burden discrete and insular minorities); Loving v. Virginia, 388 U.S. 1 (1967) (strict scrutiny for racial classifications); Levy v. Louisiana, 391 U.S. 68 (1968) (strict scrutiny for classifications burdening illegitimacy); Graham v. Richardson, 403 U.S. 365 (1971) (strict scrutiny for state classifications burdening alienage); Craig v. Boren, 429 U.S. 190 (1976) (heightened scrutiny for sex classifications); Cleburne v. Cleburne Living Ctr., Inc., 473 U.S. 432 (1985) (heightened rational basis scrutiny for classifications based on prejudice or animus).

64. For a list of problems, on which the next several paragraphs are based, see Jack M. Balkin and Reva B. Siegel, "Remembering How to Do Equality," in *The Constitution in 2020* 93, 95–96 (Jack M. Balkin and Reva B. Siegel eds., Oxford University Press 2009).

65. See Washington v. Davis, 426 U.S. 229 (1976).

66. See Pers. Admin. of Mass. v. Feeney, 442 U.S. 256 (1979).

67. Andrew Jackson, "Veto Message" (July 10, 1832), supra note 8, at 576, 590.

68. Id. at 590.

69. In fact, Gerard Magliocca has argued that Jackson's mistreatment of the Cherokee Indians gave rise to another source of the antebellum idea of equal protection. Gerard N. Magliocca, "The Cherokee Removal and the Fourteenth Amendment," 53 *Duke L. J.* 875 (2003).

It is probably not surprising that constitutional equality concepts were first developed by whites seeking equality with other whites. One of the first "equality" arguments appearing in the United States Reports is Justice Catron's concurrence in Dred Scott v. Sandford, 60 U.S. 393, 518 (1857) (Catron, J., concurring). Catron argued that the Missouri Compromise discriminated against slaveholders. Northerners could bring their property into federal territory without sanction, while southerners would lose their property in slaves. Although the Missouri Compromise did not discriminate against southerners by name and did not prohibit them from entering or settling in federal territories above the compromise line, it had a foreseeable disparate impact against them. Id. at 527. Hence, Catron argued, "the act of 1820, known as the Missouri compromise, violates the most leading feature of the Constitution—a feature on which the Union depends, and which secures to the respective States and their citizens an entire EQUALITY of rights, privileges, and immunities." Id. at 528–29.

70. Daniel R. Ortiz, "The Myth of Intent in Equal Protection," 41 *Stan. L. Rev.* 1105 (1989) (showing how the Supreme Court has relaxed the intent requirement in jury selection, education, and election cases).

71. See, e.g., Castaneda v. Partida, 430 U.S. 482 (1977); Griggs v. Duke Power, 401 U.S. 424 (1971).

72. See Grutter v. Bollinger, 539 U.S. 306, 332 (2003) (O'Connor, J.) ("In order to cultivate a set of leaders with legitimacy in the eyes of the citizenry, it is necessary that the path to leadership be visibly open to talented and qualified individuals of every race and ethnicity"); Reva B. Siegel, "From Colorblindness to Antibalkanization: An Emerging Ground of Decision in Race Equality Cases," 120 *Yale L. J.* 1278 (2011).

73. Jack M. Balkin and Reva B. Siegel, "The American Civil Rights Tradition: Anticlassification or Antisubordination?" 58 *U. Miami L. Rev.* 9, 16, 24–28 (2003)

74. Lawrence v. Texas, 539 U.S. 558 (2003); id. at 579 (O'Connor, J., concurring in the judgment) (equal protection argument); Romer v. Evans, 517 U.S. 620, 634 (1996); Cleburne v. Cleburne Living Center, 473 U.S. 432 (1985); U.S. Dep't of Agric. v. Moreno, 413 U.S. 528, 534 (1973).

75. 517 U.S. at 624.

76. Id. at 632. The Court continued: "First, the amendment has the peculiar property of imposing a broad and undifferentiated disability on a single named

group, an exceptional and, as we shall explain, invalid form of legislation. Second, its sheer breadth is so discontinuous with the reasons offered for it that the amendment seems inexplicable by anything but animus toward the class that it affects; it lacks a rational relationship to legitimate state interests." Id.

77. 539 U.S. at 577.

78. Justice O'Connor's concurrence in *Lawrence* also seems consistent with the principles against class and caste legislation. Id. at 579 (O'Connor, J., concurring in the judgment). O'Connor would have struck down the ban on same-sex sodomy on the authority of *Romer v. Evans*, arguing that "[a] law branding one class of persons as criminal solely based on the State's moral disapproval of that class and the conduct associated with that class runs contrary to the values of the Constitution and the Equal Protection Clause, under any standard of review." Id. at 585.

79. Skinner v. Oklahoma ex rel. Williamson, 316 U.S. 535, 541 (1942). On the history of *Skinner*, see Victoria F. Nourse, *In Reckless Hands: Skinner v. Oklahoma and the Near-Triumph of American Eugenics* (W. W. Norton 2008).

80. See Akhil Reed Amar and Jed Rubenfeld, "A Dialogue," 115 *Yale L. J.* 2015, 2019–34 (2006) (debating whether equality principles in the Fourteenth Amendment can extend to political rights).

81. United States v. Carolene Prods. Co., 304 U.S. 144 (1938).

82. Id. at 152 n. 4.

83. Id.

84. The House and Senate passed slightly different versions of the Fifteenth Amendment, each of which would have protected the right of officeholding. See *Cong. Globe*, 40th Cong. 3d Sess. 1318 (1869) (Senate); id. at 1428 (House). The House version did not restrict the national government, and in addition to prohibiting discrimination on the basis of "race," "color," or "previous condition of servitude," prohibited discrimination on the basis of "nativity, property, [or] creed." Id. When a joint conference committee reconciled the two versions, the reference to office-holding was dropped. Id. at 1563–64, 1623. Senators held an extensive debate on whether the omission meant that officeholding was not protected, or whether the right to hold office was implied in the right to vote. See id. at 1624–41. They did not reach a definite conclusion and simply voted for the final version. Id. at 1641. The amendment was considered in the lame-duck session of the 40th Congress, and the 41st Congress would have fewer Republicans. Supporters may have assumed that the conference version, which was ambiguous on rights of office-holding, was the best that could be achieved under the circumstances. See id. at 1626–27 (statement of Sens. Wilson and Morton).

85. See Vikram David Amar, "Jury Service as Political Participation Akin to Voting," 80 *Cornell L. Rev.* 203, 227–34 (1995) (arguing that the debates show that officeholding was covered by the right of suffrage); Reva B. Siegel, "She the

People," supra note 22, 1019–20 (discussing cases immediately following ratification of the Nineteenth Amendment holding that the new amendment gave women the right to hold office and serve on juries). I am not aware of any court decision holding that women had equal rights to serve in state militias as a result of the Nineteenth Amendment.

86. See Jamin B. Raskin, "Legal Aliens, Local Citizens: The Historical, Constitutional and Theoretical Meanings of Alien Suffrage," 141 *U. Pa. L. Rev.* 1391 (1993); Sanford Levinson, "Suffrage and Community: Who Should Vote?" 41 Fla. L. Rev. 545 (1989).

87. 383 U.S. 663 (1966).

88. Voting Rights Act of 1965, Pub. L. No. 89-110, § 10, 79 Stat. 437, 442–43 (codified as amended at 42 U.S.C. § 1973(b) (2006)); see Bruce Ackerman and Jennifer Nou, "Canonizing the Civil Rights Revolution: The People and the Poll Tax," 103 *Nw. U. L. Rev.* 63, 108–11 (2009).

89. Akhil Reed Amar, "The Central Meaning of Republican Government: Popular Sovereignty, Majority Rule, and the Denominator Problem," 65 *U. Colo. L. Rev.* 749 (1994).

90. *Cong. Globe,* 39th Cong., 1st. Sess. 2542 (statement of Rep. Bingham). It is worth noting, however, that Bingham's example of where the Fourteenth Amendment would provide a remedy was extreme: "where treason might change a State government from a republican to a despotic government, and thereby deny suffrage to the people." Id. Indeed, immediately prior to the debates over the Fourteenth Amendment, the Republicans had excluded southern representatives from Congress on the ground that these states were not republican forms of government because, by denying blacks the right to vote, they prevented a very large proportion of their free adult male populations from participating in governance. Amar, *America's Constitution,* supra note 29, at 368–78; William M. Wiecek, *The Guarantee Clause of the U.S. Constitution* 194–207 (Cornell University Press 1972).

91. 48 U.S. (7 How.) 1 (1849).

92. Id. at 43–45. Chief Justice Taney also offered a second reason, in dicta: it would be very difficult for courts to prove who voted in the various elections and their respective qualifications at the time of the election, because the Court could not take a census or decide the qualifications of each individual voter in a judicial proceeding. Id. at 41–42. No doubt this language encouraged the view that the guarantee clause could not be the source of voting rights claims. But this theory was unnecessary to the holding; moreover, there are many voting rights claims that do not require courts to conduct a census, decide who voted at a particular election, and determine the qualifications of each and every voter at the time of the election.

93. Baker v. Carr, 369 U.S. 186 (1962).

94. 377 U.S. 533 (1964).

95. Id. at 582; Wesberry v. Sanders, 376 U.S. 1 (1964).

96. See, e.g., Harper v. Virginia Board of Elections, 383 U.S. 663 (1966) (holding unconstitutional poll tax requirement in state elections); Kramer v. Union Free School District, 395 U.S. 621 (1969) (holding unconstitutional limitation of voting rights in public school district to persons owning or leasing real property).

97. See, e.g., Bush v. Gore, 531 U.S. 98 (2000) (holding unconstitutional the use of disparate and discretionary methods for counting votes in different counties in presidential elections). This aspect of *Bush v. Gore* is distinct from (and even in tension with) the remedy the Court ordered in that case. See Jack M. Balkin, "*Bush v. Gore* and the Boundary between Law and Politics," 110 *Yale L. J.* 1407, 1429–31 (2001) (arguing that equal protection theory is inconsistent with the Court's remedy).

98. See, e.g., Reynolds v. Sims, 377 U.S. 533 (1964); Wesberry v. Sanders, 376 U.S. 1 (1964).

99. See, e.g., Miller v. Johnson, 515 U.S. 900 (1995); Shaw v. Reno, 509 U.S. 630 (1993); Gomillion v. Lightfoot, 364 U.S. 339 (1960) (racial gerrymandering); Davis v. Bandemer, 478 U.S. 109 (1986) (plurality opinion) (some political gerrymandering claims justiciable).

100. See Michael W. McConnell, "The Redistricting Cases: Original Mistakes and Current Consequences," 24 *Harv. J. L. & Pub. Pol'y* 103, 106 (2000).

101. On the importance of viewing voting rights cases through the lens of fair structures of political competition rather than individual rights, see Samuel Issacharoff, "Gerrymandering and Political Cartels," 116 *Harv. L. Rev.* 593 (2002); Samuel Issacharoff and Richard H. Pildes, "Politics as Markets: Partisan Lockups of the Democratic Process," 50 *Stan. L. Rev.* 643, 645 (1998); and Pamela S. Karlan, "Nothing Personal: The Evolution of the Newest Equal Protection from *Shaw v. Reno* to *Bush v. Gore,*" 79 *N.C. L. Rev.* 1345, 1346 (2001). Something resembling *Reynolds*'s "one person, one vote" principle might be consistent with the guarantee clause, but states and local governments might have broader discretion to depart from strict numerical quotas if they could show that the apportionment served other goals of representativeness. See, e.g., McConnell, "The Redistricting Cases," supra note 100, at 114 ("The gravamen of a Republican Form of Government challenge is not that individual voters are treated unequally, but that the districting scheme systematically prevents effective majority rule").

102. U.S. Const. amend. XIV, § 1.

103. See Williams, "The One and Only Substantive Due Process Clause," supra note 1, at 424–26, 460–66; Ely, "The Oxymoron Reconsidered," supra note 1, 328–45 (1999) (focusing on vested rights); Saunders, "Equal Protection, Class Legislation, and Colorblindness," supra note 1, at 258–59 & n. 58 (focusing on special or partial laws); Michael Les Benedict, "Laissez-Faire and Liberty: A Reevaluation of the Meaning and Origins of Laissez-Faire Constitutionalism," 3 *L. & Hist. Rev.* 293 (1985); Stephen A. Siegel, "*Lochner* Era Jurisprudence and the

American Constitutional Tradition," 70 *N.C. L. Rev.* 1, 52–61 (1991) (divesting of property rights or taking property for private purposes); see, e.g., Wynehamer v. State of New York, 13 N.Y. 378 (1856); Hoke v. Henderson, 15 N.C. 1 (1833); Trustees of the University of North Carolina v. Foy and Bishop, 5 N.C. (1 Mur.) 53 (1805).

104. Bloomer v. McQuewan, 55 U.S. (14 How.) 539, 553–54 (1852). ("[A] special act of Congress, passed afterwards, depriving the appellees of the right to use [machines for which they had purchased patent licenses], certainly could not be regarded as due process of law.")

105. 60 U.S. (19 How.) 393 (1857) (holding Missouri Compromise of 1820 violated due process clause).

106. In fact Mark Graber has pointed out that the Supreme Court repeatedly enforced the prohibition on taking from A and giving to B in a series of land cases during the antebellum era, although it did not invoke the due process clause as justification. See Mark A. Graber, Dred Scott *and the Problem of Constitutional Evil* 64 (Cambridge University Press 2006); Mark A. Graber, "Naked Land Transfers and American Constitutional Development," 53 *Vand. L. Rev.* 73 (2000). In Wilkinson v. Leland, 27 U.S. (2 Pet.) 627, 658 (1829), Justice Story stated that the principle against taking from A to give to B was so basic to constitutional government that it applied whether or not a state had a due process or law of the land clause. See also Calder v. Bull, 3 U.S. (3 Dall.) 386, 388 (1798) (Chase, J.) (arguing that "a law that takes property from A. and gives it to B." "cannot be considered a rightful exercise of legislative authority" because "it is against all reason and justice").

107. 198 U.S. 45 (1905).

108. The term *substantive due process* does not appear to have been widely used until well after the *Lochner* era, and then mostly by its critics. See Ely, "The Oxymoron Reconsidered," supra note 1, at 319; G. Edward White, "Holmes and American Jurisprudence: Revisiting Substantive Due Process and Holmes's *Lochner* Dissent," 63 *Brooklyn L. Rev.* 87, 107–10 (1997).

109. See, e.g., Gitlow v. New York, 268 U.S. 652, 666–67 (1925).

110. See Griswold v. Connecticut, 381 U.S. 479 (1965), Eisenstadt v. Baird, 405 U.S. 438 (1972); Roe v. Wade, 410 U.S. 113 (1973); Carey v. Population Servs. Int'l, 431 U.S. 678 (1977); Lawrence v. Texas, 539 U.S. 558 (2003).

111. See Williams, "The One and Only Substantive Due Process Clause," supra note 1, at 452–57 (arguing that the phrase was often used to refer to the process and proceedings of courts, including procedural requirements like presentment and indictment).

112. 59 U.S. (18 How.) 272, 277 (1856) ("We must examine the constitution itself, to see whether this process be in conflict with any of its provisions").

113. *Cong. Globe,* 39th Cong., 1st Sess. 1089 (1866) (statement of Rep. Bingham).

114. See Murray's Lessee v. Hoboken Land & Improvement Co., 59 U.S. (18 How.) 272, 276 (1856); Ely, "The Oxymoron Reconsidered," supra note 1.

115. Ely, "The Oxymoron Reconsidered," supra note 1, at 332–33; Wallace Mendelson, "A Missing Link in the Evolution of Due Process," 10 *Vand. L. Rev.* 125, 126–27, 136 (1956) ("Separation [of powers] with its procedural connotations had been a ready, if narrow, bridge between orthodox procedural due process and the doctrine of vested rights in an age when legislatures habitually interfered with property by crude retrospective and special, i.e., quasi-judicial, measures"); see also Williams, "The One and Only substantive Due Process Clause," supra note 1, at 423–24; Nathan N. Frost, Rachel Beth Klein-Levine, and Thomas B. McAffee, "Courts Over Constitutions Revisited: Unwritten Constitutionalism in the States," 2004 *Utah L. Rev.* 333, 382; but cf. John Harrison, "Substantive Due Process and the Constitutional Text," 83 *Va. L. Rev.* 493, 521–24 (1997) (noting that "Nineteenth century believers in vested rights due process seem clearly to have embraced the structural principle . . . and to have associated their reading of the Due Process Clauses with it" but arguing that their views were confused).

116. Compare BiMetallic Inv. Co. v. State Bd. of Equalization, 239 U.S. 441 (1915) (due process clause allowed countywide change in property assessments through rulemaking) with Londoner v. Denver, 210 U.S. 373 (1908) (specific road improvement assessment that only affected a few individuals required a hearing under the due process clause).

117. This is probably what Chief Justice Taney was getting at in *Dred Scott v. Sandford* when he made the infamous argument that the Missouri Compromise banning slavery in northern federal territories violated due process of law. See 60 U.S. at 450 ("[A]n act of Congress which deprives a citizen of the United States of his liberty or property, merely because he came himself or brought his property into a particular Territory of the United States, and who had committed no offence against the laws, could hardly be dignified with the name of due process of law").

The argument that settlers had a right to bring property with them into federal territories was not especially controversial in 1857. Antislavery Republicans, including Abraham Lincoln, agreed. See Graber, Dred Scott *and the Problem of Constitutional Evil,* supra note 106, at 62–64. What was controversial was its application to slavery, which Republicans regarded as a disfavored form of property that was not recognized in free jurisdictions. See Dred Scott, 60 U.S. at 549–50 (MacLean, J., dissenting) ("[A] slave is not property beyond the operation of the local law which makes him such"); Id. at 625–27 (Curtis, J., dissenting) (arguing that property is a creation of local law and when people travel to a new jurisdiction they must obey the property laws there); see also Downes v. Bidwell, 182 U.S. 244, 274–75 (1901) ("The difficulty with the Dred Scott Case was that the court refused to make a distinction between property in general and a wholly exceptional class of property").

118. Trustees of Dartmouth College v. Woodward, 17 U.S. (4 Wheat.) 518, 581 (1819) (argument of counsel); the Supreme Court quoted parts of Webster's speech almost verbatim in Truax v. Corrigan, 257 U.S. 312, 332 (1921). See Williams, "The One and Only Substantive Due Process Clause," supra note 1, at 425, 462, 464, 480, 491, 493 (showing the influence of Webster's "general law" formulation in the work of later judges and commentators).

119. See Ely, "The Oxymoron Reconsidered," supra note 1, at 337–38; Saunders, "Equal Protection, Class Legislation, and Colorblindness," supra note 1, at 258–59 & n. 58; Siegel, "*Lochner* Era Jurisprudence and the American Constitutional Tradition," supra note 103, at 56, 59–60. The ban on special, partial, or class legislation evolved naturally out of the idea that due process required protection of vested rights and fair legislative process. Fair legislative process meant that legislatures would create impartial rules of law that served the public good. Laws that destroyed vested rights in property or transferred property from one private person to another were obvious examples of legislation that singled out particular individuals for unfair treatment and therefore were not general and impartial.

120. See Yudof, "Equal Protection, Class Legislation and Sex Discrimination," supra note 1, at 1376.

121. *Cong. Globe,* 39th Cong., 1st Sess. 2766 (1866) (statement of Sen. Howard).

122. See *Cong. Globe,* 39th Cong., 1st Sess. 1034 (statement of Rep. Bingham); William W. Crosskey, "Charles Fairman, 'Legislative History,' and the Constitutional Limitations on State Authority," 22 *U. Chi. L. Rev.* 1, 16–17, 25–26 (1954) (noting Republican theory that Fifth Amendment's due process clause included equal protection of the law). See also Akhil Reed Amar, "Intratextualism," 112 *Harv. L. Rev.* 747, 772 (1999) ("for the framers and ratifiers of the Fourteenth Amendment, the words of its Equal Protection Clause were not expressing a different idea than the words of the Due Process Clause but were elaborating the same idea: the Equal Protection Clause was in part a clarifying gloss on the due process idea").

123. The Ninth Amendment may be either a rule of construction noting the existence of unenumerated rights, which is the view I prefer (see Chapter 10, note 116), or a substantive guarantee of (some of) these rights. These unenumerated rights, in turn, may include fundamental rights, rights of lesser standing, or some combination of the two.

However we interpret the Ninth Amendment, we should read it in conjunction with the later-enacted privileges or immunities clause of the Fourteenth Amendment, which asserts that there are certain "privileges or immunities of citizens of the United States." As argued in Chapter 10, these rights form a template of basic rights enjoyed because of national citizenship. Because they are privileges or immunities of *citizens of the United States,* they should be binding on the national government as well as on the states. To the extent that some of these privileges or immunities are not enumerated in the Constitution, they form a subset of the rights referred to by the Ninth Amendment.

124. See *Cong. Globe,* 39th Cong., 1st Sess. 2766 (1866) (statement of Senator Howard) (The first and fifth sections of the Fourteenth Amendment will prevent the states "from passing laws trenching upon those fundamental rights and privileges which pertain to citizens of the United States, and to all persons who may happen to be within their jurisdiction").

125. See Gillman, *The Constitution Besieged,* supra note 13. See also Barry Cushman, "Some Varieties and Vicissitudes of Lochnerism," 85 *B.U. L. Rev.* 881, 885–95 (2005) (noting the overlap between due process and equal protection concepts in the late nineteenth and early twentieth centuries).

126. 347 U.S. 497 (1954).

127. Id. at 499.

128. Id. at 500.

129. See, e.g., Cass Sunstein, *Radicals in Robes: Why Extreme Right-Wing Courts Are Wrong for America* 2, 72, 131 (Basic Books 2005) (using originalists' inability to explain *Bolling* as an argument against constitutional "fundamentalism"); Mark Tushnet, *Taking the Constitution Away from the Courts* 156 (Princeton University Press 1999); Paul Brest, "The Misconceived Quest for the Original Understanding," 60 *B.U. L. Rev.* 204, 224, 233 (1980).

130. Robert H. Bork, *The Tempting of America: The Political Seduction of the Law* 83–84 (Macmillan 1990). Bork argues that judicial intervention was unnecessary because there would have been enormous political pressure for the federal government to end segregation by ordinary legislation. Id. at 83–84. But a contrary result in *Bolling* might have made it far more difficult for the justices to reach a unanimous decision in *Brown.* Indeed, if the Court reaffirmed the continuing authority of *Plessy v. Ferguson* in federal territories, this might have given additional leverage to southern resistance and actually undermined the struggle for black civil rights.

131. Michael W. McConnell, "Opinion Concurring in the Judgment," in *What* Brown v. Board of Education *Should Have Said: The Nation's Top Legal Experts Rewrite America's Landmark Civil Rights Opinion* 165–68 (Jack M. Balkin ed., NYU Press 2001). Nevertheless, McConnell is understandably uncomfortable with the conclusion that the federal government could maintain Jim Crow in the nation's capital; therefore he argues that segregation of public schools was *ultra vires.* Id. at 168. The *ultra vires* argument seems a bit of a stretch; Congress had accepted segregated schools in the District for decades prior to *Bolling.* Moreover, as noted above, southern senators would have strongly resisted any attempt to change the status quo through federal legislation.

132. *Cong. Globe,* 39th Cong., 1st Sess. 1034 (1866) (statement of Rep. Bingham); see Chapter 10, note 23 (Committee of Fifteen notes).

133. See *Cong. Globe,* 39th Cong., 1st Sess. 1094 (1866) (statement of Rep. Bingham) ("[D]ue process of law—law in its highest sense . . . is impartial, equal, exact justice"); id. at 1292 ("[I]n respect to life and liberty and property, the people by their Constitution declared the equality of all men, and by express limitation forbade the Government of the United States from making any discrimination"); Williams, "The One and Only Substantive Due Process Clause," supra note 1, at 480–81 ("Bingham's rhetoric . . . echoes Daniel Webster's *Dartmouth College* argument and, along with Bingham's apparent equation of 'due process of law' with 'equal protection,' suggests a substantial degree of overlap [with] the general law reading endorsed by numerous courts in the pre-Civil War era"); William W. Crosskey, "Charles Fairman, 'Legislative History,' and the Constitutional Limitations on State Authority," supra note 122, at 16–17 (noting that both Bingham and "a great many other Republicans of the period" believed that "the Due Process Clause of the Fifth Amendment comprehended 'equal protection of the laws' ").

134. *Cong. Globe,* 39th Cong., 1st Sess. 2766 (1866) (statement of Sen. Howard) ("Without this principle of equal justice to all men and equal protection under the shield of the law, there is no republican government and none that is really worth maintaining").

135. *Cong. Globe,* 39th Cong., 1st. Sess. 2539 (statement of Rep. Farnsworth); see also id. at 2961 (statement of Sen. Poland) (due process and equal protection are "the very spirit and inspiration of our system of government, the absolute foundation on which it was established [and] essentially declared in the Declaration of Independence and in all the provisions of the Constitution").

136. See Jacobus tenBroek, *Equal Under Law* 50–54, 116–21, 139–44 (Collier 1965); Michael Kent Curtis, *No State Shall Abridge: The Fourteenth Amendment and the Bill of Rights* 46–47 (Duke University Press 1986); Randy Barnett, "Whence Comes Section One? The Abolitionist Origins of the Fourteenth Amendment," 3 *J. Legal Analysis* (forthcoming 2011), available at papers.ssrn.com/sol3/papers.cfm?abstract_id=1538862 (February 22, 2010).

137. See *National Party Platforms, 1840–1968*, at 27 (Kirk H. Porter and Donald Bruce Johnson eds., 3d. ed., University of Illinois Press 1966) (Republican Platform of 1856); id. at 32 (Republican Platform of 1860); tenBroek, *Equal Under Law,* supra note 136, 140–41 & nn. 5–6.

138. Act of June 19, 1862, 12 Stat. 432 (territories); Act of Apr. 16, 1862, § 1, 12 Stat. 376 (District of Columbia). Because no territorial legislatures recognized slavery, the June 19th act was largely symbolic. See Barry Friedman, *The Will of the People: How Public Opinion Has Influenced the Supreme Court and Shaped the Meaning of the Constitution* 119, 441–42 (Farrar, Straus and Giroux 2009).

139. *Cong. Globe,* 37th Cong., 2d Sess. 1638–39 (1862) (statement of Rep. Bingham).

140. See *Cong. Globe,* 39th Cong., 1st. Sess. 2539 (statement of Rep. Farnsworth).

141. Amar, "Intratextualism," supra note 122, at 772.

142. See *Cong. Globe,* 39th Cong., 1st Sess. 2896 (1866) (statement of Sen. Howard).

143. See *Cong. Globe*, 39th Cong., 1st Sess. 1294 (1866) (statement of Rep. Wilson).

144. Act of May 31, 1870 (Enforcement Act of 1870), ch. 114, §§ 16, 18, 16 Stat. 140, 144.

145. *Report of the Joint Committee on Reconstruction* (Gov't Printing Office 1866); see Laurent B. Frantz, "Congressional Power to Enforce the Fourteenth Amendment against Private Acts," 73 *Yale L.J.* 1353, 1354, & nn. 10–13 (1964) (collecting examples in the report of discriminatory legislation and private violence).

146. See Balkin, "The Reconstruction Power," 85 *N.Y.U. L. Rev.* 1801, 1846–56 (2010) (discussing Republican theories of congressional enforcement of equal protection).

147. See, e.g., Richard Primus, "Bolling Alone," 104 *Colum. L. Rev.* 975, 976–77 & n. 7 (2004) (describing the theory of reverse incorporation and criticisms of it). Amar's intertextual argument is not, strictly speaking, a reverse incorporation argument; instead, Amar argues that the *adoption* of the Fourteenth Amendment changed how subsequent interpreters should interpret the Fifth Amendment. Amar, "Intertextualism," supra note 122, at 772–73.

148. See, e.g., *Cong. Globe*, 39th Cong., 1st Sess. 2766 (1866) (statement of Sen. Howard) (explaining that purpose of section 1 of the Fourteenth Amendment is "to restrain the power of the States and compel them at all times to respect these great fundamental guarantees" that apply to the federal government); id. at 2459 (statement of Rep. Stevens) ("[T]he Constitution limits only the action of Congress, and is not a limitation on the States. This amendment supplies that defect . . ."); id. at 1088–94 (statement of Rep. Bingham) (noting that the central purpose of the Fourteenth Amendment is to give Congress power to enforce the Bill of Rights against the states).

149. Gibson v. Mississippi, 162 U.S. 565, 591 (1896) (emphasis added). In this formulation Justice Harlan combined the ideas of due process and equal protection: "The guaranties of life, liberty, and property [i.e., a reference to the due process clause] are for all persons, within the jurisdiction of the United States, or of any state [a reference to the equal protection clause], without discrimination against any because of their race." Id. Note also Harlan's focus on equality in political and civil rights, as opposed to issues of social equality.

150. If we focus on only the rights of citizens, the argument for *Bolling v. Sharpe* is even more powerful. It is based on the citizenship clause and the privileges or immunities clause.

First, the citizenship clause applies to *both* the federal government and the states, and its purpose is to secure a single class of American citizens of equal status. Put differently, the citizenship clause prevents both the federal government and the states from creating first- and second-class citizens. See Balkin, "The Reconstruction Power," supra note 146, at 1819–20 (discussing the theory of the citizenship clause).

Second, although the privileges or immunities clause is directed to states, it asserts the existence of "privileges or immunities of citizens of the United States"— that is, rights that all citizens are entitled to by virtue of being United States citizens. If a right is a privilege or immunity of *citizens of the United States,* it stands to reason that it should bind the federal government as well as the states, because, among other things, all of the privileges or immunities of citizens of the United States should apply in federal territories.

As explained in Chapter 10, equal protection of the laws is one of these privileges or immunities. See Amar, *The Bill of Rights,* supra note 16, at 283; Harrison, "Reconstructing the Privileges or Immunities Clause," supra note 3, at 1411–13. All of the justices in the *Slaughter-House Cases* agreed that equal protection was a privilege or immunity of national citizenship. See Slaughter-House Cases, 83 U.S. (16 Wall.) at 80 (Miller, J.) (privileges or immunities include the rights of equal protection "secured by . . . the other clause of the fourteenth" amendment); id. at 118 (Bradley, J., dissenting) ("[E]quality before the law is undoubtedly one of the privileges and immunities of every citizen").

The declaratory theory of privileges or immunities leads to the same conclusion. Is equal protection by the federal government something that Americans have come to expect as one of the rights they enjoy because they are citizens? Certainly the Reconstruction Republicans thought so, as do Americans today.

12. Texts and Principles

1. Akhil Reed Amar, "Intertextualism," 112 *Harv. L. Rev.* 747 (1999).

2. Bolling v. Sharpe, 347 U.S. 497 (1954). The due process clause is also a good example of how older constitutional language may be reenacted or incorporated by reference in new constitutional provisions. When this happens, the original text may stand for new principles and new constructions that no one expected at the time of enactment. This is the central claim of Akhil Reed Amar, *The Bill of Rights: Creation and Reconstruction* (Yale University Press 1998).

3. Charles Black, *Structure and Relationship in Constitutional Law* 39–45 (Louisiana State University Press 1969).

4. See, e.g., Richard Hofstadter, *The American Political Tradition: And the Men Who Made It* 4 (Knopf 1948) (describing complaints about democracy by delegates to the Philadelphia convention, including Edmund Randolph, Elbridge Gerry, Roger Sherman, and William Livingston); Gordon S. Wood, *The Creation of the American Republic, 1776–1787,* at 165–67 (W. W. Norton and Co. 1972) (noting that concerns about the excesses of democracy in state governments led to calls for a new constitutional convention).

5. See Christopher L. Eisgruber, "Should Constitutional Judges Be Philosophers?" in *Exploring Law's Empire: The Jurisprudence of Ronald Dworkin* 5, 11 (Scott Hershovitz ed., Oxford University Press 2006).

6. See, e.g., Bruce A. Ackerman, "Liberating Abstraction," 59 *U. Chi. L. Rev.* 317 (1992); Frank H. Easterbrook, "Abstraction and Authority," 59 *U. Chi. L. Rev.* 349 (1992); Laurence H. Tribe and Michael C. Dorf, *On Reading the Constitution* 73–80 (Harvard University Press 1991); Laurence H. Tribe and Michael C. Dorf, "Levels of Generality in the Definition of Rights," 57 *U. Chi. L. Rev.* 1057, 1065–67 (1990); Mark V. Tushnet, "Following the Rules Laid Down: A Critique of Interpretivism and Neutral Principles," 96 *Harv. L. Rev.* 781, 791 (1983); Raoul Berger, "A Response to D. A. J. Richards' Defense of Freewheeling Constitutional Adjudication," 59 *Ind. L. J.* 339, 370–72 (1983); Paul Brest, "The Fundamental Rights Controversy: The Essential Contradictions of Normative Constitutional Scholarship," 90 *Yale L. J.* 1063, 1090–92 (1981); Ronald Dworkin, The Forum of Principle, 56 *N.Y.U. L. Rev.* 469, 498–500 (1981).

7. Andrew Kull, *The Color-Blind Constitution* 82–87 (Harvard University Press 1992); Benjamin B. Kendrick, *The Journal of the Joint Committee of Fifteen on Reconstruction* 82–85, 106–7 (Columbia University Press 1914).

8. See Raoul Berger, *Government by Judiciary: The Transformation of the Fourteenth Amendment* (Harvard University Press 1977) (using such statements to argue that the scope of the Fourteenth Amendment was limited to protecting the rights guaranteed by the Civil Rights Act).

9. Jed Rubenfeld has made this point in terms of constitutional commitments. Jed Rubenfeld, *Revolution by Judiciary: The Structure of American Constitutional Law* (Harvard University Press 2005); Jed Rubenfeld, *Freedom and Time: A Theory of Constitutional Self-Government* (Yale University Press 2001). Rubenfeld argues that when people create constitutional texts, they commit themselves and those who come after them to certain principles. When they do so in abstract language, we should read them as committing to results in a certain set of basic or paradigm cases and to general principles to be worked out later on. However the principles are worked out, they must still account for the earlier, paradigm cases. This could be an absolute requirement—as Rubenfeld suggests— but it might also merely be a rule of thumb that helps ensure that there is a continuity of commitment that allows different generations to identify with each other over time. See the discussion of Rubenfeld's theory in Chapter 2, n. 23.

10. Leonard Levy's work emphasized the speech restrictive features of law at the founding, criticizing the previous portrait offered by Zachariah Chaffee. See Leonard W. Levy, *Emergence of a Free Press* (Oxford University Press 1985) (rev. ed. of Leonard W. Levy, *Legacy of Suppression* (Harvard University Press 1960)); Zechariah Chafee, *Free Speech in the United States* (Harvard University Press 1941). Levy's critics have pointed out that actual practices were far more equivocal. See David A. Anderson, *"Levy vs. Levy,"* 84 *Mich. L. Rev.* 777 (1986); David M. Rabban, "The Ahistorical Historian: Leonard Levy on Freedom of Expression in Early American History," 37 *Stan. L. Rev.* 795 (1985); Philip Hamburger, "The Development of the Law of Seditious Libel and the Control of the Press," 37 *Stan. L. Rev.* 661 (1985); William T. Mayton, "Seditious Libel and the Lost Guarantee of a Freedom of Expression," 84 *Colum. L. Rev.* 91 (1984); David A. Anderson, "The Origins of the Press Clause," 30 *UCLA L. Rev.* 455 (1983). Philip Kurland and Thomas Emerson noted that the historical evidence is mixed and that it is difficult to draw any firm conclusions from it. Philip B. Kurland, "The Original Understanding of the Freedom of the Press Provision of the First Amendment," 55 *Miss. L. J.* 225 (1985); Thomas I. Emerson, "Colonial Intentions and Current Realities of the First Amendment," 125 *U. Pa. L. Rev.* 737 (1977).

11. I am indebted to Ronald Dworkin for this formulation.

12. See Mitchell N. Berman, "Originalism and Its Discontents (Plus a Thought or Two about Abortion)," 24 *Const. Comment.* 383, 392 (2007). Indeed, given the demographics of the country at the time of the founding, the original intention might have been narrower still: to protect against discrimination among various Christian sects, perhaps extended to all religions within the Judeo-Christian tradition. It is worth noting, however, that of the state constitutions in force at the time of the founding, only Delaware's and Maryland's explicitly limited protection to Christians, while five others restricted their protections to believers in God. See Michael W. McConnell, "The Origins and Historical Understanding of Free Exercise of Religion," 103 *Harv. L. Rev.* 1409, 1455 n. 237, 1457 n. 242 (1990) (collecting state constitutional provisions).

13. Mitchell N. Berman, "Originalism and Its Discontents," supra note 12, at 392.

14. I have tried to explain the project of interpretive charity toward the past in this way:

> When the Constitution speaks in grand general phrases like "equal protection," or "due process," it speaks to generations long after those who drafted it. It asks those future generations to look beyond the compromises and hesitancies that are inevitable in any age, and to do justice in their own time. We must regard the grand phrases of due process and equal protection as promises that we have made to ourselves as a people. They are promises, made in times of injustice, that respond to injustice, albeit

haltingly and imperfectly. They are promises that cannot always be carried out fully in their own era; but they are promises that we nevertheless pledge ourselves to as a people so that someday they may redeemed by future generations. In this way our Constitution becomes more than a collection of rules and doctrines: it becomes a document of redemption.

Just as we may see the concrete practices of justice of those who framed and ratified the Constitution as compromised and imperfect, so we must recognize that others will someday see our own attempts at justice as equally flawed and deficient. That is why we owe it to previous generations to understand and apply their constitutional aspirations in their best light. We must carry on the work that they could only begin. If we read this document as fulfilling their best aspirations rather than chaining us to their worst fears, we do them greater honor than any slavish adherence to their concrete practices could; and perhaps, if we are fortunate, we may merit an equal charity from the generations that come after us.

Jack M. Balkin, "Judgment of the Court," in *What* Brown v. Board of Education *Should Have Said: The Nation's Top Legal Experts Rewrite America's Most Famous Civil Rights Opinion* 77, 81 (Jack M. Balkin ed., NYU Press 2001).

15. Compare Abraham Lincoln's famous speech on the *Dred Scott* decision, in which he treats the Declaration of Independence with similar charity:

Chief Justice Taney [and] Judge Douglas argue that the authors of [the Declaration] did not intend to include negroes, by the fact that they did not at once, actually place them on an equality with the whites. Now this grave argument comes to just nothing at all, by the other fact, that they did not at once, or ever afterwards, actually place all white people on an equality with one or another. . . . I think the authors of that notable instrument . . . did not mean to assert the obvious untruth, that all were then actually enjoying that equality, nor yet, that they were about to confer it immediately upon them. In fact they had no power to confer such a boon. They meant simply to declare the right, so that the enforcement of it might follow as fast as circumstances should permit. They meant to set up a standard maxim for free society, which should be familiar to all, and revered by all; constantly looked to, constantly labored for, and even though never perfectly attained, constantly approximated, and thereby constantly spreading and deepening its influence, and augmenting the happiness and value of life to all people of all colors everywhere.

Abraham Lincoln, "Speech on the Dred Scott Decision at Springfield, Illinois (June 26, 1857)," in 1 *Abraham Lincoln, Speeches and Writings* 390, 398 (1832–1858) (Don E. Fehrenbacher ed., Library of America 1989).

16. See Jack M. Balkin, "How New Genetic Technologies Will Transform *Roe v. Wade*," 56 *Emory L. J.* 843 (2007); Victoria F. Nourse, *In Reckless Hands: Skinner v. Oklahoma and the Near-Triumph of American Eugenics* (W. W. Norton and Co. 2008).

17. Randy Barnett, "Underlying Principles," 24 *Const. Comment.* 405, 412–13 (2007).

18. See Jack M. Balkin, "Deconstructive Practice and Legal Theory," 96 *Yale L. J.* 743, 758–61 (1987) (applying Jacques Derrida's theory of the "dangerous supplement" to legal argument).

13. Rethinking Living Constitutionalism

1. See, e.g., David A. Strauss, *The Living Constitution* (Oxford University Press 2010) (arguing that living constitutionalism is a common law method that both constrains judges and permits evolution); Lawrence B. Solum, "Constitutional Possibilities," 83 *Ind. L. J.* 307, 315 (2008) ("In the choice between originalism and living constitutionalism as general methods of interpretation, it's the method or practice (ranging across an action type) and not the individual decision (or action token) that counts"); Mitchell N. Berman, "Originalism and Its Discontents (Plus a Thought or Two About Abortion)," 24 *Const. Comment.* 383, 391–95, 400–404 (2007) (discussing the method of living constitutionalism and its superiority to originalism and the method of text and principle); William J. Brennan Jr., "The Constitution of the United States: Contemporary Ratification," 27 *S. Tex. L. Rev.* 433, 438 (1986) (arguing that courts must look to what the Constitution's words mean today); Barry Friedman and Scott B. Smith, "The Sedimentary Constitution," 147 *U. Pa. L. Rev.* 1, 10 (1998) ("'Living constitutionalism,' . . . is the practice of interpreting the Constitution, usually in a nonhistorical way, to meet the needs of the present"); see also Charles A. Reich, "Mr. Justice Black and the Living Constitution," 76 *Harv. L. Rev.* 673, 735–36 (1963) (arguing that judges must adapt constitutional provisions as society changes or the provisions will atrophy); cf. Home Bldg. & Loan Ass'n v. Blaisdell, 290 U.S. 398, 442–44 (1934) (Hughes, C. J.) (arguing that "the great clauses of the Constitution must [not] be confined to the interpretation which the framers, with the conditions and outlook of their time, would have placed upon them," and calling for interpretation of the Constitution in light of changing times, and "a growing recognition of public needs").

2. See Robert H. Bork, *The Tempting of America: The Political Seduction of the Law* 251–53 (Macmillan 1990) (explaining that nonoriginalist theories require judges to impose their moral views on democratic majorities in the absence of moral consensus and without any satisfactory theory of why judges have authority to do so); William H. Rehnquist, "The Notion of a Living Constitution," 54 *Tex. L. Rev.* 693, 693, 695 (1976) (versions of living constitutionalism which see judges as "the voice and conscience of contemporary society" allow judges to impose their personal and subjective moral views on the public); Antonin Scalia, "Common-Law Courts in a Civil-Law System," in *A Matter of Interpretation: Federal Courts and the Law* 38–39 (Amy Gutmann ed., Princeton University Press 1997) (living constitutionalism empowers judges to engage in common law reasoning based on their views of desirable outcomes);

see Antonin Scalia, "Originalism: The Lesser Evil," 57 *U. Cin. L. Rev.* 849, 863 (1989) (nonoriginalism leads judges to mistake their preferences for fundamental rights and values).

3. The *locus classicus* of the living Constitution metaphor appears in Missouri v. Holland, 252 U.S. 416, 433 (1920), in which Justice Holmes compared the Constitution to an "organism" and argued that the words of the text "have called into life a being the development of which could not have been foreseen completely by the most gifted of its begetters." In Edwards v. Canada (Attorney General) [1930] A. C. 124, holding that women were eligible to serve in the Canadian Senate, the Canadian Supreme Court self-consciously adopted an organic metaphor to explain its version of living constitutionalism, which has come to be known as the "living tree" doctrine.

4. Paul Brest, Sanford Levinson, Jack M. Balkin, Akhil Reed Amar, and Reva B. Siegel, *Processes of Constitutional Decisionmaking* (5th ed., Aspen L. & Bus. 2006).

5. See Robert C. Post and Reva B. Siegel, "Democratic Constitutionalism," in *The Constitution in 2020* (Jack M. Balkin and Reva B. Siegel eds., Oxford University Press 2009); Robert C. Post and Reva B. Siegel, "*Roe* Rage: Democratic Constitutionalism and Backlash," 42 *Harv. C.R.–C.L. L. Rev.* 373, 374–76 (2007); see also Barry Friedman, *The Will of the People: How Public Opinion Has Influenced the Supreme Court and Shaped the Meaning of the Constitution* (Farrar, Straus and Giroux 2009) (arguing that the history of the Supreme Court demonstrates democratic constitutionalism); Larry Kramer, *The People Themselves: Popular Constitutionalism and Judicial Review* (Oxford University Press 2004) (explaining how the institution of judicial review emerged under the assumption that there would be popular checks).

6. It is also a consequence of the Constitution's hardwired rules. As noted in Chapter 4, Sanford Levinson has argued that we should no longer have faith in the Constitution because these hardwired rules have made democratic self-government impossible. Whether or not Levinson's diagnosis is correct, we should not forget the effects of the basic constitutional framework on possible constitutional constructions.

7. See Keith E. Whittington, *Constitutional Construction: Divided Powers and Constitutional Meaning 5* (Harvard University Press 1999); Keith E. Whittington, *Constitutional Interpretation: Textual Meaning, Original Intent, and Judicial Review* (University Press of Kansas 1999).

8. See Richard H. Fallon Jr., *Implementing the Constitution 5–12* (Harvard University Press 2001) (arguing that much of the judiciary's work involves creating doctrines and tests to give meaning to constitutional values); Richard H. Fallon Jr., "Judicially Manageable Standards and Constitutional Meaning," 119 *Harv. L. Rev.* 1274, 1276, 1317–18 (2006) (noting the existence of gaps be-

tween constitutional meaning and judicially enforceable rights that must be filled in through doctrinal implementation).

9. See William N. Eskridge Jr. and John Ferejohn, *Republic of Statutes: The New American Constitution* (Yale University Press 2010) (offering a theory of constitutional statutes and their entrenchment over time); Bruce Ackerman, "The Living Constitution," 120 *Harv. L. Rev.* 1737, 1742 (2007) (noting the importance of "landmark statutes that express [a new constitutional] regime's basic principles"); William N. Eskridge Jr. and John Ferejohn, "Super-Statutes," 50 *Duke L. J.* 1215, 1215–16 (2001) (offering an account of durable "super-statutes" that "seek[] to establish a new normative or institutional framework for state policy" and have "broad effect[s] on the law"); Ernest A. Young, "The Constitution Outside the Constitution," 117 *Yale L. J.* 408, 411–13 (2007) ("[M]uch of the law that constitutes our government and establishes our rights derives from legal materials outside the Constitution itself").

10. Cf. Robert A. Dahl, "Decision-Making in a Democracy: The Supreme Court as a National Policy-Maker," 6 *J. Pub. L.* 279, 294 (1957) (arguing that the "main task of the Court is to confer legitimacy on the fundamental policies of the successful coalition").

11. Howard Gillman, "The Collapse of Constitutional Originalism and the Rise of the Notion of the 'Living Constitution' in the Course of American State-Building," 11 *Stud. Am. Pol. Dev.* 191 (1997).

12. See, e.g., Wickard v. Filburn, 317 U.S. 111 (1942) (upholding regulation of wholly intrastate, noncommercial activity if such activity, viewed in the aggregate, would have a substantial effect on interstate commerce); United States v. Darby, 312 U.S. 100 (1941) (holding that Congress can regulate employment in manufacturing under the commerce clause); Steward Machine Co. v. Davis, 301 U.S. 548 (1937) (upholding the unemployment compensation provisions of the Social Security Act of 1935); NLRB v. Jones & Laughlin Steel Corp., 301 U.S. 1 (1937) (upholding the National Labor Relations Act).

13. In his model of constitutional change, Bruce Ackerman originally treated the key Supreme Court decisions of the New Deal as "amendment analogues" that amended the Constitution outside of Article V. Bruce Ackerman, 1 *We the People: Foundations* (Harvard University Press 1991). In his more recent work, he has come to see constitutional amendments arising out of an interaction between what he calls "superprecedents" and "landmark statutes" like the National Labor Relations Act and the Social Security Act. See Bruce Ackerman and Jennifer Nou, "Canonizing the Civil Rights Revolution: The People and the Poll Tax," 103 *Nw. U. L. Rev.* 63, 65, 67–69, 83, 86–88, 108–9, 124 (2009); Ackerman, "The Living Constitution," supra note 9, at 1750–53. My view is that these achievements of twentieth-century constitutionalism are constitutional constructions, not constitutional amendments.

14. See Lucas A. Powe Jr., *The Warren Court and American Politics* 214–15, 490–94 (Harvard University Press 2000); Jack M. Balkin, "What *Brown* Teaches Us about Constitutional Theory," 90 *Va. L. Rev.* 1537, 1538–46 (2004); Lucas A. Powe Jr., "The Politics Of American Judicial Review: Reflections on the Marshall, Warren, and Rehnquist Courts," 38 *Wake Forest L. Rev.* 697, 719–20 (2003). As Keith Whittington notes, the Warren Court's legislative reapportionment decisions were welcomed by liberals who believed that as cities grew larger, legislative malapportionment favored more conservative rural voters over more liberal urban voters. Keith E. Whittington, *Political Foundations of Judicial Supremacy: The Presidency, the Supreme Court, and Constitutional Leadership in U.S. History* 127 (Princeton University Press 2007).

15. See cases cited infra notes 68, 69; see also Bd. of Trs. of the Univ. of Ala. v. Garrett, 531 U.S. 356 (2001) (Eleventh Amendment barred damage suits against states for violations of the Americans with Disabilities Act); Kimel v. Fla. Bd. of Regents, 528 U.S. 62 (2000) (Eleventh Amendment barred damage suits against states for violations of the Age Discrimination in Employment Act); United States v. Morrison, 529 U.S. 598 (2000) (striking down a section of the Violence Against Women Act as beyond Congress's powers under the commerce clause and section 5 of the Fourteenth Amendment); Alden v. Maine, 527 U.S. 706 (1999) (expanding state sovereign immunity from damage suits under the Tenth Amendment); Printz v. United States, 521 U.S. 898 (1997) (holding that, under the Tenth Amendment, the federal government may not compel state executive officials to administer a federal regulatory program); Seminole Tribe v. Florida, 517 U.S. 44 (1996) (Eleventh Amendment immunity applies to legislation passed under Congress's Commerce Power); United States v. Lopez, 514 U.S. 549 (1995) (striking down a ban on guns near public schools as beyond Congress's powers under the commerce clause); New York v. United States, 505 U.S. 144 (1992) (holding that, under the Tenth Amendment, the federal government may not compel state legislatures to enact a regulatory program).

16. See Whittington, *Political Foundations of Judicial Supremacy,* supra note 14, at 105–20 (showing the different ways that the Supreme Court enforces the values of the existing regime); see also Balkin, "What *Brown* Teaches Us," supra note 14, at 1538–46 (explaining how the Court enforces the national values of the dominant coalition against outliers in state and local governments); Michael J. Klarman, "Rethinking the Civil Rights and Civil Liberties Revolutions," 82 *Va. L. Rev.* 1, 16–18 (1996) (arguing that the Supreme Court is more likely to invalidate old statutes that no longer reflect the preferences of current national majorities). Because I emphasize the role of partisan entrenchment, my account does not assume that there will always be a close connection between Supreme Court decisionmaking and contemporaneous public opinion. Nevertheless, at least since the New Deal, the two are often connected, especially when viewed in the medium to long run. See Barry Friedman, *The Will of the People,* supra note 5;

Terri Jennings Peretti, *In Defense of a Political Court* 80–132 (Princeton University Press 1999); Barry Friedman, "Mediated Popular Constitutionalism," 101 *Mich. L. Rev.* 2596, 2601–13 (2003).

17. 539 U.S. 558 (2003).

18. William N. Eskridge, *Gaylaw: Challenging the Apartheid of the Closet* 130, 139, 168, app. B2 (Harvard University Press 1999); Michael J. Klarman, "*Brown* and *Lawrence* (and *Goodridge*)," 104 *Mich. L. Rev.* 431, 443–45 (2005).

19. 347 U.S. 483 (1954).

20. See Balkin, "What *Brown* Teaches Us," supra note 14, at 1539–40. See generally Michael Klarman, *From Jim Crow to Civil Rights: The Supreme Court and the Struggle for Racial Equality* 173–96 (Oxford University Press 2004) (describing broader changes in legal understandings concerning race following World War II).

21. 163 U.S. 537 (1896).

22. Klarman, *From Jim Crow to Civil Rights,* supra note 20, at 210. The Justice Department made this request in a trio of cases decided in 1950. See Brief for the United States at 35–49, Henderson v. United States, 339 U.S. 816 (1950) (No. 25); Memorandum for the United States as Amicus Curiae at 9–14, McLaurin v. Oklahoma State Regents, 339 U.S. 637 (1950) (No. 34); Sweatt v. Painter, 339 U.S. 629 (1950).

23. Kevin J. McMahon, *Reconsidering Roosevelt on Race: How the Presidency Paved the Road to* Brown 198–201 (University of Chicago Press 2004) (noting the importance of the Eisenhower Justice Department's support for the position taken by the Truman administration, despite Eisenhower's attempts to publicly distance himself from the controversy).

24. Whittington, *Political Foundations of Judicial Supremacy,* supra note 14, at 23.

25. Mark A. Graber, "The Countermajoritarian Difficulty: From Courts to Congress to Constitutional Order," 4 *Ann. Rev. Law Soc. Sci.* 361, 366–67 (2008).

26. Whittington, *Political Foundations of Judicial Supremacy,* supra note 14, at 21–27, 82–160, 287–92.

27. Id. at 22–23.

28. Graber, "The Countermajoritarian Difficulty," supra note 25, at 366–67.

29. Whittington, *Political Foundations of Judicial Supremacy,* supra note 14, at xi.

30. Id. at 105, 117.

31. Id. at 166–67.

32. Graber, "The Countermajoritarian Difficulty," supra note 25, at 367.

33. See id. at 368 ("At the very least, a majority in at least one elected branch of the national government has historically thought government by judiciary

more attractive politically than presidential authority to determine constitutional meanings").

34. Alexander M. Bickel, *The Least Dangerous Branch: The Supreme Court at the Bar of Politics* 17 (Yale University Press 1962).

35. Id. at 16.

36. Powe, *The Warren Court,* supra note 14, at 492.

37. See Jack M. Balkin and Sanford Levinson, "The Processes of Constitutional Change: From Partisan Entrenchment to the National Surveillance State," 75 *Fordham L. Rev.* 489 (2006); Howard Gillman, "Party Politics and Constitutional Change: The Political Origins of Liberal Judicial Activism," in *The Supreme Court and American Political Development* 138–61 (Ronald Kahn and Ken Kersch eds., University of Press of Kansas 2006); Howard Gillman, "How Political Parties Can Use the Courts to Advance their Agendas: Federal Courts in the United States, 1875–1891," 96 *Amer. Pol. Sci. Rev.* 511 (2002); Jack M. Balkin and Sanford Levinson, "Understanding the Constitutional Revolution," 87 *Va. L. Rev.* 1045, 1066 (2001). See also Ran Hirschl, *Towards Juristocracy: The Origins and Consequences of the New Constitutionalism* (Harvard University Press 2004) (analyzing the patterns and effects of judicial entrenchment in different constitutional democracies).

38. See Lawrence Baum and Neal Devins, "Why the Supreme Court Cares About Elites, Not the American People," 98 *Geo. L. J.* 1515 (2010); Lawrence Baum, *Judges and their Audiences: A Perspective on Judicial Behavior* (Princeton University Press 2006).

39. See, e.g., B. Dan Wood, *The Myth of Presidential Representation* (Cambridge University Press 2009).

40. See Steven Teles, *The Rise of the Conservative Legal Movement* 11–14 (Princeton University Press 2008); Charles R. Epp, *The Rights Revolution: Lawyers, Activists, and Supreme Courts in Comparative Perspective* 20–22 (University of Chicago Press 1998).

41. See Richard H. Pildes, "Is the Supreme Court a 'Majoritarian' Institution?" *2010 Supreme Court Review* (forthcoming 2011), at papers.ssrn.com/sol3/papers.cfm?abstract_id=1733169.

42. See Lucas A. Powe and H. W. Perry Jr., "The Political Battle for the Constitution," 21 *Const. Commentary* 641 (2004) (noting that the Supreme Court's decisions do not correspond to the constitutional vision of either major political party).

43. Balkin and Levinson, "Understanding the Constitutional Revolution," supra note 37, at 1074–75.

44. See Mark A. Graber, "The Nonmajoritarian Difficulty: Legislative Deference to the Judiciary," 7 *Stud. in Am. Pol. Dev.* 35, 37 (1993) ("Elected officials in the United States encourage or tacitly support judicial policymaking both as a means of avoiding responsibility for making tough decisions and as a means

of pursuing controversial policy goals that they cannot publicly advance through open legislative and electoral politics").

45. For discussions of institutional constraints on judges, see Barry Friedman, "The Politics of Judicial Review," 84 *Tex. L. Rev.* 257, 270–329 (2005).

46. See Balkin and Levinson, "The Processes of Constitutional Change: From Partisan Entrenchment to the National Surveillance State," supra note 37, at 490–506 (2006); Balkin and Levinson, "Understanding the Constitutional Revolution," supra note 37, at 1066–83 (2001).

47. On the concept of a "constitutional culture," see Robert C. Post, "The Supreme Court 2002 Term: Foreword: Fashioning the Legal Constitution: Culture, Courts, and Law," 117 *Harv. L. Rev.* 4, 8–11, 53–56 (2003). On the idea of "off-the-wall" and "on-the-wall" constitutional interpretations, and their importance to constitutional theory, see Jack M. Balkin, *Constitutional Redemption: Political Faith in an Unjust World* (Harvard University Press 2011); Jack M. Balkin, "How Social Movements Change (or Fail to Change) the Constitution: The Case of the New Departure," 39 *Suffolk U. L. Rev.* 27, 28 (2005); Jack M. Balkin, "*Bush v. Gore* and the Boundary between Law and Politics," 110 *Yale L. J.* 1407, 1444–47 (2001).

48. 554 U.S. 570 (2008).

49. See Steven G. Calabresi and James Lindgren, "Term Limits for the Supreme Court: Life Tenure Reconsidered," 29 *Harv. J. L. & Pub. Pol'y,* 769, 777–789 (2006).

50. For a discussion of various proposals, see *Reforming The Court: Term Limits For Supreme Court Justices* (Roger C. Cramton and Paul D. Carrington eds., Carolina Academic Press 2006). The specific proposal mentioned in the text, drafted by Paul Carrington and Roger Cramton, is discussed in Jack M. Balkin, "Reforming the Supreme Court," *Balkinization*, February 19, 2009, at balkin.blogspot.com/2009/02/reforming-supreme-court.html; Paul Carrington, "Four Proposals for a Judiciary Act," February 9, 2009, at paulcarrington.com/Four%20Proposals%20for%20a%20Judiciary%20Act.htm.

51. For an account of how the proposed system would work in practice, see Jack M. Balkin, "The Rotation of the Justices: A Thought Experiment," *Balkinization*, May 20, 2009, at balkin.blogspot.com/2009/05/rotation-of-justices-thought-experiment.html.

52. See Whittington, *Constitutional Construction,* supra note 7, at 5–6, 107–12.

53. See Judiciary Act of 1789, ch. 20, § 35, 1 Stat. 73, 92–93 (codified as amended at 28 U.S.C. § 503 (1994)) (creating the office of the Attorney General). Congress did not provide the attorney general with a clerk until 1818. See Act of April 20, 1818, ch. 87, § 6, 3 Stat. 445, 447.

54. Act of June 22, 1870, ch. 150, 16 Stat. 162 (codified as amended at 28 U.S.C. §§ 501, 503, 509 note (1994)). This Act also created the office of the Solicitor General. Id. at § 2.

55. National Security Act of 1947, Pub. L. No. 253, ch. 343, 61 Stat. 495 (codified as amended in scattered sections of 50 U.S.C.) (reorganizing the military and intelligence services and creating the Department of Defense, the National Security Council, and the Central Intelligence Agency).

56. See Whittington, *Constitutional Construction,* supra note 7, at 65–71 (discussing constructions arising from the failed impeachment of Supreme Court Justice Samuel Chase).

57. See Bruce Ackerman and David Golove, *Is NAFTA Constitutional?* (Harvard University Press 1995) (describing the rise of the use of congressional-executive agreements); Whittington, *Constitutional Construction,* supra note 7, at 20–71, 113–57, 162–201 (describing controversies over impeachment, budgeting, and national security).

58. See Paul Frymer, *Black and Blue: African Americans, the Labor Movement, and the Decline of the Democratic Party* 70–97 (Princeton University Press 2008) (describing twentieth-century creation of the "Legal State," which enforces rights through building up judicial procedures and remedies).

59. See, e.g., United States v. Darby 312 U.S. 100, 119–20 (1941) (Congress may regulate activities which have a substantial impact on interstate commerce); United States v. Carolene Prods. Co., 304 U.S. 144, 152 (1938) (legislation will be upheld under the due process clause if it has a rational basis); Steward Mach. Co. v. Davis, 301 U.S. 548, 589–92 (1937) (use of federal funds to induce state participation in unemployment compensation scheme did not violate the Tenth Amendment where it did not unduly coerce states to participate and states were free to end participation).

60. Administrative Procedure Act of 1946, Pub. L. No. 404, ch. 324, 60 Stat. 237 (codified as amended at 5 U.S.C. §§ 551–59, 701–6 (1994)).

61. 17 U.S. 316 (1819).

62. 312 U.S. 100 (1941).

63. 384 U.S. 641 (1966).

64. Boumediene v. Bush, 553 U.S. 723 (2008) (holding that constitutional habeas applies to the detention center at Guantanamo Bay, Cuba); Hamdan v. Rumsfeld, 548 U.S. 557 (2006) (holding that Bush administration military commissions violated the Uniform Military Code of Justice and the Geneva Conventions); Hamdi v. Rumsfeld, 542 U.S. 507 (2004) (holding that the president may detain enemy combatants consistent with the laws of war and must afford due process protections); Rasul v. Bush, 542 U.S. 466 (2004) (holding that statutory habeas applied to the detention center at Guantanamo Bay, Cuba).

65. See, e.g., Kennedy v. Louisiana, 554, U.S. 407 (2008) (holding that a statute that prescribed the death penalty for rape of a child under twelve years of age is unconstitutional); compare id. at 2657–58 (concluding that there is a national consensus against the death penalty in these circumstances), with id. at

2665–67, 2672–73 (Alito, J., dissenting) (denying the existence of consensus and arguing that the trend might even be in the opposite direction).

66. See, e.g., Erznoznik v. Jacksonville, 422 U.S. 205 (1975) (declaring facially invalid an ordinance making it a public nuisance and a punishable offense for a drive-in movie theater to exhibit films containing nudity, when the screen is visible from a public street or place); Miller v. California, 413 U.S. 15 (1973) (announcing a three-part test for obscenity); Stanley v. Georgia, 394 U.S. 557 (1969) (holding that mere possession of obscene materials cannot be a crime); Memoirs v. Massachusetts, 383 U.S. 413 (1966) (holding that a book with literary value was not legally obscene).

67. See, e.g., Carey v. Population Servs. Int'l, 431 U.S. 678 (1977) (striking down a prohibition of distribution of contraceptives to minors); Eisenstadt v. Baird 405 U.S. 438 (1972) (holding that the right of reproductive privacy extended to single as well as married persons); Griswold v. Connecticut, 381 U.S. 479 (1965) (striking down a state law that prohibited the dispensing or use of birth control devices to or by married couples).

68. See Zelman v. Simmons-Harris, 536 U.S. 639 (2002) (upholding voucher scheme for private schools under the establishment clause); Mitchell v. Helms, 530 U.S. 793 (2000) (plurality opinion) (upholding direct government aid in materials and equipment to religious schools); Agostini v. Felton, 521 U.S. 203 (1997) (holding that a federally funded program providing instruction to disadvantaged children in parochial schools did not violate the establishment clause); Zobrest v. Catalina Foothills Sch. Dist., 509 U.S. 1 (1993) (holding that the establishment clause did not prevent a school district from furnishing a student with a sign-language interpreter to facilitate his education at a sectarian school).

69. See Good News Club v. Milford Cent. Sch., 533 U.S. 98 (2001); Rosenberger v. Rector and Visitors of Univ. of Va., 515 U.S. 819 (1995); Lamb's Chapel v. Ctr. Moriches Union Free Sch. Dist., 508 U.S. 384 (1993).

70. See United States v. Morrison, 529 U.S. 598 (2000).

71. 60 U.S. 393 (1857).

72. In fact, the practice was more common than generally supposed. See Mark A. Graber, "Naked Land Transfers and American Constitutional Development," 53 *Vand. L. Rev.* 73, 78, 116–17 (2000).

73. See Dred Scott, 60 U.S. at 452.

74. Whittington, *Political Foundations of Judicial Supremacy,* supra note 14, at 134–38; Mark A. Graber, "The Nonmajoritarian Difficulty: Legislative Deference to the Judiciary," supra note 44.

75. 410 U.S. 113 (1973).

76. See Keith Whittington, "'Interpose Your Friendly Hand': Political Supports for the Exercise of Judicial Review by the United States Supreme Court," 99 *Am. Pol. Sci. Rev.* 583, 591 (2005). In order to ensure passage of the 1996

Telecommunications Act, a reform he greatly desired, President Clinton acquiesced to the addition of the Communications Decency Act (CDA), which made it a crime to make available on the Internet indecent material that minors might be able to access. Although both the Justice Department and the Clinton administration argued that the measure was unconstitutional, President Clinton signed the bill anyway. As one administration official put it, "No way are you going to get yourself in a position where the President isn't willing to go as far as a Democratic Senator in restricting child pornography on the Internet in an election year." Id. The bill, however, also provided for expedited judicial review of the CDA, and after a three-judge district court initially struck it down, the Supreme Court declared it unconstitutional in Reno v. ACLU, 521 U.S. 844 (1997). This gave President Clinton and certain members of Congress who voted for the bill the best of both worlds; they got credit for getting tough with Internet pornography while letting the Court protect First Amendment values they shared.

77. Ackerman and Nou, "Canonizing the Civil Rights Revolution," supra note 13, at 108–9

78. 383 U.S. 663 (1966).

79. Frontiero v. Richardson, 411 U.S. 677, 687–88 (1973) (plurality opinion) ("Congress itself has concluded that classifications based upon sex are inherently invidious, and this conclusion of a coequal branch of Government is not without significance to the question presently under consideration").

80. Gonzales v. Carhart, 550 U.S. 124 (2007) (upholding federal Partial-Birth Abortion Act of 2003 and distinguishing Stenberg v. Carhart, 530 U.S. 914 (2000) (striking down a state law banning partial birth abortion)).

81. See, e.g., Bork, *The Tempting of America,* supra note 2, at 8, 16–18; cf. John Ferejohn, "Independent Judges, Dependent Judiciary: Explaining Judicial Independence," 72 *S. Cal. L. Rev.* 353, 369 (1999) ("[H]owever well motivated [judges] may be, they are likely to bring to their work the perceptions of an upper middle class, educated, largely male, and largely white elite").

82. See Larry M. Bartels, *Unequal Democracy: The Political Economy of the New Gilded Age* 285 (Princeton University Press 2008) (affluent citizens have disproportionate impact on social policy outcomes, while "the preferences of persons in the bottom third of the income distribution have *no* apparent impact on the behavior of their elected officials")(emphasis in original).

83. Klarman, *From Jim Crow to Civil Rights,* supra note 20, at 366 (noting that southern filibusters had blocked civil rights legislation between the 1920s and the 1957 Civil Rights Act); Michael J. Klarman, "The Racial Origins of Modern Criminal Procedure," 99 *Mich. L. Rev.* 48, 93–94 (2000) ("[F]rom the 1920s through the 1950s, the Supreme Court probably was a better gauge of national opinion on race than was a United States Congress in which white supremacist southern Democrats enjoyed disproportionate power because of Senate seniority and filibuster rules").

84. See cases cited supra note 12.

85. See, e.g., Kevin J. McMahon, *Reconsidering Roosevelt on Race*, supra note 23 (arguing that Franklin Roosevelt deliberately appointed judges deferential to presidential power and receptive to civil rights claims, especially when made by the Executive).

86. Balkin, "What *Brown* Teaches Us," supra note 14, at 1539; Klarman, *From Jim Crow to Civil Rights,* supra note 20, at 344–45, 445; see Mary Dudziak, *Cold War Civil Rights: Race and the Image of American Democracy* 80–81 (Princeton University Press 2000); Gerald Rosenberg, *The Hollow Hope: Can Courts Bring About Social Change?* 42 (University of Chicago Press 1991).

87. Harper v. Va. Bd. of Elections, 383 U.S. 663 (1966); see also Ackerman and Nou, "Canonizing the Civil Rights Revolution," supra note 13.

88. Powe, *The Warren Court,* supra note 14, at 492 (arguing that the Warren Court's criminal procedure decisions imposed national standards on local and state police officers, prosecutors, and judges); Klarman, "Rethinking the Civil Rights and Civil Liberties Revolutions," supra note 16, at 60–66 (connecting the Warren Court's criminal procedure revolution to changing attitudes about poverty); cf. Corinna Barrett Lain, "Countermajoritarian Hero or Zero? Rethinking the Warren Court's Role in the Criminal Procedure Revolution," 152 *U. Pa. L. Rev.* 1361, 1451 (2004) (arguing that Warren Court decisions reflected shifts in national public opinion and changing attitudes about police misconduct, race, poverty, and perceived rates of crime).

89. See Goldberg v. Kelly, 397 U.S. 254 (1970) (holding that due process requires a hearing before the termination of welfare benefits); Shapiro v. Thompson, 394 U.S. 618 (1969) (striking down, on equal protection grounds, a statute that denied welfare benefits to residents who had not been in the jurisdiction for at least one year); Harper, 383 U.S. 663 (striking down poll tax in state elections).

90. Graham v. Richardson, 403 U.S. 365 (1971).

91. 300 U.S. 379 (1937).

92. Id. at 391.

93. See Ronald Dworkin, *Law's Empire* 52, 166, 227–28, 255, 265, 363–68 (Harvard University Press 1986).

94. See Howard Gillman, *The Constitution Besieged: The Rise and Demise of Lochner Era Police Powers Jurisprudence* 10–14, 175–93 (Duke University Press 1993).

95. See Ferguson v. Skrupa, 372 U.S. 726 (1963); Williamson v. Lee Optical Co., 348 U.S. 483 (1955); United States v. Carolene Prods. Co, 304 U.S. 144 (1938); West Coast Hotel Co. v. Parrish, 300 U.S. 379 (1937).

96. Ackerman, "The Living Constitution," supra note 9.

97. Bruce Ackerman, "Revolution on a Human Scale," 108 *Yale L. J.* 2279, 2287–89 (1999) (proposing a ten-year test for revolutionary change). This

compressed time horizon helps ensure that the American people have focused self-consciously on the changes and assented to them.

98. Ackerman, 1 *We the People: Foundations,* supra note 13, at 131–62 (1991) (describing intergenerational synthesis and offering *Brown v. Board of Education* and *Griswold v. Connecticut* as examples).

99. Ackerman, "The Living Constitution," supra note 9, at 2283–85 (emphasizing self-consciousness of actors in moments of revolutionary change); see, e.g., Ackerman, 2 *We The People: Transformations* 358–59 (Harvard University Press 1998) (arguing that ordinary Americans understood the events of the New Deal as a constitutional revolution, confirmed by the consolidating election of 1940); Ackerman, 1 *We the People: Foundations,* supra note 13, at 290 (revolutionary agendas must seek "to gain the deep, broad and decisive support of the American people").

100. Franklin D. Roosevelt, "Address on Constitution Day, Washington, D.C. (Sept. 17, 1937)," in John Woolley and Gerhard Peters, *The American Presidency Project,* www.presidency.ucsb.edu/ws/?pid=15459 ("You will find no justification in any of the language of the Constitution, for delay in the reforms which the mass of the American people now demand. . . . [N]early every attempt to meet those demands for social and economic betterment has been jeopardized or actually forbidden by those who have sought to read into the Constitution language which the framers refused to write into the Constitution").

Roosevelt's public rhetoric during this period does not match Ackerman's model of self-conscious constitutional transformation. Roosevelt did not urge the public to accept anything like an amendment outside of Article V. Instead, Roosevelt spoke and reasoned like a framework originalist, arguing that the Constitution was deliberately designed as "a charter of general principles" that used "general language capable of meeting evolution and change." Id.

Roosevelt used the language of constitutional redemption rather than constitutional revolution: The Supreme Court, Roosevelt insisted, had disregarded the Constitution's text and its central principles; they were "reading into the Constitution words and implications which are not there, and which were never intended to be there." Franklin D. Roosevelt, "Fireside Chat Discussing the Plan for Reorganization of the Federal Judiciary, March 9, 1937," in John Woolley and Gerhard Peters, *The American Presidency Project,* www.presidency.ucsb. edu/ws/index.php?pid = 15381. Thus, he called for the restoration of the true Constitution: "We must take action to save the Constitution from the Court and the Court from itself. We must find a way to take an appeal from the Supreme Court to the Constitution itself." Id.

101. Ackerman, 2 *We The People: Transformations,* supra note 99, at 9, 22, 82, 120, 154 (discussing the role of unconventional adaptations in higher lawmaking); id. at 187 (unconventional adaptation by political elites allows them

to test the assent of the public). Ackerman's idea of unconventional adaptation better fits constitutional controversies during the founding, the Jeffersonian revolution, and Reconstruction; in the case of the New Deal, he argues that lawyers' use of Supreme Court opinions as amendment analogues is an unconventional adaptation, id. at 270–71, although it does not fit into his five-part scheme in the same way as in the previous historical examples. These opinions appear at the last stage of consolidation rather than setting up the key moment of popular decision for or against revolutionary change. See id. at 187–88. Although Ackerman does not address the point directly, presumably the use of both landmark judicial decisions and landmark statutes as amendment equivalents is the characteristic unconventional adaptation of the civil rights revolution. See Ackerman, "The Living Constitution," supra note 9, at 1760–61, 1770–71 (arguing that the 1964 Civil Rights Act, like the Fourteenth Amendment during Reconstruction, placed the question of revolutionary change before the public).

102. Ackerman, 2 *We The People: Transformations,* supra note 99, at 20, 26, 359 (discussing the procedural preconditions for legitimate change); id. at 166, 207, 211 (noting the signaling act of illegality by the Convention/Congress, resistance by conservative branches, recourse to the people through a triggering election, the unconventional threat of presidential impeachment, and eventual capitulation in the Reconstruction period); id. at 359 (noting the structure of New Deal revolution involving a triggering election, the unconventional threat by President Roosevelt, transformative appointments, a ratifying, consolidating election, and consolidating judicial opinions); Ackerman, "The Living Constitution," supra note 9, at 1762 (describing the five-stage process for civil rights revolution); Ackerman, "Revolution on a Human Scale," supra note 97, at 2298–99 (noting the pattern of signaling, proposing, triggering, and ratifying by the Federalists).

103. Ackerman, "The Living Constitution," supra note 9, at 1741, 1790.

104. Bruce Ackerman, "Interpreting the Women's Movement," 94 *Cal. L. Rev.* 1421, 1426 (2006) ("It was the Court's understanding of the evolving requirements of Equal Protection which shaped its response to the women's movement, not the other way around"); id. at 1434 (arguing that the Court worked out the implications of the commitment to racial equality for gender stereotyping).

105. Ackerman, 2 *We The People: Transformations,* supra note 99, at 270 (describing *Darby* and *Wickard* as "amendment analogues"); Ackerman, "The Living Constitution," supra note 9, at 1761 ("I will be presenting the landmark statutes of the 1960s as functionally equivalent to the constitutional amendments of the 1860s"); id. at 1788 ("The legal landmarks emerging from this moment of popular sovereignty should not be denigrated merely because they took the form of statutes rather than formal amendments").

106. Ackerman, "The Living Constitution," supra note 9, at 1753–54 & n. 38.

107. Ackerman does not disagree. See id. at 1788–89. However, he character-izes the issue differently: he argues that "an all-out assault on the Civil Rights Act, or the Voting Rights Act, could not occur without a massive effort comparable to the political exertions that created these landmarks in the first place." Id. at 1788. Because these landmark statutes are constitutional amendments outside of Article V, it would seem to follow from his reasoning that the same five-stage process would be required *legitimately* to repeal these statutes. This is not my view.

108. Balkin and Levinson, "The Processes of Constitutional Change," supra note 37, at 510–13 (explaining why the Rehnquist Court's federalism revolu-tion did not fundamentally reshape New Deal precedents).

109. See Jack M. Balkin and Reva B. Siegel, "The American Civil Rights Tra-dition: Anticlassification or Antisubordination?" 58 *U. Miami L. Rev.* 9, 28–32 (2003) (explaining how political countermobilizations reshaped antidiscrimina-tion law); Balkin, "What *Brown* Teaches Us," supra note 14, at 1563–68 (ex-plaining how changes in American politics altered *Brown*'s practical meaning); Reva B. Siegel, "Equality Talk: Antisubordination and Anticlassification Values in Constitutional Struggles over *Brown*," 117 *Harv. L. Rev.* 1470, 1547 (2004) (showing how the "anticlassification principle was not the [original] ground of the *Brown* decision, but instead emerged from struggles over the decision's en-forcement"); David A. Strauss, "Discriminatory Intent and the Taming of *Brown*," 56 *U. Chi. L. Rev.* 935 (1989) (arguing that 1970s equal protection jurispru-dence limited the transformative potential of *Brown*).

110. Sanford Levinson and I have distinguished the constitutional canon as understood by citizens from the canon as understood by legal professionals. See J. M. Balkin and Sanford Levinson, "The Canons of Constitutional Law," 111 *Harv. L. Rev.* 963 (1998). However, these inevitably overlap and influence each other.

111. Id. at 1018–19; see also Jamal Greene, "The Anticanon," 125 *Harv. L. Rev.* __ (forthcoming 2011); Richard A. Primus, "Canon, Anti-Canon, and Judicial Dissent," 48 *Duke L.J.* 243 (1998).

112. Social Security Act of 1935, ch. 531, Pub. L. No. 74-271, 49 Stat. 620 (codified in scattered sections of 26 U.S.C. and 42 U.S.C. (2006)).

113. U.S. Const. art. I, § 9, cl. 5.

114. Pub. L. No. 82-352, 78 Stat. 241 (codified as amended in scattered sec-tions of 28 and 42 U.S.C.).

115. 198 U.S. 45 (1905).

116. See Jack M. Balkin, "'Wrong the Day It Was Decided': *Lochner* and Constitutional Historicism," 85 *B.U. L. Rev.* 677 (2005) (noting the changing meanings of *Lochner* in the constitutional canon).

117. E.g., Craig v. Boren, 429 U.S. 190 (1976) (requiring intermediate scru-tiny of all sex classifications); Frontiero v. Richardson, 411 U.S. 677 (1973) (plu-rality opinion) (sex classifications are inherently invidious and subject to strict

judicial scrutiny); Reed v. Reed, 404 U.S. 71 (1971) (statute preferring male over female executors of estates was an arbitrary choice forbidden by the equal protection clause).

118. See Balkin and Siegel, "The American Civil Rights Tradition," supra note 109, at 28–32 (2003); Balkin, "What *Brown* Teaches Us," supra note 14, at 1563–68; Siegel, "Equality Talk," supra note 109, at 1547.

119. See Mark A. Graber, "Settling the West: The Annexation of Texas, the Louisiana Purchase and *Bush v. Gore*," in *The Louisiana Purchase and American Expansionism* 83, 85 (Sanford Levinson and Bartholomew Sparrow eds., Rowman and Littlefield 2006) (noting that serious constitutional questions regarding the Louisiana Purchase and the annexation of Texas were settled not by courts, but when opponents of these measures conceded defeat in the political arena).

120. 312 U.S. 100 (1941).

121. 317 U.S. 111 (1942).

122. 301 U.S. 548 (1937) (upholding the unemployment compensation provisions of the Social Security Act of 1935).

123. 381 U.S. 479 (1965).

124. 405 U.S. 438 (1972).

125. Voting Rights Act of 1965, Pub. L. No. 89-110, 79 Stat. 437 (codified as amended at 42 U.S.C. § 1973 (2006)).

126. NAMUDNO v. Holder, 129 S. Ct. 2504 (2009).

127. See Jack M. Balkin, "The Constitutional Catechism," *Balkinization*, Jan. 11, 2006, balkin.blogspot.com/2006/01/constitutional-catechism.html.

128. See David J. Garrow, *Liberty and Sexuality: The Right to Privacy and the Making of* Roe v. Wade 671 (MacMillan 1994); Lackland H. Bloom, "Twenty-Fifth Anniversary of *Griswold v. Connecticut* and the Right to Privacy: The Legacy of *Griswold*," 16 *Ohio N.U. L. Rev.* 511, 542–43 (1989); David J. Garrow, "Abortion before and after *Roe v. Wade*: An Historical Perspective," 62 *Alb. L. Rev.* 833, 843 (1999); Reva B. Siegel, "Constitutional Culture, Social Movement Conflict and Constitutional Change: The Case of the De Facto ERA," 94 *Cal. L. Rev.* 1323, 1409 (2006).

129. Ackerman, 2 *We the People: Transformations,* supra note 99, at 16–23; Ackerman, "The Living Constitution," supra note 9, at 1754, 1761, 1775.

130. See Howard Gillman, "How Political Parties Can Use the Courts to Advance Their Agendas," supra note 37, at 515–17 (showing how late nineteenth-century Republicans expanded federal court jurisdiction to promote their policy goals and entrench their party); cf. Ran Hirschl, *Towards Juristocracy*, supra note 37, at 39 (noting how politicians in many different countries profit "from an expansion of judicial power").

131. See Steven Teles, *The Rise of the Conservative Legal Movement*, supra note 40, at 6–21, 265–74.

132. See Bruce Ackerman, "The Living Constitution," supra note 9, at 1738–44 (2007) ("We have lost our ability to write down our new constitutional commitments in the old-fashioned way").

14. Change and Legitimacy

1. Jack M. Balkin, "What *Brown* Teaches Us about Constitutional Theory," 90 *Va. L. Rev.* 1537, 1546 (2004).

2. Ronald Dworkin, *The Forum of Principle,* 56 N.Y.U. L. Rev. 469 (1981).

3. For general discussions of this point, see Balkin, "What *Brown* Teaches Us," supra note 1; Michael Klarman, *From Jim Crow to Civil Rights: The Supreme Court and the Struggle for Racial Equality* (Oxford University Press 2004).

4. The story is told in Klarman, *From Jim Crow to Civil Rights,* supra note 3.

5. 163 U.S. 537 (1896).

6. See Klarman, *From Jim Crow to Civil Rights,* supra note 3, at 210.

7. See, e.g., Perez v. Lippold, 198 P. 2d 17 (Cal. 1948) (holding that an antimiscegenation law violated the federal equal protection clause).

8. United States v. Carolene Prods. Corp., 304 U.S. 144, 152 n. 4 (1938).

9. See Balkin, "What *Brown* Teaches Us," supra note 1, at 1551–58; Klarman, *From Jim Crow to Civil Rights,* supra note 3, at 450.

10. Klarman, *From Jim Crow to Civil Rights,* supra note 3, at 100–103.

11. Mary Dudziak, *Cold War Civil Rights: Race and the Image of American Democracy* 80–81 (Princeton University Press 2000).

12. Congress sent the ERA to the states in 1972 by a vote of 354–24 in the House and a vote of 84–8 in the Senate. 117 *Cong. Rec.* 35815 (1971) (House); 118 *Cong. Rec.* 9598 (1972) (Senate).

13. 261 U.S. 525, 553 (1923) (striking down a minimum wage law for women under the due process clause, while noting "the great—not to say revolutionary—changes which have taken place . . . in the contractual, political and civil status of women, culminating in the Nineteenth Amendment").

14. 335 U.S. 464 (1948) (upholding prohibition on female bartenders).

15. 368 U.S. 57 (1961) (upholding the automatic exclusion of women from juries).

16. 554 U.S. 570 (2008).

17. 48 Stat. 1236 (1934) (codified at 26 U.S.C. §§ 5801–22 (2006)).

18. "MacNeil/Lehrer NewsHour: Interview by Charlayne Hunter-Gault with Warren Burger" (PBS television broadcast, Dec. 16, 1991) (Monday transcript #4226), available in LEXIS, News Library, NewsHour with Jim Lehrer File.

19. Id.

20. The Omnibus Crime Control and Safe Streets Act of 1968, Pub. L. 90-351 (codified at 42 U.S.C. § 3711 (2006)).

21. The paragraphs that follow draw on the excellent discussion in Reva B. Siegel, "Dead or Alive: Originalism as Popular Constitutionalism in *Heller*," 122 *Harv. L. Rev.* 191 (2008).

22. Id.

23. Id.

24. See, e.g., Staff of Subcomm. on the Constitution of the S. Comm. on the Judiciary, 97th Cong., *The Right to Keep and Bear Arms* (Comm. Print 1982).

25. See Nicholas J. Johnson, "A Second Amendment Moment: The Constitutional Politics of Gun Control," 71 *Brook. L. Rev.* 715, 779–83 (2005).

26. Siegel, "Dead or Alive," supra note 21, at 228–29.

27. Id. at 230–31.

28. Id. at 231–32.

29. See, e.g., Linda Greenhouse, "U.S., in a Shift, Tells Justices Citizens Have a Right to Guns," *N.Y. Times,* May 8, 2002, at A1. Meanwhile an outpouring of new legal and historical scholarship began debating the individual rights interpretation in the 1990s and 2000s, and the third edition of Professor Laurence Tribe's treatise, *American Constitutional Law,* published in 2000, argued—in contrast to the two previous editions—that the Second Amendment protected an individual right. Laurence H. Tribe, *American Constitutional Law* § 5–11, at 901–2 n. 221 (3d ed., Foundation Press 2000).

30. District of Columbia v. Heller, 554 U.S. 570, 625, 635 (2008) (restricting the right to "law-abiding" citizens).

31. See, e.g., Mark Tushnet, *Out of Range: Why the Constitution Can't End the Battle over Guns* 25–26 (Oxford University Press 2007) (noting that evidence at the founding for a "pure" individual right of self-defense unconnected to citizen militias is equivocal but evidence of some form of republican or citizen-militia theory is far stronger); Akhil Reed Amar, "*Heller, HLR,* and Holistic Legal Reasoning," 122 *Harv. L. Rev.* 145 (2008) (noting evidence for republican or citizen-militia theory at the founding and only indirect evidence for incorporation of common law right of self-defense).

32. See Heller, 554 U.S. at 605-619 (describing nineteenth-century evidence); David B. Kopel, "The Second Amendment in the Nineteenth Century," 1998 *BYU L. Rev.* 1359. Both Kopel and Justice Scalia, it should be noted, believe that this evidence helps prove the case for the founding as well.

33. See Akhil Reed Amar, *The Bill of Rights: Creation and Reconstruction* 52, 145–62, 257–68 (Yale University Press 1998) (noting an increasingly individualist interpretation of the Second Amendment in the years leading up to Reconstruction); Amar, "*Heller, HLR,* and Holistic Legal Reasoning," supra note 31 (arguing for constitutional right to self-defense under the Fourteenth Amendment's privileges or immunities clause).

34. Heller, 554 U.S. at 626 ("[N]othing in our opinion should be taken to cast doubt on longstanding prohibitions on the possession of firearms by felons and the mentally ill.")

35. Id. at 627-28. ("It may well be true today that a militia, to be as effective as militias in the 18th century, would require sophisticated arms that are highly unusual in society at large. Indeed, it may be true that no amount of small arms could be useful against modern-day bombers and tanks. But the fact that modern developments have limited the degree of fit between the prefatory clause and the protected right cannot change our interpretation of the right.")

36. Id.

37. For an argument along these lines, see Richard A. Posner, "The Supreme Court, 2004 Term—Foreword: A Political Court," 119 *Harv. L. Rev.* 31 (2005).

38. One additional feature concerns federalism. To the extent that the federal courts tend to impose the values of national politicians and the dominant national political coalition on regional majorities, the federal courts and the Supreme Court in particular are not so much countermajoritarian as they are nationalist. See Balkin, "What *Brown* Teaches Us," supra note 1, at 1538–46. However, the values of a national political majority, as James Madison argued, may often be more moderate and better protect the rights of minorities than those of a smaller, more homogeneous political community. *The Federalist* No. 10 (James Madison).

39. For example, the Supreme Court's Eleventh Amendment jurisprudence beginning with Hans v. Louisiana, 134 US 1 (1890), seems to be inconsistent with the constitutional text: "The judicial power of the United States shall not be construed to extend to any suit in law or equity, commenced or prosecuted against one of the United States by citizens of another State, or by citizens or subjects of any foreign state." U.S. Const. amend. XI. See Blatchford v. Native Vill. of Noatak, 501 U.S. 775, 779 (1991) ("[W]e have understood the Eleventh Amendment to stand not so much for what it says, but for the presupposition of our constitutional structure which it confirms"). Current doctrine reads "citizens of another State" to include citizens of the same state, Seminole Tribe of Fla. v. Florida, 517 U.S. 44, 54 (1996), and also allows suits in equity through the fiction of suits against the state's attorney general, Ex parte Young, 209 U.S. 123 (1908). Perhaps the best defense of some kind of state immunity is a structural argument for protection of state sovereignty under the Tenth Amendment, see Alden v. Maine, 527 U.S. 706, 713–15 (1999), but it is not at all clear why structural considerations should produce the doctrine we currently have.

40. See Ronald Dworkin, *Law's Empire* 239–40 (Harvard University Press 1986); Ronald Dworkin, *Taking Rights Seriously* 105–30 (Harvard University Press 1977).

41. Learned Hand, *The Bill of Rights* 73 (Harvard University Press 1958) ("For myself it would be most irksome to be ruled by a bevy of Platonic Guardians, even if I knew how to choose them, which I assuredly do not").

42. *The Federalist* No. 10 (James Madison).

43. See, e.g., Keith E. Whittington, *Constitutional Interpretation: Textual Meaning, Original Intent, and Judicial Review* 111 (University Press of Kansas 1999) (arguing from popular sovereignty and noting that "[t]raditional defenses of originalism often employ some version of a popular sovereignty argument").

44. For arguments emphasizing the importance of positive constitutional theory to understanding the legitimacy of judicial review, see Balkin, "What *Brown* Teaches Us," supra note 1, at 1537, 1574–77; Barry Friedman, "The Importance of Being Positive: The Nature and Function of Judicial Review," 72 *U. Cin. L. Rev.* 1257, 1257–58, 1270–83, 1290 (2004); Mark A. Graber, "Constitutional Politics and Constitutional Theory: A Misunderstood and Neglected Relationship," 27 *Law & Soc. Inquiry* 309, 312, 317–29 (2002).

45. Lawrence Lessig, "Fidelity in Translation," 71 *Tex. L. Rev.* 1165 (1996).

46. Id. at 1184–85; see also Lawrence Lessig, "Fidelity in Translation: Fidelity and Constraint," 65 Fordham L. Rev. 1365, 1376 (1997) ("Our aim has, for the most part, been to extract normative significance from an ancient constitutional text and preserve that significance as much as possible"); Goodwin Liu, Pamela S. Karlan, and Christopher H. Schroeder, *Keeping Faith with the Constitution* (Oxford University Press 2010)(offering an interpretive theory that draws on Lessig's model of translation and the method of text and principle).

47. See, e.g., Lawrence v. Texas, 539 U.S. 558, 602, 604–5 (2003) (Scalia, J., dissenting) (arguing that the Court, dominated by elite culture, "has largely signed on to the so-called homosexual agenda" and "that the Court has taken sides in the culture war"); see also Robert C. Post and Reva B. Siegel, "Originalism as a Political Practice: The Right's Living Constitution," 75 *Fordham L. Rev.* 545, 566–68 (2006) (noting that Scalia in particular has "mobilized conservative constituencies to bring political pressure to bear on the development of constitutional law"). Scalia's constitutional theory holds that judges should not decide constitutional questions based on contemporary social values. See Planned Parenthood of Southeastern Pa. v. Casey, 505 U.S. 833, 1000 (1992) (Scalia, J., dissenting) ("How upsetting it is, that so many of our citizens . . . think that we Justices should properly take into account their views, as though we were engaged not in ascertaining an objective law but in determining some kind of social consensus"). Nevertheless, his arguments often mesh with the values of conservative elites; indeed, he owes his Supreme Court appointment to the success of movement conservatism.

48. See Charles Epp, *The Rights Revolution: Lawyers, Activists, and Supreme Courts in Comparative Perspective* (University of Chicago Press 1998) (emphasizing the role of resources devoted to litigation and directed litigation campaigns in

producing constitutional change); Steven Teles, *The Rise of the Conservative Legal Movement* (Princeton University Press 2007) (emphasizing the role of nonelectoral competition by elites and institutions of civil society in reshaping constitutional culture).

49. Jack Balkin and Reva B. Siegel, introduction to *The Constitution in 2020* (Jack M. Balkin and Reva B. Siegel eds., Oxford University Press, 2009).

50. Abraham Lincoln, "Speech in Reply to Senator Douglas (July 10, 1858)," in 1 *Abraham Lincoln: Complete Works* 247, 255 (John G. Nicolay and John Hay eds., The Century Co. 1902) (1894).

51. Reva B. Siegel, "Constitutional Culture, Social Movement Conflict and Constitutional Change: The Case of the De Facto ERA," 94 *Cal. L. Rev.* 1403–19 (2006).

52. See Balkin, "What *Brown* Teaches Us," supra note 1, at 1563–68 (describing the refashioning of constitutional claims through politics); Jack M. Balkin and Reva B. Siegel, "Principles, Practices, and Social Movements," 154 *U. Pa. L. Rev.* 927 (2006) (describing the role of social movements in shaping and reconfiguring constitutional claims in new factual contexts); Siegel, "Dead or Alive," supra note 21 (describing changing social movement conceptions of the right to bear arms); Reva B. Siegel, "The Right's Reasons: Constitutional Conflict and the Spread of Woman-Protective Antiabortion Argument," 57 *Duke L. J.* 1641 (2008) (describing changing forms of anti-abortion argumentation); Siegel, "Constitutional Culture, Social Movement Conflict and Constitutional Change," supra note 51 (describing the effects of 1970s mobilizations and countermobilizations on sex equality claims); Reva B. Siegel, "Equality Talk: Antisubordination and Anticlassification Values in Constitutional Struggles over *Brown*," 117 *Harv. L. Rev.* 1470 (2004) (describing the effects of political struggle on the meaning of *Brown v. Board of Education*).

53. See Mark Graber, Dred Scott *and the Problem of Constitutional Evil* (Cambridge University Press 2006) (arguing that in interpreting constitutions justice must be sacrificed to secure a stable democratic politics); Jack M. Balkin, "Agreements with Hell and Other Objects of Our Faith," 65 *Fordham L. Rev.* 1703 (1997) (describing the problem of constitutional evil as how to be faithful to a constitution that might permit or require great evils).

54. Memorandum from John C. Yoo, Deputy Assistant Att'y Gen., U.S. Dep't of Justice Office of Legal Counsel, to William J. Haynes II, Gen. Counsel, U.S. Dep't of Defense (Mar. 14, 2003), available at www.aclu.org/pdfs/safefree/yoo_army_torture_memo.pdf (arguing that statues or treaties limiting interrogation and detention practices, including torture, would violate the president's authority as commander in chief); Memorandum from the U.S. Dep't of Justice Office of Legal Counsel to Alberto R. Gonzales, Counsel to the President (Aug. 1, 2002), available at www.washingtonpost.com/wpsrv/nation/documents/dojinterroga tionmemo20020801.pdf (same).

55. Id.

56. Dred Scott v. Sanford, 60 U.S. 393 (1857).

57. Plessy v. Ferguson, 163 U.S. 537 (1896).

58. Buck v. Bell, 274 U.S. 200 (1927).

59. See Jack M. Balkin, "Reductio Ad Dictatorem," *Balkinization*, Apr. 7, 2006, balkin.blogspot.com/2006/04/reductio-ad-dictatorem.html.

60. See David J. Barron and Martin S. Lederman, "The Commander in Chief at the Lowest Ebb—Framing the Problem, Doctrine, and Original Understanding," 121 *Harv. L. Rev.* 689, 695–97, 800–804 (2008); David J. Barron and Martin S. Lederman, "The Commander in Chief at the Lowest Ebb—A Constitutional History," 121 *Harv. L. Rev.* 941, 947–51, 1057–59, 1100 (2008); David Luban, "On the Commander in Chief Power," 81 *S. Cal. L. Rev.* 477 (2008).

ACKNOWLEDGMENTS

Several chapters of this book began as a series of articles, all of which have been extensively rewritten for publication. Chapter 1 is based on the first section of "Abortion and Original Meaning," 24 *Const. Commentary* 291 (2007), and on "Fidelity to Text and Principle," in Jack M. Balkin and Reva B. Siegel, eds., *The Constitution in 2020* (Oxford University Press 2009). Chapters 2, 13, and 14 are drawn from "Framework Originalism and the Living Constitution," 103 *Nw. L. Rev.* 549 (2009). Portions of Chapters 3 through 7 and Chapter 12 appeared in "Original Meaning and Constitutional Redemption," 24 *Const. Commentary* 427 (2007). Chapter 9 is based on "Commerce," 109 *Mich. L. Rev.* 1 (2010).

My wife, Margret Wolfe, has been a steady source of support as I labored over these chapters over the course of many years. Nothing seems possible without her; everything seems possible with her love.

Many friends and colleagues have commented on the various parts of this book as I developed its ideas over the years. In particular I would like to thank Bruce Ackerman, Larry Alexander, Akhil Amar, Randy Barnett, Mitchell N. Berman, Steve Calabresi, Michael Kent Curtis, Barry Friedman, Jeff Goldsworthy, Mark Graber, Mark Greenberg, Dawn Johnsen, Ken Kersch, Kurt Lash, Gary Lawson, Thomas Lee, Ethan Leib, Sanford Levinson, Gerard Magliocca, John O. McGinnis, Tom Merrill, Mike Paulsen, Rick Pildes, Robert Post, Michael Rappaport, Adam Samaha, Alexander Schwab, Scott Shapiro, Reva Siegel, Larry Solum, Keith Whittington, Kenji Yoshino, and Mariah Zeisberg, as well as participants at the New York University Colloquium in Legal, Political and Social Philosophy, the Georgetown Law Center Advanced Constitutional Law Colloquium, the Originalism Works-in-Progress-Conference at the University of San Diego, the Fordham Law School faculty workshop, and the Yale Law School faculty workshop.

Thanks also to Thomas Colby and Peter Smith, who were the embodiment of graciousness when I told them that the title of this book would be the same as that of their 2009 article, "Living Originalism," 59 *Duke L. Rev.* 239 (2009). Elizabeth Knoll, my editor at Harvard University Press, knew exactly how much balm and advice to apply at strategic moments.

Several people deserve special mention for helping me improve the book by hosting forums where very talented scholars could criticize its ideas. In 2006, Mike Paulsen arranged a symposium in *Constitutional Commentary* based on an early draft of the first chapter, which led me to revise and expand my views considerably and ultimately made this book possible. Ken Kersch put together a panel at the New England Political Science Association to critique substantial portions of the book. Last but not least, Larry Solum and Kurt Lash organized an entire conference at the University of Illinois to discuss and critique a draft of the completed manuscript.

This book is dedicated to two of my Yale colleagues, Reva Siegel and Robert Post. I am inspired by their vision of a truly democratic Constitution, which grows in response to popular mobilizations and changes in constitutional culture. And I am enriched every day by their warmth and friendship. They have been dear friends and a source of constant blessings to me for many years. This book is for them.

INDEX

Abortion: rights, 9, 95, 214–219, 245, 249, 303, 304; as a coalition-splitting issue delegated to courts, 288, 303

Ackerman, Bruce: on higher lawmaking, 60; on myth of rediscovery, 97; on New Deal, 139, 439n13; on Twenty-Fourth Amendment, 303–304; theory of constitutional moments, 309–312; on nationalization of amendment process, 317; on Roosevelt and unconventional adaptation, 448–449nn100,101; on civil rights statutes as amendments, 450n107

Adair, Douglass, 152, 153

Adams, John, 288

Adaptation, unconventional, 310, 448–449nn100–101

Addington, David, 337

Administrative action, 5, 67, 68

Administrative Procedure Act (1946), 5, 301

Administrative (and regulatory) state, 5–6, 91, 109, 121, 139, 142, 143, 261, 318, 368n13

Affirmative action, 234–235

Agriculture, 153–154, 164–165, 383

Alexy, Robert, 349n12

Aliens and noncitizens, 198, 306; the Fourteenth Amendment and, 185, 192–193, 194, 198, 221, 249, 404n74; political rights and, 224, 239

Alito, Samuel, 396n153

Amar, Akhil, 141, 155, 202, 252, 257, 403n52, 418n23

Amendment 2 (Colorado), 236

Amendment(s), 113–114, 168, 261, 282–283, 439n13

"Among the several states," 140, 159, 160

Antidiscrimination law, 166–171, 250, 392n123. *See also* Equal protection clause; Fourteenth Amendment; Privileges or immunities clause

Apportionment, 242–244, 357n23

Aristotle, 106

Arms: right to bear, 120–121, 205–207, 218–219, 271, 322–324, 413n143; possession of, near schools, 171–172; regulation of, 393n134

Article I: section 3, 48; section 8, 47, 139, 375n25, 376–377n27; section 9, 55, 157, 202; section 10, 47–48

Article IV: section 2, 193–195, 208–209; section 4, 37, 240–244

Article V, 48, 60, 70, 139, 318–319

Articulation, supplementation and consistency with the text, 270–273

Ashcroft, John, 324

Aspirationalism, constitutional, 60, 62, 85, 96, 406n84

Baker v. Carr, 242

Barnett, Randy: on original meaning, 104; on faint-hearted originalism, 111–112; on New Deal, 138; on Resolution VI, 145, 376–377n27; on "among the several states," 160; on reading text and principle together, 271; on construction by the judiciary, 341n2; on commerce and navigation, 381n49; on multiple meanings of commerce, 389n94

Barron v. Baltimore, 189, 194

Basic law, 59–62, 66, 85, 268

Bedford, Gunning, 144, 376n27

Milton Keynes UK
Ingram Content Group UK Ltd.
UKHW031222141124
451167UK00003B/113